Baseball's Hall of Fame

COOPERSTOWN

Where the Legends Live Forever

Books of similar interest
from Random House Value Publishing:

Only the Ball Was White
Sports Illustrated: Baseball
The Ultimate Yankee Baseball Quiz Book

Baseball's Hall of Fame

COOPERSTOWN

Where the Legends Live Forever

Written by **Lowell Reidenbaugh**

Edited by **Joe Hoppel**

Revised and Updated by the **Editors of The Sporting News**

Gramercy Books
New York

This 2001 edition is published by Gramercy Books™, an imprint of
Random House Value Publishing, Inc. 280 Park Avenue,
New York, N.Y. 10017, by arrangement with *The Sporting News*,
a division of Times Mirror Magazines, Inc.

Gramercy Books™ and colophon are trademarks of
Random House Value Publishing, Inc.

Book and jacket design by Robert Yaffe

Random House
New York • Toronto • London • Sydney • Auckland
http://www.randomhouse.com/

Library of Congress Cataloging–in–Publication Data

Reidenbaugh, Lowell.
    Cooperstown : Baseball's Hall of Fame / written by Lowell
Reidenbaugh ; edited by Joe Hoppel. — Rev. and updated / by the
editors of Sporting news.
        p.   cm.
    Rev. ed. of: Baseball's Hall of Fame, 1997.
    ISBN 0-517-19464-3 (hardcover)
    1. Baseball players—United States Biography.   2. Baseball—
Records—United States.3. National Baseball Hall of Fame and
Museum.   I. Hoppel, Joe.   II. Reidenbaugh, Lowell. Baseball's Hall
of Fame.   III. Sporting news.   IV. Title.
    GV865.A1R43   1997
    796.357'092'273—dc21
    [B]   99-20480
                                                   CIP

Printed and bound in the United States of America.

8 7 6 5 4 3 2 1

CONTENTS

Doubleday Field, located two blocks from the Baseball Hall of Fame, is the site of the annual Hall of Fame Game.

Baseball's Hall of Fame

COOPERSTOWN

Where the Legends Live Forever

INTRODUCTION

A small minority of mortals is blessed with the ability to hammer a speeding white ball an amazing distance, or to propel it with extraordinary velocity and accuracy, or to perform with uncommon grace and agility in catching it. Such gifts can be appreciated by the millions of people who have attempted to hit a curve ball or catch a sizzling line drive, reaping only futility for their efforts.

Superbly endowed as they were with physical talents, they also had the fierce determination to succeed and were willing to devote long hours of practice to master the intricacies required of major league performers.

Behind the plaques at Cooperstown are hours of bumpy bus rides, countless blue-plate specials in sleazy all-night eateries, dingy motels in forgotten hamlets and numberless games on corduroy fields rimmed by unpainted grandstands.

Despite their early career tribulations, the future Hall of Famers persisted because it was a livelihood that offered the hope for princely salaries and universal adulation.

Some, like Frank Frisch, Bob Feller and Al Kaline, leaped directly to the major leagues from the sandlots. Others, like Carl Hubbell and Dazzy Vance, drifted in the minors for years before their courses were reversed. Hubbell was discarded by the Detroit Tigers, Joe Cronin by the Pittsburgh Pirates and Vance by Pittsburgh and the New York Yankees before, at age 31, he found his niche as a strikeout king for the Brooklyn Dodgers.

Not all of the immortals attained stardom at their original positions. Babe Ruth, George Sisler and Bill Terry were pitchers before their batting talents demanded that they play daily. Jimmie Foxx started as a catcher, Hank Aaron as an infielder and Frank Chance as a catcher.

Terry, the young head of a family, questioned baseball as a profession until the Giants made him an irresistible proposition. He played the game on his own financial terms. Edd Roush was of a similar cut. When his terms were not met, he took a one-year sabbatical from the game.

While they were idols on the baseball field, many demonstrated human frailties during their off hours. Paul Waner made no effort to conceal his affinity for the flowing grape and grain. But his unconventional lifestyle never interfered with his ability to bat .300, or to compile more than 3,000 major league hits. When he was asked to go on the wagon in order to set an example for young players, he readily agreed. But when he failed to collect a hit in an entire week, he was ordered to revert to old habits, and base hits barked again.

Throughout his incomparable career, Babe Ruth defied all dietary directives. Chocolate ice cream and pickled eels between games of a doubleheader never dimmed his effectiveness. A pint of bourbon with steak, eggs and hash browns for breakfast only served to fuel an afternoon of prodigious clouts.

They tippled in public and they tippled in private, much in the manner of those who made the turnstiles whirl, thereby producing the players with the handsome salaries that provided the means for excessive tastes.

They were human-the players, the managers, executives and umpires. The blacks, many of them denied the opportunity to enjoy major league acclaim, were great, famous and gifted in their own universe.

This volume is directed toward the humanizing of the immortals whose performances have illuminated all phases of baseball since its inception. They emerged on the national conscience as unknowns. For varying periods they flashed spectacularly. Some faded with dignity, others departed in tragedy.

Roberto Clemente perished on a mission of mercy just months after rapping his 3,000th hit. Lou Gehrig, the seemingly indestructible Iron Horse, was forced into retirement at age 36 by a disabling affliction that came to be known later as "Lou Gehrig's Disease." He died two years later.

Ed Delahanty plunged to his death through an open drawbridge and Addie Joss, in his prime, was cut down by tubercular meningitis. Ross Youngs, termed by his manager, John McGraw, as the finest outfielder of his experience, was cut down by Bright's disease when barely 30 years old.

Even in retirement, there were those who walked with misfortune. Baseball has known no more poignant a scene than Babe Ruth, racked by cancer, waving farewell to Yankee Stadium fans. Automobile accidents terminated too soon the lives of Mel Ott and Frisch. Foxx choked to death on a piece of meat at the dinner table.

Some died as princes, some as paupers. Ty Cobb enjoyed a millionaire's luxury because of investments in General Motors and Coca-Cola. Hack Wilson, the major-league RBI king, went to a penniless grave, clad in a suit and laid in a coffin donated by a charitable mortician.

They spanned the spectrum of humanity, these members of baseball's shrine. But, as different as they were in many respects, they were united in their mastery of and devotion to the game that made them celebrities for all time.

HANK AARON

The pressure was almost suffocating. Everywhere he went, cameras focused on him. Every step he took was followed by a coterie of newsmen that would have made an oil prince proud. Hank Aaron was living in a goldfish bowl, at center stage and under blinding spotlights.

Whether another public figure could have retained his composure under such circumstances is doubtful. Aaron was in methodical pursuit of Babe Ruth's lifetime major league home run record of 714, held sacred since the Babe's retirement in 1935, and the closer he drew to the mark the less privacy he enjoyed.

"The thing I'll always remember," said an Atlanta teammate, "is the way he handles himself. And something else, none of this has changed him."

The pressure on the Braves' outfielder started to build during the 1973 season when he clouted 40 home runs, climbing within two of breaking Ruth's all-time standard. Aaron was 39 and in his 20th major league season.

On the first swing of the next season, Aaron tied Ruth's mark by tagging a Jack Billingham pitch for a home run at Riverfront Stadium in Cincinnati. Aaron sat out the second game of the series, then failed to connect in the third game.

Braves officials, wanting Aaron to both equal and surpass Ruth's record at Atlanta Stadium, had at one point announced their intentions of holding Aaron out of the entire Cincinnati series. Overruled by Commissioner Bowie Kuhn, the Braves lost out on "hosting" No. 714 but retained a shot at No. 715 with a home-opening series coming up against Los Angeles.

And the man and the hour did meet in Atlanta Stadium -on April 8, 1974. In the fourth inning, with the outfield clock standing at 9:07 p.m., Aaron belted a pitch from AI Downing over the left-field fence and into the Braves' bullpen, where it was caught by reliever Tom House.

Pandemonium rounded the bases with Hammering Hank. After touching home plate, he trotted to a box seat where a female spectator clasped him in a bear hug. Later, among popping Champagne corks in the clubhouse, Aaron conceded: "I didn't know Mom was that strong."

Aaron hit 18 more home runs in 1974, but was not yet ready to call it a career. He returned to Milwaukee, where he had launched his magnificent big-league career in 1954, and served the American League Brewers for two years as an outfielder and designated hitter. He socked 22 more home runs for an overall total of 755.

A young, hopeful Henry Aaron handled second base duties for the Jacksonville Braves in 1953.

Aaron, a native of Mobile, Ala., was a skinny shortstop with Indianapolis in the Negro American League when he was discovered by Dewey Griggs, a scout for the Braves. For $10,000, the National League club acquired Aaron on June 14, 1952.

After two seasons as an infielder with Eau Claire of the Northern League and Jacksonville of the Sally League, Aaron won a regular outfield berth with the Braves in

Hank Aaron had plenty of company (above) as he rounded the bases for the record-breaking 715th time in his illustrious career on April 8, 1974, in Atlanta. Aaron finished his career in 1976 (left) with the Brewers in Milwaukee, site of many of his early-career exploits.

1954 when Bobby Thomson fractured an ankle during a spring exhibition game. Three years later, Hank was the league's Most Valuable Player, leading the Braves to a pennant and World Series upset over the New York Yankees.

Next to his home runs that tied and broke Ruth's record, Aaron's most satisfying hit may have been an infield single at Cincinnati on May 17, 1970. Before the largest Crosley Field crowd in 23 years, Aaron beat out a bouncer against Wayne Simpson in his first at-bat in the second game of a doubleheader.

With that safety, Aaron became the first major leaguer to collect 3,000 hits and 500 home runs.

As Aaron crossed the bag, a figure leaped over the fence behind first base and trotted toward the infield. It was Stan Musial, Aaron's boyhood idol and the only living member of the 3,000-hit club.

"It was getting awfully lonely," said The Man. "Congratulations, Henry."

The slugging outfielder would have preferred to hit a home run for his 3,000th hit. Ironically, he connected on his next at-bat. It was No. 570.

All-Star Game honors gravitated early to Aaron. At the finish, he had appeared in 24 midsummer classics, 23 for the National League and one for the American. Curiously, the career home run king clouted only two All-Star homers, his first in Detroit in 1971 and his second in Atlanta in 1972.

GROVER CLEVELAND ALEXANDER

In 79 years of World Series competition, there have been few dramatic moments to match what occurred on October 10, 1926, at Yankee Stadium.

With the bases loaded and two out in the seventh inning of Game 7 and the Yankees attempting to overcome a 3-2 St. Louis lead, a 39-year-old righthander shuffled out of the Cardinals' bullpen and struck out rookie slugger Tony Lazzeri.

The aged reliever, who had pitched the Cardinals to a Series-tying 10-2 victory the previous day, was Grover Cleveland Alexander-known familiarly as Old Pete or simply Alex.

For the remainder of the contest, the Yankees swung ineffectually at Old Pete's offerings. They failed to collect even one hit and when Babe Ruth was thrown out on an attempted steal to end the game, the righthander from St. Paul, Neb., was truly Alexander the Great in St. Louis.

Alexander joined the Phillies in 1911 after winning 29 games the previous year for Syracuse of the New York State League. Purchased by the National League club for $500, Alex was promised that he would earn $250 monthly with the Phils if he made the grade.

Alex hurled his first game for the Phils in a City Series exhibition contest with the defending world champion Athletics in bandbox Baker Bowl. "You'll pitch five innings," informed catcher Pat Moran. "They'll be murder, but you'll learn something."

The game proved more of a learning experience for the A's than for Alexander, however. In five innings, the 24 year-old rookie allowed no runs and no hits, nor did he walk a batter.

Alex was scheduled to make his regular-season debut in New York, but a fire that destroyed the grandstand at the Polo Grounds the night of April 13 caused the game to be postponed. He bowed in at Boston, losing 5-4 in 10 innings. Curiously, Old Pete pitched his final game in Boston 19 years later, hurling the last two innings of a 5-1 defeat that was charged to the Phils' Phil Collins.

After his initial setback in Boston, Alexander won 28 games in 1911 to establish a modern major league rookie record that still stands. He lost 13 games overall that season.

One of the most distinguished efforts of his freshman season was a 12-inning marathon against Cy Young, who at age 44 was pitching his final major league game. Young, trying for his 512th victory, struggled through 11 scoreless innings before the Phils touched the Boston veteran for the game's only run.

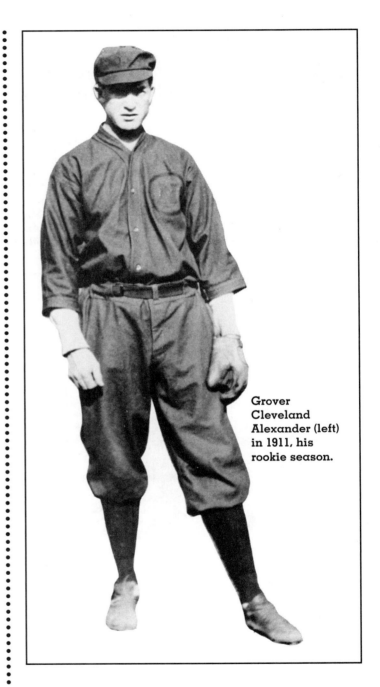

Grover Cleveland Alexander (left) in 1911, his rookie season.

Alex enjoyed his finest overall season in 1915 when he compiled a 31-10 record and a 1.22 earnedrun average. Despite the short dimensions of his home park, Alexander registered 12 shutouts.

In the opening game of the 1915 World Series at Baker Bowl, Alex scattered eight hits and defeated the Boston Red Sox, 3-1.

On May 22, 1926, Alexander (above, shaking hands) was honored by the Cubs. Just over a month later, he was waived to, St. Louis after repeated run-ins with Manager Joe McCarthy. Alexander (below) was sent to France in 1918 as a member of the 89th Infantry Division.

Alexander's best season was 1915, when he finished 31-10 with a league-leading 1.22 ERA for the Phillies.

Old Pete chalked up 33 victories (including 16 shutouts) in 1916 and 30 in 1917 for a three-year total of 94.

Despite his valiant efforts, the Phils were runners-up in both the 1916 and 1917 pennant races.

In 1917, Alexander hurled a Labor Day doubleheader in Brooklyn, winning the opener, 5-0, and taking the nightcap, 9-3.

Shortly after the close of the season, Alex, at his Nebraska home, read in the daily papers that he and catcher Bill Killefer had been traded to the Chicago Cubs for two players and $60,000.

After pitching only three games at the start of the 1918 season, Alex joined the Army and was sent to France where he served as an artillery sergeant. When he returned home, Alex was a changed man; he suffered fits of epilepsy throughout the remainder of his life.

Alexander won 27 games one season with the Cubs and 22 in another. On June 22, 1926, Alexander was waived to the Cardinals. He had run afoul of Chicago Manager Joe McCarthy with excessive drinking habits stemming from his epilepsy.

Alex, who posted 21 victories for St. Louis in 1927, tried to recapture some of his old magic in Game 2 of the 1928 World Series. But he yielded six hits and four walks in $2\frac{1}{3}$ innings against the Yanks, and was charged with a 9-3 defeat. Relieving in the fourth and final game, Alex gave up four hits in $2\frac{2}{3}$ innings.

WALTER ALSTON

Walter Alston's only major league plate appearance came at the end of the 1936 season when he batted against the Cubs at Sportsman's Park.

Speculation ran wild on the identity of the new Brooklyn manager. When media people crowded into the Dodger offices on Montague Street on November 24, 1953, the popular candidate was shortstop Pee Wee Reese, who had declined the post once before.

When the door to the inner sanctum swung open, President Walter O'Malley, seated at his desk, pointed to a balding stranger at his side and announced: "This is Walter Alston. I've hired him as my manager to beat the Yankees next season."

Alston succeeded Chuck Dressen, who had failed to defeat the Yankees in the 1952 and '53 World Series. Dressen also had demanded a multi-year contract to pilot the Dodgers. Such a practice was foreign to O'Malley's policies and Dressen was deposed.

Alston, sometimes known as Smokey because of the fastball he displayed as a youthful pitcher, was a virtual unknown. Even in his little hometown of Darrtown, OH, he was not a familiar figure.

A graduate of Miami (OH) University and an off-season science teacher and basketball coach, Alston appeared in one major league game, for the Cardinals, on the final day of the 1936 season. In his only at-bat, he struck out against Lon Warneke of the Cubs. In two chances at first base, he committed one error.

Alston did not appear in a major league uniform again until opening day of 1954 when the Dodgers, despite two home runs by Roy Campanella, lost to the Giants, 4-3.

In the 18-year interim, Walter completed his playing career (at Pueblo in 1947) and launched his managerial career (at Portsmouth, OH, in 1940).

In 1947, Neal Hobbs, general manager of Pueblo (Western), conferred with Branch Rickey, then the Mahatma of Montague Street, over a manager for the Class A club. After a dramatic contemplation, Rickey removed the cigar from his mouth and announced, "I'm going to give you Walter Alston as your manager."

"Who is Walter Alston?" asked Hobbs.

"Alston is the man we're grooming to manage the Dodgers someday," advised Rickey, who had moved on to the Pittsburgh Pirates before Walter arrived in Flatbush.

By 1950, Alston was manager of the Montreal Royals. He had engraved impressive records at every stop, and Montreal was no exception. He won pennants in 1951 and 1952 and, after finishing second the next year, his Royals defeated Buffalo and Rochester in the '53 International League playoffs before beating Kansas City, a Yankee farm club, in the Junior World Series.

A direct opposite to Dressen, his pepperpot predecessor, the strong and unemotional Alston spoke little. He conducted no pep rallies, engaged in no dramatic confrontations with umpires.

Alston did not make a show of discipline, but enforced it in his own style. When Don Newcombe refused to pitch batting practice, Alston ordered him to remove his uniform and leave the park. Newk was back a day later, minus several hundred dollars in penalties and lost pay.

Alston did not win the pennant in 1954, but he finished first in 1955 and followed with a dramatic World Series conquest of the Yankees that gave Brooklyn its only world title. His Dodgers repeated as league champions in '56. When the Dodgers transferred to Los Angeles in 1958 and Walter's "Boys of Summer" were past their prime, Alston fell to seventh. He rebounded in '59, however, guiding the Dodgers to a World Series title over the White Sox.

The Quiet Man never gloated in victory, nor bled in defeat. Unemotionally, he conducted postgame interviews regardless of the fortunes of the day. When the Dodgers lost a heartbreaking third game in the 1962 playoffs to the Giants, Alston answered inquiries outside the clubhouse while protecting his players from the press.

Working always on one-year contracts, Alston won seven pennants and four World Series titles in 23 years.

On September 27, 1976, Walter announced his retirement. Only Connie Mack and John McGraw had managed one club for a longer time.

GEORGE "SPARKY" ANDERSON

George "Sparky" Anderson wasn't much of a player. But he was an all-time great as a manager. A .218 hitter for the Phillies in 1959 (his lone major league season as a player), Anderson turned to managing five years later and embarked on a career that established him as the only man to guide teams from both the National League and American League to World Series crowns. In Anderson's 26 years as a big-league manager, his teams won five pennants and three Series championships and had a stretch of 17 consecutive winning seasons.

The son of a house painter, Anderson grew up in the Los Angeles area and learned to play baseball from his father and uncle. Rod Dedeaux, coach at the University of Southern California and bound for greatness as the Trojans' field leader, also helped out by making young Anderson batboy for his team. Anderson, a middle infielder, played ball at Dorsey High School before signing with the Brooklyn Dodgers organization in 1953. He spent six seasons in the Dodgers' system—the last three in Class AAA—and won praise as a good-fielding second baseman with competent offensive skills.

Traded to the Phillies in December 1958, Anderson won the Phils' second base job the next spring. Still steady afield, he was overmatched by big-league pitching in '59. He had only 12 extra-base hits for Philadelphia in 152 games and played himself out of the majors, never to return as a player.

Anderson spent the next four seasons as the second baseman for Class AAA Toronto, then at age 30 was handed the managerial reins of the International League club in 1964. He managed in the minors for five seasons overall, capping his run with a Southern League pennant at Asheville in 1968. He then took a coaching position in 1969 with the expansion San Diego Padres under manager Preston Gomez. Anderson's stay in San Diego was a short one. He was named manager of the Reds after the '69 season—and made an immediate impact. Cincinnati won 102 regular-season games and the National League pennant in 1970, only to lose to the Orioles in the World Series. Two years later, Anderson's Reds swept to another N.L. pennant, this time falling to the A's in the Fall Classic. But make no mistake: Anderson had most of the key parts of his Big Red Machine in place. Those parts included Johnny Bench, Pete Rose, Joe Morgan and Tony Perez.

By 1975, Anderson had put together a true juggernaut, one that rolled to 108 regular-season victories (the Reds won the N.L. West race by 20 games) and a seven-game World Series triumph over the Red Sox. The 1976 Reds won 102 games and wiped out the Yankees in four straight in the Series. Having won 502 games from 1972 through 1976, Cincinnati appeared primed for continued domination. But the Reds "slumped" to second-place divisional finishes in 1977 and 1978, and Anderson was let go as manager in a stunning move.

Known for his prematurely gray hair, mangling of the English language and ability to win baseball games at an amazing rate, Anderson wasn't out of the dugout for long. He spent some time as a broadcaster before resurfacing in June 1979 as manager of the Tigers. In five years, he had Detroit on top of the baseball world.

Anderson's 1984 Tigers got off to a 35-5 start, won 104 regular-season American League games, swept the Royals in the playoffs and then dismantled the Padres in five games in the World Series. Sparky's key players were Kirk Gibson, Jack Morris, Alan Trammell and Lou Whitaker.

Anderson won only one more divisional title, in 1987, and he retired after the 1995 season with a glittering career record. He wound up with 2,194 regular-season victories as a major league manager, trailing only legendary Connie Mack and John McGraw, and was inducted into the Baseball Hall of Fame in 2000.

Sparky Anderson, who managed Cincinnati's Big Red Machine powerhouse, is the only man to direct teams from both leagues to World Series titles.

CAP ANSON

The first of baseball's superstars, Cap Anson compiled impressive batting statistics whether pitchers threw from 45 feet, or 50 feet, or 60 feet, 6 inches.

The first baseman for Chicago's National League club was the first player to collect 3,000 hits in his career, the first to hit three consecutive home runs in a game, the first to clout five home runs in two consecutive games and the first to rap four doubles in a single contest. As a first baseman, he also was the first to complete two unassisted double plays in one game.

The reflexes of the 6-foot-1, righthanded hitter were so quick, it was said, that he never was hit by a pitched ball —no matter what the pitching distance.

Legend attributes to Anson the honor of being the first white child born in Marshalltown, LA. As a teenager, Anson played with his father and brother on a town team that was the scourge of the state.

In 1869, Anson attended Notre Dame and is generally credited with organizing the university's first baseball team. He was a third baseman and captain.

Anson played five years with the Athletics of the National Association before shifting to the Chicago club —the White Stockings—of the fledgling N.L. in 1876. He was a third baseman and batted .343 for the first N.L. championship team.

Anson played the outfield and second base and also caught before concentrating on first base in 1879, the year he commenced his 19-year reign as manager of the team.

Cap was "neither the greatest, nor the most agile first baseman," one historian wrote. "Anson played only a few feet from the base and fresh, young Chicago infielders would throw the ball low to first so as to further bark his bruised shins.

"They enjoyed seeing him squirm, but Cap seemingly swallowed liberal doses from the Fountain of Youth and at times it looked as though he would go on forever . . . Fans in Chicago loved him and rooted for him whenever he came to bat. He also brought out the customers on the road, so they could root against him."

Anson won four batting championships, twice with averages over .400 and once with a .399 mark, and he managed the Chicagoans to pennants in 1880, 1881, 1882, 1885 and 1886.

Cap, also known as "Pop" before he stepped down as Chicago manager after the 1897 season, is frequently credited with being the father of spring training. In 1886, Anson shepherded his players to Hot Springs, Ark., to "boil out" after a winter of loading and swilling beer as hometown heroes.

Major league baseball's original superstar was Cap Anson, the first player to amass 3,000 career hits and to hit three consecutive home runs in one game.

Anson also pioneered inside baseball, coordinating infield and outfield play and originating other scientific maneuvers quickly adopted by other clubs. A powerful figure himself, he showed the way in slugging for a purpose, not merely to drive the ball out of the park. At the plate, he stood with heels together and swung probably the heaviest bat of all time.

After leaving the Chicago club, Anson accepted an invitation to manage the Giants during the 1898 season. After three weeks, however, he quit. Anson said he couldn't accede to Owner Andrew Freedman's directives on the use of his personnel, nor could he accept a ban on talking to newspapermen.

Anson died in 1922, shortly after being appointed manager of a new golf club.

LUIS APARICIO

By the mid-1960s, Luis Aparicio was one of baseball's top shortstops and performing his magic for the Orioles.

In major league baseball's first 110 years, few players, regardless of position, were accorded accolades so generously as was Luis Ernesto Aparicio, whose 18-year major league career consisted of American League stops at Chicago, Baltimore and Boston.

Observers competed constantly for superlatives to describe the skills of the diminutive shortstop from Venezuela.

Marty Marion, "Mr. Shortstop" of the 1940s and Luis' first major league manager, readily conceded that Aparicio's talents exceeded his own. "He must be better," Marion asserted. "He covers twice as much ground as I did."

Casey Stengel, manager of the Yankees, added this tribute: "If that kid gets any better you might as well call in the second baseman and third baseman because he gobbles up everything within a mile of him."

Not long after Luis was named the American League's Rookie of the Year in 1956 for his .266 batting average and fielding brilliance with the White Sox, a 50-year observer of the major leagues added further praise.

"That kid is the greatest shortstop of all time," said Donie Bush, who had seen them all since the heyday of Honus Wagner. "What makes Aparicio so outstanding are his lightning reflexes. They're the greatest I've ever seen. He breaks fast and is so quick with his hands that his glove is right there no matter how erratic or sharp the ball may hop."

In Luis' prime it was not uncommon for fans to arrive at the park in time for fielding practice and to cheer wildly when Aparicio defied a coach's effort to drive a baseball past him.

The name of Aparicio was familiar to Venezuelans long before Luis was born. For 25 years his father reigned as the foremost shortstop in the country. He retired only when his son shoved him aside.

Reports of the teenage wonder filtered northward in the early 1950s and touched off a heated contest for his services. The White Sox won the bidding over the Cleveland Indians when Chicago General Manager Frank Lane advised his agent in Venezuela, "Tell the owners of the team (the Venezuelan club for which Aparicio was playing winter ball) that we'll send no more players down there if we don't get Aparicio."

The strategy worked, although by 1957 Lane had cause for regret. By the time Luis had completed his two-year apprenticeship at Waterloo (Three-I League) and Memphis (Southern Association) and was making breathtaking plays for the White Sox, Lane, the newly

Luis Aparicio's consistent bat and baserunning abilities sparked the Chicago White Sox for many years and he combined with second baseman Nellie Fox (left) to form a potent double-play combination.

appointed front-office chief of the Indians, was bemoaning his earlier success.

White Sox executives realized early that they possessed an extraordinary prospect in the 5-foot-8, 155-pound Aparicio. Conversations with officials of other teams invariably contained the query: "What will you take for that kid shortstop at Memphis?"

That "kid shortstop" was an immediate sensation on the South Side of Chicago. When the Sox blossomed as the "Go-Go" team of the majors, it was Aparicio who led them on the basepaths.

When the White Sox broke the Yankees' four-year grip on the A.L. pennant in 1959, Aparicio stole 56 bases, one of nine consecutive seasons he led the league in steals. In the World Series, won by the Los Angeles Dodgers in six games, Luis batted .308 with seven singles and a double.

In 1966, when the Orioles swept the Dodgers in the Series, Aparicio fielded virtually flawlessly for Baltimore and batted .250.

As a youngster, Luis worked diligently to polish his skills as a fielder and it was not until he achieved major league stardom that he devoted hours to improving his hitting. Dividends followed almost instantly. From a previous high mark of .277, attained in 1960, Luis climbed to .280 in 1969 and contended for the A.L. batting title for much of the 1970 season before finishing at .313.

A year later, however, Aparicio's batting touch was gone. In one stretch with his new club, the Red Sox, Luis went hitless in 44 at-bats. When the slump ended with a single, Fenway Park fans gave Aparicio a standing ovation.

Several days later a letter, written on White House stationery, was dropped into Luis' mailbox. In it, President Richard Nixon complimented Aparicio on his gentlemanly conduct during the hitless period and expressed gratitude for the countless thrills he had provided the chief executive through the years.

The nation's fans took little note of Aparicio's batting deficiencies in '71 and voted him a starting berth in that summer's All-Star Game, one of 10 appearances Luis made in the midsummer classic.

Aparicio was 39 when he called it a career at the close of the 1973 campaign. Even at that advanced stage he was able to bat .271.

LUKE APPLING

In his heyday as a shortstop for the Chicago White Sox, Luke Appling possessed perhaps the sharpest eye among major league batters.

He could foul off pitches almost at will, as the club secretary discovered on the day that he refused Luke's request for two new baseballs to give to admirers. "They cost $2.75 apiece," chided the secretary.

Appling held his tongue in disappointment, but the first time he came to bat that afternoon he worked the count to 3-and-2 and then fouled 10 pitches into the stands.

Looking toward the secretary sitting in a box seat, Appling shouted, "That's $27.50, and I'm just getting started."

Before he finished, the story goes, Appling distributed 23 souvenirs throughout the stands.

If Appling wasn't slicing baseballs into the stands, he was complaining about aches and pains that never seemed to forsake him. For years, he answered to "Old Aches and Pains," but the chief sufferers of his many, fancied maladies were opposing pitchers who felt the sting of Luke's bat.

Appling was a sophomore—and a three-sport star—at Oglethorpe University in Atlanta, with no intention of turning professional, when he suddenly found himself the shortstop for the Atlanta Crackers of the Southern Association in 1930. Before the end of the summer, he ws acquired by the White Sox, with whom he played through 1950 (except for nearly two years of service in World War II).

The .310 lifetime hitter once declared that he owed his prowess as a batter to Lefty Grove, the hardthrowing lefthander of the Philadelphia A's.

In his first at-bat against Grove, Appling recalled, a high inside pitch nearly struck him. I decided then," Appling noted, "that anybody who can duck away from his fastball doesn't have to worry about being beaned."

Luke's hitting accomplishments, which included two American League batting championships, were once attributed to his "studied carelessness" and the following incident was cited:

One day, while lounging around the batting cage, Appling noticed Bill Dickey of the Yankees draw his hand across his shirt in a gesture to his batterymate of the day. Luke interpreted the maneuver as a sign to pitch Appling inside.

On his first at-bat, Appling fell back from an inside change-up and doubled down the left-field line. Luke was a notorious right-field hitter for a righthanded batter.

Luke Appling's batting stroke was still producing base hits in the late 1940s (above), but the 75-year-old former shortstop displayed a new dimension to his game in 1982 when he muscled up and hit a ball out of RFK Stadium during the Cracker Jack Old Timers Baseball Classic.

On his next trip, Appling watched a fastball go by, then belted the second pitch, also a change-up, into the leftfield stands.

When the bewildered pitcher later asked Appling if he had stolen the Yankees' signs, the shortstop replied:

"Tell Dickey to keep his hands in his pocket or conduct his meetings in the clubhouse."

In his 17th year with the White Sox, Appling was tendered a day at Comiskey Park.

During his major league career, Appling hit only 45 home runs. However, in the Cracker Jack Old Timers Baseball Classic, played at Robert F. Kennedy Memorial Stadium in Washington in 1982, the 75-year-old Appling drove a Warren Spahn pitch over the fence to feature a 7-2 A.L. victory.

RICHIE ASHBURN

Richie Ashburn was considered one of the great outfielders of all-time, but he could hit, too. He finished with a .308 career average.

Most rookies reporting to spring training are content to remain in the background, hoping they get enough opportunity to impress the manager but being realistic enough to know how much of a chance they have to win a starting position.

When Richie Ashburn arrived at spring training as a rookie for the Phillies in 1948, he was not at all sure of what to expect. He was a centerfielder, and the incumbent at that position, Harry "the hat" Walker, had won the NL batting title the previous season by a margin of 46 points.

Not one to be easily intimidated, Ashburn took advantage of an opening when Walker fouled a ball off his foot one day, an injury that kept him out of the lineup through May. By then, Ashburn was hitting .346 and had become the Phillie's centerfielder, a position he would hold for the next 12 years.

The only rookie voted to the 1948 All-Star game, Ashburn responded with two singles and a stolen base. A broken finger suffered in August did little to mar a rookie season that included a 23-game hitting streak (the rookie record which stood until 1987), a .333 average, 32 stolen bases and recognition as the NL's Rookie of the Year. Walker became expendable, and found himself playing for the Cubs in 1949.

Ashburn's rookie campaign was an indication of what kind of player he would be during his 15-year career. Born in Tilden, Neb., in 1927, the 5-10, 175-pound Ashburn, who hit lefthanded and threw right, became an impact player on both offense and defense.

A prototype leadoff hitter, Ashburn did not hit for power. Only 29 of his career 2,574 hits were homers (in 2,189 games), and his season high of seven came in his final year, 1962, when he played for the expansion Mets in the Polo Grounds and he became the team's inaugural All-Star selection. What Ashburn did was figure out a way to get on base; his career onbase percentage was .397 and six times he topped the .400 mark, leading the league four times.

Critics once said of Ashburn's offense, "He's not hitting .333, he's hitting .133 and running .200 and there was some truth to that statement. A lifetime .308 hitter—better than the career averages of Pete Rose, Willie Mays and Hank Aaron, to name only a few—produced nine .300 or better seasons. Only in two years did his average drop below .282, On one memoral day, May 20 , 1951, Ashburn reeled off eight singles in a doubleheader.

Ashburn won two batting titles, hitting .338 in 1955 and a career-high .350 in 1958. He finished second in the batting race three other times, and three times led the league in hits, collecting 221 hits in 1951, 205 in 1953 and 215 in 1958. He also led the NL in walks four times, including a career-best of 125 in 1954.

Equipped with an excellent eye at the plate and good patience, Ashburn never struck out more than 50 times in a season in which he was coming to bat 500 or more times.

Ashburn, whose nickname Whitey was placed on him because of his light-colored hair, also used his running speed to his full advantage. He twice led the league in triples, and stole 234 bases in his career, topped by his rookie mark of 32.

Ashburn still holds the Phillies' team record for most consecutive games played, 731.

Ashburn was just as good and exciting a player on defense as he was offensively, and it was in the field that perhaps the biggest single highlight of his career occured.

The Phillies led the Dodgers by one game in the standings going into the final day of the 1950 season, when the two teams met at Ebbets Field in Brooklyn. The score was tied 1-1 in the bottom of the ninth when Cal Abrams of the Dodgers tried to score from second on a single to center by Duke Snider. Ashburn's throw cut him down by 20 feet, setting the stage for teammate Dick Sisler's homer in the 10th which clinched the pennant for the Phillies, their first title in 35 years.

On defense, Ashburn set records by recording 500 or more putouts four times and topped the 400-mark in putouts in nine seasons. He is tied with Max Carey for leading the majors in putouts nine times and ranks fifth among outfielders for all-time putouts and total chances.

The 1950 Whiz Kids' success marked Ashburn's only appearance in the World Series and it turned out to be a major disappointment as the Phillies were swept by the Yankees and Ashburn was just 3-for-17, a .176 average. Selected for five All-Star games, he played with the Phillies through 1960, when he was traded to the Cubs.

Quick on his feet, Ashburn twice led the National League in triples and had 234 career stolen bases.

He played two years in Chicago, then joined the Mets for their inaugural year in 1962.

Completing his playing career, Ashburn quickly moved into the broadcast booth for the Phillies in 1963. He remained there, a fan favorite in Philadelphia for 35 consecutive years until his death in 1997. He was elected to the Hall of Fame in 1995.

EARL AVERILL

No American League player had hit a home run in his first major league plate appearance until April 16, 1929. On that date, Cleveland's Earl Averill connected against Earl Whitehill, a crafty Detroit lefthander.

Averill had been acquired from the San Francisco Seals of the Pacific Coast League several months earlier. Billy Evans, general manager of the Indians, visited the West Coast to scout Roy Johnson, a teammate of Averill and more highly regarded as a major league prospect.

The longer Evans watched Johnson, the better he liked Averill. "There was something about the nonchalant Averill that won you over," Evans said. I guess it was the easy, steady manner in which he did his work, without any great show."

The Indians took an option to purchase both outfielders. However, when Evans learned that the Tigers had offered $65,000 and two players for Johnson, he waived his option and bought Averill for $50,000.

Johnson proved a solid major leaguer, posting a lifetime batting average of .296. Averill, though, was an immediate star. And Earl compiled a .318 career average.

That initial home run remained Averill's foremost thrill throughout his 13-year major league career—no other Hall of Famer has homered in his first big-

league plate appearance—but there were other remarkable achievements. Averill hit for the cycle at Philadelphia in 1933, and on September 17, 1930, he clouted four home runs in a doubleheader against Washington, three in one contest, and drove in 11 runs in the twin bill.

Earl was irked at day's end after the three-homer game. After all, he had just missed a record-tying fourth homer in the game when a long drive curved foul.

In 1931, Averill drove in seven runs in one contest, hit two home runs in a game three times and hit for a total of 10 bases twice and eight bases four times.

It is little wonder that on August 2, 1931, Boston pitchers decided that discretion was the better part of their repertoire and walked the lefthanded-hitting slugger all five times he appeared at the plate.

Averill played in five All-Star Games and numbered a double and a triple among his four hits. But the most-remembered All-Star play involving Averill did not include a hit.

In the 1937 classic at Washington's Griffith Stadium, Earl slammed a pitch from Dizzy Dean off the St. Louis hurler's foot. Attempting a comeback before the foot was healed completely, Dean put an unnatural strain on his arm, ending his career prematurely.

Averill, a product of Snohomish, Wash., a sawmill town in the big timber country, was named to Cleveland's alltime outfield in baseball's centennial year of 1969 along with Tris Speaker and Shoeless Joe Jackson.

Cleveland's Earl Averill crosses the plate after a Red Ruffing single during a six-run fifth inning for the American League during the 1934 All-Star Game at the Polo Grounds. Averill had reached base with a two-run double.

HOME RUN BAKER

As a major leaguer, John Franklin Baker hit 96 career home runs, a reasonably good three-year total for a latterday slugger, but hardly the kind of figure to inspire a nickname of "Home Run." But homers on successive days in the 1911 World Series did earn Baker such a sobriquet.

The Philadelphia A's third baseman rapped 11 home runs in the dead-ball season of 1911. The total was good enough to lead the American League, but incapable of stirring the public. What Baker accomplished on October 16th and 17th, though, caught the fans' fancy.

The Giants won the Series opener and the teams were deadlocked in the sixth inning of Game 2 when Baker walloped a Rube Marquard fastball over the right-field wall in Philadelphia to account for a 3-1 victory.

The next day's New York newspapers featured a column by Christy Mathewson in which the Giants' ace criticized Marquard for the way he pitched to Baker. That afternoon, when Matty was within two outs of a 1-0 shutout, Baker homered into the right-field seats at the Polo Grounds and the A's went on to win, 3-2, in 11 innings. From that day forward, the Maryland farm boy was known as Home Run Baker.

Baker was a member of one of baseball's most illustrious units, the "$100,000 infield," which included Jack Barry, Eddie Collins and Stuffy McInnis.

In six World Series, Baker batted .363, compared with his regular-season lifetime mark of .307. He was devastating in the 1913 Series when he batted .450 and clouted another homer off Marquard.

After the A's four-game debacle at the hands of the Miracle Boston Braves in 1914, a Series in which Baker batted only .250, Owner-Manager Connie Mack didn't offer Baker a raise and the Philadelphia slugger sat out the 1915 A.L. season (playing semipro ball in Upland, Pa.). The following February, Baker was traded to the Yankees, for whom he appeared in the 1921 and 1922

Home Run Baker, who hit only 96 career homers, was a member of the Philadelphia A's in 1912.

Series (after voluntarily retiring in 1920 and again playing for Upland).

Aside from his home runs in 1911, Baker is remembered as the Yankee whose sharply hit grounder between first and second base was converted into a 4-3-5 double play by the Giants that wrapped up the 1921 Series.

Although no gazelle, "Home Run" posted impressive stolen-base totals of 38 in 1911, 40 in 1912 and 34 in 1913.

Baker joined the A's late in the 1908 season at the conclusion of the Reading (Tri-State) campaign. He encountered Mack in the dining room of a Chicago hotel and announced: "Mr. Mack, I'm here."

"I see that you are," was the terse rebuttal.

To Baker's dismay, he discovered that Ed Walsh, the formidable spitballer, was scheduled to pitch that day's game. But Baker did not remain dismayed for long. "I fouled off a pitch, then Walsh threw me a ball, then I doubled over Fielder Jones' head in left field," Baker said.

Toughened by years of toil, Baker yielded to no intimidator. One year, when Ty Cobb slid into third base with spikes high, Baker went after the fiery Tiger and precipitated a near riot at Shibe Park. The A's and Tigers were deadly enemies thereafter.

Despite his differences with Mack in 1915, Baker remembered his old manager in 1924 when he spotted a burly, 17-year-old catcher in Maryland.

Mack was not instantly impressed. "We have enough catching," Connie told Baker.

"Play him anywhere," responded the old third baseman. "He has more power than anyone I've ever seen, inclucling Babe Ruth."

Mack agreed to take a look, then several more. The prodigy was Jimmie Foxx, who hit 534 home runs in the majors.

Baker retired from the major leagues after the 1922 season. He managed briefly for Easton (Eastern Shore) and later served a one-year stint as president of the club.

He died in 1963 at age 77 after suffering a series of strokes.

DAVE BANCROFT

No shortstop, it was said, was better than Dave Bancroft at fielding bad-hop ground balls or cutting off outfield throws and hanging up runners between bases.

On all-time, all-star teams of the first half of the 20th century, Honus Wagner was the choice at shortstop. Bancroft ranked second—and only because the Flying Dutchman was a superior hitter.

As a rookie in 1915, Bancroft sparked the Phillies to their first National League pennant. He made the difference between the sixth-place club of 1914 and the pennant-winning performance of a year later, insisted Manager Pat Moran.

Bancroft, known as "Beauty" because of his superlative play, spent five years with the Phillies before Giants Manager John McGraw decided in June of 1920 that he needed Bancroft on his club.

The Polo Grounders, beaten out for the 1919 flag by the Cincinnati Reds, were deep in the second division after two months of the '20 race. Moreover, the Yankees were packing 'em in with their new hitting sensation, Babe Ruth, while the Giants were playing before expanses of empty seats.

At McGraw's suggestion, Giants President Charles Stoneharn telephoned William F. Baker, president of the Phillies, and offered aging shortstop Art Fletcher, young pitcher Wilbur Hubbell and $100,000 for Bancroft. Baker was incredulous. No would-be trader had made such an extravagant offer in the immediate postwar period.

Baker hesitated to ask Stoneham to repeat the offer for fear it would be different the second time around. Stoneham demanded an answer, until Baker finally found his tongue and said: "I'll take the 9 o'clock train tomorrow and will be in your office at 11, when we can discuss the trade."

Good as his word, Baker, accompanied by the National League attorney as a witness, was in Stoneham's office on schedule and the deal was completed.

While the Giants failed to win the 1920 pennant with Bancroft in the ranks, they captured the next three flags with Dave at shortstop.

The new acquisition already had taken his position in the field for his first game as a Giant when catcher Pancho Snyder summoned Bancroft to a conference on the mound. "Maybe I should explain our signs to you," Snyder volunteered.

"Why, have they changed?" replied Bancroft. "If not, I know them already." Having mastered the system while with the Phils, Dave clearly was McGraw's type of brainy player.

Dave Bancroft was a hopeful youngster in 1909 when he played shortstop for Duluth-Superior.

One day in 1923 Bancroft reported to the Polo Grounds with a high fever, but insisted on playing. At game's end he collapsed in the clubhouse and the team physician was summoned. "Call an ambulance," the doctor ordered, "this man has pneumonia."

"Imagine," marveled McGraw, "he played nine innings with pneumonia."

Despite his extreme admiration for Bancroft, McGraw agreed to trade him after the 1923 season so that Dave could manage the Boston Braves.

Through no fault of his own, but because the club was lacking in talent, Bancroft failed to inspire the Braves to great heights. After four seasons, he was dismissed by Judge Emil Fuchs, the club owner.

Bancroft caught on with the Brooklyn Dodgers for a couple years before returning to the Giants as a coach under McGraw. Whenever Little Napoleon was indisposed, Bancroft handled the managerial chores without loss of effectiveness. But his future as a Giant was sealed when McGraw retired in June of 1932. Dave finished the year under new Manager Bill Terry, then departed.

Bancroft briefly managed Minneapolis in the American Association and guided clubs in the low minors in his native Midwest before retiring to pursue his favorite pastimes, hunting and fishing.

ERNIE BANKS

When the Chicago Cubs acquired Ernie Banks from the Kansas City Monarchs in 1953, they obtained more than a highly promising prospect. They acquired one of baseball's foremost good-will ambassadors.

In 19 years of major league competition, the shortstop-first baseman never lost his youthful enthusiasm, proclaiming regularly, "It's a great day for baseball, let's play two."

Banks could well appreciate the bounties derived from big-time baseball. He succeeded the hard way, through Negro league ball in which his salary was based on a percentage of the gate. "The most I ever got was $20 for a game in Hastings, Neb.," he recalled.

The Cubs bought Banks and a long-forgotten pitcher for about $25,000, but other clubs were well aware of the potential contained in the lithe and limber 22-year-old.

The White Sox made serious inquiries about Banks, but were unable to pin down Monarchs Owner Tom Baird on a price. Their ardor cooled when Banks, performing in a Negro all-star contest at Comiskey Park, failed to distinguish himself.

On the day that Banks donned a Cubs uniform for the first time, the club knew it had something special. Ernie walloped the first batting-practice pitch into the left-field bleachers at Wrigley Field, and never changed the tempo thereafter.

Before long, one American League executive said: "If I were permitted to pick one player out of the National League, it would be Banks."

Other experts hailed Banks for his good hands, his deadly aim and his ability to smother bad hops. "And how many shortstops can hit you a home run in the clutch?" asked Mel Ott, Hall of Fame outfielder.

In his second full season with the Cubs, Banks blasted 44 home runs. His most productive year in homers was 1958 when he socked 47 of his career total of 512.

Early in his career, Banks played 717 consecutive games, but removed himself from the lineup for fear that the pressures would jeopardize his career. He was shifted to first base in 1961 when an ailing knee reduced his mobility.

Mr. Cub, who did not play high school baseball because his Dallas alma mater did not field a team, was coveted frequently by rival clubs. One offer of $500,000 by the Cardinals received a flat "No" from Cubs Owner P.K. Wrigley.

One of Banks' more memorable days occurred on May 12, 1970, when he became the ninth member of the 500

The booming bat of Ernie Banks produced 512 career homers, but never was enough to carry the Cubs to a pennant.

homer club. The milestone was reached against Atlanta's Pat Jarvis in the second inning of a 4-3 Chicago victory.

During a standing ovation, Banks let his thoughts drift back to his first homer, a blast off Gerry Staley in St. Louis on September 20, 1953.

Throughout his career, which ended in 1971, Ernie was highly respected for his even temperament. But there was a time, in 1959, when he accused an opponent of deliberately hitting him with a pitch. It was the third time during the season that Jack Sanford of San Francisco had nicked Banks and he was angry enough to announce on a postgame radio show that "his control is too good for him to have to do that."

While still at the height of his career, the Cubs' star tried his hand at politics, running as a Republican against the incumbent Eighth Ward alderman in Chicago. Ernie was soundly trounced, but not bitter. He consoled himself with the assurance that he had finished second which, at the time, was higher than the Cubs had finished during his career.

Banks approaches the plate and tips his hat to the Wrigley Field crowd (right) after hitting home run No. 500 in 1970. Number 14's defensive play (below) matched his hitting prowess and Banks was rewarded in 1982 by becoming the first Cub to have his uniform retired (above).

AL BARLICK

Al Barlick was probably the most colorful umpire of his era.

Bill Klern was baseball's greatest umpire in the first half of the 20th century. However, in one instance, his ability to judge umpiring talent was just as great as his ability to call balls and strikes.

In the late 1930s, as his own illustrious career as a National League umpire was winding down, Klem was asked by league president Warren Giles to give his assessment of Albert Joseph Barlick, then a young umpire working in the minor leagues.

"This boy Barlick has a love of his work, a pride in it," Klem said. "I know he has the physical qualifications.

"He'll be the best umpire baseball's ever had."

Klem's opinion was astonishing, especially since he had given it without ever having seen Barlick work a game. He had merely spoken with the youngster about their common line of work.

Based in no small part on Klem's recommendation, Barlick was hired by the N.L. in September 1940 as a full-time member of the league's umpiring staff. At age 25, he became the youngest arbiter in baseball history. Ironically, Barlick eventually became the league's replacement for Klem, who was forced to end his own 37-year career because of a knee injury after the 1941 season.

The son of a Springfield, Ill, coal miner, Barlick seemed destined for a life spent in the Illinois mines before a miners' strike in the mid-1930s steered his career

path into a decidedly different direction. Barlick, who had dropped out of school a few years earlier to work in the mines to help support his family, began umpiring semi-pro games in and around the Springfield area to make a little money during the work stoppage. Although he had played a little baseball himself, Barlick's decision to umpire games and not play in them was easy: the umpires were paid $1 per game; the players often weren't paid at all.

The man who operated the Springfield leagues, John Rossiter, was so impressed by Barlick's work that he recommended the 20-year-old youngster to Joe Bertig, then president of the Northeast Arkansas League. Barlick worked in the NAL in 1936 before moving on to the Piedmont (1937), Eastern ('38) and International ('39) leagues in later years. He was working in the International League at the time he was brought up to the National League in 1940.

And once Barlick arrived on the big-league scene, there would be no going back.

"The players up here are more experienced, easier to get along with, and the conditions are much better," he said in his rookie campaign.

Of course, that would not always be the case. Like most umpires, Barlick had his share of run-ins with players and managers (for whom abusive language led to automatic ejections). And on the field, he didn't hesitate to let others know

Barlick worked seven All-Star Games, the most of any umpire, and in seven World Serles.

After a particularly bitter altercation with New York Giants manager Leo Durocher in 1952, Barlick told The Lip: "We have another game here tomorrow night, and either you or I are going to be absent." Afterward, in his postgame report to the league office, Barlick said that if Durocher wasn't suspended for what he did, then he (Barlick) would quit his job. N.L. president Ford Frick immediately suspended Durocher for five days.

In 1963, Barlick quit for five days in a dispute with league officials, whom he felt were not supporting the umpires in their confrontations with players and managers. N.L. president Giles quickly talked his best umpire into returning.

"There are two types of umpires," Cubs manager Elvin Tappe said in 1961. "Some of them demand that you show them respect. Others command your respect by the way they do their job. Al is in that second group."

Barlick was probably the most colorful umpire of his era. His loud, booming voice on balls and strikes often could be heard outside the ballpark. He worked seven All-Star Games (the most of any umpire) and in seven World Series.

Barlick's World Series work, in fact, left an indelible impression on Casey Stengel. When the former Yankee

Hired by the National League in 1940 at age 25, Barlick became the youngest arbiter in baseball history.

Eighteen years after his retirement, Barlick was inducted into Cooperstown.

field boss was managing the expansion New York Mets in the early 1960s, he warned his young charges: "Don't fool around with that fellow. I remember him from the World Series. He's dead serious."

Indeed, Barlick viewed umpiring as a serious endeavor, not something to be taken lightly.

"We're out there neither as dictators nor to be pushed around," he once told a group at a luncheon in San Francisco. "And we take just as much pride in making decisions right as Willie Mays, trying to hit one over the fence, or Jack Sanford pitching a no-hitter."

Barlick took exception to having his skills as well as those of other umpires judged by people outside the fraternity. In 1961, in a poll of managers, coaches and players conducted by The Sporting News, he was voted the best and "most respected" umpire in the National League. Instead of being flattered, Barlick denounced the poll and questioned the qualifications of the voters.

"What do the writers know about it?" he said angrily. "All they know is what they hear or are told. They're not out on the field where they can judge an umpire."

Maybe not, but in 1989—18 years after Barlick's retirement—the Veterans Committee of the Baseball Writers' Association of America voted him a spot in baseball's Hall of Fame.

And no one can dispute the accuracy of that call.

ED BARROW

If Edward Grant Barrow had accomplished nothing more, he would deserve a niche in the Hall of Fame for the influence he exerted on two of the first five players to be elected to the shrine.

In the mid-1890s, Barrow spotted a youngster with long, sweeping shoulders and bowed legs standing on the railroad tracks near Pittsburgh and heaving rocks into the Monongahela River. That chance discovery started Honus Wagner on the way to diamond immortality.

And, as manager of the Boston Red Sox, Barrow determined that one of his front-line pitchers possessed greater potential as a hitter than on the mound. There came the day in 1919 when he "called in Mr. Ruth and told him from now on you're an outfielder."

Barrow, a native of Springfield, Ill, and a boyhood resident of Nebraska, arrived in the major leagues in 1903 as manager of the Detroit Tigers. By 1918, he was manager of the Red Sox and produced a World Series championship at the expense of the Chicago Cubs.

In addition to converting Babe Ruth into an everyday slugger, Barrow wielded further influence on the Bambino in his Boston years.

On one occasion, the hot-tempered and poorly disciplined Ruth threatened to punch his boss in the eye. Barrow, although 50 years old, ordered Ruth into the clubhouse, bolted the door and started to remove his coat.

"Was there something you wanted to do?" began Barrow.

"No, Ed. I was just popping off," replied Ruth, half Barrow's age.

After the Babe socked 29 homers in 1919, he was sold to the Yankees for $125,000. Two years later, Barrow followed as business manager, having been recommended by Boston Owner Harry Frazee to Colonel Til Huston, co-owner of the New York club.

It was in the role as front-office chief that Barrow achieved his foremost success, organizing and developing the farm system that established the Yankees as the all-time kings of baseball.

To the New York media, Barrow was "Cousin Ed," but the title was not intended in the popular baseball sense, as a soft touch. He was a hard-headed businessman as well as an astute judge of talent. Under his leadership, the Yankees hired the most discerning scouts who signed the most promising prospects.

Barrow's influence on the Yankees was instantaneous. The players, who had flouted Miller Huggins' authority for three years, were told in no uncertain terms by

Edward Grant Barrow poses with Mrs. Babe Ruth.

Barrow that the little skipper was their boss in the clubhouse, in the dugout and on and off the field.

The Yankees won pennants in the first three years of the Barrow administration. Before Barrow retired in 1945, they had captured 14 pennants and 10 world championships.

In constructing the Yankee empire, Barrow conceded that he took chances, but the two greatest risks were the purchase of Tony Lazzeri and Joe DiMaggio. Tony had been the sensation of the Pacific Coast League, but was known to suffer from seizures. The Cubs and the Reds passed up the chance to buy the second baseman, but Barrow assigned a scout to follow Lazzeri for a period and, on the agent's recommendation, arranged for his purchase.

DiMaggio also was a PCL sensation, but suffered a knee injury that threatened his career. While other clubs were scared away by the injury, Barrow arranged for DiMaggio to undergo a physical examination. When the report showed no permanent damage, Barrow bought the San Francisco outfielder for $25,000.

At the depth of the Great Depression, Barrow created a national sensation by signing Ruth for $80,000, a salary peak that other players aspired to for two more decades. "And to think," Barrow mused years later, I signed him for $7,500 in 1918."

Barrow was elected to the Hall of Fame by the Committee on Veterans on September 28, 1953, less than three months before his death in a Port Chester, N.Y., hospital.

JAKE BECKLEY

Jake Beckley made up for his notorious scatter-arm with a bat that produced .300-plus averages 13 times.

By all measurements, Jake Beckley was one of the finest early-day players in the majors. In 20 years of major league competition, the lefthander batted more than .300 13 times. When he was on a hitting rampage, his cry of "Chickazoola" sounded a warning to pitchers that Beckley was after their scalps.

Great as Beckley was as a hitter, he also was the original scatter-arm. Any time Jake needed to throw the baseball, runners automatically headed for the extra base.

In the early 1900s, Beckley was tending first base for the Cardinals in a game against the Pirates, for whom Beckley had played some years earlier. When third baseman Tommy Leach of the Bucs laid down a bunt, Jake fielded the ball cleanly and tossed to pitcher Jack Taylor, covering the bag.

To nobody's surprise, the ball sailed a yard over Taylor's head and into foul territory.

Beckley lumbered after the ball as Leach raced around the bases. Instinctively, Jake knew that Leach would try to score, but he did not trust his erratic left arm with a throw to the catcher, so he did the only thing a smart first baseman would do. He retrieved the ball and ran toward the plate, sliding in head-first from one direction as Leach slid feet-first from another.

Leach not only was out, but he suffered two broken ribs in the collision. When Leach recovered from his injury, he became an outfielder—all because of Beckley's erratic throwing arm.

Despite his weakness as a thrower, Jake stayed around long enough to set a major league record for first basemen by playing in 2,368 games.

Beckley played only 34 games in his third minor league season, with St. Louis of the Western Association, before he was sold to Pittsburgh for $100 (regarded as a high price in 1888). In 71 games during the remainder of that National League season, Old Eagle Eye batted .343, one point less than Cap Anson, the league batting champion.

A dashing individual, Beckley was a crowd favorite with his bizarre style of play.

Once, when he disagreed with an umpire's decision that awarded a triple to Roger Bresnahan of the Giants, Jake grabbed the ball from the umpire and fired it toward the backstop screen. This time, his aim was unerring. Unfortunately for Jake, time had not been called. As the ball rebounded crazily, Bresnahan walked home with the run.

During his big-league career, Beckley developed a hidden-ball trick that was a bit different from other similar plays. He concealed the baseball under one corner of the bag, extracted it and then tagged out the runner.

It was a slick maneuver until the day Jake lifted up the wrong corner of the base-no ball. As Beckley scrambled to locate the ball, Honus Wagner took second base.

COOL PAPA BELL

Exaggeration may be the only way to illustrate the blinding speed that Cool Papa Bell possessed during his 27 years in the Negro leagues.

Satchel Paige delighted in telling how Bell, on a smash through the box, was struck by the ball as he slid into second base.

Hyperbole, sure, but there were instances when Bell completely flabbergasted the opposition with his speed afoot.

One year, while opposing a major league all-star team on the West Coast, Bell took off from first base with the pitch. As Paige bunted down the third-base line, Bell reached second and continued toward third. And as Roy Partee set to throw to first, Cool Papa brushed past him to score.

Partee was a major league catcher. The pitcher was Bob Lemon, a future Hall of Famer. At the time, Bell was 45 years old.

Bell once was credited with circling the bases in 13.1 seconds, four-tenths of a second faster than the accepted major league mark set by Evar Swanson.

"The field was wet," Cool Papa recalled almost apologetically. "I once did it in 12 seconds."

Because of his burning speed, Bell was able to play a shallow center field. While with the Homestead Grays, he teamed with catcher Josh Gibson to pick runners off second base.

When Maury Wills was on his way to a modern major league record for stolen bases in a season in 1962, Cool Papa pointed out to the Dodger speedster that if teammates stood deep in the batter's box the catcher would, by necessity, retreat a step, thereby giving Wills an edge in swiping bases.

"I never thought of that," Wills acknowledged.

"That's how we played in the Negro leagues," replied Bell, who is said to have stolen 175 bases in one 200 game season.

Incomplete statistics credit Bell with hitting over .400 several times, and competent observers insisted he would have been outstanding in the American League or National League if the color ban had been lifted earlier.

One gauge to Bell's abilities against major league pitching is his performance in barnstorming games against Bob Feller, Dizzy Dean, Bob Lemon, Earl Whitehill and Bucky Walters. Bell batted well over .350 against big-league pitching.

A native of Starkville, Miss., Bell turned professional in 1922 at age 19 when he joined the St. Louis Stars. Seeking to make the youngster's debut as easy as possi-

By 1940, Cool Papa Bell was in his late 30s, coaching and playing for the Kansas City Monarchs.

ble, Manager Frank Duncan cautioned him against nervousness.

Bell assured Duncan: "Back home I played before crowds that sometimes were as large as one thousand."

A teammate standing nearby observed: "He's a cool one, isn't he?"

"Yeah," replied Duncan, "a cool papa." The name stuck.

According to John Holway, premier historian of Negro baseball, Cool Papa once yielded a Negro league batting championship to Monte Irvin under extenuating circumstances.

In 1946, Jackle Robinson's first year in Organized Baseball, Bell and Irvin went into the final day's doubleheader with Bell leading in the batting race, .402 to .398. Bell needed to play two games to qualify for the title.

After rapping two singles in as many official at-bats in the opener, Bell sat out the nightcap, forfeiting the championship to Irvin.

"The fans were mad," recalled Bell, "but they didn't know what we were doing. We wanted to give Irvin a chance to go to the majors. We would rather pass something on to a young guy to help the future of the black man. And I'm not the only older guy who kept his average down. We didn't have a future. We were too old."

JOHNNY BENCH

While growing up in Oklahoma in the late 1950s, Johnny Bench's hero was Mickey Mantle, a native Oklahoman who at the time was a star centerfielder with the New York Yankees. There was a lot to idolize: Mantle won the American League Triple Crown in 1956 and the Yankees were perennial World Series participants.

Little did Bench know then that in less than a decade, other kids would view him as he viewed Mantle.

"People keep telling me that they've got kids who idolize me," Bench said in 1969, his second full major league season, "and I find it a little hard to comprehend. I know the feeling, though. When I was growing up, I worshipped Mickey Mantle. He was my idol. But it's hard to grasp the idea that there are kids today who have the same feeling toward me. I guess part of the reason is because it's been such a short time since I was on the other end."

Indeed it was, as a 20-year-old catcher for the Cincinnati Reds in 1968, Bench took the baseball world by storm, belting 15 homers and driving in 82 runs en route to winning the National League Rookie of the Year award. Bench caught 154 games that year, a rookie record that still stands. Before his career ended in 1983, Bench's resume included 389 home runs (including a record 327 hit as a catcher), 1,376 runs batted in, a .267 batting average and 10 Gold Glove awards.

Bench owned two National League Most Valuable Player awards before he was 25 years old and drove in more runs (1,013) during the 1970s than any other player.

For his stellar performance, Bench was elected to Baseball's Hall of Fame in 1989, his first year of eligibility. He was named on 96.42% of the ballots cast that year (431 of 447), the third highest percentage in history at the time. Only Ty Cobb (in 1936) and Hank Aaron (in 1982) enjoyed loftier percentages. Bench was only the 18th player to be elected in his first year of eligibility, and his election was so certain that some observers wondered if Bench would become baseball's first unanimous choice.

"I ask myself, 'How could anyone not vote for him?'" said former teammate Pete Rose. "But I guess there's always somebody who won't vote for you. They'll say, 'Well, even Babe Ruth wasn't unanimous.' But that don't make it right."

Bench and Cooperstown seemingly were on a collision course ever since he broke into pro baseball as a 17-year-old prospect with Tampa (Florida State) in 1965. Bench

Rocket-armed Johnny Bench earned 10 Gold Glove awards during his 17-year career.

Bench drove in more runs during the 1970s than any other player.

played one season there, another at Peninsula (Carolina League) in '66 and one at Buffalo (International League) in 1967 before coming up to the Reds late that year. Along the way, he left an indelible impression on those who saw him.

"Wait until you see this kid catcher the Reds have— Johnny Bench," Dave Bristol, then a minor league manager, said at the 1966 winter meetings. "He's a winning type ballplayer. And he's smart, strong, and what an arm! Wait until you see him. You won't believe he's real."

Bristol, who later became Bench's first Reds manager, stated the obvious: that Bench was a winner. The Reds won four National League pennants during his tenure behind the plate, including World Series titles in 1975 and 1976.

In 1976, Bench hit .533 (including two homers, a triple and a double) and captured Most Valuable Player honors while leading Cincinnati's Big Red Machine to a four-game World Series sweep over the Yankees. After the Series, Reds Manager Sparky Anderson was asked to compare Bench with Yankees catcher Thurman Munson, who had hit .529 in a losing effort.

"Please," Anderson pleaded, "don't embarrass any catcher by comparing him to Johnny Bench."

Munson was insulted by Anderson's remark, but it was true. Bench was not only the greatest catcher of his era, but arguably the greatest ever to play the position. In addition to his ability to hit for power and drive in runs (Bench led the National League in RBIs three times), his rocket throwing arm gave many would-be basestealers second thoughts. After Lou Brock opened the 1969 season with 21 consecutive steals, Bench gunned down the St. Louis speedster on his next attempt. In 45 Championship Series and World Series games, opponents stole just two bases with Bench behind the plate.

Bench was a durable and innovative catcher, too. He set an N.L. record by catching at least 100 games in 13 consecutive seasons from 1968–80. He also was the first catcher to catch one-handed, use the sweep tag and wear a protective helmet behind the plate.

"I don't think you'll ever see catchers with round gloves again, and all catchers wear helmets," he once said.

Although Bench spent his first three seasons exclusively behind the plate, he played some outfield, first base and third base in later years. When Atlanta's Henry Aaron recorded the 3,000th hit of his career on May 17, 1970 in Cincinnati, Bench caught the first game of a Braves-Reds doubleheader and played center field in the second game. When the nightcap went into extra innings, Bench returned behind the plate and belted a two-run homer to help the Reds prevail, 7-6, in 15 innings.

That season was the best of Bench's illustrious 17-year career, all spent in Cincinnati. He achieved career highs in both homers (45) and RBIs (148) and was named Major League Player of the Year by *The Sporting News*. That same honor had been bestowed on his idol, Mickey Mantle, 14 summers earlier.

CHIEF BENDER

Born on a reservation near Brainerd, Minn., educated at the Carlisle Indian School and a major league starting pitcher at age 19 . . . that was the story of Chief Bender, the crafty Chippewa who starred for the Philadelphia Athletics for more than a decade.

Before the start of the 1903 season, A's Manager Connie Mack was asked about the team's prospects. About his pitching, Mack said: "I think I will be able to put together a good staff. Albert Bender, who pitched for the Harrisburg A.C. last season under the name of Charles Albert, should help us."

Mack often referred to the Chief as Albert.

The 1903 season was only a couple hours old when Bender received a chance to display his wares. On opening day in Boston, Bender relieved Eddie Plank with the A's trailing, 6-0, and held the Red Sox at bay while the A's pulled out a 10-7 victory over Cy Young.

In his first starting assignment, against the New York Highlanders at Columbia Park in Philadelphia, Bender outpitched Clark Griffith, 6-0.

Chief appeared in five World Series and collected a winners' share three times. His two most notable performances were a four-hit, 3-0 victory over the Giants in 1905 when all five Series games produced shutouts, and a three-hit, 4-1 triumph agaiinst the Cubs in 1910.

Bender pitched his only big-league no-hitter in 1910, blanking Cleveland, 4-0. Cleveland's lone baserunner, aboard with a walk, was nailed by 20 feet while trying to steal.

The Chief never asked to be taken out of a game. He was durable and rarely missed a turn. In 1905, when he was 21, Bender shut out the Washington Senators in the first game of a late-season doubleheader. When the Nats forged an early 3-0 lead in the nightcap, Mack called on the Chief again, and he won that contest, too, as the A's rallied to win the game and the pennant.

Speaking of Bender, Mack once said, "If I had all the pitchers I ever handled, with one game coming up that I simply had to win, I would call on the Chief. He was my greatest money pitcher."

Prior to the start of the 1911 Series, Mack informed Bender: I expect you to win the Series (against the Giants)." The manager then asked, "Albert, how much do you owe on your house?"

"None of your business," replied the Chief, smiling.

Eventually, he admitted there was $3,500 remaining on his mortgage.

Bender lost the Series opener to Christy Mathewson,

Chief Bender, the crafty Chippewa who starred for Connie Mack's Philadelphia A's, was a rookie in this 1903 photo.

but went on to win two games, including the 13-2 clincher. The next morning, Mack presented him with a check for $3,500.

Bender's top salary with the A's was $5,000. After the 1914 season, in which Bender suffered one of the A's four Series defeats to the Miracle Braves, Federal League agents intensified their efforts to lure major leaguers to the new outlaw circuit.

A $5,000 signing bonus and an $8,500 annual salary made Bender a member of the Baltimore team in 1915.

"It was the biggest mistake of my life," he conceded. "If I had had somebody to advise me, I probably wouldn't have done it." Bender was 4-16 in 1915 for a Baltimore club that finished 47-107.

The Chief returned to Philadelphia in 1916—as a member of the Phillies—and appeared in his final major league game in 1925 when, at 41, he hurled one inning for the White Sox, yielding a walk and a home run.

Bender managed New Haven of the Eastern League for two seasons under George Weiss, later a Yankee executive.

In 1927, Bender was named manager of Johnstown (Middle Atlantic) for the second half of the season. He won seven games during the remainder of the campaign, including a one-hitter.

YOGI BERRA

Probably no major leaguer has had more anecdotes, real or fancied, told at his expense than the son of Italian immigrants who grew up in St. Louis hoping to become a Cardinal.

When folks joshed him by saying he'd never be mistaken for a matinee idol, Yogi Berra grunted: I hit with a bat, not with my face."

As a young catcher with the Yankees, Yogi roomed with Bobby Brown, about to embark on a medical career. One night, Brown closed his medical tome at the same time Yogi closed his comic book, leading Berra to inquire: "How did yours turn out?"

Hitting and catching were Yogi's game, and he might have been a Cardinal except for $500, the bonus the Cardinals paid to his boyhood chum, Joe Garagiola, who preceded Berra to the majors.

When the Cards refused to match the bonus, Berra cast his lot with the Yankees. He went on to hit 358 career homers for the Yanks, then became the club's manager.

At a press conference announcing his appointment as manager for the 1964 season, Yogi was asked what he needed to find out about his new job.

"If I can manage," he replied straight-faced.

How had he prepared for the position, another wondered.

"You can observe a lot by watching," was the retort.

Yogi's replies created waves of laughter, but there were no guffaws when Berra stepped into the batter's box. He was a natural with a bat in hand. He helped propel the Yankees into 14 World Series, in which he batted .274, socked 12 homers, drove in 39 runs and earned about $100,000.

A compassionate sort, Berra cuffed Don Newcombe for three home runs in the 1956 Series. As he rounded the bases after one wallop, he glanced at the Brooklyn pitcher, a picture of despair, and shouted, "I hit a good pitch, Newk."

Yogi, who derived his nickname from a movie character, was not a selective hitter. He functioned on the theory that if he could reach a pitch with his bat, he should swing at it. A base on balls was something abhorred.

Berra was always a menace at the plate, but particularly when an opposing club walked a preceding batter to pitch to him.

In a game against Boston during Casey Stengel's regime, Yogi and Ol' Case had a difference of opinion on the bench. Stengel bet a beer that the opposition would

Yogi Berra is welcomed home by Mickey Mantle after hitting a home run in the first game of the 1953 World Series against the Dodgers.

walk Mickey Mantle intentionally to load the bases so that a lefthanded reliever could be brought in to pitch to the lefthanded-swinging Berra. Yogi took the wager.

With the bases jammed, righthander Skinny Brown was replaced by lefthander Bill Wight.

"Okay," said Berra, "you win the bet, but I'm gonna change my stance."

"What stance you gonna use?" Stengel wondered.

"My home run stance with the bases loaded," Berra responded, and two pitches later he drove the ball over the right-field fence.

Berra also clouted a grand slam in the World Series (1956), was the first player to pinch-hit a Series homer (1947) and established dozens of other marks, most of which still stand.

The three-time Most Valuable Player managed the Yankees to the American League pennant in '64, but was deposed after losing the Series to the Cardinals. He won an N.L. flag as skipper of the Mets in 1973 and again was on the losing end of a seven-game Series, to the Oakland A's.

By 1972, Berra was giving umpires his two-cents worth as manager of the New York Mets.

Berra gathers in a foul pop during the third game of the 1949 World Series at Brooklyn's Ebbets Field.

If the pitch was within reach, Yogi could be counted on to take his Hall of Fame swing.

JIM BOTTOMLEY

One of the most popular players to wear a Cardinal uniform, Jim Bottomley starred on four pennant-winning clubs, two of which (the 1926 and 1931 teams) also captured World Series titles.

With a touch of swagger, a constant smile and a cap perched at a rakish angle, Bottomley came by his nickname of "Sunny Jim" honestly and, in his bachelor days, he was certain to attract thousands of extra customers to Ladies Days at Sportsman's Park.

Bottomley owed his professional baseball career to the fact that a St. Louis policeman was sitting in the stands on an afternoon in 1919 when Jim belted two home runs and three triples for a Nokomis, Ill., semipro team that paid the young first baseman $5 a game.

The policeman recommended Bottomley to Branch Rickey, manager of the Cardinals. Within a few years, Jim was a Redbird regular, one of the first products harvested in Rickey's budding farm system.

Bottomley's most memorable day as a major leaguer occurred on September 16, 1924, at Ebbets Field in Brooklyn.

Batting with the bases loaded in the first inning, Bottomley singled home two runs.

In the second, he doubled to left, driving in another run.

In the fourth inning, with Cardinals on second and third base, Brooklyn Manager Wilbert Robinson offered an intentional walk to Rogers Hornsby, probably figuring that the next batter, Bottomley, already had his quota of hits for the day.

Jim pulled a drive over the right-field wall and four runs scored.

In the sixth, one runner was aboard when Bottomley homered again, raising his runs-batted-in total for the day to nine.

When Bottomley singled in the seventh, two more runners crossed the plate. In the ninth, another single produced his 12th RBI, an all-time major league mark, and gave him a 6-for-6 day.

The old big-league record of 11 RBIs had been set, ironically, by Robinson in 1892.

Bottomley was voted the National League's Most Valuable Player in 1928 when he tied for the home run leadership (31), batted .325 and drove in 136 runs for the pennant-winning Cards. And in 1931 he enjoyed another 6-for-6 day (only two other players in big-league history have turned the trick twice).

A series of injuries forced Jim to the bench several times in '31. However, when his replacement, Rip Collins, also was shelved by injury in early August, Bottomley

Sunny Jim Bottomley's constant smile didn't relieve the agony he imposed on opposing pitchers.

returned to the lineup in spectacular style. He collected 12 hits in four games and went on to wage a blistering battle with teammate Chick Hatey and Bill Terry of the Giants for the batting title. Hafey finished at .3489, Terry at .3486 and Bottomley at .3482.

After the 1932 season, Bottomley was traded to Cincinnati, a chronic tail-ender. Though troubled with arthritis, he survived three seasons with the Reds, then was traded to the St. Louis Browns. When Hornsby was fired as the Browns' manager in July of 1937, Bottomley was named to succeed him, and he finished out the campaign.

After a minor league managerial stint at Syracuse, Bottomley retired from the game. However, in 1957, he signed with the Cubs as a scout and later was appointed manager of the Pulaski farm club in the Appalachian League.

Two games into his term as pilot, he suffered a heart attack and retired from baseball for good.

LOU BOUDREAU

Lou Boudreau was a performer whose brains matched his clutch bat. Boudreau was a rookie in 1938 (right) and Cleveland's manager by 1942 (left), when he led off the All-Star Game at the Polo Grounds with a home run.

Spectators rubbed their eyes in disbelief in 1946 when four Cleveland infielders suddenly took position on the right side of the diamond and the left fielder played deep shortstop.

The exaggerated deployment was designed by Cleveland Manager Lou Boudreau to blunt the slugging talents of Boston's Ted Williams, who had devastated Indians pitching in the first game of a doubleheader.

Boudreau was willing to concede a bunt single down the third-base line, if Williams' immense pride would permit, to deny a possible extra-base hit. The "Boudreau Shift" had its desired effect. Too proud to settle for a bunt single, Williams continued to swing away—into a subpar performance.

A graduate of the University of Illinois, the inventive Boudreau was a full-fledged major league shortstop at age 22. In his first full season, 1940, he led American League shortstops in fielding—a feat he also accomplished in seven of the next eight years.

Boudreau was a brainy performer, with a keen sense of anticipation. He also was capable of playing in pain. One time he played four weeks with what he thought was a pulled stomach muscle. It turned out to be appendicitis.

In 1948, Boudreau sat out several games to rest a badly injured ankle, but at a crucial spot in a critical game with the Yankees he inserted himself as a pinch-hitter against Joe Page, the premier reliever of his time.

Boudreau singled through the box to drive in the deciding run, limping all the way to first base.

Boudreau was an assistant basketball coach at his alma mater in the winter of 1941-42 when he wrote to the president of the Cleveland club applying for the managerial post vacated by Roger Peckinpaugh.

Lou was interviewed by the board of directors and was awarded the job chiefly on the recommendation of an 82-year-old board chairman of a large paint company who insisted that the team needed new blood.

When he took over the Indians in 1942, Boudreau, at

Boudreau argues (above) after umpire Bill Stewart had called Boston's Phil Masi safe on a pickoff attempt in Game 1 of the 1948 Series. Boudreau was out (below) in Game 4 when he tried to stretch a double into a triple.

24, became the youngest manager to head a team from the start of a major league season.

In 1948, the shortstop-manager drove Cleveland to a first-place tie with the Red Sox, then clouted two homers and two singles as he inspired the Tribe to an 8-3 victory in a one-game playoff for the American League pennant at Fenway Park.

Boudreau's .355 average and 106 runs batted in earned him the American League's Most Valuable Player award. In the Tribe's six-game World Series triumph over the Boston Braves, Boudreau contributed four doubles.

As a result of his achievements—and the fact that the Indians set a major league mark with an attendance of 2.6 million—President Bill Veeck tore up Lou's $50,000 contract and gave him one for $75,000.

The love affair between Cleveland and Boudreau ter-minated two years later when a new general manager, Hank Greenberg, released Lou. Within a week, Boudreau signed with the Red Sox as utility infielder. One year later, he succeeded Steve O'Neill as manager.

Boudreau tried to revive the old Philadelphia Athletics in their first three seasons at Kansas City (1955-57), but the players were not of a contending caliber and the A's finished as high as sixth only once.

In 1960, Boudreau took his baseball knowledge into the Cubs' radio booth. And when Owner Philip K. Wrigley made a managerial change, he called on the old shortstop. Lou replaced Charley Grimm, who took Boudreau's job in front of the microphone.

Lou completed the season on the field, but after a 54-83 record he retired permanently from an active role and returned to the broadcast booth.

ROGER BRESNAHAN

It was not true that Roger Phillip Bresnahan was born in Ireland, although for years he was known as the "Duke of Tralee," a monicker that he did very little to discourage.

But it is true that the Toledo-born catcher introduced shin guards to the big leagues. After taking foul tips on the shins and nursing cuts inflicted by baserunners' spikes, Bresnahan appeared on the field in 1907 with a protective device borrowed from cricket players.

The jeering was long and loud. Fred Clarke, manager of the Pirates, insisted that the guards represented a menace to runners sliding into the plate. Roger survived the ridicule, and that winter shin guards received formal approval from league officials.

Bresnahan was the batterymate of Christy Mathewson with the New York Giants when Matty enjoyed some of his greatest seasons. "I could've caught him sittin' in a rockin' chair," Bresnahan said of the fadeaway artist.

Although he gained his greatest fame as a catcher, and also played the infield and outfield, Bresnahan made his major league debut as a pitcher with the Washington club of the National League on August 27, 1897. Roger celebrated the occasion with a six-hit, 3-0 victory over St. Louis. He won three more games (losing none) that season.

Despite his impressive start, Bresnahan dritted back to the minors before surfacing to play in one game with the Cubs in 1900.

When John McGraw placed an American League club in Baltimore in 1901, Bresnahan jumped to the new organization. When McGraw tangled with A.L. President Ban Johnson in 1902 and accepted the manager's job with the New York Giants as a consequence, Bresnahan accompanied his boss to Gotham.

Bresnahan starred for the pennant-winning New York clubs of 1904 and 1905, catching superbly, batting leadoff and running the bases with excellent speed.

When the Cardinals were casting about for a new manager after the 1908 season, McGraw offered Bresnahan in a trade that stripped the St. Louis club of pitcher Bugs Raymond, outfielder John Murray and catcher George Schlei.

The Duke of Tralee lifted the Cardinals one notch in the standings in his first season and in 1911 St. Louis was in the thick of the race most of the year before winding up fifth.

Roger's work, nevertheless, pleased Owner Helene Robison Britton so much that she awarded her manager a five-year contract-and a civil contract calling for 10 percent of the club's profits.

When the Cardinals dropped to sixth place in 1912,

Mrs. Britton wanted some questions answered. Bresnahan replied in syllables worthy of his crusty old mentor, McGraw, and was fired.

Subsequently, Bresnahan received a $20,000 settlement for the unexpired portion of his contract and a $26,000 bonus to sign as a catcher with the Cubs.

In 1915, Roger was named the Cubs' manager, but he lasted only one season.

Bresnahan invested $40,000 of his baseball earnings in the Toledo club of the American Association, serving as a playing manager. He concluded his playing career in 1918 at age 39 and sold the franchise in 1922.

The Duke of Tralee pulled on the catching gear for the last time in 1943 when he was 64. Appearing in a war-bond game in New York, Bresnahan, for the first time, caught the pitches of Walter Johnson, former Big Train of the Senators, who was 56.

"He must have been quite a pitcher," Bresnahan said of the longtime standout, "because he's still fast."

Roger Bresnahan (shown in 1906), tired of bruised legs, introduced the shin guard to the major leagues in 1907.

GEORGE BRETT

Though he was an excellent defensive player, Brett made his mark at the plate, finishing his career with 3,154 hits and a .305 average.

When George Brett learned he had been selected in the second round of the 1971 baseball draft by the Kansas City Royals, he was disappointed. He had hoped to go to a team with a storied past, like the Los Angeles Dodgers or the Boston Red Sox. Instead, he was joining a team born in expansion only three years earlier. It was his brother Bobby who told Brett that going to Kansas City might turn out well for him, noting he could perhaps have a greater opportunity to advance more quickly to the major leagues.

"He was right," Brett said.

Brett spent less than three years in the minors before making his major-league debut on Aug. 2, 1973. He was 20 years old, youngest Royal to make an appearance until Clint Hurdle in 1977. His first hit came that night off Stan Bahnsen of the White Sox. After going back and forth to Triple A Omaha the rest of the season and the first part of 1974, Brett arrived back in Kansas City to stay.

Born May 15, 1953, in Glen Dale, West Virginia, Brett grew up in southern California. His older brother Ken became a successful major-league pitcher. Along with brothers Bobby and John, the Brett boys now own two minor-league baseball franchises and a minor-league hockey franchise.

In the early days of his career, Brett's goal wasn't to become an owner, it was to become the best player he could. He knew only one way to play, giving 100 percent all the time, which immediately made him a fan favorite. He hit .282 and finished third in the Rookie of the Year voting in 1974.

That was a good indication of things to come. In 1975, the lefthanded hitting Brett topped the .300 mark for the first time, finishing the year at .308. He led the A.L. with 195 hits and tied for the league lead with 13 triples. He was ready to take his place on the national stage.

Working under the guidance of hitting coach Charlie Lau, the 6-foot, 200-pound Brett won the first of his three batting titles in 1976, collecting three hits on the final day of the season to wrest the title away from teammate Hal McRae and the Twins' Rod Carew. In six consecutive games in May, he collected three hits in each game, the longest such streak in history. Brett was selected to play in his first All-Star game that year, and led the Royals to the first division championship in franchise history.

Beginning with that title in 1976, the Royals won three consecutive A.L. West crowns, but each time lost the League Championship Series to the Yankees. In the 1978 playoffs, Brett hit three homers in Game 3 off Catfish

Hunter, but it still wasn't enough to lift Kansas City to victory.

The finest season of Brett's 20-year career came in 1980, when he almost became the first hitter since Ted Williams in 1941 to crack the .400 plateau. He raised his average above .400 on August 17 and was still above the mark as late as September 19 before finishing at .390, still the highest average by a batter in either league since Williams. Brett won the MVP award and capped his year by finally leading his team past the Yankees and into the World Series for the first time. His dramatic three-run homer off Goose Gossage in Game 3 secured the A.L. pennant for the Royals. He posted a .375 average in the World Series, but the Royals lost to the Phillies in six games.

Of all of Brett's 317 regular-season career homers, the most infamous was the so-called pine-tar homer hit off Gossage at Yankee Stadium on July 24, 1983. After his two-run homer put the Royals ahead in the top of the ninth, Brett was called out when umpires ruled he had too much pine tar on his bat. A Royals protest was later upheld and Kansas City was awarded the victory.

Brett got another chance at World Series glory in 1985, this time leading the Royals to victory over Toronto in the A.L. playoffs and then beating cross-state rival and former manager Whitey Herzog and the Cardinals in seven games.

Brett, who also won his first Gold Glove that season, often credited Herzog for helping him develop as a baseball player and as a man. "If I did anything for George, I didn't teach him how to play baseball," Herzog told the Kansas City Star. "I taught him how to take care of himself and how to get his rest and what he should do more of off the field than he was doing on it."

"I taught him how to hunt quail. He didn't know what the heck we were shooting at when they first got up. But about a month later, he was as good a quail shooter as there was."

Brett always was the type of player who responded well to challenges, and it was former Royals co-owner Avron Fogelman who captured Brett's attention in 1984 by saying he didn't think Brett was taking good enough care of himself and was not allowing himself to become the best player he could be. Brett was determined to show Fogelman and others he could do that, and he did —helping the Royals to its first World Championship the following season.

"It hit me hard," Brett said of Fogelman's advice. "I went out that winter and I worked my tail off and got in the best shape of my life. And 1985 turned out to be the best year of my life when we won it all. Avron gave me the greatest inspiration ever given me.

"I really believe that's why I played 20 years. In 1984, I got a wake-up call."

Brett is the only player in history with 3,000 hits, 300 home runs, 600 doubles, 100 triples and 200 stolen bases.

Brett hit .335 in 1985 and established a career high with 30 homers. He also drove in 112 runs, one of four years in which he topped the 100-RBI mark. He also scored 100 or more runs four times in his career, including 108 runs in that 1985 season.

His ability to swing a bat prompted more than one manager or executive to get creative when he was asked to talk about Brett. Former Kansas City General Manager John Schuerholz said, "George Brett could roll out of bed on Christmas morning and hit a line drive." Added former Royals manager Jim Frey, "George Brett could get good wood on an aspirin."

In 1987, Brett moved from third base to first, while continuing to produce big numbers on offense. He captured his third and final batting title in 1990 with a .329 average, becoming the first player in history to win batting crowns in three different decades. At age 37, he became the third oldest player in history to lead his league in batting—only Ted Williams and Honus Wagner did it at an older age.

Brett's next career milestone came on Sept. 30, 1992, when he singled off Tim Fortugno of the California Angels for the 3,000th hit of his career.

By the time he retired after the 1993 season, there was no doubt about Brett's status as the greatest player in Royals history. He was named the team's player of the year eight times, and is the team's career leader in nearly every offensive category. He finished with 3,154 hits and a career average of .305, topping the .300 mark 11 seasons. A 13-time All-Star, Brett is the only player in major league history with 3,000 hits, 300 homers, 600 doubles, 100 triples and 200 stolen bases. The only other players in history to have 3,000 hits, 300 homers and 200 stolen bases are Hank Aaron, Willie Mays and Dave Winfield. Along with all of those accomplishments, however, he wanted to be known as a guy who ran all-out to first base on routine grounders and who tried to break up a double play sliding into second base every chance he got. If records were kept for either category, Brett's name would be right near the top.

Besides his regular-season accomplishments, Brett also holds the American League Championship Records for highest slugging percentage, home runs, triples, extra base hits and total bases.

Brett was named the vice president of baseball operations of the Royals following his retirement and in 1999 became the first player elected to the Hall of Fame on the strength of his accomplishments as a member of the Royals. He received 98.19 percent of all ballots cast, the fourth highest percentage in Hall of Fame voting history, in his first year of eligibility.

"Everyone who has ever played this game, from Little League on up, has a dream," Brett said. "That dream is to someday make it to the Hall of Fame. That's what makes this so special."

LOU BROCK

The St. Louis Cardinals were en route from Los Angeles to Houston in mid-June 1964 when General Manager Bing Devine turned to his companion in the next seat and revealed that the Cards, in search of an outfielder since the retirement of Stan Musial the previous fall, had an opportunity to acquire Lou Brock from the Chicago Cubs.

"What are we waiting for?" Manager Johnny Keane replied. On the strength of that conversation, St. Louis took a giant step toward three pennants in a five-year period and Brock took a huge stride toward the Hall of Fame.

To the untrained eye, the trade lacked headline quality. In giving up Ernie Broglio, a former 20-game winner who had notched 18 victories in 1963, and two others for Brock, a .251 hitter at that juncture of the '64 season, and a couple of others, there was little to excite hopes for the first St. Louis pennant since 1946.

How little the critics knew! Broglio won only seven more games in his major league career. Brock, at 25, proved to be an all-time bargain on baseball's flesh mart, a record basestealer, collector of 3,000 hits and a Hall of Fame selectee in his first year of eligibility.

Louis Clark Brock, a native of El Dorado, Ark., was an unheralded student at Southern University in Baton Rouge, La., in 1958 when he reported for the baseball team and almost immediately collapsed in the outfield under a hot sun.

A medical examination revealed he was suffering from a lack of salt. The youngster confessed he had not been eating regularly and was subsisting mainly by dropping into friends' homes at mealtime.

With his dietary habits corrected, Lou batted nearly .500 in his sophomore and junior seasons and then accepted a $30,000 bonus to sign with the Chicago Cubs organization in 1960.

In 1961, the 5-foot-11, 170-pound prospect played for St. Cloud (Northern League), where he won the batting championship of the Class-C league with a mark of .361 and was tops in games, hits, runs and doubles. Late in the year, he joined the Cubs and singled off Robin Roberts of the Phillies on his first trip to the plate in the big leagues. Lou made two errors in that game, though, and failed to get another hit during the late-season stint (finishing with one hit in 11 at-bats).

In two full seasons with the Cubs, Brock did little to generate public acclaim. His batting averages were below .265 and he struck out much too often. In 1963, he fanned 122 times while drawing only 31 walks. In the field, he left much to be desired. Bleacherites assailed him with

In 1965 (above), Lou Brock was a first-year Cardinal beginning the long journey to the 3,000-hit milestone, which ended with a tip of the cap in 1979.

cries of "Brock, as in rock." A rival manager insisted that "Brock double-dribbles everything hit to him."

"I did not feel that I belonged in the major leagues," Lou remembered years later, "until one day early in 1964. A player lined a long drive to right-center field. I raced over from my position in right field and leaped against the brick wall. I didn't think I had a chance to make the catch, but when I came down the bail was in my glove. Then and there I decided I could play in the major leagues."

Installed as the regular left fielder for the Cardinals, Brock batted .348 for the balance of the 1964 season and raised his mark for the year to .315. He climaxed the season with a .300 average (9 for 30) in the World Series as the Cardinals upset the Yankees in seven games.

For the next 15 years Lou played a dominant role in the major leagues. When he stole 63 bases in 1965, it marked the first of a record 12 consecutive seasons in which he swiped 50 or more sacks.

The Cardinal star made his first All-Star Game appearance in 1967 and, although he went hitless in two at-bats in that game, he compiled a .375 batting average in five midsummer classics.

After batting .299 in 1967 and posting career highs of 21 home runs and 76 runs batted in, Brock led the Cardinals to a World Series triumph over the Red Sox with a .414 batting average and a record seven stolen bases. One year later, in the 1968 World Series against Detroit, Lou batted .464 and again stole seven bases. His career Series batting average of .391 established a record for players with at least 20 games.

Brock was 35 years old when he attained one of his most cherished goals in 1974. His 118 stolen bases eclipsed the major league record of 104 set by Maury Wills of the Los Angeles Dodgers in 1962.

With the season stolen-base record secure—at least until it was surpassed by Oakland's Rickey Henderson eight years later—Lou set his sights on two more goals. He achieved the first in the seventh inning of a game at San Diego on August 29, 1977, when he stole his 893rd base to pass the lifetime major league mark established by Ty Cobb. (He finished his career with 938 steals.)

Brock appeared in only 92 games in 1978, however, and batted .221. Seeking to disprove a "washed-up" tag, he made a determined effort to close on a high note in 1979. At age 40, the outfielder played in 120 games, during which he became the 14th player to register 3,000 big-league hits (getting the milestone hit August 13 against Dennis Lamp of the Cubs), and he finished the season with a batting average of .304.

On that glittering performance, the onetime poor farm boy was voted *The Sporting News'* N.L. Comeback Player of the Year and he called it a career.

Lou Brock raised plenty of dust and more than a few eyebrows with his baserunning success.

DAN BROUTHERS

Like Babe Ruth of a later generation, Dan Brouthers started his career as a pitcher. Unlike the Bambino, however, Brouthers shifted to first base rather than the outfield.

Also unlike Ruth, Dan never acquired even a small degree of fame on the mound. Pitching for Troy of the National League, Brouthers was victimized by 23 of his teammates' errors in one of his rare mound appearances.

Brouthers' tremendous power at bat became evident early, even to the most casual observer. Dan hit 14 home runs in 1884, a high figure for those times.

As the "Babe Ruth of his day," Brouthers set standards for long-distance hitting. In 1886, while playing for Detroit, Dan walloped a pitch out of Capitol Park in Washington that for years was recognized as the grand-daddy of all prodigious pokes.

A Brouthers blow also sailed out of the Boston park in '86 and struck a structure known as Sullivan's Tower. That incident, in itself, was of little note, but when the impact unseated fans who were obtaining a cheap view of the game, it became a widespread news item.

A native of Sylvan Lake, N.Y., Dan made his major league debut in June of 1879 for Troy.

By 1881, Brouthers was with Buffalo of the National League and soon gained recognition as a member of that club's "Big Four" along with utility man Hardie Richardson, third baseman Deacon White and shortstop Charlie Rowe.

Brouthers won batting championships in 1882 and 1883, becoming the first player to win consecutive crowns, but a sprained ankle in 1884 contributed to his batting decline to .325.

Brouthers enjoyed one of his most explosive days at the plate on September 10, 1886, when he clouted three homers, a double and single against old friend Jim McCormick in a game at the West Side grounds in Buffalo.

Several weeks later, after Dan completed the season with a .370 average, fans were stunned by the news that the financially strapped Buffalo club had sold the "Big Four" to Detroit. The price reportedly was $7,500, a sensationally high figure for that era.

When the Wolverines, as N.L. champions, won a post-season series from St. Louis, king of the American Association, in 1887, Brouthers was able to participate in only one of the 15 contests because of illness. Upon receiving his $200 winner's share, Dan requested that the money be divided among his teammates because he was of minimal importance to his club in the series. The offer was declined.

Dan Brouthers was known as the "Babe Ruth of his day," which spanned the 1880s and 1890s.

During the same season of '87, Dan joined John Montgomery Ward and Ned Hanlon in presenting several player requests to management. A meeting was held to discuss the reserve clause and to ask that a player's full salary be spelled out in every contract.

Ownership rejected the contract plea, and in 1890 Brouthers jumped to the Players League.

An American Association campaign (1891) followed, then the old warrior spent five more years in the N.L. before going to the minors.

At the request of his old friend, John McGraw, Brouthers joined the Giants in 1904, but was unproductive in five at-bats.

Brouthers' association with Little Napoleon did not terminate when Dan took off his uniform for the last time, however. In 1907, Brouthers signed as a scout for the Giants and for more than 20 years served as a night watchman and press-box custodian at the Polo Grounds.

MORDECAI BROWN

Because of two accidents, Mordecai Brown gained Hall of Fame stature as a major league pitcher. The first mishap occurred when Brown was in his childhood. He stuck his right hand in a feed chopper on an uncle's Indiana farm and lost all but about an inch from his right index finger.

As a young man, Mordecai was playing third base when the pitcher on a semipro team fell and injured his shoulder. Pressed into duty as a pitcher, Brown attained immediate success.

Brown frequently asserted that his handicap was actually an advantage to him as a pitcher because it imparted a sharper break to his curveball.

Mordecai made his professional debut in 1901 with Terre Haute (Three-I) in his native Indiana after he was recommended to the club president by a brother of Cy Pfirman, later a National League umpire. Brown never signed a contract with Terre Haute, but received $40 a month.

After winning 23 games for Terre Haute and then 27 for Omaha in 1902, Brown went to the big leagues.

The righthander, called Three Finger by the fans but Brownie by his teammates, was a sub.-500 hurler with the eighth-place St. Louis Cardinals of 1903. However, he quickly became a mainstay of the Chicago Cubs' staff following his trade to Frank Selee's team after his rookie major league season.

The pitching duels between Brown and Christy Mathewson were historic engagements.

Brown's best-remembered triumph was pitched on October 8, 1908, in a game in which he was not the starter.

The contest was a replay of a game in which Fred Merkle earned undying notoriety for his failure to touch second base as the potential winning run crossed the plate. The earlier game—a 1-1 tie—had been called after nine innings when fans streamed onto the field.

Jack Pfiester was the Cubs' starter in the replay, but was lifted when the Giants scored one run in the first inning. Brown took over and held the Giants to four hits the remainder of the game and picked up a pennant-winning 4-2 decision over Mathewson.

Three years earlier the two righthanders had hooked up in a no-hit struggle for eight innings before the Giants nicked Brown for two ninth-inning safeties to pull out a 1-0 victory.

Matty gained the no-hitter. Brown never achieved the goal of all pitchers, although he posted seven one-hitters.

Mordecai Brown already was among baseball's premier pitchers in 1909 when he finished 27-9 for the Cubs.

The two old titans of the mound bade farewell to major league pitching on September 4, 1916, battling head-on when Matty was manager of the Reds and Brown was wearing a Cubs uniform again after stints with three other teams. It was a sentimental matchup of Mathewson, 36, and Brownie, 39, with the younger one staggering to a 10-8 victory.

Brown scored his first World Series win against the Hitless Wonder White Sox of 1906, beating Nick Altrock, 1-0, in Game 4 after losing the opener to Altrock, 2-1.

But Brown's most satisfying achievement may have been his first appearance against Ty Cobb in the 1907 Series. The Detroit star had boasted he would hit .800 against Chicago pitching. Cobb went 1-for-4 against Brown and finished the Series with a .200 batting average.

The following year was Brown's most productive season in victories. Pitching 312 innings in 1908, Mordecai captured 29 decisions and walked only 49 batters.

MORGAN BULKELEY

When the National League was founded in 1876, Morgan G. Bulkeley, a man highly regarded in the worlds of finance and politics, was named president. Bulkeley was exactly what was needed to head a league of professional baseball clubs, a unit viewed with an air of suspicion in some quarters.

Officially, the election was conducted by the time-honored system of drawing names from a hat. Bulkeley's name was the first to be drawn. The second, Nicholas E. Young, was named secretary-treasurer.

Bulkeley accepted the office with the understanding that his term would be for one year only, after which he would be permitted to resign to devote his energies to other interests.

While Bulkeley was the nominal head of the new circuit, the force behind the chair was William A. Hulbert. A Chicagoan, Hulbert represented the brains behind the throne. Because he insisted that Bulkeley accept the presidency, Hulbert has never been enshrined at Cooperstown. Conversely, Bulkeley occupies a niche on the strength of his one-year presidency.

Bulkeley was a New England blueblood, descended from Mayflower settlers. An ancestor, the Rev. Peter Bulkeley, was said to have been the first settler of Concord, Mass.

Morgan's father had been an attorney and member of the state legislature before founding the Aetna Life Insurance Co. in 1850.

Morgan attended public schools in Hartford, Conn., where the family moved in the 1840s, but instead of pursuing his education and attending Yale, as his parents wished, he left school at age 14 and took a job as an errand boy at Aetna. Eventually, at 51, he received an honorary master of arts degree from Yale, and, in 1917, Trinity College conferred upon him an LL.D.

In 1852, Bulkeley left Hartford for Brooklyn, N.Y., where he obtained employment in his uncle's dry goods store. Seven years later, he was a partner in the business. At the outbreak of the Civil War, Morgan enlisted in the 13th New York Volunteers and saw action with General George B. McClellan in the Virginia Campaigns.

At the conclusion of the National League's first season, Bulkeley, as promised, yielded the president's chair to Hulbert. Bulkeley did not even attend the league meeting at which the Mutuals and Athletics were expelled for failure to complete their schedules.

Bulkeley founded and served for seven years as president of the United States Bank of Hartford. In 1879, he was elected president of Aetna and later head of Aetna's two subsidiary companies.

From 1880 to 1888, Morgan served as mayor of Hartford, donating his salary to the city's poor fund.

Bulkeley then served as governor of Connecticut from 1888 to 1893. He was elected U.S. senator in 1905, serving until 1911.

He was a delegate to the Republican national convention from 1888 to 1896, being present for the nomination of William McKinley in '96. Bulkeley, himself, received 39 votes for the vice-presidential nomination.

Bulkeley was a member of the Grand Army of the Republic, being founder and department commander; a member of the Massachusetts Commandery of the Loyal Legion; Society of the Cincinnati Sons of the American Revolution; Society of Mayflower Descendants; Society of Colonial Wars, and Society of the War of 1812.

On Bulkeley's death, N.L. club owners, on the motion of Charles Ebbets of Brooklyn, adopted a resolution calling for the league to "inscribe on its records its appreciation of the invaluable aid rendered by him as a founder of the national game and . . . give expression of our honor to the man and of the deep regret at his death, we now convey these sentiments to the members of his family, and to those who were closely associated with him during his successful life."

Morgan Bulkeley, a heavyweight in the worlds of finance and politics, became the first N.L. president in 1876.

JIM BUNNING

When Jim Bunning learned he would be pitching on Father's Day in 1964 against the Mets at Shea Stadium in New York, he decided it would be nice if his wife Mary and daughter Barbara could join him for the day. Little did anyone in the Bunning family or elsewhere in the crowd realize it was going to be a Father's Day to remember.

Bunning, in his first year with the Phillies, turned in a perfect game against the Mets, retiring all 27 batters he faced in a 6-0 victory while striking out 10. The no-hitter allowed Bunning to become only the second pitcher in history to pitch a no-hitter in each league, having earlier pitched a no-hitter for Detroit against Boston in 1958.

The only other pitcher to hurl no-hitters in each league was Tom Hughes, who threw one for the Yankees in 1910 and for the Boston Braves in 1916.

One trivial fact about both of Bunning's no-hitters was that each came in the first game of a doubleheader.

In his gem against Boston, Bunning allowed only three baserunners on two walks and a hit batsman, striking out 12.

Bunning's 17-year career was split almost evenly between the American and National leagues. He pitched for the Tigers from 1955-1963, for the Phillies from 1964-67 and again from 1970-71, for the Pirates in 1968-69 and for the Dodgers in 1969.

Pitching in both leagues for so many years allowed Bunning to become the first pitcher since Cy Young to win 100 or more games in each league and record more than 1,000 strikeouts in each league. At the time of his retirement in 1971, Bunning's total of 2,885 strikeouts ranked second all-time to Walter Johnson.

Born in Kentucky in 1931, the 6-foot-3, 195-pound Bunning was especially difficult against righthanded hitters because of his unusual delivery, a big sweeping sidearm style that saw him finish his motion with his glove hand touching the ground in front of the mound.

Bunning won 20 games only once in his career, when he went 20-8 for the Tigers in 1957, but he could have topped the mark on other occasions with a little luck. He won 19 games for the Tigers in 1962, and then hit the 19 mark again for three consecutive years with the Phillies, in 1964, 1965 and 1966. The next season, 1967, Bunning won 17 games but had the distinction of setting a major-league record by losing five games by the score of 1-0.

Bunning led the A.L. in strikeouts twice, in 1959 and 1960, and the N.L. once, in 1967, and finished his career with a 224-184 record and a 3.27 ERA. An eight-time All-Star, six in the A.L. and twice for the Phillies in the N.L., Bunning started the game for the A.L. three times.

Jim Bunning earned 224 wins in his 17-year career. He was elected to the Hall in 1996.

As a player, Bunning was involved in the startup of the Player's Association and used the knowledge of his college degree in economics, from Xavier (Ohio), to become instrumental in the establishment of the player's pension fund.

After his playing career, Bunning became a manager in the Phillies' minor-league system for five years before deciding to return to his native Kentucky and go into politics.

The father of nine children, Bunning was elected to the state legislature and then made an unsuccessful try for governor. He then turned his attention to the federal level, and was elected to Congress in 1986 as a Republican from a heavily Democratic district.

Bunning was elected to the Hall of Fame in 1996.

JESSE BURKETT

There was a game in the New England League early in the century when Manager Jesse Burkett approached the plate as a pinch-hitter.

Who ya batting for," asked the umpire politely.

"None of your business," growled Burkett, in his late 30s.

Turning to the spectators, the umpire called: "Burkett batting for exercise."

Through incidents such as that, Burkett came by his nickname of "The Crab" legitimately. Jesse did not display his dour disposition daily though, and he generally was a congenial person, especially among young fans.

But the 5-foot-8, 155-pound Burkett was a scrapper. He once declared that he was forced to fight to succeed in a game of huskier athletes.

Once, while playing for the Cleveland Spiders in a National League doubleheader at Louisville, Burkett was ejected from both games. With teammates, he was escorted off the field by a police cordon. The next day he was fined $200 in police court for inciting a riot.

Burkett carried his short fuse to the American League after jumping from the St. Louis Cardinals to the Browns in 1902. An exchange of epithets with Manager Tommy Lottus of Washington led to Burkett punching his adversary in the nose. The next day he drew a $50 assessment.

Burkett, who was adept at bunting, shares with Ty Cobb and Rogers Hornsby the distinction of being the only players to hit .400 three times in the majors.

Jesse was past his 70th birthday when he attended a morning practice of Red Sox players in Boston. Noting that the players had difficulty laying clown bunts, Burkett stepped into the batting cage and ordered the pitcher to throw as hard as he could.

The first pitch was bunted deftly down the third-base line, the second down the first-base line and the third was smacked on a line over second base.

As a star outfielder with Cleveland and St. Louis, Burkett amassed 200 or more hits in six of seven consecutive seasons (and had 199 in the other).

Jesse did not possess exceptional speed. Generally, he occupied the leadoff spot and reached base through his deftness with the bat. In a year in which he batted .400 (.402 in 1899), Burkett failed to win the batting title because Ed Delahanty of the Phillies batted .408. But Burkett did win championships with marks of .423 (1895), .410 (1896) and .382 (1901).

When his major league playing days were over, Burkett settled in Worcester, Mass., where he had played in 1889. In his adopted city, he led the team to four con-

Jesse Burkett, a member of the Cleveland Spiders through most of the 1890s, was known as "The Crab."

secutive New England pennants and was an excellent hitter (leading the league in 1906 at .344). He also coached at Holy Cross from 1917 through 1920.

ROY CAMPANELLA

Roy Campanella and umpire Bill Stewart are the picture of concentration as runner and ball converge on the plate during a 1951 game at Ebbets Field.

Baseball's all-time record crowd of 93,103 thronged the Los Angeles Memorial Coliseum in 1959—not for a World Series game, not for a decisive contest in a pennant race.

The fans flocked into the huge arena out of admiration and affection for a paralyzed ballplayer. The date was May 7 and the occasion was a benefit night for Roy Campanella.

From his wheelchair, the onetime catcher for the Brooklyn Dodgers intoned: I thank God that I'm living to be here. I thank . . . every one of you from the bottom of my heart. It is something l'll never forget'

Nor will Campy's contributions ever be forgotten. A three-time Most Valuable Player, the rugged player was the heart of the Dodgers' lineup that dominated the National League in the 1950s. When the Yankees and Dodgers played the 1959 benefit in Los Angeles, they were performing for one of the most popular athletes ever.

When Campanella was injured in an automobile accident in January of 1958, he had turned 37 and Dodgers President Walter O'Malley had only recently announced that the club would shift from Brooklyn to Los Angeles for the '58 season. The catcher, driving toward his Long Island home in the early morning hours of a cold night, struck a slick spot in the road and his car slammed into a utility pole. Roy was pinned in the wreckage. Two vertebrae were fractured and Campanella was paralyzed below the waist. His career was over.

The son of an Italian father and a black mother, Campy joined a team known as the Bacharach Giants at age 15 for weekend games through Pennsylvania, New York, New Jersey and Connecticut. He performed for the Baltimore Elite Giants—spending winters in the Latin American leagues—before joining the Brooklyn organization in 1946, playing at Nashua (New England).

One of Campanella's favorite expressions was, "You gotta have a lot of little boy in you to be a good ballplayer," and he never lost his enthusiasm for the game. He bounced around behind the plate, chirping in his high-pitched voice. He caught every pitch with consummate ease and he swung the bat with an energy that bespoke a man in love with his work.

Campanella won Most Valuable Player awards in 1951, 1953 and 1955. He earned his first citation despite a series of injuries that would have crushed a less-determined spirit.

Before spring training, a hot-water heater exploded in his face. During spring training, he suffered a thumb frac-

ture. Roy was beaned early in the '51 campaign, and he incurred lesser hurts during the season. With it all, the durable catcher played 143 games, batted .325, clouted 33 homers and batted in 108 runs.

When the Dodgers won the final game of the 1951 regular season in Philadelphia, Campanella pulled a leg muscle running out a triple. His attempts to run thereafter were painful caricatures of the real Campy. He was sidelined after the first N.L. playoff contest against the Giants, a situation that might have had a more serious effect on the Dodgers' loss to the Giants than any other incident during the season.

When Campy received his third MVP plaque after the 1955 season, he announced: "When you win the first award, you're happy. When you win the second, you're very happy. But when you win the third, you're overwhelmed."

Campanella, a three-time MVP, was a tough competitor whether at bat or catching, as the Phillies' Richie Ashburn would have attested after his 1950 collision (above) with Campy at the plate. Campanella (below left with catcher's mitt) is pictured with teammate Jackie Robinson and (below right) with former teammates Robinson, Don Newcombe (36) and Pee Wee Reese at an old timers game in 1964, six years after his crippling accident.

ROD CAREW

Rod Carew was a craftsman at hitting. His batting stroke and use of the entire playing field is what set him apart from his peers over his 19-year major league career.

And what a career it was. Carew won seven batting titles, the same number as Hall-of-Famers Rogers Hornsby and Stan Musial, and a figure exceeded only by fellow Cooperstown inductees Ty Cobb and Honus Wagner. In the process of accumulating those titles, Carew eclipsed the 3,000-hit plateau, a feat accomplished by only 17 other major league players through the 1992 season. By the time his career had concluded in 1985, Carew had amassed 3,053 hits and compiled a .328 batting average while playing 12 years for the Minnesota Twins (1967-78) and seven seasons for the California Angels (1979-85).

Carew reached the zenith of his career in 1977, batting a big-league best .388, collecting 239 hits (the most in a season in 47 years), 128 runs, 16 triples, 14 home runs, 100 RBIs and winning American League Most Valuable Player honors.

While Carew's effortless style created the impression that he didn't have to work hard to hit well, in reality his success was derived from constant experimentation and alterations in his stance.

"The difference between guys who hit .300-plus and guys who hit .200-plus are the adjustments they make," noted California teammate Tim Foli, "Most guys wait until they go 0-for-10 before they make an adjustment. Rod makes adjustments during an at-bat." Others were equally impressed. "He stays within himself so well," said California teammate Bobby Grich. "He doesn't try to hit home runs. Because of that, there are hitters who can cause more damage and can carry a team further, but for getting on base and getting base hits, he's the best ."

Like all great hitters, Carew took great care of his bats. He bathed them with alcohol, removing the buildup of pine tar used to tighten a player's grip on the bat.

"I can't stand a dirty bat," Carew once explained. "Some guys leave pine tar on their bats and never clean them off. I can't understand that. How can they get a feel for the wood?"

Bats were so valuable to Carew that a locked closet next to the clubhouse sauna was reserved for his lumber when he played for Minnesota. The heat of the sauna "bakes out the bad wood," as Carew put it. He also kept a supply of bats in his locker when he played for the Twins, safely distant from the other players' bat bin in the tunnel leading to the dugout.

"I see guys bang their bats against the dugout steps after they make an out," Carew said. "That bruises them, makes them weaker, I couldn't do that. I baby my bats, treat them like my kids, because using a bat is how I make my living."

When he was born, it would have been hard to imagine Carew making a living as a baseball player. Born on a train in his native Panama, Carew was a sickly child who contracted rheumatic fever when he was 12. His resulting

Rod Carew accepts 1967 American League rookie of the year honors from the league and *The Sporting News*.

weakness drew his father's alternating scorn and disinterest. Consequently, his uncle became a kind of foster father, taking Rod to baseball games in Panama and encouraging his athletic pursuits.

When Rod was 15, his mother moved to New York City and, after finding a home and a job, sent for Rod and his older brother. In high school, he did not go out for sports because his afternoons were occupied by a part-time job in a grocery store to help support his family.

But he played baseball on local sandlots, and it was there he was discovered by a Twins scout. When Minnesota came to New York for a series against the Yankees, Carew was given a tryout in Yankee Stadium. He performed so well that Twins Manager Sam Mele, fearing a New York scout would spot Carew, ordered him out of the batting cage: "Get him out of here before somebody sees the kid!" One month later, Rod signed with the Twins for a $5,000 bonus.

Carew spent less than three years in the minor leagues before he was given the starting second base job with the Twins in 1967. He proceeded to bat .292 and earn American League Rookie of the Year honors. That same season, he earned his first of what would be 18 consecutive trips to the All-Star Game. Two years later, he stole home seven times (tying the major league record) and hit .300 (.332) for the first time in his career, which led the league and began a string of 15 straight seasons in which he would bat .300 or better,

I taught him how to steal home," said Billy Martin, who managed Carew in 1969. "That's all I ever taught him. As for hitting, he knew how to do that all by himself. And he could bunt .330 if he tried."

Although renowned for his batting stroke. Carew also was a steady defensive player.

Aside from excellent play, Carew's early years in the majors earned him a reputation for moodiness. He was a loner who made friends slowly. As a second baseman in 1970, a runner crashed into him while trying to break up a double play. Carew underwent surgery for torn knee cartilage and, thereafter, was gun-shy on the pivot. Carew acknowledged his fear and tried to conquer his anxiety on the field. The fact that Minnesota Manager Bill Rigney publicly questioned his courage didn't help matters.

Consequently, in 1976 Carew was shifted from second base to first, where he became a steady defensive player. The loner also became a mature team leader, and he never requested any special privileges.

But Carew's tenure in Minnesota ended after the 1978 season. A quiet man who didn't need the spotlight, Carew might have finished his career in Minnesota but for the fact that team Owner Calvin Griffith was a penny pincher. As a result, Carew was traded to California for four players in February 1979.

Carew failed to win a batting title while playing with the Angels, but he hit .300 for the first five of his seven seasons in California. In his final campaign with the Angels, Carew collected his 3,000th career hit. He earned the ultimate honor a baseball player can receive in 1991 when he was elected to the Baseball Hall of Fame on the first ballot.

Beginning his rookie year. Carew made 18 consecutive trips to the All-Star Game.

MAX CAREY

Maximilian Carnarius had every intention of making his mark in life as a Lutheran minister. But as the years unfolded, he discovered he was destined for baseball immortality under the name of Max Carey.

Carey was a student at Concordia College in Fort Wayne, Ind., when, in the summer of 1909, he and a friend attended a Central League game in Carey's native Terre Haute. Max took one look at the South Bend shortstop and allowed that he could play the position more effectively.

The next day, Carey presented himself to the South Bend manager. He displayed a medal he had won as a sprinter and offered his services.

The offer was accepted, but the young theologian changed his name to protect his amateur status. He appeared in 48 games and although his statistics were unimpressive, he was invited back the following season.

By the next spring, however, Max had been replaced by a better fielding shortstop and he was shifted to the outfield, where he remained for the remainder of his career.

On August 20, 1910, Carey was purchased by the Pirates and saw action in two games in the closing days of the race. He made his major league debut in St. Louis on October 3, rapping two hits, including a triple, and scoring two runs.

Carey played 122 games in 1911, and proceeded to fall below the 100-game mark only once until his final year as an active player, 1929.

The break in his streak occurred in 1919 when he was limited to 66 games because of illness. Even so, Carey stole 18 bases and batted .307.

A switch-hitter, Carey enjoyed perhaps his most remarkable game on July 7, 1922. In an 18-inning game against the Giants, Max collected six hits and walked three times in nine trips to the plate. In addition, he stole three bases, including a theft of home. Despite his performance, the Pirates lost.

Carey's finest hour as a money player occurred in Game 7 of the 1925 World Series. The Pirates, who lost three of the first four games to the Senators, fell behind by four runs in the first inning of the deciding contest. But led by Carey's three doubles, a single and a stolen base, the Bucs rallied to defeat Walter Johnson.

There was a story behind the Pirates' manhandling of Johnson. As Carey explained years later: "Johnson beat us twice (in the first four games) and gave us just one run. He didn't figure to pitch again. After the fourth game, Jack Onslow (Pirates' coach) got into a cab with Bobby Veach (Washington) and asked how he had hit Johnson so well when he was with Detroit.

"Veach thought the Series was just about over, naturally,

The switch-hitting Max Carey enjoyed his best season in 1925, hitting .343 at age 35.

and never dreamed Johnson would pitch again. He told Onslow that when Johnson pulled his arm all the way back in his windup, it was a fastball; when he shortened his delivery, it was a curve."

Armed with that information, the Pirates solved Johnson for 15 hits in a 9-7 victory.

As a base stealer, Max was at his best in 1922 when he swiped 51 bases in 53 attempts for a .962 percentage. He was adroit at timing and getting a jump on the pitcher. He swiped bases cleanly, without the need to bowl over a fielder.

Good as he was as a hitter, Max maintained that he might have been even better if he had seen Ty Cobb play before 1924, when the Pirates and Tigers played an exhibition game.

Holding the bat almost vertically with his hands separated on the handle, and bent forward, Cobb was able to hit any type of pitch with a flick of the wrist.

Carey adjusted his style. And, the following year, when he was 35, Max enjoyed his finest season at the plate by batting .343.

STEVE CARLTON

Steve Carlton actually arrived in Cooperstown in 1966 at the age of 21.

Pitching in the minor leagues in Tulsa at the time, Carlton's manager, Charlie Metro, gave him the news that he was going to Cooperstown. Carlton, reportedly responded, "I'm going to the Hall of Fame already?"

He was, but only for a day to pitch for the Cardinals in the annual Hall of Fame game following the induction ceremonies. His performance in that game, however, was a factor when the Cardinals decided to promote him to the majors later that season and Carlton was in the majors to stay.

Carlton won 14 games for the World Champion Cardinals in 1967 and began to repay the faith shown in him by then-pitching coach Howie Pollet. When Pollet learned the Cardinals had let Carlton return home to Florida after a tryout without signing him, he offered to put up the $5,000 bonus money himself.

By 1969, Carlton had earned enough recognition to be named the start pitcher for the N.L. in the All-Star game, one of 10 appearances he was to make in the game. He also set a then major-league record by striking out 19 Mets in a nine-inning game, which he ironically lost on a pair of homers by Ron Swoboda.

A contract dispute kept Carlton out of spring training in 1970, and he lost 19 games. He rebounded to win 20 games for the first time in his

Steve Carlton—Lefty, as he was known—accomplished two magic numbers for pitchers: He amassed more than 300 victories, finishing with 329, and more than 4,000 strikeouts, finishing with 4,136.

career in 1971, but that only set up another contract dispute with Cardinals' owner

Gussie Busch, and this time the result was the trade that sent Carlton to the Phillies for Rick Wise.

Carlton and the Cardinals were less than $10,000 apart in their negotiations in the spring of 1972 when Busch tired of the episode and ordered GM Bing Devine to make the best possible deal. He got Wise in a one-for-one swap.

"Both are capable, winning and productive pitchers," Devine said at the time, "One is lefthanded, one is right-handed."

The deal turned out to be a disaster for the Cardinals, Motivated by the trade, Carlton won a career-best 27 games for the last-place Phillies and became the first pitcher in history to win the Cy Young Award while with a last-place team. The Phillies won only 32 more games the entire season other than the wins produced by Carlton, who led the league in ERA (1.98), innings pitched, complete games and strikeouts (310).

It was perhaps fitting that Carlton's 100th and 300th career victories came against the Cardinals, who might have won one or two pennants in the 1970s had he still been pitching in their rotation.

Carlton became known for more than just becoming an outstanding pitcher in his career. His workout routine, which included twisting his arm in a bucket of rice, earned him a great

Steve Carlton won four Cy Young awards, in 1972, '77, '80 and '82.

deal of attention as did his decision to stop speaking with reporters when he became angered by stories in the Philadelphia newspapers about his off-field activities.

Always an extremely focused and intense competitor, some observers believed that not speaking with the media actually made Carlton focus more on his pitching and made him even more effective.

Carlton won 20 or more games in a season six times, and his career total of 329 wins is the second highest for a left-hander in history, trailing only Warren Spahn. He also ranks second on the all-time strikeout list with 4,136, more than any pitcher except Nolan Ryan.

Carlton also led the Phillies to division titles in 1976, 1977 and 1978 and to their only World Championship in 1980, winning 24 games in the regular season (and his third

Cy Young award) and then beating the Royals twice in the World Series.

Carlton won the Cy Young again in 1982, but three years later went on the disabled list for the first time in his career with a shoulder strain, the beginning of the end of his great career. The Phillies asked him to retire, but he refused and was released, He spent time with the Giants, White Sox, Indians and Twins before ending his career in 1988 at the age of 43.

Perhaps the only accomplishment Carlton missed during his career was pitching a no-hitter. He did come close, pitching six one-hitters. The closest he came to tossing a no-hitter was two outs in the eighth inning, which he did twice.

In 1994, Carlton was elected to the Hall of Fame in his first year of eligibility.

ALEXANDER CARTWRIGHT

In 1938, while the Hall of Fame commission was finalizing preparations to celebrate baseball's centennial the following year at Cooperstown, N.Y., and establish Abner Doubleday as the father of the pastime, members were shocked by word from Hawaii that the game's legitimate parent was an almost forgotten gentleman named Alexander Joy Cartwright Jr.

The incontrovertible evidence included a diary, clippings and other materials supplied by Cartwright's grandson Bruce. The information detailed Alexander's role in formalizing the first rules of the game.

Because the commission was too far along in its planning to turn back, the Doubleday myth was allowed to stand, but Cartwright's contributions were acknowledged and he was named to the shrine the same year.

A descendant of British sea captains, Cartwright spent his early years in New York City where he participated in the English game of rounders and other contests involving a ball and bases.

By 1842, when he was 22, Cartwright was one of a group of young executives who participated "in a new game called "base ball" on 27th Street (where Madison Square Garden would be built later).

As the city expanded into the open spaces, the young gentlemen moved to a lot at Lexington Avenue and 34th Street. After three years of informal play, the group organized into the "Knickerbockers" club in 1845.

By 1846, Cartwright formulated a new set of rules for the game, dropping the rounders regulations that provided for a runner to be retired by being hit with a thrown ball. The new rules provided for foul lines, nine players to a team and nine innings to a game.

After several Sundays of practice, the Knickerbockers announced they were ready to meet any team that was willing to play under the new set of rules. The first challenger was the New York Nine. The site for the contest was an old cricket playground, Elysian Field, in Hoboken, NI, a ferry ride across the Hudson River. The date was June 19, 1846.

Although he was the best Knickerbocker player, Cartwright umpired in the historic first game. Among his decisions was a six-cent fine against a player for swearing, payable on the spot.

Without Cartwright's talents, the Knickerbockers bowed, 23-1.

The discovery of gold in California aroused Cartwright's adventuresome spirit and, in the company of a dozen friends, Alexander set out for the West Coast. At Pittsburgh, the group purchased a covered wagon and shipped it, along with supplies, to St. Louis, where the travelers arrived 42 days after leaving home.

The extended travel time was created by frequent stopovers devoted to demonstrations of the game called base ball.

The party arrived in San Francisco in July of 1849, but five weeks later, weary of the gold rush, Cartwright decided to book passage on a ship bound for New York by way of China.

Before reaching Hawaii, Cartwright fell sick and was put ashore at Honolulu. While convalescing, he became infatuated with the islands and decided to make his home there. In 1851, he was joined by his wife and three children.

Alexander Joy Cartwright, the legitimate "Father of Baseball," played a big role in formalizing the first rules of the game.

A born organizer, Alexander soon formed the first fire department and became its chief engineer. He was president of the Chamber of Commerce and the stock board. For many years he was the administrator for the estates of Hawaii's king and queen and pioneered in baseball for the remainder of his life.

An imposing figure at 6-foot-2 and 210 pounds, the white-bearded Cartwright frequently visited the elementary schools and with chalk and blackboard explained to the children the game he had done so much to organize decades earlier in the United States.

Cartwright died on July 12, 1892. His death went virtually unnoticed in his native country.

ORLANDO CEPEDA

The "Baby Bull" from Puerto Rico led the N.L. with 46 homers and 142 RBIs in 1961.

Despite having watched Orlando Cepeda tear up the minor leagues for three seasons, the San Francisco Giants were a little reluctant to promote Cepeda to the major leagues as the team moved west from New York in 1958.

However, when first baseman Bill White was inducted into the Army, they had no choice. Cepeda made the team and was in the Opening Day lineup for the first major-league game ever on the West Coast, between the Giants and the Los Angeles Dodgers, on April 15, 1958 at Seals Stadium.

Cepeda, even if he never accomplished anything else in his career, quickly made it into the record book that day by homering to help the Giants beat Don Drysdale 8-0.

Of course, Cepeda also made certain that would not be the only reason his career would be memorable. The homer began a monstrous rookie season which saw Cepeda hit 25 homers, lead the National League with 38 doubles, drive in 96 runs and post a .312 average. That was enough for him to be a unanimous choice as the league's Rookie of the Year.

To those who had followed Cepeda's minor-league performance and knew of his family's heritage, the success wasn't surprising.

Cepeda was born Sept. 17, 1937 in Ponce, Puerto Rico. He was the second son of Pedro "Perucho" Cepeda, one of the greatest baseball players in Puerto Rico's history. The elder Cepeda, a shortstop, earned the nickname "the Bull" and was recognized as "the Babe Ruth of Puerto Rico." He twice hit .400 and won numerous home run titles, but was never able to play baseball out of his native country.

His son, nicknamed "the Baby Bull," was not much of a baseball player as a youngster. He played basketball, and when he was 15, injured his knee so severely that doctors said he might never play sports again. He underwent surgery and was hospitalized for two months. Cepeda wasn't certain what he would do with his life. Not long after he had been released from the hospital, he went with a friend to a pickup baseball game one day, started hitting, and began to like baseball. With the help of a growth spurt, he was hitting well and was asked to join one of the top amateur teams in the area.

When he was just 17, Cepeda signed with the Giants organization and was sent to Salem, Va., a Class D team, to begin his professional career.

Less than a month later and three days before he was to play his first game, Cepeda's father died.

Cepeda struggled when he did begin to play, in part because he was missing his father and because of the

transition from Puerto Rico to the United States. He knew no English, and he ate most of his meals in cafeterias, where he simply could point to the food he wanted. The Giants hoped a change of scenery might help, so they moved him from Salem to Kokomo, Ind., another Class D team.

The move worked—in 92 games Cepeda hit 21 homers, drove in 91 runs and batted a league-high .393.

The tone was set. In 1956, Cepeda moved to St. Cloud, Minn., in the Northern League and won the Triple Crown —leading the league with 26 homers, 112 RBIs and a .355 average in 125 games. Another solid season followed in 1957 at Minneapolis, and Cepeda—despite being only 20 years old—thought he was ready for the majors.

Still, Cepeda might have been forced to return to the minors if White's induction into the Army had not created a spot for him. It didn't take Cepeda long to make the most of the opportunity.

He also proved that he was not a one-year wonder, by turning in an even better performance in his second year in the majors, 1959, when he hit 27 homers, drove in 105 runs and posted a .317 average.

Cepeda made the first of his nine All-Star appearances that season. The 6-foot-2, 210-pound Cepeda spent eight years with the Giants.

His best season came in 1961, when he led the N.L. with 46 homers and 142 RBIs. He also hit .311, but lost the

MVP race to Frank Robinson, who led the Reds to the N.L. pennant. He helped the Giants win the pennant in 1962 and reach the World Series, where they lost to the Yankees.

In his first seven seasons in San Francisco, Cepeda averaged 32 homers, 107 RBIs and a .309 average before a knee injury forced him to miss all but 33 games of the 1965 season.

Returning in 1966, Cepeda fell out of favor with the Giants management and was traded in May to the Cardinals for pitcher Ray Sadecki. The trade produced a new opportunity for Cepeda and he made the most of it by winning Comeback Player of the Year honors in 1966 and leading the Cardinals to the N.L. pennant and the World Series title over Boston in 1967.

The right handed hitting Cepeda hit 25 homers and led the N.L. with 111 RBIs while hitting .325 as he became a unanimous selection as the league MVP. He was the first N.L. player selected as the unanimous MVP since Carl Hubbell in 1936 and the only player in history to win unanimous awards as both the Rookie of the Year and MVP.

"What made our club click can be summed up in one word: Cepeda," said former St. Louis teammate Tim McCarver.

Cepeda, who also earned the nickname "Cha Cha" during his days with the Cardinals because of his love of Latin music, again helped the Cardinals to a pennant in 1968. But this time they lost the World Series to the Detroit Tigers. His average slumped to .248 and he was traded again the following spring training, this time to the Atlanta Braves in exchange for Joe Torre.

Cepeda played well enough to help the Braves reach the playoffs with the first N.L. West division title, but they lost to the Miracle Mets. It was the final post-season appearance for Cepeda, who moved to the American League and played for Oakland, Boston and Kansas City before closing out his 17-year career in 1974.

Cepeda thought his career was over after the 1972 season when he was released by Oakland, but the American League voted to begin using the designated hitter—and he quickly signed with Boston. He won the first award as the Designated Hitter of the Year, hitting 20 homers and driving in 86 runs for the Red Sox.

In his career, Cepeda posted nine .300 seasons and finished with a career average of .297. He also had nine seasons in which he hit 25 or more homers en route to his career total of 379. He drove in 1,365 runs in his career, including nine seasons in which he drove in 90 or more. He also hit 417 doubles, hitting 25 or more 13 times.

Despite also having bad knees, Cepeda had 141 stolen bases in his career, including 23 in his second season with the Giants, in 1959.

"He was the type of player who had no fear, the type

of player you wanted playing behind you," said former teammate and Hall-of-Fame pitcher Juan Marichal.

Cepeda hit three homers in a game on July 26, 1970, and hit four doubles in a game on Aug. 4, 1973.

Following his career, Cepeda ran into problems off the field. He was arrested in Puerto Rico in 1975 on charges of trying to pick up a package that contained 160 pounds of marijuana. He was convicted and sentenced to five years in prison. He served 10 months before he was released, but that cloud affected his chances of reaching the Hall of Fame for years.

In 1994, in his 15th and final year of eligibility by the Baseball Writers Association of America, he fell seven votes shy of the 75 percent required for induction.

Cepeda has spent the last several years working for the Giants as a community releations representative, regularly visiting inner-city schools in the Bay Area to warn of the dangers of drug abuse.

"I've been through good things and bad things, but I was very blessed to be born with the talent to play baseball," Cepeda said.

In 1999, he was elected to the Hall of Fame by the Veterans Committee. Cepeda joined Roberto Clemente as the only Hall of Famers born in Puerto Rico. The Giants also announced they would retire the number 30 uniform worn by Cepeda during his career in San Francisco.

Orlando Cepeda was the only player in history to win unanimous awards as both Rookie of the Year and MVP.

HENRY CHADWICK

In 1857, the baseball writer for the *New York Clipper* a daily newspaper devoted to sports and the theater grew so disgusted with the method for scoring a baseball game that he designed his own system.

By assigning numbers to the various positions, he was able to record the game play by play. At game's end, he could tally the statistics for each player and present to his readers an easily understood box score that provided a major boost to the meteoric rise of baseball as the national pastime.

The young inventor was Henry Chadwick, a British-born journalist whose first love was cricket but whose paramount interest was baseball.

Chadwick was born in Exeter, England, the son of the editor of the *Western Times*. Unquestionably, Henry's association with England had much to do with his position in filing a minority report in the early years of the century when a commission denoted Cooperstown, N.Y., as the birthplace of baseball.

Chadwick stoutly maintained that baseball was descended from the English game of rounders and never accepted what he referred to as the "Cooperstown myth."

Henry was 13 when, in 1837, he migrated with his family to the United States. For the next 71 years Chadwick called Brooklyn his home, an association that was linked to the borough's passionate love for baseball through the next century.

Chadwick joined the *Clipper* in 1857 and was sports editor until 1880 (except for the period when he served as a Civil War correspondent).

While with the *Clipper*, Henry also served as baseball writer for the *Brooklyn Eagle*. The job lasted 30 years, during which time he acquired the nickname of "Father Chadwick." The journalist terminated his affiliation with the *Eagle* in 1894.

Chadwick's writing style was trenchant and fearless and he was quoted nationwide. Like Judge Kenesaw Mountain Landis after him, Chadwick attacked gambling in baseball with all his energies. One chronicler asserted that baseball's freedom from scandal is a direct result of Chadwick's untiring efforts.

In Chadwick's heyday, virtually no baseball writers bylined their stories. Editors believed that anonymity assured more objective reporting.

Henry sought no such protection. Disdaining the use of a typewriter, he composed his essays in a handsome penmanship reflective of his English origins.

Chadwick served as editor of the *Spalding Baseball Guide* for 20 years. In 1904, he was presented a medal by

Henry Chadwick, a former baseball writer, is credited with developing the modern method of baseball scoring.

the St. Louis Exposition, the only newspaperman to be honored by the World's Fair.

Later, President Theodore Roosevelt honored Chadwick as the "Father of Baseball."

Chadwick authored a number of books, including "Beadle's Dime Base Ball Book" in 1880, "Haney's Base Ball Book of Reference" (from 1866 to 1870) and "DeWitt's Base Ball Guide" (from 1869 to 1880).

In Chadwick's declining years, National League club owners discussed a motion to award him a $500 annual pension. The move was vigorously opposed by Andrew Freedman, owner of the New York Giants. Freedman insisted that Chadwick was biting the hand that fed him.

In response, Chadwick boycotted Giants games during Freedman's ownership and A.G. Spalding, the publisher of the baseball guides, launched a move to oust Freedman from baseball, a move that proved successful.

Despite a fever, Chadwick attended opening day at the Polo Grounds in 1908. Pneumonia developed, and Chadwick died on April 20. In tribute to the man who had done so much for baseball, flags were flown at half staff at all major league parks.

Chadwick's close friend, Spalding, erected a handsome marker at the old writer's gravesite in Greenwood Cemetery in Brooklyn, and for years Dodgers President Charles Ebbets led an annual pilgrimage of old-timers to Chadwick's grave for wreath-laying ceremonies. The practice was followed faithfully until Ebbets' death in 1925. Fittingly, Ebbets also was buried in Greenwood, near the remains of his longtime friend.

FRANK CHANCE

Immortalized as the first baseman in Franklin P. Adams' lyrical lament of "Tinker to Evers to Chance," Frank Chance attained prominence as the "Peerless Leader" who managed the Chicago Cubs to four pennants and two world championships from 1906 through 1910.

Chance was a student at Washington College in Irvington, Calif., in 1898 and intent on becoming a dentist when Bill Lange, former major league outfielder, recommended him to the Cubs.

A catcher at the time, Chance made his major league debut on April 29 that year by playing the final inning of a 16-2 victory over Louisville.

Chance batted for the first time on May 11 and went hitless in two at-bats against Cy Young of Cleveland. The following day, the young catcher known as "Husk" collected his first major league hit, a single against Frank Wilson.

Chance continued to catch, with an occasional game in the outfield, until 1903. En route to Chicago from the club's training base in California, Bill Hanlon—projected as the Cubs' regular first baseman—quit the team. Chance was asked by Manager Frank Selee to fill in temporarily "until I can find a regular."

As a catcher, Chance had the unhealthy habit of sticking his fingers in the path of foul tips and was sidelined frequently. Such dangers did not exist at first base, and Chance adjusted quickly to the new position.

On August 1, 1905, ill health forced Selee to resign and Chance was named his successor by Jim Hart, who was in the process of selling the Cubs to Charles Webb Murphy. At the time of the change the Cubs were in fourth place, but Chicago played inspired baseball under Chance's dynamic direction and finished third.

Chance demonstrated his leadership qualities to the fullest in 1906 when he led the Cubs to a record 116 victories and a 20-game spread over second-place New York.

The Cubs were favorites entering the World Series, but were upset by their cross-town rivals, the White Sox, in six games.

As a manager, Chance was a scrapper and would drive umpires and opposition to distraction.

Chance, nicknamed the "Peerless Leader" by Chicago baseball writer Charley Dryden, also produced flags in 1907 and '08, scoring World Series conquests both years against the Detroit Tigers and their outfield phenom, Ty Cobb. The second year, Chance cuffed Detroit pitching for a .421 average and stole five bases.

The Cubs had a golden opportunity to capture a fourth consecutive pennant in 1909 but—despite winning 104 games—finished second to Pittsburgh. A large share of the blame for their "failure" was laid at the feet of catcher

By 1910, Frank Chance, of "Tinker to Evers to Chance" fame, was known as the "Peerless Leader" of the Cubs.

Johnny Kling, who chose to stay in Kansas City, to tend to his billiard parlor and play semipro ball rather than accept a salary offer from management.

With Kling back in harness in 1910, the Cubs annexed their fourth flag under Chance but were beaten by the Philadelphia A's in the five-game World Series.

Chance played only 92 games in 1909 and never again reached the 100 mark, mainly because of headaches that were attributed to frequent beanings. He also became deaf in his left ear.

Frank remained the Cubs' manager until late September of 1912 when Owner Murphy announced succinctly: "Frank L. Chance is through as manager." Chance not only had made the Cubs the dread of the National League, he also had made Murphy a millionaire.

Chance, 35, was claimed on waivers by the Cincinnati Reds, but when an opportunity arose for Frank to manage the New York Yankees, the Reds stepped aside and the veteran first baseman was sold to the American League club for $1,700.

Serving the Yankees for two of the three years on his contract, Chance finished seventh and tied for sixth. Frequent friction with President Frank Farrell added to Chance's unpleasantness in New York.

After staying out of baseball for one season, Frank purchased the Los Angeles club of the Pacific Coast League and operated the franchise for two years before selling it at a profit.

Chance, who managed the Boston Red Sox in 1923, died of tuberculosis in 1924.

HAPPY CHANDLER

When major league club owners started to vote for a successor to deceased Commissioner K.M. Landis on April 24, 1945, the name of a United States senator from Kentucky led from the first ballot.

The owners, meeting in Cleveland, reduced the list of candidates to three, then to two—the senator and Bob Hannegan, chairman of the Democratic National Committee. In the runoff, the Kentuckian was ahead, 12 votes to 4, when the executives—in a move for unity—decided to make the vote unanimous.

Albert B. (Happy) Chandler inspired ringing accolades from the owners.

"He'll give us a good administration," said American League President Will Harridge.

"He's the best choice we possibly could have made," added Senators Owner Clark Griffith.

Jack Zeller, representing the Tigers, chortled, I think we've made a wise decision."

Yet within six years of the auspicious start, Chandler was on his way back to the Bluegrass State to resume his political career. On December 11, 1950, at a meeting in St. Petersburg, Fla., the owners voted down a new contract for Happy.

"It was the only election I ever lost where I got the majority of votes," Chandler said after receiving nine of the 12 votes required for reelection.

Between the starting gate and the finish line, Chandler ran a stormy race. Few, if any, decisions were universally endorsed.

Chandler made his first major decision less than a year after taking office. From his desk in Cincinnati, he announced that all players jumping to the Mexican League would be suspended automatically from Organized Baseball for five years. Three years later, all jumpers were granted amnesty.

When Branch Rickey, majordomo of the Brooklyn Dodgers, sought to introduce Jackie Robinson to the all-white major leagues in 1947 and owners voted 15-1 against the move, Chandler gave the blessings of his office. The commissioner's stand against discrimination opened a new and profitable era to the game.

While Happy won the admiration of the players by supporting their efforts for a pension plan, he angered executives with other actions. Del Webb, co-owner of the Yankees, and Fred Saigh, owner of the Cardinals, were openly hostile to the commissioner. Both were investigated for possible conduct detrimental to baseball.

Early in his reign, Chandler suspended Leo Durocher for an entire season for slugging a fan under the stands after a game in Brooklyn and for associating with known gamblers.

"I had to suspend him before he killed somebody," Chandler explained years later. In the same decision, Chandler suspended Dodgers coach Charley Dressen for 30 days and fined the Yankees and Dodgers undisclosed amounts for airing a dispute publicly.

In 1949, after Durocher had become manager of the Giants, the New York club was fined $2,000 and the Lip and coach Fred Fitzsimmons were penalized $500 each as a result of a tampering case involving Fitzsimmons while he was employed by the Boston Braves. The same year, Leo was suspended briefly while Happy investigated allegations that he had struck another fan. Durocher was restored to good standing when the probe found Leo blameless.

The New York press, almost to a man, launched a full-scale attack on Chandler. "They even found fault when I said I love baseball," Happy quipped.

When Leslie O'Connor, general manager of the White Sox, signed a high school player, he was fined $500. His refusal to pay led to O'Connor's suspension and some heated words before the matter was settled.

After leaving office in 1951, Chandler returned to Kentucky where he was born (Corydon) and where he went to college (Centre). A life-long Democrat, he won two terms as governor and was instrumental in the construction of the University of Kentucky medical center that bears his name.

Chandler was elected to the Hall of Fame by the Veterans Committee in 1982.

A.B. (Happy) Chandler, newly elected baseball commissioner, officially opens the 1945 World Series in Detroit.

OSCAR CHARLESTON

Oscar Charleston (left), shown with Hall of Famer Josh Gibson, displayed his vast talents in the Negro leagues.

To be compared favorably with Ty Cobb is a supreme compliment for any baseball player. But to be likened to Ty Cobb AND Tris Speaker is an extravagance known but to a few.

Among that choice minority is Oscar Charleston. The one who gazed upon Oscar and saw the Georgia Peach and the Gray Eagle "rolled into one" was Judy Johnson, a veteran of Negro league competition and a longtime major league scout.

By virtually every yardstick, Charleston was a complete player. James (Cool Papa) Bell, himself a Hall of Famer, assayed Oscar in this manner:

"I could outrun Charleston a bit and maybe others might do this or that better than him. But putting it all together—the ability to hit, run, field, throw and hit with power—he was the best I ever saw."

Charleston's career was spent in the Negro leagues, where statistics were kept with a quaint indifference.

In 1925, for instance, playing for the Harrisburg (Pa.) Giants, "Charlie" was credited with a .430 average and 14 homers, both tops for the league. In 1929, with the Philadelphia Hilldale Daisies, he reportedly batted .392 with 98 hits in 250 at-bats and collected 37 extra-base hits. He also stole 22 bases in '29 and—like Cobb—slid with spikes gleaming.

"He was so fast," trumpeted an ancient publicity release, "that he makes Ty Cobb look like Ham Hyatt." (Hyatt was a slow-moving first baseman-outfielder with several major league clubs in the pre-World War I era.)

The seventh of 11 children, Oscar was 15 when he followed an older brother's example and enlisted in the Army. As a member of the 24th Infantry in the Philippines, the teenager developed his sprinting talents. When he was discharged in 1915, he was ready to unleash his blinding speed for a baseball team and chose the Indianapolis ABCs in his native city.

Charleston was not only a speedster on the basepaths, he also moved briskly from one club to another. From the ABCs, his course led to the Lincoln Stars of New York, Chicago American Giants, St. Louis Giants, St. Louis Stars, Harrisburg, Philadelphia Hilldale, Homestead Grays and Pittsburgh Crawfords.

But, regardless of where he spent his summers, Oscar always headed south for the winter—to Cuba, where he was a national hero, or other Caribbean countries. He was a 12-month player.

As a rookie with the ABCs, Oscar earned $50 a month. The next season it was $350 monthly. As his paycheck swelled, so did Charleston's reputation on the diamond. He was particularly adept at the swinging bunt.

In the field, Charleston never ceased to dazzle and amuse spectators, frequently doing a backflip after making a circus catch.

But his power was the favorite subject among his legion of admirers.

In 1921, the St. Louis Giants, featuring Charleston, engaged in a five-game, postseason series with the Cardinals. The National Leaguers won three contests, but Oscar won the headlines, clouting four home runs in one game, two off Redbird ace Jesse Haines.

As the years started to take their toll on his once-svelte figure, Oscar shifted from the outfield to first base, where he finished his playing career. In 1932, Charleston was appointed playing manager of the Crawfords, an independent club that also numbered Bell, Johnson, Paige and Josh Gibson, all future Hall of Famers. Approaching his 36th birthday, Oscar still batted .363 with 13 homers.

Charleston managed the Philadelphia Stars from 1941 to 1944 and, at age 48, was a member of the Brooklyn Brown Dodgers in '45. The Brown Dodgers folded after one season, and for a number of years Charleston worked in the baggage department of the Pennsylvania Railroad in Philadelphia.

In 1954, Charleston returned to managing, joining the Indianapolis Clowns. The Clowns had barely completed their schedule when Oscar suffered a heart attack. He died at Philadelphia General Hospital on October 5, 1954, nine days before his 58th birthday.

JACK CHESBRO

O f all the wild pitches thrown in the major leagues, none bore so heavily on a pennant race nor created so much lasting notoriety as the errant delivery that sailed over the catcher's head in New York on October 10, 1904.

The unbridled pitch was uncorked by Jack Chesbro and enabled a Boston player to score the run that clinched the American League pennant for the Red Sox.

Chesbro was an instant goat. Almost forgotten were the righthander's 41 victories, a record for the 20th Century. Virtually ignored, too, were his six shutouts, a one-hitter, a two-hitter, a three-hitter, eight tour-hitters, six five-hitters and a 14-game winning streak. To many, Chesbro had thrown away New York's first A.L. pennant, for which fans would have to wait 17 more years.

Chesbro's wild pitch occurred in the ninth inning of the first game of a doubleheader between the Highlanders, later the Yankees, and the Red Sox, who were seeking their second consecutive pennant.

The teams were deadlocked 2-2, and New York was 2 games behind Boston at day's start-needed to sweep the twin bill to win the title.

Chesbro, making his 55th appearance of the season, battled Bill Dinneen evenly for eight innings, but in the ninth Boston catcher Lou Criger beat out an infield single. A sacrifice and infield out moved him to third base. Chesbro worked the court on Freddie Parent to 0-and-2, then fired the next pitch over catcher Jack Kleinow's head as Criger danced home.

The Highlanders won the second game, but it was scant solace for the 30,000 fans who jammed the park and ringed the outfield 12 deep.

Chesbro refused to blame anyone else for the crucial mistake. Some critics insisted Kleinow should have made a better effort to catch the ball, while others stoutly maintained it was uncatchable.

Chesbro, nicknamed Happy Jack because of his positive personality while working at a mental institution in Middletown, N.Y., in 1894, was in his second season with the Highlanders, having jumped from the Pittsburgh Pirates when the American League transferred the Baltimore franchise to Gotham.

He never again approached the brilliant performance of 1904. From a 41-13 record, he slumped to 19-13 in 1905 and was 24-16 in 1906.

An ankle injury contributed to his 10-10 log in 1907.

Struggling gamely to reach the 200-victory mark, Happy Jack posted a 14-20 record in New York's cellar season of 1908. He then suffered tour losses in as many

One wild pitch diminished the glory of Jack Chesbro's 41-victory season in 1904.

decisions in 1909, the last one after being traded to the Red Sox, and finished with 198 career victories.

Chesbro coached the Amherst College team in 1911 while continuing to pitch in semipro games. He attempted a comeback with the Highlanders in 1912, but was no more impressive than he had been in 1909 and did not appear in a regular-season game.

In 1924, Clark Griffith, Jack's former New York skipper who had become president of the Washington Senators, hired his old ace as pitching coach, but the club's financial straits led to Chesbro's early release.

Jack retreated to his Conway, Mass., home, where he stabled some trotting horses and spent idle hours hunting abundant wildlife.

Chesbro was preparing for his daily chores on November 6, 1931, when he died of a cerebral hemorrhage.

NESTOR CHYLAK

"Hustle is the answer to being a good umpire."

I f Nestor Chylak had been asked to make a prediction about his future the day he umpired his first professional game, he likely would have been wrong.

On July 1, 1947, Chylak called his first game in Hamilton, Ontario, Canada in the Class D Pennsylvania-Ontario-New York (PONY) League. The bases were loaded, and the hitter grounded into a force out at the plate. But Chylak, umpiring behind the plate, called the runner safe because he had not been tagged by the catcher. Chylak quickly realized his mistake and corrected it, but wondered if this was going to be the occupation for him.

Chylak never really intended to be an umpire anyway. He played baseball at Rutgers before entering the Army in 1942. He became a machine gun instructor at Fort Benning, and when they asked for volunteers for the Rangers, Chylak signed up. He saw combat duty as a platoon sergeant in Europe, and was wounded in the Battle of the Bulge. He spent nearly a year in hospitals because of injuries to his face and left shoulder before he finally returned home. He was awarded both a Silver Star and a Purple Heart for his services.

Chylak enrolled at his hometown school, Scranton University, where he earned his degree in mechanical engineering. He was still in school when a friend asked him to umpire a local college game.

"I got enough troubles," Chylak said. "People hate umpires. Who wants to be an umpire?"

The friend persisted—and mentioned that the umpire would be paid $25. Chylak changed his mind, never realizing his career path was about to change as well.

Bob Stedler, a sports editor in Buffalo and the president of the Pony League, was at the game and was impressed by how well Chylak handled himself. He offered Chylak a six-week assignment as an umpire for the rest of the Pony League season. His salary was $175 a month, plus seven cents a mile for transportation, split between two umpires.

Chylak advanced through the minor leagues for seven years, working the Canadian-American League, the New England League, the Eastern League and finally two years in the International League, which included the Junior World Series between Montreal and Kansas City in 1953. He had many exciting moments as he rose toward the majors, including Opening Day of the 1952 season, when as the home plate umpire he yelled "Play Ball," before he realized he had forgotten his mask.

One of Chylak's biggest thrills came on a January day in 1954, when he received a letter from the American League informing him that the league had purchased his contract and he would become a major-league umpire. He had never attended a major-league game in person.

After reporting to spring training, Chylak's first thought was, "What am I doing here?" Almost immediately, though, he told himself, "I've eaten hot dogs and slept in my car and in sleazy hotels for seven years. I'm here and they're going to know I'll be around."

Chylak, who was born May 11, 1922 in Olyphant, Pa., quickly proved to be an excellent umpire. In 1972, he was honored as the Umpire of the Year from the Al Somers Umpire School.

Chylak credited the older umpires with helping advance his career, but he also knew he was successful because of his personal philosophy.

"Hustle is the answer to being a good umpire," he once said. "Bear down every second, be part of the game, and there's nothing to worry about."

During his 25-year career in the American League, Chylak worked six All-Star games, three League Championship Series and five World Series. He worked the first night game in World Series history.

He was also the crew chief during a June 14, 1974 game in Cleveland on 10-cent beer night. When unruly fans stormed the field, Chylak declared the game a forfeit and awarded Texas the victory, despite the fact the game was tied 5-5 in the ninth inning at the time.

"Everyone looked up to him and I developed more respect every time I saw him in a World Series or All-Star game," said former major-league Commissioner Bowie Kuhn.

A mild stroke forced Chylak to give up umpiring in 1978. He served as assistant supervisor of umpires until 1981 and died on Feb. 17, 1982.

Chylak was elected to the Hall of Fame by the Veterans Committee in 1999.

FRED CLARKE

The management of the Savannah baseball team had ample reason to be distressed during the 1894 season. The Southern League club was in Memphis, railroad and hotel creditors were screaming for payment and the club's coffers were dry. No ninth-inning, bases-loaded jam was ever so ominous.

When spirits were at their lowest, relief arrived from an unexpected source. In Louisville, Barney Dreyfuss, owner of the local National League club, offered to pick up the tab for one small consideration—the contract of outfielder Fred Clarke. Circumstances did not invite bargaining. The offer was accepted, and the 21-year-old Clarke was on his way to Louisville.

Clarke joined the Colonels on June 30. While teammates suited up for the game against Philadelphia, the newcomer sat implacably in the clubhouse. He had been promised a $100 bonus, he revealed, and until Dreyfuss paid up, he had no intentions of playing.

Shortly, Clarke was $100 richer. Swinging an undersized bat he had brought with him, he ambled toward the field as others jeered: "Pitchers will saw that thing off in your hands."

For this one time, the fiery youngster held his tongue. And three hours later, teammates were wondering what manner of prodigy had been acquired in exchange for hotel and railroad debts. For the only time in major league history, a rookie broke in with a 5-for-5 performance in a nine-inning game. Clarke belted four singles and a triple in a 13-6 loss.

As a youngster in Iowa, Clarke delivered a Des Moines newspaper, the circulation manager of which was Edward Barrow (later the architect of Yankee dynasties). "He never stopped hustling," Barrow once recalled.

At age 19, Clarke read an advertisement in *The Sporting News* seeking players for the Hastings team in the Nebraska State League. He made the club and two years later he was in the majors.

In mid-season of 1897, Dreyfuss appointed his 24-year old star as manager of the Louisville club. Fred failed to produce an instant miracle, but he did excite Kentucky fans with his .406 batting average (the highest mark of his career). The average, however, was good for only second place in the N.L. race. Willie Keeler of Baltimore batted .432.

Ball parks made little difference to Clarke in his super season. He batted .407 at home, .404 on the road. Fred was more than a hitter; he could patrol left field with the best. He made four assists in one game, and he registered 10 putouts in another.

In 1903, Fred Clarke hit .351 and managed the Pittsburgh Pirates into the first modern World Series.

When the N.L. went from 12 to eight clubs in 1900, Dreyfuss shifted his franchise to Pittsburgh, where Clarke became an immediate favorite and the team, known as the Pirates, became an instant power in the league.

The Pirates captured pennants in 1901, 1902 and 1903, capping the last season with an appearance in the first modern World Series (which they lost to the Boston Red Sox).

The club's post-season fortunes were better in 1909 as the Bucs beat the Detroit Tigers in seven games.

Clarke, who was replaced as the Pirates' manager after the 1915 season, appeared at the plate for the last time on "Fred Clarke Day," September 23, 1915. Nearly 43, the old warrior played four innings and batted twice. He collected one single, his 2,703rd major league hit, (off Dick Rudolph of Boston), then called it a career.

Fred came out of retirement to serve as a Pirate coach in Pittsburgh's world-championship season of 1925, and the next year he was a club vice president and assistant manager.

Clarke retired to his Winfield, Kan., farm, "the Little Pirate Ranch," where he lived until his death at age 87 in 1960.

JOHN CLARKSON

Great as he was, John Clarkson was not an easy player to handle. He was walking testimony to the maxim that a manager, to be successful, must be able to handle all types of temperaments.

At Clarkson's death in 1909, his old Chicago manager, Adrian (Cap) Anson, exclaimed: "Clarkson was one of the greatest pitchers of all time, certainly the best Chicago ever had. Many regard him as the greatest, but not many know of his peculiar temperament and the amount of encouragement needed to keep him going. Scold him, find fault with him and he could not pitch at all. Praise him, and he was unbeatable. In knowing exactly what kind of ball a batter could not hit and in his ability to serve up just that kind of a ball, I don't think I have ever seen the equal of Clarkson."

Fortunately for Clarkson and the Chicago White Stockings, Anson was enough of a psychologist to create a premier pitcher.

The son of a well-to-do manufacturing jeweler, John was one of three brothers to pitch in the major leagues.

A handsome youth, Clarkson, it was written, "seemed to have at all times a reserve of strength that never failed him. In the early days his speed was his big asset and when his famous fastball fell by the wayside, he developed a curveball with a peculiar drop and cultivated a change of pace. In his later years his wonderful control and precise knowledge of the batter who faced him still enabled him to continue to pitch winning ball long after his famous curve and fastball were but memories."

Anson discovered Clarkson pitching for Saginaw in 1884 and acquired him immediately. John won 10 games the remainder of that season and followed with marks of 53-16 and 35-17 as the club won consecutive pennants.

After winning 38 games in 1887, Clarkson was sold to Boston for $10,000, an astronomical price in that era. The previous winter, batterymate Michael (King) Kelly had been peddled to the same club for the same price.

In 1889, Clarkson worked 629 innings, earning $2,000 on a contract that spelled out a system of fines ($25 for the first offense, $50 for the second and $100 for the third) if John overindulged in spirituous liquors.

John was not above injecting a trace of merriment into a game. Once, when an umpire refused to call a game because of darkness as Clarkson thought he should, the pitcher threw a lemon to the batter. When the umpire ruled the pitch a strike, and the catcher held up the piece of citrus, the game was called.

In 1890, while many of his teammates were jumping to the Players League, Clarkson remained loyal to the

John Clarkson, pictured in 1885, won 53 games that season for the Chicago White Stockings.

National League. Some maintained that John's loyalty was purchased for $10,000. Clarkson maintained that his responsibilities as baseball coach at alma mater Harvard necessitated his remaining in the Boston area. Whatever the reason for his posture, Clarkson found his popularity plummeting among his peers.

John closed out his career in 1894 when he split 16 decisions with Cleveland, finishing with 327 lifetime victories.

The previous January, Clarkson and his close friend, catcher Charley Bennett, were riding a train westward on the first segment of a planned hunting trip.

When the train stopped at Wellsville, Kan., Bennett alighted to stretch his legs on the station platform. As the train pulled out, Bennett slipped on the icy boards and fell beneath the wheels of the cars. Clarkson remained with his buddy through the harrowing experience that cost Bennett part of both legs.

Clarkson was never the same mentally thereafter. For a while he operated a cigar store in Bay City, Mich., but the mental sharpness of his youth was gone.

While visiting relatives in Cambridge, Mass., in 1909, Clarkson died of pneumonia on February 4 at age 47.

In a tribute to the old master, Editor Francis Richter of *Sporting Life* wrote: "On all counts the deceased will always rank in history as one of the few great masters of the art of pitching."

ROBERTO CLEMENTE

On September 30, 1972, Roberto Clemente collected his 3,000th major league hit, a double off Jon Matlack of New York at Three Rivers Stadium.

Three months later, the 11th member of the "3,000 Hit Club" forfeited his life in dedication to the welfare of mankind. The Puerto Rican star and two others were killed when their cargo plane carrying food, clothing and medical supplies to earthquake-stricken Nicaragua crashed only moments after takeoff from San Juan.

Clemente was one of baseball's all-time best bargains. Roberto had batted .257 in 87 games for Montreal (International) in 1954, his first professional campaign, and the parent Brooklyn Dodgers were so confident that the young outfielder would slip unnoticed through the player draft that he was left unprotected.

The Dodgers erred. Brooklyn's onetime front-office chief, Branch Rickey, selected Clemente for the Pirates, paying $4,000 for his contract. Roberto was a Pittsburgh regular for the next 18 years.

Renowned as a hitter (.317 lifetime average), Clemente was equally accomplished as a fielder. His arm ranked among the strongest of his era. On one occasion at Forbes Field, he caught a drive against the gate in right center field and rifled the ball to the plate, 460 feet away. It arrived on the fly.

Another time, Roberto threw out a runner on a bunt. It was a freak play, of course. With runners on first and second base and a sacrifice in order, the Pirates' strategy was for the third baseman to break for the plate and the shortstop to cover third for a forceout.

When the batter botched the bunt and popped a fly to the vacated shortstop position, the runners held up momentarily, only to discover that Clemente had raced in from right field, grabbed the ball and fired to third base ahead of the lead runner.

Throughout a large part of his career, Clemente complained of back pains. The aches were widely discounted by teammates, who cited his superior performances as being inconsistent with a player in pain.

However, a chiropractor confirmed that Roberto did suffer from an arthritic spine, the result of a whiplash from an auto accident some years earlier.

Another pain, although unrelated to the playing field, was Roberto's resentment toward media representatives who never ceased shouting the praises of Willie Mays while consigning the Pirate star to a considerably lesser role. Both players caught fly balls basket-style and both possessed strong, accurate arms. If the Giants' star had any edge, it was in his flamboyant personality.

When Roberto Clemente connected for his 3,000th career hit, a double off the Mets' Jon Matlack at Pittsburgh's Three Rivers Stadium in 1972, nobody realized it would be his last.

In 1964, Clemente (left) led the National League with a .339 average. Though Clemente missed connections (above) on a 1969 play at Chicago's Wrigley Field he was known as one of the game's premier defensive outfielders throughout his career.

The son of a sugar plantation foreman, Clemente was still in high school when he started playing for Santurce of the Puerto Rican Winter League. Representatives of 10 major league clubs attended Clemente's high school commencement, one offering the young star $30,000 to sign with the Milwaukee Braves.

But Roberto kept an earlier commitment and accepted a $10,000 bonus from Brooklyn scout Al Campanis.

Clemente, a four-time batting champion in the majors, captured five assist titles, including one as early as 1958 when he threw out 22 runners. While most runners accorded him total respect, there were still some venturesome souls as late as 1967 when Roberto led outfielders in assists for the last time.

Clemente appeared in two World Series, both seven-game events. In 1960, he hit safely in every game as the Pirates scored their storybook upset of the Yankees, but he was even more impressive in 1971.

Again, Roberto hit safely in each contest. He hit safely twice in each of the first two games, both defeats in Baltimore against the favored Orioles. He contributed five hits when the Bucs swept three games at Three Rivers Stadium and added three more back in Baltimore, including a second home run that accounted for the Series-deciding tally in a 2-1 triumph. Roberto's .414 average, with two homers and two doubles, earned the Series Most Valuable Player Award for the 37-year-old superstar.

In recognition of Clemente's baseball accomplishments and his humanitarian efforts, a special election was conducted among baseball writers in 1973. Roberto was named to the Hall of Fame without the customary five-year wait.

During the '73 season, Pittsburgh players wore patches on their sleeves displaying their former teammate's uniform No. "21" within a black circle.

TY COBB

When the first Hall of Fame balloting was conducted in 1936, Ty Cobb polled 222 of 226 votes to lead all candidates from the 60-year-old major leagues. While many pondered the qualifications of those who left the Georgia Peach off their ballots, others interpreted the results as positive proof that Cobb was the greatest player of all time.

Throughout his illustrious career and into retirement, Cobb insisted that he was not superbly endowed as an athlete, only that he had greater desire. That flaming determination was expressed to a minor league roommate in 1905. When Nap Rucker, later a Brooklyn pitcher, returned to the hotel room first and bathed ahead of Cobb, Ty censured him.

"Oh," said Rucker, "did you want to be first today?"

"I've got to be first all the time-in everything," snapped Cobb.

Ty paid a steep price for success. He would practice sliding until his legs were raw. He would place blankets along the base line and practice bunting a ball dead on the blanket. During winter months he hunted through daylight hours in weighted boots so that his legs would be strong for the upcoming campaign. He overlooked no opportunity to gain an edge over opponents, most of whom disliked Ty personally but admired his drive to succeed.

Cobb appreciated the value of a dollar and engaged in annual haggles with Detroit executives before signing his contract. One season he did not sign until May 1. These protracted encounters did not stem from avarice, only Ty's appreciation of his value to the Tigers.

Cobb's earnings were invested wisely, chiefly in General Motors and Coca-Cola stocks, which made him a wealthy man and probably baseball's first millionaire.

But Cobb's intimidating playing style, his spikes-high slides and his brawls were what many remembered best. A photo of airborne Cobb sailing feet-first toward a catcher

The notorious baserunning techniques of Ty Cobb victimized many infielders and catchers, including St. Louis Browns' catcher Paul Krichell in 1912. The sharpened spikes (inset) were a Cobb trademark.

Cobb's brilliant bat produced 4,191 hits and made him one of the two dominant hitters of his era. The other, of course, was New York's Babe Ruth, who posed (above right) with Cobb in 1928.

did nothing to dispel Ty's ferocity. Nor did an overzealous slide into third baseman Frank (Home Run) Baker of New York. There was no mistaking Cobb's intentions when he filed his spikes on the dugout steps before a game.

Perhaps his most violent fight was with Buck Herzog, longtime National Leaguer, after an exhibition game in Dallas. Herzog, who had been spiked by Cobb in a play at second base that afternoon, went to Cobb's hotel room

that evening and challenged the snarling Tiger to a fight. Cobb did not decline.

With furniture placed against the walls, and Detroit catcher Eddie Ainsmith serving as referee, Cobb (nearly 6-foot-1) and Herzog (5-11) slugged it out in primitive brutality.

"I got the hell kicked out of me," Buck mumbled, "but I knocked him down and with that swelled head of his, he'll never get over the fact that a little guy did that to him."

Ty also took on umpire Billy Evans, but his most notable brawl was with a grandstand heckler at Hilltop Park in New York in 1912. Cobb stormed into the stands and punched the spectator. When the Tigers arrived in Philadelphia, Cobb was notified by league offices that he had been fined and suspended.

Rallying behind their star outfielder, Detroit players voted to strike. The Tigers, facing a $5,000 fine if they failed to field a team the next day, recruited sandlotters to wear Detroit uniforms. The A's crushed the quasi-Detroiters, 24-2. The strike lasted for only one game.

If Cobb could inflict pain, he also could endure it. Grantland Rice wrote: "I recall when Cobb played a series with each leg a mass of raw flesh. He had a temperature of 103 and the doctors ordered him to bed for several days, but he got three hits, stole three bases and won the game. Afterward he collapsed at the bench. . . ."

It was little wonder that Tyrus Raymond Cobb, the son of a Georgia schoolmaster and state senator, departed the game in 1928 with countless records engraved in granite.

MICKEY COCHRANE

The Philadelphia Athletics were in desperate need of a catcher after the 1924 season. Cy Perkins, the A's No. 1 catcher, was coming off a .242 season.

The best prospect in the minor leagues was a 21-year-old fireball with Portland of the Pacific Coast League.

"They wanted $100,000 for him," the A's Connie Mack recalled three decades later, "and we were ready to pay it. But we discovered the whole franchise could be had for $120,000, so we bought the club."

The bright prospect was Mickey Cochrane, once likened to an incendiary bomb. In the 1920s and early 1930s he was the king of catchers, driving the A's to three pennants and managing the Tigers to two more, all within seven years.

Cochrane possessed the ability to carry a team, a trait he demonstrated during his years at Boston University. Intercollegiate football at the time was in its infancy at BU, and Mickey served as coach, trainer, punter, passer, ballcarrier and spiritual leader.

When Cochrane arrived at his first training camp with the A's, veteran third baseman Jimmie Dykes took one look at him and snorted, "If that guy's worth $100,000, I'm worth $300,00."

Through endless hours of toil (Mickey chased pop fouls until he "caught 'em in my sleep"), Cochrane soon proved his 100-grand value.

Cochrane scaled his first peaks from 1929 through 1931 when the A's won pennants each season. From his No. 3 spot in the lineup, the lefthanded-hitting catcher batted .331, .357 and .349. He averaged 129 games a season and 87 runs batted in.

When Mack was forced to sell his high-salaried stars in the depths of the Great Depression, Cochrane was sold for $100,000 to Detroit, where he was named manager.

Cochrane produced a pennant winner in his first season, 1934, but the Tigers lost the seven-game World Series to the St. Louis Cardinals' Gas House Gang.

The next season Mickey caught 100 games for the last time and batted .319. As in '29, Cochrane faced the Cubs in the World Series.

The Tigers won three of the first five games and were deadlocked, 3-3, in the ninth inning of the sixth contest when Cochrane rapped a one-out single, moved up on an infield out and scored the winning run on Goose Goslin's single.

"It was my greatest day in baseball," the playing manager declared later.

A new Yankee steamroller dethroned the Tigers in 1936, a year before Cochrane's career ended with dra-

Mickey Cochrane was a tough scrapper who had the ability to literally carry his team.

matic and tragic suddenness on May 25, 1937. Mickey came to bat with a runner on first base and ran the count to 3-and-1 against Yankee righthander Bump Hadley. Crowding the plate for a better chance to pull the ball, Mickey lost sight of the next pitch when it was about six feet from the plate.

The ball struck Cochrane on the right temple, about an inch above the eyebrow. Mickey collapsed at the plate and was unconscious for 10 days with a fractured skull. He never batted again.

Forced to manage from the bench, Mickey was no longer the inspirational force he was while active. He was replaced as pilot in August of 1938.

Cochrane served as a Navy officer in World War II and coached and scouted in succeeding years. He served as general manager of the A's in Mack's last season as manager (1950) and for a while operated a dude ranch in Wyoming. He died in 1962 at age 59.

EDDIE COLLINS

When a young shortstop named Sullivan broke in with the Philadelphia Athletics on September 17, 1906, handling six chances flawlessly and rapping a single off Ed Walsh of the White Sox, few suspected that he was playing under an assumed name or that he would blossom into one of the most brilliant second basemen of all time.

According to one account, Eddie Collins acquired his pseudonym the day he joined the A's. Connie Mack was chatting with Tim Murnane, a former major league pitcher who, in 1906, was a Boston sportswriter.

Fearing that Murnane would recognize Collins as the quarterback of the Columbia football team, thereby endangering Eddie's amateur status, the quick-thinking A's manager addressed him as "Sullivan."

The details may be apochryphal, but ironically Eddie discovered when he returned to Columbia for the fall semester that he had lost his eligibility—not for having been discovered as a member of the A's, but for having played semipro ball earlier to finance his education.

The six games that Eddie played in 1906 represented the start of the longest major league playing career, 25 years, in the 20th century. Collins remained active through the 1930 campaign.

Whether Collins was history's finest second baseman will never be resolved satisfactorily. But Mack, who managed in the majors for more than half a century, termed him "the finest infielder of all time."

Ty Cobb, an opponent for many seasons and a teammate for two years (1927-1928), declared flatly that Collins was the premier keystoner. In addition to a lifetime batting average of .333, Collins was a greyhound on the bases. Twice he stole six bases in one game, and his lifetime total of 743 thefts ranks behind only Lou Brock and Cobb on the modern list. Collins stole 67 bases in

1909, 81 in 1910 and 62 in 1912. He shares with Brock the career World Series stolen base record of 14.

Collins was a member of the "$100,000 Infield" that sparked the A's to four pennants in five years (1910-14). He won the Chalmers Award as the league's Most Valuable Player in 1914.

At the end of the 1914 season, after the A's were upset by the Miracle Braves in the four-game World Series, Eddie was sold to the White Sox for $50,000. He remained with the Sox for 12 years, managing them in 1925-26 before returning to the A's.

Upon joining Chicago, Collins negotiated a contract for a reported $15,000, double the salary of any teammate. His relatively high pay accentuated Eddie's unpopularity with some teammates, notably shortstop Swede Risberg and first baseman Chick Gandil, who never talked to the man playing between them.

Eddie, nicknamed "Cocky" for his aggressive style of play, performed for the Sox in the World Series of 1917 and 1919. In Game 6 of the 1917 Series, he gained the spotlight as the baserunner who was chased across the plate by third baseman Heinie Zimmerman of the Giants. Collins noted the plate had been left unprotected.

In 1919, Collins was one of the Chicago players who made an honest effort to beat the Reds in the Series. Eight other players—so called "Black Sox"—were accused of trying to fix the classic.

Collins was a playing coach with the A's when the Yankees offered him the post as manager following the death of Miller Huggins in 1929. Eddie declined, having been assured that he was being groomed as the successor to Mack (then in his late 60s). Mack, though, ended up managing the A's through 1950.

Eddie Collins, shown in 1926, was Ty Cobb's pick as the best second baseman of his era.

When Tom Yawkey offered the general managership of the Red Sox to Eddie in 1933, Mack insisted that he take it. In that post, Collins built the Sox from chronic tail-enders into pennant contenders. He personally scouted second baseman Bobby Doerr at San Diego and acquired an option to purchase Ted Williams from the same club.

Collins continued to occupy the general manager's chair until 1951 when he suffered a cerebral hemorrhage and died.

JIMMY COLLINS

Jimmy Collins, pictured with heavyweight fighter John L. Sullivan, revolutionized the art of playing third base.

If Walter Preston had played third base in a more acceptable fashion, Jimmy Collins may never have had the opportunity to become a Hall of Famer.

Preston was playing for Louisville of the National League in 1895 when the Baltimore Orioles—featuring John McGraw, Willie Keeler and Hughey Jennings—laid down seven successive bunts, all of which Preston misplayed.

After the seventh tantalizer, Manager John J. McCloskey summoned Fred Clarke into a conference. "I'll give you $50 more a month if you'll play third base," McCloskey told his left fielder.

Clarke wanted no part of the position, but he had a suggestion. "Why don't you move that fellow Collins from center field?" asked Clarke. "I understand he played third base at Buffalo."

Collins was a third baseman thereafter. He had been purchased only recently from the N.L.'s Boston club for $1,500, with the understanding that he could be repurchased for the same amount at the close of the season.

Collins later recalled that day in Louisville: "McGraw bunted and I came in as fast as I dared, picked up the ball and threw it underhanded to first base. He was out. Keeler tried it and I nailed him by a step. I had to throw out four bunters in a row before the Orioles quit bunting."

In a game against Boston, Collins collected four hits and handled 16 chances. Boston newspapers raised such a clamor that the local club exercised its option to reacquire Collins.

Collins had made his professional debut with the Buffalo (Eastern) club on May 25, 1893, contributing two singles to his club's 11-inning, 8-7 victory over Erie.

Back with Buffalo the next season, Collins became an instant favorite with the fans. Possessing quick, sure hands, he revolutionized the playing style of third basemen. He was the first to play away from the bag, and the first to play shallow in bunting situations so he could race in, grab the ball barehanded and, in one fluid motion, fire to first base ahead of the runner.

An ankle injury limited Collins to 83 games for Boston in 1896, but he batted .300. He was a member of the foremost infield of the 19th century, a unit also consisting of Fred Tenney at first base, Bobby Lowe at second and Herman Long at shortstop. The foursome pioneered numerous defensive strategies that soon were adopted by other teams.

In five seasons with the Beaneaters, Jimmy failed to register 300 assists only once and totaled 376 one year.

One of Jimmy's assists was a show-stopper in Philadelphia when Collins, it was said, dived toward the bag, grabbed an Ed Delahanty smash with his bare hand and threw out the hometown hero. The game was interrupted until the crowd ceased cheering.

When the American League emerged as a new major circuit, Collins accepted an offer to serve as manager-third baseman for the Red Sox. Jimmy's first contract called for a $5,500 salary, but later he earned $18,000 a year, a princely salary based on a $10,000 salary and 10 percent of the club's profits over $25,000.

After directing Boston to second-place A.L. finishes in 1901 and 1902, Collins directed a pennant winner in 1903. In the first modern World Series that followed, the Sox won five of eight games from the Pittsburgh Pirates.

The Red Sox won the A.L. title again in 1904, but there was no World Series because John McGraw did not consider the newcomers worthy of facing the proud Giants, pennant winners in the N.L.

By 1905, the Sox were a fourth-place club and when they hit the bottom the next season, Collins was dismissed as manager. Jimmy remained with Boston as a player until June of 1907 when he was traded to Philadelphia, where he closed out his major league career in 1908.

After managerial ventures at Minneapolis (American Association) and Providence (Eastern), Jimmy returned to Buffalo, where he lived comfortably off real estate investments until the Depression of the 1930s wiped him out. Thereafter he worked for the city's Park Department.

Early in 1943, Collins fell on the sidewalk near his home. Pneumonia developed during his hospitalization, and Jimmy died 12 days later.

EARLE COMBS

It is doubtful that any Hall of Famer suffered through so horrendous a debut in professional baseball as Earle Combs.

Combs had been an elementary school teacher in the Cumberland Mountains and then had taken a $40-a-month job with a coal company. In turn, he played with a semipro team in Lexington, Ky., where he was discovered by Cap Neal, a scout for the Louisville team of the American Association.

Combs won the center-field position with the Colonels, but after the first game he wasn't sure that he wanted the job. He committed two errors on ground balls early in the contest and in the ninth inning, with the Colonels leading by one run, a batter grounded up the middle.

I'll stop this if it kills me," Combs promised himself before the ball skipped through his legs and rolled to the wall as the batter and two other runners circled the bases.

In the clubhouse, sitting dejectedly in front of his locker, Combs was consoled by his manager, Joe McCarthy. "I know how you feel," McCarthy began. "But don't feel that way anymore. You're my center fielder. It won't be long before you know how to field ground balls."

With that pat on the back, Combs developed into a superlative ballhawk and, with batting averages of .344 and .380, was sold to the Yankees for $30,000 after the 1923 season.

Combs demonstrated his preparedness by batting .400 in his first 24 games as a Yankee. A fractured leg sidelined him for the rest of the season.

In Louisville, the swift Combs had been known as the "Mail Carrier," but in New York he was the "Waiter," waiting to be driven around the bases by the explosive bats of Murderers' Row. As a leadoff batter, he could wangle a base on balls, if necessary, but he also could bunt in all directions and he could drill the ball with the best. In his first complete season, Earle rapped 203 hits and batted .342.

In 1926, the Kentucky Colonel batted .299—and there's a story that partially explains that figure.

The Yankees clinched the pennant in St. Louis on a Saturday and the next day clowned through a meaningless doubleheader with the Browns, who, entering into the spirit of the occasion, let anyone pitch.

Not to be outdone in the shenanigans, Combs struck out deliberately. When the official averages were released, it was discovered that the strikeout had cost Earle a .300 mark. The following year, he batted .356.

The '27 season was climaxed by the Yankees' four-game World Series sweep over the Pirates. Combs scored the deciding run in the final game when Johnny Miljus uncorked a wild pitch in the last inning.

Combs and his first manager, McCarthy, were reunited in New York in 1931 when Joe took over the Yankees. And McCarthy was in the dugout on a steamy July afternoon in 1934 when Combs crashed into the concrete wall at Sportsman's Park in St. Louis.

The outfielder suffered a fractured skull and a broken collarbone and arm, but thanks to the surgical wizardry of Dr. Robert F. Hyland, Combs was repaired sufficiently well to play one final season for the Yankees, in 1935.

After coaching for the Yankees, Browns, Red Sox and Phillies, Combs returned to Kentucky where, among other interests, he served as a state banking commissioner and a regent at his almamater, Eastern Kentucky.

Earle Combs, one of the more overlooked elements of the Yankees' devastating 1927 machine, takes a healthy cut at a pitch during the second game of the 1927 World Series against the Pittsburgh Pirates.

CHARLES COMISKEY

Charles A. Comiskey, alias the Old Roman, is pictured with his grandson at his summer home in Eagle River, Wis.

In more than 50 years of baseball experience, Charles A. Comiskey scaled the loftiest peaks and plumbed the lowest valleys of emotion, all created by championships and scandal-racked ball clubs.

Comiskey was a pitcher when he arrived in St. Louis to play for Chris Von der Ahe's Browns in 1882. After two games, he developed a sore arm and was about to be dismissed when he convinced the owners he was a better first baseman than the incumbent.

Comiskey was not long in proving his point. He revolutionized the style of play at the position. Playing yards off the base, he taught pitchers how to cover the bag on ground balls hit to the right side.

By 1883, Comiskey was managing the Browns, whom he led to American Association pennants from 1885 through 1888. In those four seasons, Comiskey arranged championship series with the National League titlists. The first year, the Browns and Chicago Colts split the first six games and the seventh and last contest resulted in a tie.

The following year, the Browns defeated Cap Anson's Chicago team, four games to two. St. Louis then lost to Detroit in 1887, 10 victories to five, before bowing to New York, four games to two, in 1888.

After a second-place finish in 1889, Comiskey accepted the managerial reins of the Chicago entry in the Players League. However, he returned to St. Louis in 1891 when he replaced his old boss, Von der Ahe, as manager.

When the N.L. absorbed the A.A. in 1892, Comiskey was named manager of the Cincinnati Reds. Three seasons with the Reds proved uneventful, but they did afford an opportunity to meet Byron Bancroft Johnson, a local sportswriter. Together, the two men plotted the birth of a new major league, the American, which emerged from the old Western League in 1901. Comiskey was given the franchise in his native Chicago.

One of Comiskey's first acts was to induce Clark Griffith to jump from Chicago's N.L. club, and Griffith pitched the White Sox to the first A.L. pennant.

About this time, Chicago journalist Hugh E. Keough referred to Comiskey as the "Old Roman," a name that followed him the rest of his life.

In 1906, the White Sox, with a team batting average of .228, won the pennant and then stunned the baseball world by upsetting Frank Chance's lordly cross-town Cubs.

By 1915, Comiskey and John McGraw of the Giants were ready to spread the baseball gospel around the world. At the conclusion of a global tour that played to crowned heads and commoners, Comiskey hosted a banquet for 700 in Chicago.

Comiskey was a generous host, and loved to invite as many as 100 congenial spirits to his summer home in Eagle River, Wis. He paid tuition at Notre Dame for the sons of pitcher Ed Walsh and catcher Billy Sullivan, and gave 10 percent of his revenue to the American Red Cross in World War I, but his players—even the superstars— were grossly underpaid. A $15,000 salary to Eddie Collins in 1915 was double the pay of any other Chicago player.

The White Sox won the 1917 World Series over the Giants and were league champions again in 1919. Before the first game of the 1919 Series in Cincinnati, rumors were rampant that gamblers had gotten to some Chicago players.

After the Chisox lost the first two games, performing in a most suspicious fashion, Comiskey was crushed. "I blame Ban Johnson for allowing the Series to continue," he blurted tearfully a short time later. "If ever a league president blundered in a crisis, Ban did."

The Series was permitted to continue, to a Cincinnati victory, and eight Chicago players were banished from Organized Baseball for their roles in a conspiracy to fix the outcome.

Comiskey never recovered from the blow; some observers said the Black Sox episode even affected his health.

At age 72, Comiskey died in 1931 at his summer home in Eagle River.

JOCKO CONLAN

Jocko Conlan, shown making a call at the plate during a 1959 game, was a small man with a big heart.

It was apparent from the way he walked, from the manner in which he thrust his chin and chest forward, that Jocko Conlan was an umpire—and one of the best.

Conlan's ability to umpire a flawless game was emphasized best perhaps in a letter he received early in his career from Bill Klem, the patron saint of umpires. "You are one man," wrote the Old Arbitrator, "who could have umpired in the old days."

In "the old days," only one umpire officiated a game.

Jocko was a legend long before he retired in 1964. Every player had a favorite tale to tell of the jaunty little fellow who wore his chest protector on the outside of his jacket and could keep up a running line of chatter with the most garrulous of persons.

The colorful career of John Bertrand Conlan was born the day in 1935 that Red Ormsby was felled by a sunstroke and was unable to work a White Sox game in St. Louis. Jocko was a Chicago outfielder who had been sidelined by a thumb fracture suffered in a clubhouse wrestling match.

Managers Jimmie Dykes of Chicago and Rogers Hornsby of St. Louis settled on Conlan as a fit replacement. Conlan performed in such grand style—he even called out teammate Luke Appling on an attempted triple—that his course was clearly set for the future.

When Conlan arrived as an umpire in the National League in 1941 after a five-year apprenticeship, the old circuit brightened perceptibly. The little fellow took on all comers and nobody ever gained a decision over him. Jocko, for instance, engaged in a shin-kicking episode with Leo Durocher. The Lip was bruised twice in that encounter—once by the league president and once when his toes banged into Jocko's shin guards.

Durocher was perhaps one of Jocko's ongoing dislikes. Once he invited Leo to take a punch at him. "Why?" asked Durocher. "So I can knock your block off," shot back Conlan.

Conlan was not above editorializing on occasion. In the ninth inning of the final game of the 1951 N.L. pennant playoffs, he sauntered to the mound to determine Brooklyn Manager Chuck Dressen's decision on a pitching change. Starter Don Newcombe was faltering.

"Branca," said Dressen.

"Branca!" snorted the incredulous Jocko, "a fastball pitcher? "

Branca it was, rather than curveballers Clem Labine or Carl Erskine, and Bobby Thomson socked the pitcher's second pitch for a three-run homer that won the pennant for the Giants.

Jocko insisted on abiding by the rules, usually. When a Cincinnati organist insisted on performing during game action, Jocko delivered an ultimatum that said, in effect: "Play between innings, otherwise shut up."

Conlan was asked if there was a league rule on the matter.

"There sure is," he said. I just made it.'"

If fan reaction ever alarmed Jocko, he never admitted it. He did confess, however, that his worst rhubarb was at the Polo Grounds in his rookie year of 1941. Missiles of all manner sailed out of the stands after Conlan ejected all-time favorite Mel Ott for protesting a strike.

Conlan had the utmost admiration for Walter O'Malley, president of the Dodgers. During a game at Ebbets Field, a foul tip struck Jocko on the throat. For 48 hours he was hospitalized while a throat specialist and nurses, all at O'Malley's expense, stood guard at the umpire's bedside.

When Jocko revealed in 1964 that he was about to retire, he was accorded farewell salutes in virtually every city he visited.

In Chicago, where Conlan grew up as a South Side rooter for the White Sox, N.L. President Warren Giles declared: "I know of no one who has been more dedicated to his profession, more loyal to the game in which he has been such a big part, and I hate to see him hang up his spikes."

TOMMY CONNOLLY

Tommy Connolly held the distinction of umpiring the first American League game in 1901.

Tommy Connolly, who never played a game of baseball, officiated at the first American League game in 1901, the first games at Comiskey Park, Shibe Park, Fenway Park and Yankee Stadium and, with Hank O'Day, called the first World Series in 1903.

A native of Manchester, England, Connolly was a cricket player when, as a teenager, he migrated with his parents to the United States and settled in Natick, Mass. There he appointed himself a batboy for a local baseball team. He graduated to the New England League where, on April 28, 1894, he called a game between Fall River and Portland.

Tim Hurst, famed 19th century umpire, spotted Connolly and recommended him to Ban Johnson when the former Cincinnati sportswriter organized the American League.

Connolly's first assignment was the Cleveland-Chicago season opener at the White Sox's ball park. Because all other A.L. openers were rained out, Connolly earned the distinction of umpiring the first game in the new major league. The Sox won, 8-2, in 1 hour, 30 minutes.

Tommy was known as Mr. Connolly by generations of players. He wore high, hard collars and his tie was always held in place by a jeweled stickpin. He dressed neatly and conservatively, figuring he was a prominent part of an American subculture.

Everything Connolly did was to upgrade his profession. He was quiet and subdued. He did not cater to the crowd or engage in theatrical gestures. He believed that the most efficient umpire was the one who attracted the least attention. He enjoyed the respect of all the players, and in one 10-year period did not eject a single player.

Babe Ruth once felt the sting of Tommy's temper and ever after greeted the arbiter with: "Hi ya, Tommy, you old son of a gun. Remember the day you tossed me?"

Tris Speaker once made the mistake of accusing Connolly of prejudice in making a decision against his Indians.

"I'll never forget the way Tommy looked at me," remembered Speaker. "His face turned purple and I thought his neck was about to burst. But his voice was almost a whisper. 'Tris,' he said, 'of course, you're out of the game. And unless you change your way of thinking, you'll be out of baseball for life.' "

Ty Cobb said of the umpire: "You can go so far with Tommy, but when you see his neck get red, it's time to lay off him."

It was against Cobb that Connolly made one of his most unpopular decisions. In the heat of a pennant race, the first-place Tigers were trailing the second-place team late in a game. A runner was on second base and the pitcher was attempting to walk Cobb intentionally. On the third pitch, Cobb stepped across the plate and smacked an apparent triple.

"What could I do but declare Cobb out and send the runner back to second base?" asked Connolly. I thought the players and fans would attack me, but fortunately there were a lot of police there and the Detroit newspapers the next day backed me up."

Of Connolly it was written that "he probably knew more firemen than any man in America." In his off-hours, the umpire frequented fire stations where his Irish wit and eagerness to talk baseball made him a popular visitor.

Connolly also demonstrated a willingness to help a young player over rough spots.

Once, when bench jockeys were hassling a rookie over the way he was toeing the rubber, Connolly called time, strolled to the mound and advised the pitcher: "Son, there are right and wrong ways to pitch in this league. Let me show you the right way. I'll take care of that wrecking crew in the dugout and from what you've shown me today, you'll be up here a long time." Eddie Plank was forever grateful.

After 30 years of active service, Connolly was appointed umpire-in-chief by American League President Will Harridge in 1931. He held the post until his retirement in 1954, seven years before his death at age 90.

ROGER CONNOR

History does not record the direction of Jim Mutrie's gaze when the New York manager shouted to his players, "Come on, you Giants," but there is an excellent chance that he was looking at Roger Connor.

Connor, a 6-foot-2, 210-pound first baseman, was a giant in more ways than one. A bat was a genuine shillelagh for the Connecticut Irishman, who clouted 132 home runs from 1880 through 1897 in an era when the homer was a rarity and almost held in disrepute.

Until the advent of Babe Ruth and the lively ball, Connor reigned as the all-time home run king. One of his homers was especially memorable. It was socked at the old Polo Grounds at 110th Street and Fifth Avenue and sailed over the right-field fence onto 112th Street.

Several members of the New York Stock Exchange, occupying box seats, were so smitten by the Herculean clout that they took a collection for the slugger known as "Dear Old Roger."

When the contributions were totaled, the fans were able to present a $500 gold watch to their hero.

Home runs weren't Connor's only claim to fame. Roger's career total of 227 triples was exceeded only by Sam Crawford, Ty Cobb, Honus Wagner and Jake Beckley.

Roger was one of eight children born to Irish immigrants in Waterbury, Conn., his lifelong home. A younger brother Joe, a catcher, played for Cleveland, Milwaukee and New York in the American League and Boston in the National.

Connor entered professional baseball as a lefthanded third baseman, and became a first baseman only because of a dislocated shoulder that handicapped his throwing.

Connor enjoyed one of his biggest days at the plate on May 9, 1888, when he clouted three home runs against Indianapolis. On May 31, 1890, while playing for the New York team in the Players League, Connor was one of three players who homered in the same inning against Pittsburgh hurler John K. Tener, later governor of Pennsylvania.

Roger's most productive game occurred on June 1, 1895, when he was a member of the St. Louis Browns. Playing against his old teammates, the Giants, handsome, mustachioed Roger rapped two doubles, a triple and three singles in a 6-for-6 performance that highlighted a 23-8 rout against Jouett Meekin, who pitched the entire game.

Connor left the majors in 1897 and the following season purchased the Waterbury club of the Connecticut League. There Roger served as manager-first baseman, his wife worked in the box office and his adopted daughter sold tickets.

Roger batted .319 in 1898 and the next season, at 42, led the league with a .392 average.

In 1902, when Connor was managing and operating the Springfield club in the Connecticut League, a young umpire officiated a game with Meriden. First, the arbiter's calls angered Meriden players, then the umpire incurred the wrath of the Springfield players with more unpopular calls.

At game's end, the young umpire feared the worst from the bespectacled, fierce-looking Springfield pilot. But Bill Klem was relieved when Roger extended his hand and declared: "Young man, let me congratulate you for umpiring a fine ball game."

After retiring from baseball, Connor served as a school inspector for the city of Waterbury.

Late in Connor's career, the slugger's wife gave Roger a handsome weather vane fashioned from two baseball bats. The vane was a Waterbury landmark for years, even after one of the bats was broken in a storm and the home was sold by the Connors.

Roger Connor (pictured in 1887) was one of baseball's biggest power threats in the 1890s.

STAN COVELESKI

In 1921, when the Cleveland Indians were in spring training at Dallas, Tex., Manager Tris Speaker arranged an outing for the players at his farm in nearby Hubbard.

As Speaker was preparing the barbecue, pitcher Stan Coveleski suggested to young shortstop Joe Sewell that they take a rowboat ride on a nearby lake. Sewell consented.

As they approached the middle of the lake, Coveleski asked Sewell if he could swim. "No," replied Joe.

"Now's as good a time as any," chirped Coveleski, shoving Sewell overboard a quarter mile from shore.

Sewell nearly drowned before a rescue party got to him. The near tragedy was nothing but good, clean fun to Coveleski.

Born Stanislaus Kowalewski in the coal-mining town of Shamokin, Pa., Stanley was preceded to the major leagues by older brother Harry (who acquired a reputation as a "Giant killer" in 1908 when the Phillies' hurler defeated New York three times in a five-game series).

Harry later starred for the Detroit Tigers, and for a period of 20 years the family name appeared regularly in major league box scores.

Curiously, the brothers faced each other on only one occasion.

"I was with Lancaster of the Tri-State League and Harry was already in the majors," Stanley remembered. "We faced each other in an exhibition game and when neither team scored in five innings our managers took us out.

"Harry refused to pitch against me in the majors. He told the Detroit manager never to use him when I was pitching. He explained to me, 'Win or lose, it would take something away from us. If I lose, they'll say I was laying down on purpose so you could win. If I win, they'll say you were laying down.'"

The younger Coveleski did little "laying down" during his major league career. The spitballer was especially brilliant in the 1920 World Series against Brooklyn.

In the first game he made 72 pitches, winning 3-1. In his second appearance, he made 78 pitches and won, 5-1. Coveleski's third outing in the nine-game Series was a 3-0 shutout in which he made 82 deliveries. In each contest, he yielded only five hits.

Control was Coveleski's foremost asset. In one regular season game, he reportedly did not pitch a ball out of the strike zone until the seventh inning. In 1920, when he won 24 games, the righthander issued only 65 walks in 315 innings, an average of less than two every nine innings.

Coveleski was one of 17 spitball pitchers permitted to

Cleveland's Stan Coveleski was one of 17 pitchers permitted to throw the spitball after its ban in 1920.

use the moist delivery after it was banned in 1920 and he capitalized on it fully.

Ordinarily, Stan did not try for strikeouts, but he altered his style in a game against Washington after Sam Rice led off an inning with a triple.

"I threw spitballs to the next three batters and they struck out," he recalled. "Steve O'Neill was our catcher, the greatest I ever played with, and those balls were breaking so much he didn't catch a single one. But he did block them and we got out of the inning without them scoring."

Coveleski, who threw the spitter "about once in every five pitches," was traded to Washington after the 1924 season and responded with a 20-5 record for the pennant-winning Nats of 1925.

A rawboned righthander who once worked for $3.75 a week in the coal mines, Coveleski settled in South Bend, Ind., after retiring in 1928. He operated a service station for several years before settling into an easier lifestyle that afforded plenty of time for fishing.

SAM CRAWFORD

Charley Dryden, the noted baseball wit of the early 1900s, delighted in composing fictitious interviews such as the one that appeared in the *Philadelphia North American*.

"To what do you attribute your tremendous physique?" the writer allegedly asked Sam Crawford.

"Whacking wind-whipped whiskers in Wahoo," was the alliterative answer by the Detroit outfielder.

While readers chuckled over Dryden's fertile imagination, Crawford, the hardest-hitting barber to come out of Wahoo, Neb., was scarcely a laughing matter to pitchers.

"There never was a better hitter than Sam Crawford," declared Ed Barrow, the famed Yankee executive who was manager of the Tigers in 1903. "He was the Lou Gehrig of his day."

Sam was a product of Wahoo (pop. 2,100), where his father, operator of the general store, was reputed to be the strongest man in the town.

Nobody did more than Sam to popularize his home-town. For years a billboard on the outskirts of the community proclaimed, "The Home Town of Sam Crawford." The player's plaque at Cooperstown lists his nickname as Wahoo Sam.

The young Crawford wasted no time in reaching the major leagues. One summer he was accompanying about 12 other youths, riding a farm wagon across the Nebraska plains and playing games against other town teams wherever they could be found. One year later Crawford was in the majors, having played only 103 games in the minor leagues.

Sam joined the Cincinnati Reds in September of 1899, and immediately engaged in an unusual doubleheader. In the first game against Cleveland, Crawford drilled two singles; in the second game, against Louisville, the left fielder rapped two more singles and a triple. It was the first of Sam's record 312 triples, a mark that appears likely to withstand the ravages of time.

Tales of Sam's slugging prowess are endless. When League Park was built in Cleveland, a 45-foot-high screen was erected atop the right-field wall as a deterrent to Crawford's clouts. Sam paid it little heed. He simply lofted drives over the screen.

Although no speed merchant, Sam knew how to run bases. He stole 367 bases in his 19-year career, including 37 in 1911 and 41 in 1912.

During the war between the National and American leagues, Crawford signed contracts for 1903 with both

Wahoo Sam Crawford, pictured during his 1910 season with Detroit, fell 36 hits short of the magic 3,000 level.

Cincinnati and Detroit. When the leagues signed a peace agreement, Sam was awarded to Detroit, where he batted behind Ty Cobb.

For several periods during their years as teammates, Crawford and Cobb did not speak to each other.

But when Hall of Fame electors failed to enshrine Crawford as quickly as Cobb thought they should, the old Georgia Peach campaigned vigorously for Sam.

After batting .173 in 61 games in 1917, Crawford departed the majors. He played four years for Los Angeles of the Pacific Coast League and, at age 41, was still capable of banging 199 hits for a .318 average in 1921.

When he was named to the Hall of Fame in 1957, Sam was living in a beach cabin in Pearblossom, Calif. He subscribed to a simple lifestyle, unrecognized by his neighbors as a former celebrity. He had no telephone "because people are always calling and wanting to talk." His spartan dwelling had an outside shower, constructed by Sam's own hands, and a television set, the gift of friends. The TV was not connected.

JOE CRONIN

Horatio Alger would have loved him. Hollywood could have done wonders with his story. He was the embodiment of the pluck-and-luck theme that transformed shoeshine boys into wealthy and influential magnates.

He even married the boss's daughter, but that wasn't important to the phenomenal success saga of Joe Cronin.

The son of Irish immigrants, Cronin grew up in the Mission District of San Francisco and attended the same high school that had launched Gentlemen Jim Corbett and Harry Heilmann toward athletic fame.

Joe attained his initial athletic prominence when, at age 15, he won the junior tennis championship of San Francisco.

But baseball transcended all other interests. Cronin was 18 when Joe Devine, Pittsburgh scout, signed him for the Johnstown (Middle Atlantic) club. Three years later, the young shortstop was with Kansas City (American Association), having been sold outright by the Pirates, who were happy with shortstop Glenn Wright.

Enter Joe Engel, a scout for Washington. Kansas City's shortstop caught the scout's eye, and Engel arranged a deal with Blues Owner George Muehlebach to purchase the player for $7,500.

When Cronin joined the Senators, Owner Clark Griffith was not immediately impressed with the .242-hitting rookie. The Old Fox's personal choice for shortstop was Bobby Reeves, but every morning's paper revealed that Cronin was playing the position while the Nats were on the road.

Griffith wired his manager, Bucky Harris: "Reeves will never learn to play shortstop if you don't play him."

"Neither will Cronin," replied Bucky by return wire.

Harris admired Cronin's spirit, his willingness to take morning batting practice and field grounders by the hour.

By 1930, the Californian was regarded as the best all-around shortstop in the American League. With a batting average of .346 and 126 runs batted in, the 24-year-old Cronin was named the American League's Most Valuable Player.

At the close of the 1932 campaign, while he was recovering from a tonsillectomy in Washington, Joe was named manager of the Senators, succeeding Walter Johnson.

The next season, Cronin guided Washington to the American League pennant, although the Senators dropped a five-game World Series to the Giants.

Joe Cronin was a shortstop for the Washington Senators (above) in 1934 and the president of the American League (below) 25 years later.

After a seventh-place finish in injury-riddled 1934, Cronin was in his native San Francisco on his honeymoon when he received a call from Griffith. Tom Yawkey, young and wealthy owner of the Red Sox, had dazzled the Old Fox with his checkbook and offered $250,000, plus shortstop Lyn Lary, for Cronin, who would be named manager.

"Make the deal," said Cronin. "You can't afford not to."

Cronin was 36 in 1943 when he established an AL record with five pinch home runs, two with the bases loaded.

A fractured leg ended Cronin's playing career in April of 1945. He managed the Red Sox to a pennant in '46. In 1948, Joe was appointed the club's general manager, a position he held for 11 years, until he was elected president of the American League. He occupied that chair until 1974 when, completing his Alger-like climb, he was named chairman of the A.L.

CANDY CUMMINGS

Any youth walking along the beach in Brooklyn in the 1860s was apt to pick up a clam shell and give it a robust heave.

But young William Arthur Cummings, called Arthur by his family, was different from others his age. Watching the shells follow an irregular course as they flew across the water, Arthur grew curious. What accounted for the shells' unpredictable behavior, he wondered.

Curiosity led Cummings to the conclusion that a baseball could be made to act similarly if proper forces were applied.

Shortly, he was baffling players on neighborhood lots. Arthur's breaking pitch may have defied the laws of physics to his contemporaries, but they were unable to make contact with it while swinging wildly at the plate.

On the testimony of baseball historian Henry (Father) Chadwick, Arthur (Candy) Cummings invented the curveball and thereby earned a niche in the Hall of Fame.

Pitching in the face of the wind, Candy drove his catcher to distraction as the batterymate tried to corral the erratic pitches barehanded. To his dismay, Cummings learned his pitches were only routine tosses when the wind was at his back.

The young inventor's first recognition outside his hometown was gained in 1867 when the Excelsiors of Brooklyn visited New England where they opposed, among other teams, the "Harvards of Cambridge."

The Excelsiors' regular pitcher was indisposed, so Candy, a term of admiration in the 1860s, was nominated to pitch. The wind was again blowing toward the pitcher's mound, and Candy gave his new pitch a good workout.

After the game, the baffled Harvards asked Cummings: "What were you pitching us? It came at us and then it went away from us."

Candy's "horizontal whip of the wrist" soon found countless imitators. His secret was in the public domain.

Candy joined the "Stars of Brooklyn" in 1868, launching a four-year career with the aggregation that advertised itself as "the championship team of the United States and Canada." Cummings pitched the majority of the Stars' games, including a 24-12 victory over the Mutuals of New York, a professional organization like the Stars.

When Cummings defeated the Mutuals, 14-3, in an 1871 game, his reputation exceeded all bounds. Limiting an opponent to three runs in that era was exceedingly rare.

The prestigious Mutuals acquired Candy's services in 1872 when that club was a member of the National Association, forerunner of the National League. Player

Candy Cummings baffled many an opposing batter after discovering how to make a baseball curve.

contracts were taken lightly in the 1870s, and Cummings signed with three other clubs before deciding that the Mutuals offered the best vehicle for his talents.

Cummings was with Baltimore and Philadelphia the next two seasons before signing with the Hartford Dark Blues in the NL's baptismal season of 1876. Inexplicably, Candy did not appear in any games from May through August, but compiled a 16-8 record in September and October. On September 9, the 120-pound righthander became the original "iron man" of baseball, hurling the Dark Blues to a doubleheader sweep over the Cincinnati Reds.

In 1877, Cummings was a member of the Cincinnati staff, but his touch was gone and the local journals blasted him unmercifully for his deficiencies. One paper editorialized: "This thing of examining scores of games in which the Cincinnati Reds play, and seeing from 18 to 25 hits each day being piled up against Cummings' record, is getting sickening. His presence on the team is demoralizing. Unless the evil is remedied, the club on its return will not attract 100 people to the games. No change could be for the worse."

Cummings' career ended in 1878 with the Forest City club of Cleveland. Candy returned to his native Massachusetts where, in the town of Athol, he opened a paint and wallpaper business in 1902. He sold the store in 1920, four years before his death.

KIKI CUYLER

In the opinion of one highly respected scout, he was "a righthanded Ty Cobb . . . but more gentlemanly."He could do more things with his glove than Cobb, could throw better, could pick up ground balls better and was one of the most graceful players of all time.

Kiki Cuyler's double won the deciding game of the 1925 World Series against Washington, yet two years later Kiki remained on the bench as the Pirates lost the Series to the Yankees in four games.

The mystery of Cuyler's absence in the Series was never discussed publicly by Cuyler or Manager Donie Bush, but many years later Paul Waner, a member of the 1927 Bucs, revealed the circumstances leading up to the strange treatment.

It all started when Bush promoted Cuyler from the No. 3 spot in the batting order to the No. 2 position, according to Waner. Cuyler seethed over the change, maintaining that as an undisciplined hitter he was ill suited to bat second.

After a Pittsburgh victory in which Cuyler went hitless, Bush tried to console his outfielder. "Tough luck, Kiki," he said, "but don't worry about going hitless. We won and you'll start finding the holes."

"The hell with winning," Cuyler exploded. I didn't get a hit and that's what counts."

Bush waited 30 seconds, then declared: "Cuyler, you have played your last game for this club as long as I'm manager."

Bush was as good as his word. While fans chanted "We want Cuyler" and banners bearing the same message fluttered around Forbes Field, Bush never glanced in Cuyler's direction, not even to pinch-hit. Shortly after the '27 season, Owner Barney Dreyfuss traded Cuyler to Chicago for Sparky Adams and Floyd Scott.

A native of Harrisville, Mich., Cuyler attended the United States Military Academy during World War I. He gained instant acclaim on the football field, but withdrew from the academy at the close of hostilities in Europe.

He obtained a job at the Buick plant in Flint, Mich., but when he was reduced to part-time work in the postwar recession, Cuyler turned to professional baseball and joined the Bay City club in the Michigan Ontario League.

Kiki Cuyler was as graceful afield as he was devastating with his bat.

In a 1921 doubleheader, Cuyler drove a ball over the left-field fence and batted in virtually all his team's runs. Still, a Detroit scout turned thumbs down on Cuyler because he reported—and Cuyler later confirmed—Kiki could not hit a curveball.

A Pittsburgh scout detected no such weakness and recommended his purchase. Two years later, while playing for Nashville, Cuyler mastered the curve. He also won an automobile as the most valuable player in the Southern Association and acquired the nickname that followed him the remainder of his life.

For years he had answered to the name of "Cuy." At Nashville, when a fly ball was hit toward center field, the shortstop, and then the second baseman, would cry "Cuy," signifying that Cuyler was to make the catch.

In turn, the spectators picked up the cry until a sportswriter tagged him phonetically with Kiki.

Cuyler was a full-fledged star by 1925, his second full major league season. He batted .357 and scored 144 runs, then a league record, to finish second to Rogers Hornsby in the National League's Most Valuable Player voting. Ten of his 220 hits came in succession.

In the '25 World Series, Kiki's home run clinched Game 2. And in Game 7, Cuyler made a spectacular catch before hitting a bases-loaded double off Walter Johnson that drove in the deciding runs.

In 1928, his first season with the Cubs, Cuyler ran into the wall and for weeks was unable to grip a bat properly. But he was the Cuyler of old in 1929 when he batted .360 and drove in 102 runs to help the Cubs beat Bush's Pirates for the pennant.

Stints at Cincinnati and Brooklyn closed out Kiki's career. Cuyler became a successful minor league manager and he was a coach for the Red Sox under Joe McCarthy, his old Chicago boss, in 1949.

An ardent outdoorsman, Cuyler suffered a heart attack while ice fishing near Harrisville the following winter. Ten days later, while en route to a hospital in Ann Arbor, Mich., he was stricken fatally.

RAY DANDRIDGE

Ray Dandridge's first fling with Organized Baseball came in 1949 at age 36 for the Minneapolis Millers.

In the summer of 1949, when black players were still a curiosity in major league baseball and club executives were timid, almost reluctant, to participate in the great social experiment, a telephone call was placed to the manager of the New York Cubans, a black team touring the Midwest.

The caller was Alex Pompez, owner of the Cubans and a scout for the New York Giants. On the other end of the line, Manager Ray Dandridge waited expectantly for the message. Perhaps Señor Pompez wished to discuss club policy, maybe a young prospect who could strengthen his team.

The owner came right to the point. "Would you like to play in the major leagues before you quit?" he asked.

Dandridge was equally direct. "Yes," he replied.

That being the case, Pompez resumed. "Pack up and catch the first plane to Minneapolis," he said.

Turning the Cubans over to an assistant, Dandridge flew to Minneapolis. He was well aware that Minneapolis had no major league franchise. But it was a New York farm club in the American Association, which was only a short hop from the Polo Grounds. According to reports, Monte Irvin, an old friend of Dandridge, was already high on the list of black prospects in the Giant organization.

Upon his arrival at the Minneapolis airport, Dandridge was met by a representative of the Minneapolis Millers, who whisked him to Nicollet Park, where the team was engaged in a losing battle against the Louisville Colonels. Suitcase in hand, Ray ambled into the dugout. "When did you play last?" asked Manager Tommy Heath by way of a greeting.

"Yesterday."

"How would you like to go up and hit?" inquired the rotund skipper.

Dandridge glanced quickly at the mound, from where a tall and skinny 20-year-old lefthander was firing fastballs past befuddled batters. He was Maurice (Mickey) McDermott, who had set a league record a few weeks before by fanning 20 batters in a single game. Obviously, McDermott was good, but it made no difference to an experienced batter who had faced Satchel Paige and Max Lanier in their heydays.

I'll go up and try," Dandridge replied.

The southpaw's first pitch whizzed under the batter's chin. Dandridge was undisturbed. Dusters were commonplace where he came from. He moved back about an inch and awaited the second offering. This one he met solidly and lined it to the right side. At the last possible moment, the second baseman stabbed the ball with an acrobatic leap.

The 5-foot-6, 180-pounder appeared in 98 more games as a rookie and batted .362, six points below the mark of the batting champion.

Though he never was given the chance to play major league baseball, Dandridge enjoyed his moment in the sun when he was inducted into the baseball Hall of Fame in 1987 at Cooperstown.

At first, the newcomer was stationed at second base. After 18 games, however, he was switched to third. That suited Dandridge, who was widely known as the pre-eminent black third sacker of all time.

Though Ray's batting average slipped to .311 in 1950, his all-around excellence left a favorable impression with the league press corps. When the most valuable-player ballots were tabulated in September, Ray Dandridge won a close vote over teammate Bert Haas and Columbus' Solly Hemus.

Those who had watched the bow-legged Dandridge dominate the black leagues for more than a decade were not surprised at the distinction. Monte Irvin, for one, lavished praise on his old Newark teammate. "You could hardly get a baseball past him," asserted Irvin, a part-time third baseman himself. "He made very few errors and was flashy. He came in on swinging bunts, grabbed the ball bare-handed, threw to first without looking and got his man."

Brooklyn catcher Roy Campanella enthused in a similar vein. "I played with Billy Cox and saw Brooks Robinson," said the three-time National League MVP. "Believe me, Dandridge could match 'em all."

Raymond Emmett Dandridge was born in Richmond, Va., in 1913. He was a Golden Gloves boxer and quarterbacked his high school football team until an opposing lineman laid him low with a savage tackle, after which he concentrated on baseball.

In 1933, Dandridge accepted an offer to turn professional with the Detroit Stars. He was an outfielder then, but an all-wise manager spotted infield potential and switched the youngster to third base. Ray also was urged to swing a heavier bat, a suggestion that helped him blossom into a .333 hitter.

Dandridge joined the Newark Dodgers, forerunners of the Eagles, in 1934. When the Mexican League operators sounded their siren song of pesos in 1940, the third baseman hastened South of the Border. Playing for Vera Cruz, he hit safely in "29 or 30 straight games" for a league record and was presented a plaque bearing the inscription, "He Came, He Conquered."

At this stage of his career, Ray Dandridge played baseball throughout the year. One year he played on a championship club in Venezuela. "Then I went to Mexico," he said, "and played two months and we finished first. I finished the same year in Cuba and vie were nosed out by half a game."

Unfortunately for Dandridge, the racial barriers in the United States remained in place through his prime. He was 36 when he joined Minneapolis. Chances of gaining a major league opportunity were diminishing with his advancing years. Reports that major league clubs other than the Giants sought his services never materialized. While younger blacks entered the ranks of Organized Ball and went on to spectacular careers, Dandridge was left to wonder what might have been had the racial barrier been broken 10 years earlier.

He was watching a movie in Sioux City in 1951 when a message appeared on the screen, advising his roommate, Willie Mays, to report to the box office. Mays was off, with his .477 batting average, to New York, while Dandridge was left behind to bat .324 for the Millers.

Ray was traded to Sacramento of the Pacific Coast League in 1952 and wound up his career with Oakland in the same circuit in 1953, when he batted .268 in 87 games. He was 40 when he retired.

GEORGE DAVIS

George Davis was one of the central players in the battle between the National and American leagues in the early years of the 20th century, and his personal desire to remain in the National League almost destroyed the tenuous peace between the two leagues.

Davis was a switch-hitting sensation for the New York Giants, posting averages of .306 or better for nine consecutive years between 1893 and 1901. On Aug. 15, 1895, he went 6-for-6 in one game. He also hit three triples in a game on two occasions (both extra-inning games), hit 26 triples in one season and 167 for his career, both records for a switch-hitter. His best season was in 1893, when he posted a career-high average of .373.

Born in Cohoes, N.Y. on Aug. 23, 1870, Davis began his professional career in Albany in 1889. A 5-foot-9, 180-pounder, Davis joined Cleveland, a National League team, in 1890 and played three years, first as an outfielder and then as an infielder. In March 1893, Davis was traded to the New York Giants for Buck Ewing, considered by many at the time the greatest catcher of his day—and a future Hall of Famer.

Davis became a star on the Giants, hitting in 33 consecutive games in 1893, a record at the time, and even became the player-manager on two occasions—part of the 1895 season and from 1900-1901—compiling a record of 107-139.

In 1902, Davis jumped to the Chicago White Sox of the American League, but dissatisfied with owner Charles Comiskey's pay structure, he immediately jumped back to the Giants before the 1903 season began. Peace was declared between the two warring leagues early in 1903, and as part of the settlement, Davis was "awarded" to the White Sox. Davis was upset by the ruling and refused to play for the White Sox. In June of that year, he returned to the Giants and played in four games before Comiskey obtained a court injunction ordering Davis not to play for the Giants until the matter was resolved.

In the ensuing legal battle, Davis was represented by John Montgomery Ward, who immediately became an enemy of Ban Johnson, the president of the American League. Their personal feud continued for years and eventually resulted in Johnson blocking an attempt to name Ward president of the National League in 1909.

On July 15, 1903, Ward's attempt to keep Davis with the Giants was unsuccessful, and the labor peace was preserved, with Davis reluctantly agreeing to join the White Sox. He played six more seasons as the White Sox shortstop, but never regained his prior offensive form and never batted better than .278. However, he did help

the so-called "Hitless Wonders" win a world championship in 1906, collecting six RBIs in the six-game victory over the Cubs.

Davis finished his career as player-manager with Des Moines in the Western League in 1910. He later served as the baseball coach at Amherst College in Massachusetts from 1913-1918.

For his career, Davis played in 2,377 games over a 20-year span and finished with 2,683 hits, 454 doubles, 73 homers, 1,544 runs, 1,435 RBI and a career average of .297 during a period known as the Dead Ball Era. Defensively Davis led his league in double plays five times and led in total chances and fielding percentage four times.

The legal battle was a likely reason Davis was overlooked for Hall of Fame consideration for many years, despite the fact his career performance was arguably better than the careers of Bobby Wallace and Rabbit Maranville, both Hall-of-Fame shortstops from Davis' era.

Little is known about Davis' life after he left the Amherst College coaching job. Research by the Hall of Fame failed to find out anything about Davis' whereabouts until 1968, when a woman claiming to be a niece of Davis showed up in Cooperstown. She provided the name of Davis' sister, who informed Lee Allen, the Hall-of-Fame Historian, that her brother had died in the Philadelphia State Hospital in Philadelphia in 1934.

A search for the death certificate found that Davis' sister had the right place but the wrong date. Davis had been confined to the state hospital in 1934 and died there on Oct. 17, 1940.

Davis was elected to the Hall of Fame by the Veterans Committee in 1998.

During his career, George Davis played in 2,377 games over a 20-year span.

LEON DAY

A 1941 publicity release from the Newark Eagles described Leon Day as 'the most versatile and outstanding player on the team" and "the most desirable player on any club." It would be hard to dispute either statement.

During his career in the Negro Leagues in the 1930s and 1940s, the righthanded Day was the league's most consistent pitcher, but he didn't limit his work to the mound. He was the Eagles' opening day starter in 1941, but when the regular center fielder was drafted into the military, Day played that spot for most of the season. Later in the year, an injury to an infielder opened a spot at second base, and Day moved there, forming a formidable double-play combination with shortstop Monte Irvin.

The 5-foot-10, 180-pound Day also was used frequently as a pinch-hitter, and was a consistent .300 hitter during his 20-year professional career, which included stints in the Mexican League, the Venezuelan League and the minor leagues.

Day missed two prime years of his career, in 1944 and 1945, while serving in the Army in World War II. Part of his duty came with an amphibian unit which landed on Utah Beach during the Allied invasion of France.

After he was discharged from the Army in February 1946, Day returned to the Eagles and promptly pitched a no-hitter on opening day against the Philadelphia Stars. For the season he led the league in strikeouts, innings pitched and complete games, and led the Eagles to the pennant with a 13-4 record.

Even though he was suffering from a sore arm, Day started two games in the World Series against Kansas City and also made a game-saving catch while playing centerfield in another game as the Eagles won the series in seven games.

Noted for his quick wit and sense of humor, Day also was a highly competitive player who seemed to perform best in crucial situations. Using a no-windup, short-arm delivery, Day appeared in a record seven East-West All-Star games between 1935-1946, and won the 1942 game, striking out five of the seven hitters he faced. Earlier that season he established what is regarded as the Negro League record for most strikeouts in a game, 18, against the Baltimore Elite Giants.

He also is considered to hold the strikeout record in the Puerto Rican league and for the East-West All-Star game. In a Puerto Rican game in 1941, Day struck out 19 batters in an extra-inning game and in January 1941, had 15 strikeouts in a nine-inning game.

Day played baseball as a youngster growing up in the

Leon Day, elected to the Hall in '95, was the most consistent pitcher of his day in the Negro Leagues.

Mount Winan's district of Baltimore. He quit school after 10th grade and played sandlot ball with a local athletic club. He was playing second base for a semipro team in 1934 when he signed in midseason with the Baltimore Sox for $60 a month. He moved to the Brooklyn Eagles in 1935, where he was made pitcher and posted a 9-3 record.

Day joined the Newark team in 1936 when Abe Manley bought the Brooklyn Eagles and consolidated it with the Newark Dodgers. In 1937, Day's record was a perfect 13-0 during league play, with his only loss coming in an exhibition game. After missing most of the 1938 season with an arm injury, Day returned to post a 16-4 record in 1939.

He pitched in Venezuela in 1940, compiling a 12-1 record and leading Vargas to the league championship. He spent the rest of the year pitching for Veracruz in Mexico, adding a 6-0 record and another league championship.

One of Day's personal career highlights came against the Monarchs in 1942. The Monarchs were playing the Homestead Grays in the World Series and won the first three games. At that point, the Grays imported Day and three other players, adding them to their roster. Day pitched the fourth game, and beat Satchel Paige and the Monarchs 4-1, allowing only five hits. The Monarchs filed a protest, denying that they had allowed the Grays to add extra players because of injuries. The protest was upheld and the game was thrown out. The Monarchs won the series.

Day's last full season in the Negro Leagues was 1949, when he pitched for the Baltimore Elite Giants and celebrated another league championship. Day's playing career concluded in 1954. He was elected to the Hall of Fame in 1995, but died at age 78 just months before the induction ceremony.

DIZZY DEAN

Broadcaster Dean amused listeners with his peculiar use of the English language.

Almost every story told about Dizzy Dean, incredible as it may sound, contains an element of truth. The "Great One" did nothing to discourage the legends that sprouted in his footsteps. Frequently, the stories were embroidered, but they were told in such a folksy, good old-boy fashion that everyone subscribed willingly.

Like the day Dean stopped in front of the Boston dugout and proclaimed: "No curves today, fellas, just hard ones." He then shut out the Braves on three hits.

Or the day he wagered he could strike out Vince DiMaggio four times. He fanned the eldest DiMaggio three times and had a two-strike count on the batter when DiMaggio lifted a high pop foul. As the catcher prepared to make the catch, Dean raced in from the mound, shouting, "Drop it! Drop it!"

The catcher did as ordered, whereupon Dean fanned DiMaggio. He won the bet—all of one dollar.

Before the start of the 1934 season, Dean announced that "me 'n' Paul's gonna win 45 games." He erred slightly. They totaled 49 victories, with Diz accounting for 30.

When the Cardinals arrived in Detroit for the start of the '34 World Series, Dean, still in street clothes, strolled into the batting cage while the Tigers were taking practice. Grabbing the bat from Mickey Cochrane, the Tigers' catcher-manager, Diz clouted a pitch over the fence, then

informed the flabbergasted Cochrane, "I'm the worst hitter on our club."

In Game 4 of the Series, Dean was inserted as a pinchrunner. It was an ill-advised action. Dean was knocked unconscious when struck on the head by an infielder's throw. But he was back in form for Game 7 when he blanked the Tigers, 11-0.

A native of Arkansas with only a fourth-grade education, Dean served in the United States Army where he learned the rudiments of pitching. At a Cardinals tryout camp in Texas, he dazzled the supervisors by striking out three batters on nine pitches. He was called back for a second look and repeated his earlier feat to earn a contract with St. Joseph (Western).

Dean progressed rapidly—about as speedily as the fastball he fogged past bewildered batters. On July 30, 1933, en route to 20 wins and 199 strikeouts, he set a major league record by striking out 17 Cubs.

But 1934 was the year of years for the big righthander. His 30-7 record, with 195 strikeouts, earned him the National League's Most Valuable Player award. Only Denny McLain, in 1968, matched Dean's victory total in the next half-century.

Ol' Diz was a constant thorn to Manager Frankie Frisch in that pennant-winning season of '34. He staged a brief strike because brother Paul was earning only $5,000 as a rookie. He missed exhibition games and was in headlines constantly with other capers, on and off the field.

But Frisch was not blind to Dean's superb talents.

"Dean was a natural," the manager declared. "He was the best fielding pitcher I ever saw. He

Dizzy Dean (seated left) and brother Paul (right) in 1935 when they accounted for 47 victories as members of St. Louis' Gashouse Gang.

Dean, pinch running in game 4 of the 1934 World Series, goes down after being hit in the head by a throw from Detroit shortstop Billy Rogell. Dean was carried off on a stretcher.

could run the bases and when he was right, you didn't have to give him instructions, just the ball."

Dean wanted to bypass the 1937 All-Star Game because of fatigue, but yielded to Owner Sam Breadon's importunities and reported to Griffith Stadium in Washington. A line drive off the bat of Earl Averill struck and fractured Dean's toe in the third inning of the N.L.'s 8-3 loss.

Trying to pitch before his toe healed, Diz put an unnatural strain on his arm. He was pitching in Boston when something snapped. His arm was dead. In April of 1938, he was traded to the Cubs for three players and $185,000.

Dead-armed Diz enjoyed one last moment in the sun during the 1938 World Series. Pitching with nothing more than his old craftiness, Dean held a 3-2 lead over the Yankees until Frank Crosetti and Joe DiMaggio tagged him for late-inning home runs that gave New York a 2-0 edge in their World Series sweep.

Dean hung on for two more seasons before switching to the radio booth. He was broadcasting St. Louis Browns games in 1947 and criticizing pitchers regularly when management, as a promotional stunt, signed Dean for the last game of the season. In typical Dean manner, he blanked the Chicago White Sox for four innings.

Dean's peculiar use of the mother tongue sorely distressed the nation's English teachers. Fractured syntax was bad enough, but his past-tense forms were even worse, like slud for slid and throwed for threw.

After retiring from broadcasting, Dean made his home in Wiggins, Miss. He was in Reno, Nev., in 1974 when he suffered a fatal heart attack at age 63.

Dean's powerful right arm produced 150 wins against only 83 losses.

ED DELAHANTY

Big Ed Delahanty is the only man in major league history to lead both the American and National leagues in hitting.

One of five brothers to play in the major leagues, Ed Delahanty is the only player in big-league history to lead both majors in hitting. Big Ed injected a lot of life into the dead ball.

Delahanty made his professional debut with Mansfield (Ohio State) in 1887. After his purchase for $1,900, considered a record at that time, he batted ninth and went hitless when he made his major league debut as a second baseman for the Phillies one year later.

Big Ed rapped his first single off George Borchers of Chicago, May 23, 1888; his first double off John Clarkson of Boston, on May 25; his first home run off Sam Moffet of Indianapolis on June 13, and his first triple off Frank Gilmore of Washington on June 19.

Delahanty enjoyed his most productive day at the plate in the Chicago White Stockings' old West Side Park on July 13, 1896. In the first inning, against Adonis Bill Terry, Delahanty lined a home run into the left-field bleachers.

In his second at-bat, he homered to right field. The next time, he lined a single. On his fourth trip, he homered to dead center. With Terry still on the mound, and the Chicago fans cheering wildly, Big Ed homered to the clubhouse roof, thereby matching Bobby Lowe's four-homer record for one game.

Delahanty's demonstration was hardly an inspiration to his teammates, who collected only three additional hits in losing, 9-8.

Twice, Delahanty enjoyed 6-for-6 performances. He first accomplished the feat with Cleveland in the Players League on June 2, 1890. He belted a triple, a double and four singles off Marcus Baldwin of Chicago.

He repeated the feat on June 16, 1894, with the Phillies, rapping a double and five singles against Cincinnati.

Delahanty was one of eight players to achieve a .400 batting mark in two seasons. Curiously, in one such year (1894), his .400 average was good for only fourth place. He trailed Hugh Duffy, Tuck Turner and Sam Thompson. Turner and Thompson were Delahanty's teammates on a club that compiled a season average of .349.

Delahanty, a righthanded slugger, gained his first batting title in 1899 when he posted a .408 mark. Three years later, after jumping to the new American League, he batted a league-leading .376 for Washington.

Along the way, Big Ed clouted four doubles in one game and also reeled off 10 consecutive hits in two days, July 13-14, 1897.

For several years, Delahanty earned $2,400 annually, the maximum allowed by the National League, but in 1901 he was earning $3,000.

As an inducement to jump to Washington's AL club, Delahanty was offered $4,000, which he accepted. But disenchantment quickly set in when John McGraw made overtures from New York and advanced Ed $4,500 to return to the National League as a member of the Giants.

Peace between the two leagues before the 1903 season locked Delahanty to the Washington club, which only added to his discontentment. He was batting .338 when Washington played in Cleveland on June 25. Ed did not show up for the game.

Delahanty continued to travel with the team, then disappeared again on July 2. For nearly a week there was no word of his whereabouts. Eventually, the district superintendent of the Pullman Company reported that a man answering Delahanty's description had created a disturbance aboard a Michigan Central train the night of July 2.

The man, it was reported, had five drinks, then brandished an open razor, terrifying passengers on the sleeping car. When the train reached Bridgeburg on the Canadian side of Niagara Falls, the conductor put the man off the train.

A night watchman on the International Bridge spotted Delahanty trying to walk across the span, exchanged angry words with him and ordered him back to shore. Big Ed never made it.

The player's body was discovered on July 9, about 20 miles from the bridge. Money and jewelry worth $2,000 that Delahanty reportedly carried were never found.

BILL DICKEY

While Babe Ruth and Lou Gehrig earned bolder headlines and compiled more impressive home run and runs batted-in statistics, the one Yankee of the late 1920s and early '30s whom many opposing pitchers feared the most was a durable catcher whose bat always seemed hottest in the clutch.

Bill Dickey was quiet, courteous and possessed a memory as long as some of his hunting treks across the hills of Arkansas.

For 13 consecutive years—1929 through 1941—Dickey caught 100 or more games a season, an accomplishment that has been matched only by Johnny Bench.

Dickey forgot his manners only once while in uniform. That lapse occurred on July 4, 1932, when the Yankees and Senators were embroiled in a typical donnybrook of that era. When Carl Reynolds, husky Washington outfielder, barreled across the plate and then started back to be certain that he touched the plate, Dickey mistook his actions as a signal for a fight. Bill got in the first punch, and Reynolds went down with a fractured jaw. Dickey received a $1,000 fine—out of his $14,000 salary—and a 30-day suspension.

At no time thereafter was Dickey able to explain his blowup.

But Bill had his moments to cherish against the Senators, too. There was the day that Walter Johnson, Nats manager, twice moved his center fielder as Dickey approached the plate. In each instance, Bill sliced a triple to left-center field.

When Dickey batted a third time, Johnson repeated his move, and Bill belted what should have been a record-tying third triple. But the humor of the occasion got to Dickey first. Laughing heartily, he was unable to get past second base.

Dickey possessed a steel-trap memory bank for the right way to pitch opposing batters. In 1943, a few hours after his two-run homer had wrapped up the five-game World Series against the Cardinals, Dickey stepped onto an elevator in a St. Louis hotel.

A serviceman was already aboard the lift. Turning to Dickey, he said: "I'll bet you don't remember me."

Dickey studied the soldier for a moment, then confessed: "I don't recall your name, but I remember we pitched you inside and high."

Bill Dickey was the first of two No. 8s to handle Yankee catching chores with Hall of Fame distinction.

As a catcher, Dickey had an uncanny memory for the weaknesses of opposing hitters.

The man was Joe Gantenbein, who had played two seasons with the Philadelphia Athletics.

A native of Bastrop, La., Dickey spent his early years in Arkansas where he attended Little Rock College. He was a member of an athletic family that included older brother Gus, a semipro player, and younger brother George, or Skeets, who played with the Red Sox and White Sox.

Signed by the local Southern Association club, Dickey was performing for Jackson (Cotton States) when Yankee scout Johnny Nee crossed his path.

"If this boy doesn't make it," Nee wired the New York front office, I'll quit scouting."

Dickey had played in his eighth World Series and had batted .351 in limited service during the regular season when, at age 36, he enrolled in the Navy's officers candidate school late in 1943. After serving for two years in the Pacific, he returned to New York in 1946, only to find that the organization had undergone a drastic transformation.

Larry MacPhail was in command and while Joe McCarthy still was manager, the atmosphere was totally different. The season was young when Dickey, who had

been approached about managerial jobs with the Phillies and the Boston Braves, was named to replace McCarthy.

Before the season ended, Dickey himself was succeeded by Johnny Neun. Bill's record as pilot was 57-48. Dickey tried his hand at managing the hometown Little Rock (Southern) club in 1947, but when the Travelers finished last with a 51-103 record, he washed his hands of further managerial chores.

In the spring of 1949, Dickey took a leave from his job with an investment banking firm in Little Rock to spend time with the Yankees again. His assignment was to refine the catching skills of his young successor, Yogi Berra.

"Do you think you can help Berra?" Bill was asked when he arrived for the start of spring training.

"If I didn't think so, I wouldn't be here," he replied.

Dickey's success was obvious. Not only are Dickey and Berra both in the Hall of Fame, but in 1972 the Yankees retired uniform No. 8—the numeral that Bill and Yogi had worn with distinction through their extraordinary careers.

As a hitter, Dickey was at his best when the game was on the line.

MARTIN DIHIGO

Of all the players who could perform capably at more than one position, there was none, according to qualified observers, who could match Martin Dihigo.

John McGraw, a regular off-season visitor to Cuba, termed Dihigo the greatest natural player he had seen in his long and storied career.

Buck Leonard, who preceded Dihigo into the Hall of Fame, paid the following tribute to the big fellow who could play every position except catcher:

"He was the greatest all-around player I know. I say he was the best ballplayer of all time, black or white. He could do it all. He is my ideal ballplayer, makes no difference what race either. If he isn't the greatest, I don't know who is. You take your Ruths, Cobbs or DiMaggios. Give me Dihigo. Bet I'd beat you almost every time."

Renowned for his powerful arm, the 6-foot-3 Dihigo was credited with the first no-hitter in the Mexican League, was the first Cuban named to the Cooperstown Hall of Fame and the first player to be honored in the baseball shrines of Cuba, Mexico and the United States.

Dihigo made his initial appearance in the States as a second baseman in 1923, performing with the touring Cuban Stars. He had difficulty with the curveball at that time.

Two years later, however, he hit .307 in Negro league competition and in 1927, when he tied for the league lead in homers with 18, Dihigo posted a .331 mark. As a pitcher that year, he won four games and lost two.

Despite Martin's success as a pitcher, he would have been an even greater outfielder if he had concentrated on that position, according to many of his admirers. Ted Page of Pittsburgh, a Negro league outfielder whose opinions are respected universally, asserted: "He might have been an outfielder like Oscar Charleston (the Willie Mays of his day). And he had perhaps the finest throwing arm in baseball. As much as I liked Roberto Clemente, I liked Dihigo better."

As Dihigo matured, his statistics shot upward. In his homeland, his winter batting average skyrocketed from .179 to .300 to .344 to .415 to .450.

One year the league batting race between Willie Wells and Dihigo went down to the final day. Wells, batting third, went 4-for-4. Dihigo, batting behind him, went 5-for-5, including a home run in his final at-bat, to edge his teammate.

Dihigo's pitching performances were equally spectacular. In his heyday in Cuba, Dihigo posted marks of 11-2, 14-10, 11-5 and 14-2. In Mexico, in 1938, his record was

Martin Dihigo, the first Cuban in the Hall of Fame, was one of the best all-round players in history.

18-2. In 1942, Martin went 227, led the league in strikeouts and earned-run average and batted .319.

Dihigo enjoyed his top season in 1935 when he managed the New York Cubans to their best record, batted .372 and won two of three pitching decisions.

Dihigo also was the leading vote-getter for the All-Star Game in which he played the outfield and pitched.

In the championship series between the Cubans and the Pittsburgh Crawfords, headed by Josh Gibson, Oscar Charleston and Cool Papa Bell, the Cubans won three of the first five games and enjoyed a substantial lead in the late innings of the sixth game. Unaccountably, Dihigo substituted himself for the starting hurler.

Underneath the stands, Cubans Owner Alex Pompoz was counting the receipts and estimating the winners' shares when the crowd roar tipped him off that the Crawfords had tied the score. Infuriated, Pompoz fired a roll of $500 bills across the room. His ire was not lessened when the Crawfords won and clinched the title the next day.

An easy-going individual with a gentle sense of humor and a penchant for practical jokes, Dihigo mastered the English language quickly and was extremely popular with American players.

Dihigo was living in Cuba when Fidel Castro came into power, and a mystery surrounds his last years. Whether he opposed or supported the Castro regime is unclear. It is generally believed, however, that Dihigo held the post of minister of sports at the time of his death at Cienfuegos in 1971.

JOE DIMAGGIO

Few players, if any, earned the admiration and respect of all levels of society—and retained the popularity longer—than Joe DiMaggio, the son of a San Francisco fisherman.

In Yankee pinstripes or in retirement decades later, the Clipper was the cynosure of eyes and the symbol of professional class.

If fans were not reciting his miraculous catches in center field or warbling the catchy lyrics to "Jolting Joe DiMaggio," they were reminiscing about his incomparable batting streaks.

Joe was 17 when he broke in at shortstop with the San Francisco Seals of the Pacific Coast League in 1932, and he was still shy of his 19th birthday when he unreeled his 61-game batting streak one year later.

An outfielder at this point, DiMaggio launched his string with a single on May 28 and was stopped on July 25 by Ed Walsh, son of the White Sox immortal, who was pitching for Oakland. During the PCL streak, Joe went 104-for-257 for a .405 average.

In 1941, the Yankee Clipper posted an even higher average, .408, during his 56-game American League streak that caught the attention of the entire nation.

Again he started with a single, against the White Sox on May 15. After rapping 91 hits in 223 at-bats, DiMaggio was halted at Cleveland by Al Smith and Jim Bagby, pitchers who received assistance from third baseman Ken Keltner (who made two fine plays on DiMaggio). After the streak, DiMaggio hit safely in the next 17 games. Mainly on the strength of the record streak, DiMaggio won a second Most Valuable Player award (he also was honored in 1939), beating out Ted Williams, who had hit .406.

Despite Joe's lofty batting averages as a minor leaguer, scouts were cool to him as a prospect. A knee injury created doubts and when the Pirates and Red Sox lost interest, the Yankees bought DiMaggio for $25,000 and assigned him back to San Francisco, where he tuned up with a .398 average in 1935.

DiMaggio, or Joe D. as he came to be known shortly thereafter, was not in the Yankees' lineup on opening day, 1936. He suffered a burn from a heat lamp while undergoing treatment on a twisted ankle and did not make his debut until May 3, when he appeared in right field.

Joe, who was joined in the majors by older brother Vince and younger brother Dominic, starred on world champion clubs during his first four years with the Yankees. He was the popular successor to Babe Ruth and a favorite of the Italian community.

Joe DiMaggio was a young outfielder for the San Fransisco Seals in 1934.

DiMaggio was a superstar by 1950, when his 10th-inning homer beat the Phillies in Game 2 of the World Series.

The DiMaggio brothers, Vince, Joe and Dom (left to right), reunited at a PCL old timers game in 1956.

After three years of military service in World War II, DiMag rejoined the Yankees in 1946. His average dipped below .300 that season, but he rebounded for a third MVP trophy in another world-championship season of '47.

For several years, Joe had suffered from a bone spur on his right heel. The condition worsened after the 1948 season and the gifted outfielder was forced to miss the first two months of the 1949 race. He played his first games under Manager Casey Stengel at Boston in mid-June and demonstrated his ability to rise to the occasion. In a three-game series, the Jolter socked four homers in what he later designated as his most satisfying experience.

With another young star, Mickey Mantle, about to blossom, DiMaggio announced his retirement after the Yankees clinched the 1951 World Series title, Joe's ninth.

In 1968, Charlie Finley, owner of the Oakland A's, talked Joe out of retirement. The old star served for two years as batting instructor and vice president.

DiMaggio was married twice, each time to an actress. His first wife was Dorothy Arnold, his second Marilyn Monroe. The second marriage collapsed in less than a year, but the pair remained close friends. For 20 years after Miss Monroe's death, Joe arranged for red roses to be placed at her grave twice weekly.

The grace and style exhibited by No. 5 earned him a special niche in the hearts of Yankee fans.

LARRY DOBY

O f the countless number of people who watched Jackie Robinson's performance with the Brooklyn Dodgers early in the 1947 season, probably none paid closer attention than Larry Doby.

Doby was starring for the Newark Eagles in the Negro Leagues and scouts were watching. Just 11 weeks after Robinson became the first black player to appear in the major leagues, Doby became the first black player in the American League, signing with the Cleveland Indians. Doby, who later said he received no signing bonus from owner Bill Veeck, made his debut on July 5, 1947, appearing as a pinch-hitter in a game against the White Sox at Comiskey Park in Chicago. He struck out on three pitches.

Fortunately, that was not an indication of things to come, though Doby did struggle in his transition to the majors. He played in only 29 games in 1947 and hit just .156.

But the Indians were determined to give him a legitimate chance, knowing all too well his record of success in the Negro Leagues. Veeck had paid the Newark club $20,000 for Doby's contract.

In 1948, Doby began to restore Cleveland's faith. He hit .301 in 121 games, including 14 homers and 66 RBI as the Indians won the American League pennant. He also performed well in the World Series, hitting a key homer in the fourth game off Johnny Sain to help Cleveland to a 2-1 win before a crowd of 81,887 fans at Municipal Stadium. Doby hit .318 in the series.

Doby was born on Dec. 13, 1924 in Camden, S.C. He moved with his mother to New Jersey following the death of his father. In high school, he starred in baseball, football, basketball and track, but had his greatest success in baseball. Doby led East Side High School in Paterson, N.J., to the city championship and was elected captain of the baseball team his junior and senior years.

Doby attended Long Island University before joining the Newark Eagles. His career was interrupted when he entered the Navy in 1943. Following his discharge in 1946, he rejoined the Eagles and sparked the team to the 1946 Negro League championship, defeating the Kansas City Monarchs in the league playoffs.

After joining the Indians, Doby knew he could have success on the field, but he also had to learn to conquer the challenges of being a minority player off the field. He said the only difference between himself and Robinson was that Robinson received all of the publicity.

"You didn't hear much about what I was going through because the media didn't want to repeat the same story," Doby said years later. "I couldn't react. My reaction was to hit the ball as far as I could."

Larry Doby, with 253 career homers, was the first black player in the American League.

Doby did that often. The 6-foot-1, 180-pound lefthanded hitter led the American League with 32 homers in 1952 and 1954 and hit 20 or more homers nine consecutive seasons. He also led the AL with 126 RBI in 1954, the year he made his second appearance in the World Series after leading the Indians to a record-setting 111-win season. He topped the 100-RBI mark five times, hit three homers in a game on Aug. 2, 1950 and hit for the cycle on June 4, 1952.

Doby was selected to the All-Star team each year between 1949 and 1955, and delivered a pinch-hit homer in the 1954 game.

Following the 1955 season, Doby was traded to the White Sox where he played for two years before rejoining the Indians for the 1958 season. He finished his major league career in Detroit and Chicago in 1959 and later played a year in Japan.

Doby retired with a career average of .283 with 253 homers, but his service to the game was not over. He spent a year in Japan working for the State Department as a player, teacher and good-will ambassador. He spent another year touring the United States giving clinics on behalf of the Vice President's Council on Physical Fitness.

He moved back into baseball in 1969, working for Montreal, Cleveland and the White Sox as a coach, minor-league instructor and scout before he was named the manager of the White Sox in June 1978 by his former owner in Cleveland, Bill Veeck. Doby became the second black manager in major-league history, compiling a 37-50 record.

Doby was elected to the Hall of Fame by the Veterans Committee in 1998.

BOBBY DOERR

Of all natural phenomena, an earthquake would seem to be the least likely to promote a professional baseball career. Subterranean upheavals and the play-for-pay sport do not appear to have any logical connection-with one notable exception. That variant is Bobby Doerr.

Robert Pershing Doerr, born in April 1918 while General John J. Pershing was commanding the American Expeditionary Forces in France, was a high school student in Los Angeles when a tremor toppled a telephone pole. In falling, the pole brushed Odie Brannon, the second baseman for the Hollywood Stars of the Pacific Coast League.

Brannon escaped serious injury, but played thereafter as though he was expecting another pole to descend upon him momentarily. A replacement was tried. He was no improvement. In desperation, Manager Oscar Vitt turned to his employer. "The kid who can do the job for us is that Doerr," he suggested. "Why don't we sign him now?"

The proposition was laid before Bobby's father, Harold. The elder Doerr had coached the American Legion team on which Bobby had starred along with future major leaguers Mickey Owen and Steve Mesner. The senior Doerr already had a son in the professional ranks, but objected to Bobby following suit. At 16, contended the head of the household, Bobby was entirely too young.

Vitt would not accept the verdict. He persisted until the elder Doerr relented. He approved on one condition: that Bobby receive a guaranteed two-year contract at $200 a month. It proved to be a landmark bargain for Vitt and all of baseball.

Within three years, Bobby Doerr was a .342 hitter for San Diego and was leading the Pacific Coast league in base hits with 238. He also was part of a dazzling double-play combination, teaming with George Myatt, four years his senior. Glowing reports of the youngster's achievements filtered eastward and excited the curiosity of major league executives.

Among those interested parties was the general manager of the Red Sox. Eddie Collins had been a crackerjack second baseman for more than 20 years, and if anyone was qualified to pass judgment on an infielder, that man was Collins. A personal inspection tour was the only way to satisfy his curiosity.

Eddie arrived in San Diego, the new home of the Hollywood franchise, and watched both Myatt and Doerr. He liked Myatt, but he loved Doerr, despite Bobby's erratic fielding in his first game. Collins attributed the defensive

Bobby Doerr handled second-base duties and carried a big stick for the Red Sox in the 1940s.

Doerr (right) and teammate Ted Williams formed the heart and soul of the 1940s Red Sox.

lapses to nervousness brought on by the awareness that Bobby was under scrutiny.

Eddie remained in California for several more days and when he departed, his club owned the rights to Bobby Doerr.

Bushy-browed Bobby joined the Red Sox in 1937 and impressed Manager Joe Cronin as much as he had Collins. From his shortstop position, Cronin brought Doerr along slowly. The kid displayed a remarkable aptitude until halted by injury. He was beaned in an exhibition game and saw only limited action that season. Two years later, however, he was a .318 hitter and, in 1940, rapped 22 homers and drove in 105 runs.

Bobby remained a keystone kingpin until 1951. In 1944, he was named the American League Player of the Year by *The Sporting News*. He was voted to the All-Star team eight times and, in 1943, sparked the AL to triumph at Philadelphia with a three-run homer off Mort Cooper. He appeared in one World Series, batting .409 in the Sox's seven-game loss to the 1946 Cardinals.

The 180-pound Californian established a league mark in 1948 by handling 414 consecutive chances flawlessly and led the league second basemen five times in double plays.

Had it not been for Doerr, a .288 lifetime hitter, Bob Feller would have hurled five no-hitters rather than three. On May 25, 1939, and again on July 31, 1946, Bobby played the spoiler role with second-inning singles against the Cleveland fireballer. Doerr belittled the 1939 safety, maintaining, I hit the ball off my ear and broke the bat."

Modesty was Doerr's hallmark. His steadiness precluded flair that attracted more attention to players less generously endowed. In the dugouts, however, both friend and foe knew him for what he was.

When Joe McCarthy managed the Red Sox he commented, "I thought while managing the Yanks that

Joe Gordon was as valuable a second baseman and as fine a team man as I ever saw. But I couldn't pick him over Doerr after what Bobby has shown me."

Bucky Harris, a brilliant second baseman during his playing days with Washington, echoed McCarthy's sentiments. He placed Doerr "in a class by himself" and added, "It will be a long time before you see his equal. You take him for granted now. You won't realize his greatness until after he's through and somebody else is trying to play second base."

In 1946, when the Red Sox won their first pennant since 1918, Babe Ruth showered additional praise on the second sacker. "Doerr, and not Ted Williams, is the No. 1 player on the team," said the Bambino. "He rates the Most Valuable Player in the American League." The MVP went to Williams.

During much of Bobby's career, a debate flourished about the relative merits of himself and Joe Gordon of the Yankees. Neither principal could be drawn into the argument. Invariably, they heaped praise on one another and visited the other's home for dinner when in the rival city. The issue never was settled satisfactorily or conclusively, though Doerr compiled better batting and fielding statistics.

Mild-mannered and with his emotions well concealed, Doerr spent 15 years in the majors without being ejected from a game. One of the few times he showed a flash of temper occurred in 1948. After Ted Williams and Vern Stephens tagged Joe Page for consecutive home runs, the Yankee lefthander fired the next pitch at Bobby's head. "Knocking me down for something somebody else does, that's what gets me," he said with a touch of heat.

Doerr collected his 2,000th hit in July 1951. Three months later, hampered by chronic back problems, he called it quits and retired to his farm in the wilds of Oregon.

Doerr was one of the steadiest pivot men ever to play major league baseball.

DON DRYSDALE

O ff the field, he was the soul of congeniality, but when he toed the pitching mound, the 6-foot-6 righthander could be as mean as the proverbial junkyard dog.

Few players could match Donald Scott Drysdale as a Jekyll-and-Hyde personality—or as a pitcher. In 14 seasons as a Dodger, he won 209 games, established a record for consecutive innings of scoreless pitching and ignited a brawl or two with an intimidating style born of competitive fire.

He was described as "having the face of a choirboy, the physique of Goliath and the competitive instincts of a tarantula."

To another, Big D had "the image of an ogre, a man who would knock his mother down on Mother's Day if there were anything at stake and a man who would kick a small dog just because it got in his way."

Walter Alston, Don's only major league manager, remarked, "I've never seen a pitcher so unafraid of batters."

Another commented, "He has a private war with anybody who stands up at the plate; he'll knock down anyone who tries to take advantage of him."

Two such batters were Johnny Logan of the Braves and Frank Robinson of the Reds. Their direct action against Big D triggered bench-clearing brawls.

To Roy Campanella, his catcher at the start of his big-league career, Drysdale was "sweet and mean—a sweet pitcher and a mean competitor."

Drysdale, who did not pitch until his senior year at Van Nuys, Calif., High School and then won nine of 10 decisions, acquired his master's degree in mound methodology from Sal (The Barber) Maglie, who believed that a close shave for a batter was a good thing . . . for a pitcher.

The son of a repairman for a West Coast telephone company, Drysdale signed with the Dodgers' Bakersfield (California League) farm club fresh out of high school. A second season at Montreal (International) completed his apprenticeship. At age 19, Drysdale became a Brooklyn Dodger.

Don was an apt pupil for Maglie, the veteran pitcher who joined the Dodgers a month into Drysdale's rookie season of 1956. Firing a 95-mile-an-hour fastball and a wide-sweeping curve, both with a sidearm motion, Big D set batters back on their heels muttering darkly to themselves.

Drysdale made his first major league start on April 23, 1956, against the Phillies and struck out the side in the first inning. Don won his debut, 6-1.

Drysdale won four more games in 1956 and appeared

Don Drysdale's powerful right arm and ruthless determination spelled trouble for opposing batters.

in one World Series game that fall against the Yankees. He blossomed as a regular starter the next year and contributed 17 victories to the Dodgers' third-place finish.

As Drysdale matured as a pitcher, his temper tantrums showed "development" as well. No segment of the baseball community escaped his rage, not even himself. Once, yanked from a game in which he blew a 5-0 first-inning lead, he took on a bat bag, loaded with bats, and lost the kicking match.

Once, when an umpire reported to league headquarters that Don intentionally hit a batter with a pitch, for which he drew a $50 fine, Drysdale bristled. "What am I supposed to do," he stormed, "throw everything down the pike and let 'em hit it out? I can't change my style if it costs me $5,000 in fines."

Headlines clearly reflected Don's behavioral patterns. "Angry Drysdale Blasts Coaches," reported one. "Hot Drysdale Roars 'Trade Me,'" said another. Others were: "Drysdale Vows to Sue N.L. If Fined" and "Drysdale Blows Up Over Fans' Dumb Questions."

But there were other headlines, too, attesting to his greatness as an athlete, such as when he won the Cy

Dodger righthander Don Drysdale was mobbed by teammates after completing his fifth consecutive shut-out in 1968 en route to his major league-record streak of 58 straight scoreless innings.

Young Award in 1962 with a 25-9 record, or when he tied a National League season mark for home runs by a pitcher by hitting seven (Drysdale performed that feat twice), or when he established a major league record by hurling 58 consecutive scoreless innings.

That shutout-innings streak started on May 14, 1968, when Drysdale defeated the Cubs, 1-0. In quick succession, he then blanked the Astros, 1-0; the Cardinals, 2-0; the Astros, 5-0; the Giants, 3-0, and the Pirates, 5-0.

With 54 straight scoreless innings to his credit, Drysdale faced the Phillies on June 8, needing only two more shutout innings to break the record of 55⅔ straight scoreless innings set by Walter Johnson of Washington in 1913. Big D went out and blanked Philadelphia through four innings before singles by Tony

Taylor and Clay Dalrymple and a sacrifice fly by Howie Bedell snapped the string in the fifth.

Drysdale won only 14 games that season, however, and posted a 5-4 record in 1969 before calling it a career. A chronic shoulder ailment forced him into retirement at age 33.

Before the '69 season closed, the Dodgers and more than 30,000 fans tendered the big warrior a formal farewell. Gifts of all descriptions were showered on the author of 49 career shutouts and three World Series victories. Among the tributes was a wire from California Gov. Ronald Reagan that read:

"'Big D' once meant Dallas. Now it's you alone. In a day when young people are looking for heroes and too often finding the wrong kind, you are the epitome of the value of athletics."

HUGH DUFFY

Ted Williams took one glance at the 5-foot-7 septuagenarian and asked, "How did such a little fellow hit .438? Bases on balls must have counted as hits." Williams was even more perplexed when he was assured that walks did not count as hits in 1894 when Hugh Duffy, an undersized outfielder, registered his all-time major league record for a season batting average.

Duffy was 27 and in his seventh major league season when he established his record as a member of the Boston Nationals. Until his death in 1954, he expressed the hope that he would live to see Williams surpass his record. Ted's best effort fell 32 points short in 1941.

Williams would have been even more amazed to know that Hugh had hit four major league homers before he rapped a double or a triple. Playing for Cap Anson's Chicago White Stockings in 1888, Duffy walloped his first homer off Hank O'Day of Washington on July 11; another off Lady Baldwin of Detroit, July 28; a third off Ed Morris of Pittsburgh, July 30, and his fourth off Jim Galvin of Pittsburgh, August 1.

Duffy explained his failure to break into the Chicago lineup at an earlier date. When he reported to the club, Anson sized him up and snarled, "Where's the rest of you?"

"This is all there is," replied Duffy. Anson, who favored big outfielders, was so incensed he did not speak to the rookie for two months.

During his 124-game season of 1894, Duffy went hitless in only 17 games. He rapped five hits in two games, two hits in 12, three hits in 19, two hits in 47 and one hit in 27.

He opened the season with three hits in six tries, but fell into the .260 range in early May. He regained the .300 plateau on May 19 and never looked back. He zoomed past .400 with a 5-for-6 performance on July 5 and attained a .441 mark before a slight decline at the finish.

As a reward for his brilliant season, Duffy's salary was raised $12.50 a week, to $2,700 annually. For this added compensation, he also had to serve as team captain and make certain that the bats and baseballs were returned to the clubhouse at the completion of the day's activities.

"No one thought much of averages in those days," the little fellow recalled 50 years later. "I didn't realize I had hit that much until the official averages were published four months later."

Although noted primarily for his hitting, Duffy made a catch in 1897 that drew the admiration of even the opposing players. In a game against Baltimore, Duffy played shallow left field when Joe Corbett drove a pitch to deep left field. Turning with the crack of the bat, Duffy

Hugh Duffy was manager of the White Sox in 1910, 16 years after hitting a record .438.

raced within two feet of the fence, leaped and caught the ball barehanded.

While still in midair, it was reported, Duffy turned and fired to the third baseman to complete a double play.

"So miraculous were the catch and throw," it was written, "that even the Baltimore players tossed their caps into the air and joined in cheering which lasted 15 minutes—probably the longest demonstration inspired by a play."

After his playing career ended in 1908, Duffy turned to managing and scouting. He piloted the White Sox and Red Sox before signing to scout for the Red Sox in 1924.

Annually thereafter, he signed a contract as a scout. Hugh directed tryout camps throughout New England, including sessions at Fenway Park when the Red Sox were on the road.

Duffy had been ill for several months before he died at his home in Allston, Mass., 60 years after his remarkable achievements in the batter's box.

LEO DUROCHER

Of all of his accomplishments from nearly 50 years in baseball, as a player, manager and broadcaster, Leo Durocher is remembered most for creating the phrase, "Nice guys finish last."

It is included in every book of famous quotations. It is repeatedly used as a motivating tool for coaches who are trying to fire up their players and get them to be more intense and play harder. It is used when a nice guy does actually finish first, usually with the postscript, "Durocher was wrong. "

In his autobiography, which used the phrase for its title, Durocher admits he said it, but not in the same context in which it has been recorded in history.

Durocher said he was sitting on the bench one day at the Polo Grounds. He was managing the Dodgers at the time, and he was talking with reporters, when Frank Graham, a reporter from the *Journal American*, asked Durocher why he liked Eddie Stanky so much.

He was expounding on the reasons, Stanky's intangible stills more than his physical ability, when Giants' manager Mel Ott and his players walked out of the opposing dugout. Durocher said how nice a person Ott was, and ticked off the names of some of the other New York players. Then he added, "Take a look at them. All nice guys. They'll finish last. Nice guys. Finish last."

Graham reported it the way Durocher said it, but other reporters passed down the line through different generations and ran the two sentences together. In his autobiograhy, Durocher stood behind what he had said and expanded on it.

"If you're in professional sports, buddy, and you don't care whether you lose or win, you are going to finish last," Durocher said. "Because that's where those guys finish, they finish last. Last.

"I never did anything I didn't try to beat you at. If I pitch pennies I want to beat you. If I'm spitting at a crack in the sidewalk I want to beat you. I would make the loser's trip to the opposing dressing room to congratulate the other manager because that was the prop-

Leo Durocher, elected to the Hall in 1994, won 2,008 games in his 24-year managerial career.

er thing to do. But I'm honest enough to say I didn't like it. You think I liked it when I had to go see Mr. Stengel and say, 'Congratulations, Casey, you played great'? I'd have liked to stick a knife in his chest and twist it inside him."

Durocher likely always had that attitude, from the time he began playing baseball as a youth. He definitely had it when he reached the major leagues, and when he played shortstop for the Cardinals in the 1930s. It was his conversation with pitcher Dizzy Dean, again recorded by Frank Graham, that led to naming those Cardinal teams "the Gashouse Gang."

Leo Durocher, left, led the famous '41 Dodgers to 100 wins and a pennant.

The Cardinals were in sixth place at the time, and Dean and Durocher were comparing the two leagues, wondering if the Cardinals could win if they were in the American League. Durocher said, "They wouldn't let us in the other league. They would say we are a lot of gashouse ballplayers."

Graham reported the statement, other reporters picked it up, and "the Gashouse Gang" was born.

Of course, Durocher should be remembered for more than just creating two famous lines. As a player, he spent 17 years in the majors with the Cardinals, Yankees, Reds and Dodgers, and he managed for 24 years. Only seven other men ever managed more games, and Durocher's total of 2,008 wins is the seventh highest in history, trailing only Connie Mack, John McGraw, Sparky Anderson, Bucky Harris, Joe McCarthy and Walter Alston.

Durocher managed three pennant-winners, and his 1954 Giants club won the World Series.

He was a combative, feisty player and manager who frequently argued with umpires, his bosses and his players. He enjoyed agitating Babe Ruth with the Yankees in 1928. He once punched a golf caddy, was suspended by then-commissioner Happy Chandler for the 1947 season for associating with gamblers, and got into the middle of every fight he possibly could. He admitted trying to take

a rule and see exactly how far he could bend it before somebody tried to stop him.

"If a man is sliding into second base and the ball goes into centerfield, what's the matter with falling on him accidentally so that he can't get up and go to third?" Durocher said in his book. "If you get away with it, fine. If you don't, what have you lost? I don't call that cheating, I call that heads-up baseball. Win any way you can as long as you can get away with it."

He was known for those kind of antics more than his playing career. His career-high average was .286 in 1936, and his lifetime average was just .247, but he was a good defensive player who knew and understood all the nuances of the game.

As a manager, Durocher was just as colorful and controversial. He led the Dodgers to the NL pennant in 1941, and won with the Giants in 1951, losing both series to the Yankees, before finally winning his only World Series when the Giants beat the favored Indians in 1954.

After the 1955 season, Durocher began broadcasting baseball on television but returned to manage the Cubs from 1966 until 1972, and his last managerial assignment was with Houston in 1973.

Durocher died in 1991 at age 86. He was elected to the Hall of Fame in 1994.

BILLY EVANS

The Youngstown, Ohio, semipro team was ready to begin a game in 1903 when it was discovered that the umpire had failed to show up.

The managers huddled, trying to agree on a substitute, when it was suggested that Billy Evans, an $18-a-week sportswriter for the Youngstown *Vindicator*, would be a fine choice inasmuch as his stories reflected fairness and honesty.

Evans was reluctant to leave the press box until somebody reminded him that the job paid $15. That was the beginning of a career that carried Evans to the American League for 22 years, to the presidency of the Southern Association, to the general manager's chair of the Indians and Tigers and the farm director's position with the Red Sox.

Billy entered Organized Baseball in the Ohio-Pennsylvania League in 1905 and was umpiring a Niles Youngstown game when a decision on the final pitch precipitated a riot. Billy was accorded a police escort, but his courage in making an unpopular decision against the home team impressed a spectator, Manager Jimmy McAleer of the St. Louis Browns. McAleer recommended Evans to A.L. President Ban Johnson.

Billy, who was forced to withdraw from Cornell University after his sophomore year because of the death of his father, joined the A.L. staff when he was 22, the youngest umpire in major league history and the only one to jump from Class C to the majors.

Evans worked behind the plate when Walter Johnson made his major league debut, he was there when Babe Ruth hit his 60th home run and he was present for six no-hitters. He was the A.L. answer to Bill Klem of the National League.

Billy was in his second A.L. season when he was knocked unconscious by a thrown pop bottle in St. Louis. Working before an overflow crowd, Evans was conferring with Detroit Manager Hugh Jennings and left fielder Davey Jones when he was struck on the head by the bottle. He collapsed in Jones' arms and was rushed to a hospital, where he hovered near death for several weeks.

After recovery, Ban Johnson asked Billy to press charges against the culprit, but the umpire refused, saying that the 17-year-old clerk "has apologized to me one hundred times for throwing the bottle."

Evans never backed down from a challenge and when Ty Cobb invited Billy to meet him under the grandstand at Washington in 1921 to settle a dispute, the umpire accepted. "It was like fighting Joe Louis and a wildcat at the same time," Evans admitted later after a sound whipping.

Evans was quick with a soft word and a witticism. Once, when Joe Cantillon was managing Washington and coaching at third base, Billy called the first pitch of the game a ball.

From third base came Cantillon's cry: "Let's not start the game like that."

Jerking off his mask, Evans thumbed Joe.

"You've taken on too big a job," Evans told Cantillon. "You simply can't manage and umpire at the same time."

Evans was instrumental in the assignment of four umpires to World Series games. In 1909, working with Klem, Billy was required to ask bleacherites if a ball landed fair or foul. The next game, four men were on the job.

Evans was an excellent story teller and never tired of relating an anecdote involving Washington's Walter Johnson. In a close game with Detroit, Johnson permitted two ninth-inning baserunners and fired two fastballs past Sam Crawford.

"Then the most beautiful fastball I ever saw came across the plate," Billy recalled. "Unfortunately, I called it a ball. Johnson only shrugged his shoulders.

"For the only time in my life I pulled for one team, praying that Crawford would make an out, which he did on a long drive to center field."

When Johnson walked off the mound, he said to Evans, "Where was that next-to-last pitch?"

"Where do you think?" asked Billy.

"Well, it may have been a trifle low."

Evans was 71 when he suffered a fatal heart attack while visiting his son in Miami.

Billy Evans went from sportswriting to an illustrious career as an umpire and baseball executive.

JOHNNY EVERS

The middle man of the "Tinker to Evers to Chance" refrain was Johnny Evers, the Cubs' scrappy second baseman.

A t 5-foot-9 and 140 pounds, the youngster scarcely resembled a major league player, and when he was asked to wear a uniform designed for a much larger man, the dissemblance was even more pronounced.

Moreover, the kid's former manager at Troy in the New York State League had forwarded a message to the Chicago Cubs: "If you keep him, you can send me $500. If not, send him back."

Johnny Evers shunned all thoughts of going back. Only six months earlier he was working in a collar factory in his native Troy. When he was laid off, he wangled a tryout with the local baseball club, and he hung on. Now he was in the majors at age 21.

His prominent jaw proclaimed Evers a fighter from the start. He fought veterans for a chance to take batting practice. He swapped insults with teammates and opponents and even took on the Giants' John McGraw.

Before long he was a member of baseball's most celebrated double-play combination, Tinker to Evers to Chance, and he became an authority on the playing rules. In 1908, when a Pittsburgh runner failed to touch the next base on a game-winning hit in the ninth inning, Evers called the oversight to the attention of Hank O'Day.

The umpire maintained that players had been doing the same thing for years. Why change?

Later, on reflection, O'Day conceded the point to the Cub infielder. Thereafter, he said, he would call the runner out.

Fortunately for Evers and the Cubs, O'Day was umpiring at the Polo Grounds on September 23, when Fred Merkle of the Giants ran from first base to the clubhouse on what should have been a game-winning hit. Merkle was forever censured for his action; Evers, who called for the ball and forced out Merkle at second, was ever after lauded for his nimble intellect.

When the game was declared a tie, and the Cubs won the replay, Evers was credited with winning a pennant.

In 1914, Johnny provided the spark that carried the Boston Braves to the pennant. They faced the powerful Philadelphia A's, American League champions for the fourth time in five years, in the World Series.

At the instigation of Evers, the underdog Braves taunted the A's from the moment they appeared on the field. Unaccustomed to such treatment, the A's first grew angry, then disintegrated.

Before the fourth and final game, a Philadelphian told Evers, "You fellows have done a great job, you deserve a lot of credit."

Evers spat at the feet of his opponent and snarled: "We don't take praise from yellow dogs."

Johnny was too old for service in World War I, but he went to Europe as an athletic director for the Knights of Columbus.

Evers managed the Cubs in 1913 and again in 1921, and piloted the White Sox in 1924. McGraw, once a bitter enemy, hired him as a coach in 1920, and Evers served as assistant manager for the Braves from 1929 through 1932.

For years Evers was a regular spectator at the World Series. He was in Chicago when the Cubs played the Yankees in 1938. Unknown to him or to Joe Tinker, the old double-play mates—who had not spoken to each other as players and had not seen each other for years—were scheduled to appear on the same broadcast. When they spotted each other, they fell into a clinch.

"Both of us could hardly keep from crying," related Evers.

After retiring from baseball, Johnny operated a sporting goods store in Albany, N.Y., and was superintendent of city-owned Bleeker Stadium.

In 1942, Evers suffered a paralytic stroke and for a while was confined to a chair in his home, from where he could gaze out the window at his store. He recovered sufficiently to go to Cooperstown in 1946 when he, Tinker and Chance were enshrined as a unit.

A second stroke paralyzed the old warrior further before a cerebral hemorrhage proved fatal to Evers in 1947.

BUCK EWING

In 1932, when Mickey Cochrane was in his eighth season with the Philadelphia Athletics, John B. Foster, highly respected editor of the *Spalding Baseball Guide*, declared unequivocally that Buck Ewing was the No. 1 catcher in 56 years of major league baseball.

Foster fortified his thesis with the fact that Connie Mack, Cochrane's manager at the time, voted for Ewing as the game's foremost receiver.

"Buck could throw from any position," wrote Foster of the New York catcher of the 1880s. "It was not by accident that he threw fearlessly and unswervingly when he squatted down behind the batter, but because he chose to throw that way, because he knew he could and did catch runners with the same easy skill that he would have caught them if he were standing.

"Ewing could juggle the ball and still throw out the runner, and they had some fast men circling the bases in the days when he caught. He might have a 'half' passed ball and the runner on first would leave the base . . . to think that at last he had something on Ewing, only to come within two feet of second and find the baseman there with the ball."

The secret of Ewing's rifle throws was a sharp forearm snap that sent the ball with extraordinary speed to its objective, Foster stated.

Despite the speed of Buck's throws, the ball was reputed to be soft and easy to handle.

Ewing also was a diplomat behind the plate, according to Foster, who wrote: "Seldom was he critical of the umpires. He was what is known in these days as a good jollier. He had the friendship of umpires because he made life easy for them."

Ewing, nicknamed Buck by boyhood pals and credited by some historians as the first catcher to crouch behind the plate, made his major league debut with Troy on September 9, 1880, collecting a single in a 1-0 loss to Providence.

Ewing possessed only ordinary speed, but through a constant study of pitchers, he was able to achieve impressive stolen base totals. He was, said batterymate Mickey Welch, "a thinking man's player."

In one game, Ewing stole second and third base and then shouted for everyone to hear, "Now, I'm stealing home," which he accomplished with a hard slide.

The play was captured on a lithograph and became a popular novelty item among Giants fans.

When the Players League was formed in 1890, Ewing joined many others in deserting the National League. He was named manager of the New York outlaw club. The

Rifle-arm catcher Buck Ewing was a member of the New York Giants in 1887.

Giants sued for the return of their players but the courts ruled in favor of the jumpers, maintaining there was no "mutuality" in the contracts.

Back with the Giants, after the Players League collapsed at the end of one season, Ewing injured his arm in 1892, but shifted to first base and continued to hit effectively.

At the end of the '92 season he was traded to Cleveland for shortstop George Davis. Ewing was released after two seasons and signed as player-manager of the Red Stockings in his native Cincinnati. He managed Cincinnati through 1899 before returning to the Giants as manager for part of the 1900 season.

Ewing was considered a wealthy man, the result of land holdings in the West, when he retired from baseball. He was living in Cincinnati with his wife and two daughters when he died of diabetes and paralysis a week before his 47th birthday.

RED FABER

The 1917 World Series was both the best and the worst of times for Red Faber, the 29-year-old spitball pitcher from Cascade, Iowa.

The White Sox righthander won three games, one of a handful of hurlers to turn the trick in Series play. He also suffered his greatest embarrassment in his 20 years with the Sox. It occurred in Game 2 which, fortunately for Faber, the American Leaguers won, 7-2, over the Giants en route to the Series title.

Buck Weaver was the runner at second base when Faber belted an infrequent hit, a two-out single. When the throw went to the plate, Faber continued to second, assuming Weaver had scored on the play.

When the pitcher took a long windup, Faber took off for third, only to find Weaver sliding in from the other side.

"Where in the hell do you think you're going?" Weaver asked.

"I'm goin' back to pitch," Faber replied red-faced.

When the White Sox won the pennant again in 1919, Faber was unable to pitch in the World Series because of an ankle injury. Years after the Sox lost the stained Series to the Cincinnati Reds, Faber's longtime batterymate, Ray Schalk, asserted: "If Red had been able to pitch, I'm sure there would have been no Black Sox scandal."

Faber was a student at St. Joseph College in Dubuque, when he pitched so impressively against the local Three-I League team that he was offered $100 monthly to turn pro.

On August 18, 1910, Red pitched a perfect game against Davenport. It was one of his 18 victories that season. The Pittsburgh Pirates acquired his contract after the Three-I season, but Faber never appeared in a game and was sold to Minneapolis. He was purchased by Chicago for $3,500 after he won 20 games for Des Moines (Western) in 1913.

At the close of that season, Faber was asked to join the Sox for the first stage of their world tour with the Giants.

Spitballer Red Faber is pictured in 1917, the year in which he won three World Series games for the White Sox.

He was scheduled to remain with them only as far as Seattle, point of embarkation for the two clubs, so that management could appraise his talents.

When the clubs reached Seattle, however, Christy Mathewson decided not to accompany the tour overseas. John McGraw needed a pitcher. "Why not take Faber?" inquired Chicago Owner Charles Comiskey.

McGraw accepted the suggestion and the young righthander wore a Giants uniform the remainder of the trip, defeating the Sox in Hong Kong, Brisbane, Melbourne and Cairo.

After the players were at sea, it was discovered that, in the frenzied activity in Seattle, Faber was traveling without a passport.

Faber won 10 games for the White Sox in 1914 and totaled 57 victories in the next three seasons.

After a year's service in the United States Navy in World War I, Faber rejoined the Sox in 1919, weak and underweight. He captured only 11 of 20 decisions.

When the spitball was outlawed in 1920 for all pitchers except established major leaguers, Faber was one of the favored 17 and he continued to baffle A.L. batters with the pitch he learned at Dubuque. He threw only the spitter and fastball, asserting that a curveball "is too hard on the arm."

After 1920, the Sox finished in the second division for the remainder of Faber's career, yet he posted 254 career victories.

"We were a lousy team in those years," said Schalk, "otherwise Red would have won 300 games easily."

When the Philadelphia A's sold Jack Quinn to Brooklyn in 1931, Faber was the only spitball pitcher remaining in the American League. He continued until the fall of 1933, pitching mainly in relief. In his final appearance, he hurled a five-hit shutout against the Cubs in the second game of the 1933 City Series. He was 44 at the time.

Thirteen years later, Faber donned a White Sox uniform again at the invitation of his old pitching colleague, Ted Lyons, the new manager. Red served as pitching coach for three years before going into retirement again.

Death came to the old spitball master at his home in Chicago at age 88.

BOB FELLER

When Feller returned to Van Meter, Iowa, in 1948, local batters were just as helpless as before.

He burst upon baseball like a bombshell. From out of nowhere, he appeared suddenly, firing a baseball—it was said by some—with a greater velocity than it had ever been thrown previously.

The nation took its first notice of the Van Meter, Iowa, farmboy in 1936 when, as a 17-year-old, he struck out eight members of the St. Louis Cardinals in three innings of an exhibition game. Bob Feller was headline news thereafter, first as a Cleveland pitcher, then as a baseball ambassador who never feared to speak his mind.

The hard-throwing youngster was a cause celebre at the very beginning. The Indians, it developed, had signed Feller to a Fargo-Moorhead (Northern) contract. This, in itself, violated an existing regulation forbidding major league clubs from signing free agents other than college players.

In order to complete high school, Feller was advised to seek voluntary retirement in 1936, at which time his contract was transferred to New Orleans, another Cleveland farm, in the Southern Association.

When the youth subsequently appeared in a semipro tournament and scouts of other clubs learned that the phenom was unavailable because of his ties with Cleveland, Commissioner K.M. Landis conducted an investigation into the contract manipulations.

In time, Landis awarded Feller to the Indians, but they were ordered to pay $7,500 to the Des Moines (Western) club, whose owner, Lee Keyser, had charged the Tribe with violating the Major/Minor League Agreement.

A major factor in Landis' decision was the assurance by Bob and his father Bill that they were pleased with their association with the Indians.

Following his explosive debut against the Cardinals, Feller appeared a couple times in relief before receiving his first starting assignment in mid-August. The righthander turned it into a memorable occasion with a 4-1 victory over the St. Louis Browns in which he struck out 15 batters.

In September, he established an American League record and matched the big-league mark by fanning 17 Philadelphia batters. When the season ended, he returned to Van Meter to complete his high school education.

Feller won 107 games before he was 23 and was on a 300-victory course for his career when, at the close of the 1941 season, he enlisted in the United States Navy and missed virtually all of the next four seasons. He earned six battle citations as a gun crew chief.

Although he pitched a no-hitter against Chicago on opening day of 1940 (and threw two other no-hitters in his career), Feller treasured even more his season inaugural against the White Sox in 1946. It was a 1-0 three-hitter, preserved when Bob Lemon, playing center field, made a spectacular catch of a short fly ball and doubled a runner off second base in the ninth inning.

As his salary skyrocketed in the late 1940s, Feller found it advantageous to incorporate as Ro-Fel Inc. In 1947, his income was reported to be $150,000, a combination of his player's salary, personal endorsements and a barnstorming tour in which his own major league all-stars opposed black all-stars.

With a slider, developed during his military career, to supplement his curve and blistering fastball, Feller posted 26 and 20 victories in his first two years following his postwar return to the Indians, but dropped to 19 in the pennant-winning season of 1948.

Bob opened the World Series in Boston and suffered his most crushing defeat when an umpire's questionable decision on a pickoff attempt led to a 1-0 loss.

He also started Game 5 before 86,000 Cleveland fans, but yielded eight hits in less than seven innings and was tagged with a second setback.

In 1954, when the Indians set a league record with 111 victories, Feller wasn't used in the World Series as the Giants swept Cleveland.

Feller appeared in five mid-summer classics, allowing five hits and one run in $12\frac{1}{3}$ innings.

In 1948, 29-year-old Bob Feller won 19 games for the Indians, but was a two-time loser in his only World Series appearance.

Feller receives congratulations from his teammates after throwing the third no-hitter of his illustrious career on July 1, 1951, in the first game of a doubleheader against the Detroit Tigers.

RICK FERRELL

Some of the most significant facts about a player's career are not always contained in statistical summaries, but rather in yellowing magazines and newspapers. Such was true in the 18-year American League career of Richard Benjamin Ferrell, a catcher of distinction with the St. Louis Browns, Boston Red Sox and Washington Senators.

Before attaining major league stardom, Rick Ferrell won 17 of 18 professional fights and claimed the championship of North Carolina in the lightweight division.

Before he entered the majors, he was declared a free agent and accepted a bonus of $25,000 to sign with the St. Louis Browns.

As a major league star, Rick formed a battery with his younger brother, Wesley, with Boston and Washington and, late in his career, was handed the unenviable task of catching the deliveries of four knuckleball pitchers on the same club, the Washington Senators.

The fact that he was charged with 21 passed balls in one season failed to dim Ferrell's reputation as a premier catcher.

One of seven brothers born to a North Carolina farmer, Rick Ferrell became a catcher by necessity. "When several brothers decide to become pitchers," he explained, "somebody has to catch 'em, and I took the job."

Rick was a student at Guilford College in North Carolina when he accepted $1,500 to play for the Detroit organization in 1926. Later, he was ordered to join the parent club in training at San Antonio, and a telegram was sent to Tigers Manager George Moriarty to give the recruit a thorough trial.

Moriarty took one glance at the youngster, without a bat in his hands, and announced, "One look at him and you know he'll never hit a lick."

Ferrell was assigned to Columbus of the American Association for whom, in 1928, he batted .333 and attracted major league scouts in profusion. Fancy offers were made for the 21-year-old prospect.

Enter Commissioner Kenesaw Mountain Landis. The Tigers, it developed, had loaned Ferrell to Columbus on a "gentleman's agreement," whereby he would revert to Detroit at season's end. When word reached Tiger officials that Columbus was about to ignore their verbal pact, the Tigers notified Landis, who declared Rick a free agent. Moments after the announcement, Ferrell signed with the St. Louis Browns for $25,000.

It was as a Brownie that Ferrell enjoyed his most memorable days. After batting .306 for St. Louis in 1931, Rick hit a career-high .315 for the Browns in 1932.

Rick Ferrell's outstanding catching ability was his ticket to baseball's Hall of Fame.

In 1933, when the first All-Star Game was staged in Chicago, Rick was named to the American League squad and looked forward to a leisurely afternoon with Bill Dickey doing the catching. To his surprise, Ferrell, traded from the Browns to the Red Sox two months earlier, was named the starting catcher. He played the entire nine innings, handling the deliveries of Lefty Gomez, Lefty Grove and Alvin Crowder as the A.L. won, 4-2.

In sharp contrast to his tempestuous brother Wes, Rick was of a placid nature. Little disturbed him, and when he batted against his brother, who was winning 20 games regularly for Cleveland, he bore down a little harder.

On April 29, 1931, Wes was working on a no-hitter for the Indians against St. Louis when Rick cracked a sharp grounder to the left side. The shortstop's throw pulled the first baseman off the bag and the official scorer ruled an error. Wes got his no-hitter, but years later he conceded, I still think it was a hit."

When Rick completed his major league career with a lifetime batting average of .281, he had caught an American League-record 1,806 games.

ROLLIE FINGERS

When baseball historians remember Rollie Fingers, images of his signature handlebar mustache and clutch relief performances will surely pop into their minds.

Fingers was such a master of his trade that in 1992 he was elected into the Baseball Hall of Fame, an honor that only one other reliever (Hoyt Wilhelm) had achieved prior to that year. But there was a time when little fanfare surrounded Fingers.

He wasn't swamped by pro scouts after his high school career, so he enrolled at Chaffey Junior College (Calif.). But in 1964, Fingers led the Upland (Calif.) American Legion team to the national title. At the Legion World Series that year, he led all players with a .450 batting average. When he wasn't playing left field, he threw a two-hitter and, in the championship game, a three-hitter. Consequently, he was named American Legion Player of the Year that season.

A's scout Art Lilly signed him to a free-agent contract in December 1964 for a $20,000 bonus after Fingers had turned down a higher offer by the Dodgers because he didn't want to be buried in a system that was loaded with talent. Now the A's had to decide if they wanted to make Fingers a pitcher or outfielder. During his first professional spring training, the A's made Fingers a full-time pitcher, a decision the team would come to rejoice.

He began his pro career the following summer with Leesburg in the Florida State League. He toiled in the minor league for the next three seasons, enjoying success as a starting pitcher. During his four-year minor league career, Fingers never posted an earned-run average higher than 3.00, while registering double-figure win totals on two occasions. In 1968 he appeared in one game with the A's, who had moved to Oakland from Kansas City after the '67 season, before finally moving to the big leagues the following season.

But things didn't go smoothly for Fingers during his first few seasons with Oakland. Primarily a starter in 1969 and 1970, Fingers failed to post a winning record or an ERA under 3.50.

As the 1971 season opened, Fingers began the year as a starter. In fact, he was Oakland's only effective starter aside from Vida Blue, until Catfish Hunter, Blue Moon Odom and Chuck Dobson rounded into form that year. After faltering as a front-line pitcher, Fingers was banished to the bullpen in the second week of May. But he didn't complain.

"I figured I wasn't doing the job as a starter so I might as well try to do the job in the bullpen," Fingers reasoned.

In 1992. seven-time All-Star Rollie Fingers became just the second reliever elected into the Baseball Hall of Fame.

Fingers got his big break on June 11, 1971, when teammate Bob Locker came in to put out a Yankee fire but instead poured gasoline on it. That cost Locker his No. 1 bullpen job and moved Fingers ahead of him.

Fingers responded remarkably well. In six June appearances that season, he didn't allow a run en route to compiling a string of 29 2/3 consecutive scoreless innings spread over 11 appearances. Oakland Manager Dick Williams was pleased with Fingers' new-found success.

"There will be times when he'll get hit," Williams said. "But those will be rarities.

"We think he's more relaxed when he's in the bullpen. Now he doesn't know when he's going to pitch. He'd

start to get tense three days before his turn to start. "He's a cool man now. He used to be just the opposite."

Fingers finished the '71 season with 17 saves, as Oakland won the American League West title. That was the beginning of a very prosperous run for both Fingers and the A's.

In the next four seasons, Fingers helped the A's win four A.L. West titles (1972-1975), three pennants (1972-1974) and three World Series (1972-1974). He sparkled during Oakland's three World Series appearances, posting a 2-2 record, a Series record six saves and a 1.35 ERA. It was during that four-year span that Fingers became the most dominant closer in baseball.

Fingers notched his first 20-save campaign in 1972. He saved 20 or more games in three of the next four seasons before signing a free-agent contract with San Diego after the 1976 season. But for a time, it looked like Fingers was going to be member of the Boston Red Sox.

During the '76 season, Oakland Owner Charlie Finley, fearing he would lose his big-name players to free agency at the end of the year, attempted to sell outfielder Joe Rudi and Fingers to Boston for $1,000,000 each. But Commissioner Bowie Kuhn voided the deal "in the best interests of baseball" and returned the pair to Oakland. At the end of the season, however, Finley's worst fears were realized, as Fingers departed to the Padres as a free agent.

Fingers was a hit in Southern California. In his first season with San Diego, he led the league in saves (35). He was just as sharp the next year, posting a major league-best 37 saves. In 1980, Fingers closed his career in San Diego on a high note, registering 23 saves and 11 wins.

He became a key figure in an 11-player trade between San Diego and St. Louis in the off-season. But the day after he met the press as a Cardinal, Fingers was included in another blockbuster swap. This one sent him from St. Louis to Milwaukee.

During his first campaign with the Brewers, the strike-shortened '81 season, Fingers paced the big leagues with 28 saves, while posting a sparkling 1.04 ERA. For his efforts, he became the first relief pitcher to win a Cy Young Award and a Most Valuable Player honor in the same season.

"Over the long haul," said Roger Craig, who managed Fingers in 1978 and 1979 with the Padres, "he's the best relief pitcher I've ever seen."

The Fingers Express continued to roll in 1982, as he collected 29 saves with a 2.60 ERA. But an arm injury prevented him from pitching in the 1982 World Series, which the Brewers lost in seven games to St. Louis.

An arm injury prevented the seven-time All-Star from pitching the entire 1983 season, but he returned for two more years, raising his career saves total to 341, the major league record until it was surpassed by Jeff Reardon in 1992.

CARLTON FISK

W aving a home run fair in the 1975 World Series against the Cincinnati Reds may be what Carlton Fisk is best remembered for, but his 24-year career is a storied one with several major league records and honors.

With aspirations of playing professional basketball, Fisk attended the University of New Hampshire on a basketball scholarship. "What I really wanted to be was a power forward for the Boston Celtics," Fisk said. At New Hampshire, though, Fisk soon realized a professional baseball career was more likely. Fisk excelled on the diamond in college and the Boston Red Sox made him the fourth pick in the free-agent draft of 1967. Fisk spent four seasons in the Red Sox minor league organization before earning chances with the major league club in 1969 and 1971. He batted .313 in limited play at the end of the 1971 season and, in doing so, earned a shot to start for the Red Sox in 1972.

Fisk earned the starting job in 1972 and stormed onto the major league scene that year, winning A.L. Rookie of the Year and Gold Glove at catcher. He batted .293 his rookie year with 22 home runs and a league-tying nine triples. Fisk also had a stellar season behind the plate leading the league in putouts (846) and assists (72). Fisk followed up the 1972 season with another solid all-around season batting only .246, but belting 26 home runs and driving in 71 runs.

The injury bug then struck Fisk the following two years. He tore knee ligaments in June of 1974 and missed the entire season after the injury. Doctors feared the worst, saying that his career could be in jeopardy. But Fisk battled on and through rigorous rehabilitation was ready for the 1975 season. A broken forearm sidelined him the first half of the season, but he returned in the second half to help lead the Red Sox to the World Series against the Reds. He batted .331 with 10 home runs and 52 RBI in the last 79 games of the season to help propel the Red Sox into the playoffs and eventually the World Series.

Fisk took advantage of his first trip to the Series and had one of the most dramatic hits in World Series history against the Reds. With the Red Sox trailing 3-2 in the series and the score tied at 6-6 in the 12th inning, Fisk led off the 12th inning and knew something special was about to happen. "[I had] one of those feelings you get that something is afoot," Fisk said. He took a 1-0 pitch high over the Green Monster in left field—the ball hung in the air a while and Fisk knew it was close to being foul. He tried to wave the ball fair as it just sailed fair over the wall in left. Fisk leaped into the air right before first base

No one caught more major league games than Carlton Fisk, who hit 376 home runs and slugged a dramatic homer in the 1975 World Series.

and the Fenway crowd was overcome with joy. The joy was short lived as the Red Sox dropped the next game and lost the World Series. That was the only time Fisk played in the World Series.

After two injury-filled seasons, Fisk played back-to-back healthy seasons in 1977 and 1978. He excelled both years, batting .315 and .284, and hitting a combined 46 home runs with 190 RBI. Fisk spent two more seasons with the Red Sox before he left the team via free agency to sign with the Chicago White Sox before the 1981 season. He spent the rest of his career in Chicago. Fisk led the White Sox into the postseason in 1983 after another productive year at the plate. He batted .289 with 26 home runs and 86 RBI, but only hit .176 in the postseason as the Baltimore Orioles defeated the White Sox in the American League Championship Series.

Fisk put up his best power numbers of his career in 1985. He only hit .238, but had career highs with 37 home runs and 107 RBI. He battled injuries off and on the rest of his career before retiring in 1993. Before he left, Fisk broke two significant major league records in the '90s. In 1990, he hit career home run No. 328 breaking Johnny Bench's major league record for most home runs by a catcher. Fisk finished his career with 376 home runs. In 1993, Fisk also broke the major league record for most games caught. He caught his 2,226th game on June 22, 1993, and then was released by the White Sox six days later, ending his career. He had appeared in nine All-Star Games and held or shared 11 major league records. Fisk was elected to the Hall of Fame in 2000.

ELMER FLICK

Members of the Phillies had difficulty concealing their mirth when the rookie arrived at their Cape May, N.J., training camp carrying a canvas bag that contained a thick-handled bat he had turned on a lathe back home in Ohio.

But their snickers turned to smiles when Elmer Flick started drilling the ball to all corners of the field on the day early in 1898.

Initially, Flick's chances of crashing the Phils' outfield were less than favorable. Ed Delahanty, Duff Cooley and Sam Thompson were firmly entrenched. One journalist, however, was impressed with the rookie, describing Flick as "the fastest and most promising youngster the Phillies ever had."

Flick opened the season on the bench, but when recurring back problems sidelined Thompson in April, Flick stepped in and rapped two singles against Boston. Thompson returned briefly, then called it quits in May and Flick returned to the lineup as a regular.

By mid-season, fans had virtually forgotten Thompson, a .400 hitter only four years earlier. Flick's productive bat and sharp fielding made him popular, even in opposing cities.

One afternoon Flick made a catch that was described in the press as the most spectacular ever seen in Pittsburgh. It was a leaping, one-handed grab that was rewarded by a shower of silver from the appreciative bleacherites.

By 1900, Elmer was a .378 hitter, but that figure failed to win a batting title because Honus Wagner compiled a .381 average.

When the American League started to raid National League clubs in 1901, several members of the Phillies, including Napoleon Lajoie, jumped to the Athletics. Flick followed a year later. His stay with the A's was brief, however. The Pennsylvania Supreme Court ruled that defectors could perform only with the Phillies as long as they remained within the state. Elmer was sold to Cleveland.

In 1905, Flick won the batting championship with a

It didn't take long for Elmer Flick to win over Phillies fans upon arrival in 1898.

mark of .308, the lowest title-winning average in the majors until Carl Yastrzemski won with a .301 figure in 1968.

In the spring of 1907, Hughey Jennings, manager of the Tigers, proposed a trade to Owner Charles Somers of the Indians. In exchange for Flick, the Bengals offered a young firebrand who had just engaged in a brawl before an exhibition game. Jennings was weary of his rabble rouser and wished to unload him.

Somers made a counterproposal, that was rejected. Jennings offered the outfielder to two or three other clubs, none of which made satisfactory proposals. As a result, Ty Cobb remained with the Tigers until after the 1927 season.

And Flick remained with the Indians. For three consecutive years he led the A.L. in triples, a record that was matched later by only three players.

He also walloped a bases-loaded home run against Rube Waddell, the A's eccentric lefthander. "The center fielder misjudged the ball and got so mad he quit the team for a few days," Flick recalled.

In the spring of 1908, while the Indians were in New Orleans, Flick was stricken by a mysterious stomach ailment. Somers attributed the malady to drinking water, although no other players suffered similarly. Doctors were baffled. Elmer's weight dropped from 160 to 135 and he missed virtually the entire season.

When Flick came back in 1909, his speed was gone. He was only a shadow of his former self and retired from the majors after the 1910 campaign.

For years Flick was almost forgotten as he hobbled about his Warnersville Heights, Ohio home with a cane, the result of a broken hip. He did some scouting for the Indians.

When word arrived in 1963 that Elmer had been elected to the Hall of Fame, he was 87 years old, the senior living member of the shrine.

Accompanied by 17 members of his clan, Flick made it to Cooperstown in a three-car caravan and told the audience "what was in my heart."

Flick declared: "This is a bigger day than I've ever had before. And to think that this plaque will hang here until the end of time."

A lengthy illness preceded Flick's death before his 95th birthday.

WHITEY FORD

By the end of 1964, Whitey Ford was the Yankee ace and a veteran of 11 World Series.

The blocky strawberry blond had a quip for every occasion and a pitch for every situation. To him, it made little sense to pitch if you couldn't have fun while doing it.

From the time he came off the sandlots of Astoria, Queens, Whitey Ford was smart beyond his years. His twinkling blue eyes and choirboy innocence masked the guile of a veteran. With excellent reason, Casey Stengel christened him "Slick." He dominated his profession so convincingly that batterymate Elston Howard referred to him respectfully as the "Chairman of the Board."

To his last breath, Stengel insisted—although Ford denied it—that it was Whitey who telephoned the Yankees' manager and announced early in 1950: "If you want to win the pennant, you'd better call up that kid Ford from Kansas City."

Whatever the motivation, Ford was a Yankee by mid-season and won nine consecutive games before a home run by Sam Chapman of Philadelphia inflicted the only blemish on his rookie record.

After beating the Phillies in the fourth and final game of the World Series, Ford encountered Dizzy Dean in the victors' clubhouse. Dean was then a broadcaster, but 16 years earlier he had won 30 games for the Cardinals.

"No wonder you won 30 games pitching in that crummy National League," Ford saluted Ol' Diz. "I could win 40 in that league myself."

For once, Dean was speechless.

Even as a rookie, Whitey demonstrated a delightful irreverence for tradition. After defeating the Tigers in a critical game, Ford was asked if it had been the most important game of his life.

"Not really," he deadpanned. "I remember pitching the

In 1950, Edward Ford arrived in New York and promptly won nine of his first 10 decisions.

Maspeth Ramblers to a 16 to 11 victory over the Astoria Indians. That was a big one, too."

On the same trip, Stengel notified Ford several days in advance that the rookie would open a series in Chicago, hopeful that Ford and roommate Yogi Berra would devote some hours discussing the proper way to pitch to White Sox batters.

The Yankees completed their pregame workout at Comiskey Park on the day of the game before it was discovered that Ford was absent. A frantic call to the hotel roused the towhead from deep slumber. He arrived at the park barely in time to warm up—and he pitched a three-hitter.

Rival managers were quick to marvel at the gifted lefthander. "No one is better in big ball games," said one.

"He'll beat you, never beats himself," added another.

"When he's got it, the ball game's over," offered a third.

Whitey had it through most of his career, which was interrupted by a military hitch (1951-52) and blighted in the latter stages by surgery to correct a circulatory problem in his shoulder.

But other times, Ford was superb. His .690 winning percentage was the best among modern pitchers with 200 or more victories. His $33\frac{2}{3}$ consecutive scoreless innings broke a World Series record held previously by Babe Ruth when he was with the Red Sox.

Few of Whitey's 236 career victories were registered in Boston, where Fenway Park's left-field wall and the Red Sox's predominately righthanded lineup frequently spelled misfortune for a lefthanded pitcher.

"I'd like to pitch here more," Ford once said with a mischievous air, recalling, no doubt, that he was only a .500 pitcher in Fenway.

Less than a year after Ford became a Yankee, he was joined by another blithe spirit, Mickey Mantle. Together they missed planes, were late for trains and celebrated (too well) Billy Martin's birthday at the Copacabana night club in New York.

While in San Francisco for the 1961 All-Star Game, the pair accepted an offer from Horace Stoneham to use the Giant owner's membership at a local country club. Before they were aware of it, Ford and Mantle had indebted Stoneham to the amount of $400.

An offer to pay met with a counterproposal. "We'll forget it," said Stoneham to Ford, "if you can strike out Willie Mays tomorrow."

In the first inning, Ford got two strikes on Mays, then "loaded up" a pitch that started at Willie's shoulders and wound up at his belt for the third strike. From center field, Mantle raced to the infield, where he pounded Ford violently on the back.

After his retirement in 1967, and his election to the Hall of Fame in 1974, Whitey revealed how, in moments of extreme stress, he had doctored a baseball with a sticky homemade substance and a specially made rasp ring, which, he informed an inquisitive umpire, is "my wedding ring."

Yogi Berra and Mickey Mantle (above, right) share a laugh with Ford and wife Joan during ceremonies to retire Ford's No. 16 in 1974. Ford was 21 (below, left) when he posed with Binghamton teammate Tom Gorman in 1949.

BILL FOSTER

There were more famous pitchers in the Negro League than Bill "Willie" Foster, but most observers think Foster was the best lefthander ever in the league.

Dave Malarcher was Foster's teammate and manager for much of his career with the Chicago American Giants and had nothing but praise for Foster's performance and ability.

"Willie Foster's greatness was that he had this terrific speed and a great, fast-breaking curve ball and a drop ball, and he was really a master of the change-of-pace," Malarcher was quoted as saying in *Only The Ball Was White*, a history of the Negro League. "He could throw you a real fast one and then use the same motion and bring it up a little slower, and then a little slower yet. And then he'd use the same motion again, and Z-zzzz! He was really a great pitcher."

A half brother of Rube Foster, another Negro League star who was inducted into the Hall of Fame in 1981, Foster also earned praise from Hall of Fame umpire Jocko Conlon, who compared Foster to pitcher Herb Pennock, a Hall of Famer who spent much of his career with the Yankees. Foster, one of the smartest pitchers in the league, knew exactly what pitch to throw in what situation and how to use all of his pitches to his greatest advantage.

Foster's mother died when he was only four years old, and he was raised by his maternal grandparents in Mississippi. He moved to Chicago in 1918 to work in the stockyards and tried to sign on with brother Rube's Chicago team, but his brother refused to allow him to play, creating a resentment that continued throughout Foster's life.

Foster returned to Mississippi, attending Alcorn College before signing with the Memphis Red Sox in 1923. He was turned over to the Chicago squad and split time with a northern and southern team for three years. His first full season in Chicago was 1926, when he totaled 26 consecutive wins against all levels of competition, including exhibition games. In the playoffs for the pennant, the American Giants needed to win both games of a final-day doubleheader against Kansas City to win the pennant. Foster started and won both games to give Chicago the National League title. In the World Series against Baltimore, Foster pitched three complete games and relieved in another, winning twice.

In 1927, Foster had a 21-3 regular-season record and won a remarkable 32 total games. He pitched two complete games in the Series victory over the Bacharach Giants and relieved in two others.

Many consider Bill Foster (second from left) the best lefthander in the Negro Leagues. He entered the Hall in 1996.

The 6-foot-1, 195-pound Foster won 14 and 11 games respectively, in 1928 and 1929, but neither season produced a pennant-winner for Chicago and Foster was named manager of the American Giants in 1930. He led the team to a 43-51 record, but resigned the position after the season because he didn't think he could continue to pitch and manage at the same time.

He spent the 1931 season with the Homestead Grays, and after pitching the Grays to a victory over Kansas City in September, was given permission by both owners to finish the year in Kansas City.

Foster returned to Chicago and led the team to pennants in 1932 and 1933, winning 15 games in 1932. He was the starting pitcher for the West in the first East-West All-Star game in 1933, and with no rules limiting how many innings he could pitch, he turned in a complete game victory against a lineup that included future Hall of Famers Cool Papa Bell, Josh Gibson and Judy Johnson.

The American Giants were first-half champions in 1934, but lost the playoffs to the Philadelphia Stars. Foster's highlight in 1935 was a September victory over Satchel Paige and the Monarchs. He moved again to pitch for the Pittsburgh Crawfords in 1936 and he returned to Chicago in 1937, finishing his playing career in 1938. Using a tricky sidearm delivery, Foster won 137 games in his Negro League career, eight more than Hall of Famer Paige.

Foster, baseball coach and dean of men at Alcorn State College from 1960 until just before his death in 1978 at age 74, was elected to the Hall of Fame in 1996.

RUBE FOSTER

When the 22-year-old son of a Methodist minister defeated Rube Waddell, 5-2, in the spring of 1902, his teammates agreed that the best compliment they could pay the young pitcher was to give him the same nickname as the promising Philadelphia lefthander. For the 29 years remaining to him, Andrew Foster was known as Rube.

In those nearly three decades, Rube Foster was an outstanding pitcher. He managed and owned teams, organized leagues and served as commissioner. More than any other, he deserved the title of "Father of black baseball."

A native of Calvert, Tex., Foster threw batting practice for major league clubs training in Texas while still a teenager. He pitched for the Fort Worth Yellow Jackets and in 1902, when he was credited with 51 victories, Foster was a member of E.B. Lamar's Cuban Giants (actually a team of American blacks playing out of Philadelphia).

Rube's salary was $40 a month.

By 1906, Rube was at the peak of his career, mixing his overpowering fastball with a tantalizing change-up. Honus Wagner called him "the smoothest pitcher I've ever seen." John McGraw, lamenting that the color barrier prevented him from signing Foster for the New York Giants, hired him as a pitching coach of sorts. Foster is reputed to have taught his screwball to Christy Mathewson. Big Six popularized the delivery as his fadeaway.

When Foster, a 6-foot-4, 240-pounder, joined the Leland Giants of Chicago in the first decade of the century, his first act was to rename the team the American Giants. The team played in the White Sox's old park at 39th and Wentworth. Regularly, the Giants attracted 11,000 fans on Sunday in competition with the Sox, who would draw 9,000, and the Cubs, who would play to 6,000.

One year the Giants played a three-game postseason series against the Cubs, second-place finishers in the National League. Although the Giants lost each game by one run, a writer for the *Chicago Defender* wrote that "fans made fun of the way officials deliberately favored the Cubs just enough to assure victory."

Frank Chance, Cubs manager in that era, termed Foster "the most finished product I've ever seen in the pitcher's box." In Cleveland, the *Post* proclaimed: "There have been but two real pitchers who have put their feet in the Cleveland ball yard. They are Addie Joss and Rube Foster."

Foster, who addressed everyone as "Darling," except his wife, whom he called "Smoothie," managed the American Giants into the most powerful black team in the country. While operating out of Chicago, the Giants traveled widely, generally in a private Pullman car. The 1910 team won 123 of 129 games.

In the winter of 1919, Foster convened the owners of leading Negro teams and organized the Negro National League. Quickly, player salaries that had totaled about $30,000 a year rose to $275,000.

In 1920, Rube organized the team that dominated Midwest black baseball for the next decade. The team was built on speed and bunting. In one game, eight consecutive batters bunted safely for hits.

Foster not only operated the Giants in the early 1920s, but the league as well. At his own expense, he placed a team in Dayton, Ohio. When the club faltered at the gate, he shifted it to Columbus.

Wherever he traveled, Rube Foster attracted large crowds. He would reminisce at length when the Giants arrived in Kansas City, then predict what his club would do to the hometown Monarchs. On the day of the game, extra patrolmen were necessary to handle traffic en route to the ball park. Rube's showmanship guaranteed sellouts.

Foster died in 1930 at Kankakee, Illinois, at age 51.

Rube Foster managed the American Giants into the most powerful black team in the country.

NELLIE FOX

Fox did his part during the series hitting .375, but it wasn't enough to offset the superior Los Angeles pitching.

While the 1959 season was his finest hour, Fox had a distinguished career as one of the A.L.'s top second basemen during his 19 years with the Philadelphia Athletics, White Sox and his final two years in the N.L., with the Astros.

Standing just 5-foot-10 and weighing 160 pounds, Fox definitely wasn't a home run threat but what he did was develop a superior knowledge of the strike zone and realize what he had to do to make the maximum use of his skills and physical abilities.

He led the A.L. in hits four times, and made himself into a quality hitter by learning to slap the ball into the outfield. For seven consecutive years, he led the A.L. in singles.

Fox also led the A.L. in fewest strikeouts for almost his entire career. From 1950 through 1964, he never struck out more than 18 times in a season in which his lowest at-bat total was 442. For 12 of those years, he went to bat more than 600 times.

For his career, Fox struck out a remarkably low 216 times in 9,232 at-bats, the third-best percentage in major-league history.

Selected to the All-Star team 12 times and the winner of three Gold Gloves, Fox teamed first with Chico Carrasquel and then with Luis Aparicio to give the White Sox one of the best double-play combinations in the league. He led A.L. second basemen in turning double plays five times.

Fox broke into the majors with the Athletics in 1947, but played in only seven games. He played three games in 1948, but reached the majors to stay the next season, The A's traded him to the White Sox after the 1948 season for catcher Joe Tipton, beginning his 14-year stay in Chicago.

A hustling player who would do anything to win and always a spirited player who was out to help his teammates, Fox had six .300 seasons for the White Sox, topped by a .319 mark in 1954, and finished his career with a .288 average. He also proved to be an extremely durable player despite his size, setting a record for consecutive games

Nellie Fox had a 19-year career, finishing with a .288 career batting average. He led the league four times in total hits.

played at second base of 798 games. The streak began in 1956 and lasted almost until the end of the 1960 season. His uniform number 2 was retired by the White Sox.

Fox retired after playing just 21 games for the Astros in 1965. He died just 10 years later, at the young age of 47.

In 1985, Fox missed election to the Hall of Fame in the writer's balloting by two votes, the closest any player has ever missed election. He did win election in 1997 by the veteran's committee.

JIMMIE FOXX

Generally, those who knew him best discussed his genial personality or his unfortunate bankruptcy or the explosive power generated by his massive muscles when swinging a bat at a pitched ball.

Bill Dickey, longtime Yankee catcher, once remarked: "If I were catching blindfolded, I'd always know when it was Jimmie Foxx who connected. He hit the ball harder than anybody else."

One-time teammate Moe Berg asserted that Foxx "had the greatest right arm ever hung on a human being."

Jimmie's bulging biceps bespoke a superhuman power. Prodigious wallops were his trademark. One such blow, against Lefty Gomez, landed in the last section of the third tier in left field at Yankee Stadium—and had enough force to break the back of a seat.

In Chicago, Double X drove a pitch out of double-decked Comiskey Park, onto a playground, an estimated 600 feet from home plate.

Another blast, which Jimmie regarded as one of his longest, was hit at Sportsman's Park in St. Louis in Game 5 of the 1930 World Series. In the first game of the Series,

Burleigh Grimes had slipped a third-strike curve past a confused Foxx, who had been led to believe that Old Stubblebeard threw only a spitter.

In the ninth inning of the scoreless fifth game, with Mickey Cochrane on base via a walk, a smarter Foxx looked for a curve—and got it. The ball went over the fence in deep left-center field.

Later, Grimes conceded that the two curveballs to Foxx were the only ones he had thrown in the Series.

Sportsman's Park held other memories for Jimmie. On July 2, 1933, Foxx clouted two homers in the first game of a doubleheader, then came back with another pair in the nightcap, plus a triple and a double. The two lesser extra-base hits, it was said, missed the top of the wall by a total of one foot. He was that close to six homers for the day.

When Jimmie was pursuing Babe Ruth's 60-homer record in 1932, Sportsman's Park was a major deterrent in limiting his season total to 58. Jimmie socked five drives against a screen in front of the right-field pavilion. There was no screen there during Ruth's big season of 1927.

Also in '32, the Indians erected a screen in front of the left-field stands at League Park. Foxx bounced three drives off that screen. Had he played under conditions that prevailed in '27, Double X would have swatted more than 60 home runs in 1932.

A product of Sudlers-ville, Md., where he was discovered by Frank (Home Run) Baker, Foxx was 16 when he entered Organized Ball as a catcher. He was only 17 when, in 1925, he played 10 games with the A's and collected his first major league hit. Pinch-hitting for Lefty Grove, he singled against Vean Gregg at Washington on May 1.

When Jimmie won his second consecutive Most Valuable Player honor in 1933, he was asked to take a pay cut, from $16,333 to $12,000, because of the hard times. After a vigorous argument, Foxx agreed to a $16,000 contract. At Boston several years later, Foxx's top salary was about $32,000, including attendance bonuses.

When Foxx was at the peak of his game, everyone shared

Jimmie Foxx (sitting, second from right) was 13 when this picture was taken during the early 1920s.

When he joined the A's in 1925, Foxx was a catcher. Foxx (above right) is pictured in 1932, the year he hit 58 home runs and drove in 169 for the A's. Below right, Foxx was greeted by Bob Johnson after hitting a two-run homer in the 1935 All-Star Game in Cleveland.

in his opulence. Johnny Peacock, a roommate of the Maryland strong boy with the Red Sox and Phillies, once said: "Jimmie always used to pay the whole room bill no matter who his roommate was. He'd pay all telephone, valet, room service—whatever. But when we roomed together on the Phils, he let me pay my own bills."

Jimmie closed out his major league career with the Phils in 1945.

During the twilight of his career, Foxx suffered from a sinus condition. In retirement, he suffered an acute heart ailment. Trying to move a trunk, he fell down a flight of stairs and fractured a spinal disc that caused partial paralysis to his left side.

In 1963, he made an appearance in Cleveland, where he had clouted a home run and a single to help the American League win the 1935 All-Star Game. This time, he announced that he was broke, and applied for unemployment benefits.

Foxx accepted a job selling sporting goods in a downtown department store. He also served as a front man at a restaurant in Galesburg, Illinois.

The old slugger, who lost $100,000 on a golf course venture in St. Petersburg, Fla., and was in the habit of tipping $50 on a $150 tailor-made suit, never complained of any misfortunes, but said, "If I had it to do all over, I'd invest differently and not live so freely."

Jimmie choked to death in Miami in 1967 when a piece of meat lodged in his throat.

FORD FRICK

O f his countless contributions to baseball in 17 years as National League president and 14 years as commissioner, no achievement inspired greater pride in Ford Frick than his role in the founding of the Hall of Fame.

The city fathers of Cooperstown, N.Y., planned a celebration to mark the community's part in the origins of baseball and sent a representative to the N.L. office in New York to seek Frick's cooperation. The emissary suggested that major league all-star teams play a game there to focus attention on the game's reputed birthplace.

"Why do that?" replied Frick. "Why not start a baseball museum and have something that will last?"

Cooperstown accepted Frick's suggestion, and the Baseball Hall of Fame and Museum was dedicated on June 12, 1939 (three years after the first election of inductees).

A native of Indiana, Frick graduated from DePauw University and was writing sports for the *Colorado Springs Gazette* as well as teaching English courses at Colorado College when one of his sports articles came to the attention of Arthur Brisbane, New York editor for the Hearst newspapers.

Frick accepted an offer to join the *New York American*, and for a number of years he covered the Giants. Later he switched to the *Journal* and traveled with the Yankees.

He pioneered in radio sports shows and "ghosted" for Babe Ruth. Frick and the Bambino were golfing and bridge partners. Because of the close friendship, Frick found himself in one of his major controversies in 1961 when Roger Maris broke the Babe's season homer record.

When the commissioner announced that an asterisk would be placed beside Maris' name to designate a 162-game schedule, as compared with the 154 games in which Babe clouted his 60 homers, sportswriters accused him of favoritism toward his old crony.

In 1934, Frick became publicity director for the N.L. He held the post for less than one year before being elected league president, succeeding John Heydler (who was in failing health).

Frick survived his most critical moment in 1947 when Jackie Robinson broke the color line in baseball. Reacting to the epithets and threats against the Brooklyn rookie by rival players, Frick declared: "The National League will go down the line with Robinson and I don't care if it wrecks the league for five years." He said he would ban forever anyone who tried to halt the integration process.

When A.B. (Happy) Chandler was named to succeed Judge K.M. Landis as commissioner in 1945, Frick's name was entered as a candidate, although Frick did not campaign for the office. After Chandler resigned in 1951, Frick again was a candidate, along with Warren Giles, president of the Cincinnati Reds.

The 16 club owners balloted 20 times in an effort to obtain the necessary 16 votes. When the situation seemed hopelessly deadlocked, Giles withdrew from the race and Frick was elected the third commissioner of baseball.

Frick staunchly defended the reserve clause when it came under attack, but favored players earning hefty salaries. On a number of occasions, he was assailed by the press for his "That's a league matter" refrain, which was regarded as an effort to evade a decision.

Frick retired from what he described as "a lonely job" in 1965 to his Bronxville, N.Y., home, where he died in 1978 at age 83.

National League President Ford Frick (right) gets a handshake from President Franklin D. Roosevelt as baseball Commissioner Kenesaw Mountain Landis (center) looks on prior to the 1937 All-Star Game at Griffith Stadium.

FRANK FRISCH

John McGraw could either sign the collegian to a Giants contract, as the youngster requested, or the prospect would enter business with his father, a wealthy linen manufacturer in New York.

Unaccustomed as he was to acting against his will, the crusty manager acceded in this case, thereby giving baseball one of its most colorful individuals, Frank Francis Frisch.

Frisch had captained the baseball, football and basketball teams at Fordham University and was a second-team All-America halfback before he joined the Giants in 1919.

McGraw determined early that Frisch did not have the range nor the sure hands to remain at shortstop, his college position. The young switch-hitter also needed batting tips and guidance on how to slide properly. McGraw worked endless hours in polishing his prodigy, who quickly became the manager's pet.

When Frisch made his first start in September, playing third base against the pennant-bound Reds, a bad-hop smash caromed off his chest. Pouncing adroitly in pursuit, Frisch collared the ball and nipped the batter with a rifle throw to first.

"That was all I had to see," McGraw remarked. "The average youngster, nervous anyhow at making his first start, would have given up on the play."

The Flash performed at third and second base for the pennant-winning Giants of 1921 through 1924, but when the Giants slipped the next two seasons and Frisch, as captain, received a lot of verbal abuse from his frustrated manager, he packed his bags when the team arrived in St. Louis and returned home.

A breach developed between McGraw and Frisch. Two months after the close of the 1926 season, Frisch was traded with pitcher Jimmy Ring to the world champion Cardinals for Rogers Hornsby.

Frankie was not enamored with the prospect of leaving his native city, but he spent the winter at Lake Placid, N.Y., skating, skiing and walking the rugged terrain to strengthen his legs. The program paid off handsomely. Frisch handled more than 1,000 chances at second base and batted .337 for the 1927 Cardinals, but missed the Most Valuable Player award by one vote to Paul Waner of Pittsburgh.

Frisch sparked the Cardinals to pennants in 1928, 1930 and 1931 and to a world title the last year, when he also was the National League's MVP.

He homered and singled in the first All-Star Game in Chicago and a year later, in '34, when the game was played at the Polo Grounds, the Old Flash announced: "I see that I'm leading off, and Lefty Gomez is starting for the American League. He likes to throw smoke on the first pitch and if he does, I'll hit it out."

Frank Frisch was an infielder for John McGraw's Giants upon arrival in the big leagues in 1919.

Player-Manager Frisch hit .305 and guided the Cardinals to a World Series title in 1934.

Gomez was true to form and Frisch, batting right-handed, sliced a home run to right field.

Appointed manager of the Cardinals in mid-1933, Frisch drove the Gas House Gang to the pennant the following year. In the World Series against Detroit, the Old Flash enjoyed his biggest thrill when, in Game 7, the Tigers walked the previous batter to load the bases, giving Frankie an opportunity to rap a three-run double.

"It should have been a triple," he contended. "I was so fascinated watching the three runners score, I couldn't get past second. If anyone else had done the same thing, I'd have fined him."

Frisch's escapades with umpires were legion. He would draw the thumb from Beans Reardon in the afternoon, then swill beer with him at night. Once he went into a mock faint in protest of a Bill Klem decision. Running to the prostrate form, Klem barked, "Frisch, if you ain't dead, you're out of the game."

At other times, Frankie carried an open umbrella onto the field in protest of a game continuing in a drizzle. He was ejected. He made a low salaam to George Magerkurth when the umpire cleared the bench during Frank's managerial career in Pittsburgh.

But when an umpire's job was in jeopardy as the result of a Pittsburgh protest, the Old Flash withdrew his protest. "No game is worth an umpire's job," he said.

Frisch died at age 74 in Wilmington, Del., a month after suffering injuries in an automobile accident in 1973.

Cubs Manager Frisch got the thumb from umpire Augie Donatelli in 1951, only a few days before losing his job.

PUD GALVIN

His was not a household name, yet only five major league pitchers won more games in their careers than James (Pud) Galvin. He was the Walter Johnson of his time, blazing fastballs past bewildered batters.

Galvin hurled more innings—5,959—than any other pitcher except Cy Young.

He pitched two no-hitters for Buffalo, against Worcester and Detroit, and his gem against Detroit followed a one-hitter against the same club.

Galvin accounted for the first two victories scored by the Pittsburgh club in the National League, beating John Clarkson of Chicago, 6-2, and Lady Baldwin of Detroit, 8-3, in 1887.

After the powerful Providence team won 20 straight games in 1884, he shut out the Grays, beating Old Hoss Radbourn, 2-0.

Still, with his convincing credentials, it required the passage of 63 years after his death for Galvin to be elected to the Hall of Fame.

Sometimes he was called "Gentle James," in tribute to his personality. Other times he was known as "Pud," as in pudding, which, it was said, he made of opposing batters.

Galvin placed little stock in the curve as a pitching weapon, relying on his fastball and control to register 46 victories in both 1883 and 1884. In '83, he worked a staggering 656 innings.

Buck Ewing, incomparable New York catcher, insisted that "If I had Galvin to catch, no one would ever steal a base on me. That fellow keeps 'em glued to the base, and he also has the best control of any pitcher in the league."

Galvin's control was short of Ewing's high praise during one game in 1886 as he walked three consecutive batters. But to the baserunners' chagrin, they learned about Pud's knack of keeping runners "glued." Each was picked off base.

Gentle James was all but invincible for Buffalo during a six-day period in 1884. On August 2, he pitched a one-hitter. Two days later, he hurled a three-hit shutout and the next day he worked 11 scoreless innings before bowing, 1-0.

Late in the 1885 season, Pud was sold to the Allegheny (Pittsburgh) club of the American Association for $2,500, a princely sum of that day. He was given $700 from that amount, and handed a $1,000 raise by his new bosses, placing him in the $3,000 bracket.

The Buffalo owners' cash-gift generosity was in sharp contrast to their earlier treatment of Galvin. Infuriated

Pud Galvin's blazing fastball made him the Walter Johnson of the 19th Century.

that he was given no raise after a 46-22 campaign in '84, Galvin went to San Francisco and joined an independent club. Tales of his magnificent feats filtered back to Buffalo, where the Bisons were slumping dismally. On May 11, the Buffalo Express carried the welcome news: "There is great rejoicing on the baseball front. Negotiations have been opened with Gentle James."

Galvin rejoined the Buffalo club and posted a 13-19 record before being sold to Allegheny.

Although his lifetime batting average was barely above .200, Galvin played the outfield and once performed at shortstop.

An eye injury, suffered when struck by a pitched ball, made Gentle James gun-shy in later years, and a fractured leg, suffered in a collision with Cap Anson of Chicago, created idle time that boosted Pud's weight over 200 pounds by the time he retired in 1894.

Galvin umpired for one season in the National League before returning to Pittsburgh, where he opened one of the largest cafes in the city.

The father of 11—he once wisecracked that he should organize a family team and call it the "Galvinized Nine"—Galvin went broke. And, on Thanksgiving Day, 1901, he was taken sick with a stomach ailment. Less than four months later, at age 45, Galvin died.

Galvin, a friend of President Grover Cleveland, lived his final months in a rooming house on Pittsburgh's lower north side.

LOU GEHRIG

In an age when colorful nicknames were sprinkled liberally among the nation's sports heroes, no sobriquet was better suited than that of "The Iron Horse."

It symbolized durability and reliability in heat and cold, fair weather and foul, sickness and health. Yankee first baseman Lou Gehrig was every bit of that as he accumulated an almost incredible total of 2,130 consecutive games.

Then, as the locomotive yielded to more popular modes of transportation, the seemingly indestructible Gehrig yielded to an ailment that came to be known as "Lou Gehrig's disease," as incurable today as it was the day he died.

The derailment of baseball's Iron Horse occurred on May 2, 1939, in Detroit.

Before heading west on the Yankees' first trip of the season, Gehrig had made a play at Yankee Stadium that in his mind, was strictly routine. Yet, when he struggled back to first base to take a throw from Johnny Murphy, the pitcher had said, "Nice play, Lou."

May 1 was an off day, which Larruping Lou spent in his hotel room pondering his problem The next day he confronted Manager Joe McCarthy and announced his decision: "I'm taking myself out of the lineup ' "

The pilot offered no resistance, but replied: "All right, but remember that first base is your position and it is there when you want it back." But the Iron Horse never played another game.

Gehrig's first brush with fame occurred on June 26, 1920, when his Commerce High School team of New York visited Chicago to oppose Lane Tech at Wrigley Field. With the bases loaded in the ninth inning, the 17-year-old slugger walloped a home run onto Sheffield Avenue.

While at Columbia University, the son of German

At age 13, little did Lou Gehrig suspect the impact he would have on the baseball world.

immigrants was scouted by Paul Krichell and when the Yankee scout offered Lou a $1,500 bonus, he pounced on it like a fastball down the middle.

After three stints with Hartford of the Eastern League, Gehrig had a hammer lock on the Yankee first-base job by June of 1925. His consecutive game streak started with a pinch-hitting appearance on June 1. He took over at first base the next day when Wally Pipp complained of a splitting headache and was told by Manager Miller Huggins to "take the day off." The bag was Lou's for 14 years.

During that period Gehrig became Babe Ruth's running mate, laboring in the shadows of the Bambino but frequently eclipsing his luminous achievements.

In his own evaluation, Gehrig's top accomplishments were a home run off Carl Hubbell, famed Giants lefthander, in the 1936 World Series; a homer off Dizzy Dean in the 1937 All-Star Game after the great righthander had waved off a curveball and insisted on throwing a fastball, and his four-homer day in Philadelphia on June 3, 1932.

In 1931, when Lou set an American League record with 184 runs batted in, he missed out on an outright home run leadership through the blunder of a teammate. When Gehrig hit a ball into the bleachers at Washington, baserunner Lyn Lary looked up in time to see the center fielder holding the ball. Thinking that the fielder had caught the ball, rather than fielding a rebound off a bleacher seat, Lary headed for the dugout after reaching third base. Unaware of Lary's mistake, Gehrig was called out for passing a baserunner. The blow should have given Gehrig 47 homers for the season. Instead, he tied Ruth at 46.

Nobody, Gehrig least of all, grew suspicious in 1938 when Lou's home run production fell to 29 and his batting average to .295. He still drove in 114 runs and his 212-pound frame appeared as robust as ever. In the Yanks' four-game World Series sweep over the Cubs, however, Lou's four hits were singles and he had no home runs or RBIs.

On July 4, 1939, more than 61,000 fans jammed Yankee Stadium to hear the terminally ill Gehrig bid them a tearful farewell. The occasion also called for an embrace (below) from former teammate Babe Ruth.

Gehrig was a star for the Columbia University team when discovered by the Yankees.

Seven months later, Gehrig and a grieving public heard the sad news from the Mayo Clinic. Gehrig was suffering from lateral sclerosis, insidious and deadly.

The Yankees quickly arranged for a gigantic tribute to their stricken captain. On July 4, 1939, more than 61,000 fans jammed Yankee Stadium to pay homage. As mem-bers of the 1927 and 1939 Yankee teams looked on, Lou assured the world that "Today I consider myself the luck-iest man on the face of the earth."

Gehrig was appointed to the New York City Police Commission and worked diligently with youth groups until one month before his death in June of 1941.

CHARLEY GEHRINGER

Teammates poked fun at his Sphinx-like demeanor, but nobody overlooked the easy manner and stylish grace that made Charley Gehringer one of the premier second basemen of all time.

Mickey Cochrane, Gehringer's manager with the world champion Detroit Tigers of 1935, said: "He says hello on opening day and goodbye on closing day, and in between he hits .350."

Roger (Doc) Cramer quipped: "You wind him up on opening day and forget about him."

Gehringer was not flamboyant, but he handled his position with long strides, soft hands and an unerring arm. A .320 lifetime batting average contributed to his reputation as a ballplayer's ballplayer.

A native of Fowlerville, Mich., Gehringer entered baseball over parental objections. His father thought the farm afforded a good livelihood and that his youngest son should appreciate the advantage of soil, crops and livestock.

Charley felt differently and drifted onto a town team that performed at the local fair grounds. Gehringer's natural ability caught the eye of a hunting partner of Bobby Veach. "Take a look at this kid before some other club grabs him," the friend told the old Tiger outfielder.

Veach took a look and was impressed. His words to the Tigers were "Grab him." By 1925, Gehringer was a Tiger for keeps, eased into his position by manager Ty Cobb.

Gehringer's aptitude was as good for major league baseball as it had been for baseball at the country fair level. By 1929 he led the American League in stolen bases and had rapped three triples in one game.

Although he went 0-for-3 in the first All-Star Game in 1933, Charley finished with a .500 average (10-for-20) in six mid-summer classics. Seven times he collected 200 or more hits in one season, and he posted his top average of .371 in 1937 when he captured the A.L. batting title along with the Most Valuable Player award.

In a 14-year span, Charley's average sank below .300 only once. Gehringer explained: "That was the year I was going to be like Babe Ruth. I think I had eight (home runs) before he had any and I began going for the fences. I wound up getting not many homers—and not many hits either." Actually, he had 184 hits that season (1932) and a .298 average.

"I honestly believe," noted his onetime manager, Del Baker, "Charley could spot a pitcher two strikes all season and still hit within 15 points of his regular average."

With all his sterling accomplishments, Gehringer regarded a day in which he was honored by hometown admirers as his most memorable event of a distinguished career.

The occasion was scheduled for a New York-Detroit game. Such events generally produce a hitless performance for the honored athlete, or perhaps a poor demonstration on the field. Gehringer was different.

Charley hit the first pitch to him over the right-field wall. He collected three other hits and won the game for the Tigers when he stole home.

After such a performance, the lefthanded hitter could forgive his Fowler ville friends for presenting him a set of golf clubs made for a righthander.

"I just turned around and learned to play righthanded and have been playing that way ever since," he explained matter of factly.

At the close of the 1940 World Series, which the Tigers lost to Cincinnati in seven games, Charley confessed that the entire season had been torture for him and that "some days I couldn't get out of bed until noon."

He disclosed that during a spring exhibition, he had raced in for a ground ball, fielded it and was about to throw to first

Charley Gehringer's personality was not as flamboyant as the numbers he put on the board. The always reliable Gehringer shows his form as he delivers a single during action in the first game of the 1934 World Series in Detroit. The Cardinals' catcher is Bill DeLancey.

base when he noticed a young player had run into his line of fire.

"In motion and off-balance, I checked my throw at the last minute, lurched and had misery thereafter," he revealed.

After the 1942 season, in which he batted only 45 times and hit .267, Gehringer was commissioned a lieutenant and served in the Navy fitness program for the remainder of the war.

Returning to civilian life, Charley became a highly successful manufacturers agent in Detroit.

Gehringer came out of retirement in 1951 to serve as Detroit general manager at the invitation of Tigers Owner Walter Briggs. He held the post two years, then remained as a club vice president until his retirement in 1959.

BOB GIBSON

The first batter in the ninth inning had struck out and more than 54,000 throats had turned Busch Memorial Stadium into a cavern of cacophony when the message board announced that the pitcher had tied a World Series record with his 15th strikeout of the game.

From behind home plate, St. Louis catcher Tim McCarver gestured to his batterymate, suggesting that he glance at the board and learn the reason for the thunderous ovation.

The pitcher resisted. Over the din, he shouted, "Gimme the damn ball."

Bob Gibson would savor that moment later in privacy. For now, he had to retire two more Detroit batters to sew up Game 1 of the 1968 Series, which he did in the same way he had dispatched 15 other batters—via strikeouts.

Intensity was Gibson's hallmark. A psychological tunnel vision directed all his energies toward the business at hand. The opponents were his enemies and were not to be engaged in chitchat before a game. To him, such conduct was traitorous.

The attitude paid off for the righthander during his 17 years with the Cardinals. In addition to the 17 strikeouts in a Series game, other highlights included more than 3,000 career strikeouts and 13 shutouts and a 1.12 earned-run average in 1968. During one 95-inning span, Gibson surrendered only two runs.

Gibson's success as a pitcher contrasted with his humble origins in Omaha, Neb. His father died when he was 3 months old. As a child, Bob suffered from rickets and asthma and at one stage was not expected to live.

As a youngster, Gibson was a switch-hitting catcher and shortstop on a YMCA team. When he was in high school, he grew so rapidly that he needed a doctor's permission to compete in athletics because of a heart murmur.

Gibson won a scholarship to Creighton University, where he became the first member of the school's sports hall of fame. In basketball, he amazed spectators with his leaping ability by which he could touch the basket with his elbow.

Bob accepted a $4,000 bonus from the Cardinals to sign with their Omaha farm club in 1957.

Gibby's major league career was interrupted by two leg fractures. In 1962, he suffered a fracture when his spikes caught in the batter's box. In 1967, he was pitching against the Pirates when a Roberto Clemente smash struck Gibson on the left leg. Result—another fracture.

Weeks later in '67, when he returned to the clubhouse

on crutches, Bob wearied quickly of answering questions. In self-defense, he erected a sign reading: "Yes, it's off (the cast). No, it doesn't hurt. I'm not supposed to walk on it for one week. I don't know how much longer. Ask Doc Bauman (trainer). Ask Doc Middleman (team surgeon)."

Gibson returned to action in time to lead the Cardinals to a World Series victory over the Red Sox. His three victories were part of his record seven complete-game Series triumphs.

Gibson pitched his last major league game in early September of 1975, giving up a bases-loaded homer to Pete LaCock of the Cubs. "That was humiliating," Bob remembered years later. "He had never hit a foul ball—well, maybe a foul ball—off me before. I said, 'That's it, I'm finished.'"

At season's end—after 251 big-league victories—Gibson stepped into his $30,000 mobile home, a going-away gift from the Cardinals, and returned to Omaha. After 20 years in athletics, including intercollegiate play, one year with the Harlem Globetrotters and his career with the Cardinals, he was ready for an easier lifestyle. He was a network sportscaster for a time, had an interest

The competitive juices already were flowing when Gibson spent part of the 1960 season with the Cardinals.

in a radio station (which he sold), became chairman of the board of a bank and opened a restaurant-bar.

The old competitor discovered after years of retirement that he was still a coveted commodity in baseball, and he accepted a coaching position with the Mets under his old teammate, Joe Torre. He later accompanied Torre to Atlanta.

Torre was confident Gibson was the man for the job. When asked what had made Gibson a great pitcher, the former catcher-first baseman replied: "Try pride, intensity, talent, respect, dedication. . . . you need 'em all."

In 1981, at the urging of old teammate Joe Torre, Gibson came out of retirement to serve as pitching coach for Torre's New York Mets.

Bob Gibson strikes out Detroit's Norm Cash (left) en route to a World Series-record 17 in Game 1 of the 1968 classic.

JOSH GIBSON

A popular story around Griffith Stadium in Washington in the early 1930s concerned the time that Walter Johnson attended a game played by the Homestead Grays. The Big Train sat transfixed as he watched a muscular black catcher in action. At length, he turned to Clark Griffith, owner of the Senators, and said, "That boy is worth a quarter of a million dollars."

Even in those depressed times, more than a few major league clubs would have been happy to scrape up $250,000 if the unwritten rules of the day would have permitted the signing of black players.

Josh Gibson never had an opportunity to play in Organized Baseball as did Roy Campanella, Elston Howard and other black catchers of the integrated era.

A native of Buena Vista, Ga., Gibson moved to Pittsburgh at an early age. He was an 18-year-old member of the Grays in 1930 when he made his professional debut.

"It was the first night game ever played at Forbes Field," recalled his manager, Judy Johnson. "A bus in center field contained a generator and lights were placed on high extension ladders."

When the regular catcher was injured, Josh was asked if he could catch. "Yes, sir," he answered, giving birth to one of baseball's most fabulous careers.

The number of home runs that boomed off Gibson's bat never will be known. Haphazard scheduling could produce 200 games a season, some against non-league opposition. James (Cool Papa) Bell asserted once that Josh collected 72 homers in one year.

In the beginning, the 6-foot-1, 215-pound Gibson was a crude catcher, and did not learn the finer points of the position until he played winter ball, which he did regularly.

Homestead teammates referred to him as "Boxer" because, they said, he caught foul pops as though he were wearing boxing gloves. Gibson mastered this craft eventually, handling every type of pitch from the spitter to the shine ball.

Josh required no practice in his throwing. He possessed a strong, accurate arm and had the sort of speed seldom found in one his size.

In 1933, almost all of the Grays jumped to the Crawfords team of Pittsburgh. There Gibson teamed up with the legendary Satchel Paige and it became a common practice for the Crawfords to advertise that Satch would strike out the first nine batters in a forthcoming game and that Gibson would clout a home run.

After the '34 season, the Crawfords barnstormed with a team of major league all-stars featuring Dizzy and Paul Dean. The Crawfords won seven of the nine games in a series dominated by Gibson's prodigious blasts.

Josh Gibson's home run accomplishments were legendary throughout the Negro leagues.

When the Crawfords disbanded in 1936, Paige joined the Kansas City Monarchs and Gibson returned to the Grays, setting up classic confrontations between the formidable pitcher and catcher. Once, it was said, Satchel walked two batters intentionally to bring up Gibson, whom he then struck out on three pitches.

Another time, Josh rocketed a drive off the clock on the center-field wall at Chicago's Comiskey Park.

By 1946, Josh had started his descent, although he still batted .331 and led the Negro National League in homers. His weight had ballooned to 230 pounds and he took to drinking heavily. Friends detected a personality change. Some said it was due to the breakup of his marriage.

On a Saturday night in January of 1947, Josh encountered friends on a Pittsburgh street corner.

"He was like always, full of fun and kidding around," an old pal reported, but Gibson complained of a headache, went home, had a drink and went to bed.

The next morning, Josh still complained of a headache. A doctor was summoned. He gave Gibson a shot and he fell into a sleep from which he never awakened.

WARREN GILES

In August of 1923, the president of the St. Joseph club of the Western Association telephoned the offices of the St. Louis Cardinals. He had some disturbing news. The option agreement on outfielder Taylor Douthit had elapsed and, under baseball law, the minor league club was entitled to sell the St. Louis farmhand to whomever it wished.

Branch Rickey, the Redbirds' front-office chief, admitted he had forgotten about Douthit. Nor were his feelings assuaged when he learned that the Pirates had offered $10,000 for the prospect. He knew the St. Joseph club could use 10 grand, strapped for funds as it was.

But Rickey felt greatly relieved when the caller added: "I know it was an honest oversight and you can have Douthit for nothing."

Two years later, Warren Giles was rewarded for his integrity, landing the general manager's post of the Cardinals' top farm club, Syracuse of the International League.

Giles, a native of Tiskilwa, Ill., and a three-sport athlete in high school, gained his foothold in the administrative phase of baseball in 1919 when, as a recent Army officer, he attended a meeting of the stockholders of the Moline (Three-1) club. His enthusiasm and generous advice on how the club should be operated caught the ear of the others.

"In effect," he recalled many years later, "they told me that if I knew so much, why didn't I run the club. They elected me president and there I was, suddenly, totally and happily, in baseball for life."

In 1928, the Syracuse franchise was transferred to Rochester, where it won four successive pennants. By the mid-1930s, Giles was the front-office boss of the Cincinnati Reds, succeeding Larry MacPhail. One of Giles' first moves there was to lure his old Rochester pilot, Bill McKechnie, away from the Boston Braves. By 1939, the Reds were National League champions and a year later they were world champions.

In his years as Cincinnati chief, Giles frequently found fault with the quality of umpiring, but when he succeeded Ford Frick as league president in 1951, he became a staunch defender of the arbiters.

When Giles moved into the N.L. office, he was replaced at the Reds' helm by longtime lieutenant Gabe Paul.

Before long, Giles was asked to rule on a rhubarb. One umpire had overruled another, creating a donnybrook in which Reds Manager Birdie Tebbetts was ejected. Tebbets was fined $50. Irate, Gabe fired off a telegram to his old boss.

Giles was criticized for penalizing the manager, and not the umpire, who provoked the incident.

National League President Warren Giles does the honors for the Pirates' 1961 opener at Forbes Field.

When Giles and Paul met weeks later, Giles suggested that a phone call or private letter would have been more advisable than a telegram that was read by the entire office force.

Sweetly, Gabe reminded Giles of a wire Warren had sent Frick some years earlier.

"All I did was dig into the files for YOUR message," said Paul, "check off Frick's name, substitute yours and sign mine. Where is your sense of humor?"

"You dirty dog," was Giles' smiling response.

Unlike the American League system, which provides for a supervisor of umpires, Giles, with the aid of Fred Fleig, supervised the N.L. arbiters. As an old official, Giles had a feel for decision makers in athletic events. He had officiated in old Missouri Valley Conference football games.

In 18 years as N.L. president, Giles upheld only one protest. Frick, in 16 years, upheld five. Giles overruled his umpires in a Cincinnati-Milwaukee game. In the replay, the Braves won the contest, just as they had originally, but under different circumstances.

Giles retired as N.L. president in 1969 and was named president emeritus. For the next 10 years, he was "just a fan," trying to be neutral in a city (Cincinnati) that claimed his heart many years earlier, and keeping an eye on the adventures of his only child, Bill, general manager of the Phillies.

He was 83 when he died in February of 1979 after a lengthy illness and a few weeks before he was elected to the Hall of Fame.

LEFTY GOMEZ

As great as Vernon (Lefty) Gomez was—he was the only pitcher to win six World Series games without a loss, among other distinctions—the angular left-hander would have deserved a pedestal in the Hall of Fame if only for his Spanish-Irish wit that brightened baseball for more than half a century.

Known as the Gay Caballero because of his jolly and carefree manner, Gomez also was called El Goofy. He was so proud of the latter monicker that his license plates read "GOOF."

Gomez kept his teammates loose. He joked about the lordly and the lowly, a court jester in a profession that too often tended toward stodginess.

In a tense moment of a World Series he could stand in back of the mound and watch an airplane circling overhead. When he was censured by Tony Lazzeri, Lefty told the second baseman, "You take care of second base and spaghetti, I'll take care of pitching and aviation."

On another occasion, when the Yankees enjoyed a sizable lead at Detroit, Lefty fielded a hard smash by Hank Greenberg. Instead of throwing to shortstop Frank Crosetti covering second for a force out, Gomez fired to Lazzeri, who was standing 20 feet from the base.

To a dumbfounded Lazzeri, Lefty explained, "I'd heard that you were such a smart player, I just wanted to see what you'd do with it."

A notoriously weak hitter, Gomez had an annual wager with Babe Ruth, betting $50 against the Babe's $500 that Lefty would collect 10 hits for the season. One year, swinging wildly, Lefty went 4-for-4 on opening day and, he said, "Babe's eyes were big as hubcaps."

From that point, however, I went on a 42-game batting slump."

Once he attempted to take on the appearance of a hitter. Gomez swung his bat lustily as he approached the plate, gave a vigorous tug on the bill of his cap, tapped his spikes with his bat—and cracked an ankle.

There was another time when Lefty was swinging where the pitcher was pitching and he sliced a double to left field. He was promptly picked off base. "What happened out there?" Manager Joe McCarthy wondered.

"I don't know," quipped Gomez. "It was the first time I was ever out there."

But there was one hit that Gomez cherished above all others. In 1933, his single drove in the first run in All-Star Game history. The Yankee star pitched in five All-Star classics and was the winning hurler in three (1933, '35 and '37), while losing one (1938).

When Lou Gehrig's consecutive-game streak ended on May 2, 1939, and the durable first baseman and other players shed tears in the dugout, Gomez broke the tension. Laying a hand on Gehrig's shoulder, he cracked: "It took 'em 15 years to get you out of the lineup. They get me out of there in 15 minutes."

When Lefty walked off the field after beating the Giants in Game 2 of the 1936 World Series, Colonel Jake Ruppert beckoned him to his box.

"Can you pitch tomorrow, too?" asked the owner.

"If the manager wants me to," said Lefty.

He didn't, of course, but when Ruppert again signaled to him after the third game, Gomez strolled to the owner's box and shook hands. Relaxing his grip, Gomez found a check for $1,000, the amount he had been cut in salary that year.

Gomez was a prankster as well as a humorist. On a dark, dreary day in Cleveland, he walked to the plate and struck a match before facing Bob Feller.

"What's the matter, can't you see Feller?" asked umpire Bill Summers.

"Oh, I can see him," came the reply, I just want to be sure he can see me."

When Lefty joined the sales promotion department of a sporting goods company in 1948, a question on his employment form was: "Why did you leave your last job?"

He wrote: I couldn't get anybody out."

Fun-loving Lefty Gomez got his baseball kicks in more ways than one.

When Gomez reached the twilight of his career he was a veteran of five World Series.

The 1939 All-Star Game was a fitting occasion for former great Walter Johnson to visit with current great Gomez.

A youthful Gomez took the American League by storm, winning 21 and 24 games in his first two full seasons.

GOOSE GOSLIN

In the spring of 1928, the Washington Senators trained at the Fair Grounds in Tampa, Fla. While the players worked out at one end of the field, a high school track team practiced at the other.

One morning, the Senators' left fielder strolled into the track team's area, picked up a 16-pound shot and started to throw it as if it were a baseball. The next day his arm was dead.

But there was no way that Manager Bucky Harris could bench Goose Goslin—his bat was too important to the Washington attack. Every time a ball was hit safely to left field, the shortstop raced into the area and took a lob from Goslin and relayed it to the infield.

Keeping Goslin in the lineup paid off in a batting championship. As the season dwindled down to the last day, Goslin led Heinie Manush of St. Louis by one point and, as fate would have it, the Nats and Browns met in the final game.

Manush rapped two hits, and so did Goslin. In his final at-bat, Goose needed a hit, a walk or an ejection from the game. The first two pitches were called strikes, eliciting howls of anguish from Goslin. He stepped on umpire Bill Guthrie's toes, hoping for banishment, but the arbiter, aware of the stakes, did not accept the bait.

Ultimately, Goslin singled to right field and clinched the title by one point.

Goose, raised on a New Jersey farm, had been a glass blower and elevator mechanic before Bill McGowan, later a top-flight American League umpire, told the youngster he was good enough for professional ball.

Two years later, in 1921, Goose was the batting champion of the Sally League. Clark Griffith became interested in the lefthanded slugger when Jack Dunn, owner of the minor league Baltimore Orioles, revealed that he was about to bid $5,000 for Goslin.

Griffith promptly raised the ante to $6,000 and won the young prize.

In his first game for the Senators, Goslin socked a late-inning, bases-loaded triple to defeat Chicago. After the game, first baseman Joe Judge remarked idly, "I never thought we'd beat Red Faber today."

"Was that Faber?" the rookie replied innocently.

In appreciation for McGowan's good turn, Goslin asked Griffith to use his influence in acquiring McGowan for the A.L. As a result, the league benefited from 20 years of McGowan's umpiring talents.

Goslin feared no pitcher. He constantly crowded the plate until umpires threatened him with ejection unless he desisted. He swung with a gusto not unlike that of

Goose Goslin always tempted fate by fearlessly crowding the plate.

Babe Ruth and when he missed, he usually wound up on the seat of his pants.

Goose never conceded that he hit a ball with all his power. Once, when he was congratulated for hitting a line drive into the center-field bleachers at Boston, he responded, I wish I had really gotten a hold of that ball, it really would have gone places."

Goslin hit three homers in both the 1924 and 1925 World Series and another in the '33 classic. Traded to Detroit in December of 1933, he sparked the Tigers to pennants the next two years and became a Motor City hero in 1935 when his ninth-inning single drove home Mickey Cochrane to give the Bengals the world championship over the Cubs.

His last association with Organized Ball was in 1941 when he managed the Trenton (Inter-State) club.

For years, Goslin operated a successful fishing and crabbing business out of Bayside, NJ.

Goslin made it to the Hall in 1968, three years before his death on May 15, 1971. Manush had died three days earlier.

HANK GREENBERG

With five games remaining in the 1938 season, Detroit first baseman Hank Greenberg had 58 home runs. Two more would match the major league record established by Babe Ruth 11 years earlier.

The first of the five contests was played at home against St. Louis. The Tigers bombed Lefty Mills, 12-0, but the best the Detroit slugger could manage was two walks in five trips to the plate.

The next day, the record-seeking slugger again failed to hit a homer. He singled once in four at-bats.

It was on to Cleveland, where Denny Galehouse beat the Tigers without tossing a gopher pitch. A closing doubleheader the next day held the last hope for Greenberg. Bob Feller pitched the opener and struck out 18 batters. The best the Detroit muscle man could do was a double off the wall.

With shadows creeping across the field, Cleveland's Johnny Humphries and Clay Smith were holding the slugger at bay in the nightcap. After seven innings, umpire George Moriarty told Greenberg, "I'm sorry, Hank, this is as far as I can go."

"That's all right," replied Greenberg, "this is as far as I can go, too."

The son of Romanian immigrants who was raised in the Bronx, Hank might have been a Yankee but he rejected the Bombers' offer because common sense dictated

Hank Greenberg gets a big reception after hitting a game-winning homer in Game 2 of the 1945 World Series.

that his development would be stymied as long as Lou Gehrig guarded first base.

Three years after graduating from James Monroe High School, Greenberg was a major leaguer to stay. In his second season with the Tigers, he was on a league championship team that bowed to the Cardinals in the 1934 World Series.

In 1935, after 170 runs batted in and 36 homers earned a Most Valuable Player award for the 24-year-old slugger, Hank played only the first two games of the World Series against the Cubs. He suffered a broken wrist in the second game and sat out the last four games.

After driving in 112 runs and hitting 33 homers in 1939, Greenberg was stunned that winter to discover a $10,000 pay cut on his 1940 contract. When he confronted General Manager Jack Zeller, he was told that the only way to avoid the cut was to shift to left field so that a young powerhouse named Rudy York could play first base.

Recalling the years of toil and dedication that were necessary to make him a polished first baseman, Hank suggested that a new position be found for York. The notion was dismissed instantly.

Ultimately, it was agreed that if Greenberg opened the 1940 season in left field he would not only escape the $10,000 pay cut, but would receive a raise of an equal amount, to $50,000.

Hank mastered the intricacies of outfield play to earn the raise. He also won a second MVP, but the season came to a disappointing finish when the Tigers lost the seven-game World Series to Cincinnati.

Greenberg and winning pitcher Virgil Trucks celebrate after the Tigers' Game 2 win over the Cubs in the '45 Series.

Greenberg slides past Cardinal catcher Bill DeLancey with the final run of Detroit's 10-4 win in game 4 of the 1934 Series.

In early May of 1941, after playing in only 19 games, Greenberg enlisted as a private in the United States Army. He was gone four years. When he returned in July of 1945, he found the Tigers in a pennant scramble again. The race was undecided until the final day when Greenberg hit a bases-loaded homer in St. Louis to clinch the flag.

One year after listening to the World Series via radio in India, Greenberg socked two homers in the fall classic to help beat the Cubs in seven games.

Sold to the Pirates in January of 1947, Hank considered retirement but a $100,000 salary offer coaxed him into a Pirate uniform for a final fling. Moreover, Pittsburgh provided an inviting homer target, constructing a bullpen in left field that was christened Greenberg Gardens. Twenty-five home runs and 74 RBIs later, Greenberg closed the book.

Hank joined Bill Veeck at Cleveland, serving as a vice president and eventually as general manager of the Indians. When he sold his stock years later, Greenberg discovered that his original $50-a-share investment had grown to $100 per share. Later, he was a White Sox vice president (also under Veeck).

After obtaining Greenberg in 1947, the Pirates built a left-field bullpen in Forbes Field (above) and dubbed it Greenberg Gardens.

CLARK GRIFFITH

When Ban Johnson and Charles Comiskey fathered the American League, their most urgent need for credibility was a dominant player who could raid established National League clubs.

They found their man in Clark Griffith, a pitcher who had been a leading winner for Cap Anson's Chicago Colts in the 1890s and was willing to play a leading role in the formation of the new league.

Griffith had been a fighter all of his 31 years. He had spent his childhood in untamed western Missouri, where his father had been killed accidentally while hunting deer. He had battled malaria until his widowed mother, seeking a more healthful climate, moved her brood to Bloomington, Ill. There the youngster met the famed Hoss Radbourn, who taught Griffith his pitching secrets.

On May 1, 1888, Griffith made his debut in professional ball, pitching the Bloomington (Central Interstate) team to a 3-2 victory over Danville.

The 5-foot-8, 175-pounder was on his way, subduing muscular hitters with cunning and guile that led to his popular nickname of "Old Fox."

During the winter of 1900-01, the well-known Colts pitcher traipsed over the country, inducing big-name athletes to leave their N.L. clubs for more lucrative salaries. In return for his services, he was named manager of the Chicago White Sox, whom he led to the first A.L. championship in 1901.

Without Griffith, the American League would not have attained the quick success that it did.

After two years, the Johnson-Comiskey combine determined that a New York franchise was vital to the success of the league. Chicago's Comiskey agreed to release Griffith, his manager, so that Clark could oversee the New York operation and once more Griffith had a fight on his hands.

Clark Griffith (pictured in 1903) won 240 games and was instrumental in the success of the American League.

The Giants, a National League fixture in the city, took a dim view of Hilltop Park, a facility that the new club was building in the upper Bronx. The N.L. club announced it would use its influence to halt construction of subway and streetcar lines short of the site.

But Griffith, proving he was indeed an "Old Fox," arranged for some Tammany Hall chiefs to invest in his club. The transportation lines were extended to the ball park.

When an opportunity arose to buy into the Washington club in 1912, Griffith mortgaged his Montana ranch to raise the necessary funds. In time, he became the intimate of Presidents. He conceived of a chief executive tossing the first pitch to open a new season, and it was his accessibility to the White House that helped baseball operate through two world wars.

And Griffith fought on. In the 1890s, he had engaged in many skirmishes with John McGraw and the Baltimore Orioles. Once, McGraw singled off Griffith, then taunted the pitcher and umpire Joe Cantillon (standing behind the mound) with his customary invective.

"Pick him off," Cantillon whispered to the Old Fox.

"How?" asked Griff, noting McGraw's small lead.

"Balk him off."

With an outrageous balk move, Griffith fired to first and the umpire waved McGraw out. The squawk that followed was loud and profane and led to McGraw's ejection.

Griffith tried the same move on the next runner, whereupon Cantillon yelled "Balk." How come, the Old Fox wondered. "Balks only work with McGraw," said the umpire.

As an owner with meager finances, Griffith resented clubs with bottomless coffers. In the 1930s, he pushed through legislation—aimed at the Yankees—forbidding champions to trade. The regulation lasted one year.

Griffith was approaching his 86th birthday when he suffered a massive stomach hemorrhage on October 22, 1955, and died five days later.

BURLEIGH GRIMES

Old headlines tell the story best: "Facing Grimes Was a Terrifying Thing" and "Grimes Called Toughest Loser" and "Old Stubblebeard Was a Mean One."

There was nothing gentlemanly about Burleigh Grimes. He fought with opponents, teammates, managers and reporters. In the 1920s, when he was with the Dodgers, he did not speak to Wilbert Robinson, his manager. When Robinson decided it was Grimes' turn to pitch, he notified him via the clubhouse boy.

In 1930, Bill Terry batted .401 to win the National League batting crown. The first time Grimes faced Terry in 1931, he strolled off the mound and asked the Giants' first baseman, "What did you hit last year?"

"Four-oh-one," replied Terry.

"Well, you won't be hitting .400 this year," snorted Grimes, who fired the first pitch at Terry's head.

As a Wisconsin farm boy, Grimes worked in a lumber camp from dawn to dusk for $1 a day. Once while driving four horses hitched to a sled, he was buried under seven tiers of 10-foot logs when a horse tripped over a stump. Lumberjacks extricated Grimes, who was unhurt.

Burleigh was 16 when his father handed him $25 with the advice, "Son, go out into the world and make something of yourself."

Grimes reached the majors in 1916 and stayed around for 19 years, winning 270 games with a fearless determination, a fine repertoire of pitches and a one-day growth of beard that enhanced his sinister appearance.

Of the 17 established pitchers who were licensed to pitch the spitball when it was outlawed in 1920, Old Stubblebeard stayed the longest in the majors. He did not throw the moist pitch as regularly as was generally thought, but only Art Fletcher of the Phillies was able to determine when Grimes was actually loading up a baseball or when he was faking.

Grimes wore a cap a half size too small. Before every pitch, Grimes held his glove in front of his mouth to shield his true intentions. One afternoon, eagle-eyed Fletcher detected a telltale signal. When Burleigh moved his jaws to generate saliva for a genuine spitter, the muscles in his head made his cap bobble. On the fake spitter, no muscles moved. Grimes solved the problem by wearing a larger cap, and his secret was safe once more.

When Grimes was on the mound, he recognized everybody as an enemy, even a callow rookie. In 1924, when the Dodgers and Giants were embroiled in a sizzling pennant race, Grimes called the starting nine for that day's game into a huddle. "Anyone who doesn't want to play today's game to win," he started, "let me know right now."

The prospect of facing Burleigh Grimes terrified many major league hitters.

Nobody dissented. When the Cubs, who had defeated Dazzy Vance the previous day, came to bat in the first inning, Grimes' first pitch sent Art Weis, just up from the Texas League, sprawling from a head-hunter pitch. The pattern never changed. Burleigh won in the best way he knew, but the Giants won the flag.

Once, when the Cubs prepared to alight from a train in New York, a porter attempted to brush off Gabby Hartnett. "Never mind," said the catcher, "Burleigh Grimes will dust me off this afternoon."

Before he joined the Cardinals in 1930 and became a teammate of Frank Frisch, Old Stubblebeard conducted a running feud with the Old Flash. Invariably, Frankie would wind up in the dust as the first pitch sailed at his jaw.

"You have three shots at me," Frisch warned Grimes, Then you gotta pitch." Usually, Frisch drilled one of the pitches safely.

Grimes never changed, not even as a baseball oldtimer. He was 40 and a Yankee when Goose Goslin hit a homer off him. Innings later, when Goose was in the on-deck circle, Grimes low-bridged him with a pitch.

Grimes' colorful major league career ended where it had started, with the Pirates. Burleigh claimed the last of his 1,512 strikeouts on September 20, 1934, when he fanned Brooklyn's Joe Stripp.

LEFTY GROVE

The locker room at Sportsman's Park in St. Louis had been torn apart, locker-by-locker, by a man no one had dared to challenge.

In August of 1931, Lefty Grove, a tall lefthander from the coal-mining country of West Virginia, had a 25-2 record for the Philadelphia A's (who were en route to their third consecutive American League flag). He had won 16 straight games. One more would surpass the American League record shared by Joe Wood and Walter Johnson.

On the afternoon that the hard-throwing Grove tried for the record, the A's were not at full strength. Al Simmons, the regular left fielder, took the day off to seek medical treatment in Milwaukee. His place was taken by a rookie, Jimmy Moore.

In the third inning of the first game of a doubleheader, Fred Schulte singled off Grove and Oscar Melillo hit a line drive to left field. Moore misjudged the ball, which sailed over his head and permitted Schulte to score.

That was all Browns pitcher Dick Coffman needed to win the game. The A's collected only three hits and one walk, losing, 1-0.

Infuriated (not at Moore, but at Simmons), Grove exploded. His fury was heightened by the knowledge that his teammates were trampling the Browns, 10-0, behind Waite Hoyt in the nightcap.

Grove, who maintained a monastic silence for several days, compiled a 31-4 record for the season. His defeats were by scores of 7-5, 4-3, 2-1 and 1-0.

"Groves," as he was called by A's Manager Connie Mack, saved some of his most devastating performances for the Yankees when they were Murderers Row. There was the day when Grove held a 1-0 lead entering the last of the ninth inning at Yankee Stadium. Mark Koenig led off with a single, whereupon Grove struck out Babe Ruth, Lou Gehrig and Bob Meusel on nine pitches. Meusel fouled off one pitch.

"Another time in Philadelphia I replaced Jack Quirin with the bases loaded," Grove recalled in the twilight of his career. "And I struck out Ruth, Gehrig and Tony Lazzeri on 10 pitches."

Again, in Chicago, he found runners on second and third and none out when he came on in relief. He fanned the side on 10 pitches.

"The way Johnny Heving froze when he caught the last pitch, I knew he didn't see the ball," Grove said.

When the Yankees' streak of 308 games without a shutout was snapped in August of 1933, it was Grove who turned the trick, 7-0. Ruth, who socked only nine

By 1935, Lefty Grove was pitching for Boston and just warming up for his run at 300 victories.

home runs in 10 years against Grove, struck out three times, Gehrig twice.

For years, Grove was content to let the public regard him as an ill-tempered prima donna. It wasn't until years after Grove retired that a onetime employee of a sporting goods company revealed that Lefty had visited the plant frequently in the early 1930s, buying the best grade of baseballs in four- and five-dozen lots and uniforms tailored to size for a kids team that he frequently stopped to watch on his way to the ball park.

Grove was 25 when he made his debut with the A's following five seasons —the last two 27-victory campaigns—with the International League's Baltimore Orioles. He was 27 when he blossomed as a 20-game winner in 1927, launching a spectacular seven-year period in which he compiled a 172-54 record. In 1930-31, his figures were 59-9.

Traded to the Red Sox in 1934 as part of the mass exodus from Philadelphia in the Great Depression, Lefty won 20 games only once the remainder of his career.

Grove had won 286 games after his 15-4 mark led the A.L. in percentage in 1939, but it required two more seasons of cunning, rather than the blazing fastball of old, for him to reach the coveted 300-victory mark. His two-year record was 14-13, and his ERA each season topped 4.00.

Grove (right) visits with the Giants' Carl Hubbell before the first All-Star Game at Comiskey Park in 1933.

The talented Grove compiled his best semons in 1930 (above) and 1931 (left) when he won 59 and lost only 9 for the Philadelphia A's.

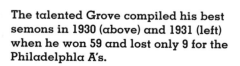

CHICK HAFEY

How good he might have been if he had been blessed with normal vision and good health will never be known, but it is generally agreed that bespectacled Californian Chick Hafey would have posted a lifetime average considerably higher than his .317.

Branch Rickey, who discovered Hafey and observed him throughout his major league career, asserted: "If Hafey had had good eyesight and good health he might have been the finest righthanded hitter baseball has ever known."

Jim Bottomley, who was a teammate of Hafey and Rogers Hornsby, declared, "Hafey hit harder than Rog. He hit with his arms and wrists. He used a long-handled bat and when he leaned on the ball you could hear the seams crack."

Hafey was a pitcher when he reported to his first Cardinals camp in 1923, but when Rickey got a glimpse of him in the batting cage, he said, "You hit the ball pretty well. 1 think you should be an outfielder."

Hafey was one of the first players in the original farm system as designed by Rickey. By 1925, he was with the Cardinals, running the bases instinctively, driving the ball with power and fielding his position impressively.

But Chick was hampered by frequent sinus attacks. During his career he underwent four operations, two in one season.

A shy and retiring individual, Hafey was, however, no pushover at the bargaining table. Prior to the 1928 season, Chick signed a three-year contract that paid him $7,000, $8,000 and $9,000. In that three-year period, he batted .337 overall, clouted 82 home runs, batted in 343 runs and scored 310. He demanded $15,000 for 1931.

After considerable haggling, Hafey signed for $12,500, with the understanding that, because he had missed much of spring training, the new contract would not take effect until the front office decided he was in condition to play. As a result, the Redbirds saved $2,100 and Hafey played for $10,400.

Despite this disappointment, Hafey produced one of his finest campaigns in 1931, winning the National League batting championship in a three-way battle with teammate Bottomley and Bill Terry of the Giants. Final figures showed Hafey with a mark of .3489, Terry .3486 and Bottomley .3482.

The following spring, Hafey and his wife drove to Florida to negotiate a new contract. The outfielder proposed a $17,000 salary that would include the $2,100 that was deducted from his 1931 pay. Rickey, general manager of the defending world champions, countered with a $13,000 offer, an increase of $500.

Chick Hafey compiled a .317 career average, despite being handicapped by poor eyesight.

Infuriated, the Hafeys jumped into their car and headed westward. "I was so mad," said Hafey, "I drove 90 miles an hour across the desert."

On April 11, he was notified that he had been traded to Cincinnati, a last-place club that paid him $15,000.

Handicapped by the flu and his old sinus problem, Hafey played only 83 games in 1932 but batted .344. He was the leftfielder for the National League in the first All-Star Game in 1933, in which he went 1-for-4, and batted .303 in the regular season.

Early in the 1935 season, the Reds and Giants played a game at the Polo Grounds in a steady drizzle. When the Reds arrived in Philadelphia that evening, Hafey got a chill that developed into the flu. Physicians were unable to cure him in the East, and he returned to his home in Walnut Creek, Calif., where he spent the remainder of the season convalescing.

But Hafey's strength did not return and he sat out the 1936 campaign. Hafey gave the game another whirl in 1937. He batted .261 in 89 games for the Reds, then called it a career.

JESSE HAINES

The righthanded knuckleballer was such a gentle person that observers found it difficult to picture him as a hard loser.

But there was the afternoon in Cincinnati when Jesse Haines tore apart the locker room at Crosley Field, even knocking over the ancient potbellied stove, because errors had cost him a victory.

And there was an earlier day when his catcher, Pickles Dillhoefer, threw wildly to a base and permitted the deciding run to score. Afterward, Haines had to be restrained by teammates from attacking his batterymate.

On the pitching mound, however, Haines was a relatively composed competitor. In his distinguished career with the Cardinals, he was ejected only twice.

Haines had a cup of coffee with the Tigers—but no pitching record—in 1915. Jesse had better fortune with Cincinnati in 1918. He appeared in one game. During the 1919 season, while winning 21 games for Kansas City (American Association), Jesse was a popular item on the playing market. Cardinals Manager Branch Rickey was among the interested parties.

The $10,000 sale price was a bit beyond the reach of the impecunious Cardinals, but Rickey turned on all of his forensic charm and talked the club's directors into investing ten grand on the 26-year-old hurler. The Redbirds never made a better investment.

Along his major league route, Haines acquired a knuckleball from Ed Rommel, an American League hurler and later an umpire in the same league. However, unlike laterday exponents who gripped the ball with their fingernails, Haines clasped the ball with his knuckles.

That pitch, mixed with a crackling fastball—and thrown in rapid sequence to intimidate the batters—helped Pop toss a no-hitter against the Boston Braves in 1924.

In 1926, Haines appeared in the first of four World Series. He relieved in the opener, hurled a 4-0 victory in Game 3 and started the seventh contest. He pitched until the seventh inning in the finale when the knuckler raised a blister and he gave way to Grover Cleveland Alexander, who preserved the 3-2 lead.

Neither the no-hitter nor the '26 Series victories produced Haines' greatest thrill. That occurred in the 1930 Series when he outpitched Lefty Grove, a 28-game winner in the regular season, 3-1, on a four-hitter.

Jesse did not pitch in the 1931 Series, having suffered a broken wrist when struck by a line drive off the bat of Babe Herman, but he was a member of the world champion Gas House Gang of 1934 at age 41.

Jesse Haines (pictured in 1930) combined a knuckleball and sizzling fastball to win 210 games for the Cardinals.

When Dizzy Dean went on his famous sit-down strike in the Polo Grounds clubhouse, sending Cardinals Manager Frank Frisch into a purple rage, it was Haines who asked permission to speak to the young righthander.

Frisch gave his okay and Jesse met with Diz.

"I keep thinking that Ol' Pop has one more chance at a World Series," Haines began, "but he can't do it without you.

Dean softened at the fatherly words and said, "All right, Pop, I'll do it for you, but not for that Frisch."

The Cardinals made it into the Series. The Dean brothers won two games apiece, and Ol' Pop pitched two-thirds of an inning in relief as the Cards defeated the Tigers in seven games.

Haines was 44 when he retired at the close of the 1937 season and he accepted a position as Dodgers pitching coach. When he ran as Republican candidate for the auditor's post in Montgomery Count, Ohio, he won and was re-elected for six consecutive four-year terms before retiring.

Haines underwent surgery for the removal of a kidney in 1970, but recovered sufficiently to attend his Hall of Fame induction that summer. He was in ill health for several years preceding his death in 1978 at age 85.

BILLY HAMILTON

By 1900, Sliding Billy Hamilton already had spent 12 seasons driving opposing defenses crazy.

The stocky Philadelphia baserunner had been a headache to the Cleveland Spiders all afternoon, running the bases almost at will as fielders tried in vain to head him off at the next base.

In frustration, the Cleveland third baseman introduced a new measure. Grabbing the runner as he approached third base, he carried him to the edge of the field and dumped him unceremoniously into the grandstand. Fortunately, the runner suffered no bodily harm; only his composure was scarred.

For 14 major league seasons, Billy Hamilton drove opponents to the brink of distraction. In 1,578 games, he stole 937 bases. Ty Cobb, by comparison, swiped 892 bases in the 3,033 games that made up his 24-year career.

A lefthanded hitter, Hamilton broke into the majors with Kansas City (American Association) in 1888. The day was a tough one for the entire K.C. club—which was held hitless and scoreless by Gus Weyhing of the Athletics.

Hamilton stole his first base as a big leaguer on August 3, 1888, at the expense of Chris Fulmer, catching for Baltimore. There was no stopping him thereafter. On September 18, he scored five runs and swiped four bases against Cleveland.

When Matt Kilroy of Baltimore picked the youngster off base three times in one game, however, Manager Dave Rowe threw reins on Billy, who had been a 10.75 sprinter in high school.

Conditions were more favorable under a new manager, however, and Hamilton stole 117 bases while batting .301 in 1889.

When the Kansas City franchise was transferred to Syracuse in 1890, Hamilton joined the Philadelphia Nationals under Harry Wright. Among Billy's teammates was Billy Sunday, who set a torrid stolen base pace for Pittsburgh at the start of the campaign before joining Philadelphia. Hamilton overhauled Sunday by August 1 and posted 102 steals for the year; the future evangelist finished with 91.

In 1894, the season he scored 196 runs in 131 games, Hamilton batted .399, but it wasn't good enough to win the batting title. He was fourth best, trailing teammates Ed Delahanty (.400) and Sam Thompson (.404) and Boston's Hugh Duffy (.438).

That same season, Billy enjoyed his best day on the basepaths. Catcher Deacon Jim McGuire of Washington watched helplessly as Hamilton stole seven bases, tying a record set by George Gore of Chicago in 1881.

After the 1895 season, Hamilton was traded to Boston, where he replaced the aging Tommy McCarthy in an outfield of Tom Bannon and Hugh Duffy. Hamilton was an instant sensation with the Beaneaters, stealing a club-record 93 bases and batting a team-leading .363.

The following season, Billy scored 153 runs for his fourth and last big-league title in that department and batted .344 on a team that averaged .319. The Beaneaters won the '97 pennant by two games in a battle with Ned Hanlon's Baltimore Orioles.

Baltimore defeated Boston in the Temple Cup Series that followed the regular campaign. Billy did not play in the fifth and deciding game; his error on a routine fly ball in Game 4 earned him a seat on the bench for the finale.

A knee injury limited Hamilton to 109 games in 1898 and another knee injury held him to 81 games in 1899. He stole 59 bases in '98, but only 19 in '99.

After scoring more than 100 runs for the 11th time in his career in 1900, Billy rejected an offer from the Red Sox in the new American League and closed out his major league career with the Beaneaters in 1901.

Hamilton remained active for another decade, however, performing for Haverhill and Lynn of the New England League and Harrisburg of the Tri-State League. In 1904, he led all of Organized Baseball with a .412 average for Haverhill.

Hamilton scouted for the Red Sox in 1911 and 1912 and ended his baseball affiliation in 1916 when he was manager and part-owner of the Eastern League club in his home town of Worcester.

NED HANLON

In the spring of 1894, manager Ned Hanlon of the Baltimore Orioles made a revolutionary decision: he gathered his team together and headed south, to Macon, Ga., for "spring training." Hanlon's team was the first ever to go south, in search of better weather, to prepare for the new season. Writers at the time described the decision as a "goofy venture." By the following year, every team headed south for spring training.

Even more important, Hanlon taught his players to perfect the hit-and-run play, a manuever that was to become a key component in the Orioles' rise from a last-place team in 1892 to championships in three consecutive years, 1894-1896.

In the season-opening series against New York, Hanlon's Orioles won four straight and executed 13 hit-and-run plays that thoroughly frustrated New York manager John Ward, who threatened to take Hanlon before the league executives, claiming he wasn't playing baseball but a new game. It was the development of that strategy, along with other decisions during his 19-year managerial career, that often earned Hanlon the title of the "Father of Modern Baseball."

Hanlon was the first manager to teach his defensive players how to move and cover for their teammates when they moved out of position, and he was the first manager to employ a full-time groundskeeper to make sure his field was in good playing condition.

Among Hanlon's pupils during his managing career in Pittsburgh, Baltimore, Brooklyn and Cincinnati were John McGraw, Hughie Jennings, Wilbert Robinson, Kid Gleason and Miller Huggins. Connie Mack later called Hanlon the best manager baseball knew prior to 1900. The Orioles' owner, Harry Vonderhorst, wore a button that said, "Ask Hanlon."

Hanlon, born in Montville, Conn., in 1857, began his playing career in the minor leagues in Providence, R.I., in 1876. He made his major-league debut with Cleveland in 1880 and moved to Detroit the next season, where he remained for eight years as the team's starting centerfielder.

The Detroit club was broken up after the 1888 season and Hanlon moved to Pittsburgh, where he took over as

Ned Hanlon managed for 19 years, compiling 2,530 wins and 1,313 losses. He entered the Hall in '96.

manager before the end of the 1889 season. He jumped to the new Players League the following year, but that effort was shortlived and he was back with the National League franchise in Pittsburgh the following year.

When the league expanded to 12 teams, Hanlon was selected to manage Baltimore and ended his playing career, which was highlighted by his defensive ability and speed on the bases. As a hitter, he usually lifted himself for a pinch-hitter when a lefthander was on the mound, becoming one of the first managers to use the strategy of matching hitters against pitchers.

He also was not above bending the rules occasionally. Playing in Detroit one day in the late innings of a close game, Hanlon was batting with the bases loaded. A pitch came inside, and Hanlon swerved away from it and fell to the ground holding his arm.

The catcher, who had caught the pitch, and the umpire looked on as Hanlon rolled around on the ground in apparent pain. Hanlon finally jumped up and started running to first base. The umpire called him back, but Hanlon showed him a red, inflamed spot on his arm and asked how he had got that mark if he had not been hit by the pitch. The umpire agreed, awarded Hanlon first and waved in the runner on third to score.

After the game, Hanlon admitted the pitch had not hit him. He made the mark on his arm by pinching it while he was rolling around on the ground.

After winning the three pennants in Baltimore, Hanlon's clubs finished second in 1897 and 1898 and he moved to Brooklyn to take over the Superbas, later known as the Dodgers. There he produced two more pennant-winners, in 1899 and 1900.

Hanlon stayed in Brooklyn until 1905, when he was fired after a last-place finish. He moved to Cincinnati for the last two years of his managerial career, which ended with a career won-loss record of 1,315-1,165.

Hanlon remained active in baseball as the president of the Orioles in the Eastern League and later became president of the Baltimore Park Board, where he encouraged the development of parks for youth leagues around the city.

Hanlon died in 1937 at age 79. He was elected to the Hall of Fame in 1996. In an obituary in *The Sporting News*, editor Edgar Brands wrote that Hanlon "was aided by an almost uncanny ability to judge players, a faculty of imparting to them his remarkable store of knowledge, a genius for inspiring his men to rise to the heights and a personality that enabled him to gain and hold the confidence of all with whom he came into contact."

WILL HARRIDGE

A.L. President Will Harridge (left) enjoys a light moment with Commissioner Happy Chandler in the late 1940s.

The young ticket agent for the Wabash railroad was dumbstruck when his superior informed him, "You have worked your last day for the railroad."

The agent's fears of dismissal were quickly allayed however. "You are not being fired," he was assured. "Next week you will start working as private secretary to Ban Johnson."

"But I don't know anything about baseball," protested Will Harridge, who had been handling the American League's ticket requirements on the Wabash for a number of years.

Harridge succeeded Robert McRoy, who had resigned as secretary to the A.L. president to join the Boston Red Sox.

"What made matters worse," Harridge recollected in later life, "was that McRoy had promised to stay on and teach me the ropes. He left the day I arrived."

Harridge's early weeks on the job were almost total chaos.

"Mr. Johnson would call for something out of the files and I wouldn't know where to look," said Harridge. I was scared to death. But I had just been married and I needed the money. That gave me the courage to see it through."

Will had been earning $90 a month. His starting salary with Johnson was $50 a week.

Harridge was well-established and highly respected when Johnson, climaxing a series of clashes with club owners, resigned in 1927. Ernest Barnard of Cleveland was elected successor to the league founder.

Barnard died suddenly in March of 1931 and the presidency was offered to Harridge, who demurred briefly.

"I told the owners I'd continue as acting president for a year," He said, "and then, if they felt I had done a good job, they could consider me for the job."

The suggestion fell on deaf ears. Charles (Old Roman) Corniskey, owner of the White Sox, proposed that Will be elected immediately. On March 27, 1931, Harridge was elected president for a three-year term.

Dignified and soft-spoken in contrast to the stormy Johnson, Harridge faced his first crisis in 1932 when Bill Dickey broke Carl Reynolds' jaw in an altercation at Washington.

Harridge fined Dickey $1,000 and suspended him for a month in the heat of a pennant race. The action enraged Yankees Owner Jake Ruppert, who did not speak to Harridge for nearly a year.

Gentle Will also demonstrated early that he could be firm with umpires. He fined and suspended George Moriarty after the umpire engaged in fisticuffs with Chicago players after a game.

As much as he liked Jimmie Dykes, Harridge fined the manager more than any other individual. In his career, Dykes was fined 37 times by Harridge.

Will also was a persuasive salesman. In 1933, when Arch Ward proposed a major league all-star game as an adjunct to the Century of Progress Exposition in Chicago, Will convinced his club owners that the extravaganza would be beneficial to baseball.

Harridge possessed inordinate pride in his league, but generally concealed his emotions during his reign (when the A.L. dominated the World Series and All-Star Games).

One exception occurred in 1941 after Ted Williams' ninth-inning homer gave the A.L. All-Stars a 7-5 victory at Detroit. As the ball sailed out of the park, Harridge leaped to his feet and stumbled over chairs in a hasty exit from his box. Once he fell and had to be helped to his feet. In the clubhouse, he and Williams embraced jubilantly.

"I would have kissed him," Will confessed, "if there hadn't been so many people around."

Harridge was 75 when he resigned on December 3, 1958. He still enjoyed good health, but he had seen how owners demanded Johnson's resignation when Ban's health failed in 1927, and he resolved the same would not happen to him.

Harridge, succeeded by Joe Cronin, was named to the newly created post of chairman of the board. He was 87 when he died at an Evanston, Ill., nursing home on April 9, 1971.

BUCKY HARRIS

Few opponents could boast of outsmarting John McGraw, but, the young manager of the Washington Senators earned the privilege of bragging—if he had wished—on October 10, 1924.

In an effort to chill the hot bat of the Giants' lefthanded-hitting Bill Terry, who had gone 6-for-12 in the World Series, Nats skipper Bucky Harris developed a strategy to curb the New York player's effectiveness —and maybe even get him out of the game. (Terry hadn't started games 2, 4 and 6 against lefthanders.)

While nominating righthander Curly Ogden to start Game 7, Harris had lefthander George Mogridge warming up under the stands for the Senators. After Ogden pitched to two batters, Mogridge was waved into the game. Terry went hitless in two at-bats against Mogridge, and McGraw removed Terry in favor of righthanded-hitting Emil (Irish) Meusel (and Harris soon inserted another righthanded pitcher).

The Senators went on to Win, 4-3, in 12 innings, to capture the world championship.

Harris had the baseball smarts. He was gentlemanly when the occasion required, but he also could go for blood when others set the pattern. When a Yankee pitcher started to dust off Washington batters during the 1924 season, Harris pushed a bunt along the first-base line, challenging the pitcher to cover the base. The hurler did not take the bait.

On the next pitch, Harris barreled into second with spikes gleaming. The shortstop backed off, and tempers cooled quickly.

Bucky learned to be tough in the Pennsylvania State Basketball League, a professional circuit. When action got out of hand in one game, the 5-foot-9 1/2 Harris socked a 6-foot-4 opponent, and opened a gash from ear to chin.

Bucky was a four-year veteran when, at age 27, he was named manager of the Senators in 1924. The

During his five seasons as Tigers manager, Bucky Harris played only when necessary.

appointment of one so young created banner headlines. A world championship the same season made Harris the Boy Wonder.

The news was less worthy when he rejoined the Nats in later years, twice as a manager and once as a Scout.

Throughout his career, Harris was the epitome of honesty. His word was always his bond. In 1947, when he was offered what amounted to a lifetime contract as general manager of the Tigers, he declined because he had verbally agreed to manage the Yankees (although he hadn't signed with the Yanks).

Bucky, who left school at 16 to become a breaker boy in a Pennsylvania coal mine, managed Washington for five years in his first stint there before taking over at Detroit, where he also put in five seasons. After the 1933 season, he announced his decision to resign.

Owner Frank Navin was extremely fond of Bucky, but Harris made his case by saying: "The Tigers are a ballclub now. Maybe it's because I've taken so much time in putting them together. . . . I'm tired of looking at them, or they're tired of looking at me, because neither one of us is doing as well as we could. Get a new manager and they'll win."

Under Mickey Cochrane, the Tigers won pennants in 1934 and 1935.

Harris had a winning way with his players due, in part, to the manner in which he supported them. Normally outspoken, Bucky determined on one occasion that silence was the best answer to a sticky situation.

During his first term in a Washington uniform, Harris married the daughter of a United States senator from West Virginia. After a game in which Bucky had been plunked by a pitch that forced in the winning run for the Nats, Harris had dinner with his in-laws.

"People are saying that you deliberately let yourself be hit by that pitch so the Senators would win," his bride reported.

"Stanley would never do a dishonest thing like that just to win a game, I'm sure," responded her father.

Bucky decided not to enter the conversation.

GABBY HARTNETT

Darkness was rapidly enveloping Wrigley Field on a late September afternoon in 1938. The visiting Pirates, one-half game ahead of the Cubs in the National League pennant race, were tied with the home club, 5-5. As umpires huddled and debated the wisdom of letting the game continue into the ninth inning, 34,000 fans squirmed, knowing that a tie would force a doubleheader the next day.

The go-ahead was given, and ancient Charlie Root retired the Bucs in order in the ninth. Mace Brown, Pittsburgh's redoubtable reliever, then trudged to the mound in the gathering twilight.

Brown retired Phil Cavarretta and Carl Reynolds before facing Gabby Hartnett. The catcher manager, nearing 38, swung and missed Brown's first pitch, a curve. He swung at—and fouled off—his second serve, another curve. Ordinarily, under such circumstances, a pitcher would waste a pitch. But Brown had confidence that another curve, down and away, would end the game and necessitate a twin bill.

I put it over the plate between the belt and knees," Brown lamented.

Hartnett made solid contact. The ball streaked into the left-field bleachers for the famous "homer in the gloamin'" and the Cubs were in first place—to stay.

Hartnett was 20 years old and working in a steel and wire mill in Worcester, Mass., when he was offered a contract to play for the town's Eastern League club. He reached for a pen without delay and caught 100 games before the year was out.

Reports on the hard-throwing catcher filtered into New York, where John McGraw reflected on the Giants' need for such a commodity. He instructed his scout, Jesse Burkett, to check out the prospect.

In due time, the old slugger filed a wire report: "Hartnett will never be a big-league catcher. His hands are too small."

The Cubs found no such fault with Hartnett. They bought the youngster for $2,500.

The rookie was no blushing violet when he reported to Catalina Island for his first major league training camp in 1922. He chirped constantly, until one newspaperman wondered "Who's that gabby kid I can hear no matter where I go on the island?"

Henceforth, Hartnett was known as Gabby, although teammates called him by his middle name, Leo, and to others he was "Old Tomato Face."

Gabby was in his prime when he went to training camp in 1929, but his early optimism faded when, in making one of his customary hard throws to an infielder, he felt something snap in his shoulder. He appeared in just 25 games and batted only .273 for the pennant-winning Cubs.

Gabby, who reportedly missed only three foul flies in 1,990 games behind the plate, was the N.L. catcher in the first five All-Star Games, including the 1934 classic when Carl Hubbell fanned Babe Ruth, Lou Gehrig, Jimmie Foxx, Al Simmons and Joe Cronin in order.

Gabby had the "best seat in the house" in the 1932 World Series in which Ruth allegedly "called" a homer.

"Babe was just replying to our bench jockeys," explained Gabby. "He held up one finger and said, 'It only takes one to hit.' "

Hartnett's only weakness, it was generally agreed, was his slowness afoot. "If he had had the speed of a Mickey Cochrane, he would have hit .400," insisted Pie Traynor.

In his 19-year major league career, Hartnett seldom felt censure. One exception took place in the late 1920s when Gabby was king of the Cubs and Al Capone was Chicago's reigning underworld figure. Prior to a game, Gabby was called to a box seat, where Capone asked him to autograph a baseball for his nephew. An alert photographer snapped a picture, which Commissioner K.M. Landis saw in the next day's newspapers. A non-fraternization edict was issued from Landis' office the next day.

A liver ailment proved fatal to Hartnett in Park Ridge, Ill., on his 72nd birthday.

It was generally agreed that Gabby Hartnett's only weakness was his slowness afoot.

HARRY HEILMANN

Even a faulty memory can lead to a distinguished career as a major league outfielder. At noon on a Saturday in 1913, the young bookkeeper at a San Francisco biscuit company closed his ledgers and left his office, looking ahead to some free time.

After walking a few blocks, he remembered that he had left his topcoat in the office. Retracing his steps, he met an old friend who was managing the Hanford team in the San Joaquin Valley League. The friend had a problem: his third baseman was ill. Could the bookkeeper fill in for the next day's game at Bakersfield? He was promised $10 and expenses, and accepted.

In storybook fashion, bookkeeper Harry Heilmann hit an 11th-inning double to give Hanford a 4-2 victory. Exuberant Hanford fans showered the field with money and when the hero of the day counted his new wealth he totaled $150 which, with the promised $10, represented more than a month's salary at the biscuit company.

Among the spectators at the game was a scout for the Portland club of the Northwest League. The next day the scout visited the bookkeeper's home and signed him to his first professional contract. As a bonus, the youngster received a spaghetti dinner. Three years later, Heilmann was in the major leagues to stay as an outfielder with the Detroit Tigers.

In the next 15 years, Harry failed to play as many as 100 games in only one season (part of 1918 was spent in the Navy quartermaster department).

The righthanded hitter, known to his teammates as "Slug," was not an immediate sensation with the Tigers. His emergence as one of the top all-time hitters coincided with the elevation of Ty Cobb as manager in 1921.

"Until that time, Cobb didn't care whether I hit or not, just figured it wasn't any of his business, I guess," Heilmann explained. Cobb taught Heilmann how to dis-

Harry Heilmann's 1927 batting form resulted in his fourth batting championship.

tribute his weight while batting, "with a little more weight on the front foot," and how to study pitchers.

The improvement was dramatic. A .296 hitter for the five previous years, Heilmann batted .394 in 1921 and captured the first of four batting titles. He also won hitting championships in 1923, '25 and '27, clinching the last two crowns in last-day doubleheaders.

In 1925, Heilmann came on with a rush, picking up nearly 50 points on Tris Speaker in the final month. In the opener of the last day's twin bill, Harry rapped three hits to move ahead of Speaker. Teammates urged him to go home and enjoy his newly won laurels. He refused. "I'm playing out the string," he insisted before going 3-for-3 in the nightcap and beating Speaker by four points.

In 1927, Heilmann battled Al Simmons down to the wire. Because of the time differential, Heilmann learned early in St. Louis that Simmons had gone 2-for-5 for Philadelphia and moved one point ahead of him.

Heilmann had four hits, including a home run, in the first game, lifting him one point in front of Bucketfoot Al, and again friends suggested he take off the rest of the day. Again he refused. He collected three hits in the second game, winning the title comfortably—and honorably.

Traded to Cincinnati in 1930, Harry batted .333, then was forced to sit out a year because of arthritis. He came back in '32, but gave up after 15 games.

His finances depleted by the stock market crash, Heilmann was hired by the Tigers to broadcast their games in 1933 and became an instant success.

During spring training in Lakeland, Fla., in 1951, Harry collapsed in his hotel room. He was hospitalized in Lakeland and then returned to Detroit where he made occasional visits to the radio booth.

Heilmann had been Commissioner A.B. (Happy) Chandler's first choice to broadcast the 1951 All-Star Game from Detroit, but he declined because of failing health.

Harry died July 9, 1951, of lung cancer at Henry Ford Hospital in his adopted city, the day before that game.

BILLY HERMAN

Billy Herman, traded to the Dodgers in 1941, slides safely across the plate in a game against St. Louis.

asey Stengel called Billy Herman "one of the two or three smartest players ever to come into the National League."

Carl Hubbell, lefthanded screwball artist of the Giants, was nothing more than "Cousin Carl" to the righthanded hitter after he started to use a longer, heavier bat and a delayed swing.

Herman was a marvel at stealing signs. Pee Wee Reese, his doubleplay partner at Brooklyn, recalled:

"It wouldn't take him long to break a code. As he took a lead off second base, he'd crouch to let a batter know a fastball was coming or stand straight up for a curve.

"When he coached at first or third base, it wouldn't take long before he'd tell you what the pitcher was throwing. If he yelled, 'Be ready,' you could expect a fastball. If he yelled, 'Come on,' it would be a breaking pitch."

Ruefully, Reese concluded, "Once we knew every pitch that Max Lanier (Cardinals) was throwing and he still shut us out."

Nobody ever questioned Herman's brains, although his mother may have had her doubts the day she sent Billy into town to make a mortgage payment on the family farm near New Albany, Ind. En route, the teenager spotted a game in progress and joined in. He played until nightfall, then retrieved the bag containing $250 in mortgage money that had been unattended during the game.

With his heady style of play, bat control and hit-and-run skills, Herman would have been an ideal player for John McGraw. And the Giants manager had a chance to buy Billy from Louisville, but rejected him as too small.

Billy was no more than a reserve infielder on his high school team, but he won some local acclaim after he pitched his church team to a league championship. He was 19 when he invested a dime in a round-trip fare to Louisville to sign with the American Association Colonels on the recommendation of Cap Neal, the club's colorful scout.

Neal's parting advice to Herman was, "You're an infielder, not a pitcher." Even after Neal saw infielder Herman commit five errors in a game while playing for Dayton (Central) a year later, he still insisted, "I'm not worried about that, son, and neither should you be. You're gonna be one of the great ones."

By August of 1931, Billy had progressed so impressively that the Cubs shelled out $60,000 for his contract.

Billy, who grew into a solid 5-foot-11, 195-pounder, was a fearless batter. The first pitcher he faced in the majors was Si Johnson of Cincinnati. Herman greeted him with a single and on his second at-bat was struck behind the ear by a Johnson fastball.

Herman was trundled off the field, but the next time he faced Johnson he rapped three hits.

After he was traded to Brooklyn and sparked the Dodgers to a 1941 pennant, Herman was dusted off with a major league beanball by Paul Erickson of the Cubs in the heat of the 1942 race. Billy hit the next pitch into the left-field seats, one of only two homers he had that season.

When he was traded to the Braves in 1946, the old campaigner had the satisfaction of booming a double against his former Brooklyn teammates in a 4-0 Boston victory in the regular-season finale. The loss forced the Dodgers into a tie for the pennant. They lost the playoff to the Cardinals in two games.

Herman, a star on four pennant-winning clubs overall, saved his best performances for the All-Star Game. He performed in 10 contests, starting with the 1934 game, and batted a gaudy .433 (13-for-30).

When the Pittsburgh Pirates sought a manager in 1947, President Frank McKinney polled 12 highly respected baseball persons, seeking their recommendations. Herman's name topped 11 lists and ranked second on the other.

Billy got the job, but was fired as the Bucs tied for last place. Seventeen years later, he received a second managerial chance, this time with the Red Sox. Billy was in the second season of a two-year contract in 1966 and had just returned from a successful road swing when he strode into the front office and was greeted with the announcement, "We've decided to make a change."

Some minor league managerial jobs followed, as well as coaching positions with major league clubs that wished to capitalize on the talents of a super baseball intellect.

HARRY HOOPER

The tourist was nearly 75 years old when he reminisced during a visit to the Baseball Hall of Fame in 1962, but he remembered in fine detail his memorable afternoon in a World Series game 47 years earlier.

Harry Hooper was a lefthanded batter who led off for the Red Sox in Game 5 at Baker Bowl in Philadelphia on October 13, 1915.

"In the third inning," he remembered, I solved a pitch from Erskine Mayer and drove it over the wall. We were tied 4-4 in the ninth inning. Eppa Rixey, the lefthander, had replaced Mayer by that time. I realized it was no time to wait. I picked on the first pitch and that was it—another homer."

The ball flew past the outfielders, up a ramp and into the clubhouse where a teammate was taking a shower. He retrieved the ball and presented it to Hooper, who treasured it the rest of his life.

The second homer gave the Red Sox their second world championship in four years. They had defeated the Giants in the 1912 classic in which Hooper contributed an incredible barehand catch.

With the Giants leading, 1-0, in the fifth inning of the eighth and deciding game (one had been a tie), Larry Doyle walloped the ball toward the temporary bleachers in right-center field.

"I took off for the fence when the ball was hit," recalled the Red Sox captain, "saw the ball coming over my shoulder and stuck out my hand. I felt no impact.

"I knew I had the ball, but the fence was there and I was running into it. It was low, I jumped over and the crowd opened up.

"I can still see that instant, like everything was standing still, like a movie that is stopped. I can still see the ball—right there."

The Red Sox won the game, 3-2, in 10 innings.

Harry was in his fourth full season with the Sox at that time. A product of St. Mary's College in California, he joined the Alameda club in an outlaw California league in 1907. When he was sold to Sacramento (California State), Hooper pocketed $12.50, half of his sale price as per agreement with the club.

At the end of the 1908 season, Hooper was asked by Sacramento Manager Charley Graham how he'd like to join the Red Sox.

"I'd love it," replied the youngster.

Two years later, in 1910, Hooper was a member of one of baseball's greatest outfields, teaming up with Tris Speaker in center and Duffy Lewis in left.

As a fielder, Hooper specialized in the "rump slide."

Instead of diving for a ball, Harry positioned himself feet first with one leg tucked under. It enabled him to come up instantly in position to throw.

Harry cashed his last two Series checks, both winners' shares, in 1916 and 1918.

In 1919, Hooper suggested to Manager Ed Barrow that teammate Babe Ruth be converted from a pitcher to an outfielder to capitalize on his hitting prowess.

"They'd have me investigated if I did that to the best lefthander in the game," protested Barrow.

"But you've got $60,000 invested in the club," Hooper countered. "You're interested in bringing fans out. They come out when Ruth pitches, but they come to see him hit. Play him in the outfield and they can see him hit every day."

Barrow did—and the fans did.

When Harry held out for a $15,000 salary in 1921 he was traded to the White Sox, who gave him $13,250. Hooper retired after the 1925 campaign but played one season with the Missions (Pacific Coast) before calling it quits.

He accepted a temporary appointment as postmaster of Capitola, Calif., but stayed on the job for 25 years. He was an expert bowler and spent a lot of time hunting and fishing, as well as watching the surf from his seaside home in Santa Cruz, Calif. He was the oldest member of the Hall of Fame when he died in 1974 at age 87.

By 1910, Harry Hooper was part of a great Red Sox outfield that included Tris Speaker and Duffy Lewis.

ROGERS HORNSBY

Although the 19-year-old shortstop for Denison (Western Association) had batted only .277 and made 58 errors in his second pro season, Bob Connery decided he was worth a $500 investment.

Wiring news of the purchase of Rogers Hornsby to the home office, the Cardinals' scout said, "If the boy fails to make good, you can take the money out of my salary."

Before he died more than 50 years later, Connery had the satisfaction of seeing his discovery develop into the greatest righthanded hitter of all time.

Over a five-year span (1921 through 1925), Hornsby averaged .402 as a major league hitter. In 1924, he established a modern record by batting .424 in 143 games. He missed three games in May because of a dislocated thumb and eight late-season games because of a wrenched back.

In his remarkable season of '24, the Rajah hit safely one time in 44 contests, twice in 46, three times in 25 and four times in four. He was blanked only 24 times and, curiously, the pitcher who enjoyed the greatest success against Rog was a lefthander, Johnny Cooney of Boston who shut him out three times.

Hornsby, named St. Louis manager on June 1, 1925, attained his peak of popularity in 1926 when helped the Redbirds to their first pennant and a stunning upset of the Yankees in the seven-game World Series.

But success was not without its perils. An outspoken individual, Hornsby was openly critical of Owner Sam Breadon, calling him a money-grubbing cheapskate for scheduling a late-season exhibition game at New Haven, Conn., when, Rog insisted, a day of rest would have been more beneficial to the players.

Relations between the two men strained further when Hornsby demanded a three-year contract at $50,000 a season. Shortly before Christmas of 1926, an incensed St. Louis citizenry learned that the Rajah had been traded to the Giants for Frank Frisch and Jimmy Ring.

Hornsby's blunt manner never changed. With the Giants, he quarreled with Owner Charles Stoneham and others. One evening, while Rog was at dinner with shortstop Eddie (Doc) Farrell, a newspaperman asked Hornsby if the Giants had a chance to win the pennant. "Not as long as Farrell plays shortstop," was his unsmiling reply.

After one season in New York, the Rajah was traded in 1928 to Boston, where he was named manager in May. "Can this team win the pennant?" asked Owner Emil Fuchs. "Not with these humpty-dumpties," answered Hornsby.

Rogers Hornsby, manager of the St. Louis Browns in 1936, confined most of his hitting to practice sessions. The seven-time batting champion made only five plate appearances.

Hornsby began his career as a shortstop, but by 1920 he had found his niche at second base.

Hornsby's best season was 1924 (above) when he hit .424. Hornsby (below, No. 42) was St. Louis Browns manager in 1952 when a controversial play occurred that might have cost him his job. Yankee Gil McDougald (12) missed connections with a foul pop (the ball is behind him), but the umpires ruled the batter out because of fan interference. Hornsby's mild reaction to the call angered Owner Bill Veeck, and The Rajah was fired two days later.

Rog wore out his Boston welcome in one year, too, and moved on to Chicago. By late September of 1930, he was named Cubs' manager. One afternoon when the Cubs and Braves were locked in a tie, Rog inserted himself as a pinch-hitter for Rollie Hemsley and socked a game-winning, bases-loaded homer.

In the clubhouse, Bill Veeck Sr., Cubs' general manager, greeted him by saying, "You should not have put yourself on such a spot."

"I know I'm a better hitter than Hemsley," replied Hornsby, confident to the end.

In 1932, after Hornsby was replaced in mid-season as manager, the Cubs went on to win the flag under Charlie Grimm. The players demonstrated their feelings to their old boss by cutting him out of the World Series pool.

The Rajah neither drank nor smoked, nor understood players who did. He did not attend movies for fear of possible damage to his icy-blue eyes. His only acquaintance with a newspaper was to read the averages.

But he took kindly to outfielder Jim Rivera in 1952 when Rog managed the Browns. "Haven't you heard," asked Rivera, "movies stopped flickering long ago?"

Rog openly criticized Ted Williams for failure to hit to left field when opponents shifted to the right side. "He's not a great hitter," Hornsby reasoned.

In later years, when Hornsby scouted for the Mets, his evaluations were classics in brevity. On one report, he wrote "too fat." On another, "He didn't impress me." On a third, "Glasses."

For the many precautions that he exercised to guard his vision, it was ironic that Hornsby was in a Chicago hospital for removal of cataracts when a slight heart attack and a blood clot proved fatal in 1963.

WAITE HOYT

Waite Hoyt collected 19 victories in 1921, his first season with the Yankees.

The 15-year-old youngster had pitched batting practice for the Giants for a few weeks and had grown weary of the long, round-trip ride from his Brooklyn home. Fearlessly, he approached crusty John McGraw and explained the disadvantages under which he was working.

"Get this boy a contract," the New York manager told an aide. The youngster, Waite Hoyt, was dumbfounded. All he really wanted was a raise. When he and his father signed a contract the next day, the Giants slipped Waite $5 to seal the deal.

The teenager touched the fin briefly. Outside the Polo Grounds, his father said, "Five dollars is too much for you. I'll keep it."

Hoyt, who made one relief appearance for the Giants in 1918 after three seasons in the minors, wore a Red Sox uniform when he made his first major league start in 1919 against Ty Cobb, Harry Heilmann, Bobby Veach and company. Cobb, Detroit's third batter in the first inning, screamed imprecations at the youngster from the bench before he walked to the batter's box. Hoping to unnerve Hoyt, the Georgia Peach stood at the plate for 5 minutes, with his back to the mound.

When Cobb finally stepped in, Hoyt turned around on the mound and gave Cobb 5 minutes of his own medicine. Eventually, the two squared off and Hoyt, after running the count to 2-and-2, fanned Cobb on a changeup.

Hoyt proved particularly effective against Cobb throughout their American League careers. And he was in top form in World Series competition as well, winning six games for the Yankees.

Hoyt regarded his performance in the second game of the '21 Series as his superlative effort. The game was played at the Polo Grounds, where the Yankees were tenants of the Giants.

As Waite warmed up, he heard a raucous voice inquiring, "Is this the young punk who's gonna beat us?" It was Giants outfielder Ross Youngs talking to Frank Frisch.

Hoyt held the Giants to two hits in posting a 3-0 victory. Late in the game, his old benefactor, McGraw, tossed a piece of soap at Hoyt's feet as the pitcher walked by the dugout after grounding out.

Unshaken, Waite fired the soap back with considerable speed. The missile grazed McGraw's ear.

The son of a minstrel man, Hoyt mastered the act of self expression at an early age. He could be caustic or cute as the situation demanded.

He was at his best on an afternoon that produced a sharp exchange with umpire George Moriarty. In his last outburst at the umpire, Hoyt seethed, "You should be a traffic cop so you could stand in the middle of the street with a badge on your chest and insult people with impunity."

Waite, a 237-game winner in the majors, once sought a raise from Yankees Owner Jake Ruppert, whose wealth was estimated conservatively at $10 million.

"Can't do it," retorted the Colonel. "Ruth wants a raise, Meusel wants a raise. What do you fellows think I am, a millionaire?"

Once, while pitching as a National Leaguer at Wrigley Field late in his career, Hoyt was subjected to a savage riding from the Cubs' bench. It was after the Yankees had beaten the Cubs four straight in the 1932 World Series.

Hoyt tolerated the abuse for awhile, then silenced his hecklers by yelling, "If you don't shut up I'll put on my old Yankee uniform and scare you to death."

As a pal of Babe Ruth and an all-night reveler, Hoyt knew that the Bambino would have approved a remark made on a hot day when Waite and former teammate Joe Dugan stood by Babe's grave.

"I'd give anything for a cold beer," muttered Dugan.

"So would the Babe," said Hoyt.

CAL HUBBARD

To be a good umpire, Cal Hubbard once commented, it is necessary to maintain discipline and know the rules. He could have added that 265 pounds on a 6-foot-2½ frame also was desirable.

With such dimensions, the hulking Hubbard had little difficulty keeping order. Neither players nor managers saw fit to engage Cal in prolonged dispute, although Yogi Berra once went about as far as he dared.

For several innings, the Yankee catcher found fault with Hubbard's ball-and-strike decisions until Cal yanked off his mask and addressed his critic.

"There's just no sense in both of us umpiring this game," he told Berra. "The unfortunate part of the situation from your standpoint is that I'm being paid to stand behind the plate and umpire. You're not. You're only being paid to catch. One of us is obviously unnecessary and has to go. It breaks my heart to say so, but the guy who's gonna go is you."

"C'mon, Cal," screamed a suddenly contrite Yogi, I'll be quiet, I promise." Hubbard let him stay.

Another catcher who got Cal's message was Mike Tresh of the White Sox. Hubbard lectured the carping catcher thusly: "If you don't shut up, I'm gonna hit you so hard on the top of your head it'll take a derrick to get you back to ground level."

Another catcher, Gene Desautels of the Red Sox, was responsible for Cal's most embarrassing moment. Desautels bickered frequently with Hubbard in spring exhibitions, but Cal held his temper, figuring his chance would come to crush the receiver.

In a regular-season game at Detroit, Desautels doubled. The next batter smashed a hard liner that second baseman Charley Gehringer caught with a spectacular leap. His throw to shortstop Billy Rogell arrived just as Desautels slid back into the base in a cloud of dust. "Yer out," shouted Cal as the runner came up beefing.

"So you want to give me trouble again," growled Hubbard. "Okay, I'll call it again. 'Yer out.' "

"But," yelled the runner, "I've got the ball."

Big Cal Hubbard is a two-sport Hall of Famer.

A native of Missouri, Hubbard was a nationally known sports figure long before he became a major league umpire. He was an outstanding football lineman at Centenary College under Bo McMillin. When Bo transferred to Geneva College in Beaver Falls, Pa., Cal followed. "I followed my heart," explained the big fellow.

At Geneva, Hubbard earned All-America honors while starring on a team that, among other achievements, upset Harvard.

Even then, Hubbard knew the rule book. "I've seen him hold up games three and four times while he corrected officials," recalled McMillin. "He knew more about rules than the officials because he spent more time studying them."

After leaving Geneva, Cal played two seasons with football's New York Giants and then was traded to Green Bay, where his size, strength and speed earned him all-league recognition.

While most pro players were earning $50 or $75 a game, Hubbard was drawing $175, and ultimately $200, as the highest-paid player in the National Football League.

Cal began his umpiring career while still in his prime as a football player. He began in the Piedmont League in 1928 and called 'em in the Southeastern and Sally leagues and the Western Association before joining the International League in 1931.

When he joined the A.L. in 1936, veteran arbiters said he was the best freshman umpire in league history. He had studied the baseball rules book as avidly as he had the football book.

Hubbard umpired in four All-Star Games and three World Series until he was forced to retire after the 1951 season. While Cal was hunting, a shotgun pellet ricocheted off a rock into his left eye. Blurred vision forced him to retire. He accepted a position as assistant to Tommy Connolly, supervisor of American League umpires. When Connolly stepped down in 1954, Cal stepped up. In turn, he yielded the post to Dick Butler in 1970.

When Hubbard was elected to the baseball Hall of Fame in 1976, it gave him the distinction of being the only man elected to the college and pro football and the baseball shrines.

Cal was 76 when he died of cancer on October 17, 1977, at St. Petersburg, Fla.

CARL HUBBELL

Dick Kinsella, a Giants scout, was an Illinois delegate to the Democratic national convention at Houston in 1928. One humid afternoon, when convention business dragged on endlessly, Kinsella forsook the political arena for the baseball arena and visited the local Texas League park where the Buffs were playing Beaumont.

The Beaumont pitcher, an angular lefthander, quickly drew the scout's attention. When Kinsella returned to his hotel, he telephoned New York and told John McGraw, "This afternoon I saw another Art Nehf. He beat Houston, 1-0, in extra innings."

The comparison to the Giants' lefthanded pitching star of earlier championship years was sufficient recommendation for McGraw, who bought Carl Hubbell for $30,000, a record price for a Texas League player.

Hubbell had been the property of the Detroit Tigers, but in two spring camps with the American League club he had pitched only one inning, in a "B" game against the University of Texas. When he was optioned to Beaumont, Carl told his manager that he would not return to Detroit. If he was not sold to another major league club, he would quit professional baseball and work for an oil firm that offered an opportunity for year-round employment and a chance to pitch for the company team.

The screwball that was to be his trademark with the Giants was not a part of Hubbell's repertoire in 1928. As Tiger property, he had experimented with the delivery and had attained proficiency with it before coach George McBride warned him of possible damage to his elbow.

Hubbell did not throw the pitch again until one afternoon while facing the Cardinals. With two runners on base and a count of 3-and-1 on righthanded slugger Chick Hafey, Carl's batterymate, Shanty Hogan, signaled for a fastball. "I threw a screwball," reported Hubbell, "and it fooled Hafey. Hogan called for another fastball and I threw another screwball and Hafey struck out."

"I don't know what that pitch was," Hogan said, "but keep throwing it."

From then on the screwball was Hub's bread-and-butter pitch, and Carl was the "Meal Ticket" of the Giants.

Control was one of Hubbell's major assets. In July of 1933, before 50,000 fans at the Polo Grounds, he defeated the Cardinals, 1-0, in 18 innings. In what amounted to two nine-inning shutouts, Hubbell did not walk a batter, struck out 12 and allowed only six hits. In his 16 years with the Giants, he averaged fewer than two bases on balls per nine innings.

After five seasons in the minors, Carl Hubbell brought his screwball to New York and dazzled N.L. hitters.

In 1935, Hubbell won 23 games and was just one season away from his career-best 26-6 mark.

Hubbell gets a handshake and a gold watch from crosstown great Babe Ruth in 1930.

The long shutout game was not his finest effort, contended Hub. Nor was his no-hitter against the Pirates in 1929, nor any of his 24 consecutive victories over a two-year period. It was a one-hitter against the Dodgers at Ebbets Field in 1940. The only Dodger hit was a single by Johnny Hudson, who was retired on a double play.

"Control made that the most memorable game for me," said Hubbell. "Every pitch went just where I wanted it to go. I never had such control before or afterward. I can't explain it. I made only 81 pitches. I faced only 27 batters and only three balls were hit to the outfield."

In the 1933 World Series, King Carl pitched 20 innings without allowing an earned run. In the opening game, he struck out the first three batters—Buddy Myer, Goose Goslin and Heinie Manush—and beat the Washington Senators, 4-2. He won the fourth game, 2-1, in 11 innings. That same season he had hurled 46 consecutive shutout innings.

Carl launched his 24-game unbeaten streak with a 6-0 victory over the Pirates on July 17, 1936. It was the only shutout of his streak, which was snapped by the Dodgers, 10-3, on Memorial Day of 1937.

For all his glittering efforts in championship play, Hubbell always will be remembered best for his spectacular pitching in the second All-Star Game played at the Polo Grounds in 1934. After the first two batters reached base, catcher Gabby Hartnett instructed Hubbell, "Just throw that 'thing.' It'll get 'em out. It always gets me out."

Carl followed orders, striking out Babe Ruth, Lou Gehrig and Jimmie Foxx to end the inning. Only Foxx made contact, hitting a harmless foul.

In the second inning, the Meal Ticket fanned Al Simmons and Joe Cronin, yielded a single to Bill Dickey and then struck out Lefty Gomez.

Throughout his 535 major league games, the two-time Most Valuable Player never forgot his manners. Veteran umpire Babe Pinelli recalled: "Only once did he complain and then I don't think the fans realized it. With the count 2-and-2 on the batter he threw a pitch he thought was a strike. I called it a ball and on the next pitch the batter hit a home run. As he walked by me at the end of the inning he said, 'Babe, I thought that third ball was a pretty good pitch.' I answered, 'Carl, I thought it was a little inside.'" After retiring in 1943, Hubbell was named farm director of the Giants.

MILLER HUGGINS

At 5-foot-4 and 146 pounds, he had to be a scrapper. And he spent many of his 49 years proving he belonged and that he could hold his own among those who were better endowed physically.

Miller Huggins battled for an opportunity to gain a foothold as a major league second baseman, and succeeded admirably. He battled as manager of the Cardinals, fought an owner's prejudice against men who wore caps and fought the likes of Babe Ruth, Joe Dugan and Joe Bush to demonstrate his ability to manage the strong-willed Yankee players of the 1920s.

Hug, an excellent leadoff batter during his 13 years in the majors, was named successor to Roger Bresnahan as the Cardinals' manager in 1913 and led the club to two third-place finishes in five years.

All the while, American League President Ban Johnson was squirming in his Chicago swivel chair as the Yankees lagged in the second division. He was convinced that a strong New York franchise was necessary to take the play away from the solidly entrenched Giants.

On a visit to St. Louis, Johnson asked his friend, J.G. Taylor Spink, publisher of *The Sporting News*, to sound out Huggins. Would Hug be interested in managing the Yankees? The answer was affirmative. Miller was instructed to visit the Yankees' offices on his next visit to New York to negotiate with club President Jacob Ruppert.

After numerous delays, which included time to convince Ruppert that cap-wearing gentlemen could be managerial giants, Huggins was offered the job. But now he imposed a condition. He demanded that Bob Connery, the Cardinal scout who discovered Rogers Hornsby, accompany him to the Yankees.

Eventually, that issue was resolved and, in January of 1918, Little Hug was signed for the position that produced his greatest fame.

The diminutive Miller Huggins, manager of the great Yankee teams of the 1920s, is flanked, and dwarfed, by his two great sluggers, Babe Ruth (left) and Lou Gehrig, during spring training in 1928.

Huggins poses with big Frank Chance, manager of the Red Sox, during the 1923 season.

Despite his size, Huggins achieved respectability as a second baseman before becoming Cardinals manager in 1913.

He won his first pennant in 1921 and followed with five in the next seven seasons.

A native of Cincinnati, Huggins graduated from the University of Cincinnati Law School. Although he was admitted to the bar, he never practiced law.

While attending college, Miller played for Mansfield (Inter-State) under the name of Proctor and in the summer performed as a second baseman for the team that yeast king Julius Fleischmann ran for his own amusement in the Catskills. The catcher on the team was Red Dooin, later manager of the Phillies. A pitcher was Doc White, later an outstanding lefthander with the White Sox.

Still using the alias, Huggins played for St. Paul (Western Association) in 1901. After a successful season, he notified his father that baseball—not law—was to be his profession. Thereafter he played baseball under his legal name.

Miller joined the Reds in 1904 and scored 96 runs his first year before tallying a career-high 117 in his second season. A sore arm and batting slump limited Hug to 46 games in 1909, after which Manager Clark Griffith traded him to St. Louis.

In 1913, Schuyler P. Britton, owner of the Cardinals, named Huggins manager.

By the time Huggins led the Yankees to their first world championship in 1923, Ruppert had dropped his bias against caps. After saluting Ruth and all his teammates at the victory celebration, the Colonel declared: "And lastly, I give credit where credit is mostly due, to that great manager of a great team, little Hug."

Huggins finished in the second division only once as a Yankee skipper. In 1925, the year Ruth suffered his spring collapse and later was fined $5,000 after a run-in with Hug, the Yanks finished seventh.

The Yankees were running second to the Philadelphia A's in September of 1929 when Huggins arrived at Yankee Stadium for the last time. Instructing coach Art Fletcher to take over for him, Little Hug entered a hospital, where he died of crysipelas five days later. He was buried in his native Cincinnati.

At his death, Huggins was worth approximately $400,000. He frequently had advised players on investments. In his later years he and Connery had owned the controlling interest in the St. Paul (American Association) club.

WILL HULBERT

One hundred and thirteen years after his death in 1882, William Hulbert's contributions to baseball were finally rewarded with his election to the Hall of Fame.

Partially because of his own desire to remain in the background, Hulbert's contributions to the founding of the National League and development of the game were unfairly overlooked for more than a century. Writing in *Sports Illustrated* in 1990, Steve Wulf said, "He deserves to be in Cooperstown as much as any baseball executive, not just because he organized the National League but also because he brought stability to that shaky enterprise and helped rid the game of the influences of gambling and booze."

To pacify other owners from Eastern teams, Hulbert, who was from Chicago, insisted that Hartford owner Morgan Bulkeley become the first president of the National League when the league formed in 1876. Bulkeley served as figurehead president for a year, even though Hulbert was really running the league, and Bulkeley was selected for the Hall of Fame in 1937.

Hulbert had been afraid that other teams, especially those from Eastern cities, would not pull out of the National Association and jump to his new league if he was in charge. Bulkeley's selection did insure the other teams involvement in the league, and the National League was born.

Hulbert was born in New York state in 1832, not far from Cooperstown. His family moved to Chicago when he was two, and he grew up to become a stockbroker and a baseball fan. He became involved with the White Stockings in the National Association, and by 1875 was selected as the team's president. Upset by the team's performance, he recruited pitcher Albert G. Spalding and other players to move from Boston back to his native Illinois. He reportedly told Spalding, "I'd rather be a lamppost in Chicago than a millionaire in any other city."

At the same time, Hulbert was upset by the league's problems with gambling, drinking and incomplete sched-

William Hulbert was elected to the Hall of Fame in 1995 by the Committee on Veterans.

ules. In signing Spalding and three other players under contract to Boston, he knew the White Stockings would be kicked out of the National Association. That's when Hulbert decided to form his own league. He and Spalding drew up the league constitution, then brought a group of National Association owners together, locked the hotel room door so they could not leave, and outlined the new league for them.

A year later, when Hulbert officially replaced Bulkeley as president, one of his first actions was to kick the New York Mutuals and Philadelphia Athletics out of the league for failing to complete their 1876 schedules. He later threw the Cincinnati Red Stockings out of the league for their refusal to ban the sale of beer on Sundays in their park.

In 1877, when the Louisville club began to lose a 3 ½ game lead in August, Hulbert supported an investigation that uncovered evidence of game fixing. Four members of the Louisville club were accused of throwing games—Jim Devlin, Bill Craver, George Hall and Al Nichols. Hulbert banned them for life. In his 1911 book, *America's National Game*, Spalding wrote that one of the players, Jim Devlin, came to see Hulbert years later and begged him for another chance. Hulbert became emotional, according to Spalding, and pulled out a $50 bill and handed it to Devlin but refused his request to be reinstated.

"That's what I think of you personally," Spalding quoted Hulbert as saying. "But damn you, you are dishonest and you sold out a game. I can't trust you. Now go on your way, and never let me see your face again, for your act against the integrity of baseball never will be condoned as long as I live."

Hulbert also was the driving force behind the hiring of the first impartial umpiring staff. Before, the hiring of the umpires had been the job of the home captain and the scores of the day's games were sometimes known in advance.

Hulbert likely would have made even more decisions that would have shaped the game of baseball for years to come, but he died at the early age of 49, from heart failure, prior to the start of the 1882 season. He had lived long enough, however, to see his new National League survive for six years and become stable enough to ensure its long-term success.

CATFISH HUNTER

During that improbable era when the Oakland A's flourished on a diet of uncommon skills and unconventional conduct, a round-faced pitcher from the coastal plain of North Carolina stood bastion-like amid the tumult.

Back home in the peanut-corn-and-soybean country, he was known as Jimmy. Along the baseball pathways, he answered to Catfish. On the birth rolls of Perquimans County, he was listed as James Augustus Hunter.

Catfish Hunter embodied all the virtues generally associated with Smalltown, U.S.A. The Hertford farmboy also was blessed with a strong arm, acute baseball acumen and the business sense that would help him convert those assets into startling success.

By any reckoning, Catfish Hunter was a singular individual. That point was driven home by his affiliation with a big-city insurance tycoon who introduced him to fame and fortune at an early age. The benefactor was Charles O. Finley. A full-blown non-conformist with manners that were sometimes querulous, Finley launched Hunter into national prominence. It was Finley who supplied the youngster's first financial windfall and it was Finley who later hassled the hurler, broke faith with him and eventually sent him forth to reap unprecedented wealth with a rival club.

This unusual relationship began in 1964 after A's scout Clyde Kluttz informed Finley of the Carolina wunderkind who was baffling high school and American Legion opponents with a repertoire that almost defied description.

Jimmy Hunter was phenomenal, Kluttz told Finley. He already had pitched a bunch of no-hitters and several major league clubs had offered him a signing bonus of $50,000. But the kid wanted more. Then the scout offered a suggestion. "Why not visit Hertford and see for yourself how good the kid is?" he told his boss.

Finley liked the idea. By plane and limousine, he arrived at the small town (population about 2,000) and saw Jimmy pitch in a high school tournament. I saw his curve and couldn't believe it," Finley said later. It was better than any pitcher on my own club had."

From the tournament, Finley moved on to the Hunter farm, where he found Jimmy's mother hoeing weeds in the peanut patch and his dad rearranging ham and bacon in the smokehouse.

A family conference was called with the visiting dignitary occupying the seat of honor. Before the discussions had gone far, Jimmy removed his right boot and exhibited a foot that was minus its little toe and was filled with

Catfish Hunter was the toast of the town after pitching his 1968 perfect game against the Minnesota Twins.

about 30 pellets from a shotgun blast delivered accidentally by his brother the winter before.

When the discussions ended, Finley had two hams as gifts of the family, while Jimmy had a check for $75,000 as well as a nickname. Finley recalled the circumstances.

"After we signed the contract, I told him we had to have a good nickname for him. Looking around this country setting, I came upon 'Catfish.' I told him that we would tell the press he had been missing one night and that his folks found him down by the stream with one catfish lying beside him and another on his pole. He looked at me and smiled and said in that drawl of his, 'Whatever you say, Mr. Finley, it's OK with me.'"

As Catfish Hunter, the righthander made his professional debut at Chicago on May 13, 1965. It was an impressive start. In two innings of relief, he allowed neither a hit nor a run.

The Cat won eight games his first season, nine the next and 13 in each of the next two. The high point of his illustrious career occurred May 8, 1968, exactly one month after his 22nd birthday. Facing the hardhitting Minnesota Twins, Hunter mixed fastballs and sliders with three changeups and one curve in a perfect, 4-0 no-hitter—the

Hunter's strong right arm carried him to 224 major league victories and a 3.26 career ERA.

When Hunter won his freedom from the A's in 1974, the New York Yankees won the bidding war for his services.

first regular-season perfecto in the American League since 1922.

After his classic performance, Catfish received a congratulatory phone call from the club owner. "But you cost me $5,000," said Finley.

"I'm sorry," replied Catfish. "Who got it?"

"You," advised Charlie. "It'll be in your new contract."

Hunter scaled the 20-win mark for the first time in 1971 when the A's won their first of five straight divisional titles. In the world championship years of 1972, '73 and '74, Hunter produced 67 victories. In the same period, he won three League Championship Series decisions and posted a perfect 4-0 record in World Series conquests of the Reds, Mets and Dodgers, respectively. He earned the Cy Young Award in 1974 after posting a 25-12 record.

Hunter terminated his Oakland ties the same year. Relations between the pitcher and Finley had soured over the years, primarily because of an interest-free loan of $150,000 that the club owner had given Hunter to buy farm acreage in North Carolina.

In the ensuing months Finley badgered Hunter about repayment of the loan. Such demands usually were made on days that Catfish was scheduled to pitch. The hurler finally sold off 80 percent of his acreage to pay off the loan and announced that all future agreements with Finley would be spelled out clearly with legal blessings.

The strained relations between executive and pitcher snapped in 1974. Under terms of the player's contract, Finley was to pay $50,000 of the player's salary to an insurance company as an annuity. When Finley failed to comply, Catfish laid the matter before an arbitrator. On December 2, 1974, the arbitrator ruled that the contract had been breached and that Hunter was a free agent.

The decision ignited an instant furor. Every major league club except San Francisco sent representatives to North Carolina seeking the pitcher's services. Probably the most popular delegation was composed of Gene Autry and Dick Williams. While the California club owner handed out autographed record albums, the manager talked baseball with townfolk on the street corners.

When all the bids were in, however, Hunter chose the Yankees; not because their offer was the most lucrative, but because of his long friendship with Kluttz, the former A's scout who now worked for the Bombers. Whether the terms of the five-year contract called for $2.85 million or $3.75 million was of secondary consequence. Of greater importance was the fact that Catfish became the wealthiest pitcher of his time.

The Cat won 23 games for the Yankees in 1975 and 17 in the pennant-winning season of 1976. But chronic shoulder problems forced his retirement in 1979 at age 33. He retired with 224 major league victories and a 3.26 career ERA.

MONTE IRVIN

The outfielder for the Newark Eagles was dejected. It was 1948, and his contemporaries in the Negro National League were entering Organized Baseball while he was being ignored.

Jackie Robinson, the first modern black in the white man's game, was still at UCLA in the early 1940s when the Newark slugger batted .432 and hit 41 home runs. Those who knew the Eagles player and his accomplishments were as puzzled as he.

"Eventually," said Monte Irvin, I made up my mind to forget that they'd overlooked me. I was in good physical shape and saw no reason why I couldn't play my kind of ball."

Twenty-five years later, when Irvin was enshrined at Cooperstown, his former adversary, Roy Campanella, asserted, "Monte was the best all-round player I ever saw. As great as he was in 1951 (at age 32) when the Giants won the pennant, he was twice that good 10 years earlier in the Negro league."

Irvin almost became a Brooklyn teammate of Campanella. While playing in the Cuban Winter League, Monte was scouted by Fresco Thompson of the Dodgers and signed a St. Paul (American Association) contract.

When Mrs. Effa Manley, owner of the Eagles, reminded the Dodgers that the player was under contract to her team, the Dodgers offered to buy him for $2,500. The offer was rejected as inadequate. He was purchased by the Giants in 1949 on the recommendation of scout Hank DeBerry.

One of 10 children of an Alabama farm couple who moved north in the 1920s, Monte was a four-sport high school star in Orange, N.J., before he turned pro at 17. In the next decade, he estimated, he averaged .350 at bat.

One year, he batted .397 and was named the Most Valuable Player in the Mexican League.

Irvin was in his first full season with the Giants when he sparked them to the 1951 pennant in "The Little Miracle of Coogan's Bluff." When the Giants and Dodgers ended the 154-game race in a tie, Monte was encountered by a newsman.

"How ya feeling?" he was asked.

"I feel so good," came the reply, "that I've a mind to give a month's rent free to my neighbors if we lick Brooklyn."

Bobby Thomson's ninth-inning home run in the third playoff game took a sizable slice from Monte's paycheck, but during the World Series with the Yankees—after Irvin went 4-for-5 in the first game and 3-for-4 in the second— Monte found time to pose for a newspaper photo with his neighbors, who were cheering their benefactor.

Soft-spoken, modest Monte batted .458 in the Series and drove in two runs to go with the 121 that he amassed to lead the National League in the regular season.

Irvin was 33 when he went to training camp in 1952. As was their annual custom, the Giants barnstormed eastward with the Cleveland Indians. On April 2, the teams stopped at Denver for a game. In the second inning, Monte led off with a walk, then sped to third when Willie Mays lined a single to right-center field. The throw from the outfield went to second base, but Irvin slid needlessly into third and "something popped like a paper bag."

Irvin's spikes had caught in the dirt. His right ankle was fractured. Monte did not return to action until late July, but he rebounded in 1953 to bat .329.

He was still a solid man for the world champion Giants of 1954, but he was 35 at the time and retired after the '56 season (which he spent with the Cubs).

Monte accepted a position as a special assistant to Commissioner Bowie Kuhn. In 1973, his boss introduced him to the media as a new member of the Hall of Fame.

Yankee shortstop Phil Rizzuto is late with the tag as the Giants' Monte Irvin steals second base during Game 2 of the 1951 World Series in Yankee Stadium.

REGGIE JACKSON

Reggie Jackson's mighty swings resulted in some of the Most memorable home runs ever.

Even in his own era, there were other players who drove in more runs, some who hit for a higher average and many more who were better fielders. But when the games were their most important and the pressure was on, few players in baseball history were more proficient than Reggie Jackson.

In 1977, Jackson, then a 31-year-old right fielder for the New York Yankees, described his role on the club as that of "the straw that stirs the drink." It was an arrogant statement, one that caused dissension among his teammates, but performance makes arrogance more palatable.

And Jackson performed. He played for four teams in a 21-year career that spanned 1967-1987. Eleven of his teams won division titles, six of them advanced to the World Series, and five of them won it. When he retired, only five players in history had hit more home runs than Jackson's 563. He also struck out more times than anyone else (2,597), but Jackson was proof of the adage nothing ventured, nothing gained.

"Sure, I strike out a lot," he said in 1968, the first of four consecutive seasons he would lead the American League in whiffs. "If I strike out 90 times in a row, if I get my swings, that's OK. You don't have a chance if you don't swing. A lot of guys will strike out only 10 times a year. But how many home runs will they hit?"

Jackson's mighty swings often resulted in some of the most memorable home runs ever. In the 1971 All-Star Game, he slugged a mammoth drive off Pittsburgh's Dock Ellis that struck a transformer on the right-field roof at Detroit's Tiger Stadium. Few people remember that the American League won that game; no one who saw Jackson's blast will forget it.

Jackson played in 12 All-Star Games during his career, but he left his mark in postseason play. A .262 hitter during the regular season, Jackson hit .357 in 27 World Series games. He set 12 Series records and tied eight others. He hit three home runs on three consecutive pitches from three different pitchers in Game 6 of the 1977 World Series against the Los Angeles Dodgers. Babe Ruth is the only other player to accomplish that feat. Jackson hit 10 homers in 98 World Series at-bats and six more in Championship Series play.

Jackson became one of baseball's first big-money free agents in November 1976 when he signed a five-year contract with the Yankees worth $2.9 million. However, unlike some players who became lesser talents after signing for big money, Jackson earned every penny. The Yankees had not won a World Series in 15 seasons when he arrived in 1977. They won it that year, thanks in large measure to Jackson's record five home runs. Four of those homers came on consecutive pitches, an unprecedented feat.

Jackson's post-season prowess earned him the nickname "Mr. October," and it was a moniker every bit as deserved as Ruth's "Sultan of Swat" or Lou Gehrig's "The Iron Horse."

"I've played against him, coached against him and managed against him," Jeff Torborg, a Yankees coach in the early 1980s, said. " But I never knew what a money player he is. I should have known, but I didn't."

Jackson's flair for the dramatic was legendary. In Game 2 of the 1978 World Series, he struck out after a nine-pitch duel against Dodger pitcher Bob Welch. There were two men on base and two out in the ninth inning at the time and New York lost the game 4-3. Six days later against the same pitcher in Game 6, Jackson homered in the Yankees' title-clinching victory.

On April 27, 1982, in his first game back at Yankee Stadium after signing with the California Angels as a free agent, Jackson homered to lead his new team to victory against his old one. A packed Yankee Stadium crowd chanted "Reg-gie! Reg-gie! Reg-gie!" throughout the at-bat.

Although Jackson played for four teams, his five seasons with the Yankees were his most famous. or infamous. In a nationally televised game at Boston's Fenway Park on June 18, 1977, Jackson and Manager Billy Martin nearly came to blows in the New York dugout after Martin thought Jackson dogged a ball in right field (the runner stretched a single into a double on the play). Martin sent out a substitute player to replace Jackson in the middle of the inning and, upon Jackson's return to the dugout, the two men approached each other with fire in their eyes. Coaches Elston Howard and Yogi Berra had to step between the two to head off a fight.

Immediately after the game, rumors began to fly that Jackson or Martin would have to go, that no clubhouse could handle two egos as huge as theirs (Martin, a former Yankee star himself, had opposed the signing of Jackson in the first place). Since it was likely that no other team would be willing to assume Jackson's big contract, Martin seemed the obvious one to go.

Later that evening, sensing what might happen, Jackson told team owner George Steinbrenner, I don't want to be the cause of a manager's firing. Don't fire him."

Steinbrenner, who would hire and fire Martin five times as the Yankee manager, held off on this occasion.

Jackson, the A.L. Most Valuable Player in 1973, led or tied for the American League lead in home runs four times and drove in over 100 runs six times. He also led or tied for the lead in errors by outfielders five times. He was, at best, adequate as a fielder.

The huge egos of Jackson and Billy Martin often caused player and manager to clash.

"He's so set on doing well that he feels defeated if anything goes wrong," said Frank Robinson, who managed Jackson one winter in Puerto Rico. "He'll be thinking about a strikeout while he's in the field and he'll get so down he won't charge a ball that's hit to him."

Jackson's passion, however, was hitting home runs and winning World Series rings—not Gold Gloves—and he ended up in the Hall of Fame because of it.

"There isn't any feeling in the world like that," he once said of hitting home runs. "No feeling. That's what I play for. To feel that ball take off. To circle the bases. To know you've done it alone. You've conquered."

TRAVIS JACKSON

John McGraw was enjoying the comforts of his Memphis hotel suite in 1922 when he received a visitor, Kid Elberfeld, who had been a shortstop for New York's American League club years earlier when Little Napoleon was winning pennants with the Giants.

McGraw was in Memphis because the Giants made an annual stopover there en route from their training camp in San Antonio to New York. Elberfeld was there to promote an 18-year-old shortstop performing for the Little Rock (Southern Association) club that he managed.

"You'd like him," said the Kid. "He's skinny with not much power at the plate just now, but he'll get better as he goes along. But he can hound the ball, and you never saw a shortstop with a better arm. Have somebody look at him. He should be ready for you after one more year in this league."

"If anyone should know a shortstop, you should," McGraw replied. The reports that McGraw received from Dick Kinsella, his one-man scouting board, were as flattering as Elberfeld's and before the season was out Travis Jackson had played three games for the Giants.

Elberfeld saw Jackson for the first time when the native of Waldo, Ark., was 14 years old. Jackson's uncle, a Little Rock druggist and a friend of Elberfeld, introduced the youth to Kid. Four or five times a summer, Jackson visited Little Rock, where Elberfeld batted ground balls at him by the hour. "There wasn't anything about playing shortstop that Elberfeld didn't teach me," Jackson remembered. "And when I got to the Giants at 18, John McGraw never had a criticism of my fielding."

In June of 1923, Dave Bancroft, the Giants' regular shortstop, was stricken with pneumonia and missed nearly two months of the season. During his absence, Jackson filled in with a steady glove and an active bat that was good for a .275 average.

At the end of the season, Bancroft was traded to Boston, where he was appointed manager of the Braves.

"Who's gonna play shortstop next season, Jackson?" a reporter asked McGraw, who only smiled.

"Do you think that such a young fellow is ready for such a big job?"

"Do you think," replied McGraw, "that I would have let Bancroft go if I thought he wasn't ready?"

Throughout his career, Jackson was hindered by injury. At Little Rock, he collided with the center fielder while they were chasing a Texas Leaguer at full tilt. Both were knocked unconscious and were hospitalized. Jackson suffered a deep gash on his foreheaded. The center fielder lost an eye.

Early in his major league career, Jackson injured his knee while running the bases and was periodically handicapped thereafter. In 1932 and 1933, he appeared in barely over 50 games each season, but a Memphis surgeon rebuilt his knee during the winter and Travis gave it a rugged workout the next spring. Cautioned by teammates, he responded, "If the knee holds up, fine; if not, I'll go back to Waldo."

The knee not only held up in 1934, but Jackson played 137 games, drove in 101 runs and was the starting shortstop in the All-Star Game at the Polo Grounds.

Jackson was named captain of the Giants in the spring of 1928 when he motored to Hot Springs, Ark., to see the batterymen work out in advance of the regulars. On arriving at the camp, Jax was greeted by McGraw's announcement: "From now on, you're captain of this club."

After concluding his career as a third baseman in the 1936 World Series, Jackson managed minor league clubs for many years and served at other times as a coach for the Giants. He retired from baseball after managing Davenport (Midwest) in 1960. I just got tired of the bus rides," he explained.

When he was elected to the Hall of Fame in 1982, Jackson joined the three other members of the 1927 Giants' starting infield—Bill Terry, Fred Lindstrom and Hornsby.

Travis Jackson (right) with Manager John McGraw in 1932, McGraw's last season with the Giants.

FERGUSON JENKINS

As a boy growing up in Chatham, Ontario, Canada, Ferguson Jenkins' first athletic love was hockey, which didn't set him apart from most Canadian youth. However, by the time his athletic career ended some 25 years later, it was baseball—not hockey—that set Jenkins apart from the rest of his countrymen.

In 1991, after a stellar 19-year pitching career, Jenkins became the first Canadian-born player inducted into baseball's Hall of Fame. The vote was close, as Jenkins received the 75 percent of the vote he needed by just a single tally.

The closeness of the balloting didn't surprise him.

"After all, I won and lost a lot of one-run games," Jenkins said.

That he did. If any pitcher could ever file a lawsuit for non-support against his teammates, Jenkins could. In 1968, while playing for the Chicago Cubs, the 6-foot-5, 205-pound righthander lost five 1-0 games to tie a major league record. Jenkins still won 20 games that season, but better run support easily could have swelled that victory total to 25.

"Every time I lost one of those 1-0 games," Jenkins remembered, "I had to keep telling myself that I've got to try harder next time."

Few pitchers tried as hard or pitched as regularly as Jenkins. He led the majors in complete games four times and finished 267 of his career starts (an average of 14 per season). In addition, Jenkins was a durable pitcher who suffered only one severe injury in his entire career: a torn Achilles tendon in his right heel in 1976.

"I never iced my arm, and I think I had one cortisone shot in my life," he said.

Although Jenkins' achievements-284 victories, six straight 20-win seasons and 3,192 strikeouts rank favorably with other pitchers of his era, he rarely received the national acclaim of such other dominant pitchers as Bob Gibson, Tom Seaver and Juan Marichal. The probable reason: those pitchers played for successful teams that won pennants and World Series. Jenkins, who spent more than half his career with mediocre Cub teams, never pitched for a pennant-winner, or in the World Series.

"It means a lot to the individual player to get into a World Series," Jenkins said in 1971, his best season. "Everything is centralized in a World Series, and therefore there is a lot of national recognition. People put a lot of stock in World Series performances."

Jenkins' success stemmed more from exquisite control than an overpowering fastball. He is the only pitcher in baseball history to amass more than 3,000 strikeouts with fewer than 1,000 walks.

Because, he never pitched for a pennant-winner, Ferguson Jenkins rarely received the acclaim bestowed other dominant pitchers of his era.

"My game plan is simple," he once said. I throw strikes and make 'em hit the ball. And if they don't, I got another strikeout. The idea is to throw strikes and let the batters do the work."

Jenkins began his major league career with the Philadelphia Phillies in 1965. However, the Phillies, thinking Jenkins didn't throw hard enough to win, traded him to the Cubs the following spring. Although Chicago manager Leo Durocher used his new pitcher in relief immediately after acquiring him, Durocher started Jenkins in seven games late in the 1966 season. Jenkins impressed enough in those games to end his days as a reliever.

It was with the Cubs that Jenkins achieved his greatest success. For six seasons from 1967-72, he never won fewer than 20 games. In his best year, 1971, he won a league-high 24 games and walked only 37 batters in 325 innings en route to winning the National League's Cy Young Award.

After Jenkins' streak of six straight 20-win seasons ended in 1973 (he was 14-16 that year), the Cubs traded their ace to the Texas Rangers for infielders Bill Madlock

In 1971, Jenkins won a league-high 24 games and walked only 37 batters In 325 innings en route to winning the National League's Cy Young Award.

and Vic Harris. Jenkins, who had asked to be traded, was stunned when the Cubs shipped him to baseball's worst team, the Texas Rangers. In 1973, the Rangers lost a major-league-high 105 games and finished 37 games out of first place in the American League Western Division.

"I looked on the trade to Texas as a great challenge," Jenkins said. "The Cubs said I was 30 years old, that I had a bad back and a bad arm. They said I was all washed up."

Jenkins, however, was anything but washed up. In 1974, his first season in the American League, he won a career-high 25 games (tying Catfish Hunter for the A.L. lead). He also led the league with 29 complete games and was named A.L. Comeback Player of the Year. And the Rangers, the laughing stock of baseball the previous year, increased their victory total by 27 games en route to finishing second to the powerful Oakland A's in the West

Division. In four starts against the A's that year, Jenkins allowed just three runs (two of them earned) in 36 innings while posting a 4-0 record.

Although his propensity for giving up home runs was something Jenkins could have lived without (he led his league in that category five times), the only true black mark against him came in 1980, when he was arrested for drug possession in Toronto. The charges were later dropped, but Commissioner Bowie Kuhn's quick suspension of Jenkins in September of that year (before a trial could even be held) stained the pitcher's image in the minds of many people. It is commonly believed that the controversy surrounding the drug charges may have delayed Jenkins' Hall of Fame induction by a couple of years and resulted in a close vote when he did get in.

Regardless, Ferguson Jenkins made it to Cooperstown in 1991, and deservedly so.

HUGHEY JENNINGS

"Ee-yah" was the battle cry of Hughey Jennings, whose greatest fame came as Tigers manager.

A former breaker boy from the hard-coal mines of Pennsylvania, he was red-haired, freckled, smiling, cocky and tough, a candidate for immortality among the old Baltimore Orioles who terrorized the National League in the 1890s.

Hughey Jennings was so tough that he survived three skull fractures. But above all, Jennings was intelligent. He earned a law degree from Cornell, coached baseball at Cornell and Georgia and managed the Tigers to three consecutive pennants at a time when they were less intent on winning than they were on abusing a young firebrand named Ty Cobb.

The son of Scotch-Irish parents, Jennings was a catcher for a semipro team in Lehighton, Pa., in 1890 when his 15 putouts, four assists and five hits in one game caught the eye of the manager of the Allentown club of the Eastern Interstate League. After 13 games, the league collapsed and Hughey rejoined Lehighton.

At Louisville the following season, Jennings started out as a first baseman, switched to third base on June 30 and to shortstop on July 4. He became a major leaguer in 1892 when Louisville entered the National League. Following a trade, he made his Oriole debut on Independence Day in 1893, after which he developed rapidly under the tutelage of Ned Hanlon.

After three pennants and one Temple Cup championship in the mid-1890s, Jennings, Hanlon, Willie Keeler and Joe Kelley transferred, in 1899, to the Brooklyn Superbas who were under the same ownership as the Orioles. The quartet formed the nucleus of the team that won pennants in 1899 and 1900.

After obtaining his law degree, Jennings retired from professional baseball for a short while. However, when the Phillies offered him the opportunity to captain their club in 1901, he jumped at the chance to return to the diamond.

Hughey was playing with Baltimore, now in the Eastern League, in 1906 when the Tigers sought to buy him. Hanlon demanded $5,000. Frank Navin, secretary of the Tigers, politely declined, then drafted Jennings for $1,000.

Jennings' foremost asset and most painful headache at Detroit was Cobb, then in his second full season. Driven by a fierce determination to succeed, Cobb engaged in clubhouse brawls almost daily. The Georgian was no boxer and bore numerous bruises and scars from his escapades. No matter how badly he had been beaten up the previous day, Cobb kept coming back for more until Jennings stepped in.

"This has gone far enough," Hughey told the Tiger veterans. "I'm convinced that the kid has as much guts as I thought he had. By this time he should have proved it to you. Now let him alone. He's not going to be driven off this club if I have to tire everybody else. The next guy who taunts him or lays a hand on him will have to answer to me."

The warning restored order, and with Jennings plucking grass from the coaching box and shouting his mysterious "Ee-yah" at his players, the Tigers won flags in 1907, '08 and '09. Each year, however, they were beaten in the World Series.

Jennings remained on the job until 1920 when he stepped down in favor of Cobb. He rejoined his old buddy, John McGraw, as a coach for the Giants and enjoyed four consecutive pennants all the more because of the light responsibilities that he carried.

In the winter of 1923, Hughey and his wife accompanied the McGraws on a tour of Europe, and a year later Jennings visited the continent as a member of the Giants/White Sox tour.

In 1925, when McGraw was taken ill, he turned the reins over to Hughey, who brought the club home in second place.

After the season, Jennings, a Scranton lawyer, suffered a nervous breakdown. He recovered in Asheville, N.C.

The old Oriole suffered an attack of spinal meningitis in January of 1928 and died the next month at age 57.

BAN JOHNSON

The son of a Cincinnati educator, descended from old New England stock, Byron Bancroft Johnson was the premier organizer in baseball.

Johnson organized the American League, numbering among the foremost planks in his platform the elimination of rowdyism and staunch support of his umpires. Within a few years, he had built his circuit into such a powerful force that the National League was forced to recognize it and accept it as an equal.

Barely a quarter of a century later, Johnson locked his desk in his Chicago office and closed the door for the last time, broken in health and spirit and nearly blind.

Johnson was targeted early in life for the ministry, but that parental hope was abandoned when Ban rebelled against compulsory chapel attendance at Oberlin College and transferred to Marietta College. As a collegian, he was said to have been so outstanding a catcher that he was offered a contract by Cleveland of the National League.

Johnson graduated from the University of Cincinnati Law School and practiced the legal profession for a while. Inadequate compensation left him to forsake law in favor of a reporter's job with the Cincinnati *Commercial-Gazette* that paid $25 a week.

He advanced to city editor, but when the sports editor's job became available, he eagerly sought—and obtained that position. Ban was serving in that capacity when Charles (Old Roman) Comiskey arrived in town to take over as manager of the Reds.

Johnson and Comiskey developed a close friendship, from which was born the Western League in 1894 and the American League a few years later.

Johnson, Comiskey and allies changed the league's name from Western to American in 1899, and operated as a minor circuit in 1900. The following year, with strong franchises in Chicago, Boston, Detroit, Philadelphia, Baltimore, Cleveland, Washington and Milwaukee, the league fathers announced they were ready to operate as a second major loop and would raid established N.L. clubs for playing talent.

Johnson was elected president for a 10-year term. With the club owners' approval, he barred the sale of liquor in ball parks. Profanity on the field was forbidden. Umpires were vested with total authority. And there was no $2,400 salary limit such as prevailed in the N.L. In that infant season of 1901, more than half of the new league's players were former National Leaguers.

By 1903, the N.L. was ready to sue for peace. Johnson helped to forge the National Agreement that brought the two leagues into harmony and provided for the National Commission, the ruling board that consisted of the two league presidents and Garry Herrmann, president of the Cincinnati Reds.

With the transfer of the Milwaukee franchise to St. Louis in 1902 and the Baltimore franchise to New York in 1903, Johnson's organization flourished instantly. With the lure of former N.L. stars and the advent of young players such as Ty Cobb, the league not only attained equality but superiority.

But success took its toll on the Johnson-Comiskey friendship. The old drinking cronies who had organized the league in a room off the bar-lounge in the Fisher Building drifted apart for reasons never fully explained.

The estrangement deepened with the Black Sox scandal of 1919. Comiskey accused Johnson of negligence in not canceling the World Series after the first two games aroused suspicions of a fix.

The election of Judge K.M. Landis as the first commissioner terminated the National Commission and eliminated much of Johnson's traditional power. Ban started to quarrel with club owners. He rejected a suggestion by Clark Griffith of Washington and Jake Ruppert of New York that he take a leave of absence. But, on October 17, 1927, the rugged individualist, accompanied by a coterie of newsmen, walked from the Fisher Building for the last time.

Johnson retired with his wife to Spencer, Ind., and died of diabetes in St. Louis at age 67.

Ban Johnson was the prime force behind the organization and success of the American League.

WALTER JOHNSON

In the summer of 1908, the Washington Senators arrived in New York for a series with the Highlanders at Hilltop Park.

The visitors were among the weakest teams in the league and would finish seventh, 22 $\frac{1}{2}$ games behind the pennant-winning Tigers.

But the Senators did have one magnificent asset, a 6-foot-1, 200-pound righthander from Coffeyville, Kan., who had been discovered a year earlier in an Idaho semi-pro league.

On Friday, the 20-year-old pitched a four-hit shutout. The next day astonished spectators watched him hurl a three-hit shutout. Because Sunday baseball had not been legalized in New York, the next game was played Monday. The script was changed only slightly, as the phenom charged to the pitching mound again and blanked the home club on a two-hitter.

Joe Cantillon, Washington manager, was tipped off to Walter Johnson in 1907. A friend in Idaho wrote to Pongo Joe extolling the talents of the pitcher who neither smoked nor drank, but threw a blinding fastball.

The Senators had no scouts, but Cantillon had an injured catcher-first baseman, Cliff Blankenship, who could serve in that capacity.

Cantillon instructed Blankenship to go to Wichita and check on a swift young outfielder, Clyde Milan, later a Senators star.

"And while you're out there," Cantillon added, "you might as well run up to Idaho and see about that young pitcher."

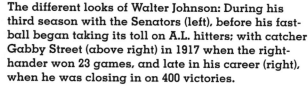

The different looks of Walter Johnson: During his third season with the Senators (left), before his fastball began taking its toll on A.L. hitters; with catcher Gabby Street (above right) in 1917 when the right-hander won 23 games, and late in his career (right), when he was closing in on 400 victories.

Johnson, who had just shut out the Pirates in Game 4 of the 1925 World Series, gets a handshake from brother Leslie (right). Before he was finished, Johnson had struck out 3,508 major league hitters.

Blankenship recommended the acquisition of both players. Before Johnson signed, however, he made one stipulation. If he failed to make the grade, the Senators would have to pay his transportation back to Idaho. The condition was met immediately.

Johnson won five games for the Nats in his first season, including the first two shutouts of his record total of 110. The youngster pitched a five-hitter in his debut on August 2, but lost to the Tigers, 3-2.

Before long, Johnson was christened "Big Train" and opponents stood awestruck at the plate as his fastball shot past.

Ping Bodie of New York, a good fastball hitter, stood motionless as three pitches rocketed through the strike zone.

"You can't hit what you can't see," he moaned.

In his 21 major league seasons, the Big Train suffered only one sore arm, yet, curiously, it was during that time that he pitched his only no-hitter, against the Red Sox in 1920.

On at least two occasions, Johnson fanned the side on nine pitches with the bases loaded. He performed the feat against Ty Cobb, Sam Crawford and Bobby Veach of Detroit and Tris Speaker, Chick Gandil and Elmer Smith of Cleveland.

They were just six of his 3,508 major league strikeouts, all for Washington.

In 1913, Johnson hurled $55\frac{1}{3}$ consecutive scoreless innings, a record that stood until Don Drysdale of the Dodgers surpassed it in 1968. Johnson's streak would have ended 20 innings earlier except that Tris Speaker was struck by a batted ball for the third out of the inning.

Annually, Johnson pitched the season opener at Griffith Stadium. In 14 inaugurals, most of them before the President of the United States, he won nine times, seven of them by shutouts.

After 18 major league seasons, Johnson pitched in his first World Series in 1924. Walter lost two games in the Series and won one, but the victory came in the seventh and deciding contest. He pitched the final four innings of the Senators' 12-inning, 4-3 triumph over the Giants.

The Big Train defeated the Pirates twice in the 1925 Series, but lost the seventh game.

After managerial stops at Newark (International), Washington and Cleveland, Johnson retired to his 550-acre farm near Germantown, Md. A stroke, caused by a brain tumor, paralyzed his left side in April of 1946, eight months before his death at age 59.

WILLIAM (JUDY) JOHNSON

Connie Mack observed the black third baseman for several years, dreaming of what he might mean to the fortunes of the Philadelphia Athletics.

Asked for his opinion of the extraordinary fielder, .350 hitter and fleet runner, Mack replied, "If Judy Johnson was white, he could name his own price."

Johnson, son of a seaman who moved his family from Snow Hill, Md., to Wilmington, Del., in the early 1900s, was known as Billy in his younger years. He was in his early 20s when teammates started to call him Judy because, they said, he resembled Judy Gans, a veteran player.

The elder Johnson had hoped that his son would develop into a boxer. When Billy was 8, his father bought him a pair of boxing gloves, and a second pair for his 12-year-old sister, Mary Emma, the neighborhood tomboy.

Obediently, Billy went along with his dad's program until he grew tired of his sister's thrashings and turned to less strenuous activities.

Billy performed for integrated baseball and football teams in Wilmington. At Howard High School, however, there was no sports program, so Billy terminated his formal education after his freshman year and took a job on a loading dock in Deepwater Point, N.J. He returned home after World War I and caught on with the Chester Giants in Pennsylvania. His pay was $5 a game, plus transportation.

Johnson then performed for the Bacharach Giants, still for $5 a game, but by 1920 he was with the Philadelphia All-Stars.

In 1921 he was sold to the Hilldale team, a powerful Philadelphia club, for $100. Suddenly, Judy was enjoying the affluence of $100 a month.

At this point in Judy's career, according to veteran observer Cool Papa Bell, Johnson "was the best hitter among the four top third basemen in Negro baseball. Although someone else might hit as high as Judy, no one would drive in as many clutch runs as he. He was a solid player, real smart, and the kind of player who would get the job done. He was dependable, quiet, not flashy at all, but could handle anything that came up.

"And above all, he was a gentleman on and off the field. Oh, nobody could push him around, but his quiet, easy, down-to-business manner made him a standout as a player and as a man."

Johnson was a key figure for the Hilldale club that participated in the first Negro World Series in 1924. He led all hitters in that series with a .341 mark.

The following year, although suffering a fractured arm while playing shortstop, Johnson batted .392, which he believed was his all-time high.

By 1925, Judy Johnson was among the best third basemen in Negro league history.

Judy joined the Homestead Grays as player-manager in 1929, receiving $500 a month, his top baseball salary.

Two years later, he joined the Darby Daisies, formerly the Hilldale team, and then moved again in 1932, becoming player-manager of the powerful Pittsburgh Crawfords and a teammate of Satchel Paige, Josh Gibson and Cool Papa Bell.

Johnson led the Crawfords to the league title in 1935 and the second-half championship in 1936.

Judy retired from the playing field after the 1937 season and took a job as a supervisor with the Continental Can Company in Wilmington. In 1940, he and his brother opened a general store, but a few years later Judy returned to Continental Can, where he remained until 1951 when he joined the Philadelphia A's as an instructor and scout. One of his major assignments was to ease the entry of Bob Trice and Vic Power, young blacks, into the majors. As a scout, Judy recommended the purchase of Hank Aaron from the Indianapolis Clowns for $3,500, but the financially strapped A's vetoed the suggestion.

When John Quinn, general manager of the Milwaukee Braves, switched to the Phillies in 1959, Johnson joined him and helped with the acquisition of Richie Allen.

In 1973, Judy retired to his home in Marshallton, Del.

ADDIE JOSS

To many, it was the most extraordinary game ever pitched, better than the Vaughn-Toney double no-hitter, better than the Oeschger-Cadore marathon.

What made the game of October 2, 1908, extra special was that it was pitched in the heat of a pennant race. The Cleveland Naps and the Chicago White Sox were in frenzied pursuit of the Detroit Tigers in a race that would go to the Bengals by a half-game over Cleveland and 1½ games over Chicago.

Addie Joss was seeking his 24th victory for Cleveland, Ed Walsh his 41st for the visiting Chicago team. Walsh already had hurled more than 400 innings for the Sox.

In the third inning, the Naps solved Walsh for a run. Joe Birmingham singled, went to second on a delayed steal and took third when the throw struck him on the shoulder and bounced away. A wild pitch permitted him to score.

Birmingham's single was one of four hits yielded by Walsh, who struck out 15. On this day it was Big Ed's misfortune to hook up with a pitcher who was letter perfect. Only four balls were hit to the outfield.

Joss received some sparkling help from Nap Lajoie at second base. The Frenchman raced behind the mound on several occasions to field slow-hopping balls and throw out the batter.

Pat Dougherty, leading off the eighth inning, accounted for the only hard-hit ball against Addie. The ball was a ground smash toward right field, but graceful, gliding Lajoie gloved the ball and threw out the runner.

In the seventh inning, Fielder Jones of Chicago worked the count to 3-and-2. As the next pitch crossed the plate, Jones dropped his bat and started toward first base. Umpire Tom Connolly, however, called the pitch strike three.

Jones sent in three pinch-hitters in the ninth inning in an effort to break Joss' spell. The first was retired on a grounder to Lajoie, the second on strikes. At that point, one reporter noted, "A mouse working his way along the grandstand floor would have sounded like a shovel scraping over concrete."

The third pinch-hitter was big John Anderson, powerful but slow afoot. Anderson lined the first pitch to left field, where the ball curved foul at the last instant. On the second pitch, Anderson hit a smash over third base, but Bill Bradley, who had no previous chances, collared the ball and fired toward first. The throw was low, but George Stovall scooped it up and umpire Silk O'Loughlin waved the batter out on a bang-bang play to complete the perfect game.

Joss was discovered while pitching for Toledo (Western Association) in 1901 and made his major league debut in St. Louis on April 26, 1902. He was superb on that date, too, holding the Browns to one hit in a 3-0 victory.

The only safety was a single by Jesse Burkett on a drive that the right fielder insisted he caught.

Umpire Bob Caruthers ruled otherwise.

On June 12, 1903, Joss engaged Rube Waddell in another masterful performance. The Philadelphia lefthander edged Joss, 2-1, in a 14-inning thriller reeled off in 2 hours, 10 minutes.

Joss, a former University of Wisconsin athlete, attained the 20-victory mark in four consecutive seasons, starting in 1905. He hurled a second no-hitter, also against the White Sox, on April 20, 1910, but there were a few flaws in the performance. He issued two bases on balls and one batter reached base on an error. Only five balls were hit to the outfield.

After slipping to 14-13 and 5-5 records in 1909 and 1910, Joss reported to training camp in 1911. During an exhibition game at Chattanooga, Tenn., he fainted on the bench, but dismissed the incident as insignificant after treatment at a local hospital. He maintained that he had only "pulled a baby trick."

When the team reached Cincinnati, Joss was taken ill. Doctors diagnosed his ailment as pleurisy and ordered him to his home in Toledo. On April 14, two days after the Naps opened the season in St. Louis, Joss died of tubercular meningitis. He was 31.

The funeral, at which evangelist Billy Sunday preached, was said to be the largest in Toledo history. Among the mourners were all of Joss' teammates.

Addie Joss is pictured in 1910, his final season before dying at age 31.

AL KALINE

When the skinny youngster, obviously ill at ease, stepped into the batting cage and hit a few pitches weakly past the infield, veteran Detroit players looked quizzically at one another as if to say, "Is this the kind of kid they're giving $30,000 bonuses these days?"

Manager Fred Hutchinson, however, had no reservations about 18-year-old Al Kaline, who was just out of Southern High School in Baltimore. "He'll be all right," said Hutch. "He has fine wrist action."

Ed Katalinas' scouting report was much more exciting. Among the points he emphasized were: "Showed outstanding arm, has good speed, excellent body control, is the best player I ever scouted."

Kaline was groomed by his father for a professional baseball career. At 14, he played on an iron and metal company team that competed against clubs whose pitchers had minor league experience. "As a result," Kaline said, "I learned to hit the curve and change of pace."

In three seasons of high school competition, Al batted .353, .418 and .469.

Kaline would have preferred to sign with the Washington Senators, but they did not reciprocate his affection. He could have opted for the Yankees, but chose the Tigers because of Katalinas' four-year interest in him and because the Bengals were in a youth program that had already snatched Harvey Kuenn and Billy Hoeft.

Kaline made his major league debut on June 25, 1953, one day after joining the Tigers. He relieved center fielder Jim Delsing in the eighth inning of a game at Philadelphia and flied to center field on the first pitch from Harry Byrd in the ninth inning.

In 1955, 20-year-old Al Kaline (left) became the youngest player ever to win a batting championship. Nineteen years later, Kaline received a big hug from his mother after rapping out hit No. 3,000.

The strong bat and golden glove made Kaline (pictured in 1972 above and 1973 right) one of the best all-round players during his 22 seasons with the Tigers.

Al recorded his first hit on July 8. It was a single off Luis Aloma at Chicago. His initial home run was hit on September 26. It was a ninth-inning bases-empty clout off Dave Hoskins in a 12-3 Tiger loss at Cleveland.

When Steve Souchock suffered a fractured wrist while playing winter ball in Cuba and was unable to start in right field the next spring, Hutchinson gave the job to Kaline.

Spurred by a couple of nine-game batting streaks, Kaline's average shot above the .300 mark in early May. However, a pulled thigh muscle and water on the knee that resulted from a collision with the outfield wall restricted Al to 138 games and contributed to his season-ending .276 batting average.

During the season Hutchinson introduced Kaline to Ted Williams and asked the Red Sox slugger to give the youngster some batting tips. Williams stressed exercises to develop shoulders and arms and suggested that Kaline swing a bat daily through the winter to accelerate his wrist action.

Kaline put the advice to quick advantage. He reported to spring training with 20 more pounds, up to 175, and staged one of his lustiest hitting exhibitions ait Briggs Stadium on April 17, 1955. Al lashed four hits in five at-bats, including three homers, two in one inning. It

marked the first time that an American Leaguer had homered twice in one inning since Joe DiMaggio in 1936. Only two other American League batters had ever accomplished the feat, Ken Williams of St. Louis in 1922 and Bill Regan of Boston in 1928.

Throughout the season, Kaline demonstrated increased power. From one homer as a rookie and four the next year, he exploded for 27 in '55. Only three A.L. players had more.

Kaline's emergence as a hitter led Casey Stengel to exclaim: "That feller has picked up five years of experience in two."

Al collected 200 hits in 1955, but more important, he won the league batting championship with a .340 average. He was only 20 years old, the youngest batting king in history.

Kaline became the 12th player to register 3,000 career hits on September 24, 1974. The milestone hit was a double down the right-field line against Dave McNally in Baltimore. Al was the first American Leaguer to attain that plateau since Eddie Collins of Chicago in June of 1925, nearly half a century earlier.

Kaline's final safety, on October 1, 1974, was a single off Jim Palmer of Baltimore that gave the Tiger star 3,007 career hits.

TIM KEEFE

Buck Ewing had no idea when he yanked his starting pitcher on July 16, 1888, that he would create a 20th century controversy.

His strategy was perfectly sound. New York held a 9-0 lead in the second inning and Ewing's best hurler was on the mound for the Giants. Why not switch the pitcher with the right fielder, a part-time hurler, and save the starter for another day since the game was virtually won anyway?

Tim Keefe, the starter, had won eight consecutive games previously and he would win 10 straight after July 16. By 20th century scoring rules, a pitcher must work at least five innings to receive credit for a victory. There was no such provision in the code of the 1880s, so Keefe was awarded the July 16 victory over the Chicago White Stockings for an overall 19 consecutive triumphs.

Almost from the time that Rube Marquard won 19 consecutive games for the Giants in 1912, there has been a question as to whether he tied Keefe's mark or set a record. Most authorities give Keefe credit for 19 straight inasmuch as he achieved the mark under existing rules.

Chicago snapped Tim's streak on August 14. A Polo Grounds crowd of 10,000 watched the White Stockings score two unearned runs in the fifth inning and pull out a 4-2 decision.

The next day a correspondent wrote: "After 19 victories, Keefe officiated in a losing game."

Keefe, the son of Irish immigrants, grew up in Cambridge, Mass. His father, Patrick, was a builder who was working in the South at the outbreak of the Civil War. Rather than serve in the Confederate Army, Patrick spent three years in prison manufacturing bullets for the Rebels. Two of Patrick's brothers were killed fighting for the Union.

When he returned home, Patrick found his son, then 9 years old, already deeply interested in baseball. Despite parental objections, Tim continued to pitch, firing his fastball and curve and pioneering in the development of a change of pace.

At 29, Keefe was a mainstay of the New York staff, teaming with Smiling Mickey Welch to form one of the most potent mound duos of the day.

The righthander was a quiet, gentle man off the field who, at the peak of his career, studied shorthand so he would have a skill if his arm should fail him.

In 1887, Tim missed several weeks of the season as the result of a nervous breakdown, suffered after one of his fastballs struck Boston second baseman John Burdock on the temple.

Tim Keefe was a pioneer in the use of a change of pace to complement his fastball and curve.

But Keefe came back strong the next year, which he climaxed by winning four games in a postseason series as the Giants defeated the St. Louis Browns of the American Association.

Keefe, who had held out for $2,100 when he was with Troy some years earlier, demanded $4,500 after his 1888 performance and got it. He was the highest-salaried Giant, followed by pitcher Ed Crane at $3,800 and first baseman Roger Connor at $3,500.

After closing his pitching career with the Phillies in 1893, Keefe applied to N.L. President Nick Young for a job as an umpire. He was hired, but his term was brief. The man who never complained about an umpire's decision as a player made a few unpopular calls in a game at the Polo Grounds, scene of his greatest triumphs. Branded a thief and a robber, Keefe was bombarded with dust and pebbles as he was escorted to safety by gendarmes. That night he telegraphed his resignation to league headquarters.

Keefe returned to Cambridge where he became a real-estate man. He also coached baseball at Harvard, Tufts and Princeton and attended games at Fenway Park and Braves Field on the average of once a week.

After Keefe died at age 76, Welch declared, "I never saw a pitcher better than Keefe. It is true that he did his greatest work at the old distance of 50 feet. But if he had been a modern pitcher at 60 feet, 6 inches, he would have had no superior. He was a master strategist who knew the weakness of every batter in the league. I'd put him in the class of Hoss Radbourn and John Clarkson."

WILLIE KEELER

On opening day of the 1897 season, the diminutive Baltimore outfielder lashed a single and double in five at-bats against Boston. The two hits set a pattern that was to endure for nearly two months, from April 22 through June 18. In 44 consecutive games, Willie Keeler hit safely at least once. For 44 years the old Oriole held the major league record—until Joe DiMaggio broke it in 1941.

Willie was stopped by Pittsburgh lefthander Frank Killen, after Keeler had registered one four-hit game, eight three-hit games, 19 two-hit contests and 16 in which he was held to a single safety.

The son of a Brooklyn trolley switchman, Keeler broke into professional ball with Binghamton of the Eastern League in 1892. Although a lefthanded thrower, Willie made his debut at shortstop. He handled eight of nine chances afield and contributed a single in three tries.

Late that season, Keeler was purchased by the New York Giants and made his debut at the Polo Grounds on September 30 as a third baseman. His single off Tim Keefe of the Phillies was the first of nearly 3,000 hits he would collect during his illustrious career.

Willie fractured his ankle early the next season and was sold to Brooklyn for $800 by Manager John Montgomery Ward, who maintained that the 5-foot-4½ sprite was incapable of withstanding big-league punishment.

Before the 1894 season, Keeler and first baseman Dan Brouthers were traded to Baltimore, where Ned Hanlon converted Willie into an outfielder. With his natural speed and reliable glove, Willie was in his element in right field, but it was as a batter that he gained his greatest distinction.

With Keeler batting first and John McGraw second, the Orioles became proficient in the hit-and-run play. And they perfected the "Baltimore chop," the slick maneuver in which batters drove the ball into the ground and then sprinted to first base as infielders waited helplessly for the high bounder to descend.

Bat control was Willie's specialty. If infielders played deep, he would bunt for a single. If they played shallow, he would loop the ball over their head. He was so dexterous that when he was asked the secret of his success, he replied, "Keep your eye clear and hit 'em where they ain't." Ever after, batters attempted to imitate his "hit 'em where they ain't" style.

Wee Willie also scampered wildly on the bases. He stole 30 in 1894, raised his total to 57 the next season and 73 in '96. Attempting to lead the Orioles to a fourth consecutive flag in 1897 (the Orioles finished two games back), Keeler batted .432, second only to Hugh Duffy's record .438, and stole 63 bases. His 243 hits were a record until Ty Cobb topped the mark in 1911 with 248. Keeler won another batting title in 1898 with an average of .379, then moved to Brooklyn with his manager, Ned Hanlon, and a few teammates for the 1899 season.

Willie played on championship clubs in Brooklyn in 1899 and 1900, giving him the distinction of performing for five pennant winners and two runners-up in his first seven years as a regular.

When American League clubs raided the N.L. in 1901 and '02, Willie remained loyal to the senior league. However, Frank Farrell and Bill Devery, owners of the New York A.L. club, made Willie an offer he could not refuse prior to the 1903 campaign. Limited for years by the N.L.'s $2,400 salary ceiling, Keeler jumped to the Highlanders and became baseball's first $10,000 player.

When Clark Griffith resigned as manager of the Highlanders in the 1908 season, the owners wanted to offer the job to Keeler. Willie got wind of the plan, however, and went into hiding.

Keeler was a pinch-hitter for the Giants under old pal McGraw in 1910, coached for the Brooklyn Federal League team in 1914 and scouted for the Boston Braves in '15.

He was 50 when death came in a lonely shack in Brooklyn on New Year's Day, 1923.

Willie Keeler is best remembered for his 44-game hitting streak that was a record for 44 years.

GEORGE KELL

Andy High, a scout for the Brooklyn Dodgers, took the stocky, sandy-haired kid aside one day in the early 1940s and said, "You'll never be a major leaguer until you know the disappointment of being released by some club."

Larry MacPhail, majordomo of the Dodgers, was even more negative. "Get rid of him," snapped MacPhail after watching the kid struggle at third base. "He'll never be a ballplayer."

The player was set to take a construction job at an attractive salary when his new wife stepped in and said "Don't quit."

The advice kept George Kell on the baseball trail. Cut loose as a Brooklyn farmhand, he applied for a job with the Lancaster club of the Inter-State League.

"Can you play second base?" asked Manager Tom Oliver.

"Sure," replied Kell with more confidence than honesty.

"You're on," said Oliver in the spring of 1942. Kell did not impress at second base, or shortstop, or the outfield, but an injury to the Red Roses' third baseman created a vacancy that George filled handsomely. By the end of the 1943 season, Kell was a member of the Philadelphia A's. His .396 average for Lancaster that year was the highest in Organized Ball.

Connie Mack scouted George personally. "How would you like to come to Philadelphia?" he asked Kell.

The native of Swifton, Ark., answered in the affirmative. But he was with the A's only a short while when Mack cautioned him, and coach Al Simmons concurred, "You'll never be a major league hitter."

After his earlier discouragements, not even Mack's opinion could deflate Kell. Through courage, concentration and persistence, George developed not only into an All-Star third baseman but a Hall of Famer as well.

One factor in Kell's ascent to the majors that Mack ignored was that he was jumping from Class B, and even though he made the leap during World War II, it still was a big climb. In 1946, Mack traded George to Detroit. The deal, Connie acknowledged later, was a mistake.

Kell suffered from weak knees throughout his career. As a toddler, he would pitch headlong for no apparent reason.

Slick-fielding third baseman George Kell compiled nine .300-plus seasons.

After playing a doubleheader for Lancaster, he found that his knees would not support his weight and wife Charlene spent long hours massaging his knees with hot water to relieve the pain that prevented sleep.

Despite his handicap, Kell was surprisingly agile on the basepaths and drove pitchers to distraction with false starts off the bag.

He also was a mystery to pitchers while in the batters' box, changing positions as often as four times in one at-bat. By noting the alignment of the fielders and using one of the lightest bats in the game, George learned to drive the ball to open areas.

In 1949, the Tiger third baseman—who, according to Mack, would never be a good hitter—won the American League batting championship on the final day of the season. With one game to go, Kell trailed Boston's Ted Williams by three points. A phone call from Charlene in Arkansas inspired him.

"Two hits today will win it for you," said his wife. "Get 'em."

A double and a single in three at-bats raised Kell's average to .3429. Williams, hitless, finished at .3428.

George learned how to play in pain. In May of 1948 at Yankee Stadium, he threw up his hand to deflect a Vic Raschi fastball hurtling toward his head. The sound of breaking bone—Kell's wrist was fractured—was heard in the bullpen, and doctors predicted a long recuperation for George. In 10 days, though, he was back throwing—accurately, but with intense pain.

In August of the same year, again in New York, a savage drive off the bat of Joe DiMaggio struck a pebble and smashed into Kell's jaw. Instinctively, George groped for the ball, picked it up and stepped on the base for a forceout. He then staggered to the dugout, where he collapsed in the arms of the trainer. Having suffered a jaw fracture, Kell missed the rest of the season.

Although only 35, Kell retired after the 1957 season and was hired by CBS to conduct pregame interviews on Game of the Week telecasts. In 1959, the off-season high school teacher in Swifton joined the Detroit broadcasting team as a replacement for the late Mel Ott.

George resigned his $50,000-a-year job after the 1963 season. He was quitting, Kell said, to be with his wife, son and daughter in Swifton. However, after only a year away from the game, Kell was lured back to Detroit in 1965 as a telecaster for weekend games.

JOE KELLEY

The left fielder for Ned Hanlon's fabled Baltimore Orioles of the 1890s was a mite different from most left fielders. In fact, he was unlike any other major leaguer.

The dissimilarity stemmed from a mirror that the outfielder carried with him at all times. Between pitches, it was not unusual for Joe Kelley to withdraw the mirror from his pocket and preen himself in full view of the customers.

But the spectators loved Kelley. He had a rare personal magnetism, and he could inspire the fans to heights of emotion with his behavior on the diamond.

One afternoon, Kelley stirred the fans and players to paroxysms of laughter. It had been his habit to hide a baseball in the tall outfield grass to be used when the proper moment presented itself.

On this particular day, he chased a drive in the alley, picked up the ball and fired it to the infield at the same time that center fielder Steve Brodie snatched the hidden ball and threw it to a baseman. That ended the outfielder's "hidden ball" trick.

A native of Cambridge, Mass., Kelley entertained a youthful dream of pitching for the powerful Boston club of the National League. At 19, he signed with Lowell of the New England League as a pitcher. He performed satisfactorily, too, winning 10 of 13 decisions. But he also played the outfield and batted .331. In addition, he stole 21 bases in 57 games. Such everyday talent was not to be wasted on the pitching mound. Thereafter, Joe was a full-time outfielder.

During the 1891 season, Kelley wore Boston and Pittsburgh uniforms for a total of 14 games. However, at the start of the 1892 campaign he was with Omaha (Western), where he played so well that he was sold to Pittsburgh in June. In September, he was traded to Baltimore for George Van Haltren and played 10 games before the end of the season.

Under the influence of Hanlon, Kelley became a polished player quickly. Regularly each morning when the Orioles were at home, Kelley and Hanlon reported to the

By 1908, Joe Kelley was nearing the end of a career that produced 2,245 hits.

park, where the manager worked on the player's bunting and baserunning. In 1893, Joe batted over .300 for the first of 12 consecutive seasons.

In 1894, when the Orioles completed their two-year leap from last place in the 12-team National League to first, Kelley swiped 45 bases and batted .391.

On September 3, Kelley performed a feat unequalled before or since. He went 9-for-9 in a doubleheader. In the opener, he rapped three singles and a triple. He blasted four doubles and a single in the nightcap.

During his heyday with the Orioles, Kelley spent the off-season as superintendent of a drayage business in Baltimore. On the same day that teammate Hughey Jennings took a bride, Kelley married Margaret Mahon, daughter of James Mahon, part-owner of the Orioles and a leading politician in Maryland.

Joe accompanied Hanlon and several teammates to Brooklyn in 1899 and, as team captain, batted .330 in the first of two pennant-winning seasons.

Kelley jumped to the American League in 1902, returning to Baltimore where his old crony, John McGraw, was now manager. In midseason, however, McGraw went to New York to pilot the Giants and Kelley, with Mike Donlin and Cy Seymour, defected to Cincinnati. Two weeks later, Kelley was named manager of the Reds. His 33-26 record in his first managerial effort helped the team finish fourth.

Joe managed the Reds through 1905, but stayed on as a player in 1906 when his old skipper, Hanlon, replaced him as a pilot.

A stint as manager at Toronto followed and in 1908 Kelley was back in Boston as skipper of the N.L. club. Differences with catcher Frank Bowerman and owner George Dovey led to Joe's dismissal.

Kelley managed Toronto for six more years and then scouted for the Yankees in 1915-16. As an ivory hunter, Kelley earned the thanks of the club's frugal co-owner, Colonel Til Huston, for not recommending the purchase of a single player in an entire season. His negative reports saved the club $150,000.

When Kelley quit scouting, he took a job with the Maryland Racing Commission. His last baseball connection was as a coach with Brooklyn in 1926.

The last survivor of the old Orioles had been ill for a year when death came in 1943 in his adopted city of Baltimore.

HIGH POCKETS KELLY

The tall, righthanded first baseman never could understand why John McGraw demonstrated uncommon patience with him. The 19-year-old kid out of San Francisco went hitless in his first 19 at-bats for the Giants, and often was a strikeout victim.

One journalist wrote that he would retire when the youngster got a hit "because there was nothing more to see."

But McGraw never wavered on George Kelly. His confidence in the player may have stemmed from the fact that the youth was the nephew of Bill (Little Eva) Lange, a star outfielder with the Chicago Colts of the 1890s. Or maybe it was because scout Dick Kinsella had filed a favorable report on the kid. What McGraw didn't know was that Kinsella fell asleep in a Victoria, B.C., hotel room and didn't see the player before sending in a report based entirely on hearsay.

The long drought ended for Kelly on his 20th trip to the plate. He connected with a fastball in St. Louis and smacked a triple. In any other park, it was said, it would have been a home run.

High Pockets Kelly became the Giants' regular first baseman in 1920, and there were distressful overtones to that move. Since Kelly had succeeded Hal Chase, one of the most graceful of all first basemen, the most myopic spectators could spot the difference and were quick to let Kelly know of his inadequacies.

McGraw took the 6-foot-3 Kelly aside.

"Don't listen to what they yell or what you read in the papers," he counseled. "I put you in there because I thought you could do the job. Stick in there and soon those people who are yelling will be cheering you."

By the spring of 1921, Kelly had found himself as a major league hitter. When he socked seven homers in April, New York newspapers printed daily comparisons between Kelly and Babe Ruth, who had clouted a record 54 homers for the Yankees in 1920.

The comparisons were not published long. Ruth went on to hit 59 homers; Kelly finished with 23 (but led the N.L. that season).

George drove in 122 runs during the '21 season, four coming on an August afternoon at the Polo Grounds. The Pirates arrived in New York with a 7½-game lead and were in high spirits as they opened a five-game series against the second-place club.

Pittsburgh led by three runs in the seventh inning when the Giants loaded the bases against Babe Adams. In previous trips to the plate, Kelly had been baffled by Adams' curveball and as he batted with the bases loaded, he received three straight "take" signs from McGraw. The three curves broke out of the strike zone.

After a slow start, first baseman George Kelly won the hearts of skeptical New York Giants fans.

On a 3-and-0 count, Kelly was given the hit sign. Startled by the unlikely development, Kelly looked again. The sign still indicated hit, and when Adams laid a fastball across the middle of the plate, Kelly hammered it into the stands for a grand-slam.

McGraw, smug over his correct call, announced in the clubhouse, "If my brains hold out, we'll win this thing." The brains did and the Giants did.

Constantly that year, McGraw had challenged Kelly to "pull a good play." The chance to muzzle Little Napoleon came in the ninth inning of the last World Series game. With Aaron Ward of the Yankees on first base with one out, Frank Baker slashed a grounder toward right field. Second baseman Johnny Rawlings made a spectacular stop and throw to nip Baker, but Ward—confident the ball would go through—turned second and raced for third, only to be cut down on Kelly's bullet throw to Frank Frisch. The Series was over and so was McGraw's needling about "pulling a good play."

Kelly enjoyed his biggest day as a major league batter at Wrigley Field in September of 1923, hitting a single, double and three home runs.

In 1924, Kelly divided his time between first base and the outfield so that Bill Terry could add lefthanded power to the lineup. George also filled in at second base before he was traded to Cincinnati in 1927. He was acquired by the Cubs to help out in their unsuccessful pennant bid in 1930, and concluded his major league career with Brooklyn in 1932 after playing with Minneapolis.

George toured Japan with major league all-stars in 1931 and '34. He coached the Reds and Braves, managed Wenatchee to a last-place finish in the Western International League and also coached at Oakland where, among other things, he taught Billy Martin how to throw accurately to first base.

MIKE KELLY

There was nobody quite like Michael Joseph (King) Kelly, an intelligent, handsome, mustachioed Irishman from Troy, N.Y.

"King Kel," 5-foot-10½, 185-pounder, could surpass any man going from base to base or bar to bar.

He could drink any two men under the table, arise from his perch and with top hat cocked at a rakish angle, welcome the morning sun.

Kelly also could play baseball in a singular style. He could score six runs in a game (as he did while playing for Boston against Pittsburgh on August 27, 1887), and he could steal six bases in a game (as he did for Boston of the Players League against Cleveland on May 19, 1890).

In the days of the one-umpire system, Mike was not above scoring from second base without benefit of tagging third. What the umpire did not see he could not call.

When a batter lifted a pop foul beyond the reach of the catcher and first baseman, Kelly jumped out of the dugout, shouted, "Kelly now catching for Boston," and made the grab barehanded. No rule said it couldn't be done.

Another time, he duped Jesse Burkett into a putout at the plate. With the St. Louis star on third base, the batter grounded to the shortstop, whose throw to first arrived too late to retire the hitter. Seeing Burkett approach the plate, catcher Kelly dropped his mitt and Burkett slowed down, convinced the third out had been made at first base. However, in a flash, Kelly caught the throw from the first baseman barehanded and tagged out an astonished Burkett.

Kelly was a multi-position player, but it was as a catcher that he became "The $10,000 Beauty" when, in 1887, he was traded by Chicago to Boston for that unheard of sum.

Kelly paid immediate dividends for his new team. In his first five games he made more hits, scored more runs and stole more bases than the rest of the team. The famous cry of "Slide, Kelly, slide" rang loud and often across the Boston Commons.

In Chicago, meanwhile, fans mourned the absence of their favorite. The White Stockings were virtually boycotted except on days when Boston was in town, when the fans thronged the park to cheer for the visitors and hiss the home club.

The King, who earned $3 a week as a paper mill laborer in Paterson, N.J., in his early years, earned $4,000 a season from 1887 through 1889. He supplemented that income with off-season stage appearances, once touring one of the major circuits with Billy Jerome, a leading parodist of the era.

King Kelly was as colorful both on and off the field as anybody in baseball.

The King also was an author. He wrote a book, "Play Ball," which sold for 25 cents and was dedicated to the players and fans of America.

If Kelly had a weakness, it was in "stepping on himself." Chicago journalist O.P. Caylor wrote: "His only fault was a seemingly lasting weakness to fall down without any terrestrial cause, and often while actually waiting to catch a ball, his feet seemed to go into a panic and throw him."

Once Kelly eagerly wagered $100 on himself in a foot race with a notorious slowpoke. Mike took an early lead, then sprawled ignominiously on the ground as his adversary lumbered on to victory. I knew he couldn't run that far without falling at least once," said the smiling winner.

Kelly's lifetime desire to play for a New York team was realized in 1893 when he was 35. He was just a shadow of the athlete that Cap Anson once called "as great a hitter as anyone and as great a thrower, both from the catcher's position and the field, more men being thrown out by him than any other man."

Mike played a handful of games for the Giants, then drifted to the minors.

Kelly opened a saloon in New York with umpire John Kelly (no relation) and then received a call to appear in the Palace Theater in Boston. En route by boat, he contracted a cold that developed into pneumonia.

As Kelly was being carried into a Boston Hospital, the litter bearers stumbled and he slid to the floor. "That's my last slide," cracked the once-great base stealer, who died at age 36 on November 8, 1894.

HARMON KILLEBREW

Ossie Bluege would have bet, willingly and eagerly, that he had seen all that there was to see when he received an order to scout a young slugger in Payette, Idaho, in the spring of 1954.

The farm director of the Washington Senators, a former major league player and manager, was directed by his boss, Clark Griffith, to check on the phenom in the same state where, in 1907, an earlier Washington scout had found a fireballing righthanded pitcher named Walter Johnson. Perhaps the Senators could uncover another gold mine.

Bluege was ill prepared for what he saw. In an Idaho-Oregon Border League semipro game, Harmon Clayton Killebrew clouted a 435-foot home run. Checking out the 17-year-old slugger, Bluege learned that he was batting .847 and that he had collected 12 hits—four home runs, three triples and five singles in as many at-bats.

Bluege was flabbergasted. He wired Griffith that "the sky's the limit," and the club owner, for the first time in his career, offered a bonus contract to a prospect.

Before Killebrew accepted, however, there was a matter of honor to be taken care of. Days earlier he had

As youth gave way to experience, Harmon Killebrew developed into one of the top power hitters in history.

played golf with Earl Johnson and promised the Boston Red Sox scout that he would not sign with a major league club without giving Johnson a chance to match the proposal.

Washington's three-year offer was in the form of a $30,000 package, an annual salary of $6,000, the major league minimum, and a yearly bonus of $4,000. Johnson refused to match the offer and Griffith obtained one of baseball's greatest bargains.

Soft-spoken Harmon became an instant curiosity in the nation's capital. Baseball folks were unaccustomed to seeing muscular machines at Griffith Stadium but, reported the teenager, bulging biceps ran in the family. The former all-state high school quarterback explained that his father had been a collegiate fullback and his paternal grandfather, a Civil War veteran, was reputed to be the strongest man in the Union Army.

To improve on his inherited muscles, Harmon added, he had, in his younger years, wrestled 10-gallon milk pails—full of milk. "That," he said, "will put muscles on you even if you don't try."

Killebrew was not an instant success as a major leaguer. In his early years in the pro ranks, he tried to learn discipline as a batter and to throw like a third baseman rather than like a passing quarterback.

"It took me five years to catch up with major league pitching," he noted. Those years were split between Washington, Charlotte, N.C., Indianapolis and Chattanooga. But when he did catch up, pitchers paid an enormous price.

On opening day of the 1959 season, his first year as a Senators regular, Harmon walloped a homer against Baltimore and later, during a 17-game stretch, he enjoyed five two-homer games. On the final day of the season, he clouted his 42nd homer to tie Cleveland's Rocky Colavito for the league title.

After two seasons as a Washington idol, Killebrew accompanied the Senators franchise to the Minneapolis-St. Paul area, where it was renamed the Minnesota Twins.

Harmon made the transition smoothly and homers continued to fly to distant spots. The clouts were not of the line-drive variety, but high, majestic pokes that invited measurement by public-relations people.

Killebrew won four A.L. home run titles outright, shared two crowns and hit 40 or more homers in a season eight times (reaching 49 twice, in 1964 and 1969). He appeared in 11 All-Star Games, including the 1968 contest at Houston in which, stretching for a throw, he suffered a leg injury and was limited to 100 games that year.

Killebrew was named the American League's Most Valuable Player in 1969, when he also won the first of two consecutive designations by *The Sporting News* as the A.L. Player of the Year.

The punch of Bob Allison (left) and Harmon Killebrew kept Minnesota fans happy through the 1960s.

Along the way Harmon also tied a major league record by hitting two or more homers in each A.L. park in one season (1962), equaled a league mark for most homers in a doubleheader (four) and established a league record for most lifetime homers by a righthanded batter (573).

After hitting only 13 homers in 1974, the 38-year-old slugger was released by the Twins and signed to play with the Kansas City Royals for $125,000, exceeding his top Minnesota salary by $15,000.

Appearing in 106 games (mostly as a designated hitter), Harmon belted 14 homers in 1975 and then retired. "The artificial turf took it out of my legs," he explained, "and I wanted no more of it."

Killebrew intended to enter the cattle business in the Northwest, but plans did not work out. He attended classes to obtain a securities license, and when he achieved that goal, Killebrew and several partners organized an insurance-securities company in Boise, Idaho, approximately 50 miles from his home in Ontario, Ore. Harmon also entered the broadcasting field.

As he carved out new careers, Killebrew could not help but wonder what his home run total would have been had he accepted less money to play for the Red Sox in 1954. Playing half of his games in Fenway Park, with its inviting left-field wall for righthanded hitters, could have swelled his homer total immeasurably.

"When I made my first trip to Boston," he recalled, "and walked out on the field, the wall seemed so close that I could touch it."

RALPH KINER

As a rookie in 1946, the handsome youngster from Alhambra, Calif., led the National League in home runs with 23. There was no question that his future was assured, but it would be even more luminous if he could reduce his strikeouts.

The cure arrived on January 8, 1947, when the Pirates acquired Hank Greenberg, former American League home run king, from Detroit. Greenberg asked to room with the muscular mauler, thereby affording endless hours for teacher-pupil discussions that paid off at the ball park.

Ralph Kiner listened intently as Greenberg imparted the knowledge gained from years of major league experience. Gradually, a finished ballplayer emerged. At season's end, the sophomore slugger had tied Johnny Mize of the Giants for the majors' home run championship at 51.

Greenberg not only impressed on Kiner the value of sleep as a success factor, but discussed at length the science of hitting. He suggested that Ralph spread his feet, stand closer to the plate and, above all, relax.

"In 1946," Kiner explained, I was afraid that when the pitcher got two strikes on me, the next pitch would come at me. I'd bite at the pitch and strike out. With Hank's coaching, I learned to swing only when the ball was over the plate."

Before long, Kiner clouted 15 homers with the count of two strikes.

In his youth, Kiner performed for a West Coast team known as the Yankee Juniors, and it was generally assumed that he was headed for the South Bronx. New York scouts dallied however, and Pittsburgh scout Hollis Thurston beat them to the prize. Thurston delivered Kiner to the Pirates for a $3,000 bonus and a $5,000 salary.

Ralph was 17 in the spring of 1940 when Pirates Manager Frank Frisch inserted him as a pinchhitter against the White Sox in an exhibition game at Pasadena, Calif. The prodigy blasted a 450-foot homer off Bill Dietrich, one of Chicago's better pitchers.

Ralph Kiner, a nine-year slugger in the National League, hits his first American League home run in April of 1955 as a member of the Cleveland Indians. It was the first of 18 in his final season.

By 1952, Kiner's big bat had earned the respect of the Giants (above), who employed a shift during a game at the Polo Grounds. The Pirate slugger gets a handshake from Stan Musial (right) after hitting a ninth-inning homer to send the 1950 All-Star Game into extra innings.

Kiner performed for Albany (Eastern) and Toronto (International) before enlisting in the Navy in 1943. He was a patrol bomber pilot, "but never got into action, never even saw a whale."

Ralph was ticketed for Hollywood (Pacific Coast) in 1946, but his 13 preseason homers and a batting average of well over .400 convinced the Pirates that Kiner deserved a varsity berth.

For the first six weeks of the N.L. season, he struggled badly, batting under .100. Once he found the range, however, home runs followed and his batting average climbed near .250.

Ralph exploded in 1947. He clouted home runs on four consecutive trips to the plate. He slugged five in two games, six in three and seven in four.

In his first four seasons, Kiner clouted 168 homers, more than any previous big-league hitter.

The handsome, wealthy bachelor became the first citizen of Pittsburgh. Groupies virtually demolished his convertible in their uncontrolled adulation. He received 1,000 letters a week.

"He's the franchise," acknowledged General Manager Roy Hamey.

The Pirates were a mediocre team at the time, but fans were loyal, at least until Kiner had his last at-bat of the game, after which they swarmed toward the exits.

Tales of his prodigious accomplishments sprouted around him. One afternoon the Pirates trailed the Cubs, 12-9, in the eighth inning. Kiner, with a temperature of 103, was on the rubbing table in the trainer's room when the call came, asking if he was in condition to pinch-hit.

Weak and trembling, he managed to get to the plate and hit a game-winning grand slam.

At Boston, he powered a homer that knocked the neon tubing off the new scoreboard, nearly 500 feet distant.

Kiner captured the fourth of his seven successive (outright or shared) home run titles in 1949 with 54, two short of Hack Wilson's N.L. record.

After brief terms with the Cubs and Indians, Kiner retired in 1955 and served as general manager of the San Diego (Pacific Coast) Padres.

In 1961, the articulate former slugger joined the White Sox broadcasting team. A year later he was behind the microphones for the New York Mets.

CHUCK KLEIN

One year he was working in an Indianapolis steel mill, stripped to the waist and catching white-hot ingots through an eight-hour shift with no time off for lunch.

Four years later, Chuck Klein was the Most Valuable Player in the National League, the toast of Philadelphia and recognized as the premier slugger in the N.L.

Klein, an Indiana farm boy, was playing for the Keystones Athletic Club in Indianapolis when a Prohibition agent spotted him and recommended Chuck to the owner of the Evansville club in the Three-I League.

Klein stayed with the team through the 13-day training period, but was released on opening day with the managerial admonition: "Kid, you can't time the ball right. You hit too many fouls."

Later, however, a player shortage won Klein a second chance with Evansville. He played only 14 games the remainder of the 1927 season, the result of a leg fracture suffered while sliding into second base. That winter he was sold to Fort Wayne (Central) for $200.

The 1928 season was barely half over when Burt Shotton arrived in Fort Wayne to evaluate the young slugger who had hit 26 home runs and was batting around .330.

The Phillies' manager needed only one glimpse of Klein, who propelled a 400-foot homer. The Phils bought Klein for $7,500.

Barely an hour after alighting from the train, Chuck reported to Baker Bowl, where the Phillies were playing the Cardinals. He was greeted by Shotton, who informed the rookie, "You'll room with Pinky Whitney (third baseman). Now suit up."

Klein rode the bench until late in the game. Shotton then sent him up as a pinch-hitter for pitcher Augie Walsh, and Chuck popped out to infielder Wattie Holm. But the Phils won the 16-inning contest, 7–6. The date was July 30, 1928.

The next day Klein was installed as the regular right fielder, replacing 40-year-old Cy Williams. To mark the occasion, Klein socked a double and single off Grover Cleveland Alexander, but Old Pete won handily.

Chuck Klein, Philadelphia Phillies slugger, watches the flight of the ball along with Boston catcher Rick Ferrell during action in baseball's first All-Star Game at Chicago's Comiskey Park in 1933.

Klein and Phillies teammate Lefty O'Doul take some time away from the batting cage to pose during the 1930 season.

Klein, who played in his only World Series as a member of the Cubs in 1935, scored the tying run on Augie Galan's ninth-inning fly ball during Game 3 against Detroit.

The Hoosier Hammerer turned on a full burst of power in 1929 when he belted 43 home runs, an N.L. record. The final clout, which bounced off the right-field foul pole, was off Carl Hubbell of the Giants.

After being named the No. 1 N.L. player by *The Sporting News* in 1931 and 1932, Klein enjoyed a Triple Crown season in 1933 when he drove in 120 runs, hit 28 homers and batted .368.

Chuck, who played the outfield in the first two All-Star games, was sold by the financially strapped Phils to the Cubs after the 1933 season and was with the Bruins when they unleashed their 21-game winning streak that clinched the 1935 pennant.

Klein rode the bench for the majority of those victories. However, when outfielder Fred Lindstrom injured an ankle in the World Series against Detroit, Chuck returned to action and batted .333 with a home run among his four hits.

Subsequently, Klein was traded back to the Phillies, then went to the Pirates. A third stint with the Phils—which lasted five seasons—rounded out his career.

Chuck staged the loudest hitting show of his 17 years in the majors in 1936 when he hit four home runs for the Phils in a 10-inning game at Pittsburgh, two off Jim Weaver and two off Mace Brown.

In his later years, when it was suggested he had amassed impressive statistics because of the favorable dimensions of Baker Bowl with its high wall only 280 feet from the plate, Chuck rebutted: "Those four home runs weren't hit at Baker Bowl. And while I did get some homers on high flies over the fence, I also lost a lot because line drives that would have cleared the fence in other parks ricocheted off the wall at Baker Bowl."

After retiring as a Phillies coach in 1945, Klein briefly operated a tavern in Philadelphia. An unhappy marriage led him back to Indianapolis. Due to excessive drinking and malnutrition, he suffered from a disease that affected his central nervous system and left one leg partially paralyzed.

The last game he was known to have attended was at Cincinnati in the late 1940s. Chuck spent the evening reminiscing with veteran writers.

Klein was washing his hands after working in the yard in March of 1958 when he was fatally stricken by a cerebral hemorrhage. He was 52.

BILL KLEM

In 1904, a young American Association umpire was officiating a game by himself and receiving steady verbal abuse from a rowdy outfielder.

The umpire had just called a runner safe at second base and was returning to his position behind the plate when, out of the corner of his eye, he saw the bully running toward him. By this time the umpire was at the batters' box, where he calmly drew a line in the dirt with his spikes, turned his back on the player and walked away.

Recognizing the mark as his "dead line," the outfielder drew up quickly and retreated.

The line that Bill Klem drew as a minor league umpire became his trademark and proved effective against the National League's saltiest characters.

Klem was a native of Rochester, N.Y., as was Silk O'Loughlin, an American League umpire who gave young Bill a letter of introduction to President Jim O'Rourke of the Connecticut State League. Orator Jim, former National League outfielder, also was owner, manager and catcher of the Bridgeport club.

In the heat of one game, Klem ejected the Bridgeport shortstop, bringing a torrent of abuse from O'Rourke. "You'll never umpire another game in this league," he shouted.

"Maybe so," said Bill soothingly, "but I'll umpire this one."

Klem joined the National League staff in 1905 and called 'em for 37 years, after which he became chief of staff for the final 10 years of his life.

By common agreement, managers, players, writers and executives rated Bill the best umpire in the N.L. Klem's vote made the decision unanimous.

The scoreboard at the Polo Grounds in Klem's early years was partly in fair territory, partly in foul. The right-field foul line started at the base of the wall, leaped over the scoreboard and then continued upward. One day a New York batter bounced a long drive off the board that Bill ruled foul, bringing an enraged John McGraw from the dugout.

Entering the park the next day, Klem was met by the groundskeeper who told him, "Mr. McGraw asked me to check where that ball hit yesterday. And would you believe it, I could tell by the dent in the board that it was three inches foul."

"Naturally," replied Bill. "I've never missed one in my life."

The legend that was born on that spot was softened years later when the Old Arbitrator elaborated, I never missed one in my heart."

When discussion centers on good umpires, past or present, the name Bill Klem always is mentioned first.

Klem umpired in 18 World Series, and from 1908 to 1918 he missed only two fall classics. In the 1934 Series, Detroit outfielder Goose Goslin made the mistake of calling Klem "Catfish," the one name that Klem despised.

The next day a contrite Goslin sought to apologize to Bill in a Detroit hotel elevator, but the umpire would not let him off that easily. Calling on all his purple prose, Klem berated Goslin in the packed elevator and then doggedly pursued him through the lobby—shouting invectives all the while.

When word of the incident reached Commissioner K.M. Landis, Klem was fined $50. The money was deducted from Bill's Series check.

Maintaining that he was innocent of any wrongdoing, Klem returned the check. Landis sent it back, and for nearly a year the pair played their little game until Klem cashed the check.

While working a Chicago series, Klem visited Landis' office. As he was about to leave, the commissioner remarked, "I understand you play the horses." Most baseball personalities would have trembled and melted in the face of the Judge's withering gaze, but not the Old Arbitrator.

Approaching the Judge's desk, he declared, "Yes, sir, for 35 years . . . and I've always paid 100 cents on the dollar." The subject was never broached again.

Because of the Series incident and his admission that he wagered on the ponies, Klem did not receive a Series assignment from 1935 through 1939. In 1940, though, N.L. President Ford Frick interceded with Landis, asking that Bill be allowed to work the Detroit-Cincinnati classic as a fitting climax to his illustrious career. The request was granted.

Klem retired to Miami where, after a month's hospitalization, he died in 1951 of a heart ailment at age 77.

SANDY KOUFAX

How great he might have been—and what records he might have established—had not an arthritic elbow intervened will remain a subject of speculation for decades.

He was only 30, had won 27 games and led the National League in earned-run average for the fifth consecutive season when he called a press conference and revealed that he had decided to retire rather than risk permanent damage to the arm that had made him one of baseball's all-time pitching masters.

Sandy Koufax could have accepted another fat contract from the Dodgers and made some token appearances. But, as a man of principle, he informed the world that his brilliant career was at an end. The 1966 announcement produced shock waves through-

Koufax is greeted by Manager Walter Alston (left) and trainer Wayne Anderson after throwing his second career no-hitter, an 8-0 victory over San Francisco, on May 11, 1963.

out baseball, for even though his elbow ailment was common knowledge, Koufax had pitched in pain for several years and was expected to continue in the same manner until his fastball no longer left a blue trail and his curveball no longer snapped.

"The arm is more important than any amount of money," Sandy explained.

Koufax was born Sanford Braun, but took his stepfather's name when his mother remarried following a divorce. He earned a baseball scholarship to the University of Cincinnati, where his talents drew the attention of major league scouts.

As a native of Brooklyn, Sandy would have been a natural as a gate attraction for any of the three major league clubs in Greater New York at the time. He worked out at the Polo Grounds, but, he said, "nobody seemed to care, so I left."

The Yankees displayed interest, but backed away when the youngster asked for a bonus. "I felt," Sandy said, "that if I was going to leave college and give up my scholarship to play ball, then I needed money so that if I decided to return to college, I could pay my way."

The Dodgers agreed to the bonus, signing Koufax in 1955 and paying him $14,000. As Sandy left the Dodger office, a Pittsburgh scout met him and revealed that Pirates General Manager Branch Rickey would top any offer by $5,000. Sandy had not signed a contract, but he rejected the offer. He even declined when the proposal was raised by $10,000.

Success was slow in arriving for Koufax. Wildness was a constant companion. According to pitching coach Joe Becker, the kid with the powerful shoulders "needed a loose wrist to get snap in the ball at the point of release, not more muscular tension that he was already creating. But it was hard to get that point across."

After six seasons, Koufax's record was 36-40.

Sandy's turn toward greatness occurred at an unlikely time in an unexpected place. He was with the "B" squad heading out of Vero Beach, Fla., for an exhibition game in the spring of 1961 when catcher Norm Sherry, said, "Why not have some fun today? Don't try to throw so hard and use more curves and change-ups."

The seed took root. In the next six seasons, Koufax won 129 games and lost only 47. He pitched four no-hitters, including a perfect game. He became the first pitcher to strike out 300 batters in three seasons, achieving a record 382 in 1965, and he twice struck out 18 in one game.

The traumatic arthritis that terminated Koufax's career was discovered in 1964 when, after falling on his elbow while making a pickoff throw to second base, Sandy found his elbow so badly swelled that he could neither straighten his arm nor bend it beyond the hooked position it had taken.

"I had to drag my arm out of bed like a log," Koufax reported. "I could actually hear liquid squishing round in my elbow, like there was a sponge in it."

Sandy made his final pitching appearance in the second game of the 1966 World Series, yielding six hits and four runs in six innings against the Orioles, who swept the Dodgers in four games.

Exceedingly poised and articulate, Sandy accepted a 10-year contract, at a reported $100,000 a year, to broadcast Saturday games for NBC. He fulfilled six years of the contract, then retired to the privacy he had treasured throughout his public life.

By 1965, Koufax was dominant and on his way to a shutout over Minnesota in Game 7 of the World Series.

As a second-year Dodger in 1956, Sandy Koufax was far from the dominant pitcher of later years.

NAP LAJOIE

From the time he stepped down off his hack in Woonsocket, RI, to sign his first contract, Napoleon Lajoie was the epitome of grace on a baseball diamond. To him, every play was easy, whether he glided to his left or right, or raced in to make a pickup and throw on a slow, tricky ground ball.

At bat, the big Frenchman swung with crunching force and any third baseman who played shallow in anticipation of a bunt was inviting disfigurement from a blistering smash off the righthanded hitter's bat.

Lajoie did not insist on a pitch being over the plate Once, on a hit-and-run play, he threw his bat at the ball, and singled into right field.

Nap was with Fall River of the New England League in 1896 when a Phillies scout arrived in town to check on outfielder Phil Geier. When the Phils offered $1,500 for Geier, Manager Charles Marston was so smitten by their generosity that he tossed Lajoie into the deal.

Marston's gesture indicates he was unaware of the prize property he was discarding, but the manager wasn't alone. Boston player Tommy McCarthy, sent by Manager Frank Selee to pass judgment on Lajoie, offered this report: "He'll never learn to hit."

Lajoie remained a Phil until 1901, when the promise of a salary far in excess of the National League's $2,400 limit lured Larry to the Athletics of the new American League. He promptly batted .422, which stands as the record A.L. average and ranks second in the modern majors only to Rogers Hornsby's .424.

For a number of years, record books based Larry's .422 mark on 220 hits in 543 at-bats. When an eagle-eyed mathematician notified the record keepers that the numbers figured out to .405, the average was revised without regard to the hits or at-bats. Further research revealed that a typesetter in the early century had set "220" instead of "229," so another change was authorized restoring Lajoie's missing 17 points.

The Phils sued for the return of their star second baseman, and the State Supreme Court ruled that Lajoie could not play for any Pennsylvania team other than the Phillies.

As a consequence, the Athletics traded Lajoie to Cleveland midway through the 1902 season.

Larry was appointed manager of the Cleveland club in 1905. In his honor, the team was called the "Naps," a name it retained until Lajoie departed in 1915 (when Cleveland became the Indians).

Lajoie was a participant in one of the hottest and most controversial batting races in history in 1910.

The crunching bat of Cleveland's Nap Lajoie produced 3,252 hits in a marvelous career.

Several days before the end of the season, Ty Cobb left the Detroit Tigers, confident that his average was high enough to win the championship. He did not figure on Lajoie going 8-for-8 in the final day's double-header at St. Louis.

Seven of Nap's hits were bunts, dropped in front of rookie third baseman Red Corriden, who had been told to "play deep" rather than run the risk of being maimed.

Because Lajoie was popular among his peers and Cobb was fiercely disliked, A.L. President Ban Johnson suspected collusion between Cleveland and St. Louis. But an investigation, in which umpire Billy Evans defended the Browns, cleared everybody's good name. Even with his final flourish, Lajoie just barely lost the batting title.

One of Larry's proudest moments occurred in 1912 when Cleveland fans presented him with a giant horseshoe festooned with more than 1,000 silver dollars. Earlier, he had been awarded a Chalmers car by the manufacturer after his near-miss batting race with Cobb.

Lajoie collected his 3,000th lifetime hit against the Yankees in 1914. Two years later, he closed his big-league career with a triple, hit No. 3,252.

Larry managed Toronto and Indianapolis before retiring to Daytona Beach, Fla., where he died of pneumonia in 1959 at age 83.

In 1912, Cleveland fans presented the popular Lajoie with a giant horseshoe festooned with more than 1,000 silver dollars.

Because the 1910 batting race was so close, both Ty Cobb and Lajoie received the traditional Chalmers car.

KENESAW MOUNTAIN LANDIS

In the 1920s, Will Rogers entertained audiences with his own account of how baseball came to name Kenesaw Mountain Landis as its first commissioner.

"The game needed a touch of class and distinction," drawled the Oklahoma philosopher, "and somebody said, 'Get that old guy who sits behind first base all the time. He's out here everyday anyway.'

"So," concluded Will, "they offered him a season pass and he grabbed at it."

It was true that Landis was a frequent spectator at Cubs and White Sox games and had been a baseball fan since his early years in Logansport, Ind. And he was not unknown at the time. In 1907, the federal judge had fined the Standard Oil Company $29 million in a freight rebate case.

Landis accepted an offer of $50,000 to become the commissioner of baseball, replacing the threeman National Commission that had governed the game for years. He served from 1921 to 1944.

A native of Millville, OH, Landis was the son of

Baseball's first commissioner, Judge Kenesaw Mountain Landis, acted quickly and with authority.

Abraham Landis, a Union Army surgeon who had lost a leg at the Battle of Kennesaw Mountain in Georgia. For unknown reasons, the parents dropped an "n" in their son's name.

Dropping out of high school after two years, Landis dreamed of becoming a railroad brakeman. But when the Vandalia and Southern rejected his application, Kenesaw turned his attention to bicycle riding and gained a reputation for speed at the Indiana county fairs.

He operated a roller rink with a conspicuous lack of success and eventually mastered shorthand and took a job in the South Bend, Ind., courthouse where he decided on a law career. Landis attended the Cincinnati Law School before earning his degree at Union Law School (later called Northwestern University).

In 1905, President Theodore Roosevelt appointed Landis a United States Judge for the Northern District of Illinois. During World War I, Landis imprisoned 94 members of the International Workers of the World. Weeks later, his office was bombed, but he was absent at the time.

Landis violently opposed gambling, horse racing and baseball officials who attempted to operate on the fringe of baseball law. His first decision as commissioner freed Phil Todt, a young first baseman who, Landis contended, had been "covered up" for two years by Branch Rickey of the Cardinals. Todt later signed with the St. Louis Browns.

Functioning in an era when the game was trying to recover from the Black Sox scandal, Landis banned pitcher Phil Douglas of the Giants for suggesting that he go AWOL so another club could win the pennant.

Jimmy O'Connell, a Giants outfielder, and coach Cozy Dolan were similarly banished for life for telling Phillies shortstop Heinie Sand, "It will be worth $500 to you if you don't bear down too hard against us today."

Babe Ruth and Bob Meusel of the Yankees were suspended for 40 days at the start of a season for defying the Judge's edict against barnstorming tours the preceding fall, and Landis fined Bill Klem a substantial amount when the veteran umpire loudly and profanely berated a player in the elevator and lobby of a Detroit hotel during the 1934 World Series.

In that same Cardinal-Tiger classic, Landis removed St. Louis outtielder Joe Medwick from the seventh game "for his own safety." Medwick had been the target of fruit showers from the left-field bleacherites after a spiking incident at third base.

Landis was an implacable opponent of the farm system

In the 1934 World Series, Cardinal left fielder Joe Medwick was showered with debris by irate Tiger fans. Landis conferred (above) with Medwick (center) and Manager Frank Frisch and had Medwick removed from the game.

and the hiding of players. In March of 1938, he liberated 91 Cardinal farmhands and fined minor league affiliates Sacramento (Pacific Coast), Cedar Rapids (Western) and Springfield (Western Association) amounts ranging up to $1,000. Moreover, none of the 91 players was permitted to sign with a St. Louis farm for at least three years. One of the freed players was Pete Reiser, who went on to stardom with the Brooklyn Dodgers.

On January 14, 1940, the Landis ax fell again. Once more scores of farmhands were set free, this time the property of the Detroit Tigers. Landis also ordered payments totaling more than $40,000 to a number of other players with whom the Tigers had dealt.

One player whom Landis did not free was Bob Feller. Feller's contract had been owned by several minor league clubs—none of whom he ever joined—before the pitcher broke in with the Indians. Landis based his decision on the fact that Feller and his father "zealously sought" validation of the Cleveland contract.

Landis, who voluntarily cut his salary $10,000 during the Depression, earned $65,000 during his final years as commissioner.

One of the judge's final rulings prior to his death in 1944 at age 78 was to banish Phillies Owner Bill Cox from baseball for betting on his own team.

Landis (above) officially opens the 1928 World Series between St. Louis and the Yankees at Yankee Stadium.

TOM LASORDA

Early in his career with the Dodgers, Tom Lasorda told owner Walter O'Malley that he wanted his tombstone to read, "Dodger Stadium was his address, but every ballpark was his home."

Lasorda went on to say that he wanted to continue to work for the Dodgers after he died. O'Malley asked how that would be possible, and Lasorda replied that he could put the Dodgers schedule on his tombstone, so when people came by they could check to see if the team was at home or on the road.

"Bleeding Dodger blue" became the line used to describe Lasorda during his long association with the Dodgers, which covered years as a player, scout, minor-league manager, major-league coach and 20 years as manager, from 1977 to 1996, making him only the fourth manager in history to manage one club for 20 years or longer—joining the trio of Connie Mack, John McGraw and his predecessor as manager of the Dodgers, Walter Alston.

Lasorda never was promised that he would become manager when Alston retired, in 1976, after 23 years as skipper, but he was so sure it would happen that he turned down earlier chances to manage in Atlanta, Montreal and Pittsburgh. Actually getting the job made all of the work he had done in the minors and as a coach worthwhile.

Lasorda was a lefthanded pitcher, who actually signed with the Phillies when he graduated from Norristown, Pa., High School in 1944. He was sold to the Dodgers shortly thereafter, however, and began his association that was to be interrupted only slightly over the next 52 years.

He met his wife, Jo, at a ballpark in Greenville, S.C., and used a $500 loan from former Dodger executive Buzzy Bavasi to get married in 1950.

Tommy Lasorda, only the second manager in Los Angeles Dodgers history, won 1,599 games for the Dodgers.

Tommy Lasorda led the Dodgers to seven division titles.

Lasorda reached the major leagues in 1954, pitched in four games, and was returned to the minors. He again made four appearances in 1955, and did get his name in the record book by tying the mark of issuing three wild pitches in one inning in a game against the Cardinals. What Lasorda prefers to remember about that game is that he struck out Stan Musial.

In 1956, Lasorda's contract was sold to the Kansas City Athletics and he got his longest stint of major-league experience, pitching in 18 games and compiling an 0-4 record. Combined, his major-league pitching totals were the 0-4 record and a 6.52 ERA in 26 games.

After more years bouncing around the minor leagues, Lasorda ended his playing career and was signed by Al Campanis as a Dodgers scout in 1961. He moved back to the field as a minor-league manager in 1965 and in eight years in Pocatello, Ogden, Spokane and Albuquerque, produced five pennant winners, earning another promotion to Alston's coaching staff in Los Angeles. He further prepared himself for managing in the majors by spending winter league seasons in charge of teams in Cuba, Puerto Rico, Panama, the Dominican Republic and Venezuela.

Taking over for Alston, Lasorda inherited a veteran team filled with many of the players he had managed and developed in the minors, and enjoyed immediate success by leading the Dodgers to the N.L. pennant in each of his first two seasons, 1977 and 1978, but watched them lose each World Series to the Yankees in six games.

Lasorda got his revenge, and his first world championship, three years later when the Dodgers again won the pennant and beat the Yankees in six games in the 1981 World Series.

Lasorda managed his last pennant winner, and another world champion, in 1988 when his underdog Dodgers defeated the favored Oakland A's in five games.

The Dodgers also won a division title but lost in the National League playoffs in 1983 and 1985, and lost in the division series in 1995 during Lasorda's tenure.

Lasorda had a close relationship with his players, and was concerned about their lives in baseball and at home. In exchange he expected their loyalty to the Dodgers and an all-out dedication to the game, the same desire and drive he had as a player.

"Tommy John asked me once what I would do it I ever had a player like myself," Lasorda said, "It scared the hell out of me."

Concerns about his health prompted Lasorda's retirement in 1996, and he concluded his career with 1,599 victories in the 3,039 games he managed. In his 20 years at the helm, there were more than 180 managerial changes in the major leagues.

His flamboyant style and spirited leadership helped Lasorda became one of the leading goodwill ambassadors for the game, and he made frequent appearances talking about his loyalty to the Dodgers and his love of baseball. He was elected to the Hall of Fame in 1997 in his first year of eligibility, becoming the 14th manager enshrined in Cooperstown.

TONY LAZZERI

Tony Lazzeri, who had a reputation for being one of the smartest players in baseball. "Was like a manager on the field." said teammate Frank Crosetti.

To many people, it was an injustice that Tony Lazzeri wasn't inducted into the Baseball Hall of Fame sooner.

But finally, in 1991, the Hall of Fame Veterans Committee inducted the former New York Yankee great into the hallowed Hall. He was loved and admired by all who knew him, but he was a victim of the passage of time. He was a star on a team that was loaded with superstars, including Babe Ruth, Lou Gehrig and Joe DiMaggio. As a result, he was passed over for induction to the Hall. When he finally earned entrance, he had passed away. Lazzeri had died in 1946 at the age of 42 after a fall in his San Francisco home.

"He not only was a great ballplayer, he was a great man," teammate Frank Crosetti said. "He was a leader. He was like a manager on the field."

"He was the guy who taught us what it meant to a big leaguer," Lefty Gomez said. "He taught us what it meant to be a Yankee. What was expected of us, and how we had to behave."

Lazzeri, who suffered from epilepsy, was a great hitter during his 14-year major league career. He collected more than 100 RBIs seven times, and his single-game total of 11 RBIs remains the standard in the American League. But despite those feats, he may be best remembered as a strikeout victim of Grove Alexander in the 1926 World Series. It was a highlight of the great pitcher's career.

With the bases loaded and two outs in the seventh inning of the seventh game of the 1926 World Series, the 39-year-old Alexander entered the game to face Lazzeri, who was a rookie, as the St. Louis Cardinals held a 3-2 edge. Alexander proceeded to fan Lazzeri and subsequently retire the Yankees in the next two innings to seal the victory and Series title for the Cardinals.

Despite that down moment, Lazzeri sported his share of highlights. Perhaps his greatest claim to fame was his association with the 1927 Yankees, considered by many as the greatest squad of all time.

That team collected 110 victories, a total exceeded only once in American League history, then swept the Pittsburgh Pirates in the World Series. Ruth swatted 60 home runs, while Gehrig notched 47. Lazzeri, who stood 5-foot-11 and weighed 160 pounds, held his own with the Yankee sluggers, finishing third on the team with 18 homers. That total also ranked third in the league. He batted .309 that year, the first of five years he would finish above .300.

Lazzeri had a lot of big hits in his career, too, including the second grand slam in Series history in New York's six-game win over the New York Giants in 1936. The following season, his last in pinstripes, he led all Series hitters with a .400 average.

The Yankees purchased Lazzeri's contract for $55,000 following his stellar 1925 season for Salt Lake in the Pacific Coast League, during which he batted .355 and totalled 60 home runs and 222 RBIs while playing 197 games.

Lazzeri, who was also a slick-fielding second baseman, debuted for the Yankees the next year, hitting .275 with 18 homers and 114 RBIs.

"Tony is a great natural player," said New York Manager Miller Huggins after Lazzeri's rookie season. "Make no mistake about that. This is his first year in the majors, but he's a finished player now and his hitting is no flash in the pan. He should improve."

Indeed, Lazzeri continued to get better. He batted a career-high .354 in 1929 and drove in a career-high 121 runs in 1930. He finished his career with a .292 batting average, collecting 178 homers and 1,175 RBIs. While playing in the World Series seven times, Lazzeri totalled four home runs, 19 RBIs and batted .250.

Lazzeri also had a reputation for being one of the smartest players in baseball. He often called strategies, defensively and offensively.

One day, in a game against Detroit, there was a Tiger on first base and the batter tapped a bouncer back to Gomez on the mound. Crosetti dashed to second base for a throw from Gomez, but Lefty threw the ball to Lazzeri, who was on his way to back up the shortstop.

Lazzeri called time and trotted to the mound. "What the hell was that all about?" he asked. Gomez shrugged. "I keep reading about how smart you are," Lefty replied. "I wanted to see what you would do with the ball." Gomez then took the ball from Lazzeri and proceeded to earn the win, "Tony liked a good joke," Gomez said. "But not on the field. He took baseball very seriously."

Lazzeri also looked after his own. More than any other player, Lazzeri eased the path for the remarkable flow of talented baseball players from San Francisco to Yankee Stadium.

"Tony took care of the kids from San Francisco," said DiMaggio, who teamed with Lazzeri and another Bay Area-product, Crosetti, on several great New York clubs.

That San Francisco trio made a lot of noise on the field, but away from the diamond, the three had little to say.

Lazzeri invited Crosetti and DiMaggio to drive with him from San Francisco to the Yankees' spring training site in St. Petersburg, Fla., in 1936. It was a long, quiet journey. None of the three was a big talker. Lazzeri and Crosetti alternated driving, while DiMaggio curled up in the back seat and slept most of the way.

After a couple thousand miles, it occurred to Lazzeri and Crosetti that the rookie in the back seat hadn't taken a turn driving, Lazzeri pulled the car to the side of the road and said, "O.K., Joe, it's your turn to drive." DiMaggio's eyes opened wide. "I don't know how to drive," he said.

"It got a little noisy right about then," Crosetti remembered. "That was a surprise."

In spite of his soft-spoken ways, Lazzeri was very effective at getting his point across on the field, too. "Whenever they thought I wasn't pitching as well as I should have been, Tony or Lou Gehrig would call time out and come over to the mound," Gomez recalled. "For a couple of quiet guys, they could get pretty nasty."

The slick-fielding Lazzeri was a star on a team loaded with superstars, including Babe Ruth, Lou Gehrig and Joe Dimaggio.

BOB LEMON

Cleveland and Detroit players were warming up for an exhibition game at Lakeland, Fla., in 1946 when Birdie Tebbetts of the Tigers addressed a newspaperman covering the Indians.

"What's the idea, why third base?" wondered Tebbetts, nodding to a former Navy man working out at that spot for Cleveland.

There was no special reason, Birdie was told, except that the player was a third baseman.

"You may think he's a third baseman," replied shrewd Birdie, "but I know he's a pitcher. I hit against him during the war in the Pacific and if I never have to bat against him again it will be too soon."

Cleveland Manager Lou Boudreau received more glowing reports, and by midseason Bob Lemon was given his first starting assignment. Two years later, when the Tribe won the World Series, Lemon was a 20-game winner and en route to the Hall of Fame.

Lemon's education as a pitcher was entrusted to coach Bill McKechnie. The canny Scot was not unfamiliar with conversion projects. As manager of the Boston Braves and Cincinnati Reds, he had been instrumental in transforming Bucky Walters from an ordinary third baseman into a superlative hurler.

In 1948, his first season as a full-time pitcher, Lemon joined the ranks of no-hit artists. The righthander, who for years refused to wear a toeplate as a symbol of his distaste for pitching, blanked Detroit, 2-0.

Lemon retired the first 21 batters in a 1951 game against Detroit, then grooved a slider that Vic Wertz slammed into the right-field seats. Lemon retired the next six batters in order.

As a youth in Long Beach, Calit., Lemon was a teammate of Vern Stephens, later an American League shortstop. The legion team was managed by Stephens' father.

Lemon's own father, who had played professionally, groomed his offspring for a baseball career. At 17, Bob was signed to a $100-a-month contract by John Angel, a Cleveland scout. In five seasons, he bounced around the minor leagues with only year-end glimpses of Cleveland. Three years in the Navy and competition against service

Cleveland's Bob Lemon (center) is flanked by teammates Jim Hegan (right) and Dale Mitchell after his June 30, 1948, no-hitter against Detroit.

Lemon came to the Indians in 1941 as an infielder before moving to the mound permanently in 1948.

In the 1950s, Lemon became one of a select group of pitchers to compile seven 20-victory seasons.

Lemon managed the Yankees to a World Series title in 1978, but lost to the Dodgers in 1981.

teams on Pacific islands prepared Lemon for his introduction to major league pitching.

Lemon, one of a select group of pitchers to win 20 games or more seven times, did not enjoy the publicity of more colorful hurlers, but he was highly respected by opposing batters. He was incapable of throwing a straight fastball. His pitches would dip or take off horizontally, even when he threw from third base.

Also, because of his infield experience, Bob was a superb fielder on the mound and could contribute as well from the batter's box. He hit 37 homers for the Indians.

Lemon appeared in four World Series games, beating the Boston Braves twice in 1948 and losing twice in 1954 when the New York Giants swept the Indians.

In the '54 opener, Lemon held the Giants to two runs in nine innings at the Polo Grounds. But Dusty Rhodes' 260-foot fly, a routine out most everywhere else, found the home run range in right field and pinned Lemon with a 5-2 loss. He lasted only four innings in the finale.

Lemon suffered a leg injury in 1957 and an elbow injury the following season. He concluded his career with San Diego (Pacific Coast) in 1958.

Because of his talents as a pitching instructor, Lemon was never jobless after his pitching days. He scouted, coached and managed at the minor and major league levels. In the majors, he piloted the Royals, White Sox and Yankees (getting two stints with the Yanks). He produced a world championship in his initial New York regime (1978), then lost to the Dodgers in the 1981 World Series.

BUCK LEONARD

A salary of $125 a month in the Depression year of 1933 was better than unemployment, but it did not excite a working man's visions of the finer things in life. It required a lot of skimping and a bit of conniving if you were performing in the Negro leagues that functioned in the eastern portion of the United States at that time.

"The thing to do," recalled Walter (Buck) Leonard, "was to borrow enough from the club so you'd be in debt at the end of the season. Then you could be sure they'd have you back next season. But they got wise to that, too, so after a while it didn't work."

Leonard's salary did not remain at $125, of course, but neither did it soar into the stratosphere. By 1942, Buck was earning $500 a month—for a 4½-month season—plus 75 cents-a-day meal money. In 1942, his salary was doubled to $1,000 a month, and he hit the top in 1948 when he earned $10,000 for summer and winter play.

That was the pay scale for the Negro League's top hitter (.391) in 1948 and one of the leading home run hitters (42) in 1942.

Leonard, nicknamed Buck by a brother who could not pronounce Buddy (the family's pet name for Walter), left his Rocky Mount, N.C., home in 1933 to join the Portsmouth Firefighters. In August, he joined the Baltimore Stars and a month later was with the Brooklyn Royal Giants. The next season Buck was the first baseman for the Homestead Grays, with whom he remained for 17 seasons.

The Grays originally were based in Pittsburgh, but starting in 1937 they were a two-city club, playing in Pittsburgh when the Pirates were on the road and in Washington when the Senators were out of town. In the course of a year, the Grays played 200-210 games.

"We'd play a semipro team, say, in Rockville, Md.," Buck once recalled, "and then a league game at Griffith Stadium at night. Or we'd play semipro teams around Pittsburgh. We'd start around 6:30 and get in as many innings as we could before dark. The Grays would get $75-$100 a game. But weekends was when you were really expected to make enough money to pay off your players. These were the games you played in Forbes Field, Griffith Stadium or Yankee Stadium. They were called 'Getting-Out-of-the-Hole-Days.'"

Frequently, the Grays departed by bus from Pittsburgh early on a Sunday morning, drove 220 miles to Washington and reported to the park by 11:30. If the players weren't there at the appointed hour, the gates would not be opened.

After a doubleheader—one game lasting seven innings—the Grays returned to their three hotel rooms for showers, then grabbed a bite to eat and boarded the bus to doze as well as they could until they tumbled into bed in Pittsburgh at 7:30 a.m.

Playing under such unfavorable conditions, Leonard teamed with Josh Gibson and others to lead the Grays to Negro League titles from 1937 to '45.

"If he (Leonard) batted fourth, behind Gibson," Roy Campanella once noted, "we could pitch around him and make him hit an outside off-speed pitch. He had a real quick bat, and you couldn't get a fastball by him. He was strictly a pull hitter with tremendous power."

Buck was selected for 12 all-star games in which he batted .273 and hit three home runs.

With the young black stars entering Organized Baseball, the Grays succumbed at the end of the 1950 season. Buck was offered a job by Bill Veeck with the St. Louis Browns, but he was in his 40s and declined the invitation.

Instead, the slugger (who had spent his winters playing in Cuba, Puerto Rico and Venezuela) joined the Obregon club of the Mexican League. He also performed for Jalapa in the same circuit. At 48, Buck closed out his career in 1955 with Durango of the Mexican Central League two years after playing 10 games for Portsmouth of the Class B Piedmont League.

Leonard returned to Rocky Mount, where he served as a truant officer and physical education instructor in an elementary school. He also was a director of the Rocky Mount club in the Carolina League and was president of the Buck Leonard Realty Agency.

By 1946, Buck Leonard was an aging first baseman for the Homestead Grays.

FRED LINDSTROM

One evening in the 1920s, John McGraw visited a New York hospital to cheer up his outfielder-third baseman who had suffered a broken leg.

The conversation commenced on a friendly tone. Then the Giants' manager berated Fred Lindstrom for his carelessness.

"I hope you break YOUR leg," replied the athlete.

Blind with rage, McGraw raced from the hospital into the path of a taxi and, true to his player's wish, suffered a broken leg.

Lindstrom's relations with his boss were not always acrimonious. There was one occasion when the Giants trailed Pittsburgh by two runs in extra innings. When Lindstrom came to bat, runners were on first and second with none out. Looking at the coach for a sign, Lindstrom caught no hint of whether to bunt or hit. He strolled to the dugout and asked for instructions.

"Hit a homer on the first pitch," said McGraw.

And that's what Freddie did, slicing a Babe Adams pitch into the right-field seats. Ordinarily, McGraw would have awaited the day's hero in the runway. This time, he raced onto the field to extend congratulations.

A native of Chicago, Lindstrom was an outstanding shortstop at Loyola High School. A workout with the Cubs was arranged, but at the conclusion he was told that the club was not interested. Later, Freddie learned that Manager Bill Killefer had been playing cards in the clubhouse and had not seen the workout.

"Just suppose he'd seen me," Freddie mused in later life. I might have been a Cub instead of a Giant."

A month after the workout, Lindstrom joined Toledo (American Association). The manager was George Whitted and the club president was Roger Bresnahan, onetime catching great of the Giants.

I was only 16, so young that Bresnahan wouldn't let me sit on the bench during a game," recalled Lindstrom. "The team was going so badly, however, that Whitted had to do something. 'That kid's doing us no good in the bleachers,' he told Bresnahan, 'so I'm gonna stick him in the game whether you like it or not.'"

Fred Lindstrom's first big season was 1928, when he hit .358 with 107 RBIs for the Giants.

Two years later, Lindstrom was playing third base for the Giants and batting .333 in the World Series against the Senators.

Freddie was best remembered in that 1924 classic as the third baseman who watched helplessly as a ground ball hit by Earl McNeely struck a pebble and bounced over his head, driving in the winning run in Game 7 of the Series.

A handsome blond with a delightful sense of humor, Lindstrom was the only non-complainer at one time when his teammates lamented loud and long about food and services at a hotel. Asked why he did not join the chorus, Freddie explained, "When a fellow is hitting .240, whatever he gets is much too good for him."

But Lindstrom could show displeasure, too. When the Giants purchased Johnny Vergez in the winter of 1930-31 and McGraw announced that Fred would be shifted to the outfield to make way for the young third baseman, he responded: "Taking me out and moving me to a strange position to make room for a busher . . . I don't like it."

But, just as McGraw had predicted, Lindstrom became an excellent outfielder, with speed and an unerring glove.

Lindstrom's displeasure grew in June of 1932 when McGraw resigned and Bill Terry was named to succeed him. Owner Charles Stoneham had led Freddie to believe that he would be McGraw's successor.

Outspoken as usual, Lindstrom announced to his former roommate Terry, "I'm sorry, Bill, but I can't play for you. Trade me."

Against his wishes, Memphis Bill traded Lindy to Pittsburgh. In 1935, Freddie was peddled to the Cubs, for whom he might have started his career except for Killefer's card game.

Lindstrom appeared with the Cubs in the 1935 World Series and finished his career with the Dodgers the next year. He was only 30.

Lindstrom served for years as baseball coach at Northwestern University and later was postmaster at Evanston, Ill.

He retired from the postal position in 1964 and lived in New Port Richey, Fla., prior to his death in Chicago in 1981 at age 75.

JOHN HENRY LLOYD

In a game at Augusta, Ga., in 1905, the visiting Macon team, too poor to afford proper equipment, presented the unusual sight of a catcher working behind the plate without a mask.

In the third inning, the 21-year-old player's left eye was struck by a foul tip. In the seventh, another tip closed his right eye. Unable to see, he calmly announced, "Gentlemen, I guess I'll have to quit."

The next day the wounded warrior showed up with a wire basket that he strapped over his face to finish the series. The next year, John Henry (Pop) Lloyd showed up in Philadelphia as an infielder. Before long he was performing such extraordinary feats at shortstop and at bat that he gained the sobriquet of "the black Honus Wagner."

A native of Palatka, Fla., and an elementary school dropout, Lloyd arrived in Philadelphia with $1.50 and pocket watch among his few earthly possessions. He joined the Cuban X Giants in 1906 and gained an early following by hitting a game-winning, ninth-inning double in the season opener.

In 1910, Lloyd and several teammates joined the Leland Giants of Chicago, an affiliation that lasted one season. In 1911, Pop was in the East once more, playing with the new Lincoln Giants of New York.

For three years, Lloyd starred under his old Philadelphia manager, Sol White, fielding spectacularly and posting impressive statistics at the plate.

One of the highlights of Pop's career with the Lincoln Giants was a game with the Philadelphia Phillies in 1913. The Giants pounded out 14 hits in a 9-2 victory over Grover Cleveland Alexander, a 22-game winner that season.

Explaining that "wherever the money was, that's where I was," Lloyd moved westward again in 1914, joining Rube Foster's Chicago American Giants, with whom he remained through 1917.

During the winter of 1917-18, Lloyd worked in the Army Quartermaster's depot in Chicago and refused to accompany the Giants to Florida for winter ball. Shortly, he learned he had been displaced as shortstop by Bobby Williams. Lloyd was named manager of the Brooklyn Royal Giants and frequently played first base, hinting that, perhaps, at 34, he had slowed too much to perform adequately at his old position.

From 1918 until his retirement from pro ball in 1931, Pop managed and played for the Royal Giants, the Columbus (OH) Buckeyes, the Bacharach Giants, the Hilldale club of Philadelphia and the Lincoln Giants.

Lloyd topped the .400 batting mark three times. In

John Henry Lloyd poses with fellow Hall of Famer Jimmie Foxx well after his 1931 retirement.

1911, at 27, he batted .475 for the Lincoln Giants. Twelve years later, pushing 40, he batted .415 for the Hilldales and bettered that average at .422 the following season.

Although Pop retired from professional ball in 1931, he did not hang up his spikes. He continued to play with semipro teams around Atlantic City, N.J., until he was 58.

"Pop never got mad at anything, like when people would yell things at him," said a sportswriter who knew him well. "One day a loudmouth guy was yelling at him from the stands and his manager asked him why he didn't yell back. 'Well,' said Lloyd, 'the Lord gave us two ears and one mouth, so I think he wanted us to listen more than we talked. So that's what I do.'"

Lloyd accepted a janitorial job in the post office and for years served as Atlantic City's Little League commissioner.

His adopted city honored Lloyd on October 2, 1949, by renaming the municipal athletic field "Pop Lloyd Stadium." In an emotion-packed ceremony, congratulatory telegrams were read from Jackie Robinson, Roy Campanella, Don Newcombe, Larry Doby and Satchel Paige.

After a two-year illness, Pop died of arteriosclerosis on March 19, 1965, at age 80. In 1974, he was inducted posthumously into the Black Athletic Hall of Fame at Las Vegas, Nev., together with Campanella and Roberto Clemente.

ERNIE LOMBARDI

Ernesto Natali Lombardi, more familiarly known as Ernie Lombardi, was inordinately huge, unbelievably slow and incredibly vicious when he assaulted a pitched baseball with his 46-ounce bat. One pitcher insisted that a line drive off Lombardi's bludgeon sounded like a "sizzling steak" when it passed perilously close to his ear.

Carl Hubbell, the great lefthander of the Giants, actually feared for his safety when facing the 6-foot-3, 225 pounder. Hub called Ernie "the only batter who really frightened me . . . the only guy who I thought might hurt me, maybe even kill me."

Fear was but one emotion imparted by the menacing presence of Lombardi. Amusement was another. Hubbell had to chuckle on the afternoon when the big fellow drilled one of his pitches over the center fielder's head and puffed into third base, only to find two confused teammates already there. They had been puzzled by the umpire's vague signals—was it a putout or was it a base-hit?—and precipitated a triple play on a legitimate three-bagger.

Lombardi captured two National League batting titles, one Most Valuable Player Award and thousands of hearts belonging to fans who admired his multiple skills and shuddered at his painfully slow gait that deprived him of countless infield hits.

Jibes about Ernie's slowness followed him through 17 seasons. With only slight exaggeration, it was said, "He gotta hit a triple to stretch it into a single."

The congenial catcher took the barbs in stride. It was obvious that infielders played far beyond their normal positions knowing that they could throw out Ernie on any ground ball hit in their direction. "Pee Wee Reese was in the league three years," joked Ernie, "before I realized he wasn't an outfielder."

To teammates and rivals alike, Ernie was known as "Lom." He also carried the nickname of "Schnozzola" or "Schnozz," which was bequeathed to him by Jimmy

Ernie Lombardi, alias 'Schnozz,' began his big-league career in Brooklyn.

Durante, the long-beaked comedian who conceded that Lombardi's proboscis was longer than his own. "But mine is more educated," Durante added.

Still a third sobriquet was "Botchy." This traced to Lom's youthful excellence in bocci ball, the Italian version of bowling on the green.

Pitchers seldom threw to a base to keep Lombardi close. The threat of a steal was almost non-existent. Occasionally, though, the tortoise-like hulk fooled 'em. He was credited with eight stolen bases during his career, one of which he cherished above all the others.

It happened in Philadelphia, he said. The year was 1942, when Ernie won his second batting title with a mark of .330. "I broke for second and the catcher was so surprised the ball went out to center field," he remembered, "and when the center fielder let it go through his legs, I ran to third and then made it home."

Lumbering Lom was 18 years old and was driving a delivery truck for the family grocery and produce store in Oakland in 1926 when he decided to play professional baseball. The fact that his father was on a two-week trip and was not present to dissuade his son facilitated the youth's decision.

Ernie broke in with his hometown team in the Pacific Coast League. He was used sparingly his first season, but blossomed into a .398 hitter in 1927 with Ogden of the Utah-Idaho circuit. Lom's lusty hitting carried over into the next three seasons when averages of .377, .366 and .370 earned him a promotion to the Brooklyn Dodgers.

The rookie made his major league debut on April 15, 1931. Batting twice against Harry (Socks) Seibold of Boston, Ernie rapped a pair of singles.

Lombardi batted just under .300 as a rookie. He appeared in 73 games while playing second string to Al Lopez, a second-year major leaguer. Impressive as Ernie's rookie statistics were, Wilbert Robinson envisioned even greater success for the big fellow. The Brooklyn manager had a fetish about huge pitchers and strongly recommended that Lom transfer to the other end of the battery.

Quietly but firmly, Ernie rejected the notion. "I'm a catcher," he insisted, "and before I pitch I'll go back to the Coast league."

Lombardi, pictured above being greeted by New York Giants teammates after hitting a 1946 home run, spent his most productive offensive and defensive years as the Cincinnati Reds' No. 1 catcher.

Such a retreat was unnecessary. After the 1931 season he was traded to the Cincinnati Reds in a multi-player transaction and was a member of the Ohio ensemble in the years of its reconstruction from a perennial tail-ender into a championship contender. During his 10-year tenure with the Reds, Lombardi socked four consecutive doubles in as many successive innings against Philadelphia and also collected six consecutive hits in another game. Ernie was behind the plate on both of Johnny Vander Meer's no-hitters in 1938, the same year he batted .342 and was named the Most Valuable Player in the N.L.

Big Ernie was a member of the Giants in 1947 when that club established a major league record by hitting 221 homers. His fourth round-tripper of the year tied the old mark before Buddy Kerr belted the record-setting home run.

The rugged catcher appeared in four All-Star Games and batted well over .400, using his distinctive interlocking bat grip like that of a golfer. He also played in two World Series, against the Yankees in 1939 and the Tigers in 1940.

It was against the Yanks that Lom suffered his most humillating indignity as a major leaguer. The Yankees had won the first three games, one by a single run, one by

a shutout and the third by the score of 7-3, but trailed, 4-2, after eight innings of the fourth contest. Bucky Walters, a 27-game winner, was on the mound for the Reds when he was sabotaged by his defense in the ninth inning.

Shortstop Billy Myers' error on a potential double play enabled the Bombers to tie the score and three more miscues in the 10th helped the Yanks clinch their fourth straight world championship. Frank Crosetti opened the extra frame by drawing a walk. A sacrifice advanced him to second and Myers' misplay on Charlie Keller's grounder placed runners on first and third with one out. Joe DiMaggio's single plated Crosetti and sent Keller to third. When Ival Goodman fumbled DiMaggio's hit, Keller raced for the plate. The right fielder's throw home arrived before Keller, but Lombardi dropped the ball and then was sent sprawling from the impact of Keller's collision. As Lom lay dazed, DiMaggio also rumbled across the plate, giving New York a 7-4 win.

Though the incident had no bearing on the outcome of the game, Lombardi was remembered thereafter as "Sleeping Beauty" and for "Schnozz' Snooze." His election to the Hall of Fame in 1986 occurred nine years after his death at Santa Cruz, Calif.

AL LOPEZ

Wilbert Robinson was partial to big catchers and when the Brooklyn manager spotted newcomer Al Lopez in 1928, he exclaimed, "They're sending me midgets. This Cuban ain't never gonna make a catcher. He's too small and skinny."

Uncle Robbie, it turned out, was wrong on two scores. Lopez was not a Cuban, but a Floridian of Spanish ancestry. And, for all his unimposing dimensions, Al developed into an excellent catcher and an even more outstanding major league manager.

Robbie might have looked more kindly on Lopez had he known that four years earlier, when he was a high school student of 16, the Senor had caught Walter Johnson in a barmstorming game at Tampa, Fla.

Lopez was something of a schoolboy celebrity at the time, and was selected to catch the Big Train as a means of drawing the local citizenry to the game. The gimmick worked and the youngster handled the old master with consummate ease.

Johnson's pregame conversation with Lopez consisted of: "Kid, it'll be all fastballs today except some curves that I'm saving for Ike Boone (Red Sox) and Jacques Fournier (Dodgers)."

Johnson set up both players with fastballs and struck them out with curves.

Six years earlier, at age 10, Lopez received a rough baptism to baseball. He was knocked unconscious when struck in the face by a ball. After hospital treatment to repair broken bones, he was given trolley fare to his home, where he was soundly thrashed by his father for playing hooky.

With the Dodgers, Al's start was less painful. On September 27, 1928, the final day of the season, Lopez caught a doubleheader (after appearing in one earlier contest). He went hitless in both games, but was thrilled the next day to read a quote in the newspaper by Jess Petty, Brooklyn's first-game pitcher.

"Al Lopez caught two fine contests. He knows what it's all about," Petty said.

By the time Lopez caught his last major league game, he had set a record by working more than 1,900 contests.

In 1935, the Senor was traded to the Boston Braves in an effort by the Dodgers to obtain pitching help. Al's skill behind the plate was instrumental in lifting the Braves from eighth place to sixth, one rung above the Dodgers.

But the Braves were no turnstile match for the Red Sox, who were flourishing as the "Gold Sox," and on June 14, 1940, Bob Quinn, president of the struggling National Leaguers, called a press conference, at which he

announced: "I've just sold Lopez to Pittsburgh. It was the toughest job I've had to do in 50 years in baseball."

Al closed his major league playing career with Cleveland in 1947 before beginning his illustrious managerial career at Indianapolis.

Graduating to the major leagues, Lopez was an immediate success with the Indians. Drawing from his experiences under Casey Stengel at Brooklyn and Bill McKechnie at Boston, the Senor produced a pennant winner in Cleveland in 1954 and another American League champion with the Chicago White Sox in 1959. Each year he snapped a string of pennants by his old pal, Stengel. Casey had won five consecutive flags before the Indians won in '54 and four straight titles before the Sox triumphed five years later.

Lopez was the complete manager. He knew when to gamble and when to play the percentages. His clubs consistently had the best pitching in the A.L.

He was kind, considerate and understanding. His work with pitchers was exceptional, each being treated as an individual. He was a father confessor to young players, always available to listen to their problems.

Reporters never departed from Lopez with an empty notebook. His patience and charm made him one of the most popular managers. After the White Sox lost the 1959 World Series to Los Angeles, Lopez sat in his office in full uniform, long after his players had left the clubhouse, until the last newsman's questions were answered.

Health problems led to Al's retirement to his Tampa home after the 1965 season. He was back as the White Sox manager for a brief period in 1968-69.

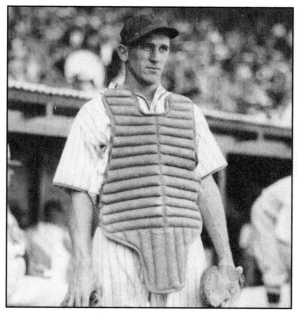

In 1930, Brooklyn's Al Lopez was just beginning his march toward a career-record 1,918 games behind the plate.

TED LYONS

In 1922, when the Philadelphia Athletics trained at Lake Charles, La., coach Harry Davis visited the home of a young pitcher who was compiling an impressive record at Baylor University.

A contract was offered—"and it was a good one," said the hurler—but Ted Lyons rejected it in favor of one tendered by the Chicago White Sox.

Seven years later, A's Manager Connie Mack encountered Lyons in the lobby of a Chicago hotel just before the A's opened the World Series against the Cubs.

"Young man," said Mack, shaking a finger at the big one that got away, "you see what would have happened if you had signed with us. You'd now be with a championship team."

Pitching in rotation with Lefty Grove, George Earnshaw and Rube Walberg, Lyons may have made the A's invincible for years. As it was, he never appeared in a World Series while serving as the backbone of the Chicago staff for nearly 20 years.

Lyons was directed to the White Sox by his college coach, Frank Bridges. In 1923, the White Sox trained in Waco, Tex., site of Baylor University. Bridges invited Chicago catcher Ray Schalk to drop by the campus and catch some pitches from Lyons. Schalk was immediately impressed and recommended Ted to Kid Gleason, his manager.

Ted made his major league debut in St. Louis, pitching one inning of relief in which he retired Urban Shocker, Johnny Tobin and Wally Gerber in order.

Although the White Sox finished in the second division more often than not during Lyons' career, Ted won 260 games. How many he might have won with a contender has long been a subject for speculation.

A gentleman off the field, Lyons was a fiery competitor on the diamond—even when he opposed a close friend. When Moe Berg, erudite Princeton alumnus, was with the White Sox, he and Lyons were the best of cronies. Traded to Washington, Berg singled in his first at-bat against Lyons, driving in the winning run. Berg

touched first base, then accelerated his pace in leaving the field because Lyons, with eyes blazing, was in hot pursuit. Ted overhauled Moe in the clubhouse, where he pounded his pal over the head with a glove and shouted, "A fine friend you are."

Lyons pitched a no-hitter against the Boston Red Sox in 1926—and it was more unusual than most no-hitters.

He walked the first Boston batter on four pitches. The next hitter smacked a vicious line drive on which outfielder Johnny Mostil made a circus catch and threw to first base for a double play. Thereafter, Ted retired every batter in order.

Another time, Lyons went the distance in a 21-inning marathon in which his mound opponent, George Uhle of the Tigers, started Ted on his way to a 6-5 loss with an infield hit.

Lyons' overall record might have been even more remarkable except for a damp and raw night in Houston in 1931.

In a spring exhibition under the lights against the Giants, Lyons suffered a shoulder injury while breaking off a curve. A 73-game winner in the four preceding seasons, Ted won only 35 in the next four.

In his last full major league season, 1942, the 41-year-old hurler started and finished 20 games, posted a 14-6 record and led the

Popular Ted Lyons salutes the White Sox fans who chipped in to buy their star a new automobile in 1940.

American League in earned-run average with 2.10.

Although he could have escaped military service in World War II, Lyons entered the Marine Corps and saw duty in the Pacific.

Twenty-three years after he made his major league debut, Lyons closed his active career in 1946 with one victory in five decisions.

On May 25, 1946, Lyons was appointed manager of the White Sox, replacing Jimmie Dykes. The team that had gone 10-20 under Dykes fashioned a 64-60 record under Lyons to finish fifth.

Ted guided the Sox to sixth place in 1947, but was dismissed after the White Sox dropped to the basement in 1948.

From 1949 through 1953, Ted coached the Detroit pitchers.

He coached for the Dodgers in 1954 and scouted for his old Chicago team for 12 years before retiring to a 750-acre rice farm in Vinton, La.

CONNIE MACK

In light of his gentle and gracious manner in later years, it seemed unlikely—even impossible—for the manager of the Philadelphia Athletics to have been ejected from a game and fined $100 for his vehement protest of a play at second base in 1895.

What was said to umpire Hank O'Day to draw a banishment and such a healthy fine was not revealed, but,

yes, Connie Mack conceded, he was a bit fiery in his youth.

As a catcher for Pittsburgh, the tall and gaunt Mack was not above tipping the bat with his glove on occasion. And if a pitch came near the bat, Connie at times would smack his tongue against the roof of his mouth, deceiving the umpire into believing that the ball ticked the bat.

Mack was born Cornelius McGillicuddy in East Brookfield, Mass., but changed his name so it would fit into a box score. He made his major league debut with Washington on October 7, 1886, hitting a triple and single in a 12-3 romp over Kansas City.

Connie Mack was 47 years old (right) when his A's defeated the Cubs in the 1910 World Series. Mack's Hall of Fame battery during the 1931 Series was catcher Mickey Cochrane (left) and pitcher Lefty Grove.

Mack was a 39-year-old "youngster" (left) in 1902, and 87 years old (above) when A.L. President Will Harridge (left) and Dodgers Manager Burt Shotton honored him for his 50 years with the A's.

Mack was playing manager of the Pittsburgh club in 1896 when he was dismissed by Owner William W. Kerr, who insisted on interfering with strategy on the field. The move proved a stroke of fortune for the 33-year-old Connie. He was invited to Chicago to meet with Ban Johnson, already envisioning a second major league.

Johnson offered Connie the managerial job with Milwaukee in the Western League. Mack accepted and a few years later was told by Johnson, "I think you're the right person to take over the Philadelphia franchise in the American League."

Again Connie accepted the advice and, with the financial backing of Ben Shibe, a sporting goods dealer, Mack established the Philadelphia Athletics. By raiding the Phillies of established stars, such as Nap Lajoie and Elmer Flick, Mack produced a contending club immediately. But when the Pennsylvania Supreme Court issued an injunction that prevented the former Phils from playing with the A's, Mack traded the one-time National Leaguers to Cleveland.

By 1902, Mack had his first flag winner. By 1905, he had another league champion. But the '05 season ended on a sour note when the A's lost the World Series to Christy Mathewson and the Giants, four shutouts to one.

By 1910, the A's were riding high behind their "$100,000 Infield" of Stuffy McInnis, Eddie Collins, Jack Barry and Frank Baker, and a pitching staff that featured Chief Bender, Eddie Plank and Jack Coombs.

Philadelphia beat the Cubs in the 1910 Series, defeated the Giants in 1911 and 1913 and lost to the Miracle Braves in a four-game upset in 1914.

Crushed by the '14 collapse, Mack disposed of most of his stars in 1915 and suffered through a 15-year dry spell until he reached the top again in 1929.

In the first game of the '29 Series, Connie shocked the baseball world, particularly his own players, by starting Howard Ehmke, a 35-year-old righthander who had seen little action late in the season. Ehmke gave his boss his greatest thrill by striking out 13 and beating the Cubs.

Behind a powerful offense featuring Jimmie Foxx, Al Simmons and Mickey Cochrane and a staff headed by Lefty Grove and George Earnshaw, the A's repeated as champions in 1930 when they defeated the Cardinals in the Series. A third flag in 1931 was followed by a Series loss to the Cards.

In his straw hat and high collar, with his scorecard that he used to wig-wag players into position, Mack was now the Grand Old Man of baseball. But the Great Depression was taking a heavy toll at the turnstiles and Connie was forced to sell his high-priced stars for a second time. The A's plunged to the bottom of the league and Mack never again enjoyed a championship.

Connie managed the American League team in the first All-Star Game in 1933 and completed a half century at the A's helm in 1950.

The 87-year-old gentleman was saluted on his final swing around the circuit, including a ticker-tape parade in New York.

A fractured hip, which Connie suffered while getting out of bed, led to Mack's death in 1956 at age 93.

LARRY MACPHAIL

He was abrasive and bombastic, but he also was base ball-smart, with a healing touch for dying franchises and the skill to make healthy clubs even healthier.

In his relatively brief time in the major leagues, Larry MacPhail made enemies, but none was a stockholder in a club that he raised from the death bed. Last rites had been performed on the Cincinnati Reds and Brooklyn Dodgers when MacPhail burst upon the scene and administered his magic potions. And he was the chief executive officer of the Yankees at the birth of a new dynasty following World War Il.

MacPhail's most memorable achievement, though, was the introduction of night baseball to the major leagues. The old guard opposed the move vigorously, but MacPhail was not accustomed to defeat. He persisted in his crusade until, reluctantly, National League club owners granted permission for arc contests in Cincinnati, one against each rival.

When the landmark game was played in 1935 and the fiscal benefits became apparent, resistance melted and the onetime Big Ten Conference football official was hailed as a Moses in baseball's wilderness.

MacPhail, a native of Cass City, Mich., attended Staunton Military Academy in Virginia, where he distinguished himself in the classroom as well as in baseball and football.

At 16, he passed the entrance exams to the United States Naval Academy. On the advice of his father and because of his youth, however, he passed up Annapolis in favor of Beloit College in Wisconsin.

Two years later, he entered the University of Michigan Law School. After another year, he transferred to the George Washington University Law School where he obtained his law degree at the age of 20.

MacPhail joined a Chicago law firm, then resigned within six months because the firm refused to make him a partner. He joined another firm, reorganized a tool company and then resigned from the law firm to join the tool company. At 24, he was president of a large department store in Nashville, Tenn.

MacPhail served in the 114th Field Artillery during World War I and participated in the abortive attempt to kidnap the Kaiser after the Armistice. However, he did obtain one of the Kaiser's bronze ash trays, which he treasured the remainder of his life.

Returning to civilian life, MacPhail settled in Columbus, Ohio, where he practiced law, owned an automobile agency and dealt in real estate. In 1930, he bought Columbus' debt-ridden American Association club and immediately pumped new vitality into it. The team was said to be the first in Organized Ball to travel by air.

In the fall of 1933, the Central Trust Co. of Cincinnati asked MacPhail to revitalize the nearly bankrupt Reds.

With the aid of night ball, a refurbished Crosley Field and shrewd player deals, MacPhail revived baseball interest and put the Reds on the road to success that produced pennants in 1939 and 1940.

By that time, however, MacPhail had moved on to Brooklyn, where he breathed new life into a moribund franchise. The team was $1.2 million in debt and had lost $500,000 from 1933 to 1937 when Larry arrived on the scene at the invitation of the Brooklyn Trust Co. Using his old formulas, MacPhail turned the Dodgers into contenders in a few years and had a pennant winner by 1941.

MacPhail's manager at the time was Leo Durocher, equally as volatile as the Redhead. "He fired me 66 times," the Lip once reported. "It was only six," Larry replied.

Before the close of the 1942 season, MacPhail resigned as president and general manager of the Dodgers to become a lieutenant colonel in the Army Services of Supply.

At the end of the year, Larry and partners Dan Topping and Del Webb bought the Yankees from the estate of Jake Ruppert. For less than $2 million, they acquired the Yankees, Yankee Stadium, four minor league clubs and the rights to 400 players. At a cost of nearly $1 million, MacPhail modernized the park with new and more comfortable seats and organized the swank Yankee Stadium Club.

Amid the Yankees' victory celebration after the 1947 World Series, MacPhail bade a teary farewell and retired to his farm in Bel Air, Md. He was 85 when he died in Miami in 1975 after a lengthy illness.

Larry MacPhail (right) poses with Yankee slugger Joe DiMaggio (left) and Manager Joe McCarthy in 1946.

LEE MacPHAIL

Lee MacPhail was named Major League Executive of the Year in 1966 by *Sporting News.*

Lee MacPhail's baseball career literally began on the ground level. Born on Oct. 25, 1917 in Nashville, Tenn., Lee's first job in the game came when his future Hall-of-Fame father, Larry MacPhail, was the owner of the Columbus, Ohio, team in the American Association. Lee worked as a member of the grounds crew.

The elder MacPhail tried to discourage his son from making baseball his career, believing he would be better off in private business. Like most youngsters, Lee was determined to strike out on his own and he first tried to make it in the game as a player. He was the third baseman on his Swarthmore College team, but his self-analysis revealed that he couldn't hit a curve ball.

Armed with an economics degree from Swarthmore, MacPhail was ready to move into the business world when he graduated in 1939, and assumed he would follow his father into a baseball front office job. His dad, however, had different ideas.

Lee MacPhail promised his father he would try something different for a year, and agreed to take a job in the livestock business. He spent the year working at a stockyard in South Carolina, where one of the things he learned was that he would much rather be working in baseball. "I got pretty good at judging weight on the hoof," he once said, "and that's why Boog Powell could never put anything over on me in spring training."

His father was working for the Dodgers and finally relented to his son's wishes, allowing Lee to begin his career as the business manager of the Dodgers farm team in Reading, Pa., the first job of what would turn out to be a 45-year front office career.

MacPhail then spent a year working as the general manager of the Toronto club in the International League before his career was interrupted by World War II. He taught American History at Deerfield Academy in Massachusetts while waiting to go into the Navy, working in the Dodgers front office on school holidays and in the summer. He entered the Navy in 1944 and served for two years, spending much of the time on active duty aboard the destroyer USS Turner in both the Atlantic and Pacific theaters, before leaving with the rank of lieutenant.

After getting out of the Navy, MacPhail became the business manager of the Kansas City Blues, the top farm team of the New York Yankees, where his father was the chief executive. MacPhail worked his way through the Yankees system to become farm director and then director of player personnel, helping the team win nine pennants and seven world championships between 1948 and 1958.

He moved to Baltimore in 1958 as president and general manager of the Orioles. He left the Orioles organization in 1965 to become an executive in the Commissioner's Office, helping ease the transition from Commissioner Ford Frick to William Eckert. For his work, MacPhail was named the Major League Executive of the Year in 1966 by *The Sporting News.*

MacPhail missed the day-to-day contact with the operations of a team, however, and a year later he returned to the Yankees as general manager and executive vice president. He served in those posts until 1973, when he began a 10-year tenure as President of the American League. During his 10 years of leadership, the A.L. expanded to Toronto and Seattle, and MacPhail helped develop the designated hitter and became known for his ability to reason and moderate disputes.

He resigned in 1983 to become president of the Major League Player Relations Committee, representing the owners in negotiations with the Players Association.

MacPhail said he never felt any pressure following in the career footsteps of his father, who was known as extroverted and tempestuous. Lee MacPhail was known for being soft-spoken and introverted, with a great love for symphony music.

"I never really felt I had to compete with him in some sort of way," MacPhail said in a 1966 interview with *The Sporting News.* "He's a forceful, colorful personality . . . I'm on the quiet side. The important thing, I've always felt, is to be yourself, to try to do your best your own way."

When he was elected to the Hall of Fame by the veterans committee in 1998, MacPhail joined his father as the first father-son duo ever elected to Cooperstown. The family legacy has now been passed on to one of MacPhail's four sons, Andy, who is the president of the Chicago Cubs after serving for several years as the general manager of the Minnesota Twins.

MICKEY MANTLE

Before the arrival of the Oklahoma Kid, nobody expended the time or effort to measure prodigious home runs. When a batter unloaded an extraordinary clout, witnesses could only gape in amazement, chatter excitedly and speculate on the approximate distance.

But that all changed in 1953 when a young superstar of the Yankees bludgeoned a pitch out of Griffith Stadium in Washington. By mathematical calculations and some leg work, an enterprising New York publicist determined that Mickey Mantle's blast had carried 565 feet. From that point, "tape measure homers" were part of baseball's lexicon.

Nobody had ever socked a fair ball out of Yankee Stadium, but Mantle came the closest. One drive struck the facade of the right-field stands, 106 feet above ground level and 390 feet from the plate.

On July 23, 1957, Mantle drove a pitch from Bob Keegan of the White Sox against a seat only two rows from the top of the right-field bleachers.

I thought it was gone," admitted Mantle, who added a single, double and triple for his only major league "cycle."
Mickey smacked a 550-foot drive at Comiskey Park, and in an exhibition game at Forbes Field in Pittsburgh he cleared the rightfield stands. Only Babe Ruth and Ted Beard had performed the Forbes Field feat earlier. At the same park in the 1960 World Series, the Yankee standout became the first to clear the wall in right-center field.

The son of an Oklahoma lead and zinc miner, Mantle was coached to be a switch-hitter from age 5. With his father pitching to him from one side and his grandfather from the other, Mickey mastered the art of swinging from either side of the plate and became the most powerful turn-around hitter in the history of the game.

Mickey Mantle, a 1951 prize Yankee rookie, works in a sliding pit during spring training. In 1950, Mantle (left) was 18 and playing for Class C Joplin.

In a high school football game, Mickey suffered a leg bruise that developed into osteomyelitis. He overcame that handicap, as well as surgery on both knees, a shoulder operation, a broken foot and an ankle so weak that it buckled under him when he batted lefthanded.

Mantle arrived at Yankee Stadium in 1951, fresh from Joplin of the Class C Western Association. After being sent to Class AAA Kansas City during the season and then recalled, Mickey was the Yankees' starting right fielder and leadoff man as the '51 Yankees-Giants World Series got under way. However, he tripped over a drain pipe in right field in Game 2 at Yankee Stadium, suffered torn knee cartilage and missed the rest of the Series.

The youngster's father, Elvin, or Mutt, was a spectator at the Series. The day after his son's injury, Mutt was taken ill and joined Mickey in the hospital. The next summer Mickey's father died of Hodgkin's disease.

Mantle roamed the outfield through 1966, after which he switched to first base for his last two years as a concession to his aching legs.

Winner of one Triple Crown and three Most Valuable Player awards, Mantle performed in 12 World Series in his first 14 seasons as a Yankee. His bases-loaded home run in the 1953 classic against Brooklyn rated as his foremost thrill.

The grand slam was hit at Ebbets Field in Brooklyn just after Dodgers Manager Charley Dressen lifted

Johnny Podres, a lefthander, and brought in righthander Russ Meyer.

Mickey's second most cherished moment occurred in the 1964 Series when his ninth-inning homer off Barney Schultz gave the Bronx Bombers a 2-1 victory over the Cardinals.

When he wasn't hammering baseballs to distant points, the Commerce Comet was burning baselines with the speed that carried him from home plate to first base in 3.1 seconds. He would steal bases at the risk of permanent injury to his legs.

A shy, reticent type, Mickey was never completely at ease among strangers, or even some media people. His happiest hours were spent in the company of Whitey Ford and Billy Martin, who shared Mantle's penchant for late-hour fun.

Mickey retired in 1969, after

In 1953, Mantle connected (above) for a grand slam against the Dodgers in the World Series.

testing his legs in spring training. At a hastily called press conference in Fort Lauderdale, Fla., he announced simply, "I'm not going to play any more baseball."

In his last official at-bat the previous September 28, he had popped up against Jim Lonborg at Fenway Park. Mickey's last hit was a single against Luis Tiant of Boston at Yankee Stadium, September 25, and his final homer came off Lonborg on September 20.

Mantle abhorred speeches, but at the retirement of his uniform No. 7, he told 60,000 Yankee Stadium fans, "Playing 18 years for you folks has to be the best thing that ever happened to a ballplayer."

Mantle abhorred speeches, but took his turn at the microphone in September of 1965 to thank Yankee fans for their support on "Mickey Mantle Day."

HEINIE MANUSH

In the sixth inning of Game 4 of the 1933 World Series, a Washington player was called out on a close play at first base. A heated argument between player and umpire Charley Moran ensued and eventually the player was ejected. Many thought the banishment resulted from the player brushing against Moran after crossing the bag. It wasn't until 31 years later, when he entered the Hall of Fame, that Heinie Manush revealed the real story behind his ejection.

"I was too smart to lay a hand on Moran when I came back to argue the call," said the former outfielder. "But when he bellied up to me and asked what I was gonna do about it, there was temptation that was too much.

"Like all other umpires of that day, Moran was wearing a little black, leather bow tie, the kind that comes ready-made with elastic around the neck. I didn't lay a hand on Moran, but I did pull the tie two feet away from his neck and let it snap back against his throat."

Manush was the last player thrown out of a Series game by an umpire because Judge K.M. Landis, who fined Manush $50 for his conduct, ruled that henceforth only a commissioner would be empowered to take such action.

The loss of Manush conceivably cost the Senators the game. With Heinie gone, Goose Goslin shifted to left field and Dave Harris took over in right field. Harris was the Nats' premier righthanded pinchhitter and would have been called on in the 11th inning when the Senators loaded the bases with one out.

Instead, the call went to Cliff Bolton, a painfully slow runner who grounded into a game-ending double play. The Nats lost the game, 2-1, and were beaten by the Giants again the next day on a Mel Ott home run.

Manush, the seventh son of a famlly of eight, was a 17-year-old student at the Massey Military Academy in Pulaski, Tenn., when he decided to strike out on his own. He went to Burlington, La., where he worked in his brother George's plumbing business. Tired of digging ditches, he drifted westward to Salt Lake City and ultimately to Portland.

Heinie was let go before he got into a Pacific Coast League game and didn't make his professional debut until he joined the Edmonton (Western Canada) club in 1921. After playing at Omaha (Western) in 1922, Manush joined the Tigers in 1923 for the start of a 17-year major league career. He was only 21.

Conditions on the Tigers were not ideal for a rookie. "Ty Cobb (manager) wouldn't even let me bat," Manush once recalled. "Every time I'd go to the plate, Cobb would yell, 'Get outta there, kid.' Finally, Harry Heilmann felt sorry for me and said, 'You can take my turn at bat.' "

Gradually, Cobb softened his attitude toward Heinie, who batted .334 in 1923 to go along with Heilmann's league-leading .403 and Cobb's .340.

"You had to get your hits to stay in there," Manush remembered. "Two hitless games in a row and you were on the bench." Waiting on the bench were Bobby Veach and Bob Fothergill, both .300 hitters.

Manush won the American League batting title in 1926, beating out Babe Ruth with six hits in nine at-bats in the closing day's doubleheader for a .378 average. After his average dipped below .300 in 1927, Heinie was traded to the St. Louis Browns.

In 1928, Heinie again hit .378, only to lose out to Goslin in a batting race that was unresolved until the last day of the season.

A lengthy salary hassle with Browns Owner Phil Ball in the spring of 1930 hastened Heinie's departure to the Senators. Manush played in his only All-Star Game (1934) as a member of the Nats.

After his trade to the Red Sox in December of 1935, Manush closed his big-league career with the Dodgers and Pirates. He managed numerous minor league clubs.

At his Hall of Fame induction in 1964, Heinie encountered Bill Terry, the Giants' first baseman in 1933 when Manush was ejected from the Series game.

"Hey, Bill," Manush said, "wasn't I safe?"

It was very close," replied Terry.

"You haven't been telling the truth for 31 years," snorted Heinie.

A lengthy bout with cancer that cost Manush the power of speech led to Heinie's death in 1971 at age 69.

Heinie Manush played in his only All-Star Game as a member of the Senators.

RABBIT MARANVILLE

Aside from the fact that he had more names than most major league players, James Walter Vincent Maranville was different from his contemporaries in other ways as well.

In 23 National League seasons, he created a legend of wild nights and zany stunts, of incredible escapades on and off the field.

The Rabbit, named for his large ears and small build (5-foot-5 and 155 pounds), led a fabled and charmed life from the time the Boston Braves bought him from New Bedford of the New England League for $1,000.

He was the shortstop of the 1914 Miracle Braves team that beat the powerful Philadelphia A's in four straight games in the World Series, Afterward, Rabbit and several teammates went on a vaudeville tour. In Lewiston, Me., Maranville croaked through a few songs, related a few anecdotes and then announced: "I will now demonstrate how I stole second base against Bullet Joe Bush in the Series."

Sprinting nimbly, he went into a picture slide. But he had miscalculated the distance. Flying over the footlights, he landed on a drum in the orchestra pit and broke his leg.

This was the free spirit of whom Manager George Stallings had said at the end of the Series, I consider Maranville the greatest player to come into the game since Ty Cobb."

One afternoon, Maranville slid between the legs of umpire Hank O'Day on a steal of second base. Stuffily, the dignified umpire checked the rules book for a possible violation. Finding none, he begrudgingly ruled Maranville safe at second.

In New York, Rabbit arranged with pitcher Jack Scott to chase him through Times Square shouting "Stop, thief!" A crowd took up the pursuit, until a breathless Maranville ducked into a saloon that, he knew from experience, had a rear exit.

In St. Louis, Rabbit dove fully clothed into a shallow pool and emerged with a goldfish between his teeth. "There's a mean fish down there that bit me," he reported.

"What did you do?" he was asked.

"I bit him right back," Maranville replied mischievously.

In Philadelphia, Maranville returned from a night on the town to find his hotel room locked and a card game

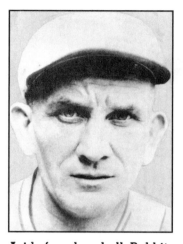

Aside from baseball, Rabbit Maranville was known best for his legendary off-field escapades.

in progress on the inside. Rabbit did not seek admittance by conventional methods. Moments later a card player heard a tapping on the window. Maranville's face was pressed tightly against the pane. Rabbit had gone to an adjoining room and climbed along a narrow ledge, 20 floors above the sidewalk.

Another time, teammates heard screams coming from Rabbit's room. There were sounds of breaking glass, some gunfire and then Maranville shouting, "Eddie, you're killing me."

When the door was broken down, Rabbit and two accomplices paraded past the astonished teammates, greeting them airily with "Hiya fellas."

Thrown out of a game in Brooklin by Bill Klem, Rabbit was observed later in full uniform hawking newspapers outside Ebbets Field and shouting, "Read all about it, Maranville and that big baboon Klem."

When Maranville was fined $100 for drunken driving and $25 for refusing to obey a patrolman's order the same evening, a judge in a Boston suburb commented, "It must have been quite a night. I observe from the record that you played baseball all the next day. Congratulations."

Maranville had one managerial experience, and it was brief. In July of 1925, he was named skipper of the Cubs. A few nights later, he marched through the Pullman car, pouring ice water on sleeping players and shouting, "No sleeping under Maranville's management, especially at night." In early September, he was fired.

The master of the vest-pocket catch was sent to the minors in 1927. The demotion had a sobering effect on Maranville—literally. He took the pledge on May 24, 1927, and never touched another drop.

In 1927, he was acquired by the Cardinals from their Rochester farm and the following season batted more than .300 in the World Series against the Yankees.

By the spring of 1934, Rabbit, now a second baseman, was back with the Braves. Maranville played his last big-league game in 1935, managed a few years in the minors, then served as director of the sandlot baseball program for the New York Journal-American.

On January 5, 1954, Maranville suffered a heart attack at Woodside, N.Y., and died at age 62, a short time before his election to the Hall of Fame.

JUAN MARICHAL

Congratulations were in order after the high-kicking Dominican pitched a no-hitter against the Houston Colt .45s on June 15, 1963. Greeting Marichal were catcher Ed Bailey and first baseman Orlando Cepeda.

From the moment he joined the Michigan City club of the Midwest League in 1958, it was apparent that the high-kicking righthander was mature beyond his years.

Juan Marichal was only 19, but he pitched overhand, three-quarter sidearm, sidearm and underhand. He possessed above-average speed and his control was almost flawless. He struck out 246 batters, walked only 50 and compiled an earned-run average of 1.87.

After one season at Springfield (Eastern) and 18 games at Tacoma (Pacific Coast), the "Dominican Dandy" made his major league debut with the Giants on July 19, 1960, hurling a one-hit, 2-0 victory against the Phillies. The losers' only hit was an eighth-inning single by Clay Dalrymple.

Twelve years earlier, Marichal was manufacturing his own baseball from a piece of rubber, threads unwound from an old silk stocking and adhesive tape. The ball was crude, even lopsided, but it provided the first essential of the deprived youngster's education in the art of pitching in the Dominican Republic.

In 1958, Juan accepted a $500 bonus from San Francisco scouts Horacio Martinez and Alex Pompez.

Marichal's features generally were creased in a smile, and to many he was known as "Laughing Boy."

In the mid-1960s, former Phillies catcher Gus Triandos noted, "The thing that I hated about him was that it seemed so easy for him. It was one thing to go hitless against pitchers like Sandy Koufax or Don Drysdale; at least you could look out there and see the cords standing out on their neck. They look like they're working—and worried. Marichal just stands there laughing at you."

During his prime, when he was winning 20 or more games from 1963 through 1966, Marichal was the dominant righthanded pitcher in the game. Some considered him a superior pitcher to the Dodgers' Koufax.

A two-time National League leader in complete games and shutouts, the Dominican enjoyed his greatest success against the Dodgers. At Candlestick Park, Juan compiled a 24-1 record against Los Angeles. Overall, he was 37-18.

The most serious blemish against Marichal's record occurred at Candlestick Park on August 22, 1965, when he swung a bat at the head of Los Angeles catcher John Roseboro. The third-inning incident followed an earlier pitch that brushed Marichal back from the plate. "You better not hit me with that ball," he told Roseboro. When Roseboro threw too closely to Marichal's ear when returning the ball to Koufax, Juan swung his bat at the catcher, inflicting a gash on his head and a lump on his hand.

Marichal was ejected from the game and subsequently was suspended for nine days and fined $1,750. It was the stiffest penalty in league history.

Marichal was named to the All-Star Game eight times. He pitched a total of 18 innings, allowing only two runs. He was the game's most valuable player in 1965 and the winning pitcher in the first 1962 game and in 1964.

Juan hurled a no-hitter against Houston on June 15, 1963, in which two walks accounted for the only base-runners.

Juan was sold to Boston after the 1973 season, and drew his release after posting a 5-1 record. He was signed by the Dodgers the following spring, but retired after two ineffective performances.

Marichal returned to his native Dominican Republic, where he owned a 1,000-acre farm. In 1983, he became the first Latin American player elected to the Hall of Fame through the regular selection process.

The blemish on Juan Marichal's career came in 1965 when he attacked catcher John Roseboro with a bat. Sandy Koufax tried to intercede.

RUBE MARQUARD

The season of 1912 was a notable year for pitchers. In the American League, Walter Johnson won 16 consecutive games for the Senators and Joe Wood won the same number in succession for the Red Sox.

But the No. 1 achievement was credited to a slim lefthander of the Giants. A few years earlier, he had been ridiculed as "the $11,000 lemon." By 1912, he had blossomed as "the $11,000 beauty."

Richard LeMarquis, a Cleveland native who was better known as Rube Marquard, won his first start of the season, beating the Dodgers, 18-3, in Brooklyn. Marquard pieced together 19 consecutive victories until, on July 8, he lost to the Cubs, 7-2, in Chicago.

"I should have had 20," Rube stoutly maintained the rest of his days. In a game against Brooklyn, Marquard relieved Jeff Tesreau with the bases loaded and none out in the eighth inning. He struck out Jake Daubert and Zack Wheat and retired a third batter on an infield grounder.

When the Giants scored a ninth-inning run to win the game, the official scorer, following the practice of the times, awarded the victory to Tesreau because he had pitched more innings than Marquard. In the more than seven decades that followed, Marquard's winning streak withstood the onslaughts of countless other hurlers.

The lefthander's surname was changed by an unknown baseball writer for a long-forgotten reason. And Richard was christened Rube because an Indianapolis newspaperman discerned a resemblance to Rube Waddell, the great and eccentric lefthander of the Philadelphia Athletics.

In 1908, Marquard was on his way to 367 innings pitched and 28 victories for Indianapolis when major league scouts picked up the scent. Just about every club was represented on September 5 when Rube took the mound at Columbus. It was announced that the Indianapolis club would accept offers at the end of the game. After the lefthander hurled a no-hitter, his hometown Cleveland club (which had been shut out by Rube, 2-0, in a spring exhibition) bid $10,500. The Giants, however, won the prize with a bid of $11,000.

Several days later, Marquard arrived at the Polo Grounds and knocked on the clubhouse door, which was opened by Cy Seymour.

"Who the hell are you?" asked the tough-talking outfielder.

"Marquard," was the answer.

"Hey, fellows," yelled Mike Donlin, "look at the bum John McGraw paid $11,000 for."

In his first start, against Cincinnati, jittery Rube hit the first batter and walked the next two.

Giants pitcher Rube Marquard is pictured in 1910, the year before his first 20-win season.

Marquard beckoned to his catcher. "Maybe I'm trying too hard," he said. "Maybe I should take something off the next pitch."

"Okay," replied Roger Bresnahan, "but don't take off too much or this guy will bust one."

Bresnahan was correct. Hans Lobert drove a pitch to the old car barns on Eighth Avenue.

By 1912, Marquard was the idol of Broadway with 26 victories. After his winning streak, in which his teammates supported him with 139 runs while he yielded only 49, the lefthander won only seven games the balance of the year. But he won twice in the World Series, which the Giants lost to the Red Sox.

Rube's popularity was at an all-time peak. Hearts fluttered wherever the 23-year-old celebrity appeared. He made a movie, and he married Blossom Seely, star of the musical comedy stage. He toured with his wife during the winter, doing dance routines with Miss Seely. The marriage was one of three for the pitcher.

After winning 23 games in 1913—for a three-year total of 73—and participating in his third successive World Series, Rube dipped below the 20-victory total. During the 1915 season he was waived to Brooklyn.

Marquard fractured a leg while sliding in 1919 and won only three games, but he came back to help the team win the pennant in 1920, just as he had done in 1916.

One season with Cincinnati and four with the Boston Braves concluded Rube's major league career. Marquard umpired one season in the Eastern League and pitched his final game with Atlanta (Southern) at age 43.

Marquard later worked as a mutuels clerk at various race tracks. He died in 1980 at age 90.

Willie Mays

Casey Stengel

Sandy Koufax

Warren Spahn

Frank Robinson

Juan Marichal

Robin Yount

Bob Gibson

George Brett

Brooks Robinson

Ernie Banks

Mickey Mantle

Nolan Ryan

Hank Aaron

Whitey Ford

Roberto Clemente

EDDIE MATHEWS

In 1949, when it was mandatory for a major league club to retain on its roster for two years any free agent who was paid more than $6,000, Brooklyn's Branch Rickey offered a young California slugger a $10,000 bonus, plus an additional $30,000 for his family, which the family could have used.

So it was more than surprising, and highly suspicious, when scout Johnny Moore of the Boston Braves obtained the youngster's signature, as well as that of his father, for $6,000.

Moore had been a fine—but not great—major league outfielder. However, the speed with which he grabbed the prodigy was of Hall of Fame quality.

Eddie Mathews was at his high school graduation dance in Santa Barbara, Calif., when, at 12:01 a.m., the first possible moment the youth could be signed, Moore arrived on the scene. The formalities were quickly completed and Mathews was headed for baseball prominence, the seventh player to sock 500 career homers.

Explaining their choice of the Boston offer, the father and son revealed they had studied major league rosters and decided that the Braves offered the best opportunity for a young aspirant inasmuch as third baseman Bob Elliott was in the twilight of his career. Moreover, Eddie had no desire to ride a bench for two years without a chance to develop.

Mathews was a triple-threat football player in high school and had dazzled college scouts in the California championship game. However, baseball was his primary interest, an interest that had been nurtured by his grandfather and father, a Western Union operator who transmitted Pacific Coast League box scores.

By the end of the 1951 season, Eddie was with Milwaukee, then in the American Association. In his first at-bat, Mathews, just weeks short of his 20th birthday, slugged a bases-loaded home run.

Eddie's first major league homer was off Phillies lefthander Ken Heintzelman and the ball sailed over the high, distant wall in right-centerfield at Shibe Park in Philadelphia.

Prodigious homers became an early Mathews trademark. He socked one past the scoreboard in center field at Wrigley Field, and another far over the right-field pavilion in St. Louis. But Eddie always felt that his most powerful blow was struck at Crosley Field in Cincinnati where the ball landed three rows from the top of the center-field bleachers and still was rising at impact.

Boston Braves rookie Eddie Mathews signs autographs before the team's 1952 home opener.

By 1959, Mathews and Hank Aaron provided the Braves with the most awesome left-right punch in baseball.

In 1959, Mathews (above) produced 46 home runs and 114 RBIs. Nine years later, Mathews was in St. Louis (below) for Game 2 of the 1968 World Series as a member of the Tigers. He retired at the end of the season.

As a rookie in 1952, Mathews rapped 25 homers, beating Ralph Kiner's freshman record set six years earlier. On the next-to-last day of the season, Eddie belted three at Ebbets Field, one off Joe Black and two off Ben Wade, to become the first rookie to hit three homers in one game.

When the Braves transferred to Milwaukee in 1953, Mathews was caught up in the civic enthusiasm that helped sweep the team to a pennant four years later. Eddie started slowly in the 1957 World Series, but his home run produced a victory in Game 4 and his high-hopping infield single led to the only run of Game 5.

In the ninth inning of Game 7, when the Yankees loaded the bases with one out, Eddie dived to his right for a backhand stab of Moose Skowron's smash and stepped on third base for a Series-ending force play.

As a thrill, said Mathews, "that play ranked right up there with breaking the 500-homer barrier. I'd made better plays, but that big one in the spotlight stamped me the way I wanted to be remembered."

Eddie was a first baseman for the Houston Astros in July of 1967 when he clouted homer No. 500. The wallop came at the expense of Juan Marichal in Candlestick Park.

Mathews hit 30 homers or more nine straight seasons before he fell one short of that total in 1962. Eddie explained the decline: "One day against Turk Farrell of Houston I took a tremendous swing, missed the ball completely, and tore all the ligaments and tendons in my shoulder. The injury was slow to heal, and even after it did, I became a defensive hitter and developed some bad batting habits. I didn't hit over 30 homers again until 1965."

Mathews finished his playing career as a part-time performer with the 1968 world champion Detroit Tigers.

Eddie managed the Atlanta Braves for part of the 1972 season, all of 1973 and a portion of 1974, until replaced by Clyde King on July 21.

CHRISTY MATHEWSON

Mathewson (right) in 1912 with fellow Hall of Famers
John McGraw (center), Giants manager, and Wilbert
Robinson, a Giants coach.

By 1909, Mathewson
was in the midst of
one of the greatest
baseball careers in
history.

When a 21-year-old pitcher wins 20 games for a
seventh-place team, it is generally agreed that he
is an artisan of inordinate skill.

But that was not the case in 1902 when the New York
Giants attempted to convert Christy Mathewson into a
first baseman, and then a shortstop.

The architect of this transformation was Horace Fogel,
a gentleman of questionable intellect, who was ushered
into the front office early in the year to make way for
George Smith as manager.

In July, Smith was replaced by John McGraw, newly
arrived from Baltimore. "You can get rid of Fogel,"
McGraw notified Owner Andrew Freedman. "Anybody
who doesn't know any more about baseball than that
doesn't have a right to the ball park."

Thus Mathewson was saved for the pitching mound,
where he performed so creditably that he was the first
pitcher elected to the Hall of Fame.

"There is no doubt that Matty was the greatest pitcher
of all time," insisted longtime batterymate Roger
Bresnahan. "He was the perfect pitcher. He always
pitched to the batter's weakness. He had all kinds of stuff
and he knew just where to use it."

Christy Mathewson, known as "Gun Boots" during his collegiate days at Bucknell, was positioned in the back row, second from the right, when this 1899 team picture was taken.

During his collegiate days at Bucknell, Mathewson was known as "Gun Boots" because of his proficiency in drop kicking a football.

Matty broke into pro ball on July 21, 1899, when, pitching for Taunton, he lost to Manchester, 6-5, in a New England League game. The next season, with Norfolk (Virginia), Matty compiled a 20-2 record by July, when he was purchased by the Giants for $2,000.

In addition to a curve and pinpoint control, Mathewson featured a fadeaway (the modern screwball) that he threw about a dozen times a game. The fadeaway, which exerted an excessive strain on his arm, broke into a righthanded batter and, naturally, away from a lefthander.

According to Grover Hartley, a contemporary of Mathewson, the righthander had such magnificent control of all his pitches that he could throw them into an area the size of a grapefruit. One season, Matty hurled 391 innings and walked only 42 batters.

If Christy had a weakness, it was in his habit of coasting with a big lead. On one such occasion, he loaded the bases with none out, bringing McGraw from the dugout. Little Napoleon raved and ranted, but Matty soothed his friend and manager by saying: "Take it easy, it's more fun this way." He then proceeded to strike out the side.

Early in his New York years, Mathewson was nicknamed Big Six after the city's most punctual and efficient fire company. Sam Crane, baseball writer for the *Journal*, attached the name to Matty when he wrote: "Mathewson is certainly the Big Six of pitchers."

In 1903, Matty beat the powerful, pennant-winning Pittsburgh Pirates eight times in as many tries, but his best performance came in 1905 when he shut out the Philadelphia A's three times in the World Series.

Mathewson's most heart-breaking game was the final contest of the 1912 World Series against the Red Sox. With the Giants leading by a run, Boston's leadoff batter in the 10th inning hit an easy fly to center field where Fred Snodgrass muffed the ball, allowing the runner to take second. One out later, a walk put runners on first and third with Tris Speaker at the plate.

Again it appeared the Giants were world champions when the Gray Eagle lifted a foul between first and the plate. First baseman Fred Merkle and catcher Chief Meyers converged, pulled up short and let the ball drop.

Speaker then singled to tie the game and the next batter drove home the winning run with a sacrifice fly.

When his arm went dead in 1916, Big Six was traded to Cincinnati, where he was appointed manager. He pitched his final game on September 4, ending the season with 373 victories, high in the National League.

Matty was an Army officer in World War I. He coached the Giants for three seasons and served as president of the Boston Braves from 1923 to 1925 before he died of tuberculosis at age 45.

WILLIE MAYS

Unquestionably, it was the most spectacular getaway in the history of the minor leagues—a .477 average in 35 games, eight home runs, 30 runs batted in, breathtaking speed and outfield catches that challenged the eye of man.

The Minneapolis Millers' 20-year-old center fielder was the rage of the American Association. Nobody doubted that he was programmed for the major leagues.

Once, in a game against Louisville, the phenom raced to the wall in right-center field, dug his spikes into the fence, leaped and somehow came down with the baseball. The batter, Taft Wright, was so confident he had hit a double that he remained glued to second until Manager Pinky Higgins trotted from the dugout to relay the sad tidings.

The prodigy was at the movies in Sioux City, La., where the Millers had stopped for an exhibition game, when a phone call came from New York: "Have Willie Mays join the Giants immediately."

Willie did not find immediate success in the National League. In his first 26 times at bat, he made only one hit, a mammoth home run off Warren Spahn.

"Boss man," Willie sobbed to Manager Leo Durocher in the depths of his slump. "I'm hurtin' this team. You'd better bench me or send me back to the minors."

"Don't worry," replied the Lip. "You aren't going anywhere. Just keep swinging because you're my center fielder if you don't get another hit the rest of the year."

Willie's drives soon started to find open spaces. For several weeks he batted at a .360 clip and his average climbed. He was on his way to becoming the Rookie of the Year, finishing with a .274 average and 20 homers.

A native of Westfield, Ala., Willie was playing for the Birmingham Black Barons when he was discovered by Giant scouts Ed Montague and Bill Harris. The Boston Braves had offered $7,500 for Mays, with another $7,500 if he made good, but the Barons' financially pressed owner needed immediate cash, and he accepted the Giants' $10,000 bid. Mays also was given a $5,000 bonus.

Two years later, Willie was a fixture in the New York outfield. Constantly, he would run out from beneath his cap and would make two catches on the same play, spearing the ball with his glove, his cap with his right hand.

Mays' miraculous fielding plays were the talk of the league. Willie made a diving catch against the left-field wall at Ebbets Field to rob Bobby Morgan of extra bases. He held a Del Ennis "triple" to a single. And he threw out Joe Adcock at second base on a sure double.

Willie Mays was well known for his fielding artistry, but one of his real masterpieces was unveiled in Game 1 of the 1954 World Series at the Polo Grounds when he made his famous catch to rob Cleveland's Vic Wertz.

But the super deluxe production was a catch and throw at the Polo Grounds against the Dodgers. With Billy Cox on third base, Carl Furillo smacked a drive to right-center field. Just making the catch would have been all that anyone could have asked. But Mays caught the ball, spun in mid-air and uncorked a line throw to catcher Wes Westrum, who tagged out Cox.

Willie was part of the "Little Miracle of Coogan's Bluff" in 1951 before spending nearly two years in military service. When he returned, the Giants captured another pennant, in 1954, when Mays won the first of two Most Valuable Player awards.

Wonderful Willie moved west with the Giants in 1958, but he never enjoyed the immense popularity in San Francisco that had been his in Gotham. In the City by the Bay, fans had vivid memories of Joe DiMaggio and, said Willie, "I was just a visitor from New York."

But Mays' sterling qualities as the complete ballplayer never suffered. The man who never had hit more than two homers in a game socked four at Milwaukee—two off Lew Burdette, one off Seth Morehead and one off Don McMahon—on April 30, 1961. On September 22, 1969, he rapped his 600th homer, joining Babe Ruth in that select group, and on July 18, 1970, he singled for his 3,000th hit, becoming only the 10th player to reach that milestone.

Willie appeared in 24 All-Star Games, compiling a .307 average. His foremost thrill was not one of his several homers, but a catch he made on a Ted Williams drive just as it was about to leave Milwaukee's County Stadium in the 1955 All-Star contest.

Mays closed his career where it had started, in New York, with the Mets in 1973. And, as he had started in 1951, he appeared in a World Series. But, at 42, he was only a shadow of the effervescent youth that brought excitement and joy to baseball fans everywhere.

Mays still had his moments as a Met in 1973, such as this catch that robbed Atlanta's Darrell Evans of a home run.

Mays (left) connects for one of his four home runs during a 1961 game against the Milwaukee Braves. Mays (right) salutes the New York fans who came out to pay tribute to their former star in May of 1963.

BILL MAZEROSKI

Hitting one of the most dramatic home runs in history is what longtime Pirates second baseman Bill Mazeroski is best known for. Yet Mazeroski was considerably more than the unlikely batting hero of the 1960 World Series. Mazeroski, in fact, is considered by many to be baseball's best fielding second baseman ever. He finished his career with eight Gold Gloves and a reputation for extraordinary sleight-of-hand while turning the double play.

Mazeroski, who was born in Wheeling, West Virginia, starred in high school ball in Tiltonsville, Ohio, before signing with the Pirates' organization in 1954. He started his professional career as a shortstop for Williamsport of the Eastern League. Despite a rough start in the play-for-pay ranks (a .235 batting average and a bushel of errors), he nonetheless began the 1955 season in the rarefied atmosphere of the Pacific Coast League—one rung below the major league level.

By this point, Maz had been converted into a second baseman. Mazeroski's offensive shortcomings were exposed in the PCL, where he hit only .170 in 21 games for the Hollywood Stars. Sent back to Williamsport, Maz—still only 18 years old —found the range at the plate and contributed a .293 average and 65 RBIs. His reward: another chance with Hollywood at the beginning of the 1956 season. This time, Mazeroski didn't disappoint. He played flawlessly at second and solved PCL pitching for a .306 batting mark and nine homers in 80 games. His reward: a midseason call-up by Pittsburgh, where he became a fixture for 15 years.

While never a feared major league hitter, Mazeroski made remarkably fast progress with the bat. After showing little pop in his half-season of play in '56, he hit .283 in 1957 with 27 doubles, eight homers and 54 RBIs. And in 1958, he really broke through as a big leaguer. He clubbed 19 home runs (a career high), played in his first

The double play was a work of art for Bill Mazeroski, a gifted fielder who won lasting fame with a World Series-winning home run in 1960.

All-Star Game and earned his first Gold Glove. Furthermore, he was a key part of a young Pirates team that vaulted to second place in the National League standings after finishing in a last-place tie in '57.

Mazeroski's mastery at second base was apparent right from the start. He earned the nickname "No Touch" for his super-quick pivot at second base, where it seemed as if he never touched the ball but merely redirected it to first base. That speed in completing the double play is reflected in the record book, which lists him No. 1 among second basemen in career double plays (1,706), double plays in a season (161) and most years leading the league in double plays (eight). He topped the league in assists nine times, also a major league mark.

Even with his consummate skill afield, it was Mazeroski's batting that etched his name into baseball history. With Game 7 of the 1960 World Series tied at 9-9 in the bottom of the ninth inning at Forbes Field, he homered off the Yankees' Ralph Terry. The magnitude of the blast—no Series had ever ended with a home run—sent Pittsburgh fans into a frenzy. Not only did the home run provide the Pirates with their first Series crown in 35 years, it ended one of the most bizarre Fall Classics in history. The Pirates had been outscored by the Yankees, 55-27, yet somehow found a way to win. Mazeroski was named Major League Player of the Year in 1960 by *The Sporting News*, chiefly for his storybook ending to the Pirates' championship season. His regular-season play was strong, too. He had led National League second basemen in fielding percentage and batted .273.

As his career wound down, Mazeroski enjoyed another World Series title in 1971 as a part-time player for a Pirates club that defeated the Baltimore Orioles. He finished his 17-year career, spent entirely with the Pirates, with a 34-game stint in 1972. Mazeroski collected 2,016 hits in his major league career. His batting average was .260, his fielding percentage .983. His home run total was 138. Mazeroski, who later had coaching stints with the Pirates and Seattle Mariners, was inducted into the Baseball Hall of Fame by the Veterans Committee in 2001.

JOE McCARTHY

In the winter of 1915-16, Ed Barrow, president of the International League, recommended a Buffalo infielder to the New York Yankees.

A deal was in negotiation when the player decided to sign with Brooklyn of the Federal League. When that outlaw league collapsed, however, the infielder signed with Louisville of the American Association.

By that curious happenstance, Joe McCarthy missed an opportunity to wear a major league uniform a decade before he took over as manager of the Chicago Cubs.

McCarthy possessed only average playing talents, but his keen mind and ability to handle players made him a superlative manager. Many superstars who were in a position to know flatly declared that Joe was the No. 1 skipper.

A native of the Germantown section of Philadelphia, McCarthy attended Niagara University for two years before launching his professional baseball career. Managerial experience at Wilkes-Barre (New York State) and Louisville prepared him for the major league call that came in 1926 from the Cubs.

Marse Joe—he was nicknamed by a Chicago writer—took over an eighth-place club and produced a pennant winner in his fourth season. In his rookie year, McCarthy demonstrated his strength as a pilot by firing Grover Cleveland Alexander after the pitcher strayed once too often.

The dismissal occurred in Philadelphia. McCarthy received quick support for his actions. A telegram from Owner William Wrigley informed McCarthy: "Congratulations. I've been looking for a manager with enough nerve to do that."

After the Cubs lost the 1929 World Series to the A's, Marse Joe was given another year to avenge the embarrassment, but when he failed in that mission in 1930, he was fired by Wrigley.

One of the Cubs' brightest stars during the McCarthy regime was Hack Wilson, a patron of night spots and John Barleycorn. Under Joe's tactful discipline, Hack batted .356 in 1930, set a major league record by driving in 190 runs and established a National League mark with 56 homers.

Under another manager in 1931, the slugging outfielder's average plunged to .261 and his homer and RBI outputs dwindled to 13 and 61, respectively.

McCarthy took over the Yankees in 1931, inheriting another touchy situation in the person of Babe Ruth, who had applied for the managerial post and was rebuffed

Joe McCarthy (left) made his major league managerial debut with the Cubs.

By the 1939 All-Star Game, Gabby Hartnett was Chicago's manager and McCarthy was leading the Yankees.

McCarthy had taken over the Red Sox by 1949, with Casey Stengel handling his old duties in New York.

with the statement, "You can't manage yourself, how can you manage others?"

But McCarthy had only one request of the Bambino "Be prompt," Marse Joe requested, and Ruth generally was.

When Joe won a flag with the Cubs in 1929, he became the first pennant-winning pilot without major league playing experience. When he won with the Yankees in 1932, he became the first to produce a champion in both leagues.

While it was not in McCarthy's nature to gloat, he derived a deep sense of satisfaction when the Yanks swept the Cubs in the 1932 Series.

The square-jawed Irishman won seven more titles with the Yankees and won six world championships. He frequently expressed his success formula as "get the players and keep them happy."

Marse Joe had his share of top-flight players who appreciated his talents as a leader. "There wasn't a day," said Joe DiMaggio, "that someone on the Yankees didn't learn something from McCarthy."

Phil Rizzuto added, "He would never say anything behind a player's back and he would never second-guess his men."

Marse Joe seldom displayed irritation, but he bristled during his Yankee heyday when Jimmie Dykes of the White Sox referred to him as "a push-button manager."

Marse Joe also flared when it was suggested that differences with Yankees President Larry MacPhail led to his resignation in 1946. It was strictly a matter of ill health, the skipper insisted.

With improved health, McCarthy accepted the managerial post with the Red Sox in 1948.

McCarthy was 90 when he died of pneumonia in 1978 at his farm in suburban Buffalo.

As Yankee manager, McCarthy cornered eight American League pennants and seven World Series titles.

TOMMY McCARTHY

O f all the colorful nicknames applied to professional baseball players, especially those of the 19th century, few can equal the designation attached to two outfielders with the Boston Nationals.

With their innovative style of play and lofty batting marks, two sons of the Ould Sod were christened the "Heavenly Twins."

Tommy McCarthy and Hugh Duffy were naturals for adulation in Boston, the seat of Irish culture in America. McCarthy, from South Boston, and Duffy, from small-town Rhode Island, were among the first practitioners of the hit-and-run play.

In addition, McCarthy pioneered in the trap play. He would race in from his outfield position, grab a line drive on the short hop and throw out a baserunner standing flatfooted. One season, McCarthy was credited with 53 assists, many of them on the trap-play maneuver.

As a player on the diamonds of Boston, McCarthy caught the attention of Tim Murnane, a prominent pitcher of the day and later a sportswriter.

Tommy received his first notice in public print in the *Sporting Life* in July of 1884: "The Boston Unions are trying a new local player of promise named McCarthy."

In his debut with the Union Association club, Tommy batted ninth and played right field in a 2-1 loss to Chicago. The Boston team collected only one hit off Hugh (One-Armed) Daily and committed nine errors, none by McCarthy.

A righthander, McCarthy also tried his luck at pitching that season but failed to post a victory in seven decisions. His best efforts came in a 2-1 loss to Kansas City and a 2-0 defeat to Milwaukee.

After seeing action with Boston and Philadelphia (both National League clubs) in the next three years, Tommy joined the St. Louis Browns of the American Association, a major league, in 1888. Under the guidance of Charles (Old Roman) Comiskey, Tommy batted .276 in 131 games and stole 109 bases in helping the Browns to their fourth consecutive pennant.

In 1890, when Comiskey jumped to the Players League, McCarthy was appointed manager of the Browns. But the experiment was short-lived, Tommy resigning with a 13-13 record.

Although the A.A. folded after the 1891 season, Browns Owner Chris Von der Ahe maintained that he still owned the rights to his players. The beer baron hired a break-and-entry artist to vandalize McCarthy's hotel room. The escapade netted $19 in cash and a watch, which Chris regarded as a debt paid in full.

Tommy McCarthy's mastery of the trap play led to later adoption of the infield fly rule.

Back with Boston (National), McCarthy registered his best batting averages and scoring statistics as he shared the spotlight with other top names like King Kelly, Bobby Lowe, Fred Tenney and Herman Long.

By this time Tommy was recognized as the master of the trap play, a tactic that umpire Bill Klem noted many years later, led to the adoption of the infield fly rule.

Tommy also was credited with being one of the first to steal a catcher's signs.

After retiring from the game, McCarthy opened a bowling alley and saloon with his "Heavenly Twin" partner. The establishment was known as "Duffy and McCarthy" and was located on Washington Street in Boston. The business prospered until Bostonians developed new Irish heroes.

Tommy scouted for Cincinnati from 1909 to 1912 and for the Boston Braves in 1914 and 1917. In 1918 he managed Newark (International), where one of his players was Ed Rommel, later an outstanding American League pitcher and umpire.

At various times, McCarthy coached baseball at Dartmouth, Holy Cross and Boston College. At Holy Cross, he converted Bill Carrigan from an outfielder into a catcher, the position Carrigan occupied when he starred for the Boston Red Sox.

Another McCarthy product at Holy Cross was Jack Barry, who entertained ideas of being a pitcher until Tommy switched him to shortstop, which Barry played as a member of the Philadelphia A's "$100,000 Infield" in the 1910-14 period.

WILLIE McCOVEY

It was June 1894 when a mere broth of a lad by the name of Fred Clarke celebrated his arrival in the National League by lashing five hits in as many times at bat. It was a record then and remains so still, probably because a tall, slender lad batted only four times in his first major league appearance 65 years later.

Willie Lee McCovey was 21 when his name first appeared in the San Francisco lineup on July 30, 1959. He stood 6-foot-4, weighed 220 pounds and was nicknamed "Stretch" for reasons that became abundantly clear when the first baseman reached for off-target throws.

Willie Lee's debut was made under less than ideal circumstances. For one thing he was wearing a steel brace on his right knee, a reminder of the surgery he had undergone several months earlier. For another, Willie Lee was bone-tired from lack of sleep.

The implausible story began at Phoenix, San Francisco's Triple-A affiliate in the Pacific Coast League, the night of July 29. Phoenix had lost a 10-inning game to Vancouver and McCovey was preparing to leave the park when he was told to see the club's chief executive officer. Wearily, the big first baseman with the .372 batting average and 29 home runs mounted the steps to Rosy Ryan's office.

"The big club wants you," announced the CEO.

"When?" asked McCovey.

"Immediately."

If McCovey would gather up his possessions, Ryan said, a ticket would be available for an early morning flight to the City by the Bay.

Driven by a sudden surge of emotion, Willie chased about the city retrieving possessions he had entrusted to friends. Some items he recaptured, some he did not. Nevertheless, he was at the airport in time to catch his flight.

In San Francisco, McCovey was met by a team chauffeur, who escorted him to Seals Stadium in a style to which he was unaccustomed. Batting practice was already underway when he was introduced to Bill Rigney.

"You ready to play?" asked the manager gazing upward.

"That's what I came for," replied the youngster peering downward through eyes that had not known sleep for more than 24 hours.

"You're in," said Rigney, reaching for a lineup card and scrawling "McCovey, 1b" in the third slot between "Mays, cf" and "Cepeda, 3b."

With that, Rigney tossed the kid to the lions, otherwise known as the Philadelphia Phillies, and Robin Roberts, whose wide assortment of pitches frustrated many a seasoned veteran, let alone a sleep-drugged youngster just off the plane.

The seemingly unfair confrontation was of little import to Willie Lee McCovey. On his first at-bat, the left-handed batter whiplashed a single to right field. Had it been hit with less velocity, it might have been a double. On his second try, he boomed a triple off the center-field wall. There was another single, again drilled too hard to permit two bases, and then a triple off the left-field fence. As Willie pulled into third base, Gene Freese of the Phils greeted him with: "Hey, kid, lighten up on us."

Willie Mac's eight total bases, three runs and two RBIs sparked the Giants to a 7-2 win and put to shame all other coming-out parties since Fred Clarke's in 1894.

One of 10 children sired by a railroad worker in Mobile, Ala., Willie signed a San Francisco farm contract as a 17-year-old. In exchange for his signature, he received $500 and a bus ticket to Sandersville, Ga. Willie

San Francisco first baseman Willie McCovey brought new meaning to the word power.

left a sizable imprint on the Georgia State League by driving home 113 runs in 107 games and was promoted to Danville, Va. A stop at Dallas followed and then Phoenix. At every spot, he evoked loud gasps with his prodigious drives. Qualified observers contended that nobody had ever hit a ball more viciously—or ever would.

McCovey batted .354 in his maiden season with the Giants and was named the National League Rookie of the Year. It was the first of numerous distinctions that would gravitate his way during a 22-year career. In 1969, his 45 home runs, 126 RBIs and .320 batting average were the major ingredients in a Most Valuable Player Award. In 1977, at the age of 39, he was acclaimed the Comeback Player of the Year.

No National League player ever hit more lifetime grand-slam home runs (18). No N.L. lefthanded slugger ever clouted more home runs (521). When he led the circuit in home runs and RBIs for two consecutive years (1968 and '69), he became only the fifth player in major league history to perform that feat.

Coiled at the plate, McCovey struck fear into the most intrepid pitchers. Discretion, not valor, was the overriding principle when a hurler gazed at the menacing mauler ready to spring just 60 feet away. Visions of imminent destruction undoubtedly accounted for his record 45 intentional bases on balls in one season (1969).

After 15 years as a Giant, Willie Mac was traded to San Diego. Dutifully, he accepted the deal, while leaving his heart behind. By 1977, however, he was back home, back in the congenial latitudes of Candlestick Park. He remained active until 1980 and retired as one of the few players to perform in four decades. In one of his last appearances, he blasted a game-winning pinch double against the Dodgers to the utter delirium of 51,000 hero worshippers.

Record books strongly emphasize Willie's right to the Hall of Fame, which he entered in 1986. Yet memory, which often times outmuscles cold statistics, preserves another image of the jolly Giant. It remembers him for the closing scene in the 1962 World Series.

With Giant runners on second and third base and the Giants trailing, 1-0, with two out in the ninth inning of the seventh game, Willie Mac strolled to the plate to face Ralph Terry. In the second game of the Series, Stretch had tagged Terry for a homer. Earlier in the crucial contest, he had cuffed the Yank for a triple. Inasmuch as first base was open and an intentional pass could not influence the outcome of the contest, Yankees brass flabbergasted 44,000 customers by ordering Terry to pitch to the big fellow.

The strategy appeared doomed when Willie Mac hoisted a long fly to right field. It drifted foul by a narrow margin. Then he rocketed a white blur toward right-center field. It was a game-winning—no it wasn't. Second baseman Bobby Richardson took a step to his right and gloved the ball head high. For want of an inch or two, Willie Lee McCovey was denied World Series adulation that comes to but few men.

McCovey and teammate Willie Mays (24) formed one of the most formidable 1-2 punches in baseball history.

McCovey joined the San Diego Padres in 1974, though he left his heart in San Francisco.

JOE McGINNITY

E ven before he pitched his first doubleheader, the husky righthander from Illinois was known as the "Iron Man."

When he joined the Brooklyn Superbas in 1900, the pitcher was asked by a sportswriter, "What do you do during the off-season?"

I work in my father-in-law's iron foundry in Oklahoma; I'm an iron man," replied Joe McGinnity who, in at least one journalist's accounts, was referred to as "Iron Man Joe."

McGinnity gained immortality as the iron man of the pitching mound in 1903 when he hurled three double headers in one month.

Joe was on his way to a 31-victory season for the Giants when he staked his claim to superior stamina and durability. He won a twin bill in Boston, 4-1 and 5-2, on August 1.

A week later, Iron Man Joe repeated the stunt at the Polo Grounds, defeating Brooklyn, 6-1 and 4-3. An excellent runner for a man his size, McGinnity stole home for the Giants' first run in the nightcap and also contributed two singles to the victory.

On August 31, Joe beat the Phillies twice at the Polo Grounds, 4-1 and 9-2.

Two other times in his career, McGinnity pitched both ends of doubleheaders, which he split.

McGinnity broke into Organized Ball with Montgomery (Southern). After pitching for Kansas City (Western), McGinnity dropped out of the professional ranks for three seasons. The nation was in the throes of a financial panic and Joe found that semipro ball in Decatur, Ill., was more profitable, especially for a newlywed.

One season with Peoria (Western Association) led to Joe's acquisition by the Baltimore Orioles in 1899. The following year, McGinnity accompanied his manager, Ned Hanlon, and several teammates to Brooklyn. He returned to Baltimore in the early days of the American League, then moved to the Giants with John McGraw in 1902.

Despite his outstanding achievements, McGinnity appeared in only one World Series. He might have added

Giants pitcher Joe McGinnity, pictured in 1908, was known for his stamina.

a second, except that McGraw refused to take on the A.L. champion Red Sox in 1904.

The following season, McGinnity faced the Philadelphia A's twice in the Series. He lost to Chief Bender, 3-0, in the second game, but defeated Eddie Plank, 1-0, in the fourth.

Iron Man Joe played a key role in the famous Fred Merkle incident of 1908. McGinnity was coaching at third base when Al Bridwell singled home what appeared to be the winning run against the Cubs. But Merkle, the runner at first base, followed the practice of the day and did not touch second. The omission was spotted by second baseman Johnny Evers, who shouted for the baseball. On the throw from the outfield, McGinnity scuffled with Chicago players. He stoutly maintained that he recovered the game ball and threw it into the stands. The ball that Cub teammates threw to Evers, who stepped on the bag for the forceout of Merkle, was, according to Joe, an extra ball supplied from the Cubs' bench.

McGinnity's departure from the majors after the 1908 season did not mean the end of pitching for Joe. As a pitcher and manager, he roamed the minor leagues and won more than 200 games in the bushes. At 52, he won 15 games for Dubuque (Mississippi Valley). He was 54 when he compiled a 6-6 record for Dubuque in 1925.

The following seasons, McGinnity returned to the Dodgers as a coach. He was stationed in the first-base box, his legs crossed and his hands shoved deep in the pockets of his sweater (which players wore in the days before windbreakers). Within weeks after the start of the season, Joe's sweater had been stretched to his knees.

When he got a sign from the bench, Joe sprang into action, uncrossing his legs and slapping his hands on his knees. His gestures brought a droll observation from his manager, easy-going Wilbert Robinson:

"Every time I give Joe a sign, it's like ringing a fire alarm. I don't know if any players are gettin' the sign, but I know everybody in the park is, including the peanut vendor."

McGinnity was an assistant coach at Williams College before he succumbed to cancer in 1929 at age 58.

BILL McGOWAN

Yankee players pursue umpire Bill McGowan during the 1947 World Series.

Bill McGowan was the most colorful and probably the best umpire of his era. When McGowan retired after the 1954 season because of heart problems, he was known to friends and ballplayers as "Number 1." Clark Griffith, who owned the Washington Senators, called him "the greatest umpire I've ever seen."

One of the things that made McGowan great was that he brought a new, vigorous and colorful style to umpiring. After joining the American League in 1925, he worked every inning of 2,541 games over $16\frac{1}{2}$ seasons. But it was the quality of his work—not the quantity—that earned him induction into the Baseball Hall of Fame in 1992.

By the time he reached the majors, McGowan had been umpiring in organized baseball for 11 seasons. A native of Wilmington, Del., he made his debut behind the plate at a college game, substituting for his brother Jack. "He suggested that I take the job," McGowan recalled years later, "but I told him I did not know the rules. Nevertheless, he talked me into going."

Two years later, McGowan was asked to umpire a game in the Tri-State League after an umpire failed to show up. From there, his career continued to build.

He subsequently worked in the Virginia League, New York State League, Blue Ridge League, International League and Southern Association. After noting his proficiency in the latter circuit, Griffith invited him to officiate Washington's spring training games in 1925. McGowan performed so well during the exhibition contests that Griffith recommended him to major league officials. McGowan was subsequently hired to work in the big leagues.

Upon arriving in the majors, the one trait that set him apart from his peers was his activity on the field. McGowan, who worked eight World Series and four All-Star Games, was so active between the lines that Connie Mack used to tell his Philadelphia Athletics, "Don't let McGowan outhustle you."

Among his major supporters was Jimmie Dykes, who held few men in blue in high regard while managing five A.L. clubs and one N.L. team over 21 seasons. "I've seen him work an entire game without missing a pitch," Dykes insisted.

As an example, Dykes recalled opening day in 1953, when his A's met the Yankees. The home-plate umpire was McGowan, who hadn't worked a game in spring training.

"The only spring training he needed was a few minutes of practicing breathing hard so he could blow up his chest protector," Dykes cracked. "Harry Greb used to say the only training he needed for a fight was a hot shower. McGowan always took hot showers, so the only workout he could get was pumping up that rubber fortress, and yet he was 56 years old and there he is on opening day. He's got the suit pressed and he looks sharp. He hasn't looked at major league pitching since October.

"(Alex) Kellner is pitching that day (and wins, 5-0, against New York's Vic Raschi), and what do you know? McGowan calls the greatest game I ever saw in my life. He doesn't miss a pitch."

Many concurred with Dykes' opinion, including Hall of Fame catcher Mickey Cochrane, who entered the American League the same season as McGowan. "[He was] the best ball-and-strike umpire I ever knew," Cochrane said in tribute.

McGowan's pugnacious nature got the best of him in 1948, when he threw his ball-and-strike indicator at Washington pitcher Ray Scarborough and allegedly cursed other Senator players, for which he was suspended and fined $500 by A.L. President Will Harridge.

Four years later, he was suspended for four days after refusing to tell St. Louis sportswriters which players he had ejected from the Detroit bench after the Tigers taunted Satchel Paige of the Browns. Some attributed these blowups to problems brought on by diabetes.

His declining health finally caused him to take a leave of absence during the 1954 season. Although McGowan had been told that a heart condition ruled out umpiring, it was not public knowledge that his career was at an end. Yet baseball people knew, and many called "Number 1" to wish him well, among them Ted Williams, who engaged the umpire in a 15-minute conversation about baseball.

At his funeral four months later, the pallbearers included six major league umpires who had been trained at his Florida umpiring school.

JOHN McGRAW

Honus Wagner was the runner at second base when the next Louisville batter stroked a single to the outfield on which the speedy Dutchman seemed certain to score. When Wagner reached the vicinity of third base, however, the fielder thrust out his hip and knocked Wagner off stride. Honus was out at the plate.

That was the way the fielder, John McGraw, played baseball. His antics could go unnoticed because the attention of the single umpire working the game was directed elsewhere.

When a runner tagged up, intent on scoring on a sacrifice fly, McGraw would slip his finger around the unsuspecting fellow's belt, delaying his start just long enough to produce a putout at the plate.

That trick worked only until Pete Browning unbuckled his belt, leaving it dangling in McGraw's hand as Pete scored.

Despite his size (5-foot-7, 155 pounds), McGraw was a scrapper from the very beginning. In his first day with the Baltimore Orioles, he was referred to as "the batboy." Veteran players crowded onto the bench until the rookie, sitting at the end, was shoved onto the ground. He came up with fists flailing and thereafter was an accepted member of the rough and rowdy crew.

The Truxton, N.Y., Irishman joined the Orioles in 1892 and was a leading actor in baseball drama for 40 years. His first Baltimore contract called for $1,500 a year, uncommonly high for a rookie.

McGraw sparked the Orioles to three pennants in the 1890s. He was as fast on his feet as he was with his fists. He was expert on the hit-and-run play and he could foul pitches off almost at will. Once he fouled off 15 consecutive pitches from Clark Griffith of Chicago. At the time, fouls were not considered strikes.

At another time against Griffith, McGraw maneuvered his knee over the plate and was struck by the ball. Umpire Hank O'Day called, "Strike one." Griffith threw again, another nick on the knee. "Strike two." The Old Fox threw again and McGraw took a third pitch off his knee. "Yer out," shouted O'Day as McGraw walked away boiling.

When Manager Ned Hanlon and several key players shifted to Brooklyn in 1899, McGraw stayed behind. He and catcher Wilbert Robinson owned a saloon-bowling

John McGraw was a 17-year-old first-year player (left) for Olean of the New York-Pennsylvania League in 1890.

By 1902, he was the player-manager of the New York Giants.

alley called "The Diamond" that needed attention and, for a second reason, John was named manager of the Orioles.

Little Napoleon played for St. Louis in 1900, then accepted Ban Johnson's suggestion that he take over the Baltimore franchise in the American League, a new major league.

But in July of 1902, the accomplished umpire baiter grew disenchanted with Johnson for the manner in which the league president backed his arbiters. McGraw accepted an offer to manage the New York Giants. His release was purchased for $10,000, which represented a dividend to McGraw, who was a Baltimore stockholder.

McGraw made his New York debut on July 19, 1902, and the Giants lost to Philadelphia, 4-3. Four days later, he posted his initial victory, 4-1, at Brooklyn.

In 30 years as the Giants' manager, McGraw won 10 pennants and three World Series. He finished out of the first division only twice.

One sure method of infuriating McGraw was to call him "Muggsy," a fact unknown to Brooklyn's Tommy McMillan. Passing McGraw during pregame activities, the rookie called out airily, "Hiya, Muggsy." McGraw unleashed a torrent of oaths on the kid, who apologized the next day after learning the seriousness of his offense. McGraw was so affected by the apology that he escorted McMillan to short-stop where he gave him pointers on playing the position.

McGraw was earning about $75,000 late in his career and also received dividends as a stockholder in the Giants. The first modern manager to win four consecutive pennants, he was a soft touch for old players, generally finding jobs for them in the organization.

He also was free with his money. When the Florida land boom burst in the 1920s—a promotion to which McGraw had lent his name—and a number of former players went broke in their investments, John gave up nearly all his salary for six years to rectify the financial setbacks.

On June 3, 1932, McGraw summoned Bill Terry into his office and offered him the managerial post. The manager and first baseman—who accepted the job—had not talked for two years after Terry openly criticized his boss' harassment of a player.

Doctors had ordered McGraw to retire as manager, but permitted him to remain as a club vice-president.

John made his last public appearance in early February of 1934 when he attended a dinner given by Giants Owner Charles Stoneham for National League club owners.

McGraw died of internal hemorrhaging at New Rochelle Hospital later that month and was buried in Baltimore.

Manager John McGraw came decked out in his special black uniform for the 1911 World Series against the A's. The Giants discarded their regular uniforms because black was what they wore in their last Series triumph in 1905. Also pictured are (from left) Bill Dinneen, Tommy Connolly, the A's Harry Davis, Bill Klem and Bill Brennan.

BILL McKLECHNIE

In the days before World War I, Frank Chance was asked why his constant off-the-field companion was a .200 hitter.

"Because he's the only guy on this club," explained the manager of the New York Highlanders, "who knows what the game is all about. He can't hit worth a hoot, but he has something under his cap."

For more than 40 years, Bill McKechnie was regarded as one of the keenest intellects in baseball. He knew how the game should be played and detected things that escaped the attention of others. He knew the capabilities of his players without expecting too much from them.

He was the only manager to win pennants with three franchises, a distinction that would have eluded him if he had won a political contest in 1929.

McKechnie won a flag with the St. Louis Cardinals in 1928, but lost the World Series to the Yankees in four games and was demoted to Rochester (International). He was crushed.

Bill sought and won the Republican nomination for tax collector in his native Wilkinsburg, Pa., promising the electorate that he would retire from baseball if he won the post.

Deacon Bill lost the race and remained in the game for another 20 years. He piloted Boston's National League club for eight seasons, winning Manager of the Year honors in 1937 for guiding a supposedly dismal team to a 79-73 record and fifth place.

A master handler of pitchers, McKechnie turned aging minor leaguers Jim Turner and Lou Fette into 20-game winners for Boston. But the club's future was bleak; Judge Emil Fuchs, the owner, was in financial straits constantly. When the call came to take over the Cincinnati Reds under wealthy Owner Powel Crosley, McKechnie accept-

Pittsburgh Manager Bill McKechnie and Senators Manager Bucky Harris join in festivities before the start of the 1925 World Series.

ed. In two years he converted an eighth-place team into a pennant winner. In 1940, he again won managerial honors by manufacturing another world championship to go with one he had produced at Pittsburgh in 1925.

The Deacon received his initial managerial opportunity as a player-manager in the summer of 1915 when he replaced Bill Phillips at the helm of the Newark club in the Federal League. The Federal League died at the end of the season and McKechnie didn't manage again until 1922, when he became the Pirates' skipper. Three years later, the N.L. champion Bucs beat Washington in the World Series.

Ordinarily, Bill was a soft-spoken, affable individual, but he was an unchained demon in Game 3 of the '25 Series when umpire Cy Rigler's decision went against Pittsburgh. In the eighth inning, with the Senators leading by one run, Earl Smith of the Bucs hit a deep fly to right-center field where Sam Rice leaped against the low fence, tumbled into the Griffith Stadium bleachers and, after a tantalizing delay, emerged with the ball. Rigler allowed the catch. The Deacon protested vehemently—but in vain.

In later years, the weight of evidence indicated that a bleacherite had slipped the ball into Rice's glove.

The incident did not influence the outcome of the Series, the Pirates winning in a dramatic seventh game.

After his second world title in 1940, when the Reds defeated the Tigers, Bill remained on the job in Cincinnati through 1946.

McKechnie accepted the role as pitching coach under Lou Boudreau at Cleveland and polished up a world championship staff in 1948. The Deacon had opportunities to manage the Chicago Cubs and White Sox, the St. Louis Browns and the Pirates, but declined the offers.

McKechnie retired after the 1949 season and several years later moved to Bradenton, Fla. The canny Scot had no financial worries. He owned oil wells, a meat-saw factory, half of a rock-bearing mountain, parcels of real estate in Pittsburgh and a tomato farm in Florida. He was 78 at the time of his death in 1965.

BID McPHEE

Bid McPhee, a standout in the 19th century, was a superb fielder—but not always a great glove man. He played much of his career without a glove.

"I have never seen the necessity of wearing one, and besides, I cannot hold a thrown ball if there is anything on my hands. This glove business has gone a little too far. . . .True, hot-hit balls do sting a little at the opening of the season, but after you get used to it there is no trouble on that score." Such were the words of Bid McPhee as he talked to a reporter about wearing a glove while playing second base.

John Alexander McPhee was born on November 1, 1859, in New York. After moving to Illinois, he left in 1877 for Davenport, Iowa, to play professional baseball. He signed with the Cincinnati Reds of the American Association after playing minor league baseball for four years. McPhee got his nickname of "Biddy" from his small stature—he was only 5'8" and weighed only 152 pounds. The nickname was later shortened to "Bid." In 1882, at the age of 22, he won the second base job with the Reds. The Reds would win a pennant in his first year; it was the only time McPhee played on a pennant winner.

In that first season, McPhee only hit .228, but he led the American Association second basemen in putouts, double plays and fielding average. By 1884, he was improving at the plate. He learned the art of drawing walks and went on to score 100-plus runs that season. It was the first of nine times McPhee would score 100-plus runs in his career. The Reds rejoined the National League in 1890. In 1893, the pitching mound was moved back to 60 feet from home plate. McPhee suddenly became a brand-new hitter. From 1894 to 1897, he hit .313, .299, .305 and .301. He hit 19 triples in 1887 and 22 in 1890. He hit three triples in one game alone. He also led the league in home runs in 1886, which included seven inside-the-park home runs.

McPhee was a notable base stealer, stealing 568 for his career. Although stolen bases had a different meaning back in *his* playing days, Bid McPhee was pretty good.

He still refused to put on a glove, and before each season, he would soak his hands in brine. This would help make his hands tougher for the upcoming season. His defense was still steady, but it was average compared to the rest of glove-wearing second basemen. Finally, on Opening Day of 1896 he put on a glove for the first time. The results were amazing. He led the league in fielding percentage again, and set a mark of .978. This was a record that surpassed the previous record by 19 points. It was also a record that would stand for 23 years before someone else would break it.

McPhee is as renowned as some of other players in his day for a few reasons. He didn't drink or get into brawls. He was never thrown out of a game. He also played in Cincinnati for his whole career, another reason he isn't as widely known. He quit playing after the 1899 season.

He came back to manage the Reds. He managed the 1901 squad but quit after 65 games into the 1902 campaign due to rumors he was going to be replaced as the manager. He later moved to Los Angeles and spent several years scouting for the Reds. He died in 1943 in San Diego. At the time of his retirement, he held the records for most hits by a second baseman and most games played by a second baseman. Both have since been surpassed. He ended his career with 2,313 hits, a career batting average of .277 and a career .355 on-base average. He was voted into the Hall of Fame by the Veterans Committee in March of 2000.

JOE MEDWICK

The 1934 World Series had just ended disastrously for the Detroit Tigers and Manager Mickey Cochrane was in the clubhouse following his club's 11-0 loss in Game 7. Reflecting on the 23-year-old left fielder of the St. Louis Cardinals, Cochrane exclaimed, "Where, oh where, do they grow fellows like that?"

Black Mike had ample cause to be impressed with Joe (Muscles) Medwick, who rapped four hits in Game 1 and 11 for the Series in which he batted .379.

Barrel-chested Joe was the son of Hungarian immigrants and a three-sport star at Carteret (N.J.) High School, where he was discovered by Charles (Pop) Kelchner, a scout for the Cardinals.

Medwick had visions of a college football career and hesitated to sign a professional baseball contract until it was suggested that he play under an alias to protect his amateur status.

As Mickey King, he broke into Organized Ball in 1930 with Scottdale of the Middle Atlantic League and batted .419 in 75 games.

A two-year stint in the Texas League was all the additional seasoning that Joe needed before joining the Cardinals in late 1932. Nicknamed Ducky because a fan thought his walking style resembled that of a waterfowl, Medwick met instantaneous success as the left fielder on the rough-and-tumble club known as the Gas House Gang.

Joe contributed generously to the National League team's reputation as a brawling aggregation. He was quick with his fists, so quick that teammate Dizzy Dean observed; "You try to argue with him and before you can say a doggone word, he bops you."

Cardinal players learned early the folly of talking impolitely to the swaggering outfielder. One day pitcher Ed Heusser censured Joe for failing to hustle after a fly ball. A punch to the jaw sent Ed to the dugout floor.

Another time, pitcher Tex Carleton, scheduled to start for the Redbirds, reported to Manager Frank Frisch with a black eye. Tex had made the mistake of walking in front of Medwick once too often as Joe posed for a photographer. "Do that once more," snarled Joe, "and I'll smack you."

The Joe Medwick controversy in Game 7 of the 1934 Series began with a hard slide into Detroit's Marv Owen.

Medwick was the last National Leaguer to win the Triple Crown, accomplishing the feat in 1937.

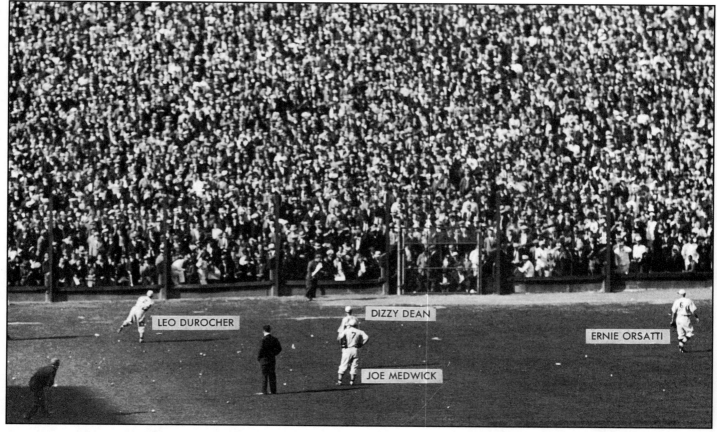

LEO DUROCHER

DIZZY DEAN

ERNIE ORSATTI

JOE MEDWICK

When Medwick (7) returned to his left-field position, irate Tiger fans showered debris onto the field , delaying the game. Commissioner Kenesaw Mountain Landis finally ordered Medwick removed from the game for his own safety.

Once, in Pittsburgh, a dispute arose between Dizzy and Paul Dean on one side and Medwick on the other. The brothers decided to teach their teammate a lesson and started for him. Grabbing a bat, Ducky announced, "One at a time, and I'll kill you both. But if you're comin' together, I'll separate you." The Deans revised their plans.

At the plate, Medwick was oblivious to the strike zone. Leo Durocher remembered that the first time he saw Joe, the kid clouted a double, two home runs and a single— "and he had to reach for every pitch."

Eldon Auker, who was victimized by Joe's hitting in the 1934 Series, lamented, "You throw him a strike and he ignores it. Throw the ball over his head and he hits a home run."

More than anything, Joe loved his base hits. At a time when Pepper Martin was in a slump, a newspaperman scattered hairpins in a hotel lobby, hoping that Martin would find the pins (each one was regarded as a base hit by superstitious ballplayers).

But Medwick came along first and started to scoop up the pieces of luck.

"Hey," said the newsman, "those are for Pepper."

"The hell with Martin," snapped Medwick, "let him find his own hairpins."

Medwick was not on the premises when the Cardinals wrapped up the 1934 World Series. In running out a triple, he had engaged in a kicking match with third baseman Marv Owen. On returning to his left-field position, Joe was bombarded with over-ripe fruit and vegetables by the bleacherites. When the fans would not desist, Medwick was removed from the game "for your own safety," according to Commissioner K.M. Landis.

At the time, Medwick had 11 hits and would have batted once more in quest of a record 12th hit. Chick Fullis, who replaced Joe, got the last at-bat-and singled.

Medwick, a Triple Crown winner and N.L. Most Valuable Player with the Cardinals in 1937, was traded to Brooklyn in June of 1940. A few days later, the Cardinals visited Ebbets Field where Bob Bowman, who had some heated words with Joe in a hotel elevator, beaned Ducky and sent him to the hospital with a concussion.

Although only 28 when the beaning occurred, Medwick never regained the savage batting style of other years.

The one-time firebrand mellowed in his later years and was welcomed affectionately at baseball gatherings. He was serving as a minor league batting instructor for the Cardinals in 1975 when he suffered a fatal heart attack at St. Petersburg, Fla., at age 63.

JOHNNY MIZE

Cincinnati Manager Charley Dressen was ecstatic about the graceful first baseman, calling him "the greatest rookie I've ever seen." It was the spring of 1935 and the kid carried a $55,000 price tag that the Reds would have to pay if they decided to keep the Cardinal prospect.

"I was willing to gamble on him," said General Manager Larry MacPhail, "but the board of directors wasn't."

The Cardinals shipped the prospect, Johnny Mize, to Rochester where, in midseason, he suffered another in a series of Charley horses that had blighted his career.

Mize was recalled by the Cards and turned over to Dr. Robert F. Hyland, famed "Surgeon General of Baseball," who discovered a growth on the player's pelvis. The doctor leveled with Mize, informing him that even if an oper-

ation were successful, it would not necessarily enable him to return to baseball. There was a possibility, too, that he could be crippled for life.

"Get the knives ready," said the big Georgian.

"He never batted an eye," reported Hyland. "I'm as proud of the results as anything I've ever done in the operating room."

Hyland's skill and Mize's determination to succeed combined to produce one of the foremost performers in the history of the Cardinals, Giants and Yankees.

Mize made his debut with St. Louis in the spring of 1936, dividing his time between the outfield and first base. Of Johnny's first 28 hits, five were home runs, four were triples and eight were doubles. Mize went on to Rookie of the Year honors with an average of .329.

By 1938, reports were circulating around the National League that Mize could be handled by a change-of-pace curve. His .250 average lent substance to the notion until the Boston Bees visited St. Louis. Jim Turner tried the slow treatment on Big John and watched three home runs sail out of Sportsman's Park.

By 1939, Johnny Mize was a bona fide slugger for the St. Louis Cardinals. Ten years later, Mize was wearing the same uniform as another slugging great, Joe DiMaggio, and nearing the end of his career.

Mize gets a warm reception from Yogi Berra after hitting a home run in the fourth game of the 1952 World Series against the Dodgers. Mize played in five Series, all with the Yankees.

A week later, the Giants repeated the slow-curve approach. Again, three home runs. Mize finished the season with a .337 average.

In addition to his hitting achievements, Mize was a fielding artist, a quality that won him his nickname of "Big Cat." One afternoon, while John was catching low throws and stopping wicked bouncers at first base, teammate Joe Orengo exclaimed, "Ain't he a wonder? Why, he's a big cat."

During his Cardinal career, Mize made two unassisted double plays in one game and set a record for first basemen by playing 61 consecutive games without making an error.

After the 1941 season, Mize was swapped to the Giants in a multi-player trade. He performed admirably in his first season at the Polo Grounds, then spent three years in the Navy in the Pacific.

When peace rumors started to circulate, Big John, who was larger than when he left the States, embarked on a major weight-loss program that returned him to the Giants at a svelte 220 pounds.

Mize slugged 51 home runs in 1947 (when the Giants socked 221), but he found himself a discard two seasons later when the Giants sold him to the Yankees because, Leo

Durocher said, the slowed-down slugger did not fit into the manager's plans for a running team at the Polo Grounds.

As a Yankee, the big fellow participated in five World Series in as many years. He was devastating in the seven game 1952 classic against the Brooklyn Dodgers.

In the ninth inning of Game 3, Mize pinch-hit for pitcher Tom Gorman and crashed a homer into the right-field seats.

The next day, in Game 4, he took over at first base for slumping Joe Collins and clouted a fourth-inning homer in Allie Reynolds' 2-0 victory.

John smacked a third homer in as many days in an 11-inning loss in Game 5, then contributed two singles in the deciding triumph in Game 7. At 39, Mize led all Series players with a .400 average.

The superlative performance earned Mize another contract with the Yankees, but he pinch-hit only three times 'in the 1953 Series and failed to hit safely.

When Dodgers catcher Roy Campanella was asked if John's 0-for-3 performance meant the Dodgers had finally learned how to pitch to the aging slugger, he quipped: "We always did know how to pitch to him, but some days when you're squatting behind the plate Mr. Mize's bat swells UP."

JOE MORGAN

At 5-foot-7 and 155 pounds, Joe Morgan was not exactly an imposing physical specimen when he made his major league debut with the Houston Colt .45s in 1963. In a game against Philadelphia that year, he stunned the Phillies by singling home the winning run in the ninth inning to give Houston a rare victory.

After the game, Phils manager Gene Mauch was livid, disbelieving that such a small player could beat his club. He scattered the post-game buffet to all corners of the Phillies' locker room and demanded an explanation from the pitcher who allowed Morgan's hit, Johnny Klippstein.

"How can you get beat by a guy who looks like a Little Leaguer?" he wondered.

Joe Morgan, who would turn 20 that month, may have looked younger than his years, but his game-winning hit that day was only the first of many he would get over the course of his baseball career. Before Morgan hung up his spikes after the 1984 season, he had played in more games, hit more homers and compiled more putouts, assists and total chances than any second baseman in history.

Ironically, Morgan's size was more of a help than a hindrance in his becoming one of the greatest second basemen of all time. His small strike zone made him difficult to pitch to (only Babe Ruth and Ted Williams drew more walks in major league history), and those pitches which did enter Morgan's strike zone often ended up on the other side of the outfield fence. The 266 home runs he hit as a second baseman are two more than the total hit by the great Rogers Hornsby.

"I always felt my size was a positive thing, because I had to work hard," Morgan said. The oldest of six children, Joe signed with Houston for $5,000 in November 1962 (the Mets and Yankees also were interested) largely because the Houston scout who pursued him, Bill Wight, never talked about Morgan's size in conversations with him.

"He had confidence I could make the major leagues, and that is what sold me," Morgan said.

A lefthanded swinger, Morgan used a distinctive batting style in which he flapped his left elbow away from and toward his body. He was taught the method by Nellie Fox, who was wrapping up his own 19-year playing career before becoming a coach in Houston as Morgan was breaking in. Fox was convinced the youngster would hit better if he kept his left elbow away from his body. The flapping was Morgan's way of reminding himself to do so.

"[Fox] also taught me never to take an error to the plate or a strikeout to the field," said Morgan, who won five Gold Gloves for his fielding prowess. He led N.L. second

Joe Morgan's 5-foot-7, 155-pound frame was more help than hindrance in his becoming one of the greatest second basemen of all-time.

basemen in fielding three times, and in 1977 tied the major league record for fewest errors (5) by a second baseman in 150 or more games. It was a far cry from 1965, when Morgan led the National League with 27 errors in his rookie season.

"The thing I'm most proud of is that I became a good defensive player through hard work," he said, "The other thing I'm most proud of is that teams were better when I was there than after I left."

Indeed. Morgan, who played for five teams, took great pride in making his new teams better and noting that his old clubs got worse. He helped the Cincinnati Reds advance to the National League Championship Series in five of the eight seasons (1972-79) he played there. In 1980, after rejoining the Houston organization as a free agent, he helped the Astros win their first N.L. Western Division title (and dethrone the Reds in the process). In 1983, as a 39-year-old everyday second baseman, Morgan helped the Philadelphia Phillies win the N.L. pennant.

His greatest years, however, came with the Reds, the team he joined after an eight-player trade between Houston and Cincinnati on November 29, 1971. Although Morgan had been a fine player in Houston, his inclusion in the blockbuster deal was not surprising. He had been labeled a "troublemaker" by Astros manager Harry Walker, a charge Morgan always resented.

"Anyone was a troublemaker who was smarter than Harry Walker," Morgan sneered. "And that didn't take much."

The Astros' loss was the Reds' gain. Cincinnati, a fourth-place team in 1971, never finished lower than second in Morgan's eight seasons there. In 1975 and 1976, he won back-to-back National League Most Valuable Player awards (the only second baseman ever to do so) while helping the Reds win consecutive World Series championships.

In the 1975 Series against Boston, after Pete Rose was intentionally walked to get to him, Morgan singled home the winning run in the top of the ninth inning of Game 7 to give the Reds a 4-3 victory and their first world title in 35 years. A year later, Cincinnati swept the New York Yankees in four games to extend its postseason winning streak that year to seven games (including three straight over Philadelphia in the National League playoffs).

"When he's healthy, he's the finest ballplayer I ever played with," said Hall of Fame catcher Johnny Bench, who played with Morgan on those great Reds teams. "He could win more ball games in more ways than anybody."

Morgan played in nine All-Star Games, seven Championship Series and four World Series. In 1990, he was inducted into the Baseball Hall of Fame in his first year of eligibility, one of fewer than two dozen players so honored.

"You know, I played 22 years and felt I wanted to leave my imprint on the game," Morgan said. "Now, I feel I didn't play all that time only to be forgotten.

"Going into the Hall of Fame assures that my imprint will be there forever."

Morgan's greatest years came with the Cincinnati Reds, who advanced to the NLCS in five of the eight seasons he played there.

Morgan's 266 home runs hit as a second baseman are the most in baseball history.

Morgan won five Gold Gloves for his fielding prowess and led National League second basemen in fielding three times.

STAN MUSIAL

In August of 1940 at Orlando, Fla., the 19-year-old center fielder for the Daytona Beach team made a diving catch of a line drive and landed heavily and painfully on his left shoulder.

A lump formed and the lefthander, who had compiled an 18-5 pitching record while not playing the outfield, saw hopes for a mound career evaporate in the months that followed.

But there was one redeeming factor. While he may have been unable to pitch, Stan Musial retained a sharp batting eye. And when it came time to distribute the wealth of talent in the St. Louis Cardinals' farm system the next spring, the fleet-footed youngster was assigned to Springfield of the Western Association.

Before the 1941 season had run its course, the dead-armed pitcher of a year earlier had batted .379 in the Class C league, .326 for Rochester (International) and .426 in 12 games for the Cardinals.

Musial was in the National League to stay for 22 seasons. On the last day of the 1963 campaign, Commissioner Ford Frick saluted the nearly 43-year-old grandfather as "baseball's perfect warrior. . . . baseball's perfect knight."

Between arrival and departure, Musial ingratiated

Stan Musial wore a Rochester uniform for 54 games in 1941 before making the jump to St. Louis.

By 1942, Musial was a Cardinal regular and well on the road to greatness.

Musial connected for hit No. 3,000 on May 13, 1958, off Cubs pitcher Moe Drabowsky during a game at Wrigley Field. Musial played five more seasons and collected 630 more hits.

himself to millions with his qualities as a player and as a person. He wore a perpetual smile and when he wasn't driving baseballs to every corner of National League parks, he was greeting folks with his trademark salutation: "Waddya say! Waddya say!"

The son of a Polish immigrant who settled in the industrial town of Donora, Pa., Stan passed up a basketball scholarship at the University of Pittsburgh to cast his lot with professional baseball.

He registered his first major league hit on September 17, 1941. It was the first of his 725 doubles and was struck against Jim Tobin, knuckleball pitcher of the Boston Braves.

In the first game of a doubleheader against Chicago that same year, Musial doubled twice and singled twice. In the ninth inning, while the Cubs' first baseman argued over a close play, Stan raced home from second base with the winning run. In the second game, he rapped two more hits and made two diving catches, leading Chicago Manager Jimmy Wilson to comment: "Nobody, but nobody, can be that good."

Musial's batting crouch was unique. It was described as resembling a small boy peeking around a corner looking for the cops. When Ted Williams imitated the stance, he hit himself on his leg with the bat when he swung.

Musial was not easily intimidated. In a game against Brooklyn, he was knocked down on the first two pitches from Van Lingle Mungo. On the third pitch, Musial tripled. As umpire Larry Goetz brushed off the plate, he yelled to the mound, "Hey, Van, you sure scared the hell out of that kid, didn't you!"

When the Pasquel brothers of Mexico raided major league clubs for talent in 1946, Musial was a prime objective. Stan, earning $12,500 at the time, was offered a $75,000 bonus and a five-year contract for $125,000. He turned it down to honor his contract with the Cardinals.

Stan could play hurt, too. In Boston, he abruptly ripped tape off his injured wrists and rapped five hits off Warren Spahn and relievers. It was his fourth five-hit game of the season, tying a record set by Ty Cobb.

Musial enjoyed his finest season in 1948 when he led the N.L. in all major offensive departments except home runs—and he missed in that department by only one rained-out homer.

Stan clouted six homers in 24 All-Star Games. His most notable drives occurred in Milwaukee in 1955 when his 12th-inning blow produced an N.L. victory, and at Yankee Stadium in 1960 when he socked a pinch homer into the third tier of the right-field stands to evoke a standing ovation.

May 2, 1954, proved a home run bonanza for Stan. Facing the Giants on an overcast Sunday at St. Louis, Musial belted three home runs in the first game of a doubleheader and two in the second.

Musial collected his 3,000th major league hit—a double—at Chicago on May 13, 1958, and closed his career with 3,630 safeties (1,815 at home, 1,815 on the road).

In lasting admiration for a superstar, the baseball writers of St. Louis erected a statue of Musial outside Busch Memorial Stadium.

HAL NEWHOUSER

It was August 1938, and the Detroit Tigers, struggling in the American League pennant race, fired manager Mickey Cochrane and named Del Baker as his replacement. It was important news, and the Tigers wanted everyone in their organization to know.

Wish Egan, a top Detroit scout, returned to his hotel room at 9 o'clock that evening after a day spent looking at prospects. He was greeted by numerous telephone messages upon his arrival, all from his secretary, and all spaced about 20 minutes apart. He proceeded to call his secretary at her home.

"Mr. Egan," she said, "I've been trying to get in touch with you all day. I have terrible news for you. Mickey Cochrane is out as manager and Del Baker is going to take his place."

Egan was nonplussed.

"A couple of years from now, the Tigers will win pennants no matter who manages them," he said, "because today I've signed the greatest lefthander pitcher I ever saw—a kid by the name of Newhouser. "

Hal Newhouser, then a 17-year-old terror in Detroit's American Legion ranks, later went on to become a terror for the city's American League team. From 1939-53, Newhouser won an even 200 games for the Tigers, leading them to a seven-game World Series triumph over the Chicago Cubs in 1945.

In recognition of his efforts, Newhouser was elected to baseball's Hall of Fame by the Veterans Committee in 1992.

For three seasons between 1944-46, Newhouser was baseball's most dominant pitcher, winning a major-league, high 80 games and losing 27. Given the nickname "Prince Hal" by a New York sportswriter, the crafty lefthander with a terrific curve was the American League's Most Valuable Player in 1944 and 1945, the only pitcher to win that honor in successive seasons.

Although Newhouser's back-to-back MVP awards were dismissed by some as the good fortune of a "wartime" pitcher (many of baseball's best players were serving duty in World War II at the time; Newhouser was rejected for service due to a heart problem), Prince Hal confounded his critics in 1946, when he tied Cleveland's Bob Feller for the league lead with 26 victories. On September 22 of that year, Newhouser outdueled Feller, 3-0 in a classic pitching duel at Cleveland's Municipal Stadium. Newhouser threw just 97 pitches and allowed only two batters to reach base (both on singles, and neither player reached second base).

Two years later, in what Newhouser later said was his most satisfying win, he outpitched Feller on the final day of the 1948 season to force a one-game playoff between the Indians and Boston Red Sox for the A.L. pennant, Newhouser worked hard at his craft, and little of his success could be attributed to luck or good fortune. In fact, just the opposite almost led a frustrated Newhouser to abandon baseball after a dismal 1943 campaign. That year, Newhouser lost 17

Hal Newhouser receives congratulations from manager Steve O'Neil and teammates after outdueling Bob Feller, 3-0, on September 22, 1946.

games, including his last 13 decisions in a row (six by a single run). He became so convinced that the Tigers' shoddy fielding would prevent him from ever becoming a big winner in his hometown, he demanded to be traded after the '43 season.

"I damn near went back to the tool and die business," said Newhouser, who viewed every mistake committed behind him as a personal affront. His violent clubhouse tantrums following such games became the stuff of legends. Detroit, in fact, almost shipped Newhouser to Cleveland for infielder Jim Bagby prior to the start of the 1944 season. But Steve O'Neill, then the Tigers' manager, nixed the deal.

Ironically, Newhouser's career turned around in a game against the Indians that very season. After being relegated to the bullpen after beginning the season 1-4 as a starting pitcher, Newhouser was summoned from the pen by O'Neill after the Indians, already leading by three runs, loaded the bases in the eighth inning. Newhouser worked out of the jam without allowing a run, and the Tigers proceeded to load the bases in their next at-bat. A reserve catcher, Hack Miller, was sent in to pinch-hit. Miller, in the first at-bat of his major-league career, lashed the first pitch he saw over the head of Cleveland right fielder Roy Cullenbine for an inside-the-park grand slam.

"My thinking changed," said Newhouser, who proceeded to win seven more games in succession after that improbable victory. "The players were for me, instead of against me."

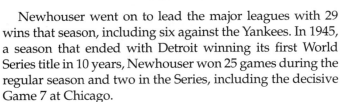

Newhouser went on to lead the major leagues with 29 wins that season, including six against the Yankees. In 1945, a season that ended with Detroit winning its first World Series title in 10 years, Newhouser won 25 games during the regular season and two in the Series, including the decisive Game 7 at Chicago.

After compiling a 17-17 record in 1947 (a performance the Tigers deemed worthy of cutting his salary $15,000), Newhouser disposed of two lucrative business ventures, feeling the distractions they created contributed to his failure to win 20 games.

"Baseball is what I should be worrying about," he said. He worried himself to a 21-12 record in '48.

A chronic sore shoulder led to Newhouser's release by Detroit in July 1953. Still only 33, he hooked on with the Indians a year later, compiling a 7-2 record that season to help Cleveland win the A.L. pennant.

After his playing days ended, Newhouser became a scout for Baltimore and Cleveland. His biggest achieve-

ment in that role was the discovery of pitcher Dean Chance, who, as a 23-year-old pitcher for the Los Angeles Angels in 1964, became the youngest player to win the Cy Young Award.

The Cy Young Award, first bestowed in 1956, did not exist during Prince Hal's 17-year playing career. If it had, he'd have won a few.

Newhouser (in 1991 photo) was the American League's Most Valuable Player in 1944 and 1945, the only pitcher to win that honor in successive seasons.

KID NICHOLS

Although not an imposing figure at 5-foot-10½ and 180 pounds, Kid Nichols had a fastball that reportedly was the equal of that thrown by Amos Rusie, famed righthander of the New York Giants.

Nichols was one of baseball's all-time bargains. He was sold by Omaha of the Western Association for $3,000 and won 20 or more games in each of his first 10 seasons with Boston's National League team. In nine consecutive years, the pitcher topped the 25-victory mark.

Nichols was a workhorse. In his first five major league seasons, his innings-pitched totals were 424, 423, 454, 414 and 417. In six of the next seven years he registered more than 300 innings.

Although he never pitched a no-hitter, Kid (so called early in his career because of his size) came as close as possible on a number of occasions. His most memorable performance occurred in his rookie season when he hooked up with Rusie at the Polo Grounds. The teams battled in a scoreless tie in the 1890 game until, with two out in the 13th inning, outfielder Mike Tiernan tagged Nichols for a home run.

It was the year of the Players League and after one of that circuit's games at a nearby park, fans swarmed into the Polo Grounds to watch the conclusion of the Nichols-Rusie struggle.

Kid pitched the Beaneaters to pennants in 1897 and 1898. He was already earning the top salary permitted by the league, $2,400. He demanded a raise for 1899 and finally accepted a $235 bonus for winning the pennant the previous year.

By this time the press was referring to Nichols as "Nervy Nick." He had defeated the Baltimore Orioles two out of three times to clinch the flag for Boston.

After three more seasons in Boston, Nichols bought a part interest in the Kansas City (Western) club. He man-

Fastballer Kid Nichols put together his final 20-victory season in 1904 for the Cardinals.

aged the team in 1902 and 1903 and pitched Kansas City to a total of 48 victories.

Nichols was pitcher-manager for the St. Louis Cardinals in 1904. Although he won 21 games, the club suffered from a shortage of talent and finished fifth.

Conditions did not improve appreciably the next season and the Cardinals won only 19 of their first 48 games before Nichols was ousted as manager in mid-June.

Frank DeHaas Robinson had hired Nichols, but Kid was dismissed by Frank's brother, Stanley.

"Somehow, I always felt that Stanley had it in for me," explained Kid. "But firing me as manager was only the beginning of my troubles. In Cincinnati one day—I think I had pitched the day before—Stanley ordered me to work on one of the gates. Players had to make themselves useful in more ways than one in those days and he wanted me to keep an eye on the tickets to see that we got an honest count.

"Anyhow, I told Stanley I wasn't going to work any gate, that I was going to the Latonia race track. He fired me off the club."

Kid joined Philadelphia and, in his first appearance, defeated the Cardinals, 2-1. "That gave me a lot of personal satisfaction," he said.

Nichols retired from the game after the 1906 season and opened bowling alleys in Kansas City. In partnership with Joe Tinker, former Cub shortstop, he entered the motion picture business. He also sold movie film in outlying areas and dabbled in real estate.

Kid also managed a 34-alley bowling emporium, one of the largest in Missouri, and he was recognized as one of the finest bowlers in Kansas City. At age 64, he won the Class A championship.

For a while, Kid coached the baseball team at Missouri Valley College in Marshall, Mo.

Nichols' finest hour came in 1949 when he went to Cooperstown to see his name enshrined in the Hall of Fame. It was an honor denied him for many years, although he always was among the leading candidates.

Nichols died in Kansas City in 1953 at age 83.

PHIL NIEKRO

Former Yankee Bobby Murcer once said trying to hit a knuckleball thrown by Phil Niekro was like eating jelly with chopsticks."

That might be the most accurate description ever of what it was like being 60 feet, 6 inches away from a pitcher like Niekro who relied on the uncertainty of his famous pitch to become one of the game's stars.

No pitcher has ever mastered the tricky knuckleball like Niekro, who lasted 24 years in the majors, until age 48, and used it to produce 318 career victories , the 14th highest victory total in major-league history.

Born in Ohio in 1939, Niekro was a boyhood pal of future basketball Hall of Famer John Havlicek. He signed as a free agent with the Milwaukee Braves in 1958 and spent six years in the minor leagues before reaching the majors with the Braves in 1964.

Niekro spent the first two seasons of his major-league career pitching out of the bullpen, and didn't move into the rotation to stay until 1967 when he was 28 years old. It was two years later that Niekro enjoyed the first big season of his career, winning 23 games to lead the Braves to a division championship.

The Braves were upset by the Mets in the N.L. playoffs, however, and it would turn out to be 13 years before Niekro and the Braves got another chance at postseason play. They also lost that N.L. playoff series, being swept by the Cardinals in three games, keeping Niekro from the World Series for his entire career. He never won a game in the postseason. Playing 24 years without appearing in a World Series also is a record that no one might ever equal.

Niekro's national attention was limited, despite his individual success, because most of his years in Atlanta came when the team was playing poorly. The Braves finished last six times during his career, and Niekro led the league in losses four times, a record.

He did record two other 20-win seasons, winning 20 games in 1974 and winning 21, and losing 20, in 1979, leading the league in both categories That was one of two years in which Niekro lost 20 games. He lost 274 games in his career, and 47 of them came on shutouts.

Phil Niekro, a 1997 addition to the Hall of Fame, was known for his trademark pitch, the knuckleball. He won 318 games in 24 seasons.

Niekro pitched for the Braves through the 1983 season before signing as a free agent with the Yankees. He earned his fifth All-Star selection in his first season in New York, on his way to a 16-8 season at age 45.

In his five All-Star selections, Niekro actually pitched only twice, for a total of 1⅓ innings, probably at least partially out of concern for how a different catcher would be able to handle the knuckleball. He once had six wild pitches in one game, four in the same inning.

Niekro's two most memorable individual highlights came 12 years apart. On Aug. 5, 1973, he pitched a no-hitter against San Diego, winning 9-0.

On Oct. 6, 1985, pitching for the Yankees, he turned in a four-hit, 8-0 shutout of Toronto that not only represented his 300th career victory (after failing in four previous starts trying to get the milestone win), but also made him, at age 46, the oldest pitcher ever to throw a shutout in the majors.

What made that game even more special for Niekro was that he made a decision not to use his famous knuckleball until he was one out away from the victory. He then used it against former teammate Jeff Burroughs and struck him out with three knucklers.

Niekro joined the Indians in 1986, and on June 28 of that year, faced Don Sutton of the Angels in a memorable matchup. It was the first time two 300-game winners had squared off since Tim Keefe faced Pud Galvin in 1892. Neither Niekro or Sutton was involved in the decision.

Niekro closed out his remarkable career in 1987 at the age of 48. He finished with 3,342 strikeouts, the eighth highest total in history, and his 5,404 innings pitched was the fourth highest of all time.

He holds the record for most wins after the age of 40, 121, and became the second oldest player to hit a homer in the major leagues when he hit one at age 43. He holds or shares 14 Atlanta career pitching records, and his number 35 was retired by the Braves in 1984. He defeated every team in the majors that he faced at least once. There was one team he never faced—the Braves.

Combined with younger brother Joe's 221 victories in the majors, the Niekros broke the combined victory total for brothers that had been set by Gaylord and Jim Perry.

Niekro was elected to the Hall of Fame in 1997.

JIM O'ROURKE

As a player for the Buffalo club of the National League in 1881, John Peters compiled an undistinguished record. But he did acquire a measure of distinction for the answer he received when he asked for a pay raise.

"I'm sorry," the team manager replied, "but the exigencies of the occasion and the condition of our exchequer will not permit anything of the sort at this period of our existence. Subsequent developments in the field of finance may remove the present gloom and we may emerge into a condition where we may see fit to reply in the affirmative to your exceedingly modest request."

Not surprisingly, Peters did not renew his request. One confrontation with Orator Jim O'Rourke convinced him that his present salary was altogether adequate.

Unquestionably, O'Rourke had a way with words. Once, when he was president of the Connecticut League and also catcher for Bridgeport in the same circuit, he became embroiled in a heated dispute with the umpire. After using profanity, O'Rourke recognized the seriousness of his offense and whipped off his mask. Addressing the crowd, he said: "As president of the Connecticut League, I hereby fine player James O'Rourke $10 for swearing at the umpire." He then resumed his position.

O'Rourke, the son of a Bridgeport, Conn., farmer, was left fatherless at a young age and played ball only when farm chores would allow. Before his mother would permit him to sign a professional contract, she insisted that the team management provide a farm laborer to pinch-hit for her son.

When the N.L. opened for business in 1876, Jim was a member of the Boston team that inaugurated the season in Philadelphia on April 22. With two outs in the first inning, O'Rourke singled to left off Lon Knight, thereby rapping the first hit in big-league history.

O'Rourke had arrived in Boston in 1873, playing for the city's team in the National Association (a professional league). Because the Irish were held in low regard at that point in Boston history, Manager Harry Wright asked Jim if he would change his surname to conceal his Gaelic origins. The suggested alias was Rourke, a poorly veiled pseudonym, but it made no difference to Jim, who replied, "Mr. Wright, I would rather die than give up my father's name. A million dollars would not tempt me."

In 1874, Jim was a member of the first missionary group to visit England. The Red Stockings and Philadelphia Athletics played 14 games in the United Kingdom, Boston winning eight contests.

O'Rourke played three seasons with the Boston

Nationals and became a local favorite. When the team sought to deduct $20 from his 1878 salary to pay for his uniform, Jim resisted adamantly. The impasse was resolved only when the fans passed the hat and raised the required amount.

Orator Jim moved on to Providence for one season, back to Boston for another, and then to Buffalo for four years before going to New York. In 1888, he played on the Giants' first flag winner.

After five more years as a big-league player, O'Rourke tried his hand at umpiring

Orator Jim O'Rourke (pictured in 1887) had a way with words and bat.

in the N.L. in 1894, but gave it up after one season.

Back in Bridgeport, he organized the Victor League, forerunner of the Connecticut League. Jim managed and caught for the local club, which played its games on a diamond constructed on the old O'Rourke farm.

In 1904, O'Rourke longed to play once more with the team for which he helped win pennants in 1888 and 1889. Manager John McGraw gave his consent and allowed the 52-year-old man to catch the Giants' pennant-clinching game. O'Rourke singled once in four at-bats.

O'Rourke sold the Bridgeport club after the 1908 season and devoted his remaining years to the practice of law. He earlier had earned his degree from the Yale Law School.

He was a member of the fire commission and the paving and street commission in Bridgeport, and he served as a director of the National League and the Arbitration Board of the minors.

On New Year's Day of 1919—"a very cold day," according to his daughter—Orator Jim walked into Bridgeport to see a client. He contracted a cold that developed into pneumonia, which claimed his life seven days later.

MEL OTT

The 16-year-old catcher from Gretna (La.) High School was heartbroken. He and his batterymate had tried out for the New Orleans (Southern) team. The pitcher had received a contract, but the catcher had not.

"You're too young," the catcher was told.

Years later, Mel Ott recalled that "I must have blubbered something in my disapointment because the owner said to me, 'If you want to play semipro ball in the country, I can fix you up with a team that plays three or four games a week. It's in a little town called Patterson, about 90 miles from here. Just tell Harry Williams that I sent you."

The sadness over his failure to make the New Orleans team evaporated when Ott learned that Williams, a wealthy lumber baron, would pay him $150 a month plus expenses, including haircuts, movies and sodas. "And whenever somebody did well," said Mel, "they passed the hat so that I was earning more in extras than I was in salary."

Before the summer was spent, Williams dispatched a telegram to his friend, John McGraw, telling the manager of the New York Giants, "I think I have a real prize for you."

"Have your prize report to me at the Polo Grounds," McGraw replied. After quieting maternal fears about his safety in the big city, the teenager boarded a train and arrived in Penn Station on schedule.

New York Giants star Ott, shown fouling off a pitch in the 1942 All-Star Game, hit four home runs in his three World Series, but never connected in any of the 11 mid-season classics in which he participated.

The rise of Mel Ott's right foot usually spelled trouble for opposing pitchers.

During his illustrious career with the Giants, Ott hit 511 home runs and produced 2,876 hits.

Getting to the Polo Grounds presented more of a problem. "I must have changed subway trains 12 times in the two hours it took me to get to the Polo Grounds, but I finally made it," he remembered.

McGraw's first decision after watching the prodigy was that he was not a catcher. Ott's stocky legs were not intended to do a lot of crouching; Mel was designed to be an outfielder.

McGraw's second decision was that Ott would remain on the bench with him, that his development would not be entrusted to a minor league manager, not even Casey Stengel.

"I could help you develop that kid Ott if you let me have him for a year at Toledo," said Stengel.

McGraw exploded. "Ott stays with me!" he bellowed in red-faced rage. "No minor league manager is going to ruin him."

McGraw feared that somebody would tamper with Ott's unique batting style, in which he lifted his right foot before striding into the pitch.

The manager took a fatherly interest in the youngster, even fining him for playing poker with Bill Terry and other veterans. "I don't want you playing cards with the men," McGraw advised.

Ott played in 35 games as a 17-year-old, 82 at age 18, 124 at 19 and 150 (all but one of the Giants' games) when he was 20.

Ott smacked the first of his 511 major league home runs on July 18, 1927. It was an inside-the-park blow on which Chicago center fielder Hack Wilson missed a shoestring catch.

Ott's last homer was hit at New York on opening day, April 16, 1946, when he connected against Oscar Judd of the Phillies.

For 22 seasons, Ott patrolled right field for the Giants, delivering crucial hits, throwing out baserunners with his rifle arm and ingratiating himself to everyone with his pleasant manner and constant smile.

He set records in wholesale lots and for many years his 511 home runs represented a National League record. He socked four home runs in three World Series, but never connected in 11 All-Star Games.

Ott succeeded teammate Terry as manager in 1942 and remained on the job until midseason of 1948 when he was replaced by Leo Durocher. Mel was too easy-going, it was generally agreed, to get the most out of his players.

He broadcast Detroit Tigers games for a while and managed Oakland (Pacific Coast) in 1951-52.

Ott was in the contracting business in New Orleans when, on the night of November 14, 1958, he was involved in a head-on automobile collision near Bay St. Louis, La.

The former home run king suffered fractures of both legs and multiple internal injuries. After emergency treatment at Gulfport, Miss., he was moved to New Orleans, where he died on November 21 at age 49.

SATCHEL PAIGE

His age was never clearly determined, but he insisted —usually when all other research failed—that he was born in Mobile, Ala., in 1906.

But his age was of little consequence when Leroy (Satchel) Paige started to throw a baseball. His control was phenomenal and stories of his accuracy mushroomed along his pathway as he meandered with his oversized feet through the Negro Leagues and, in the final stages, into the white man's major leagues.

When Bill Veeck brought him into the major leagues with Cleveland in 1948, the question arose if Satch still could thread a needle with his pitches.

"Jim Hegan grabbed a towel to brush off the plate," Paige remembered later. "I told him there wasn't any use for that and gave him a gum wrapper and told him to lay it lengthwise on the plate. After I split that wrapper a few times with my fastball, they decided I still had my control."

The life story of the rubber-armed righthander is told best in anecdotes. In 1948, when the Yankees were challenging the pennant-bound Indians for the league lead, Satch was summoned with none out in the ninth inning and Phil Rizzuto dancing off third base. As Paige passed the Scooter on his way to the mound, he told him: "Don't get nervous, little man, you ain't goin' nowhere."

After the hurler retired the next three batters on 10 pitches, Veeck accosted him in feigned disgust. "Leroy," he said, "what about that 10th pitch? Why did you waste one?"

"Don't you worry none about ol' Satch," came the reply. "He won't let you down."

That same year, when Paige would read in the bullpen before a game, fellow pitchers would chide him lightly with, "Ain't you gonna run, ain't you gonna get in shape?"

His response invariably was: "No, where I come from we throw the ball across the plate, we don't carry it across."

Paige was well known for his homespun humor and his admonition, "Don't look back. Something might be gaining on you."

Future teammates Bob Feller and Satchel Paige got together in 1946 (right) during an Indians-Kansas City Monarchs barnstorming tour. Two years later, Paige (left) was ready to make his major league debut for Cleveland.

Paige, a man of many windups, was pitching for the St. Louis Browns in 1952 (right) and came back for one final appearance in 1965, at age 59, as a member of the Kansas City A's.

He declared that "there never was a man on earth who pitched more than me. The more I pitched, the stronger my arm would get."

Satchel once started 29 games in a month in Bismarck, N.D., and insisted that he won 104 of the 105 games he pitched in 1934.

The tall, slender Paige was at his best as a member of the Pittsburgh Crawfords in 1933. Using an assortment of pitches, including a unique delivery called the hesitation pitch that was banned in the major leagues, he won 31 games and lost four. He won 21 consecutive games and registered 62 straight scoreless innings.

Satchel's family name originally was spelled without the "i," but the ballplayer explained, "The family added the extra letter to sound more high-toned."

Paige acquired his nickname, he explained, while work-

ing as a 7-year-old porter in the Mobile railroad depot.

"I rigged up ropes around my shoulders and waist," he said. "I carried a satchel in each hand an one under each arm. I carried so many satchels that all you could see was satchels. You couldn't see Leroy Paige."

In 1924, Satchel obtained a trial with the Mobile Tigers, a semipro team, and fired 10 fastballs past the manager. He had a job, and the start of an exceptional career.

In succeeding years, Paige pitched in the Negro leagues during the summer and Caribbean leagues in the winter. He faced major league barnstorming teams almost annually. Once he outpitched Dizzy Dean, 1-0. Another time he struck out Rogers Hornsby five times in one game. Joe DiMaggio called him "the best and the fastest pitcher I've ever faced."

Paige died of a heart attack in Kansas City in 1982.

JIM PALMER

He first caught the attention of the baseball world in 1966, when, as a youngster completing his first full major league season, he shut out the Los Angeles Dodgers, 6-0, in Game 2 of the World Series.

It wasn't just any victory, either. Coming just nine days before his 21st birthday, righthander Jim Palmer of the Baltimore Orioles became the youngest pitcher in history to hurl a World Series shutout. The losing pitcher that October day, Hall of Famer Sandy Koufax, never pitched another game. By the time his own career ended some 18 years later, Palmer, too, was headed for Cooperstown.

As one of the premier pitchers of his era, there was little Jim Palmer did not accomplish. He won the Cy Young Award three times and played on three World Series champions (in 1966, 1970 and 1983, enabling him to become the only pitcher to win a World Series game in three different decades). He won at least 20 games in eight of nine years from 1970-78 and more games (186) in the decade of the '70s than any other pitcher.

In 1971, he joined with Dave McNally, Mike Cuellar and Pat Dobson to give Baltimore the second quartet of 20-game winners in major league history.

"Jim had one of the most beautiful deliveries I've ever seen," said Ray Miller, Palmer's former Baltimore pitching coach. "It was almost like watching ballet."

Palmer's career and life were not without problems, however. An orphan who never knew his real parents, Palmer was adopted at a young age by a New York couple, Moe and Polly Wiesen. Moe Wiesen was a dress manufacturer and Polly Wiesen owned a boutique, enabling them to raise young Jim in luxury. However, Moe Wiesen died of a heart attack when Jim was nine years old, and mother and son moved shortly thereafter to California. Mrs. Wiesen eventually married Max Palmer, an occasional Hollywood actor. Jim took his stepfather's surname when he was 13 years old.

Palmer, who grew up in a Beverly Hills home once owned by James Cagney, became an all-state performer in baseball, football and basketball while in high school. In August 1963, the Orioles gave him a reported $60,000 bonus to sign his first pro baseball contract.

Palmer spent only one year in the minor leagues (at Aberdeen, S.D., in the Northern League) before making his major-league debut with the Orioles at age 19 in 1965. He went 5-4 that season before winning a teamhigh 15 games the following year as Baltimore won its first American League pennant en route to a stunning four-game World Series sweep of the Dodgers.

Serious back and shoulder injuries over the next two years, however, sent Palmer's career into a tailspin. In 1967, he pitched just 49 innings for Baltimore; zero in 1968. In 17 starts in the minor leagues those two seasons, Palmer won exactly one game. Baltimore left him unprotected in the 1969 expansion draft held to fill out the Kansas City and Seattle rosters.

Palmer's fortunes, however, seemed to accelerate shortly thereafter just as quickly as they had crashed two seasons earlier. After playing in Puerto Rico following the '68 season, he posted a 16-4 record for the pennant-winning Orioles of '69 despite missing six weeks due to injury. In his first start after coming off the disabled list, on August 13, he hurled an 8-0 no-hit victory over the Oakland A's.

"I was beginning to think I was a physical wreck or a hypochondriac," Palmer said. "And I know a lot of people thought most of my trouble was in my head."

Palmer's numerous ailments both real and imagined were a cause of great consternation for his teammates and his manager, Earl Weaver. Weaver and Palmer had countless run-ins about the ace righthander's ability, or inability, to fulfill his pitching assignments.

"Let's see, there was the Year of the Back, the Year of the Elbow, the Year of the Shoulder and, oh yeah, the Year of the Ulna Bone," Weaver once said, disparagingly.

Prior to Game 1 of the 1979 American League Championship Series, Palmer and Weaver got into a tiff over who should be the Oriole's starting pitcher. Palmer, who won just 10 games that year after spending a month on the disabled list, thought Mike Flanagan, a 23-game winner and Cy Young recipient, deserved the assignment. Weaver, who liked Palmer's post-season experience, preferred Palmer.

Palmer started.

"A lot of times, if Jim is not 100 percent, he won't go out there," Orioles catcher Elrod Hendricks said. "He hates to be embarrassed. He feels he'll be humiliated."

Palmer wasn't embarrassed many times in his career, but a couple of those times came in 1977, when the Boston Red Sox clubbed nine home runs off him in successive starts. Palmer had asked Weaver to lift him from both games because of fatigue, but his requests fell on deaf ears.

"If I had been taken out when I said I was tired, I wouldn't have given up the majority of those nine," Palmer said. "The problem with me is that everybody expects me to be perfect. They expect me to always win and never get hurt."

In 1991, one year after his induction into baseball's Hall of Fame, the 45-year-old Palmer made a serious, if short-lived, comeback attempt. At one workout, Palmer's wife, Joni, asked Lazaro Collazo, a University of Miami assistant pitching coach who was helping the former Orioles star, what he thought of the comeback attempt.

"For a guy going to the Hall of Fame, he has terrible mechanics," Collazo said. Jim Palmer corrected him.

"I am in the Hall of Fame," he said.

Jim Palmer won more games during the 1970s than any other pitcher.

Palmer won the Cy Young Award three times and played on three World Series champions.

HERB PENNOCK

Miller Huggins, who did not express opinions carelessly, called the slender pitcher "the greatest lefthander in the history of baseball."

There were other expressions of varying shades, but nobody disputed the fact that Herb Pennock exhibited style and class during his more than 10 years in the American League.

At his peak, Pennock threw with a free and easy manner so that batters yearned to bat against him. To their chagrin, the ball never arrived at the plate when or where they expected it.

Bucky Harris, when he was managing and playing for the Washington Senators, said of Pennock, "Nicest fellow in the world, off the field. On the field, he just stands out there and looks at you and tugs on the bill of his cap . . . and winds up and lets go. The ball is never where you think it's going to be. When you swing at it the best you get is a piece of it. You fuss and fume and sweat and holler and he stands out there and looks at you . . . and tugs at the bill of his cap and—aw, what's the use?"

A native of Kennet Square, Pa., and as comfortable riding to the hounds as he was on the pitching mound, Pennock attended Friends School in West Town, Pa., but the sports program there was inadequate for Herb so he transferred to Cedar Croft school.

Instead of matriculating at the University of Pennsylvania, as his parents wished, Herb accepted a contract with the Philadelphia Athletics. "Just sit on the bench," Connie Mack told the 18-year-old. "I won't ask you to do any pitching for a long time."

Two days later (May 14, 1912), however, when Jack Coombs was treated roughly by the White Sox, Mack called on Pennock, who allowed only one hit in four innings.

Herb registered his first of 240 major league victories on June 28 when, pitching the last two innings, he received credit for a 10-inning victory over Walter Johnson and the Senators.

Waived to the Red Sox in 1915, Pennock considered retirement from the game because of his chronic wildness. He was dissuaded, though, by Manager Ed Barrow and embarked on an intensive program to develop control.

In later years, when he was asked by young pitchers how he gained control, Pennock would explain, "When I was struggling, I pitched in games, in batting practice, before games, in morning games and during the off-season. When I couldn't get anybody to catch me, I'd throw against a stone wall or a barn door. It wasn't always fun, but I kept plugging away because it meant so much to me."

Herb discovered early that speed was not essential to

Former Yankee Manager Miller Huggins called Herb Pennock the greatest lefthander in baseball history.

success. His pitches floated to the plate, causing Gee Walker of the Tigers to observe, "The only comforting thing about hitting against him is that you don't have to be afraid of getting hurt. Even if he hits you on the head with his fastball, he won't knock your hat off."

Pennock gained his greatest fame after being acquired by the Yankees on January 30, 1923, exactly 25 years before his death. He won five World Series games without a loss, compiling an earned-run average of 1.95.

His foremost performance occurred in Game 3 of the 1927 Series. Facing the Pittsburgh Pirates, who were tough on N.L. lefthanders, Pennock retired the first 22 batters en route to a three-hit victory.

Although not much of a hitter himself, Herb was frequently consulted by Babe Ruth, Lou Gehrig, Bob Meusel and Tony Lazzeri when they went into slumps.

Pennock hit one home run he always cherished. It was stroked in Fenway Park when he was with the Red Sox. The Yankees' Ruth had difficulty picking up the ball in the tall right-field grass and Herb swan dived into the plate with an inside-the-park homer.

"It was the only time I was photographed with a bat in my hand," he beamed after cameramen snapped the hero of the day.

Pennock was vice president and general manager of the Phillies and was attending an N.L. meeting in New York when he died of a cerebral hemorrhage in 1948.

TONY PEREZ

When Tony Perez signed with the Cincinnati Reds after attending a tryout camp, the only bonus the Cuban player received was enough money to buy a visa to the United States. Perez parlayed that nominal expense into an American success story. Four decades later, he was elected to the Baseball Hall of Fame.

Perez began his professional career in 1960 at age 17, and at the time he knew very little English. Despite the language barrier and other adjustments to a new country, he quickly hit his stride on the field. In his second year in the minors, he led the New York-Penn League in hits, RBIs and batting average.

By 1965 he was well on his way to becoming a regular with the Reds. After seeing plenty of playing time at first base in his first two full seasons with Cincinnati, Perez was moved to third base in 1967—and he caught fire. He hit 26 home runs in '67, drove in 102 runs and batted .290. Then, after a so-so 1968 season, he had monster years in 1969 (37 home runs, 122 RBIs) and 1970 (40 homers, 129 RBIs). His slugging in '70 was a major factor in Cincinnati's romp to the National League pennant. Reds manager Sparky Anderson moved Perez back to first base in 1972, and the player continued to be a big run-producer. Perez was a key member—perhaps even the driving force—of Cincinnati's Big Red Machine team that captured World Series crowns in 1975 and 1976 and won five divisional titles in one seven-year stretch. "That team had a lot of leaders," Anderson said. "But only when Perez left (in a trade after the '76 season) did I realize he was the leader." Reds president Bob Howsam expressed a similar view, saying Perez "had more of an effect on our team—on and off the field—than I ever realized." Perez had six 100-RBI seasons for Cincinnati and hit 20 or more home runs eight times as a Reds fixture. He batted .435 in a losing cause in the 1972 World Series against Oakland. And despite a paltry .179 batting mark, Perez hit three home runs in the '75 Fall Classic against Boston—two in Game 5 and one in Game 7. He played in seven All-Star games as a member of the Reds. His first appearance in 1967 was a memorable one—he won the game for the National League with a 15th-inning home run off Athletics pitcher Catfish Hunter.

After the 1976 season, the Reds dealt Perez to Montreal. After three seasons with the Expos, Perez signed a free-agent contract with the Red Sox. He enjoyed one last standout season in 1980, hitting 25 homers and knocking in 105 runs for Boston. He spent two more years with the Sox before rounding out his playing career with the Phillies (1983, as a part-time player on a pennant-winning

team) and the Reds (1984-1986, as a reserve on his old team). He concluded his 23-season major league career with 379 home runs, 1,652 RBIs and a .279 average.

Perez served as a Reds coach from 1987 through 1992, then got a chance to manage Cincinnati in 1993. But after only 44 games—the Reds were 20-24—management replaced him with Davey Johnson. It was a big disappointment for Perez, who had worn a Reds uniform as a player, coach and manager. Yet no one questioned his immense contributions to the Cincinnati Reds, as Hall of Fame voters demonstrated in 2000.

Tony Perez was a key contributor for the Big Red Machine of the 1970s because of his run-production numbers and leadership skills.

GAYLORD PERRY

Gaylord Perry was, by his own admission, "an outlaw in the strictest sense of the word: a man who lives outside the law," in this case the law of baseball.

Perry was the foremost and most successful advocate of the spitball in the modern era. In *Me and the Spitter*, a book he published in 1974 and billed as an autobiographical confession, he said he doctored the baseball with a variety of substances, including saliva, slippery elm, K-Y jelly, baby oil and Vaseline.

Perry, who continued a ritual of touching virtually every part of his uniform before each delivery, claimed that he stopped throwing illegal pitches at the time he wrote his book, and at least one person confirmed it.

"In 1973, he threw a few spitters," said Dave Duncan, then his catcher with the Indians. "But in 1974, he threw just one all year. It was getting to the end of the season and (Boston's) Tim McCarver was up. Gaylord called me out and said, 'Let's throw one for old-times' sake.' McCarver hit a double off the right-center-field wall.

"People forget he had terrific stuff, not just the spitter. He had an outstanding forkball."

Yet, eight years later, while a member of the Seattle Mariners, Perry became the first pitcher in four decades to be suspended for throwing a spitball. That occurred in the same season in which he won his 300th career game and certified his place as one of the toughest competitors in his sport.

To Perry, the competition between hitter and pitcher was a mind game in which just the idea that he applied a foreign substance to the ball provided him with a psychological edge.

"The more people talk and write about my slick pitch," he said, "the more effective I get. I just want to lead the league every year in psych-outs."

Perry did well in more conventional departments, too. Twice he led the National League in victories and once he topped the American League in wins. Twice he led the N.L. in innings pitched and twice he paced the A.L. in complete games. He remains the only pitcher to receive the Cy Young Award in both leagues (1972 with Cleveland and 1978 with San Diego).

In more than two decades on major league mounds, Perry pitched 5,351 innings, completed 303 starts and posted a 314-265 record. His lone stay on the disabled list was the result of a sprained ankle, suffered while running the bases.

Perhaps Perry's best season was the 1972 campaign, when he pitched for Cleveland. En route to winning his first Cy Young Award that year, Perry compiled a 24-16 record, 1.92 earned-run average and 234 strikeouts.

During his second Cy Young campaign, in '78 with San Diego, Perry fashioned a 21-6 mark with a 2.72 ERA.

Those aren't bad statistics for the son of a dirt-poor tenant farmer who did some pitching on the side. Evan Perry was a local legend in the semipro leagues around Williamston, N.C., where he pitched in the 1940s. He passed on not only his talent and guile to two sons, but also his durability.

James Evan Perry, the eldest son of Evan, won 215 games in the majors, all in the American League, and retired at 38. He won one Cy Young Award. Gaylord Jackson Perry, two years younger than Jim, padded his victory total to 314 at the age of 44 over 22 big-league seasons. Remarkably, he won 240 games after turning 30, a figure surpassed only by Cy Young's 318 and Warren Spahn's 277.

Years earlier, it was of some concern to Perry that at age 25, with a career record of 6-8, mostly in relief, he appeared buried in San Francisco's bullpen. However, his career took a dramatic turn for the better on May 31, 1964, during an historic doubleheader between the Giants and New York Mets at Shea Stadium.

Gaylord Perry, who posted a 314-265 record in 22 big-league seasons, remains the only pitcher to receive the Cy Young Award in both leagues.

The score was tied, 6-6, in the 13th inning of the second game when Manager Alvin Dark summoned Perry. Virtually everyone except the next day's starter, Bob Hendley, had been used in one capacity or another by San Francisco. "They didn't even have a catcher left to warm me up," Perry recalled. "I figured I was going to be in there until we won or lost."

No one could have known that the game would remain deadlocked until the 23rd inning, and that the two teams were engaged in what would become the longest doubleheader in history, consuming 9 hours and 52 minutes of playing time. But even as he walked to the mound on that Sunday night, Perry understood this might be the chance of a lifetime. He decided to use the spitball he had been working on since spring training for the first time in a pressure situation.

Perry proceeded to pitch 10 shutout innings before Del Crandall, pinch-hitting for Perry, drove in the go-ahead run in an 8-6 victory. Hendley closed out the victory with one inning of relief and, soon thereafter, Perry was moved into the starting rotation. Within two years, he was a 20-game winner and synonymous with the spitball.

Perry, who confessed in a 1974 autobiography that he doctored the baseball, had a ritual of touching virtually every part of his uniform before each delivery.

Signed as a free agent by San Francisco on June 3, 1958, Perry began his professional career with St. Cloud (Minn.) in the Northern League. He made his big-league debut in 1962, compiling a 3-1 record in 13 games. By 1964 he was a fixture on the Giants' roster, and in 1966 he posted the first of five 20-win seasons (21) and sported a 2.99 ERA. In 1968 he pitched the only no-hitter of his career, besting the St. Louis Cardinals, 1-0, on September 17.

Aside from his gaudy statistics, the thing that separated Perry from his peers was a dogged determination to win. He was a fierce competitor with a measure of good-old-boy hostility.

Perry was known to glare menacingly at teammates who, in his opinion, had not pursued a batted ball with sufficient effort while he was pitching. No matter that the ball he threw might be hard to get a grip on. But he affected down-home indifference when he was approached on the spitball issue during his career.

"Ain't been no damage." And the umpires are welcome "to come out and talk with me anytime."

Perry welcomed umpires "to come out and talk" with him anytime.

EDDIE PLANK

By majority opinion, he was the king of dawdlers on the pitching mound. He fidgeted so long between pitches and his games consumed so much time that commuters, it was maintained, would shun the ball park on days he worked for fear of missing their trains home.

Eddie Collins, who played second base behind Eddie Plank for a number of years on the Philadelphia Athletics, once summarized the lefthander's modus operandi as follows:

"To some he would pitch without fussing. To others he would throw the ball only when the umpire warned him against delay.

"Plank's favorite situation was two men on and a slugger up. The better the hitter, the better Eddie liked it. For, if the man had a reputation to uphold, the fans would urge him on and he would be aching to hit.

"Plank would fuss and fiddle with the ball, with his shoes, then try to talk to the umpire.

"His motion was enough to give the batter nervous indigestion. He'd dish up something the batter couldn't reach with two bats, would follow that with an equally wild pitch—inside. Probably, the next would be a twister that the batter could reach, but could not straighten out. A couple of fouls, and he would wink knowingly at me.

"Then he would attempt to pick off the baserunners, which he frequently did.

"Then, suddenly, Plank would turn his attention to the fretting batter who would, in all probability, pop up in disgust."

A native of Gettysburg, Pa., where he worked as a battlefield guide in the off-season, Plank enrolled at Gettysburg College when he was 21. Eddie had played little, if any, baseball in his youth on the family farm, but at the suggestion of Coach Frank Foreman, he tried out for the college team. Four years later, Foreman recommended Plank to Connie Mack of the Athletics.

Plank, who threw with a three-quarter motion as well as a sidearm crossfire, made his big-league debut on May

Eddie Plank (pictured in 1905) often was called king of the dawdlers.

13, 1901, at Baltimore, yielding three runs in a four-inning relief stint. He registered the first of his 305 victories five days later, an 11-6 decision over Washington.

A humorless individual, Eddie suffered from a nasal condition that impaired his breathing. He also complained frequently of a sore arm, but teammates noticed that he pitched most effectively when the alleged pain was most severe.

Plank pitched on six pennant-winning teams, but appeared in only four World Series. There was no interleague classic in 1902 when Mack's team won its first flag; in 1910, when the A's faced the Cubs for the world title, Mack entrusted the pitching to righthanders Chief Bender and Colby Jack Coombs.

In 1905, Eddie opposed the New York Giants twice, losing to Christy Mathewson, 3-0, in Game 1 and to Joe McGinnity, 1-0, in Game 4.

He split two decisions with the Giants in 1911, beating Rube Marquard on a five-hitter in Game 2 and losing in relief in Game 5 on Fred Merkle's sacrifice fly in the 10th inning.

Plank faced Mathewson twice in the 1913 Series. He lost, 3-0, in Game 2 before coming back in the fifth and final game to pitch what many regarded as his finest game ever. He outdueled Mathewson, 3-1, on a two-hitter. The only safeties were singles by Matty and catcher Larry McLean.

In his final Series effort, Eddie suffered his fifth setback. It was a 1-0 decision to Bill James of the Boston Braves in 1914.

After the A's were upset by the Miracle Braves, Plank, Bender and Coombs were released by Mack, who was unable to compete with salaries offered by the outlaw Federal League. Coombs went to the Dodgers, Bender to the Baltimore Feds and Plank, at age 39, to St. Louis' Federal League club.

When the Federal League died after the 1915 season, Plank stayed in St. Louis as a member of the Browns.

Along with Del Pratt and $15,000, Eddie was traded to the Yankees for five players in January of 1918. He refused to report, however, choosing instead to pitch in the Bethlehem Steel League.

Plank returned to his home in Gettysburg where, on February 22, 1926, he suffered a stroke that led to his death two days later. He was 50.

KIRBY PUCKETT

Seldom affected by injuries since he arrived in the major leagues in 1984, Twins outfielder Kirby Puckett was dealt a stunning blow when he was diagnosed with glaucoma before the start of spring training in 1996. The disease caused irreversible damage to Puckett's right eye, forcing him into early retirement. "Don't take it [life] for granted," said Puckett, who was 35 years old at the time. "Tomorrow is not promised for any of us, so enjoy yourself."

Minnesota's Puckett made his mark on baseball before his premature retirement. He was a standout on two World Series championship teams, won a batting title, appeared in 10 consecutive All-Star games and earned six Gold Gloves. His enthusiasm for the game made him one of the most popular players in baseball history.

"For me, a kid from Chicago, coming out of a bad neighborhood, people never thought that I would do anything," Puckett said at his retirement news conference. "The only sad thing, the only regret that I have about this game at all, is that I know I could have done so much better if I could've played (longer)."

Puckett, born and reared in Chicago, was the third pick overall in the 1982 amateur draft and spent his entire big-league career with Minnesota. He played two years in the low minors and had a short stint with Class AAA Toledo in 1984 before being called up by the Twins. A squat 5'9", 223-pounder, Puckett stormed onto the major league scene by collecting four hits in his first game, tying a major league record. He batted .296 that season with 14 stolen bases. He also had a league-high 16 assists, quickly establishing himself as a premier outfielder.

The bubbly Puckett had a strong second season, too, but his 199 hits in 1985 included only four home runs. He hadn't homered in 128 games in '84, so Twins officials were expressing some concern—at least privately—about his power potential. But Puckett silenced his critics in 1986. Coming to spring training with a new stance and style in which he kicked up his left leg before swinging, he went on a 31-homer spree and drove in 96 runs. He

Kirby Puckett, whose upbeat personality and enthusiasm made him a favorite of fans everywhere, was a .318 hitter in a career that ended prematurely.

also hit a sizzling .328. Any suggestion that Puckett had experienced a fluke season was dashed in 1987 when he batted .332 (with 207 hits) and smashed 28 home runs. His exploits helped the Twins to their first division title since 1970. Kirby had a quiet League Championship Series against Detroit—Minnesota nonetheless won in five games—but he hit .357 in the Twins' World Series triumph over the Cardinals. The Series crown, achieved in a wild seven-game battle, was a first for the Twins.

Puckett continued his assault on American League pitching in 1988, setting career highs in batting average (.356), hits (234) and RBIs (121). In 1989, he won the A.L. batting crown with a .339 mark and led (or shared) the league lead in hits for the third consecutive season. After Puckett and the Twins labored through a 1990 season in which Minnesota tumbled into last place, things turned around dramatically in 1991. Puckett helped the Twins back into the postseason by hitting .319 with 89 RBIs, and he was MVP (.429 average, six RBIs) in Minnesota's five-game ALCS conquest of Toronto. He then used his glove and bat to help the Twins pass the Braves in a stirring worst-to-first World Series (Atlanta also had finished in the basement a year earlier). In a memorable performance in Game 6, Puckett made an extraordinary leaping catch against the wall early in the game and then drilled a game-winning home run in the 11th inning. The Twins wrapped up their second Series crown in five years the next night.

Puckett remained one of the top players in the game over the next four seasons, hitting .329, .296, .317 and .314 and averaging more than 100 RBIs per year. In the strike-shortened 1994 season, he drove in 112 runs in only 108 games. He was the All-Star Game MVP in 1993. On September 28, 1995, Puckett was struck in the face by a pitch from Cleveland's Dennis Martinez and suffered a jaw fracture and a cut inside his mouth. The at-bat proved to be Puckett's last. "He didn't do it on purpose," Puckett emphasized. "I was hanging out over the plate."

Puckett was diagnosed with glaucoma the next spring, ending a career in which he batted .318 and collected 2,304 hits in only 12 seasons. He hit above .325 five times and topped 200 hits on five occasions (and once finished at 199). The man who managed only four home runs in his first two seasons (1,248 at-bats) wound up with 207 career homers. Puckett was inducted into the Baseball Hall of Fame in 2001, his first year of eligibility.

CHARLES RADBOURN

Why Charley Sweeney quit the Providence Grays in July of 1884 has never been determined conclusively. The cause for his precipitate action may have been his removal from a game while he was ahead, or it may have stemmed from the manager's insistence that he play the outfield when not pitching, a not uncommon practice in that era.

Anyhow, Sweeney bolted the club, leaving a squad of eight players, plus Charley (Old Hoss) Radbourn, who was under suspension for cursing his catcher and firing the baseball at him and knocking him flat on his back. The catcher's offense was dropping a third strike.

As the manager convened his players and discussed the necessity of disbanding the club, Radbourn spoke up.

"Do you want to win the pennant?" he asked.

"Of course, I do," the skipper replied.

"I'll pitch every game," Radbourn volunteered. "And don't worry about my being able to do it."

In return for his Herculean performance, the Providence righthander asked some extra compensation and his free agency at the close of the National League season.

Between August 7 and September 6, the Grays won 20 straight games, with Old Hoss accounting for 18 of the victories. Providence won the flag and then polished off the New York Metropolitans, champions of the American Association, in the first fully sanctioned big-league playoff as Radbourn won all three games, 6-0, 3-1 and 11-2.

Radbourn's compensation for the extraordinary season—he posted a 60-12 record, worked 679 innings and struck out 411 batters—was $3,000.

The excessive labors took a heavy toll on the pitcher's arm. He was unable to raise his hand to his ear "even if you held a $5 bill up there." He would apply hot towels to his protesting muscles for an hour or two, then toss an iron ball underhand for several minutes. Gradually, he would toss a baseball at ever-lengthening distances until he felt ready to throw at the regulation distance, at which point the game would begin.

Radbourn, whose name for years was spelled mistakenly with a final "e," learned to pitch on the family farm in Bloomington, Ill., although, strangely, he played right field for Buffalo when he made his debut in the National League on May 5, 1880. Batting sixth, Charley hit safely once and did not commit any of the Bisons' 17 errors in a 22-3 loss to Cleveland. Radbourn was released after six games.

Old Hoss made his pitching bow on May 5, 1881, when he hurled Providence to a 4-2 victory over Boston.

Although not renowned as a hitter, Radbourn enjoyed one brief moment in the spotlight because of his slugging.

Charley Radbourn won 60 games in 1884 while working 679 innings and striking out 411.

On April 17, 1882, he clouted an 18th-inning home run to give John Montgomery Ward a 1-0 victory over Detroit.

Radbourn did not exercise his option to join another club after his taxing performance of 1884, but returned to Providence to win 26 games in 1885. When the franchise folded at the close of that season, Charley joined Boston, where he posted three more 20-victory seasons. He closed his career with a 12-12 record for Cincinnati in 1891.

With his wife and stepson, Old Hoss returned to Bloomington, where he opened a saloon and pool hall. An avid outdoorsman, he hunted regularly until an accident disfigured his face. He lost an eye and suffered partial paralysis and the loss of speech. Embarrassed to face the public, Radbourn spent his final years in a darkened rear room of his establishment. The once tireless pitcher was only 43 when he died.

In 1940, more than four decades after Radbourn's death, Clark Griffith, president of the Washington Senators and also a product of the Bloomington sandlots, unveiled a plaque in the city's cemetery that recounted the achievements of Old Hoss.

In his dedicatory speech, Griffith, who learned to throw a curve on instructions from Radbourn, said, "Charley . . . I hope your spirit is hovering near so that it may be witness to the tribute paid this day to the memory of you, the greatest pitcher of all time. . . . You gave me many lessons in how to pitch and above all instilled in me the spirit of determination and courage—to you, my dear friend, thanks."

PEE WEE REESE

From 1947 through 1956, when the Brooklyn Dodgers won six National League pennants and were in the thick of every flag race, nobody contributed more handsomely or more consistently than the shortstop known as the Little Colonel.

He was christened Harold Henry Reese, but since the age of 12 he had been known as Pee Wee, a tribute to marble-shooting skills that carried him to the finals of the Louisville championship tournament.

Reese was captain of the Dodgers. During Pee Wee's 15 seasons with Brooklyn (he also played one season for the Los Angeles Dodgers), the Dodgers won seven pennants, finished second six times and wound up in third place twice. The Little Colonel was the solid performer, the one who made the dazzling plays to choke off rallies and delivered the clutch hits to ignite Brooklyn rallies. It was Reese to whom teammates looked for counsel and advice on and off the field, the one who cooled inflamed tempers in a turbulent clubhouse.

With it all, Pee Wee was a reluctant Dodger. He had graduated from the same church league team that sent Billy Herman into professional baseball. In two seasons with his hometown Louisville team of the American Association, Reese batted in the high .270s and in his second year stole 35 bases.

In the late 1930s the Colonels were owned by the Boston Red Sox and it was assumed that Reese would succeed an aging Joe Cronin as shortstop for the American League club. Reese himself counted on the move.

But Cronin, it developed, was not quite ready to abdicate and Reese was placed on the market. When that bit of intelligence reached Brooklyn, Larry MacPhail, major-domo of the Dodgers, dispatched scout Ted McGrew to check out Reese. McGrew's report sounded too lavish for MacPhail, who ordered Andy High on a similar mission.

When High was equally as extravagant in his praise, MacPhail decided to take a look himself and his evaluation surpassed the other two. The Dodgers acquired Reese for approximately $75,000 in players and cash.

Reese was in Kansas City, preparing to play in the 1939 American Association All-Star Game, when the announcement was made. He was crestfallen. For years he had heard about the Brooklyn Daffiness Boys under Wilbert Robinson—and he wanted no part of such an organization. When Pee Wee studied the situation, however—and received $3,750 as his share of the sale price—his attitude softened. In time, he admitted that the deal "was the break of my life."

When Jackie Robinson broke the modern major league color line in 1947, Kentuckian Reese rallied to the defense of his teammate. During an exhibition game in Fort Worth where raucous, racist spectators belabored Jackie, Reese strolled to Robinson's side, draped an arm encouragingly over his shoulders and spoke a few soothing words. The harassment subsided.

A similar situation developed in Boston during the early part of the '47 season. Reese repeated his earlier actions and once more the air was cleared.

Jackie never forgot Pee Wee's kindnesses.

"I could talk about that fellow for an hour, or a day or a year," Robinson said years later. "Everybody respects and follows that fellow. In my book, there's none finer."

Reese batted .300 only once, reaching .309 in 1954. His most productive RBI season was 1951 when he drove in 84 runs, and his best power season was 1949 when he smacked 16 home runs.

Always a threat on the bases, Reese led the National League with 30 stolen bases in 1952.

Reese appeared in seven World Series, during which he batted a composite .272 and helped Brooklyn to its only Series championship in 1955. He accompanied the Dodgers to Los Angeles when the storied franchise relocated there after the 1957 season.

After concluding his playing career in 1958 with a lifetime batting mark of .269, Pee Wee served as a Dodgers coach in 1959 and then retired from baseball, declining all offers of a managerial position. At the time of his election to the Hall of Fame in 1984, the Little Colonel was a representative of the Hillerich & Bradsby Co., manufacturer of Louisville Slugger bats.

Pee Wee Reese sparked the Dodgers to seven pennants and six second-place finishes in his Hall of Fame career.

SAM RICE

One afternoon in 1915, Clark Griffith announced to the Washington press that the Senators had acquired a player by the name of Rice from the Petersburg club of the Virginia League, which had just folded.

"What's Rice's first name?" a journalist wondered.

Without hesitation and hiding the fact he had no idea of the correct answer, the president-manager of the Nats blurted, "Sam."

In such fashion was born a nickname that Edgar Charles Rice carried for the remainder of his days.

Rice was a pitcher with an 1112 record and a .301 batting average when he was acquired by the Senators for a $500 loan that Griffith had extended to the Petersburg club to meet a payroll. The preceding year, Rice bought his way out of the Navy where he had gained some success as an off-duty pitcher.

Eddie Foster, a Washington outfielder, suggested to Griffith that Rice be converted into an outfielder, a move that the Old Fox adopted after Sam collected seven pinch-hits in nine at-bats. Rice became a complete player, fast afoot with a sure glove and sharp batting eye.

A lefthanded batter, Rice hit Lefty Grove with consummate ease.

"If I can't nick Grove for a couple of hits a game," Sam once remarked, "I think something's wrong."

A native of Indiana, Rice worked in the wheat fields of the Dakotas and Minnesota, served as a railroad section hand and bottled whiskey at the Green River distillery in Louisville before drifting to Norfolk, Va., and a short-lived Navy life.

Two questions stood out about Rice's career: (1) Why did he retire with 2,987 hits when he had an opportunity to become the seventh player with 3,000? (2) Did he really catch Earl Smith's long fly while tumbling into the bleachers in the 1925 World Series?

Rice was released by the Senators at the end of the 1933 season and signed with the Cleveland Indians, whose general manager, Billy Evans, told him he could play only when Evans felt like it.

Later, Sam regretted his failure to stick around long enough to collect 13 more hits, but explained, "You must remember, there wasn't much emphasis on 3,000 hits when I quit. And to tell the truth, I didn't know how many hits I had when I retired." Another factor, of course, was his age. Rice was 44 when he retired.

Sam's controversial catch occurred in the eighth inning of Game 3 of the 1925 World Series at Griffith Stadium, where temporary bleachers were erected in center field to handle the overflow from the crowd of more than 36,000.

With the Senators leading, 4-3, Smith whacked a Fred Marberry pitch to deepest right-center field. From his position in right field, Rice raced to the spot, leaped, extended his glove and tumbled into the stands.

At least 10 seconds elapsed before Rice crawled into view holding the baseball aloft. Cy Rigler, who was umpiring at second base, ruled it a legitimate catch.

The Pirates stormed the field protesting the call. Eventually, they appealed to Commissioner K.M. Landis, who tried to pry the truth from Rice. The outfielder's only comment was: "The umpire said I caught the ball." That was his stock answer to the question until the day he died.

More than 1,600 bleacherites filed affidavits and had them notarized, giving varying views on the play. Some maintained that Rice struggled with a fan for possession of the ball, others said that a fan had picked up the ball and stuck it in Sam's glove.

Senators great Sam Rice finished his career 13 hits short of the magic 3,000 level.

After Sam's death, his widow reported that her husband had shown her a letter, to be opened after his death, which he mailed to the Hall of Fame.

After considerable searching, the missing letter was found. In the letter, Rice revealed that he indeed had made the catch, adding that "at no time did I lose possession of the ball."

The whole matter would have been much more weighty if the Bucs, after losing the game, 4-3, had not gone on to win the Series in seven games.

BRANCH RICKEY

Without much doubt, nobody exercised as profound an influence on baseball for an extended period as the Ohio farm boy who invented the farm system, broke the color barrier and, through the founding of a third major league, forced the existing big leagues to expand.

A mediocre player himself but possessed of enormous enthusiasm, Branch Rickey left his imprint on baseball with his fertile brain and active imagination. He was, said a newspaperman, "a man of many facets—all turned on."

Rickey was a superb orator who delighted in blackboard lectures to players, some of whom comprehended his message. He was a master phrase-maker. Among his best remembered adages was "luck is the residue of design."

He invented the sliding pit, originated Ladies Days and organized the Knot-Hole Gang so school children could see major league games at a moderate price.

Rickey was an indefatigable worker with a highly developed eye for raw baseball talent. At a tryout camp, he spotted a graceful prospect who walked with an unnatural stride. Investigation revealed that the youngster had nailed spikes to his badly worn street shoes.

"Judas Priest!" exclaimed Rickey, then manager of the Cardinals, "let me get you a decent pair of shoes."

The player was Sunny Jim Bottomley, longtime Redbird first baseman and a Hall of Fame selection.

The son of devout Methodist parents, Rickey promised his mother while still a young man that he would not attend a ball game on Sunday. He never violated his promise. His first major league opportunity was ended before he had a chance to play a game for Cincinnati in 1904 because he refused to play on the Sabbath.

The product of a little red schoolhouse education, Rickey earned a law degree from the University of Michigan in 1911, paying for his tuition by coaching the baseball team. By that stage of his career, he had caught for the St. Louis Browns and New York Highlanders, for whom he permitted 13 stolen bases in one game.

Rickey managed the Browns for two seasons and was vice president-business manager of the Cardinals before starting a 6½-year term as field boss of the National League team in 1919.

While with the Cards, Rickey was offered the general manager's post at Detroit because, said Tigers President Frank Navin, "He's the smartest man in baseball and also he's baseball's best salesman. He'll earn two or three times his salary in the sale of surplus players."

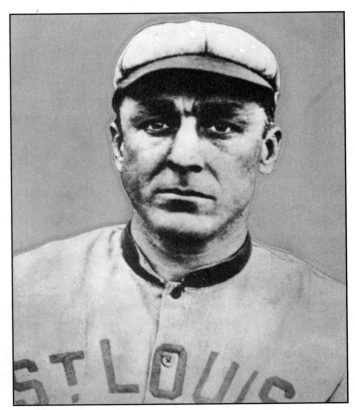

In 1905, Rickey played his first major league game as a member of the St. Louis Browns.

The deal fell through, however, when Navin was unable to match Rickey's $40,000 salary with the Redbirds.

The founding of the farm system, Rickey always said, "was not a stroke of genius, it was necessity." As the operating chief of an impoverished Cardinal club, Rickey was unable to compete with wealthier clubs on the open player market. By leaving their ball park, Robison Field, and moving into Sportsman's Park as tenants of the Browns, the Cards obtained capital to buy a half interest in the Fort Smith (Western Association) and Syracuse (International) clubs.

From those two affiliates, the Cardinal farm system grew into a productive supply source for pennant winners in 1926, 1928, 1930, 1931, 1934 and 1942.

Because of Rickey's differences with club President Sam Breadon, Branch's contract—which netted him between $75,000 and $100,000 annually—was not renewed after December 1, 1942.

Rickey joined the Brooklyn Dodgers as president-general manager and three years later announced that he had signed Jackie Robinson, a black shortstop from the Kansas City Monarchs, to a Montreal (International) contract. Robinson's success in 1946 (with the Class AAA team) and in 1947 (when he won N.L. Rookie of the Year honors with the Dodgers) paved the way for countless other blacks to achieve distinction in the major leagues.

When his co-owners protested his heavy overhead, Rickey sold them his Brooklyn stock for a reported $875,000 profit in October of 1950. Known as "The Mahatma," he moved on to Pittsburgh, where he directed Pirate operations for five years.

When the National and American leagues refused to entertain bids for new franchises in the late 1950s, Rickey and wealthy sportsmen in major league-hungry cities organized the Continental League as a third major loop. The circuit never functioned, however, as the majors began to enact expansion measures in 1960.

At age 80, Rickey was named senior consultant for the Cardinals in 1962, an office he held for three years.

Rickey suffered a heart attack on November 13, 1965, that proved fatal less than a month later.

Rickey shares a laugh with Cardinal Manager Frank Frisch (right) and Dizzy Dean in spring training of 1935.

Two baseball heavyweights, Larry MacPhail (left) and Rickey, are pictured together during their prime as top-level executives.

In 1948, Branch Rickey officiated at Jackie Robinson's second signing, a year after he broke the color barrier.

EPPA RIXEY

Charley (Cy) Rigler a longtime National League umpire, was studying law and coaching the baseball team at the University of Virginia in the early months of 1912 when he spotted a tall, gangling lefthander with a blazing fastball.

"You've got a future in professional baseball," Rigler informed the big fellow out of Culpeper, Va.

"I plan to be a chemist," the youth replied.

"I'll make a deal with you," said Rigler. "I'll arrange for the Phillies to give you a $2,000 bonus and we'll split it."

The proposition appealed to Eppa Rixey and he signed a Philadelphia contract. However, Rixey never received a cent of the promised compensation because the National League adopted a rule that an umpire could not scout for one particular team.

While Rixey got nothing, the Phils got a superb pitcher whose 266 career victories represented a record for an N.L. lefthander until the arrival of Warren Spahn.

For much of his career and through no fault of his own, the pitcher was known as Eppa Jeptha Rixey. The middle name, it developed, was the creation of Bill Phelon, a Cincinnati writer who found pleasure in bizarre nomenclature.

Easy-going Eppa Rixey never objected to the added cognomen. "It sounds," he said, "like a cross between a Greek letter fraternity and a college yell."

Although he possessed a fastball, Rixey was not a strikeout pitcher. The 6-foot-5 hurler preferred to "work" on batters and force them to swing at bad pitches. He appeared to have an unusually large number of 3-and-2 counts, yet did not issue many bases on balls. In 22 major league campaigns, he averaged only 2.1 walks per nine innings.

Eppa was not an especially good hitter. "I usually hit my weight," the 210-pounder said. But there was one day in St. Louis in 1924 that Rixey treasured forever. Batting against Jesse Haines, another future Hall of Famer, Cincinnati's Rixey clouted a home run, double and two singles. That evening he telephoned the good news to his fiancee, Dorothy Meyers, in Cincinnati.

"Goodness," she exclaimed. "Something dreadful is about to happen in St. Louis if you hit a home run."

The next day a tornado struck the Mound City.

The homer was one of three Eppa hit during his career. He belted one as a Phillie in 1920 and his last for the Reds at Boston in 1928.

Three years after joining the Phillies, Rixey appeared in his only World Series. Replacing Erskine Mayer in the

Lefthander Eppa Rixey recorded 266 career victories for the Phillies and Reds (above).

fifth and final game against the Red Sox in 1915, he allowed four hits in 6⅔ innings and was tagged with a 5-4 defeat when Harry Hooper hit a home run in the ninth inning.

Eppa served overseas in the Chemical Warfare Division in World War I. He pitched two more years for the Phils after his return to the States before he was traded to Cincinnati.

With the Reds, Rixey formed a battery with Bubbles Hargrave. Together, they represented perhaps the slowest runners in the game, so it was something of a major accomplishment when they executed a double steal against the Cubs.

"Gabby Hartnett, the best thrower in the game, couldn't believe it," related Eppa. "He just stood there open-mouthed and forgot to throw."

Eppa's finest moment as a pitcher, he often remarked, occurred in 1920 in Cincinnati when he was with the Phillies. After Edd Roush tripled to lead off the ninth inning of a tie game, Rixey walked the next two batters, then induced Greasy Neale to bounce back to the mound for the start of a double play. Eppa retired the next batter and the Phils won in the 15th inning.

Another career highlight came when Rixey hurled a two-hitter against the Giants, facing only the minimum 27 batters.

Rixey retired after recording his final six victories during the 1933 season and developed a lucrative insurance business in Cincinnati. He died of a heart attack at age 71 in 1963, one month after he was elected to the Hall of Fame.

PHIL RIZZUTO

Phil Rizzuto's path to becoming a Hall of Famer was not an easy one. Following graduation from high school in 1936, he tried out for the Dodgers and Giants but was told that at 5-foot-6 he was too small—and sent home.

After impressing a Yankees scout during a semipro game, Rizzuto tried out for the Yankees and was signed to a minor-league contract for about $75 a month. Playing in Bassett, Va., that year, he stepped in a gopher hole and injured his leg. The leg became infected and gangrene set in. Doctors were worried Rizzuto might lose his leg before they were able to save it.

Rizzuto advanced through the minor leagues and reached the majors in 1941. He was playing shortstop one day with Lefty Gomez pitching when Gomez called him to the mound.

"Kid, is your mother in the stands?" Gomez wanted to know. "Yes sir, Mr. Gomez," Rizzuto replied. 'Well, stay here and talk to me a little; she'll think you're giving advice to the great Lefty Gomez." he said.

That was the day Rizzuto hit the first homer of his career, all of which was spent playing for the Yankees. He hit .307 for his rookie campaign, and was named the league's top rookie by *The Sporting News*.

Rizzuto, who was given the nickname Scooter by a minor-league teammate, lost three prime years of his career, 1943-1945, when he enlisted in the Navy during World War II. While in the Navy, he contracted malaria and the illness continued to bother him after he returned to the team in 1946.

Rizzuto had the good fortune to play with the Yankees during their glory days. In his 13-year career, the team won nine American League pennants and won the World Series seven times. He contributed to those teams through his defensive skills and speed, and earned a reputation as one of the best bunters in the game.

It was his defensive ability that most impressed observers like Yankee manager Casey Stengel.

"He is the greatest shortstop I have ever seen in my entire baseball career, and I have watched some beauties," Stengel said. "Honus Wagner was a better hitter, sure, but I've seen this kid make plays Wagner never did."

In one stretch, Rizzuto accepted 289 consecutive chances without making an error.

Former manager Joe McCarthy was another observer who was impressed by Rizzuto's performance, especially considering his disadvantage in physical size.

"For a little fellow to beat a big fellow he has to be ter-

Phil Rizzuto had a career average of .273 and a fielding percentage of .968, and he was a key contributor to the great Yankee teams of the '40s and '50s.

rific, he has to have everything, and Rizzuto's got it," McCarthy said.

In 1949, Rizzuto was moved to the leadoff spot in the Yankees' batting order and he scored 110 runs while hitting .275 and drawing 72 walks. He finished second in the MVP voting to Ted Williams, who just missed winning his third Triple Crown.

In 1950, Rizzuto was even better. He raised his average to .324—51 points above his lifetime average—collected 200 hits, drew 91 walks, scored 125 runs and this time did win the MVP award.

A five-time All-Star, Rizzuto retired in 1956 and the next year moved into the Yankee broadcast booth with Mel Allen and Red Barber. He remained there for nearly 39 years before retiring in 1995.

Rizzuto became legendary as a broadcaster as he had as a player, developing his own style of keeping score that included notations such as WW instead of K for strikeout or BB for bases on ball. The WW stood for wasn't watching."

In 1985, Rizzuto's number 10 was retired by the Yankees and his plaque was dedicated in Monument Park. He was elected to the Hall of Fame in 1994.

ROBIN ROBERTS

As a star at Michigan State, Robin Roberts (above) was only a year away from the major leagues. After signing with the Phils, Roberts joined the parent club in 1948 (above right) after a 9-1 stint with Wilmington.

A pitching staff built around Warren Spahn and Robin Roberts most certainly would have produced more than two pennants for the Milwaukee Braves in the 1950s and '60s. However, Roberts got away because the Philadelphia Phillies' agents talked fast—and acted even faster.

Roberts' potential as a major league hurler was no secret in 1947. Robin had pitched in a Vermont summer league and was coveted by six major league clubs, including the Phils and Braves, then located in Boston.

Both clubs arranged workouts for Robin at Wrigley Field in Chicago, but, fortunately for Philadelphia, the schedule called for the Phillies to arrive first. The righthander worked out and the Phils were deeply impressed. Roberts was offered a $25,000 bonus.

Robin liked the offer, but demurred on signing because the Braves had offered his parents, living in Springfield, Ill., an expense-paid week's vacation to Chicago.

The Phils could not afford the risk, so an executive

suggested that Roberts phone his father in Springfield and discuss the matter. The elder Roberts recommended that Robin wait. His offspring countered with a promise to pay for the week-long Chicago vacation from his bonus. That clinched the matter and Robin signed with the Phils.

In his first appearance in a spring exhibition, Roberts struck out Joe DiMaggio for openers, then repeated against Phil Rizzuto.

"Did that kid throw you a fastball?" the Clipper asked the Scooter.

"I'll say he did," answered Rizzuto. "It almost flew up and hit me."

Roberts threw with an effortless motion that betrayed his fastball. The pitch arrived at the plate with deceptive swiftness, frequently freezing the bat on the hitter's shoulder.

Cardinal second baseman Red Schoendienst said the "ball seemed to skid across the strike zone as though it were on a piece of ice."

Control was never a problem for Roberts, a Michigan State graduate. He said it was a mystery to him why he had pinpoint accuracy. "I can neither understand it nor explain it," he said. "I can't comprehend why other pitchers are wild."

Robbie's chief problem after joining the Phils from a 9-1 performance at Wilmington (Inter-State) in 1948 was a needless haste between pitches. To cure the habit, coach Bennie Bengough suggested a tedious routine in which

Roberts would fondle the ball in his glove, hitch up his belt, adjust his trouser leg, tug at the bill of his cap, wipe his brow, take off his glove and maybe then take the catcher's sign.

In the 1950 National League pennant race, Manager Eddie Sawyer called on Robbie three times in the last five days. On the closing day, with everything on the line at Ebbets Field, Roberts outpitched Don Newcombe in a 10-inning struggle. Dick Sisler's homer gave Robbie his 20th victory of the year and the Phils their first flag since 1915.

Roberts pitched Game 2 of the World Series and battled Allie Reynolds into the 10th inning before DiMaggio's homer gave the Yankees a 2-1 triumph.

For six consecutive seasons, Roberts registered 20 or more victories with his explosive fastball and almost impeccable control.

He was at the crest of his career when a new manager, Mayo Smith, advised him: "You have to develop a new pitch, perhaps a sinker or a slider. You can't get by forever with just a fastball."

"I don't agree," the hurler responded. "I've gotta pitch the only way I know how."

When Roberts' speed started to fade, there was no backup pitch. Robin drifted around the majors for several years trying to win with a slowed-down fastball. But time ran out on the once-powerful righthander. He finished with 286 victories, 14 shy of the goal he might have attained with the extra pitch that he rejected.

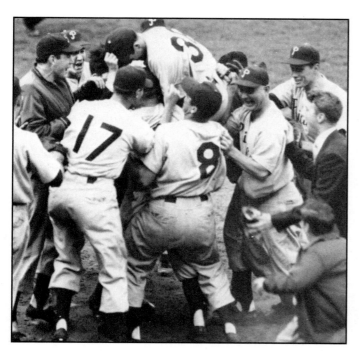

Roberts was sky high on the final day of the 1950 season when his 20th victory gave the Phillies their first pennant in 35 years.

Roberts was sold to the Yankees after the 1961 season but appeared in a New York uniform only during spring training of 1962 before being released.

BROOKS ROBINSON

Brooks Robinson in 1955, his first season with the Orioles.

Paul Richards never dreamed when he opened his mail on a February morning in 1955 that a new era was about to dawn for the Baltimore Orioles.

Among the manager's communications was a letter from a former minor league opponent, Lindsay Deal, a resident of Little Rock, Ark.

The letter trumpeted the talents of an 18-year-old high school senior who "measures up to having a good chance in major league baseball . . . he is a natural third baseman . . . his physique is outstanding for a boy his age . . . he is not a speed demon but neither is he a truck horse . . . he has a lot of baseball savvy and always is cool when the chips are down . . . seven other clubs are definitely interested in him."

Baltimore scouts followed up on the tip and confirmed Deal's judgment. For a $4,000 bonus, the Orioles acquired Brooks Robinson, an all-time great as a third baseman and as a person.

Robinson, the son of a Little Rock fireman, made his debut with the Orioles late in the 1955 season. In his first game, he rapped two singles against Washington. One of the hits, off Vibert Clarke, produced his first run batted in.

In the buoyancy of youth, Brooks told himself, "This sport was made for me."

That attitude was quickly shattered. Brooks did not get another hit in 18 remaining at bats that season. In his 22 official at-bats in '55, Robinson struck out 10 times.

By 1966, Robinson's bat was complementing his magic glove and combining with the big bat of teammate and future Hall of Famer Frank Robinson to drive the Orioles to new heights.

"That opened my eyes," he admitted. "I knew from then on I was going to have to work like blazes."

To improve all segments of his game Robbie worked in good times and bad, even through excruciating pain. Chasing a foul fly in Detroit one day, he crashed into a concrete ledge that laid open his lower jaw and chipped off parts of five teeth. In a semiconscious state, he heard the trainer say, "Call the ambulance."

The youngster leaped to his feet and demanded, "Give me my glove and let's get on with the game. Didn't you ever see anyone shaken up before?"

Almost overnight, Robbie was an accomplished third baseman.

Pie Traynor, acknowledged king of third basemen, said, "He has exceptional reflexes and even the strongest pull hitters can't get the ball by him."

Casey Stengel contributed, "Traynor was the best, but Robinson is nearly up there with him."

Brooks was at his unbelievable best in the 1970 World Series, a five-game victory for the Orioles. "Robinson beat us," groaned Manager Sparky Anderson of the losing Cincinnati Reds after Brooks batted .429 with nine hits and set a record of 17 total bases.

But Robinson's performance in the field was even more implausible. The Oriole star dived to his left and to his right, robbing Reds of sure hits. One disgruntled loser moaned, "He can field a ball with a pair of pliers."

Robinson's defense was so consistently spectacular that Cincinnati cleanup hitter Johnny Bench, a frequent victim, was incapable of anger.

"I walked back to the dugout appreciating his play for what it was-a thing of beauty," said the catcher.

While Robbie dazzled on the field, he sparkled just as brightly off it. One observer said, "Other stars had fans, Robbie made friends."

At the All-Star Game in California in 1967, Red Ruffing, the newest member of the Hall of Fame, was congratulated by only one player from the two squads. It was Brooks Robinson.

During spring training in Florida, a lady asked Brooks to pose for a photo, pure drudgery for most players. When it was discovered that the camera was out of order, Robinson took it from the lady, adjusted the mechanism, handed it back and said, "Now, see if it works."

The shutter clicked and the two parted, each smiling.

Then, too quickly, the long honeymoon was over. On September 18, 1977, Baltimore threw open its heart on "Thanks Brooks Day." A throng of 51,798, the largest regular-season crowd in the history of the franchise, jammed Memorial Stadium to say farewell to everybody's favorite player.

Gifts were few because that was the way Brooks wanted it. But there was an overflow of emotion as Robbie expressed gratitude to his wife, his parents and "to Almighty God for giving me the health and the talent."

Robinson's glove was always at its magical best during World Series, such as this 1970 diving catch against the Reds and Johnny Bench that helped the O's prevail in Game 3.

FRANK ROBINSON

S hrewd as he was as a baseball executive, Bill DeWitt was not immune to human frailties, such as errors of judgment in assessing the future of a 10-year major league veteran.

When the president of the Cincinnati Reds was asked in December of 1965 why he had traded a 30 year-old outfielder who had smashed 324 home runs and driven in 1,009 runs in 10 seasons with the club, DeWitt replied, "because he's an old 30."

The Baltimore Orioles entertained no such qualms. And in six seasons with the Birds, discarded slugger Frank Robinson dominated four pennant winners and two worldchampionship clubs.

When he retired as an active player at age 41, Robinson left behind a 21-year big-league career that produced Most Valuable Player awards in both major leagues (the only player so distinguished), 586 homers (fourth highest), a Triple Crown, a World Series MVP honor and the distinction of being the majors' first black manager.

One of 10 children, Robinson played for the Bill Erwin Legion Post team of Oakland, Calif., at a time when catcher J.W. Porter was the most coveted young player in the country. The Reds failed to land Porter, who accepted a $65,000 bonus from the White Sox and played parts of only six big-league seasons, but they did sign Porter's teammate, Robinson, for $3,000—and he was a major leaguer from 1956 to 1976.

Robinson's capabilities as a teenager were common knowledge. In 1953, when the Reds were offering five players for infielder Danny O'Connell, Branch Rickey, front-office chief of the Pirates, remarked casually, "How about throwing in that kid Robinson at Ogden?" Ogden was in the Class C Pioneer League.

The suggestion was quickly quashed by Gabe Paul, Rickey's counterpart at Cincinnati. "No way," retorted Gabe. "Robinson is the type of player you dream about. He stays."

For a fleeting moment there was some question if Robby would remain with the Reds. During spring training of 1960, irritated over Manager Fred Hutchinson's plan to make him into a first baseman, the slugger was within one step of bolting the team when Paul reminded him of the seriousness of walking out while under contract.

After his trade to Baltimore, Frank arrived at the 1966 training camp two days late. He leaped into his uniform and, without batting practice, rapped a first-pitch double in an intra-squad game.

"Hey," shouted second baseman Dave Johnson, "this guy is gonna help us."

By 1956, Frank Robinson (above) was just beginning the trek that would carry him to MVP honors for the Reds in 1961. Robinson was even better in 1966 (below) when he won a Triple Crown and MVP as an Oriole.

He sure did.

The season was barely a month old when Robinson walloped the first home run ever hit out of Memorial Stadium. The historic drive, off Luis Tiant of Cleveland, carried more than 500 feet.

Another time, during a tie game in Boston's Fenway Park, Robinson crashed into the right-field railing while making a catch that deprived slugger George Scott of a home run.

As the leadoff batter in the next inning, Frank cleverly laid down a bunt that the third baseman fielded—and nothing more.

Robinson eventually scored the winning run, but why, he was asked, did he select that spot to deliver his first bunt in 12 years.

Simple, explained Frank. He had damaged his ribs in crashing into the wall and could scarcely breathe, let alone take a full swing.

For years, Robinson spent his winters managing in the Caribbean leagues in preparation for the day when he might be tapped as the majors' first black pilot. His credentials were favorable and he got his opportunity in 1975 when he was named the player-manager of the Cleveland Indians. On opening day, the manager-designated hitter clouted a first-inning home run to help defeat the Yankees, 5-3.

But the Indians were not of contending quality and on June 19, 1977, Robby was released. Some reported he was too tough on black players, others that he was too lenient.

"I did the best I could," he commented without bitterness. "Race was not a factor."

Robinson then served as a coach with the Angels and Orioles and as manager for Rochester (International) before being appointed manager of the San Francisco Giants in 1981.

He was named the National League's Manager of the Year by United Press International in 1982 after leading the Giants to a third-place finish.

In 1972, Robinson (left) returned to the National League as a Dodger. On opening day in 1975, player-manager Robinson led the Indians to victory with his first-inning homer. He was greeted (right) by John Lowenstein.

JACKIE ROBINSON

In the aftermath of World War II, Branch Rickey decided that the social climate of the United States was at last favorable for implementing a plan that he had held in abeyance for a number of years.

The Mahatma of Brooklyn determined that the time was ripe for all-white major league baseball to admit a black player. That pioneer could not be just any black athlete, but one who measured up to the standards established by the Dodgers' president.

The player had to be a college product, a competitor, an intelligent individual with baseball talent who had the moral and physical courage to shrug off the on-field insults with remarkable displays of self-control.

Rickey's search for this extraordinary person ended with Jackie Robinson, a former three-sport star at UCLA and an Army lieutenant in World War II before joining the Kansas City Monarchs of the Negro League as a shortstop.

Rickey subjected Robinson to withering blasts of profanity and obscenity before he was convinced that the athlete possessed the discipline to hold his tongue. Only then was Jackie signed to a 1946 contract with the Montreal farm club.

Robinson won the batting championship of the International League, which ordinarily was enough of a credential for a cordial major league welcome. But the major leagues were unprepared for a social upheaval. Club owners voted 15 to 1 against the pioneering venture before Commissioner A. B. (Happy) Chandler gave his overriding approval.

Acceptance was a different matter. Once, in infield practice, Jackie was taking a blistering salvo from the opposing dugout when shortstop-captain Pee Wee Reese, a Kentuckian, laid a consoling hand on Robinson's shoulder as if to warn opponents, "He's my teammate, lay off."

Reports were circulated that the Cardinals were plotting to strike their games with the Dodgers, until National League President Ford Frick threatened lifetime banishment for anyone guilty of such actions.

Nor did all the Dodgers greet Jackie warmly. Outfielder Dixie Walker, a Georgian, was noticeably cool until he determined that Robinson was an asset to the team, at which point he gave the newcomer batting tips.

"I had to fight hard against loneliness, abuse and the knowledge that any mistake I made would be magnified because I was the only black man out there," Robinson wrote in his autobiography.

But Jackie fought fiercely, and the Dodgers won because of him. In Robinson's 10 seasons with Brooklyn, the Dodgers won six pennants and one world championship. Jackie was the Rookie of the Year in 1947 and the N.L.'s Most Valuable Player two years later when he won the batting championship.

Jackie Robinson (left) was a three-sport star at UCLA before joining the Kansas City Monarchs (center, 1944) as a shortstop. By 1948, Robinson (right) had weathered his first major league season.

Robinson was a pressure player of the highest order. On the last day of the regular season in 1951, when the Giants had already won and assured themselves of a pennant tie, the Dodgers were locked in an extra-inning game at Philadelphia. The Phillies loaded the bases with two outs in the 12th inning when Jackie made a diving catch of a wicked line drive. In doing so, however, he jammed an elbow into his stomach and was knocked unconscious.

Two innings later Robinson socked a game-winning homer that created a pennant tie (which was resolved in the historic playoff with the Giants).

If it had not been for Rickey, Jackie was set to quit baseball. "It was too dificult in the black league," he declared. "The travel was brutal. Financially, there was no reward. It took everything you made to live off."

Had he quit baseball, Robinson said, he probably "would have gone to coach baseball at Sam Houston College (in Texas). My minister had gone there. That was about the only thing a black had left then, a chance to coach somewhere at a small black college."

After the 1956 season Jackie, then 37, was traded to the Giants. Rather than report, however, he announced his retirement in a bylined article in *Look* magazine.

Robinson went on to hold numerous executive positions within the business community. He was chairman of the board of the Freedom National Bank.

Less than two weeks after Jackie was honored at the 1972 World Series, he suffered his second heart attack at his Stamford, Conn., home and died at age 53.

Daring baserunning was a Robinson trademark, such as his steal of home (above) in Game 1 of the 1955 World Series against the Yankees and catcher Yogi Berra. Robinson (below) forces out Yankee pitcher Allie Reynolds on a double-play attempt during the 1949 Series.

WILBERT ROBINSON

He was legendary in his own time, a Falstaffian figure with sound baseball instincts but renowned chiefly for anecdotes presenting him as an amiable leader of less gifted athletes.

When three Brooklyn players wound up on third base, he muttered, "That's the first time they've been together all season."

When Zack Taylor tripled to lead off the ninth inning of a tie game, his manager, coaching at third base, extended his hand. "Great going, kid," he bubbled. "Put 'er there." Taylor did as he ordered, stepped off the bag and was tagged out.

When the Brooklyn Daffiness Boys of the 1920s became unbearably zany, the pilot announced the formation of a Bonehead Club. Anyone guilty of a mental misadventure would be fined $10. He then gave the umpires an old batting order, costing the Dodgers some runs and the game.

Wilbert Robinson, known universally as Uncle Robbie, was like that, lovable but certainly not loony.

As a youth in Massachusetts, Robbie drove a fishmonger's wagon, earning

Wilbert Robinson, best known for his years as Brooklyn Dodgers manager, was a catcher for the National League Baltimore franchise in the 1890s.

him his first nickname as Billy Fish. His formal education was limited, and spelling was a constant puzzle to him.

On a day when he wished to start Oscar Roettger at first base instead of Claude Hendricks, Robinson started to fill out the lineup card. Coming to Roettger's name, he began R-o-t, then erased it. He gave it another try . . . R-e-o. In frustration he cried out "Hendricks, you play first base."

From the beginning, it appeared that Uncle Robbie's career would be different from most. While playing for the Baltimore Orioles on June 10, 1892, Robbie collected seven hits in as many at-bats and drove in 11 runs in a 25-4 victory over St. Louis. The record achievement went unnoticed in the daily newspapers the next day and remained undetected for 20 years until Heywood Broun unearthed it in a casual conversation with Robinson.

While with the Orioles, Robbie became a fast friend of John McGraw. They opened a cafe and bowling establishment known as The Diamond, where duckpins were invented. The business flourished, but it was dissolved when McGraw moved to New York as manager of the Giants in 1902.

Robbie was named player-manager of the Orioles upon

McGraw's departure. A broken finger in July of 1904 led to his quitting the game in favor of a saloon enterprise. He also operated a butcher shop and was extremely proud of his skills in that business. Many years later, when the Dodgers were given a tour of the Chicago stockyards, Robbie, on invitation, picked up an executioner's hammer and slew a steer with one well-aimed blow to the head.

Robinson returned to baseball in 1911 as a coach under McGraw. In that role, he was credited with the development of Rube Marquard and Jeff Tesreau as top-flight pitchers.

Old cronies Robinson and McGraw fell out over strategy in the 1913 World Series and Robbie moved to Brooklyn the next season where he began an 18-year reign as manager. In tribute to the new pilot, the team was renamed the Robins.

The club won two pennants under Robbie, but lost the 1916 World Series to the Red Sox and the 1920 Series to the Indians.

For the first 11 years in Brooklyn, Robinson enjoyed a pleasant relationship with Charles Ebbets. When the club president died in 1925, however, and Vice-President Ed McKeever passed away a short time later, heirs battled fiercely for control of the club. As a compromise, Robbie added the presidential duties to his managerial responsibilities. It was an impossible situation.

During spring training of 1927, the Giants threw a big party in Venice, Fla., to mark McGraw's 25 years as manager. Dodger officials were invited, but Uncle Robbie flatly refused to attend. At the last minute, he yielded to vigorous persuasion and healed old wounds.

In his later years, Robbie made his winter home at Dover Hall, Ga., where he loved to hunt and fish and sit before a roaring fire quaffing choice viands. Having undergone major surgery, he asked his doctor if he were permitted alcohol. "No more than a mouthful a day," he was told. Thereafter he would pour himself a water tumbler full. When he was queried about the excessive amount, he would reply, "That's a mouthful—a cow's mouth."

Robinson's death at 70 was followed by burial at Sea Island, Ga., in close proximity to the graves of his beloved hunting, fishing and drinking buddies, Col. Til Huston, former co-owner of the Yankees, and Bill McGeehan, noted New York sportswriter.

BULLET ROGAN

One of the first people to judge the outstanding base-ball ability of Wilbur "Bullet" Rogan was Casey Stengel, at the time decades away from making himself a household name in the game.

Rogan had joined the Army in 1911 and remained in the service for eight years, being selected as the captain of camp baseball teams while stationed in the Philippines, Hawaii and Arizona. He caught Stengel's eye while play-ing with the infantry team based at Fort Huachua. Stengel recommended Rogan to J. L. Wilkinson, owner of the All Nations baseball team.

Based on Stengel's opinion, Wilkinson signed Rogan for his team in 1917, though Rogan was still in the Army. Rogan played with the team that season as a pitcher, out-fielder and shortstop. He also played that year in a win-ter league for the Los Angeles White Sox where, though he was a pitcher, he was placed fifth in the batting order.

Wilkinson also owned the Kansas City Monarchs club, and when that club was placed in the Negro National League in 1920, Rogan moved to that team and began an association that lasted for 19 seasons.

Born on July 28, 1889 in Oklahoma City, Rogan grew up in Kansas City, Kan., and began his baseball career as a catcher with Fred Palace's Colts in 1908. He also played for a year with the Kansas City Giants and helped that team to 54 consecutive wins against semipro and local competition.

Bullet Rogan was considered the finest fielding pitcher in the Negro League.

Rogan earned his nickname because of his outstanding fastball, which helped him become one of the most respected pitchers in the Negro League, despite the fact that he was not intimidating physically, standing just 5-foot-9 and weighing 175 pounds.

Another member of the Monarch staff, Chet Brewer, compared Rogan to legendary pitcher Satchel Paige and said, "Rogan should have been put in the Hall of Fame before Satchel. Rogan could throw a curveball faster than most pitchers could throw a fastball."

Said fellow Hall of Famer Judy Johnson, "Satchel Paige was fast, but Rogan was smart."

Rogan, also considered the finest fielding pitcher in the Negro League, had a .721 winning percentage in his career, a record of 113-45, the highest winning percentage in league history. He used a no-windup delivery and his pitch assortment included a forkball, palmball and a legal spitter in addition to his fastball and curveball. He led the league in wins in 1924, 1925 and 1927.

Rogan was a workhouse who averaged 30 starts a year for a decade, and when he wasn't pitching, he usually played the outfield. He led the league with 16 homers in 47 games in 1922 and also consistently hit over .300, twice topping the .400 mark, and finished his career with a .343 average.

In 1924, he led the Monarchs to the Negro League World Series by leading the league with 16 wins and hit-ting .411. In the World Series against Hilldale, he pitched three complete games, going 2-1, and relieved in another, compiling a 2.57 ERA. He played in the outfield the other six games, hitting at a .325 clip to lead the Monarchs to the championship. With Rogan unable to pitch the fol-lowing year because of an injury, the Monarchs lost to Hilldale. Rogan became the Monarchs player-manager in 1926, and the team reached the playoffs against the Chicago American Giants. He started both games of a doubleheader on the last day of the playoff, but lost both games to Willie Foster, who also pitched both games.

The Monarchs won their fourth league title in seven years in 1929, and after the team disbanded and then reformed in 1931, Rogan came back as manager and remained in that job until 1938. He then became an umpire and worked in the Negro American League through the 1946 season.

He continued to play exhibitions against major lea-guers, compiling a .329 average in 25 games. He made his final appearance at the age of 48, playing left field against the Bob Feller All-Stars and collected three hits.

"Old Rogan was a showboat boy, a Pepper Martin-type ballplayer," said Hall of Famer Dizzy Dean. "He was one of those cute guys, never wanted to give you a good ball to hit."

After his baseball career, Rogan worked in the post office in Kansas City. He died on March 4, 1967. He was elected to the Hall of Fame by the Veterans Committee in 1998.

EDD ROUSH

In 1920, Edd Roush was coming off one of his two batting championships as a member of the Cincinnati Reds.

The atmosphere on the Giants' bench was tense as John McGraw picked up a bat that had been flicked away by a batter. "Whose is this?" he snarled.

"Don't say anything," coach Hans Lobert advised the guilty party.

"That's my bat," said the kid from Indiana, ignoring the advice.

"Don't ever let me catch you using that bat again," growled the manager.

"Sh-h-h-h," Lobert advised again.

"This is the first damn league I ever played in where the manager picked the bat for you," came the rejoinder.

"What league did you ever hit .300 in?" McGraw wanted to know.

"Every league I ever played in," replied the not-quite-honest rookie, Edd Roush, "and I'd do it in this league, too, if I'd play regularly."

Roush was an original. Nobody, not even the belligerent McGraw, intimidated him. Edd detested spring training and he knew his value as a player, even if it meant holding out all season in defense of a principle.

Edd's initial "J" did not stand for a name. Roush's grandfather's were named Jim and Joe and so not to show favoritism, his parents settled on the initial.

Shortly after his clash with McGraw in 1916, Roush was traded to Cincinnati, and McGraw spent the next decade trying to buy him back.

In Roush's opinion, the lengthy spring training periods were unnecessary. When he was asked when he could be expected to join his teammates, Edd would reply, "Just before you break camp." Generally, he did not sign his contract until he reached camp. There was one exception and it was, said Roush, "my biggest mistake."

That was in his first year with the Giants when McGraw invited Edd to Mineral Wells, Tex., the Giants' training site, to "talk it over." Roush complied. When the manager would not budge, Edd realized that a return home would be at his own expense, so he signed. Thereafter he held out in his hometown of Oakland City, Ind.

His first day in camp, Edd would take batting practice to sharpen his eye. The next day he would field infield grounders to flex some muscles. The third day he would field flies in the outfield, and by then he was ready to go. One year he did not report until July, then banged three hits in his first game.

Roush swung a 48-ounce bat, the heaviest manufactured by the makers of Louisville Sluggers. He insisted he never broke a bat. He ordered six at the start of each sea-son. By closing day they were gone, given away by Edd or the clubhouse boy.

The Giants reacquired Roush in January of 1927 and, as customary, the player held out. McGraw wired an invitation to meet him in Chattanooga—at the manager's expense.

"Don't you want to play for me?" asked McGraw.

"Hell, no," shot back Roush.

"I won't climb over you or call you names," McGraw promised. "I'll leave you alone. I can't pay the $30,000 you demand, but I'll give you a three-year contract for $70,000." Roush accepted.

When the Giants sought to cut his pay $7,500 in 1930, Edd stoutly resisted, announcing, "I never got a $7,500 raise, so I ain't taking a $7,500 cut." He stayed out of the game that year.

Back with Cincinnati in 1931, he played 101 games, then retired.

During his big-money days, Roush was not a spend-thrift. While others were buying drinks for the house, Roush went to a local brewery "where I could drink as much beer as was good for me."

Out of his relatively high earnings, and with a frugal lifestyle, Edd invested heavily in General Motors, Procter and Gamble and Sears & Roebuck, as well as in government bonds. As a result, he was able to live and travel as he pleased during his retirement.

RED RUFFING

One afternoon in 1929, a Boston Red Sox pitcher was hitting fungoes to outfielders in pregame drills when the Yankees' manager called him aside.

"I understand," said Miller Huggins, "they are trying to make an outfielder out of you. Don't let 'em do it. Someday you may be with us."

The next season Red Ruffing was with the Yankees. Huggins, though, had died in September of 1929.

Ruffing remained a pitcher for the remainder of his career. The absence of four toes from his left foot, the result of a mine accident, restricted his running speed. His productive bat was limited to pinch-hitting appearances and to those days when he was wheeling his fastball and sharp curve from the mound.

At age 15, Ruffing played first base on a mine company team managed by his father in Nokomis, Ill. After the mine mishap cost him his toes, the youngster just about abandoned hopes for a major league career.

"I couldn't run a lick," he remembered, "but one day our team was to play against another mine team which was loaded with ringers and our pitcher developed a sore arm.

"Everybody on the team said I should pitch and I only lost the game, 3-2, in the 10th inning because our left fielder dropped a fly ball. In my next game I struck out 16.

"The foot bothered me the rest of my career and I had to land on the side of my left foot in my follow-through."

The youngster's success with the mine team caught the attention of the owner of a Nokomis semipro team.

Asked how much his father paid him per game, Ruffing said, "My dad doesn't pay any of his players."

"I'll give you $75 to play three games next week," the club owner told Ruffing. "My dad just lost a pitcher," the redhead replied.

By the time he was 19, Red was with the Red Sox, who were struggling to attain respectability after a previous owner disposed of the club's stars. In a little more than five seasons, Ruffing won only 39 games and lost 96. He lost 25 games one year and 12 straight the following season while en route to 22 defeats for the campaign.

Ruffing's fortunes improved dramatically with the Yankees. In time, Bill Dickey would say, "If I were asked to choose the best pitcher I've ever caught, I would have to say Ruffing."

Red topped the 20-victory mark four times. And generally, the big righthander opened the World Series for the Yankees, as he did in 1942 against the Cardinals in St. Louis. It was Red's most memorable Series performance although, strangely, he was not around for the finish of the game.

In 1936, Red Ruffing embarked on a string of four 20-victory seasons for the Yankees.

Ruffing issued two walks in the first inning, but then mowed down the Redbirds with regularity until, after six innings, he said to a teammate, "You guys don't have to be so damn quiet. I know I've got a no-hitter, and if I get through the eighth I'll keep it."

But, with two out in the eighth, Terry Moore broke the spell with a single. Ruffing had a 7-0 lead with one out in the ninth, but the Cards scored four runs and Spud Chandler came on to preserve the lead.

Overall, Ruffing posted a 7-2 Series record.

After two years in military service, Ruffing rejoined the Yankees in 1945.

In 1946, he had a 5-1 record when he suffered a broken kneecap when struck by a line drive and was sidelined for the remainder of the year. He concluded his active career with the White Sox in 1947.

The winner of 273 games scouted for the White Sox and Indians and also managed several minor league clubs before his appointment as the first pitching coach for the Mets in 1962.

In September of 1973, Ruffing suffered a stroke that confined him to a wheelchair. Despite his handicap, Red still managed to travel from his Cleveland home to Cooperstown, N.Y., for the Hall of Fame installation ceremonies.

AMOS RUSIE

The powerful righthander came out of Indiana in 1890 and because of his blinding speed he was immediately nicknamed the "Hoosier Thunderbolt."

Amos Rusie was the first genuine sports idol of New York City. Actress Lillian Russell asked to be introduced to him. Comedians Weber and Fields wrote a skit in his honor. A hotel bar concocted a cocktail that bore his name, and small boys everywhere saved their pennies—25 of them—so they could buy a paperback titled "Secrets of Amos Rusie, the World's Greatest Pitcher, How He Obtained His Incredible Speed on Ball."

Whether Rusie's fastball attained greater velocity than those of later pitchers in problematical, but in the 1890s it was regarded as second only to the speed of sound.

One of Amos' pitches struck Hughey Jennings on the head, knocking the Baltimore shortstop unconscious for four days. Another of Rusie's fastballs was lined back to the mound where it struck the pitcher on the ear and damaged his hearing permanently.

Partly because of Rusie's speed, the pitching distance was increased from 50 feet to 60 feet, 6 inches. The change was not only a safety measure for batters, but was an aid to Amos as well, inasmuch as it provided the extra distance needed to put the break on his overpowering curveball.

Amos Rusie was the first genuine sports idol of New York City.

Rusie, who quit school at an early age to work in a lounge factory, made his baseball debut as an outfielder with a team in the Indianapolis City League. When the regular pitcher was knocked out of a game, teammates suggested that Amos replace him. Rusie never again played the outfield.

The hard-throwing pitcher's reputation led to a contract with the Indianapolis (National) club. In his first appearance, Amos opposed the New York Giants. It was, observers agreed, an unfair test for the young hurler, but Amos took it in stride. He struck out the first batter on three pitches (none of which, the victim said, he saw).

Rusie himself became a Giant in 1890 when the Indianapolis franchise was transferred to New York, where he became an instant hero.

Differences between Rusie and Owner Andrew Freedman created a sticky situation, though. When Rusie rejected a young pupil because "he was a smart aleck" and unwilling to learn, Freedman fined the pitcher $100.

Later, when Amos insisted he was in bed at 11 p.m., the owner accused him of being out all night. A second $100 fine resulted.

When he received his 1896 contract, which did not restore what he considered unjust fines, Rusie refused to sign. Freedman stood firm. The pitcher sat out the entire season, after which he sued Freedman for $5,000.

Rather than have the case come to trial, other N.L. owners, in a meeting at Indianapolis, voted to make up the amount of the suit. As a consequence, Rusie earned $2,000 more by remaining idle than if he had pitched.

Rusie signed his 1897 contract, but then it was Freedman's turn. He issued orders that Amos should not be issued a uniform.

Shortly, the owner relented to the point that Rusie was given a uniform and ordered to sit in the bullpen. When the Giants lost a number of games and fans started to cry for Freedman's scalp, the owner yielded and Amos came on to snap the losing streak.

In 1898, after compiling a 20-10 record, Rusie attempted to pick off Chicago's Bill Lange without first moving his foot toward first base. Something "like a jolt of electricity" shot through his arm. The pain was blinding. He did not know that Lange had been called out, nor was he able to catch the ball when it was returned to the mound.

Amos finished the game, however, throwing "floating curves." The next day he commenced a series of visits to doctors, none of whom could diagnose his problem.

Rusie remained out of baseball for two years, then was traded to Cincinnati in a deal that sent Christy Mathewson to the Giants. Amos pitched three games for the Reds in 1901 and was kayoed each time. At 30 he was washed up.

Rusie worked in a Muncie, Ind., paper and pulp mill for three years until it closed. He moved to Vincennes, Ind., and engaged in fresh water pearling in the Wabash River.

In 1911, Amos got a job as a steamfitter in Seattle, working in that capacity for 10 years and eventually becoming foreman. In 1921, John McGraw, learning of Rusie's whereabouts, offered him a job as superintendent of the Polo Grounds.

He resigned in 1929 and returned to the Northwest, where he bought a small ranch and raised chickens and engaged in farming on a small scale. In 1934, he suffered multiple injuries in a car accident that handicapped him until his death in 1942 at age 71.

BABE RUTH

In the after-stench of the Black Sox scandal, when baseball urgently needed a magnetic personality to restore public confidence in the game, there emerged a bulbous figure with an explosive bat who, more than any other player, set the game soaring to unprecedented popularity.

On and off the playing field, Babe Ruth was a man of gargantuan achievements. He was a symbol of that deliriously wacky age known as the "Roaring Twenties," and he roared louder than his contemporaries.

When he wasn't setting home run records, Ruth was shattering all known gastronomic marks. A quart of chocolate ice cream and pickled eels were standard fare between games of a doubleheader. A breakfast might consist of a pint of bourbon and ginger ale, a porterhouse steak, four fried eggs, fried potatoes and a pot of coffee.

Ruth did everything in a style unknown to lesser mortals. He could party all night, drive cars at break-neck speed, consume enormous portions of food and drink and then perform as the demigod of the diamond.

Babe was in a class by himself as a gate attraction.

After establishing records as a lefthanded pitcher, he became a symbol for majestic, dramatic home runs and for equally majestic, dramatic strikeouts, all of which earned him adulation from the spectators.

A Baltimore waterfront waif who learned to sip beer and chew tobacco before he was 7, George Herman Ruth entered St. Mary's Industrial School, where he learned a degree of discipline and the rudiments of baseball.

When Ruth was 18, his tutor, Brother Mathias, recommended him to Jack Dunn of the Baltimore (International) Orioles. The owner was impressed and signed the kid, immediately named Babe, as a pitcher. By the end of the 1914 season, Ruth was purchased by the Boston Red Sox.

For five years he was a mainstay of the Sox's pitching staff, appearing in three World Series. Gradually, however, as his batting talent became apparent, he saw more action as an outfielder. By the time he was traded to the Yankees in 1920, Babe's days as a pitcher were virtually ended.

Aided by a new, lively ball, the Bambino won a nation's heart by slugging 60 home runs in 1927 and a career total of 714. At other times, he flouted the authority of club management as well as the commissioner of baseball.

When he collapsed on the Asheville, N.C., railroad platform in 1925, suffering from "the world's largest belly ache," Babe was fined $5,000 by the Yankees for breaking training rules and curfew.

A young Babe Ruth, standing (left) with the catcher's mitt and mask, poses with his teammates at St. Mary's Industrial School, where he learned the rudiments of baseball.

Another time, he ignored Commissioner K.M. Landis' edict against postseason barnstorming and drew a 30-day suspension as well as a fine.

Meanwhile, home runs flew in abundance. Ruth swatted three in one World Series game against the Cardinals in 1926 and duplicated the feat against the same team in 1928. In his 10th and last Series, against the Cubs in 1932, the Babe walloped two homers, including a controversial shot that may, or may not, have been called.

As Ruth's homer totals soared, so did his salary—until it reached $80,000 annually. During Herbert Hoover's administration, Ruth once was a holdout. Seeking to break the impasse, a writer friend reminded Ruth that he was already earning more than the President.

"I had a better year than he did," grunted Ruth.

Several years earlier, while all the Yankees were being introduced to Calvin Coolidge at a Washington opener, Babe broke the routine with: "Geez, it sure is hot, ain't it, Prez."

The Babe eagerly sought the Yankees' managerial job before the appointment of Joe McCarthy in 1931, but Owner Jake Ruppert passed him by.

The Sultan of Swat was released after the 1934 season and joined the Boston Braves as vice president, assistant manager and outfielder. Babe socked six homers in the National League, the final three in a May 25, 1935 game at Pittsburgh. He retired after appearing in 28 games.

His once-powerful frame shriveled by cancer, Ruth died in 1948 at age 53.

Ruth watches the flight of his 60th home run in 1927, the homer that stood as a baseball standard until 1961.

Ruth (center) was a strong-armed lefthanded pitcher for the Red Sox during his early years. By 1926, Ruth was making headlines with his bat (left) and colorful off-field exercises (right).

NOLAN RYAN

Pat Jarvis and Greg Myers have something in common that they might not realize. Jarvis, a pitcher for the Atlanta Braves, was the first strikeout victim in the major leagues of Nolan Ryan on Sept. 11, 1966. Myers, a catcher for the California Angels, was the last, on Sept. 17, 1993.

Including those two strikeouts—27 years and a week apart—the Ryan Express struck out 1,174 other batters a total of 5,714 times on his way to stardom that included seven no-hitters and 53 major league records.

No other pitcher in history has matched Ryan's performance, which included 324 victories and almost every strikeout record imaginable. No other player, neither pitcher nor position player, appeared in 27 different seasons and the only pitcher who started more games than Ryan's total of 773 was Cy Young with 815. The only athlete in any of the major professional sports who spent more time as an active player was Gordie Howe in hockey, who was active for 32 years.

Ryan was born Jan. 31, 1947 in Refugio, Texas. He grew up in Alvin, Texas, and after high school was drafted by the New York Mets in the 10th round of the 1965 amateur draft and was signed by scout Red Murff. He made his professional debut that year in Marion, Va., in the rookie Appalachian League, going 3-6 in 13 games.

Ryan gave an indication of his future ability in 1966, pitching at Greenville, S.C., when he went 17-2. After three games at Williamsport, he was called up to New York in September, pitching in two games for the Mets. He missed most of the 1967 season because of military obligations and a sore elbow, but arrived back in New York in 1968 and was in the majors to stay.

Ryan pitched five seasons with the Mets before he was traded on Dec. 10, 1971 to the California Angels with pitcher Don Rose, catcher Francisco Estrada and outfielder Leroy Stanton in exchange for infielder Jim Fregosi. Ryan spent eight years with the Angels before signing as a free agent with Houston before the 1980 season.

After nine years with the Astros, Ryan again became a free agent after the 1988 season and this time signed with the Texas Rangers, where he completed his career. Before expansion in 1993, he was one of nine pitchers in history to defeat every major league team and recorded at least one win in 31 of the 35 stadiums he pitched in during his career.

Ryan was most widely known for his huge strikeout totals and his no-hitters, more than any pitcher in history. Six times in his career he struck out more than 300 batters in a season, topped by the major league record of 383 strikeouts for the Angels in 1973. He led his league in

Nolan Ryan's jersey number, 34, was the first ever retired by the Rangers.

strikeouts 11 times and struck out 200 or more batters 15 times.

He averaged 9.55 strikeouts per nine innings in his career, becoming the only pitcher other than Sandy Koufax to average a strikeout an inning among pitchers with at least 1,500 innings pitched. He is 1,578 strikeouts ahead of Steve Carlton, second on the all-time list, the widest percentage differential between first and second place in any major statistical category.

Ryan struck out 10 or more batters a record 215 times. Koufax is second with 98. Ryan struck out 19 batters in a game four times, three of those in extra innings. His 19 strikeouts in a nine-inning game on Aug. 12, 1974, was a record until Roger Clemens struck out 20 in 1986. He had 26 games in which he struck out 15 or more batters, another record, and struck out the side in an inning 331 times in his career.

He became the oldest player to ever lead the American League in a major statistical category when he led the league in strikeouts in 1990 at the age of 43. He is the only pitcher to strike out 16 or more batters after the age of 40, and he did it three times. His strikeout victims included eight father-and-son combinations, 12 sets of brothers, and 27 members of the Hall of Fame (through the 1999 election).

Ryan's most frequent victim was outfielder Claudell Washington, whom he struck out 39 times. Among Hall of Famers, his favorite victim was Rod Carew, who fanned 29 times.

Ryan, the first player in history to earn $1 million a season, broke the previous career record of 3,508 strikeouts set by Walter Johnson on April 27, 1984 when he struck out Montreal's Brad Mills.

The 6-foot-2, 195-pound righthander was most known for a blazing fastball. One of his catchers, Jeff Torborg, said one time he got a vivid reminder of just how fast Ryan threw.

"In 1973 against the Red Sox, Nolan threw a pitch a little up and over my left shoulder," Torborg said. "I reached up for it and Nolan's pitch tore a hole in the webbing of my glove and hit the backstop at Fenway Park."

Torborg was the catcher for Ryan's first career no-hitter, on May 15, 1973, for the Angels at Kansas City. He pitched three other no-hitters for the Angels: on July 15, 1973, at Detroit, on Sept. 28, 1974, against Minnesota, and on June 1, 1975, against Baltimore.

Ryan had one no-hitter while pitching for the Astros, on Sept. 26, 1981, against Los Angeles. His final two no-hitters came in a Texas uniform, on June 11, 1990, at Oakland, and on May 1, 1991, against Toronto. Ryan also pitched 12 one-hitters in his career, tying Bob Feller's record, and he had five potential no-hitters broken up in the ninth inning.

An eight-time All-Star, Ryan pitched in five games. He was the starting pitcher in the 1979 game at Seattle. He was the winning pitcher in his final All-Star appearance, in 1989, when he became the oldest pitcher to win an All-Star game and the second oldest to appear in one.

Nolan Ryan averaged 9.55 strikeouts per nine innings, the only pitcher—among those with 1,500 or more innings pitched —other than Sandy Koufax to hold that record.

For most of his career, Ryan pitched for teams that were not in playoff contention. He made it to the postseason five times, losing the 1981 divisional series to the Dodgers, and three times losing in the league championship series, with the Angels in 1979 and the Astros in 1980 and 1986. His only appearance in the World Series came early in his career, for the Mets in 1969, when he earned a save in Game Four in his only appearance as New York upset the Orioles in five games.

Ryan's first career win came on April 14, 1968 against Houston. He became the 20th pitcher to win 300 games with a victory over Milwaukee on July 31, 1990.

Ryan, who made 16 trips to the disabled list during his career, accomplished almost everything possible in his career, except for winning a Cy Young award. He won 21 games or more on two occasions, for the Angels in 1973 and 1974, and won 19 games in both 1972 and 1977. Ryan's final win came on Aug. 15, 1993, at Cleveland.

He made his final appearance on Sept. 22, 1993 at the Kingdome in Seattle. He tore the ulnar collateral ligament in his right elbow on a 1-1 pitch to Dave Magadan in the first inning. His jersey number 34 was the first-ever retired by the Rangers, and made Ryan one of four players and a manager to have a jersey retired by two teams. California retired Ryan's number 30 in 1993. The other players so honored by two teams are Hank Aaron, Carew, Rollie Fingers and manager Casey Stengel.

As a player, Ryan made two visits to the Hall of Fame in Cooperstown, playing with the Angels and Astros in the annual exhibition game that is part of the induction weekend. He said he never thought while he was there that he would one day be back, enshrined as a member of the Hall.

"When I was an active player, I concerned myself with the job I had to do," Ryan said in an interview with the *Dallas Morning News*. "In the offseason, I was always preoccupied with the next season, working out, or dealing with what my daily life consisted of.

"I was never one who reminisced or reflected back on what had happened in their career. I was the type that always concerned myself with today and what I had to do for tomorrow. That's pretty much the way I've lived my life."

Since his retirement, Ryan has continued to work for the Rangers as an assistant to the president, helping the team with baseball operations, marketing and public relations on a part-time basis. He also is active in the ranching and banking business in his hometown of Alvin.

When Ryan was elected to the Hall of Fame in 1999 in his first season of eligibility, he was named on 491 of 497 ballots cast, a percentage of 98.79. The only player to receive a higher percentage was Tom Seaver, 98.84.

RAY SCHALK

When the Milwaukee team of the American Association needed a catcher immediately in 1911, the Detroit Tigers agreed to let the Brewers have a teenager on whom they had acquired an option for $750.

The young player was with Taylorville in the Illinois-Missouri League. The following season he joined the White Sox, starting a 17-year career with Chicago that earned him recognition as one of the game's all-time best catchers.

Ray Schalk was one day short of his 20th birthday when he reported to the White Sox at Comiskey Park on August 11, 1912. Schalk arrived a few hours before the start of a Sunday doubleheader and was greeted by Manager Jimmy Callahan, who told him, "Here's your pitcher, Doc White. You're catching the first game."

The youth handled White like an old pro and rapped a single off Chief Bender, but the Sox lost to the Athletics, 3-1.

When and how Schalk obtained the nickname of Cracker was never determined satisfactorily. One version insisted it stemmed from a remark of a veteran player who, seeing Schalk, asked, "Who's that little cracker?"

Another explanation traced the name to the fact that Ray cracked the whip over the Chicago pitchers. The catcher could shed no light on the matter.

Fast for a catcher and ever alert, Schalk generally was credited with being the first catcher to run to first base behind the batter to guard against an overthrow.

At the suggestion of first baseman Hal Chase, Schalk also covered third base to make putouts and once surprised a runner with a putout at second.

"One day," Schalk related, "a ball was hit over the infield and in front of the center fielder. I had a hunch it would fall safely, so I ran out over the pitcher's mound and when the ball dropped in I yelled to Eddie Collins, who threw the ball to me in time to tag the runner as he slid in (at second). We worked the play two or three more times."

Schalk also was credited with making a catcher out of Moe Berg, who was a shortstop when he graduated from Princeton.

Cracker was managing the White Sox at the time and was incapacitated by a fractured thumb when a foul tip split the hand of Buck Crouse, the No. 2 catcher.

"Any one of you fellows ever a catcher?" asked Ray, surveying the bench.

"I thought I was once," said Berg, "but somebody told me I wasn't."

"Who was that?" asked Schalk.

"My high school coach in Newark," replied Moe.

By 1920, White Sox catcher Ray Schalk had developed into one of the premier receivers in baseball history.

"Well, as long as he isn't around, how about getting in there and trying it again?" suggested the manager.

"If you can stand it, I can," answered Moe, a catcher thereafter.

Schalk received a winner's share in the White Sox' World Series victory over the Giants in 1917 and also appeared in the 1919 Series when he was believed to be the first to sense that some teammates were not making an all-out effort to defeat the Reds.

While he flatly refused to discuss the Black Sox scandal in subsequent years, Ray did declare that "we could have won if Red Faber had not been sick."

Schalk caught four no-hitters in his tenure with the White Sox, including Charley Robinson's perfect game at Detroit in 1922.

Ray ended his affiliation with the White Sox midway through the 1928 season. He had managed the club for $1\frac{1}{2}$ years and the team had compiled a 32-42 record in '28 when he stepped down from his $25,000-a-year job. He had expected to remain as a player for $15,000, but when Owner Charles Comiskey offered approximately half that amount, the Cracker severed his Chicago connection.

For years Schalk operated a Chicago bowling establishment and served as an assistant baseball coach at Purdue University.

He succumbed to a long siege of cancer in 1970 at age 77.

MIKE SCHMIDT

If Philadelphia fans had it to do all over again, the cheers for Mike Schmidt likely would drown out the boos.

Schmidt spent his 18-year playing career trying to do the impossible, to please the hardest group of fans in the country. No matter how much he accomplished on the field for the Phillies, Schmidt just couldn't become a fan favorite in the city of brotherly love.

The three MVP awards—in 1980, 1981 and 1986—quieted some of his critics, as did his performance in winning the MVP award in the Phillies' 1980 World Series victory. Through all of the home runs, All-Star selections and Gold Gloves, however, Schmidt heard critics say that he could do more, that he could be better.

Looking back on the career of perhaps the greatest third baseman in major-league history, that doesn't seem possible.

Schmidt was selected by the Phillies in the second round of the 1971 draft from Ohio University, where he had been named shortstop on *The Sporting News'* College All-America team. He played less than two years in the minors, 205 games, before he was called up to the majors by the Phillies in September 1972.

That's where he remained until his 1989 retirement, when his career totals included 548 home runs, the seventh best total of all time, 509 coming as a third baseman, the most ever in history.

Schmidt hit 30 or more homers 13 times in his career; the only player ever to do it more often was Hank Aaron (15). Schmidt hit 35 or more homers 11 times; the only player to top that total was Babe Ruth, who did it 12 times.

Many baseball observers consider Mike Schmidt the best third baseman of all time. He entered Cooperstown in '95, getting 96.5 percent of votes that year.

Schmidt led the N.L. in homers a record eight times, and hit a career-best 48 in 1980. He hit four consecutive homers twice in his career, in one game in Chicago on April 17, 1976 and in 1979, when he homered in his final at-bat on July 6 and in his first three at-bats on July 7.

He led the league in RBI four times during his career, and nine times drove in more than 100 runs in a season. He was selected to 12 All-Star teams, starting eight times, and won 10 Gold Gloves for his defensive work at third base.

Schmidt likely brought some of the criticism he received on himself because he never performed to please the fans, and didn't want the attention that was heaped on him because of his ability and status as the team leader.

Speaking to the *Philadelphia Daily News* in 1995, Schmidt said there were things he would do differently if he had a second chance.

"I would have been a little more political about it,"

Schmidt said. "I'd have realized that hey, you've got to show these people that you want it more.

"Maybe I would have dived back into first base when I didn't have to. Get that uniform dirty. Lead off a little bit and then fall back into the base, and hey, my uniform is dirty for the rest of the game. And everybody would think, 'Wow, he's really grinding. He likes to get dirty.'

"I think you play with your God-given personality, but if I had it to do all over again, I'd probably figure out a way, in this media age, to realize the value of people's perceptions and what it would mean to me down the road, what it would mean off the field. And maybe I'd do things a little differently."

Schmidt was named captain of the Phillies in 1978, but didn't like the role and enjoyed it more the following year when Pete Rose arrived and brought some of the media and fan attention with him.

Rose, for one, always appreciated Schmidt's accomplishments.

"I've played with a lot of great players, but Mike is the best I've ever played with," Rose said. "He was right up there with the best of them, with the Hank Aarons and Roberto Clementes."

Schmidt was able to rise to stardom after a disastrous rookie year in 1973, when he hit .196—striking out 136 times in 367 at-bats. He spent that winter playing in Puerto Rico, and came back in 1974 to hit 36 homers and drive in 116 runs.

"I found a swing that made things happen," Schmidt said of his winter in Puerto Rico. "I was standing at the plate nice and relaxed and that sucker went off my bat a mile."

Schmidt led the Phillies to three consecutive division titles from 1976 to 1978, but each year they lost in the league championship series. Schmidt failed to homer in 43 at-bats, and in the 1977 and 1978 losses to the Dodgers, he was a combined 4-for-31.

He also hit poorly in the 1980 playoff series against Houston, but the Phillies won anyway and Schmidt got a chance to shine in the World Series against Kansas City. He hit .381, hit two homers, and drove in the decisive runs in the clinching game six.

The Phillies again reached the World Series in 1983, but this time they lost to Baltimore in five games as Schmidt again struggled, going 1-for-20.

Some disappointing numbers in the postseason can't remove the fact that he joined Stan Musial and Roy Campanella as the only players to win three N.L. MVP awards. He led the N.L. in homers for the final time in 1986, as he won the third MVP crown.

Schmidt retired in 1989, and his uniform number 20 was retired by the Phillies. He was elected to the Hall of Fame in his first year of eligibility in 1995.

Mike Schmidt was a three-time Most Valuable Player in the National League.

RED SCHOENDIENST

Schoendienst was a member of the 1958 Milwauke Braves team that held a three-games-to one lead over the New York Yankees before losing the World Series in seven games.

As a youngster growing up in Germantown, Illinois, a small town about 40 miles east of St. Louis, Albert (Red) Schoendienst loved one thing more than anything else: playing baseball.

One evening in June 1942, Schoendienst and a boyhood chum, Joe Linnemann, were hanging out in the Germantown pool hall. They heard a radio announcer mention that the St. Louis Cardinals would be holding a tryout camp for boys between 17 and 23 years of age at Sportsman Park.

"You know, Joe, we ought to go over there," the 19-year-old Schoendienst said. "Wouldn't do any harm. Besides, if we work out we'll get to watch the Cardinals play that big series with Brooklyn."

Schoendienst, who had never seen a major league game, wouldn't see any of that Dodgers-Cardinals series in '42, either. He so impressed the scouts at the tryout that the Cardinals had him signed to a minor-league contract within a week.

The scouts weren't wrong. Within three years, Schoendienst was in the big leagues, playing both the outfield and infield as a rookie with the Cardinals in 1945. It would be the first of 48 consecutive years (including 1992) in which Schoendienst wore a big-league uniform.

Schoendienst, who was elected to baseball's Hall of Fame in 1989, adapted quickly to professional baseball.

In his first full season, 1943, he led the Class AA International League in batting with a .337 mark, becoming the first 20-year-old to lead the International League in that department since Willie Keeler in 1892. In 1944, Schoendienst hit .373 in 25 games at Rochester (his season was cut short due to military service) to earn a promotion to the big leagues the following year.

Although Schoendienst's rise to the major leagues was hastened by World War II (Cardinal outfielders Stan Musial, Enos Slaughter and Terry Moore all missed the 1945 season due to military service), he quickly showed he belonged. Schoendienst led the league in stolen bases (26) and committed only five errors in left field despite being a shortstop by trade.

The shortstop job in St. Louis, however, was occupied by Marty Marion, the National League's Most Valuable Player in 1944. So, new Cardinals manager Eddie Dyer moved Schoendienst to second base at the start of the '46 season, selecting him as the team's starter over incumbent Emil Verban and prospect Lou Klein. Klein, who saw the writing on the wall, fled with pitchers Max Lanier and Fred Martin to the upstart Mexican League in

May. Schoendienst, still only 23 years old, proceeded to lead N.L. second basemen in fielding (.983) and helped the Cardinals win that fall's World Series in seven games over the Boston Red Sox.

A slick fielder who possessed good range, Schoendienst led or tied N.L. second basemen in fielding seven times, a record that still stands.

A switch-hitter, Schoendienst's best year at the plate was 1953, when he hit a career-high .342 with 15 homers and 79 runs batted in. His batting average was just two points shy of league-leader Carl Furillo of Brooklyn and that year was one of the rare times the great Musial did not lead St. Louis in batting.

Schoendienst, who hit just 84 home runs in his career, hit a memorable one on July 11, 1950, when his 14th-inning homer against Detroit's Ted Gray was the decisive blow in the National League's 4-3 victory in that summer's All-Star Game. Schoendienst's blow landed in the upper left-field stands at Chicago's Comiskey Park.

Illness and misfortune, however, kept Schoendienst from achieving even more as a player. While playing for the Milwaukee Braves, he came down with a case of tuberculosis in May 1958 that left him weak during most of that season and prevented him from playing all but a handful of games in 1959 as well.

"There wasn't one time that I even felt like stooping over to field a ground ball," Schoendienst said after the 1958 World Series, which the Braves lost in seven games to the New York Yankees. "In the World Series, of course, you put out a little extra something, but I'll admit now that I'd had it after the seventh game.

"If there had been an eighth game, I never would have made it." Remarkably, the gritty Schoendienst hit .300 and started every Series game.

Schoendienst entered a St. Louis hospital for treatment of his tuberculosis after the World Series ended. (For Schoendienst, a hospital was not an unfamiliar place. As a 17-year-old kid in 1940, he spent 10 weeks in one to receive treatment after a nail accidentally struck his left eye. The eye was saved, but his vision was affected enough to force the former righthand-hitting-only batsman to try swinging from the left side, thus creating a switch-hitter). During his convalescence from TB, Schoendienst received thousands of get-well letters, including one from President Dwight Eisenhower.

Schoendienst rebounded to play 68 games for Milwaukee in 1960 before finishing up his playing career as a player-coach with the Cardinals from 1961-63. On November 19, 1964, he succeeded Johnny Keane as St. Louis manager, a position he went on to hold longer than any man in franchise history. In Schoendienst's managerial tenure, the Cardinals won two N.L. pennants (in 1967 and 1968) and one World Series championship (1967).

Schoendienst crosses the plate after his 14th-inning homer became the decisive blow in the 1950 All-Star Game.

Schoendienst, who was elected to baseball's Hall of Fame in 1989, wore a big-league uniform for 48 consecutive years.

Slick-fielding Red Schoendienst led or tied National League second basemen in fielding seven times, a record that still stands.

TOM SEAVER

The year was 1969, and New York Mets righthander Tom Seaver came within two outs of pitching a perfect game against the Chicago Cubs, a performance he would later describe as "the best game I ever pitched." A few days afterward, he was introduced to Mrs. Babe Ruth.

"I'm glad that you didn't get that game," said the widow of baseball's greatest player. "Something like that always seems to bring bad luck."

Seaver was dumbfounded.

"She mentioned Don Larsen, and I was about to mention Sandy Koufax, but I didn't," Seaver said. "How much bad luck did he have? I found it odd that the wife of a great baseball hero would have an opinion like that."

Bad luck, it seems, is about the only thing Seaver's career did not have. It lasted 20 years, spanned three decades, produced three Cy Young Awards, 311 victories and 61 shutouts. And, yes, it included a no-hitter, a 4-0 victory over St. Louis on June 16, 1978.

Seaver's only no-hitter came while he was pitching for the Cincinnati Reds, but his greatest seasons came as a member of the New York Mets. Beginning in 1967, a year he won a club-record 16 games and was voted the National League's Rookie of the Year, Seaver helped transform a laughable franchise into a world champion.

"When I came to New York in 1967, there was a feeling of futility," the native Southern Californian said. "Too many guys were content to simply go through the motions and collect their pay. But I wouldn't accept that feeling. I not only wanted to win, but I wanted everybody else to want to win, too."

In 1967, Seaver won 16 games for a team that finished 40 games under .500. Two years later, he went 25-7 for a club that won 100 games and stunned the heavily favored Baltimore Orioles in five games to win the World Series. In 1973, the Mets won the Series again as Seaver won 19 games and posted a league-leading 2.08 earned-run average.

"A good pitcher doesn't win 12 one year and 27 the next," he once said. "If you are better than ordinary, you do the job every year."

Seaver was certainly better than ordinary, a fact that became evident in 1992 when he was voted into the Baseball Hall of Fame in his first year of eligibility If the highest tribute that can be paid to a player is a plaque in Cooperstown, N.Y., Seaver is in the stratosphere. He garnered 98.8 percent of the votes cast that year, the largest percentage in the Hall's 56-year history Seaver's percentage eclipsed the previous mark of 98.2 set by Ty Cobb in 1936, the Hall of Fame's first year.

The key to Seaver's success is that he pitched more to his strengths than to the batter's weakness. He treated pitching as an art form, using the plate as an easel and painting the corners with fastballs and sliders to make opposing hitters blue. He threw as hard as any pitcher of his era, and his 3,640 strikeouts rank third on the all-time list. He struck out at least 200 batters in nine straight seasons (1968-76), a record that still stands.

Seaver was never better as a strikeout artist than he was on April 22, 1970, when he fanned 19 San Diego Padres—including the final 10 of the game—in a 2-1 Mets victory. The 19 whiffs tied Steve Carlton's major-league record set the year before and the 10 straight strikeouts established a new standard.

"He was fantastic, outstanding," said Johnny Podres, who had shared the previous record of eight consecutive strikeouts with three other pitchers. Podres, then a minor league pitching instructor with San Diego, witnessed Seaver's feat that afternoon at Shea Stadium.

"There was no doubt in my mind he would break the record. He had perfect rhythm. As hard as he was throwing, he was still hitting the spots. If you didn't swing, it was still a strike."

"Some guys swinging a good bat can't wait to hit. They run up to the plate," said Al Ferrara, Seaver's last strikeout victim that day. "Seaver was running out to the mound. He couldn t wait to throw."

Few pitchers were as obsessed with greatness as Seaver. In an interview with *The Los Angeles Times*, he once said: "If that means patting my dog with my left hand, throwing logs on the fireplace with my left hand, then I do it. If it means coming to Florida and wearing a shirt so my arm doesn't get sunburned, if it means giving up a tan, I do that, too. If in the winter it means I eat cottage cheese instead of chocolate chip cookies, I do that, too.

"Some pitchers want to be the fastest. Some want to have the greatest season ever. I want to be the best ever."

Some would say he was.

Tom Seaver, who was voted National League Rookie of the Year in 1967 after winning 16 games, takes notes at that year's All-Star Game.

Seaver extended his record-setting strikeout feat to nine straight seasons, and it's a mark that still stands.

Seaver's 20-year career produced three Cy Young Awards, 311 victories and 61 shutouts.

FRANK SELEE

One of the most famous phrases in baseball history, "Tinker to Evers to Chance" might never have been spoken if not for the work of Frank Selee.

Selee was the manager of the Chicago Cubs in the early 1900s who made all of the roster moves necessary to come up with a combination of Joe Tinker at shortstop, Johnny Evers at second base and Frank Chance at first base.

That wasn't the only decision that Selee made that turned out well. He spent 16 years as a manager in the National League, 11 in Boston and five for the Cubs, between 1890 and 1905. During that time he developed a reputation as one of the best judges of talent in the game, and as someone who wasn't afraid to take chances with his players.

Selee was born on Oct. 26, 1859 in Amherst, New Hampshire. He began managing in the minor leagues in the 1880s, leading Oskosh of the Northwest League to a pennant in 1887 and Omaha to the Western Association title in 1889. It was that success which earned him a chance to manage in the major leagues, becoming the manager of the Boston Beaneaters in 1890.

Selee was able to recruit some of the best players from the Western Association, including Hall of Fame pitcher Kid Nichols, and led the team to a fifth-place finish in his first season. That would turn out to be the lowest finish of any Selee team in the majors.

Boston won the N.L. pennant in 1891, and after adding several players from the defunct American Association, repeated as the champion in 1892 and 1893. He led the team to pennants again in 1897 and 1898. His 1898 team finished the year with a 102-47 record.

In 12 full seasons in Boston, Selee's teams posted a 1,004-649 record, a .607 percentage, and only once did he finish below .500. Bobby Lowe was the second baseman on all five pennant winners, and he said Selee "was a good judge of players. He didn't bother with a lot of signals. He let his players figure out their own plays. He didn't blame them if they took a chance that failed."

Selee also was recognized for his ability to work with young players, and for being able to recognize that a player might turn out to be better if moved from one position to another. He scoured the minor leagues not only for stars, but for players who could fill holes in his lineup.

He did both of those things when he left Boston after the 1901 season and became the manager of the Cubs. Beginning at shortstop, Selee invited a dozen shortstops to spring training. One of them was Joe Tinker, who had been playing at Portland in the Pacific National League.

Manager Frank Selee was recognized for his ability to judge talent and work with young players.

Later that season, he purchased the contract of another shortstop, Johnny Evers, who had been playing at Troy in the New York State League, and put him at second base. He had two young catchers, Johnny Kling and Frank Chance, and he decided to move Chance to first base.

The first Tinker to Evers to Chance double play was turned on Sept. 15, 1902, establishing Selee's claim to fame.

Selee's Cubs won 68 games in 1902, and improved to 82 victories in 1903 and to 93 wins in 1904. He was not able to stay in his job because of illness, and turned the team over to Chance in the middle of the 1905 season. It was his moves and selection of players that formed the nucleus of the Cubs' pennant-winning teams in 1906, 1907, 1908 and 1910. Of the 13 key players that Chance inherited from Selee, eight were still regulars in 1910.

For his career, Selee managed in 2,180 games, with a record of 1,284-862, a .598 percentage. He perhaps was ahead of his time in his philosophy of managing, which was to allow his players freedom unless they proved they couldn't handle it.

"I want them to be temperate and live properly," he said of his players. "I do not believe that men who are engaged in such exhilarating exercise should be kept in strait jackets, but I expect them to be in condition to play. I do not want a man who cannot appreciate such treatment."

Twelve players from Selee's teams are members of the Hall of Fame.

Selee's illness was diagnosed as tuberculosis, and he died of the disease on July 5, 1909 in Denver, Colo., at the age of 49.

He became the 15th manager elected to the Hall of Fame when he was selected by the Veterans Committee in 1999.

JOE SEWELL

The University of Alabama graduate had played fewer than 100 games with New Orleans of the Southern Association when he was ordered to join the Cleveland Indians. It was an emergency. Shortstop Ray Chapman had just been killed by a pitched ball.

It was not the ideal spot for a 21-year-old kid to break into the majors, but the 5-foot-7 infielder not only held up in the pressure spot, he batted .329 in the 22 games remaining in the Indians' pennant-winning 1920 season.

Joseph Wheeler Sewell—he was named for the Confederate cavalry officer—stayed in the majors for 13 more seasons, earning a reputation for durability and a sharp eye at the plate.

Joe played in 1,103 consecutive games before being sidelined because of the flu. The streak would have been longer except that, in an early year with Cleveland, Sewell sat out two games while Manager Tris Speaker experimented with another infield alignment.

Sewell's primary claim to fame, however, was in laying the bat on the ball. In 7,132 major league at-bats, Joe struck out only 113 times, an average of once every 63 trips to the plate.

Swinging a 40-ounce bat that he christened Black Betsy, Sewell once played 115 consecutive games without striking out. The most troublesome pitchers for the lefthanded-batting Sewell were lefthanders Hubert (Dutch) Leonard and Pat Caraway.

Leonard, who pitched for the Red Sox and Tigers, threw a spitball that Sewell found bothersome. Caraway, a 6-4 Chicago stringbean who compiled a 22-40 lifetime record, "couldn't throw hard enough to blacken my eye," Sewell said, "but he had a floppy-armed delivery with that soft stuff and when he threw it from a white-shirted back-

Cleveland infielder Joe Sewell's primary claim to fame was his ability to get his bat on the ball.

ground, I had trouble picking it up. Struck me out twice in one game."

The only other hurler to strike out Joe twice in a game was Wally Warmoth, a rookie lefthander with Washington who accomplished the feat on May 13, 1923. In 1925 and 1929, Sewell struck out only four times.

Sewell enjoyed perhaps his biggest day against the Philadelphia A's Lefty Grove in New York in 1932, Joe's second season with the Yankees.

"I got five hits in five times up," Joe recalled, "and the last one was a home run into the right-field bleachers. When I hit it, Grove threw his glove in the air and followed me around the bases yelling at me."

Sewell recalled one of his strikeouts against George Blaeholder of St. Louis.

"Bill McGowan was the umpire and the count went to 3-and-2," he said. "The next pitch was a fastball right even with my cap. McGowan hollered, 'Strike three, oh my God I missed it' all in one breath. I looked at him, but did not say a word. The next day he apologized for missing the third strike. He was a good umpire, very capable, and I never held it against him."

Joe, who had two brothers in the majors (Tommy appeared in one game for the Cubs in 1927 and Luke was a longtime American League catcher), was released by Cleveland after the 1930 season. He signed with the Yankees and played three more seasons as a third baseman.

After retiring, Sewell coached the Alabama baseball team, worked as a good-will ambassador for a dairy and entered the hardware business, which he sold "because I wasn't too good a businessman," he explained.

"I'd upset my store manager by scooping cash out of the drawer to go fishing or hunting. Finally, I agreed to leave a note on how much money I took so he could balance the books, but doggone it, I'd forget.

"Oh, I'd remember to leave the note, all right. But my store manager was still mystified when, in my haste, I wrote only, 'I took it all.'"

AL SIMMONS

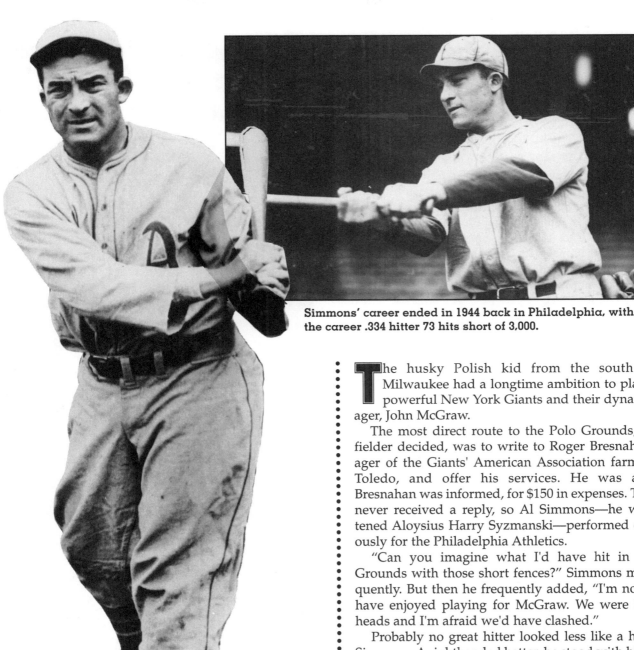

Simmons' career ended in 1944 back in Philadelphia, with the career .334 hitter 73 hits short of 3,000.

As an A's rookie in 1924, Al Simmons hit .308, a portent of things to come.

The husky Polish kid from the south side of Milwaukee had a longtime ambition to play for the powerful New York Giants and their dynamic manager, John McGraw.

The most direct route to the Polo Grounds, the outfielder decided, was to write to Roger Bresnahan, manager of the Giants' American Association farm team at Toledo, and offer his services. He was available, Bresnahan was informed, for $150 in expenses. The youth never received a reply, so Al Simmons—he was christened Aloysius Harry Syzmanski—performed conspicuously for the Philadelphia Athletics.

"Can you imagine what I'd have hit in the Polo Grounds with those short fences?" Simmons mused frequently. But then he frequently added, "I'm not sure I'd have enjoyed playing for McGraw. We were both hotheads and I'm afraid we'd have clashed."

Probably no great hitter looked less like a hitter than Simmons. A righthanded batter, he stood with his left foot pointed toward third base. When Al reported to his first major league training camp, veterans ridiculed his style.

"Let that young man alone," A's Manager Connie Mack advised. "He hit .398 at Milwaukee and .360 at Shreveport, and if he can hit like that it's all right with me if he stands on his head at the plate."

Simmons resented the "Bucketfoot Al" tag that was tacked on him and explained scientifically how he could hit outside pitches despite his unorthodox style.

"I've studied movies of myself batting," he said. "Although my left foot stabbed out toward third base, the rest of me, from the belt up, especially my wrists, arms and shoulders, was swinging in a proper line over the plate."

Simmons never swung better than he did on Memorial Day of 1930 when the A's played a morning-afternoon doubleheader against the first-place Washington Senators. The A's were losing the first game, 6-3, with two out in the ninth inning at Shibe Park when Spencer Harris and Dib Williams singled. Simmons homered to tie the score and eventually tallied the deciding run in the 13th inning.

Moments before crossing the plate, Al had dived back into third base and felt something snap in his knee. By the time Simmons reached the clubhouse, the knee was badly swollen. The doctor informed him a blood vessel was ruptured and that, while he might be able to pinch-hit in the second game, he should not consider running.

The Nats led, 7-5, in the fourth inning of the second game when the A's loaded the bases and Mack beckoned to Simmons to pinch-hit. With a count of 2-and-0, pitcher Bump Hadley threw a change-up that Al caught just right. The ball landed in the left-field seats for a grand-slam. The A's won the game, 15-11.

Months later, after the A's captured their second consecutive pennant, Washington Owner Clark Griffith told Mack, "I checked up on Simmons this year. He hit 14 homers in the eighth and ninth innings and every one figured in the ball game. We were never the same after he licked us in that doubleheader."

In the 1929 World Series, when the A's were losing to the Cubs, 8-0, in the seventh inning of Game 4, it was Simmons

In 1937, Simmons became a member of the Washington Senators, his fourth American League team.

who spoiled Charlie Root's shutout with a homer. "What a way to waste a homer," Al said to himself.

Before the inning was over, Simmons also singled and scored again as the A's tallied 10 times in the most productive of World Series innings.

Simmons, who batted .329 in four World Series and .462 in three All-Star Games, was sold along with Jimmie Dykes and Mule Haas to the White Sox after the 1932 season as Mack dismembered his second great club. He had two more stints with the A's, though, finishing his playing career with Mack's team in 1944.

Al died of a heart attack in 1956, four days after his 54th birthday.

Simmons, shown sliding into second base with one of his two doubles in the 1934 All-Star Game, was one of the five A.L. sluggers who struck out consecutively against Carl Hubbell in the same game.

GEORGE SISLER

During his .420 season in 1922, slick-fielding first baseman George Sisler was dazzling St. Louis fans with his bat and glove and was mentioned in the same breath with such heavyweight contemporaries as Yankee slugger Babe Ruth (left).

When a player bats .420, as George Sisler did for the St. Louis Browns in 1922, it is inconceivable that he could have had a superior season.

Sisler, though, regarded his 1920 performance as more satisfying. In '20, the first baseman played every inning of 154 games, established a major league record with 257 hits, scored 137 runs, drove in 122, stole 42 bases and batted .407. He had 49 doubles, 18 triples and 19 home runs.

On the final day of the season, George got three hits, scored two runs, stole three bases and, although he hadn't pitched competitively in four seasons, hurled the final inning against the White Sox.

A graduate of the University of Michigan (where he played for Branch Rickey), Sisler was a cause celebre after it was discovered that he had signed contracts with the Browns and the Pirates. The National Commission, ruling body of baseball at the time, awarded him to St. Louis, where he immediately blossomed into stardom.

Sisler entered the majors in 1915 (Rickey was his first big-league manager), breaking in as a pitcher. In one of his early games, George was matched against Walter Johnson, his boyhood idol. Sleepless the night before and nervous to a fault before the game, Sisler settled down quickly after the game started and defeated the Big Train, 2-1.

By 1918, Gorgeous George, then 25, was a full-time first baseman, dazzling with his agility afield and his skill at bat.

Sisler was mannerly and gentle, but no weakling, as pitcher Bob Groom discovered. Groom berated Sisler unmercifully on the bench for failing to catch a high throw, where upon George walked over to Groom and decked him.

Generally, his temper was in tight control, but Sisler once slapped umpire George Hildebrand with his glove and drew a short suspension.

Reports of Sisler's genius with the glove staggered the imagination, but creditable witnesses vouched for the feats. Once, George made a superlative stop of a hard smash and lobbed gently toward first base in the expectation that the pitcher would cover the bag. When the pitcher failed to arrive, Sisler raced to the base and caught his own throw for the putout.

Another time, Hal Janvrin of the Red Sox was on third base and Tris Speaker on first when the batter hit a line drive to Burt Shotton in left field. Feeling that he had no chance to get Janvrin at home plate, Shotton fired to Sisler, who tagged out Speaker and then whirled and caught Janvrin at the plate.

On a third occasion, George raced in to field a squeeze bunt, tagged out the batter and then dived for the plate to nip the runner trying to score.

After his great year of 1922, Sisler suffered a violent sinus attack that caused double vision and sidelined him for the entire 1923 season. He rejoined the Browns in 1924 and although he batted .345 one year and .340 another, he was never again—by his own admission—the same player he had been before his illness.

Sisler was appointed manager of the Browns in 1924 and held the position for three years although he was poorly suited for the job.

The Sisler name remained in the public eye. Three of the Hall of Famer's sons had ties to the game—George Jr. as a longtime minor league executive, Dick as a first baseman-outfielder for three major league clubs and Dave as a big-league pitcher.

After retiring from the game in 1932, George entered the sporting goods business in St. Louis. He returned to baseball when Rickey, then with Brooklyn, offered him a job as a scout. Sisler accompanied the Mahatma to Pittsburgh and remained active until a few years before his death at age 80.

Sisler's career started downhill in 1927, when the Browns sold him to the Washington Senators.

ENOS SLAUGHTER

Enos Slaughter literally hustled his way into the hearts of fans throughout the baseball world.

In the summer of 1959, a national magazine published a feature article that bore the heading "Last of the Old Pros." A subhead read: "For half of his 42 years, the old Warhorse has been ripping the game apart with his hustling, hell-for-leather brand of ball. If he ever runs out of gas, there won't be any more like him."

Enos Slaughter started running early. He remembered clearly the exact time and place and repeated the story frequently as an example of the benefits to be derived from his full-scale approach to the game.

Slaughter was in his second season of professional ball in 1936 and playing for Columbus, Ga., of the South Atlantic League when he started his program of constant running. Discouraged by what he considered his own inferior play, Enos walked from his outfield position toward the dugout at the close of an inning. As he crossed the foul line, he was greeted by his manager, Eddie Dyer, who barked: "Are you tired, kid? If so, I'll get some help for you."

The 20-year-old North Carolinian was stung by the remark. "I suddenly realized," he remembered afterward, "people don't care how sorry I felt for myself. That's when I started running."

The next season, with Columbus, Oh., of the American Association, the newly energized outfielder won a batting championship with a mark of .382 and gained a new nickname, "Country," which was tacked on by his manager, Burt Shotton.

The hard-driving 22-year-old joined the St. Louis Cardinals in 1938 and batted a creditable .276. But he really blossomed in 1939 when, playing with the reckless abandon of the old Gas House Gang, he batted .320, drove in 86 runs and led National League outfielders in putouts and assists.

The fact that Slaughter was able to play at all in '39 was remarkable. Hunting with his father on New Year's Day, Enos handled infected rabbits and contracted tularemia, a fever that killed his father three days later.

When spring-training time arrived, Slaughter still was suffering from chills and lightheadedness. Against the pleadings of his mother and advice of his doctor, however, he reported to the Florida camp. His manager, Ray Blades, never learned of the handicap under which the young sophomore performed.

Playing hurt was a trademark for Enos. In 1941, in an effort to avoid a collision with center fielder Terry Moore, Slaughter dived into a concrete wall and suffered a fractured collarbone. He returned to action before the injury

healed and when he swung at a pitch and missed, the skin tore and blood spurted forth.

The following season, Slaughter led the league with 188 hits and 17 triples before contracting the flu preceding the World Series. Hours in the steam room enabled him to shake the disease, but Slaughter remained weak at the start of the Series against the New York Yankees. It made little difference. The stocky right fielder scintillated on defense and delivered key hits as the Birds upset the favored Yankees.

After a three-year stint in military service during World War II, Slaughter returned to the Cardinals in 1946. He rapped 18 homers and led the majors with 130 runs batted in (establishing personal big-league highs in those departments) and sparked the Birds into the World Series against Boston. In the fifth game, a St. Louis defeat, Slaughter was hit on the right elbow. The pain brought tears to the eyes of the old Warhorse who, apparently for the only time in his career, asked to be removed from a game.

Heat packs were applied during the ensuing 24-hour train ride from Boston to St. Louis, but the Cardinals' team physician expressed doubt that Slaughter would be ready for the sixth game. A blood clot had formed. If it burst, dire consequences were predicted.

But Enos played. Swinging the bat with one hand and playing in pain, he executed a difficult catch in the sixth game. In Game 7, after belting an eighth-inning single, Slaughter raced home from first base on Harry Walker's hit to left-center field. The daring baserunning caught the Red Sox by surprise and gave the Cards a Series-clinching 4-3 victory.

Slaughter was 38 when, in April 1954, he was traded to the Yankees in a deal that sent promising minor league outfielder Bill Virdon, among others, to St. Louis. Enos remained in the major leagues for six more seasons and appeared in the 1956, 1957 and 1958 World Series with the Yankees.

HILTON SMITH

Best known as "Sartchel's relief," Hilton Smith was too close to retirement when the color barrier was broken to play in the major leagues.

With a repertoire of pitches at his disposal, right-hander Hilton Smith became one of the greatest pitchers in Negro league history. Smith had what most considered as the best curveball in the Negro leagues, complemented by a hard fastball, sinker, slider and change-up. He also threw his pitches with both a sidearm and overhand delivery, maintaining solid control with both styles. His array of pitches helped Smith compile a 161-22 record according to Negro League record books.

Smith played with Satchel Paige for the Kansas City Monarchs of the Negro leagues and was best known as "Satchel's relief." Smith would regularly come in and shut the door after one of Paige's starts. Smith pitched in the shadows of the flamboyant Paige throughout his career and did not receive the same notoriety as Paige. Bob Feller even considered Smith to be better than Paige.

Smith learned the game of baseball from his father with whom he played in a town league before heading to Prairie View A&M College in Texas. Smith began pitching in his second and final year at Prairie View and then caught on with a semipro team after his college career.

Smith spent the next few years bouncing around in different leagues playing for the Monroe Monarchs, the New Orleans Black Creoles and the New Orleans Crescent Stars. Smith began to polish his trade of pitching with all those teams and landed with the Kansas City Monarchs of the Negro American league in 1936. He spent the next 12 years with the Monarchs and ended his career with the team.

Smith put up huge numbers for the Monarchs for a team that won five pennants in the first six years of the league's existence. Playing against all types of competition while with the Monarchs, Smith won 20 or more games each year with the team and reportedly did not lose a game in 1938.

Smith also pitched in six consecutive All-Star games and he is tied with Paige on the all-time All-Star list with 13 strikeouts. Not only was Smith a dominating pitcher, he was also an accomplished hitter. The Monarchs took advantage of his batting skills by using him as a pinch hitter, outfielder and first baseman. Smith saw time in the field on a regular basis in 1945 with many regulars gone on military service. Smith hurt his arm in 1943 but bounced back and still managed to post ERAs of 2.74 and 2.31 the following two years. Smith's arm returned to health in time to help lead the Monarchs to the 1946 pennant. Smith pitched in Venezuela that winter and collected an 8-5 record with the champion Vargas team. Smith also pitched against the New York Yankees in Venezuela and held the Yankees to one hit in five innings to earn the victory. Smith had a 6-1 record in exhibition games against major leaguers.

The color barrier was broken that spring and Brooklyn gave Smith an offer to pitch, but he declined knowing that his best years had passed. Smith's age was the only thing that prevented him from pitching in the majors. Smith pitched two more years for the Monarchs before retiring in 1948 at the age of 36. Smith pitched two more years of semipro ball in New Mexico before officially closing the door on his baseball career.

After his baseball career, Smith entered the field of education as a teacher and coach. He then went on to work at Armco Steel where he worked until he retired in 1978. The Chicago Cubs employed Smith as an associate scout until his death in 1983.

DUKE SNIDER

The Pittsburgh scout was deeply impressed with the 17-year-old who was hitting and fielding spectacularly with a Navy team during World War II.

"I'll give you $20,000 to sign with the Pirates," Babe Herman told the teenager, who replied, "I'm sorry, Mr. Herman, but I've already signed with the Dodgers for a $750 bonus and $250 a month."

As an all-round sports star at Compton High School in California, Duke Snider was trailed by scouts of the Reds, Cardinals and Dodgers. He chose the Brooklyn club because it "had a couple of players named Pee Wee Reese and Pete Reiser when it won the pennant in 1941 and I was a great admirer of them."

Edwin Donald Snider, nicknamed by his father when still a tyke, earned 10 letters in baseball, football, basketball and track while in junior high school and four more monograms in $1\frac{1}{2}$ years at Compton High.

After graduation in February of 1944, Duke took off for Bear Mountain, N.Y., where the Dodgers did their wartime training. One season at Newport News (Piedmont) and a Navy hitch preceded stints at Fort Worth (Texas) and St. Paul (American Association) before Snider was ready for the Dodgers.

Even then, however, he was not fully prepared for the National League. He had one serious flaw—ignorance of the strike zone.

Inventive Branch Rickey devised a cure. He sent Duke to Vero Beach, Fla., with a special coach, George Sisler. The cure consisted of Snider standing at the plate, bat on shoulder, with an umpire on hand.

"After the ball was delivered," Duke recalled, "the ump would call it a strike or ball and then Sisler would ask my opinion. I wasn't permitted to swing even if it was right down the gut. At first we were far apart—and then I began to notice that I was calling more of 'em right. Moreover, when I got into a game I didn't lunge for pitches so much."

Snider was justifiably proud of his arm. In high school, he had tossed a football 70 yards in a throwing contest. In a game, he threw a 63-yard pass to pull out a victory in the last 15 seconds.

Once, in a pregame discussion, the subject of how far Snider could throw a baseball was raised. While the groundkeepers were tidying up Ebbets Field, and while bewildered spectators looked on, Snider stood at home plate and let fly. His first throw struck the scoreboard in right-center field. His second cleared the right-field fence, 40 feet high and at least 350 feet from home plate.

Snider insisted that his arm was even stronger when he played at Newport News in 1944. "In 1947 I didn't

When the Dodgers moved to Los Angeles in 1958, Snider's prolific slugging days were nearing an end.

warm up properly during a damp night in St. Paul and my arm hasn't been the same since," he said.

After the Dodgers moved to Los Angeles, Duke attempted to throw a baseball out of Memorial Coliseum. He strained his arm and was unable to play for one game. He was fined one day's pay, approximately $245.

Duke had brilliant and dismal World Series experiences. He struck out eight times and collected only three hits in the 1949 classic. However, Snider rapped 10 hits in the 1952 Series and walloped four home runs in both the '52 and 1955 Series.

En route to more than 2,000 hits and 400 homers in the majors, Snider enjoyed many unforgettable moments and days, but none to equal a game against the Phillies when he smashed three consecutive homers and a fourth drive that missed clearing the wall by only a foot or two.

Perhaps his most notable defensive play also was at the expense of the Phillies in Philadelphia. Snider dug his spikes into the fence in left-center field and made a leaping, one-handed catch of a Willie Jones drive as the potential winning run headed for the plate.

After completing his active career with the Giants, the onetime Major League Player of the Year scouted and managed in the minors before turning his talents to the radio booth with the Montreal Expos.

Snider celebrates after the final out of the Dodgers' win over the Yankees in Game 1 of the 1952 Series.

In 1949, Duke Snider (left) spent his first full season in a Brooklyn uniform. He was producing homers with regularity by 1955, hitting four in the World Series (including two in Game 5, right) against the Yankees.

WARREN SPAHN

Ordinarily, three years of military service when a professional athlete is in his early 20s would be regarded as unfortunate, but the shrewd pitcher who won more games than any lefthander in big-league history never regarded it as a tough break.

"People say that my absence from the major leagues may have cost me a chance to win 400 games," said Warren Spahn. "But I don't know about that. I matured a lot in three years and I think I was a lot better equipped to handle major league hitters at 25 than I was at 22. Also, I pitched until I was 44. Maybe I wouldn't have been able to do that otherwise."

Spahn was given a field commission as a first lieutenant for action in repairing the Remagen Bridge over the Rhine River. He was wounded in the same action, but shrugged it off as "only a scratch."

The native of Buffalo, N.Y., pitched for the Braves in four games in the 1942 season—two at the beginning and two at the end. The rest of the season he pitched for Hartford (Eastern). In his big-league debut, a relief appearance against the Giants, Spahn retired both batters who faced him.

In his second year back from the war, Spahn was a 21-game winner. It was his first of 13 seasons in the 20-victory circle. Only Cy Young, with 16, had achieved it more frequently.

Warren missed the 20 mark in 1948, but he helped pitch the Braves to their first pennant since 1914. Down the stretch, he and Johnny Sain seemed to pitch almost daily and New Englanders pinned flag hopes on "Spahn and Sain and pray for rain."

Spahn split two decisions in the World Series against the Cleveland Indians, then notched victory totals of 21, 21 and 22 before dropping to 14 in 1952. Boston attendance fell alarmingly in the last two years, and Spahn was asked to take a $5,000 pay cut (down from $25,000).

The pitcher refused to sign, and Braves President Lou

A 19-year-old Warren Spahn (right, left photo) played his first professional season for Bradford of the Pony League in 1940. In 1948, Spahn was congratulated by catcher Bill Salkeld (right) after winning Game 5 of the 1948 World Series with a scoreless relief stint.

Spahn delivers a ninth-inning pitch (above) en route to a September 16, 1960, no-hitter against Philadelphia, the first of two in his career. Victory No. 300 came in 1961 and earned Spahn handshakes from Hank Aaron (below right) and catcher Joe Torre.

Perini countered with an offer of 10 cents on every admission for 1953. Spahn was adamant. He had to have $25,000 and Perini ultimately yielded.

How was Spahn to know that the Braves would transfer to Milwaukee for the '53 season? Had he accepted the 10-cent proposal, he would have earned more than $150,000 from the outpouring of Milwaukee fans.

With a wide assortment of pitches, plus cunning control and a bat that smacked a total of 35 homers, Spahn piled victory upon victory. He notched two no-hitters and 63 career shutouts. He was, said Charley Dressen, his manager in 1960 and most of '61, "my go-to-sleep pitcher." Translated, that meant Charley could "go to bed the night before Spahn pitches and get a good night's sleep."

Whitlow Wyatt, a Dodger pitcher when Spahn came up, was pitching coach for Milwaukee when Spahn was the club's foremost hurler.

"I pitched against him in 1942," recounted Wyatt, "and 15 years later he reminded me that the first time I faced him I threw him a fastball, then a curve, then another fastball that he hit to the shortstop. He not only remembered the hitters, but the pitchers, too."

Spahn won his 100th game on August 15, 1951, by beating the Phillies. He gained his 200th, also over the Phils, on September 13, 1956. He reached the 300 milestone on August 11, 1961, when he defeated the Cubs. Curiously, Richie Ashburn was a member of the losing club in each game, although he did not play in the latter contest.

Spahn, who underwent three knee operations during his career, remained in shape during the offseason by swimming and working on his ranch in Hartshoren, Okla. He was 42 when he posted a 23-7 mark for Milwaukee in 1963. He was sold to the Mets after the 1964 season and finished the '65 campaign with San Francisco.

The stylish old master won his last major league game on September 12, 1965 beating Chicago, 9-2, in the second game of a twin bill. It was Warren's 363rd lifetime victory, the highest total by a lefthander and the fifth-best mark in history.

During his final major league season (1965), Spahn was a teammate of fellow Hall of Famer Willie Mays.

ALBERT SPALDING

The $5-a-week grocery clerk in Rockford, Ill., was dazzled by the offers that poured in from professional baseball clubs seeking his services in 1867.

He was only 17 when the National Baseball club of Washington made an extended tour of the Midwest. The Nationals were regarded as the strongest club in the land and readily accepted the challenge of the Forest City team of Rockford.

When the young pitcher defeated the Nationals, he became a national celebrity and salary offers up to $2,500 were received from teams in New York, Cleveland and Washington. He resisted the blandishments to remain with Forest City, but four years later the righthander succumbed to the inducements of Harry Wright, then organizing a team in Boston.

For Albert Goodwill Spalding, the die was cast. For the remainder of his life he was recognized internationally as a premier pitcher, manager, club president, founder of a worldwide sporting goods business and high-ranking counselor in the inner chambers of baseball.

Spalding was the only pitcher on the Boston roster during his first season, when he posted a 20-10 mark in 1871. He was the pitcher of record in all but one contest. Thereafter, Spalding pitched the Red Stockings to four consecutive National Association flags, climaxing the string with a 56-4 record in 1875.

During the '75 season, Spalding was approached by William A. Hulbert, a Chicago businessman who had been offered the presidency of the White Stockings, a mediocre team. Before acting on the offer, Hulbert told the Boston pitcher:

"Spalding, you've no business playing in Boston. You're a western boy . . . If you come to Chicago to play and manage next season, I'll accept the presidency of the club and we'll give those easterners a fight for their lives."

The season was only half over, but Spalding and Boston teammates Ross Barnes, Cal McVey and Deacon Jim White signed contracts secretly to play the following season for Chicago.

News of their undercover actions leaked out, however, and the quartet played out the season listening to cries of —among other things—"Your White Stockings will turn gray."

In the meantime, Hulbert grew disgusted with the way in which gamblers had infiltrated the National Association and, eyeing reform, he instituted plans to organize the National League, which made its debut the following year.

Albert Spalding's baseball career started on the mound and eventually wound through the game's inner chambers.

Al contributed 47 victories to Chicago's total of 52 in the N.L. pennant-winning season of 1876. In '77, he played first and second base as the White Stockings dropped to fifth place.

Spalding made his final Rockford appearance in uniform on Harry Wright Day, April 13, 1896, when he pitched in an old-timers' game.

In 1888, Spalding led two teams on a worldwide tour, one club named "Chicago" and the other "All-America." After launching the trip at Chicago on October 20, the travelers headed westward via San Francisco. They visited 14 countries in an effort to popularize baseball before returning in April of 1889.

Because his sporting goods company, founded on capital of $500, was demanding more of his time, Spalding severed his baseball connections in 1891 and moved to Point Loma, Calif.

In 1900, President William McKinley appointed Spalding a U.S. commissioner to the Olympic Games in Paris. In tribute to his work in behalf of international sport, the government of France made him a member of the Legion of Honor.

Spalding was called eastward in 1901 when the National League was at war with the American. Through his efforts, the old and the new leagues signed a Major League Agreement.

Spalding wrote "America's National Game," an illuminating review of baseball's early years.

Two strokes took a heavy toll on his mobility before his death in 1915 at age 65.

TRIS SPEAKER

If John McGraw's memory on October 16, 1912, extended to the spring of 1908, he could only condemn the quirks of history that made him a loser in his third World Series.

In 1908, a young outfielder offered his services to McGraw while the Giants were training in Marlin, Tex. Little Napoleon explained that he already had an abundance of outfielders in camp and could not give the newcomer a fair trial.

Maybe McGraw recalled that incident in the fall of 1912 when the same rejected player, now a brilliant performer for the Red Sox, drove in the tying run in the 10th inning of the final Series game that was won by Boston.

Speaker had played briefly with Boston in 1907, but did not receive a 1908 contract before the deadline. Realizing he was a free agent, he traveled 40 miles from his native Hubbard, Tex., to the Giants' camp.

At age 16, Speaker was a lefthanded pitcher for a semi-pro team when he was spotted by the owner of the Cleburne club of the North Texas League. Signed to a $50-a-month contract, Tris was told to report to the Cleburne team, then playing in Waco. The brash youngster awakened the manager, Benny Shelton, at 6:30 a.m. and was told to wait in the hotel lobby until a more respectable hour.

At the ball park, Speaker was ordered to warm up. He did, for 30 minutes. "Must have made 300 pitches," he recalled years later. Then Shelton ordered: "Shag flies." The kid did, throughout batting practice of both clubs. As game time approached, Shelton barked, "You're pitching today, warm up."

"Warm up," cried Speaker, "what the hell do you think I've been doing?"

Speaker allowed only two hits, but was a 3-2 loser

When the Red Sox traded him to Cleveland in 1916, Tris Speaker (left) continued his assault on AL pitchers with a league-leading .386 mark. In 1920, Speaker, now managing the Indians, posed with a floral piece prior to Game 1 of the World Series against Brooklyn.

As the 1927 season began, fellow greats Speaker (right, left photo) and Rogers Hornsby were wearing unfamiliar uniforms. Speaker, long retired by the 1939 All-Star Game, poses (right) with Yankee great Joe DiMaggio.

when Shelton, playing first base, argued a ninth-inning decision as two runners crossed the plate.

Some time later, when Cleburne's right fielder suffered a cheek fracture, Speaker announced that he also was an outfielder. He never pitched another game.

The Senators and Pirates also had opportunities to acquire Speaker, but the Red Sox, having passed him up once, bought him from Little Rock for $750 after the 1908 season. In quick order, Tris was recognized as the premier center fielder in the major leagues.

The Gray Eagle—Speaker was prematurely gray—played an uncommonly shallow center field which enabled him to catch many balls that ordinarily would fall in for hits. It also enabled him to cover second base on sacrifices and in one season, 1918, to pull two unassisted double plays. He also turned one in the 1912 Series against the Giants.

Speaker, or Spoke as he was known in the dugout, credited Cy Young with helping to make him a superb outfielder.

"Cy used to hit fungoes to me every day when I joined the Red Sox," Spoke said. "He always tried to hit the ball just one step beyond me so that I couldn't catch it unless I hustled.

"I watched him and in a few days I knew just by the way he swung whether the ball would go to my right or left. Then I figured that if I could do that with a fungo hitter I could do it in a ball game. I asked our pitchers how they pitched to each batter. I also studied the batters and when he started his swing, I knew if he would hit to my left or right and I was on my way."

Speaker played with the Red Sox through 1915, a Boston pennant season, but balked when Owner Joe Lannin asked him to take a 50 percent slash in pay, from $18,000 to $9,000, for 1916.

Tris was traded to Cleveland in April of 1916. With about two months left in the 1919 season, he was named manager of the Indians.

Speaker resigned after the 1926 season when he and Ty Cobb were under investigation by Commissioner K.M. Landis for allegedly conspiring to fix a late-season game several years earlier. Both received a clean bill of health.

After completing his major league career with the Philadelphia Athletics in 1928, Speaker managed Newark (International) for two seasons. He broadcast major league games in Chicago for two years, after which he joined comedian Joe E. Brown in ownership of the minor league Kansas City Blues. A couple of years later, he sold his interest and returned to Cleveland as a broadcaster of Indians games.

The Gray Eagle was 70 when a coronary attack proved fatal in 1958.

WILLIE STARGELL

In the waning weeks of the 1982 baseball season, a Pittsburgh television station sponsored a citywide tribute to Willie Stargell. As a memento of the occasion, a brochure was prepared in which teammates, old and new, and opponents, past and present, paid tribute to the Pirates' first baseman-captain, who was about to retire.

The comments covered a broad spectrum. They touched on Willie's leadership, his humility, his athletic talents, his gentleness and, one of the rarest commodities among professionals, his class.

Pitcher Gene Garber eulogized Stargell as "a great player, leader and competitor, but also a great person with feelings of compassion for others."

To Ken Brett, another hurler, Stargell was "that rare combination of athlete and gentleman. He is one of the very few to be a star both on and off the field."

Jerry Lynch, the redoubtable pinch-hitter during Willie's early years as a Buc, commented: "Humility and thoughtfulness are Willie's greatest assets."

Foremost among the remarks from rivals was one by Steve Garvey. "He's the quintessential gentleman and team player. That's the highest honor I can give to a team player," wrote the former Los Angeles Dodger and San Diego Padre first baseman.

"There's only one word to describe Willie Stargell," offered Dodger Manager Tommy Lasorda, "and that's class. He's been an inspiration to millions of youngsters all over America."

President Ronald Reagan, a baseball broadcaster in his earlier years and a fan since childhood, lauded the slugger for "your commitment to excellence, both on and off the field, and your humanitarian concern for your fellow man (that) embodies all that is great about the American spirit."

Commissioner Bowie Kuhn called Stargell "one of the finest and most exceptional players. . . . Baseball is richer for having had you with us. . . ."

By all reckoning, Wilver Dornel Stargell was a remarkable individual. At 6-foot-3 and 225 pounds, he was a striking figure in his Pirate black and gold. Waving his bat windmill fashion at the plate, he was just as likely to blast a ball 500 feet as he was to fan dramatically, a feat he accomplished 154 times in 1971 and 1,936 times during his career.

Throughout his score of years with the Pirates, Willie operated on the maxim: "Have fun. Work hard."

Stargell followed that principle to the ultimate. He was the prankster in the Pittsburgh clubhouse, the one who kept his teammates loose in a leadership way. When he

Willie Stargell's home run trot was a familiar sight for Pittsburgh fans in the 1960s and '70s.

worked, it was with a vigor and determination that served as a spur for those less dedicated.

A native of Earlsboro, Okla. and a product of the Oakland sandlots, the fellow they called "Pops" joined the Buccos late in the 1962 campaign after a four-year minor league apprenticeship. The lefthanded slugger carved his niche in the record book for the first time July 22, 1964, when he hit for the cycle in a 13-2 victory over the Cardinals in St. Louis. On June 24, 1965, Stargell treated 29,000 Dodger Stadium spectators to a power show. He slammed Don Drysdale and successors for three home runs, a feat he would perform three more times, in a 13-3 walkaway.

A year later, Willie unleashed his batting wrath against the Houston Astros. On June 4, he rapped four straight hits, and followed with five safeties in a row on June 5. His nine successive hits fell one short of the National League record.

"I wish you'd talk about the team instead of me," suggested Willie afterward. The remark was consistent with his oft-repeated statement that baseball is "not an 'I' game. It's 'we'. There's no one man who dominates any game."

The Bucs' resident philosopher gave Atlanta fans a sample of his clouting prowess on August 1, 1970. Starting against George Stone and continuing against Braves relievers, Willie blasted five extra-base hits, three two-baggers and a pair of homers. He tied a record achieved only twice previously, by Lou Boudreau and Joe Adcock.

Wondrous Willie was a one-man wrecking crew in 1971 when he led the league in home runs with 48. Twice in April he blasted three homers in a single game. His 11 round-trippers for the month equaled a major league record. That same year he tied a league standard by walloping 36 homers by the end of July.

Stargell enjoyed his most productive season in 1973, when the Pirates finished third in the National League East Division. "No. 8" led the league in doubles (43), homers (44) and RBIs (119). The accomplishments earned Willie second place in the N.L. Most Valuable Player Award voting behind Joe Torre of the St. Louis Cardinals.

Stargell's career appeared to be nearing a close in 1976 when his batting average dipped to .257 and his RBI total to 65. The following season he played in only 63 games, the result of a broken arm suffered while breaking up a fight between teammate Bruce Kison and Mike Schmidt of the Phillies. Willie rebounded, however, in 1978. His .295 batting average, 97 RBIs and 28 homers were worth a Comeback Player of the Year citation.

Stargell was 38 when he waged his last major assault against National League pitchers in 1979. It was the type of pennant battle that appealed to his lust for combat, a pulsating struggle down to the wire. He relished neck-to-neck encounters, even though they cost him needed sleep and raised "goosebumps big as quarters" on his torso.

Pops' home run on the final day of the regular season sparked a victory over the Cubs that clinched the division title. The victory was a dress rehearsal for even gaudier performances by Willie in post-season skirmishes.

Stargell had a big hug for teammate Dave Parker after the Pirates' had clinched the 1979 N.L. East Division title.

In the first game of the League Championship Series against Cincinnati, Stargell whacked a three-run homer in the 11th inning to produce a 5-2 win. The next day, the old warrior rapped a single and double in a 10-inning victory. He concluded his demolition act with a double, homer and three RBIs in the pennant-winning finale. For the three games, he batted .455.

The Baltimore Orioles were next. The American League champs, who had won 102 games before eliminating the California Angels in the playoffs, won three of the first four games before the Pirates, behind Stargell, struck back. Pittsburgh captured Game 5 with the help of a single and sacrifice fly by Stargell, deadlocked the Series behind the shutout pitching of John Candelaria and dismantled the Birds in the decisive contest, which was another showcase for the venerable first baseman.

Willie touched off his pyrotechnics with a single. On his second at-bat, he doubled. On his third trip to the plate, when the Pirates trailed, 1-0, he bashed a two-run homer that put them ahead to stay. Later in the 4-1 victory, Willie lashed a second double. Wrapped up in his .400 batting average were seven-game Series records for extra-base hits (7) and total bases (25).

Stargell was a runaway choice for MVP honors in the playoffs and World Series. In the balloting for the league MVP, four voters neglected to list Willie's name and he wound up as co-winner with Keith Hernandez of the Cardinals. At the end of the year, *The Sporting News* saluted Stargell as both Player of the Year and the Man of the Year.

One more distinction awaited Willie. Undoubtedly, it was treasured above all others. In recognition of his public service and his countless hours devoted to raising funds for the fight against sickle cell anemia, Willie Stargell was awarded a Doctor of Humanities degree by St. Francis College of Loretto, Pa., in 1980, two years before he retired. Stargell died in April 2000 of a stroke.

Stargell (8) with 1966 teammates (left to right) Roberto Clemente, Matty Alou and Manny Mota.

TURKEY STEARNES

Norman Thomas Stearnes was known as Turkey Stearnes. When Stearnes ran, he flapped his arms. Stearnes did a lot of flapping in the Negro leagues, where he was accustomed to tearing around the bases on doubles and triples or easing into a home run trot. The trot around the bases was a familiar one. Of the top 12 single-season home run totals in recorded Negro leagues history, Stearnes is credited with four. He hit a career-high 24 homers in 1928 and finished with 20 three times. His team, the Detroit Stars, played an average of 90 games in those four seasons.

Born in Nashville in 1901, Stearnes honed his talent on the sandlots of the Tennessee capital. After his father died, Stearnes was forced to leave school at age 15 to take a job. He took his baseball skills to Detroit in 1923 and joined the Stars. A left-handed hitter, Stearnes had a peculiar batting style that eventually drew comparisons to that of right-handed hitter Al Simmons, whose foot-in-the-bucket approach netted great results with the Philadelphia Athletics. Odd stance or not, Stearnes exhibited great power, as his six league homer titles attest.

Jimmie Crutchfield, a former teammate, called Stearnes a "quicky-jerky sort of guy who could hit the ball a mile. Turkey had a batting stance that you'd swear couldn't let anybody hit a baseball at all. He'd stand up there looking like he was off balance. But it was natural for him to stand that way, and you couldn't criticize him for it when he was hitting everything they threw at him."

Stearnes spent nine seasons with Detroit and also played for the Chicago American Giants and Kansas City Monarchs, among other teams. In 1933, he was the West team's center fielder and leadoff man in the first Negro leagues All-Star Game at Chicago's Comiskey Park. His counterpart on the East was Cool Papa Bell.

Bell, a Baseball Hall of Fame inductee in 1974, once said, "If they don't put Turkey Stearnes in the Hall of Fame, they shouldn't put anybody in." Negro leagues pitching great Satchel Paige, who entered the Hall in 1971, offered this opinion: "[Stearnes] was one of the greatest hitters we ever had. He was as good as anybody who ever played ball."

Stearnes remained in Detroit after his playing career ended, and he was often seen in the bleachers at Tiger Stadium. He died in 1979. Soon after his death, Nettie Stearnes began to lobby to have her husband admitted to the Hall of Fame roster. "I was always plugging," she said. "I never stopped." More than two decades later—and 60 years after his career ended—the Hall of Fame's Veterans Committee took Cool Papa Bell's advice. In 2000, it voted Stearnes a place in Cooperstown. Nettie Stearnes was overjoyed. "This is a moment I'll cherish for the rest of my life."

Despite an unusual batting style, Turkey Stearnes was one of the top power hitters in Negro leagues history. His best years were spent with the Detroit Stars.

CASEY STENGEL

The success and color Casey Stengel brought to the managing ranks overshadowed his abilities as a top-notch outfielder during his playing days (1922, above, with the Giants). Yankee Manager Stengel (right) clowns around during a 1952 rain delay at Yankee Stadium.

They called him the "Old Perfessor," probably because his fractured syntax, mixed metaphors and non sequiturs were totally unlike what was heard in a college classroom.

For years he was recognized chiefly for his comical behavior on a baseball field. He was 60 when the world suddenly realized that beneath his clownish veneer lay a baseball intellect capable of establishing managerial records.

His name wasn't even Casey. He was born in Kansas City, the initials of which were slurred into the world-famed nickname of Charles Dillon Stengel.

Because of his success as a manager, Stengel's playing skill was frequently overlooked. But Casey qualified as a top-notch outfielder with the Dodgers, Pirates, Phillies, Giants and Braves.

Before entering baseball, Stengel was a dentist in his native city. "I was not very good at pulling teeth," he confessed, "but my mother loved my work."

Casey's comic art was developed before he reached the majors. While playing for Montgomery (Southern), Stengel spied a manhole in the outfield. While the spec-

tators' attention was directed elsewhere, he slipped off the cover and lowered himself into the hole, leaving just enough space to observe the progress of the game.

When a ball was hit in that direction, Stengel arose majestically from the depths, circled under the ball and made the catch.

"Boy, was the manager mad," he said.

Ol' Case probably was remembered best for his stunt at Brooklyn after he had been traded to the Pirates. Jeered lustily on his first at-bat, Stengel made a grand, sweeping bow and doffed his cap as a liberated bird soared out of Ebbets Field.

Casey played in three World Series. His last was in 1923, when he socked two home runs in the Giants' losing cause to the Yankees. On Stengel's second homer a syndicated writer described how the 33-year-old outfielder limped and hobbled around the bases. In California, the parents of Casey's fiancee wondered what sort of antique their daughter was about to marry.

Edna Lawson Stengel was her husband's loyal companion for more than half a century, tolerating his escapades and furnishing a steadying influence.

By 1963, Stengel (left) was pulling the strings for the hapless Mets. Former Yankee stars Whitey Ford (center, right photo) and Yogi Berra were on hand in 1970 when the Yankees retired Stengel's number.

Casey began his managerial career at Worcester (Eastern) in 1925, also serving as club president and right fielder. It was not an auspicious season. On the final day, Stengel, as manager, released Stengel the player. As president he fired Stengel the manager, and then resigned as president.

Ol' Case managed Brooklyn and Boston from 1934 to '43, never finishing higher than fifth in the National League. When he was struck by a cab in Boston and suffered a broken leg, it appeared Stengel was ready to call it a career. He was wealthy from oil holdings in Texas and real estate and banking interests in California.

In 1944, however, he managed the Milwaukee (American Association) club as a favor to a friend. It was the turning point of his career. A year at Kansas City and three at Oakland prepared him for his appointment, in 1949, as skipper of the Yankees.

Casey might have earned the Yankee position earlier except that Ed Barrow, then front-office chief, recalled how Stengel, in his home run hobble of 1923, had thumbed his nose at the heckling Yanks before more than 62,000 Yankee Stadium spectators.

Stengel lost no time in convincing doubters that his clowning days were far behind. He won a world championship his first year in New York, and extended the World Series title string to five straight. He introduced the platoon system to baseball, a highly unpopular move with the players but a popular strategy with his bosses.

After 10 pennants in 12 years—he was beaten only by his oil partner, Al Lopez, in 1954 at Cleveland and in 1959 at Chicago—Casey was retired by the Yankees at age 71.

Stengel was unemployed only one season. When his old boss, George Weiss, took charge of the expansion Mets in 1962, he tapped his former sidekick, then 72, as the franchise's manager. Not even Casey was up to this challenge. His first three Met teams compiled 40-120, 51-111 and 53-109 records and the '65 club was on the way to 112 losses when Stengel stepped down at mid-season.

The Old Perfessor died in 1975 at age 86.

DON SUTTON

When Walter Alston retired after managing the Los Angeles Dodgers for 23 years, he left a copy of his book for pitcher Don Sutton, with a special inscription.

"To Don," the inscription read, "when it is on the line, I want you to have the ball."

"I will never forget that," Sutton said.

Sutton was not the most famous pitcher on the great Dodgers staffs of the 1960s—there were a couple of future Hall of Famers named Sandy Koufax and Don Drysdale ahead of him—but his longevity was remarkable. He pitched in the major leagues for 23 years, winning a total of 324 games, the most by a righthanded pitcher since Grover Alexander.

Sutton was born on April 2, 1945 in Clio, Ala. A graduate of Tate High School in Pensacola, Fla., Sutton played at Gulf Coast Community College in Florida, Mississippi College, Southern California and Whittier College before signing with the Dodgers as a free agent in 1964.

He spent only one year in the minor leagues, 1965, posting a combined record of 23-7 at Class-A Santa Barbara and Double-A Albuquerque, where he was named the Texas League Player of the Year.

The 6-foot-1, 185-pound righthander started the 1966 season with the Dodgers, winning his first game on April 18, a 6-3 decision over Houston. He won 12 games that year, but more impressively, struck out 209 batters, the most by a National League rookie since 1911. He was named the N.L.'s Rookie of the Year by *The Sporting News*.

He spent that season as the fourth starter in the distinguished Dodgers rotation, behind Koufax, Drysdale and Claude Osteen. Each member of the quartet posted 40 or more shutouts during their careers, an accomplishment no other starting rotation can match.

Sutton pitched for the Dodgers through the 1980 season. In the eight-year span from 1969 through 1976, he won at least 15 games each season. He posted a career-high 21 wins in 1976, the only season in which he topped the 20-win mark.

Sutton twice won 19 games, in 1972 and 1974, and struck out 200 or more batters five times in his career.

Without ever having the dominating ability and recognition of a Koufax or Drysdale, Sutton still became the Dodgers career leader in wins, games pitched, strikeouts, innings pitched and shutouts. He was the opening-game starter seven times for Los Angeles.

Almost as impressive as his individual accomplishments is the performance of the pitching staffs and teams of which Sutton was a member. Seven times he was a

According to Phil Niekro, ". . . with Don, you never knew what you'd get on any count. The longer he went, the stronger he'd get. He was an artist."

starter on the pitching staff with the best ERAs in the league. In 18 of his 23 seasons, his club finished with a winning record.

Sutton pitched in five League Championship Series and four World Series and also made four All-Star appearances—1972, 1973, 1957 and 1977. He did not allow any earned runs in eight innings of All-Star competition and was the starter, winner and MVP in the 1977 game.

Sutton led the N.L. in ERA in 1980, which turned out to be his final full season in Los Angeles. Sutton became a free agent after that season, and with a future desire to become a broadcaster, was interested in signing with the Atlanta Braves. He flew into town and met with team owner and broadcasting entrepreneur Ted Turner, but Turner surprisingly didn't offer Sutton a competitive contract.

It turned out Turner had been getting criticized by other owners for overpaying free-agent outfielder Claudell Washington a few weeks earlier, and he didn't want to sign Sutton and incur more wrath. Instead, Sutton signed with the Astros. Had he joined the Braves, he would have become one of three future Hall of Famers on the Braves 1981 staff, joining Phil Niekro and Gaylord Perry.

Niekro always was a firm admirer of Sutton's ability.

"When you pitched against him, you always knew you had to have your 'A' game," Niekro said in an interview with the *Atlanta Journal-Constitution*. "He was a great competitor. He had a great curveball, one of the best I ever saw.

He had a good changeup and a good fastball, too, although not overpowering. He had great control and spotted the ball well. He always seemed to have to pitch out of jams, not that he got into many jams against us.

"With some pitchers, hitters walk to the plate knowing what they will get. With Don, you never knew what you'd get on any count. The longer he went, the stronger he got. He was an artist."

One hitter who could tell early in Sutton's career that he was going to develop into a great pitcher was Niekro's teammate, Hank Aaron, the all-time home run champ, who remembers hitting a home run against Sutton the first time he faced him in 1966.

"I told somebody in the dugout that day, 'This guy has a chance to win a lot of ballgames; he doesn't back down,'" Aaron said. "I never had much more luck against him after that."

Indeed, in the nine remaining years that their careers overlapped in the National League, Aaron hit only two more homers off Sutton.

Sutton stayed with the Astros for less than two seasons, before moving on to Milwaukee, Oakland, California and back to Los Angeles before retiring in 1988. Traded to the Brewers in hopes of helping them win the pennant in 1982, he beat Baltimore's Jim Palmer on the final day of the season to clinch the division title.

At age 41, he won 15 games for the division champion Angels in 1986, including his 300th career win on June 18, 1986. The final victory of his career came on May 14, 1988, leading the Dodgers over the Phillies.

He defeated every major league team at least once during his career, but Sutton does hold the record for

Don Sutton was the Dodgers career leader in wins, games pitched, strikeouts, innings pitched and shutouts.

most consecutive games lost to one club—the Cubs—at 13, from April 23, 1966, to July 24, 1969.

Sutton made four League Championship Series appearances with the Dodgers, in 1974, 1977 and 1978, posting a combined 3-1 record. He also started and won a game for the Brewers in 1982 and started a game, but was not involved in the decision, for the Angels in 1986. His career record in LCS play was 4-1 with a 2.02 ERA. He holds the record for most innings pitched in a four-game series, 17, in 1974, the same year he tied the N.L. record for wins and strikeouts in a four-game series.

Sutton's team reached the World Series in 1974, 1977 and 1978 (Los Angeles) and 1982 (Milwaukee). He won one game in 1974 and 1977, but was 0-2 in the 1978 Series and 0-1 in 1982.

It took Sutton five tries to win an election to the Hall of Fame. Some voters apparently had the misconception that Sutton "hung on" too long to win his 300th game, but he actually won only 44 games after celebrating his 40th birthday before he retired at the age of 43.

"People don't understand just how hard it is to win 300 games," said pitcher Bruce Sutter. "It's like Pete Rose's hit record."

One of the most memorable starts of his career came on June 28, 1986, when Sutton was with the Angels. His start against the Indians and Phil Niekro was the first matchup between 300-game winners since Tim Keefe and Pud Galvin faced one another in 1892. Neither Sutton nor Niekro was involved in the decision.

Sutton never won a Cy Young award or pitched a no-hitter, but he was consistent and durable. A fanatic about conditioning, he never spent a day on the disabled list until the final two months of his 23-year career. He pitched five one-hitters, tying the N.L. record, and nine two-hitters.

He won 10 or more games 21 times, missing only in 1983, when he won eight for Milwaukee, and in his final partial season in 1988. He became the first pitcher to win 300 games and only win 20 games in a season once. He finished with 178 complete games and 58 shutouts.

He surpassed the 3,000-career strikeout mark much the same way. He struck out 100 or more batters each of his first 21 seasons, then struck out 99 in 1987, topped by a career-high of 217 in 1969. He finished with a career total of 3,574 strikeouts.

Eight times Sutton posted an ERA of less than 3.00, including his league-leading mark of 2.20 in 1980. He pitched in a career total of 774 games, starting 756.

At the time of his retirement, Sutton ranked among the career leaders in games started (second), strikeouts (fourth), innings pitched (sixth), shutouts (ninth) and losses (sixth).

After retiring, Sutton did finally make it to Atlanta, joining the Braves as a broadcaster in 1989. He was elected to the Hall of Fame in 1998.

BILL TERRY

Progress had been frustratingly slow for the young lefthander, so when he and his wife sat down to breakfast in a Shreveport, La., coffee shop in 1917 they made a decision. If the major leagues did not beckon at the end of the coming season, pitcher Bill Terry would return to Memphis, Tenn., and enter a more rewarding business.

Terry won 14 games in the Texas League during the ensuing months. Still, no scouts gave him an offer and he returned to Memphis where, as a 15-year-old school dropout, he had worked in a railroad yard.

This time, Bill entered the oil business. Prospects were encouraging, and when he wasn't at work he was playing first base for a semipro team.

A few years later, when the Giants made their annual spring stop in Memphis, a friend tipped off John McGraw to the young oil man.

McGraw invited the local hero to meet him at the Peabody Hotel. For several hours the Giants' manager expounded on the honor of playing for the Giants under his leadership, finally suggesting that his guest sign a contract with the Toledo farm club.

"For how much?" Terry asked.

After McGraw recovered from the shock caused by such monumental ingratitude, he and Terry haggled for a time before Bill agreed to play for $5,000.

Memphis Bill put in two seasons in the American Association and, although only 24, managed the Mud Hens for a portion of the 1923 campaign.

Terry was not a complete first baseman when he joined the Giants in 1924. His chief flaws were in making the first-to-shortstop-to-first double play and throwing to the plate. Through diligent morning practice, however, the

By 1930, Bill Terry was a bona fide Giants star, both with bat and glove (left and center). Terry and Yankees Manager Joe McCarthy posed together (above) prior to a World Series game in 1936, Terry's final season.

weaknesses became strengths and Terry evolved into one of baseball's all-time great first basemen.

Bill played only half the schedule in 1924, being platooned with righthanded-hitting George Kelly, but he was a regular in 1925.

Annually, his salary wrangles with McGraw were explosive affairs. One year, the exasperated manager told Bill to make a deal for himself.

"Make your own deals," shot back Terry. "I have enough trouble playing first base."

A shrewd businessman who had come up the hard way, Terry knew his own value and did not mind expressing his views even to McGraw, who inspired only fear in others.

During a McGraw clubhouse diatribe against a player whose misplay had resulted in defeat, Terry bristled and told Little Napoleon publicly, "You've been blaming other people for the mistakes you've been making for 20 years."

Another time, Terry and Irish Meusel were three minutes late for the 11:30 p.m. curfew. A movie, Terry explained, had run longer than they had anticipated. But McGraw made no exception. Bill was fined $50, and was not in the starting lineup the next day.

Taking a seat at the end of the dugout, Terry removed his shoes and was in sweet repose when, late in the game, a teammate whispered that McGraw wanted him to pinchhit. Stirring slowly, Terry shuffled to a spot in front of the manager, leisurely put on his shoes and then strode to the plate, leaving behind an infuriated skipper.

Terry responded with a game-winning homer. That evening McGraw refunded his fine and invited Bill to his suite for some Prohibition beer.

Terry won the 1930 batting title with a .401 mark—he is the last National Leaguer to achieve that plateau—and finished second in a three-way battle with Chick Hafey and Jim Bottomley in 1931.

McGraw and Terry had not spoken for two years when, on June 3, 1932, Muggsy summoned Terry into his office. "I was expecting to be notified I was traded," Bill said.

Instead, Bill was offered the managerial job—and he accepted. Almost immediately, he earned unpopularity with some writers for refusing to give out his private telephone number. He also denied permission for a newspaper to photograph his family, maintaining it was an invasion of privacy.

Terry managed the Giants to three pennants before turning over his job to Mel Ott in 1942. Memphis Bill remained with the club as farm director for one year, then resigned to devote his energies to an automobile agency in Memphis. Later, he moved to Florida, where he eventually operated three lucrative dealerships.

In 1939, Terry was managing the Giants and Leo Durocher (left, left photo) was managing the Brooklyn Dodgers. Ten years later, Terry was hitting coach for the Cincinnati Reds as spring training began.

SAM THOMPSON

Carpenters in Danville, Ind., were earning $2.50 a day in 1883 when the Detroit Wolverines of the National League arrived for an exhibition against the town team.

Scurrying about the village to round up all the players, the manager discovered an outfielder perched on a house roof making repairs. The 23-year-old was interested in playing, but first he wanted a full day's pay for a half day's work. He got it. He also received an encouraging appraisal that earned him a shot at minor league ball in 1884.

By July of 1885, Sam Thompson was in a Detroit uniform. He replaced the regular right fielder, who had been injured. In two at-bats, Thompson collected one hit and scored a run.

The lefthanded hitter used a unique batting style. From a crouch, he would leap up when the pitch was delivered and lash out viciously at the ball. Because of the small, lightly padded gloves of the time, infielders were reluctant to stand in the direct path of his savage smashes.

The first time Thompson faced Boston, he found second baseman John (Black Jack) Burdock in a shallow position. From behind the plate, the Boston catcher yelled to his teammate: "Better play back, Birdie."

Burdock would have none of it, replying, "Nobody can knock 'em through Birdie."

Seconds later, Birdie jacknifed to the turf to escape decapitation by Big Sam's rifle shot.

At 6-2 and 207 pounds, Thompson was the game's foremost slugger in an era when power hitters were regarded as untalented players.

The Spalding Guide of the 1890s asserted that Thompson "belongs to that rutty class of slugging batsmen who think of nothing else when they go to the bat but gaining the applause of the groundlings by the novice's hit to the outfield for a homer, one of the least difficult hits known to batting in baseball as it needs only muscle and not brains to do it."

Some folks' low opinion of the home run did not disturb Sam. According to one observer, "he took the fans' breath away with his hitting and fielding." Thompson's throws from the outfield were strong and accurate. One source credited him with originating the one-hop throw to the catcher to head off baserunners attempting to score.

In the 1887 world championship playoff between Detroit, champion of the N.L., and the St. Louis Browns, American Association titlists, Thompson became the first player to hit two homers in one game in a post-season series.

In the first 11 games of the tournament, at which point

Big Sam Thompson was a power hitter in an era when such players were looked down upon.

Detroit won a decisive eighth time, Sam had 19 hits, including the two homers and two doubles. In Game 7, he saved a 3-1 victory by catching a long line drive with two on and two out.

Despite his build, Thompson was not particularly slow. He stole 33 bases one season and 235 during his career.

A sore arm limited Thompson to only 55 games in 1888 and he was sold to the Philadelphia Phillies at the end of the season. In Philadelphia, he teamed up with Billy Hamilton in center field and Ed Delahanty in left to form a future Hall of Fame outfield.

In his first season with the Phils, Thompson belted 20 home runs, a personal record. During his career, he socked 126.

Thompson played more than 100 games in 1896, but a back ailment sidelined the big slugger after only three games the following season. He attempted to play again in 1898, but was forced to retire after 14 games.

Sam made his home in Detroit, and he was on call in 1906 when Tigers Manager Bill Armour sought a temporary replacement for injured Sam Crawford. In his first game back, the 46-year-old Thompson was standing on the right-field foul line adjusting his sunglasses when the pitcher made his first delivery. The batter hit a drive down the line where Sam, far out of position, reached up to make the catch.

At various times in later life, Sam served as a U.S. Marshal, sold real estate and worked as a bailiff. He died of heart disease in 1922 at age 62.

JOE TINKER

The Cubs' Joe Tinker usually saved his best for superstar pitcher Christy Mathewson and the Giants.

Most batters considered it cause for great rejoicing if they got a scratch single off Christy Mathewson, famous fadeaway pitcher of the New York Giants.

But Cubs shortstop Joe Tinker, who had a lifetime average of .264, batted over .350 against Matty in 1902 and topped .400 against the Giants' star in 1908.

Tinker earned his reputation as a steady shortstop for the Cubs under Peerless Leader Frank Chance in the first decade of the 20th century. To the Giants, however, he was cyanide—taken internally.

In 1908, the season that Fred Merkle's failure to touch second base forced the Giants and Cubs into a pennant-deciding makeup game, Tinker left his imprint on the Polo Grounders as follows:

May 25—Batted in the deciding run in a 10-inning, 8-7 victory.

July 17—Homered off Mathewson in a 1-0 triumph.

July 18—Drove in the deciding run in the ninth inning as the Cubs won, 5-4.

August 8—Saved the Cubs from a shutout with a sacrifice fly in 4-1 loss.

August 10—Rapped three hits off Mathewson and scored a run in a 3-2 Cub defeat.

August 11—Drove in half of the Cubs' runs in 4-0 victory.

August 30—Scored the deciding run in the fifth inning of 2-1 victory.

September 23—Homered for the Cubs' only run in the famous Merkle game, a 1-1 tie.

October 8—Led the assault on Matty with a triple as the Cubs defeated the Giants, 4-2, to win the pennant in a replay of the Merkle game.

Tinker's greatest renown, however, was earned as the front man of the Tinker-to-Evers-to-Chance doubleplay combination that was immortalized by Franklin P. Adams.

Tinker was a $35-a-month shortstop for a Coffeyville, Kan., team in 1899 when he played in an exhibition game against Kansas City. The 19-year-old performed so elegantly that the Kansas City manager recommended him to Denver (Western), where his pay was $75 monthly. Two years later, Joe was a member of the Cubs.

After the 1912 season, Tinker was traded to Cincinnati, where he served one year as manager. Joe batted .317, his highest major league average, but the Reds finished seventh. The season was a series of confrontations between Tinker and club President Garry Herrmann, who allowed Tinker no voice in trade negotiations and sent a representative on team trips to keep an eye on the players.

At the end of the 1913 season, the Reds traded Tinker to Brooklyn, but the shortstop refused to report. Instead, he accepted the managerial position with the Chicago Whales of the Federal League. Tinker was the first player of note to join the new league.

A popular figure in Chicago, Joe led the Whales to a second-place finish in 1914 and to a pennant in '15. The team played its games in a park that in 1916 became the home of the Cubs.

After the Federal League folded Tinker remained in Chicago as manager of the Cubs in '16, but was released after a fifth-place finish. For several years he owned an interest in and managed the Columbus (American Association) club before migrating to Orlando, Fla., in the early 1920s.

Joe, who was associated with numerous minor league franchises in the decade that followed, acquired extensive land holdings during the Florida boom (during which his wealth was estimated at more than a million dollars). He was wiped out, however, when the boom collapsed.

In the depth of the Depression, Tinker operated a billiard parlor in Orlando. After the repeal of Prohibition, he opened the city's first barroom and the establishment became the popular headquarters for the local sporting gentry.

Joe suffered greatly in his last years from diabetes, which led to the amputation of his left leg. The old shortstop, for whom Orlando's ball park, Tinker Field, is named, died in 1948 on his 68th birthday.

PIE TRAYNOR

How he acquired his unusual nickname never was determined satisfactorily, but there never was any doubt that Harold Joseph (Pie) Traynor was one of the finest third basemen in major league history.

One version of the origin of his nickname dates to the long-ago day when he returned home after hours of vigorous activity, covered from head to foot with dirt and grime. His father, a printer, reportedly took one glance at his offspring and announced, "You look like pied type."

By another account, the youth played regularly on a local parish playground. At the end of the day, the priest, in recognition of cooperation and fair play, asked each youngster what he would like for a treat.

Invariably, the one who resembled pied type replied, "I'll take pie."

Regardless of the origin, Traynor imparted to his nickname superior quality as a gentleman and third baseman for the Pittsburgh Pirates.

A resident of Somerville, Mass., the youthful Traynor developed a deep affection for the Red Sox, but it was a Braves scout who found him and invited Pie to Braves Field for a tryout. Unfortunately, the scout failed to notify George Stallings. When the miracle manager of 1914 spotted the unidentified teenager on the field, he ordered him off the premises.

"I ran halfway back to Somerville," Pie said.

Traynor was scouted by the Philadelphia A's and his favorite club, the Red Sox. When the manager of the Portsmouth club of the Virginia League wired Pie an offer, the youth showed it to Boston Manager Ed Barrow, who advised him, "Go ahead, we have a working agreement with Portsmouth and if you do well, we'll buy you."

Pie batted .270 in his first pro season, earning a glowing report from Pittsburgh scout Tom McNamara. Although other clubs were interested, Pie was sold to the high-bidding Pirates for $10,000.

Traynor made his major league debut on September 15, 1920, playing at shortstop. He had two assists in as many

Pie Traynor was a slick-fielding third baseman for the Pittsburgh Pirates.

fielding chances and doubled once in two at-bats as the Pirates bowed to the Boston Braves, 4-1.

On July 22, 1937, he singled twice in five at-bats against the Dodgers for his last major league safeties. Pie played his final game against the Cardinals on August 14, 1937, scoring in a pinch-running role in the ninth inning.

Between his first and last appearances, Traynor was regarded as the king of third basemen. His only serious competition as the all-time best at the hot corner was Jimmy Collins, who stood out for the Red Sox in the early 1900s.

Pie was particularly adept at fielding bunts and slow hoppers. He dived to either side with equal agility and speared hot smashes with a glove that contained a felt interior, rather than leather. "With the felt lining, a hard-hit ball, if not caught cleanly, will drop at your feet," he explained. "With a leather liner, it will glance off for a base hit."

Traynor did most of his hitting with discarded bats. In 1927, he and Paul Warier used a thickhandled bat cast away by a member of the San Francisco Seals. Warier batted .380 to win the league batting title and Traynor hit .342.

Gentlemanly Pie was ejected from only one game. "He said he was sick," reported umpire Pete McLaughlin, ". . . sick and tired of my lousy decisions." In truth, Traynor had thrown the ball to the ground in protest to a call and, said McLaughlin, umpires were "instructed to put out of the game any player who makes a gesture indicating disrespect."

Traynor never learned to drive a car. He was an inveterate walker. In the early 1950s, Pie ate breakfast at his New York hotel on 34th Street, then walked to Yankee Stadium, more than 100 blocks away, for a World Series game.

The saddest walk Traynor ever took was in Chicago in 1938 when, as manager of the Pirates, he strolled from Wrigley Field to the Bucs' downtown hotel after the Cubs had knocked Pittsburgh out of first place on Gabby Hartnett's historic homer. With him was the club trainer and a young writer. Not a word was spoken the entire route. "If either one had said a word, I'd have slugged him," Pie said.

A respiratory ailment took Traynor's life in 1972 while Pie was visiting a friend in Pittsburgh. He was 72.

DAZZY VANCE

Dazzy Vance was a 10-year minor league veteran before he got a legitimate shot with Brooklyn.

Tales of the hard-throwing righthander are legion, but all attest to the fact that he was in a class by himself when it came to blinding speed.

He was pitching for a National League all-star team against American Leaguers in California one autumn when he broke off three explosive curveballs to Baby Doll Jacobson of the St. Louis Browns. On the third strike, Jacobson was flat on his back.

"Strike three, yer out," cried the umpire.

"And damn glad of it," replied Jacobson.

In St. Louis, the pitcher was informed by a writer before a game that "Rogers Hornsby hasn't struck out this season."

"That so? Well, save that story until after the game."

"Why?"

"Because I'm pitching."

That afternoon, Dazzy Vance fanned the Rajah three times and retired him the fourth time on a foul pop.

Vance, who gained his nickname in Nebraska from mimicking a cowboy's pronunciation of "Daisy," was a minor league vagabond for 10 years and reached the majors to stay only because the Dodgers were forced to take him. Brooklyn wanted Hank DeBerry from New Orleans, but the Pelicans refused to sell the catcher unless the National League club also took Vance. The Dodgers were easily coerced—and never regretted it.

When Dazzy arrived with DeBerry in his first training camp, he was greeted warmly by virtually everyone in sight. Curious about Vance's wide circle of acquaintances, DeBerry was told, "Why, my boy, these are old friends of mine. We've played with or against each other here, there, everywhere. I'd bet one hundred bucks that if I dropped in on every minor league camp in the country—and I wouldn't care how small the league—I would know at least three guys in every one of them."

Vance, who had pitched in a total of 11 big-league games for the Pirates and Yankees before joining the Dodgers in 1922 at age 31, led N.L. pitchers in strikeouts in '22 and repeated the next six years. In 1924, he registered a 28-6 record, which could have been 32-2 with a little more support.

The following spring, the Dazzler held out until mid-March. Arriving at the Clearwater, Fla., camp in an aged touring car, he used the steering wheel for a desk and signed a three-year contract calling for $47,500.

Dazzy proceeded to win 22 games in 1925 and he pitched a no-hitter against the Phillies. He lost his shutout —Brooklyn won, 10-1—on an error.

By 1928, Vance was earning $20,000 and the next year the Dodgers' foremost gate attraction was earning $25,000 as the highest-paid pitcher in baseball at that time.

During Dazzy's heyday, the Brooklyn club was known as the Robins, in tribute to Manager Wilbert Robinson. But the team also was called the Daffiness Boys, acknowledging the bizarre events that frequently marked their style of play. It was Vance who was the lead man when three Brooklyn players wound up on third base. He also was the president of an off-hour group of revelers known as the "Night Prowlers," whose vice president was the inimitable Rabbit Maranville.

Vance took his pitching seriously, though.

When Wally Berger was a fine young outfielder with the Braves, Vance fanned him on his first at-bat with three curves. On Berger's second appearance, Dazzy fanned him on three fastballs.

"What kind of pitching is that?" grumbled Berger. "You learn how to strike me out one way and then you ignore what you've learned to strike me out another way. I don't understand it."

"Someday you will, my friend," said Vance. "The unexpected pitch is still the best pitch anyone can throw."

Dazzy threw the "unexpected pitch"—strike three— past 2,045 major league batters. But his hopes for 200 victories were dashed when, after two short hitches with the Cardinals and one with the Reds, he was released by the Dodgers in 1935, several months after appearing in his only World Series (with the Cards). He was 44 when he signed to pitch with the Bushwicks, a famed New York semipro team of that period.

For many years, Vance operated a hunting and fishing lodge in Homosassa Springs, Fla., where he died of a heart attack in 1961 shortly before his 70th birthday.

ARKY VAUGHAN

In the 1941 All-Star Game at Detroit, Arky Vaughan cracked two-run homers in the seventh and eighth innings, and when the National League carried a 5-3 lead into the last half of the ninth inning, few in the crowd of 54,000-plus would have doubted that the Pittsburgh shortstop would be the hero of the contest.

But a four-run American League rally, capped by Ted Williams' dramatic three-run homer, sent the senior circuit to a 7-5 defeat and left Vaughan's achievement all but forgotten.

The incident typified the career of Joseph Floyd Vaughan, a superlative performer who labored for many years away from the spotlight. His .318 lifetime batting average, speed and excellent arm were frequently overlooked in favor of less-talented athletes. Vaughan engaged in no colorful antics and uttered no spicy comments, letting his natural talents speak for themselves.

Arky, so named by a California playmate when he learned that Vaughan was born in Arkansas, might have become a Yankee great if it had been possible for a New York scout to be in two places at once. Arky was a young shortstop for a semipro team in Fullerton, Calif., and had started to attract notice when Bill Essick, a Yankee scout, drew up his schedule for a Sunday near the holiday season. Essick had a choice. He could check out either Vaughan in Fullerton or a young catcher in Long Beach. He chose the latter course. Eventually, he signed the backstop, Willard Hershberger, who went on to play for the Cincinnati Reds until his death by suicide in 1940.

When Essick checked on Vaughan at a later date, he learned that the shortstop had been signed by Art Griggs, president and manager of the Wichita club of the Western League.

One season of schooling was all Arky required for advancement to the majors. A .338 batting average, 21 homers and 81 runs batted in convinced the Pirates that he was ready, and they never had cause to reconsider their decision.

In 10 seasons with Pittsburgh, Vaughan never batted below .300 and attained his high-water mark of .385 in 1935 when he won the National League batting championship and was named the league's Most Valuable Player by *The Sporting News*. He drove in more than 90 runs four times, topped by 99 in 1935. He also tied an N.L. record by leading the league in bases on balls for three consecutive years, 1934 through 1936.

After a decade with the Pirates, Vaughan was traded to Brooklyn, where he spent two seasons before going

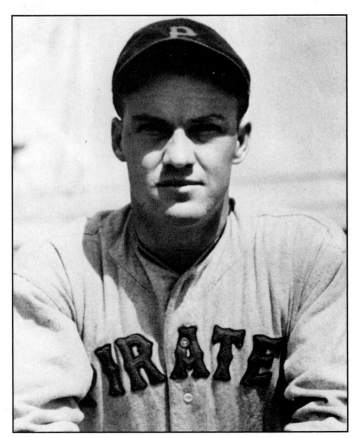

Arky Vaughan's potent bat and quick hands helped solidify Pittsburgh's infields in the 1930s.

into voluntary retirement. World War II was in progress and, with a younger brother in the military service, Arky's full-time attention was demanded on his 2,000-acre ranch in Potter Valley, Calif.

In 1947, after selling all but 400 acres of his spread, Vaughan felt baseball's siren song again. He was only 35 and had remained trim by maintaining the rugged outdoor life style he had favored since childhood. He was a part-time third baseman and outfielder in 1947 and '48 for the Dodgers, batting .325 and .244 before drawing his release. One season with San Francisco (Pacific Coast League) completed his career.

In retirement, Arky loved to spend hours fishing near Eagleville, Calif., on Lost Lake, a deep body of water in the crater of an extinct volcano. On August 30, 1952, after promising his wife he would return in time to accompany her and three of their children on a drive to a neighboring town, Arky set out on another fishing expedition, his last. When a companion made a vigorous cast, their boat capsized. Vaughan was an excellent swimmer, but both anglers disappeared about 65 feet from shore. The 40-year-old former player was believed to have suffered a heart attack while trying to rescue his friend. Both men drowned.

BILL VEECK

No one can say that Bill Veeck didn't have fun. As the owner of the Cleveland Indians (1946-49), St. Louis Browns (1951-53) and Chicago White Sox (1959-61 and 1976-80), Veeck brought color to the sport. And consequently, baseball was better for it

"I want to create the greatest enjoyment for the greatest number of people, not by detracting from the ball game, but by adding a few moments of fairly simple pleasure," Veeck said.

The quality in Veeck that set him apart was not his success as a baseball executive. Plenty of others had taken two teams to the World Series, as he did with the 1948 Indians and 1959 White Sox. His promotional skill didn't make him unique, although he consistently did more at the gate with less product than any baseball executive in history. Above all else, the thing that made Veeck stick out from others was his courage.

It has been said that courage is a man's chief virtue because it makes all the other virtues possible. Veeck always had the courage to follow his instincts. And

Veeck chats with commissioner Bowie Kuhn in 1975.

Veeck's instincts told him to not be consumed with winning, but to savor the sport of baseball.

Veeck began his career is baseball with the Chicago Cubs in the late 1920s as a part-time jack-of-all-trades. It was natural that he work for the Cubs, since his father, Bill Sr., was president of the team. As a youngster with the organization, Veeck planted the now-famous ivy that lines the outfield walls at Wrigley Field.

When his father died in 1933, Veeck left college to work full-time in the Cubs' ticket office. He had become the team's treasurer by the early 1940s, when he quit to strike out on his own by buying a nearly bankrupt minor league baseball team in Milwaukee.

He was able to implement some radical promotional ideas with the club before World War II intervened. Veeck joined the Marines and was sent to the South Pacific. While there, the recoiling breechblock of an anti-aircraft artillery piece crushed his lower right leg, which was amputated in 1946 after he had returned to civilian life and purchased the Cleveland Indians.

Veeck's peg leg became a personal badge and one of his trademarks, and it didn't seem to handicap him in his non-stop efforts to promote teams in then-unorthodox manners.

For that, he was labeled an anarchist by some owners for introducing such gimmicks as giveaway days and sewing players' names on the backs of uniforms so fans "wouldn't have to buy a program." But those were just a few trademarks Veeck left on baseball.

One of Veeck's most noted accomplishments came while he was the owner of the Indians. In July 1947,

Colorful Bill Veeck was never consumed with winning, only with savoring the sport of baseball that he truly loved.

Veeck played the first black player in the American League, Larry Doby. If Veeck had had his way, Doby would have broken the color barrier before Brooklyn's Jackie Robinson. In 1943, he made plans to buy the down-trodden Philadelphia Phillies with the intention of stocking their roster with black players, a move that might have earned the team several pennants during the war years. But he made the mistake of telling Commissioner Kenesaw Mountain Landis, who reportedly told Philadelphia's owner to find another buyer.

Veeck didn't stop with signing Doby. In the middle of the 1948 season, he inked Negro League legendary pitcher Satchel Paige. Some wondered how smart it was to sign a 42-year-old pitcher, but Paige posted a 6-1 record and helped the Indians win the World Series that year.

Veeck left the Indians after the 1949 season and acquired the Browns in 1951. While in St. Louis, Veeck orchestrated one of the zaniest moments in major league history. In 1951, Veeck had 3-foot-7 Eddie Gaedel bat. The midget walked on four straight pitches and was replaced by a pinch-runner. The stunt sent shock waves through baseball, as Gaedel was banned from baseball the next day and a rule was passed that stated all player contracts must be approved by league presidents.

Veeck wanted to move the Browns to Baltimore in 1952, but the league wouldn't let him. A year later they relented, on the condition that Veeck sell the team.

Veeck was out of baseball for several years, until he acquired the White Sox in 1959. The team won the A.L. pennant that year and set an attendance record. But his front-office judgment became suspect, as he broke up the speed and defense nucleus of the Go-Go Sox for a few sluggers in 1960. Finally, ill health forced him to sell the club midway through 1961. But while he was with the Sox, he introduced the exploding scoreboard that lit the night whenever a Chicago player hit a home run.

After that stint in Chicago, Veeck went into semi-retirement on an estate in Maryland, then bought a horse racing track in Boston and wrote a book about racing. Thanks to treatment at the Mayo Clinic, Veeck was well enough by 1975 to jump back into baseball. He headed up a group that purchased the financially ailing White Sox and prevented them from moving to Seattle.

Veeck turned Comiskey Park into a carnival of activities. He outfitted the club in uniforms reminiscent of those worn at the turn of the century. Fans were treated to wild promotions, including the ill-fated Disco Demolition Night in 1979 that resulted in the White Sox forfeiting the second game of a doubleheader to Detroit due to the damage caused to the field during the between-game promotion.

But Veeck soon found it difficult to operate under the game's new rules—specifically free agency. He could not and would not pay the high salaries that players were

Veeck, who bought the Chicago White Sox in 1959, throws the ceremonial first pitch at the team's home opener in Comiskey Park that season.

demanding. He knew the game had changed forever when a six-figure offer was not enough to sign the 18-year-old the team had picked in the second round of the 1980 amateur draft. So after the 1980 season, he sold out.

After he sold the White Sox, Veeck was seen frequently at Cubs games. Typically, he preferred to sit in the bleachers at Wrigley Field. After battling a multitude of physical problems almost from the time he entered baseball, Veeck died of cardiac arrest in January 1986.

RUBE WADDELL

Connie Mack always insisted that the finest pitcher in his experience was the one who gave him his biggest headaches.

Mack, who piloted the A's for 50 years, treasured the memory of the husky lefthander who pitched like a superman but whose child-like nature required infinite managerial patience and tact.

"The pitcher who had the best combination of speed and curve was Rube Waddell," said Mack, who managed the eccentric player around the turn of the century. "I saw Rube throw curves that came up waist-high and watched Nap Lajoie and Ty Cobb swing while the catcher dug the ball out of the dirt.

When Waddell was not pitching, he likely was fishing, chasing fire engines, shooting marbles with youngsters or enjoying himself at the local saloon.

His fascination with fire engines started when he was 3 years old. He ran away from home and was discovered asleep in the fire house.

Rube, known to his friends as Eddie, may have loved fishing even more than pitching. When Waddell was with Milwaukee playing minor league ball for Mack in 1900, the manager proposed to him, "If you pitch both games today, I'll give you three days off."

The opportunity to get away to his favorite fishing hole was too attractive for Waddell to pass up. Rube scattered 13 hits in the 17-inning opener, winning, 3-2, then allowed one hit in the 1-0 nightcap victory halted by darkness after five innings.

Demon rum, though, created many problems for Waddell. Usually without funds, Waddell would whisper to a bartender, "Give me a drink and I'll give you the ball I used to beat Cy Young in 20 innings."

The ruse worked regularly and hundreds of bartenders across the country displayed what they believed to be the historic souvenir.

On one occasion, the distraught pitcher told Mack, "I've lost my watch charm, the one I got for winning the pennant."

"Offer a reward for it," Mack told the penniless pitcher, "and if someone finds it, I'll pay the reward."

After the 1907 season, A's Manager Connie Mack traded Rube Waddell to the St. Louis Browns.

The next day, Rube phoned his boss from a nearby saloon. "A fellow found the watch charm," he reported. "Come over and give the guy his money."

Mack complied. He recognized the finder as a bartender. "As soon as my back was turned," said Connie, "the fellow turned the $10 over to Rube."

Rube might have had a long career with the Pirates except that Manager Fred Clarke was unable to handle him. In 1901, the Bucs traded Waddell to the Cubs. That fall, the lefthander accompanied an all-star tour to the West Coast and remained in Los Angeles to pitch the next year. Mack, who had moved from Milwaukee to Philadelphia, sent Rube a wire, early in 1902, inviting him to join the A's.

"Send $100 and transportation," the pitcher wired back.

Connie obliged—and waited. He learned that Waddell had boarded an eastbound train, but that a Californian had found him and delivered an impassioned speech focusing on Rube's "betrayal" of his loyal Los Angeles subjects. Waddell got off the train, weeping profusely.

Mack put Pinkerton detectives on his trail. The A's were in St. Louis when Mack received word that Waddell was in custody of the detectives, who were heading for Kansas City. Connie grabbed a train and met his elusive pitcher there.

In September of 1905, the playful hurler engaged in some horseplay with teammate Andy Coakley and fell on his left shoulder. The next morning Rube was unable to lift his arm high enough to attach his collar and missed the remainder of the season, including the World Series, which the A's lost to the Giants in five games.

Mack traded Waddell to St. Louis after the 1907 season. Rube made his first 1908 appearance against the A's in Philadelphia on May 19 and beat his old teammates. On July 29, in St. Louis, Rube boasted to the A's that he would set a strikeout record against them that afternoon; he fanned 16 to equal the existing modern record.

By 1911, Rube was pitching for Minneapolis (American Association). He was befriended by Manager Joe Cantillon and was at Joe's home in Hickman, Ky., in the spring of 1912 when the Mississippi River went on a rampage. Waddell responded to the emergency and stood for hours in icy water up to his armpits helping to place sandbags.

He contracted a severe cold and, although he pitched through 1913, he came down with tuberculosis that claimed his life in San Antonio in 1914 at age 37.

HONUS WAGNER

While discussions may rage about the greatest all-time players at other positions, a unanimity prevails on the foremost shortstop in the first century of baseball.

He was thick-chested with massive shoulders. His legs were bowed like parentheses. A barrel, it was said, could be rolled through his legs, but a baseball, never. His arms were so long, cracked Lefty Gomez, that he was the only player who could tie his shoelaces without bending over.

Honus Wagner was colorful, quick and complete as a ballplayer. Awkward in appearance, he nevertheless performed with a speed that earned him the nickname of the "Flying Dutchman."

One of nine children born to a Bavarian immigrant,

Wagner quit school at age 12 to work in the western Pennsylvania coal fields at $3 a week. When the opportunity arose at 21 to play baseball professionally, he leaped at the chance and performed for five teams in his first two seasons. A year later, however, Honus was in the majors, playing for Louisville of the National League.

The first time Wagner faced the Baltimore Orioles, the scourge of the league, he hit what should have been a stand-up triple. As Honus rounded first base, Jack Doyle gave him the hip. At second, Heinie Reitz "nearly killed me," Wagner said. "Hughey Jennings tripped me at short and John McGraw was waiting for me with everything but a shotgun at third."

"Don't let 'em get away with that. Knock 'em over," bawled Manager Fred Clarke when Honus returned to the bench after being tagged out by McGraw.

The Dutchman heeded the advice. On his next triple against Baltimore, he toppled infielders like tenpins, knocking McGraw halfway to the dugout as he charged

Honus Wagner is considered by many the best shortstop of all time. Wagner was en route to a .329 average in 1902 (above), the sixth in a string of 17 straight seasons in which he compiled a .300-plus mark. In 1909 (right), Wagner was working on his fourth consecutive batting championship.

into third base. From that point, Wagner owned the respect of the Orioles. To his last breath, McGraw maintained that Honus was the greatest player he had ever seen.

When Barney Dreyfuss transferred the Louisville franchise to Pittsburgh in 1900, nobody was happier than Wagner. The shortstop was born in nearby Carnegie, Pa.

Wagner won the first of his eight batting titles in 1900 and he soon was coveted by the new, free-spending American League clubs. Clark Griffith, manager of New York Highlanders starting in 1903, placed a score of $1,000 bills before Honus, but he declined without even asking Dreyfuss for a raise.

The Pirates won pennants in 1901, 1902, 1903 and 1909. In '09, Wagner had his only confrontation with Ty Cobb.

The first time the Detroit star reached first base in the World Series, he cupped his hands and, after prefacing his remarks with a slur, shouted his base-stealing intentions at Wagner.

"I'll be waiting," replied the Dutchman who, a few seconds later, took the catcher's throw and applied a none-too-gentle tag on Cobb's lip that brought blood.

In his early major league seasons, Wagner earned $2,400 annually, the maximum allowed by the N.L. By 1909, his salary had escalated to $10,000. When contract-signing time arrived in subsequent years and Dreyfuss asked what Honus wanted in salary, the invariable answer was, "Same as last year." The owner would produce a blank contract, Wagner would sign and Dreyfuss would insert the figure.

As Honus' baseball stature increased, babies were named for Wagner, as well as a cigar and brands of beer. But the use of his photo with a cigarette advertisement was another matter.

A Pittsburgh sportswriter was offered $10 to obtain the Dutchman's permission to publish his picture with the product. Wagner's written answer was: "I don't want my picture with cigarettes, but I don't want you to lose the $10 either, so I'm sending you a check for the sum." The letter was never destroyed, nor the check cashed.

A line-drive hitter with power to all fields, Honus solved the great pitchers as well as the lesser breed. Against Nap Rucker, he batted over .350; against Christy Mathewson, Wagner hit over .300.

The Flying Dutchman ended his active career in 1917, the same season he managed the Pirates for four days. Named to succeed Jimmy Callahan on July 1, he turned the job over to Hugo Bezdek on July 4.

Wagner coached baseball and basketball at Carnegie

Wagner and Ty Cobb (right) discuss hitting techniques at the 1909 World Series.

Tech for a while, served as sergeant-at-arms for the Pennsylvania Legislature and, with Pie Traynor, owned a sporting goods store.

Honus was a coach for the Pirates from 1933 through 1951, during which time he amused younger folks with outrageously funny yarns of his superhuman accomplishments as a player.

Wagner was 81 when he died in 1955.

BOBBY WALLACE

Connie Mack, who accepted congratulations graciously, also could chuckle when reminded of his failures.

When Bobby Wallace, a 5-foot-8 shortstop of the St. Louis Browns, crossed paths with Mack, the Philadelphia manager would grin and mutter, "Too small, huh?"

Mack's smile indicated that he remembered that day in 1893 when he was manager of the Pittsburgh club and an 18-year-old Scot obtained a tryout. At the conclusion, Mack issued his "too small" edict and promptly forgot about Wallace, who had earned recognition in western Pennsylvania semipro ranks as a pitcher.

Even so perceptive an individual as Mack was unable to detect shortstop possibilities in Wallace, who won 24 games for Cleveland before switching to third base and ultimately to shortstop, where he starred for many years.

The first American League shortstop to be elected to the Hall of Fame, Wallace was earning $45 a month, plus board and lodging, with the Franklin (Pa.) semipro club when the financial panic struck in 1893. The Franklin team folded and Bobby was considering returning to his brother-in-law's feed store—where he had once wrestled 100-pound sacks of corn and oats—when he received a wire from Pat Tebeau.

The manager of the Cleveland team was desperate for a righthanded pitcher. Would Bobby be interested?

The answer was yes, and Wallace made his major league debut on September 15, 1894. In a game shortened to six innings by rain, Bobby yielded 14 hits in suffering a 7-2 loss to Boston. He defeated Philadelphia in his second outing.

Bobby compiled a 12-13 record in 1895 and a 10-7 log in '96, when the Spiders qualified to meet the Baltimore Orioles in the Temple Cup Series, forerunner to the modern World Series. Bobby lost his only start, 7-2, and made two pinch-hitting appearances in the four-game Baltimore sweep, but at the completion he was richer by $117.

Although he had been a winning pitcher, Bobby was

Connie Mack's evaluation of Bobby Wallace was way off the mark.

informed abruptly at Louisville in 1897 that "You're on third today." In 1899, after the Spiders had been moved to St. Louis, Wallace was shifted to shortstop, a position he dominated for the next decade. "We were in Philly when Tebeau shifted me," he recalled. "Right off, I knew I had found my dish."

Wallace was credited with pioneering the scoop-and-toss style of playing shortstop. Instead of fielding a ground ball, coming erect and throwing, as predecessors had done, Bobby fielded and threw in one continuous motion.

"I noticed more and more runners were beating out infield hoppers by a fraction of a second," he related. "It was apparent that I had to learn to throw from the ankle and off-balance as well."

When the American League opened for business in 1901, Wallace was a prime target for the agents raiding the established league.

On assurance that he was receiving top dollar, Wallace agreed to sign with the new league and received a dollar to seal the agreement. Later, on learning that other players were receiving four and five times the amount paid him, he abrogated the contract, returned the one dollar and stayed in the N.L. By 1902, though, Wallace had jumped to St. Louis' new American League team. He played more than 100 games in each of the next 10 seasons.

In 1911, Bobby was offered the managerial post and accepted reluctantly. However, after an eighth-place finish, and with the club in last place in June of 1912, he was relieved of his job.

A broken hand in 1912 and burns suffered in an accident in 1914 sharply limited Wallace's activity. Bobby regained his old position in 1915, but quit on June 1 to try his hand as an A.L. umpire. He was teamed with Billy Evans, premier umpire, but resigned on August 1, 1916. He rejoined the Browns and played 14 games the remainder of the season.

Wallace started the 1917 season as manager of Wichita (Western). By June, however, he had experienced enough and obtained his release to join the Cardinals. Bobby played eight games for St. Louis that year and 32 in 1918 before retiring for good.

Back in California, Wallace devoted his hours to golf, billiards and model sailing ships. He died in 1960, one day before his 86th birthday.

ED WALSH

In the closing days of the American League pennant race in 1908, one pitcher stood a head taller than the others. In fact, there may never have been another performance to match that of the Chicago righthander who hurled 41 $\frac{1}{3}$ innings in an eight-day span in a futile effort to bring a pennant to the White Sox.

Ed Walsh started his incredible iron-man pitching on Tuesday, September 29, when he defeated Boston in both halves of a doubleheader. He allowed three hits in the first game and four in the second.

Big Ed returned to the mound on Friday, facing Cleveland which, like Chicago, was in the midst of a hectic flag race. Walsh drew Addie Joss as his mound opponent. Although Walsh struck out 15 batters and allowed only four singles, one hit was converted into a run on a stolen base, error and passed ball. Nothing more was needed by Joss, who pitched a perfect game.

Walsh, a spitball artist, returned to the mound on Saturday, October 3, relieving Frank Smith with one out and the bases full of Indians in the seventh inning. The first batter to face Walsh was Bill Hinchman, who grounded into a forceout at the plate.

Larry Lajoie, Cleveland's manager and hard-hitting second baseman, was up next. Years later, Walsh remembered what happened:

"Lajoie fouled off the first two spitters I threw him,

Ed Walsh gave his spitball and arm a severe test during the 1908 season.

one a screamer to left field, the other back into the stands. Billy Sullivan signaled for another spitter, but I just stared at him. Then Sully walked out to the mound. 'What's the matter?' Bill asked me. 'I'll give him a fast one,' I said, but Billy was dubious. Finally, he agreed. I threw a fastball and Larry watched it come over without even an offer. 'Strike three,' roared umpire Silk O'Louglin. Lajoie sort of grinned, tossed his bat toward the bench without even a word. That was the high spot of my baseball career, fanning Larry in the clutch without him swinging."

After finishing the Saturday game, Walsh rested for one day. He defeated the Tigers on a four-hitter on Monday, October 5, and followed with 3 $\frac{1}{3}$ innings of relief the next day in a 7-0 loss to the Tigers, who thereby clinched the pennant.

The victory in the Monday contest was the 40th of the year for Walsh. The final-game stint raised his season total of innings pitched to 464, a modern major league record.

Big Ed's salary for his remarkable season was $3,500. Later, when the White Sox were relaxing at the Wisconsin lodge of Charles Comiskey, the owner slipped Walsh a check for $3,500 in appreciation for his magnificent pitching. But when Ed opened the envelope containing his 1909 contract a few months later, he was distressed to find it called for the same figure as in '08.

Walsh boarded a train for Chicago and argued his case before Comiskey. The Old Roman was adamant and on opening day Ed, still unsigned, was about to catch a train for his Connecticut home when a messenger arrived with the news that Comiskey would pay him a $1,500 bonus for his signature. Walsh agreed, but at the end of the season he was hard-pressed to extract the promised bonus from his penny-pinching boss.

The youngest of 13 children born to Irish immigrants, Walsh worked in the coal fields of Pennsylvania before starting his professional career. By 1904, he was a rookie with the White Sox and drew Elmer Stricklett as his spring training roommate in Marlin, Tex. Stricklett, an early exponent of the spitball, taught the moist delivery to the youngster, but Walsh did not use it until 1906. That season, Big Ed won 17 games, 10 of them shutouts, as the Hitless Wonders won the flag and then upset the powerful Cubs in the World Series.

Walsh won two decisions in the six-game '06 Series. He captured Game 3, 3-0, on a two-hitter.

After his grueling 1908 season, Walsh slipped to 15 victories in 1909, engendering rumors that overwork had taken its toll. In 1911 and 1912, however, he posted 27-victory seasons.

Walsh concluded his active career with the Boston Braves in 1917, after which he briefly tried his hand at umpiring in the American League.

The Hall of Famer made his last appearance at Comiskey Park on Ed Walsh Day, June 22 1958. He died in 1959, at age 78.

LLOYD WANER

Pirate third baseman Pie Traynor took one look at the Pittsburgh rookie in the spring of 1927 and immediately pronounced him "too small, too thin and too scrawny."

For years Lloyd Waner made a practice of confounding folks with his lack of size. When he joined the Pirates, Lloyd was a 132-pounder. But he scooted like a jackrabbit on the plains of his native Oklahoma.

"Oh, he was fast," Traynor remembered 40 years later. "He was the fastest man in the league and got a tremendous jump on balls hit to center field."

On his first at-bat in the major leagues, Waner grounded to the shortstop, who made a seemingly routine play only to discover that Waner was four steps past first base when the throw arrived.

Lloyd was three years younger than his Hall of Fame brother Paul, with whom he played in the Pittsburgh outfield for 14 years. But according to Lloyd, neither of the brothers was the best hitter in the family.

"Our sister Alma was the best," Lloyd acknowledged on the day he was enshrined at Cooperstown. "We used to soak corncobs in water so they wouldn't fly so far when we hit 'em. Alma was the first to hit one far enough to break a window in the barn."

Like Paul, Lloyd broke into professional baseball with San Francisco (Pacific Coast), but he was released after six games in 1926. The release puzzled Paul, then an established star with the Pirates, who interceded with Pittsburgh Owner Barney Dreyfuss. "He's a better player than I am," insisted Paul in a slight exaggeration.

Dreyfuss invited Lloyd to Pittsburgh and, despite the 20-year-old's unimpressive size, signed him to a Columbia (Sally) contract. A .345 batting average earned Lloyd a promotion to the Pirates, for whom he became an instant starter. He collected more than 200 hits in his rookie season and shared the National League lead in runs. He batted .355.

Although the Pirates lost the '27 World Series to the Yankees in four games, Lloyd batted .400 and Paul .333. Together they collected 11 hits.

After the Series, which was dominated by Babe Ruth and Lou Gehrig, the Waners embarked on a cross-country vaudeville tour, Paul playing the saxophone and Lloyd the violin. The act played 16 weeks in major theaters in New York, Pittsburgh, St. Louis, Los Angeles and San Francisco. The brothers were paid $2,100 weekly, far in excess of their pay with the Pirates.

Part of their act that never failed to bring down the house consisted of Paul playing the sax and Lloyd arriving on the stage breathlessly. "Where ya been?" Paul would ask. "I've just finished chasing the last ball hit by Babe Ruth," cracked Lloyd.

Lloyd earned a $1,000 raise after his spectacular rookie season, but never made more than $13,500—even in his prime.

Early in his career Lloyd acquired the nickname of "Little Poison," while Paul was tagged "Big Poison."

The names traced to an afternoon in Brooklyn, Lloyd explained. A press-box habitue with a heavy accent referred to the pair as big and little person, but to others it sounded like poison, which the brothers were to the opposition.

Lloyd was extremely difficult to strike out, fanning only 173 times in the majors.

Although Lloyd did not share in Paul's reputation as an all-night creature, he could perform with distinction in the wee hours. Anyone encountering the brothers in a hotel lobby at 8 a.m., it was said, could not be sure if they were coming in or going out.

An appendectomy forced Lloyd to miss almost half of the 1930 season, but he bounced back to lead the N.L. in at-bats and hits the following year.

Little Poison was traded to Boston early in the 1941 season. Before the season ended he was acquired by the Reds. He was with the Phillies in 1942, then decided to retire when shipped to Brooklyn during spring training of 1943.

When the player pinch grew tighter during World War II, however, Waner had a change of heart and joined the Dodgers. He was released after 15 games and received an offer from his old club, the Pirates, the next day. A hero's welcome was accorded Little Poison when he was introduced at Forbes Field. Used primarily as a pinch-hitter, Waner batted .321 in 1944 and .263 in '45 before calling it a career.

Lloyd, who scouted for the Bucs and Orioles and then served as field clerk for the municipal government in Oklahoma City, died in 1982 at age 76.

Though "too small, too thin and too scrawny," Lloyd Waner produced Hall of Fame numbers.

PAUL WANER

It was May 20, 1932, and the Pirates were in Chicago to play the Cubs at Wrigley Field. As the 29-year-old Pittsburgh outfielder wobbled to home plate, he said to catcher Gabby Hartnett, "I didn't get too much sleep last night and won't be able to follow the flight of the ball too well. Please see that the pitchers don't throw too close to my head."

Assured that Hartnett would signal for no pitches high and tight, Paul Waner lashed four doubles to tie a major league record.

Big Poison was not a temperance group's shining example on the evils of drink. He thrived on all-night conviviality and made no attempts to hide his habits. Once, as a favor to his manager, he went on the wagon and promptly fell into a horrendous slump. A return to his old lifestyle seemingly restored his batting eye.

Paul's middle name was Glee, and no parents ever selected a more appropriate name for an offspring because fun was paramount to Waner. After an all-night tour of New York watering holes, he arrived at the Polo Grounds for a doubleheader with eyes glazed and head throbbing. In the first game, he clouted a double, homer and single; in the second contest, Paul hit two doubles, a homer and a single.

Fred Lindstrom, a teammate in the 1930s, once arrived at the Waner home for a morning golf date and was advised by Mrs. Waner: "Paul's gone to the store for a loaf of bread."

Lindstrom waited and waited. With patience all but exhausted, Lindstrom inquired, "When did he leave for the store?"

"Last night," replied Mrs. Waner, accustomed to her husband's antics.

Paul, a three-time National League batting champion, stood with his feet close together in the batter's box, about five inches from the back line. When attacking a pitch, he took a full stride, raising his right foot about four inches. Line drives rattled off his bat to all sectors of the field.

Power was not the forte of the 153-pounder. He hit only 113 home runs in his illustrious career, but he racked up large totals of doubles and triples because of his dazzling speed. Waner led the N.L. in triples in his first two seasons and, as a sophomore, topped the N.L. in hits, 237, and batting average, .380.

Paul, who was joined in the Pittsburgh outfield by younger brother Lloyd in 1927, possessed unusual eyesight. Uncle Wilbert Robinson, then managing Brooklyn,

By 1928, Paul Waner was indeed "Big Poison" to opposing National League pitchers.

once remarked that the brothers "have cats' eyes . . . probably can see in the dark."

Yet a specialist recommended that Paul wear glasses because he was unable to read the scoreboard from home plate. But Waner wore spectacles for only a few days. "With glasses," he said, "the pitch appears the size of a baseball. Without them, it's as big as a grapefruit."

Casey Stengel once suggested that Waner "hits from memory," which seemed reasonable in that Big Poison piled up more than 3,000 hits. He was the seventh major leaguer to top that mark.

By 1928, Paul Waner was indeed "Big Poison" to opposing National League pitchers.

Paul Warier's speed and strong left arm complemented his blazing bat and baserunning abilities.

The Waner brothers, Paul (right) and Lloyd, patrolled the Pirates outfield together for 14 seasons.

Waner was a member of the Boston Braves when he registered his 3,000th hit on June 19, 1942. Earlier in the series at Braves Field, Waner had signaled to the press box that he did not want credit for the milestone hit when he beat out an infield roller that could have been ruled a hit or an error.

The Braves were playing the Pirates when Paul reached No. 3,000. Old teammate Rip Sewell walked Waner on his first two at-bats, but in the fifth inning Big Poison rapped a clean, run-scoring single to center field.

Minutes later, a note was delivered to the Boston press corps. "Let's have a party tonight," read the message, signed by the player who never tired of all-night parties.

Waner rapped 3,151 hits as a National Leaguer and one in the A.L., a single with the Yankees in 1944.

Waner tried his hand at managing, but one year convinced him he was not cut out for the job. He was hired as a batting instructor by the Milwaukee Braves and was credited with making superior hitters out of a number of key players on the World Series championship club of 1957. Later, he served in a similar capacity with the Cardinals and Phillies.

Paul was 62 when he died, in 1975, of pulmonary emphysema, complicated by pneumonia, at his home in Sarasota, Fla.

JOHN MONTGOMERY WARD

When the Penn State student forsook his education to try his hand in professional baseball, his hometown newspaper commented negatively. To the Bellefonte (Pa.) *Democratic Watchman*, John Montgomery Ward had violated the sacred memory of his forebears.

On July 13, 1877, the ever-vigilant *Watchman* observed: "Monte Ward, youngest son of the late, lamented James and Ruth Ward of this place, a young man of talent and whom we expected to see as scholar and statesman, perhaps, has become a hired baseball pitcher. There is no reason why a baseball pitcher should not become eventually a great man, but the chances for Monte's sake, we are sorry to say, are against it, and trust he will pause and reconsider.

Mr. Ward pitched a trial game for the Philadelphia Athletics on Saturday, last week, and won high praise, we believe. Nevertheless, Monte, quit it and go to your books again."

If Monte read the counsel, he did not heed it. His back was turned forever on his birthplace as he became one of the game's finest pitchers, a reliable hitter, a manager, union organizer, club owner and, after retirement, a highly respected attorney.

The *Watchman* later softened its attitude. "There is nothing WRONG in pitching ball any more than there is in making shoes or picking type," the paper said, "and when the motive is a good one as this is (earning money to complete his education), we think the individual is to be commended."

Ward, by this time, had moved westward to Wisconsin where he had received a $75 bonus and a $20-a-week contract.

In 1878, the 18-year-old righthander joined Providence of the National League. He made his debut on July 20, blanking Indianapolis, 4-0, on a two-hitter.

Monte played five seasons with the Grays, dividing his time between the mound, the infield and outfield. One of his most memorable performances took place on August 17, 1882, when he hurled an 18-inning, 1-0 victory over Detroit. The only run was scored on a homer by Hoss Radbourn, playing right field that day.

After Monte's trade to the Giants, the *Watchman* reported on August 3, 1883: "Ward . . . gets $3,000 for this season's work. They paid him $1,000 down when the bargain was made, and $1,000 when he commenced work with them—

John Montgomery Ward, pictured in 1885, didn't restrict himself to pitching.

the remainder to be paid when the season is about half over."

By 1884, Ward's arm was dead and he became a full-time infielder. When the manager was dismissed late in the season, Ward handled the Giants for the last two weeks.

Ward was not only adroit defensively, but was a jackrabbit on the bases. He led the N.L. three times in stolen bases, once swiping 111.

As a member of the Giants, Monte attended night law classes at Columbia University. At graduation exercises in 1885, he was awarded a $50 second prize in the department of political science.

In 1887, Ward authored a magazine article denouncing baseball's reserve clause. Shortly thereafter, he laid the groundwork for the Brotherhood of Professional Base Ball Players. In 1890, approximately 100 members formed the Players League, which operated one season in competition with the National League.

Ward managed Brooklyn for two years following the peace agreement. During this period, when betting was an accepted part of the game, he won 20 shares of Giant stock on a wager. It created the unusual situation of a Brooklyn player being a shareholder in a rival club.

After two years with Brooklyn (the club was in the N.L. in 1891), Ward wanted to return to the Giants. A deal was agreed upon, but the Giants lacked the necessary cash. As a result, Brooklyn agreed to take a portion of the Giants' gate in exchange for the player's contract.

In 1894, John Montgomery led the Giants to a sweep of the Baltimore Orioles in the Temple Cup Series. Cantankerous Owner Andrew Freedman fired the manager a short time later and although he was only 34, Ward retired from baseball to devote his energies to his law practice.

Much of his practice involved ballplayers' suits. Ward won a cash settlement for pitcher Fred Pfeffer, who had been suspended illegally by Freedman.

John Montgomery was a member of the triumvirate that purchased the Boston Braves in 1911. His partners bought out Ward in July of 1912.

Ward, who earlier had denounced the reserve clause, defended it frequently in later years and remained in close contact to the game as a member of the rules committee. He contracted pneumonia and died in 1925 at age 65.

EARL WEAVER

Earl Weaver, who won 1,481 games as Orioles manager, entered the Hall of Fame in 1996 by way of the Committee on Veterans.

Earl Weaver became famous as the type of manager who liked to sit back and wait for a three-run homer, much as former Ohio State football coach Woody Hayes was known for a running game that produced a lot of three-yard runs up the middle. Weaver never disputed that. "If you play for one run, that's all you get."

More often than not during Weaver's 17 years managing the Baltimore Orioles, the strategy worked. His teams won six division titles, four American League pennants and the 1970 World Series. Five of Weaver's teams won 100 or more games, making him the only manager other than Joe McCarthy to be able to make that claim. Twelve times his team won 90 or more games.

Weaver's intense and combative style of managing produced a career .583 winning percentage (1,480-1,060). At the time he retired in 1986 he ranked fifth all-time among 20th century managers with 10 or more years of service.

Weaver was born in St. Louis in 1930, and dreamed of playing for the hometown Cardinals, He signed with the organization after graduating from high school, and spent 13 years as a player in the minor leagues, mostly in the St. Louis organization, but never advanced higher than Double A. Weaver, a second baseman, was named MVP in three minor leagues and was a five-time All-Star but never earned serious consideration for a promotion to the majors.

He was playing at independent Knoxville in the Class A South Atlantic League in 1956 when he got his first chance to manage at age 26, taking over a last-place team when the manager was fired late in the season. Under Weaver, the team finished the year 10-24.

His managing skills were noticed by the Orioles, who hired him as a manager at Fitzgerald in the Class D Florida-Georgia League the following season, beginning a trek that would take him to Dublin, Ga., Aberdeen, S.D., Fox Cities, Elmira and Rochester before reaching the major leagues in Baltimore in 1968.

Weaver was coaching for the Orioles when he was named to succeed manager Hank Bauer, and he remained on the job for 14½ seasons before retiring at the end of the 1982 season. After a two-year retirement, Weaver came back to manage the Orioles in 1985 for two years, retiring again, for good, in 1986.

His Orioles won three consecutive division titles in 1969, 1970 and 1971. His 1969 club, with stars such as Brooks Robinson, Frank Robinson and Jim Palmer—all future Hall of Famers—was favored to win the World Series, but lost to the Miracle Mets.

In 1970, the Orioles won their only World Series under Weaver, beating the Cincinnati Reds in five games after having scorched the rest of the American League in the regular season, winning 108 games.

In their third consecutive trip to the Series in 1971, the Orioles lost to the Pittsburgh Pirates in seven games and Weaver was blamed by many critics for his refusal to bench first baseman Boog Powell, who was playing with a broken wrist and hit just .111 in the series.

Frank Robinson was traded following that season, beginning the decline of the Orioles' dynasty, but they did win two more division titles in the next three seasons, in 1972, 1973 and 1974, but each year lost to Oakland in the A.L. championship series.

Weaver's fourth World Series appearance came in 1979, when the Orioles again took the series to seven games before losing to Pittsburgh.

As famous as Weaver was for his style of managing, he was probably even more notorious as one of the leading baiters of umpires in the game's history. Never one to avoid an argument, Weaver was ejected from games nearly 100 times during his career and was suspended six times by the American League for run-ins with the men in blue.

That was the style that made him successful, and Weaver has the honors to show for it. He was named Manager of the Year twice by *The Sporting News*, and his uniform number 4 was retired by the Orioles in 1982.

Weaver became the 13th manager to be honored as a Hall of Famer when he was elected in 1996.

GEORGE WEISS

To some, he was cold and dispassionate, a heartless creature who never left his office without a briefcase and who lived by the maxim: "There are no hours in baseball."

In the opinion of others, he was a shy individual, a workaholic who could, in the proper environment, engage in delightful conversation while playing host in his 200-year-old Greenwich, Conn., home that overflowed with baseball nostalgia.

The spotlight was for others because George Weiss preferred it that way. He was content to stand in the shadows while others less deserving took the bows and uttered bits of wisdom about world championship teams designed by a master architect in the front office.

Weiss, the son of a New Haven storekeeper, engaged in baseball promotion while still a student at Yale. As head of a semipro team known as the Colonials, Weiss scheduled Sunday games with major league clubs who were prohibited from playing Sabbath contests in their own cities. The Colonials played in an island park known as Rocky Point.

When Sunday ball was legalized in New Haven in 1920, Weiss, with a $5,000 loan, bought an Eastern League franchise and was on the road that led to four Major League Executive of the Year Awards (including three in succession).

In 1922, Weiss and his manager, Bill Donovan, produced a championship New Haven team that defeated the Baltimore Orioles, International League champions, twice in a three-game series. When the Orioles went on to defeat St. Paul in the Junior World Series, Weiss claimed the minor league championship for his Class A club and invited a Pullman car full of New York writers to New Haven for a banquet to celebrate the fictional title.

More than a year later, Weiss and Donovan were in a sleeper bound for the winter meetings in Chicago. Weiss, 28, had the lower berth, but generously offered it to the older Donovan. A train wreck during the night killed Donovan.

In the winter of 1928-29, Weiss visited Baltimore to arrange spring exhibition dates with the Orioles.

One of George Weiss' first moves as Yankee G.M. was to hire Casey Stengel as manager.

Legendary Jack Dunn had died some months earlier, leaving the club affairs in disarray. During the discussion on spring dates, the attorney for the estate suddenly asked Weiss, "How'd you like to be general manager?"

George accepted, and for three years he conducted a profitable operation. His shrewd deals attracted attention among major leaguers, particularly Col. Jake Ruppert. The owner of the Yankees had differences with Weiss years earlier when the Yanks arrived in New Haven for an exhibition game without Babe Ruth, whose appearance had been advertised widely by the club president.

His promotion damaged, Weiss refused to pay the Yankees. Ruppert squawked, but developed a firm admiration for George. When the Colonel tired of paying exorbitant prices for minor league players on the open market and decided to build his own farm system, he turned to Weiss. Ruppert signed him secretly on December 31, 1931, and phoned Ed Barrow, telling his general manager, "I hope you fellows get along."

Although the two were never chummy, Weiss and Barrow were compatible professionally most of the time. One major clash occurred when Weiss proposed the purchase of Joe DiMaggio from San Francisco of the Pacific Coast League. Barrow objected to the deal, but Weiss took a carload of top Yankee scouts to French Lick, Ind., where Ruppert and Barrow were vacationing, and convinced the two that DiMaggio was a bargain at $25,000.

During Weiss' years as farm director, the Yanks won nine pennants and eight world championships. When Dan Topping, Del Webb and Larry MacPhail bought the club in 1945, Weiss was given highsounding titles that pointed him toward the general managership that Barrow had relinquished earlier. In the hysteria that followed the 1947 World Series triumph, MacPhail fired Weiss, then offered his resignation to his partners, who promptly rehired Weiss as general manager. In that role, Weiss produced 10 pennants and seven world championships.

One of George's first moves after gaining complete control was to hire Casey Stengel.

Weiss and Stengel were pushed aside in the Yankees' youth movement following the 1960 season. After one year of unemployment, they surfaced with the Mets.

Weiss, associated with the Mets until December of 1971, died the next year at age 77.

MICKEY WELCH

The little fellow standing watch at the bleacher entrance to the Polo Grounds in the second decade of the 20th century was a popular figure with fans who wanted to reminisce about the emerging years of baseball.

Smiling frequently, the oldtimer recalled how he had won more than 300 major league games, pitching from distances of 45 and 50 feet.

Mickey Welch, an Independence Day baby in 1859, learned the rudiments of baseball on the streets and sandlots of his native Brooklyn before traveling up the Hudson River to play for the Poughkeepsie Volunteers in 1877. The 5-foot-7 righthander was 18 at the time.

After two seasons with Auburn and Holyoke, both of the National Association, Welch entered the National League as a member of the Troy (N.Y.) Haymakers in 1880. He was an instant sensation, winning 34 games in 574 innings of work. Mickey did not possess blinding speed, but he made the most of a good curve, a change of pace and an early version of the screwball popularized by Christy Mathewson and Carl Hubbell in the next century.

Welch, nicknamed Smiling Mickey by cartoonist E.V. Munkitrick, reduced his innings of work in 1882, but he completed all of his 40 starts for a two-year figure of 104 consecutive complete games. The string was snapped at 105 in 1883.

John B. Day, who had owned the New York club of the American Association, purchased the Troy franchise in '83 and transferred it to New York where, as the Maroons, the club played in the original Polo Grounds next to the northern edge of Central Park.

In '83, Mickey pitched more than 400 innings. Before signing for '84, he insisted that his contract contain a clause stipulating that he could pitch more frequently than every other day. For the remainder of his career, the clause was a standard part of his contract.

Welch completed 62 of 65 starts in '84 and struck out 349 batters. He also walked 141, tops in the league.

By 1885 the New York club was known as the Giants. The nickname stemmed from a cry by Jim Mutrie. After an especially sweet victory, the manager shouted, "My big fellows, my giants." The name caught on and Welch, despite his lack of brawn, was a Goliath among them.

Welch once fanned the first nine Cleveland batters to face him, and between July 18 and September 4, 1885, Mickey won 17 straight games, including four shutouts and four one-run games. The string was snapped on September 5 when Welch, pitching out of turn because Tim Keefe was ill, lost to Charley Ferguson of Philadelphia, 3-1.

Although earned-run averages were not a part of statistics at the time, an examination of boxscores indicated that Mickey's ERA would have been around 1.70.

Asked after his 44-victory season of '85 to what he attributed his success, Welch cracked, "To drinking beer."

With Welch and Keefe accounting for 61 of the team's 84 victories, the Giants won their first pennant in 1888. The club boasted only one .300 hitter, Buck Ewing, and had a combined batting average of .242.

In a postseason series against the St. Louis Browns, champions of the American Association, the Giants won six of 10 games. Welch split two decisions, losing his first to Elton Chamberlain, 3-0, on October 17, and beating the same pitcher, 12-5, on a three-hitter, on October 22.

By winning 17 of their last 20 games, the Giants edged Boston for the 1889 pennant. In the postseason series against Brooklyn, New York prevailed—six games to three.

Smiling Mickey remained loyal to the Giants during the Brotherhood War of 1890, but he won only five of 14 decisions in 1891.

Because Ewing, his regular catcher of earlier years, was sidelined much of the '91 season, Welch was unable to develop a winning stride, creating friction with Manager Pat Powers (who took over the club in 1892). After one game in '92, Mickey was sent to the Giants' farm club at Troy, where he terminated his active career.

After retirement, Welch moved to Holyoke, Mass., where he served for a long time as steward of the Elks club. He returned to New York in 1912 when John McGraw offered him a job at the Polo Grounds.

Mickey was visiting a grandson in Nashua, N.H., in 1941 when he was taken sick. He died at age 82.

In his later years, Mickey Welch enjoyed reminiscing about his 307 career wins.

WILLIE WELLS, SR.

Willie Wells, one former player said, "he didn't have a strong arm, but he could always get that man at first."

One of the major contributions Willie Wells made to baseball had nothing to do with trying to be a pioneer—he was merely trying to protect himself.

Wells was a frequent target of opposing pitchers during his career in the Negro League. Playing for the Newark Eagles in 1936, Wells was hit in the temple by a pitch from Baltimore spitballer Bill Byrd and knocked unconscious.

Doctors advised Wells not to play for the remainder of the series, but he was back in the lineup the following day, wearing a modified construction worker's hard hat to give his head extra protection. He had invented the forerunner of today's batting helmet.

Born in Austin, Texas, Wells grew up playing on the sandlots of Texas and was playing for the San Antonio Black Aces in 1923 when he was discovered by both Rube Foster of the Chicago American Giants and Dr. George Keys, who owned the St. Louis Stars. Wells decided to sign with the Stars, and began his Negro League career in St. Louis in 1924.

A 5-foot-9, 160-pounder, Wells earned the nickname "the Devil," establishing himself as the best shortstop in black baseball in the 1930s and early 1940s before giving the title away to Jackie Robinson. He was an outstanding fielder and was a surprisingly effective hitter for a man his size. He hit 123 career home runs, including 27 in just 88 games in 1929.

He was not gifted with a strong arm, but overcame that weakness with another pioneering feat, studying the opposing hitters and learning the importance of proper positioning of the defense. His arm was accurate, and he used his outstanding speed and good hands to full advantage. Hall of Famer Buck Leonard once said of Wells, "he didn't have a strong arm, but he could always get that man at first."

Wells made himself into an effective hitter, and led the Stars to National League championships in 1928, 1930 and 1931. He led the league in hitting in 1929 and 1930, improving on his .368 average in 1929 by hitting .404 in 1930. He established a career average of .334 during 20 Negro League seasons, and in exhibition games against major-league teams posted an even more impressive mark of .392.

The Stars folded after the 1931 season, and Wells bounced around before finally joining the Chicago American Giants in 1933. He was selected for the first East-West All-Star game that season, and contributed two hits in the West's 11-7 victory. Wells appeared in eight All-Star games in his career.

Wells left Chicago in 1936 and joined the Newark Eagles, where he was paired on the left side of the infield with future Hall of Famer Ray Dandridge. In his four seasons in Newark, Wells hit .357, .386, .396 and .346 but failed to help the team win a pennant.

He also spent winters playing in Latin America, and in seven years playing in Cuba established a career average of .320 and led three teams to championships. He was selected the league MVP in 1939 after hitting .328 to lead Almendares to the league championship.

Wells played in Mexico in 1940 and 1941, but returned to the Newark Eagles in 1942 as a player-manager. An intelligent player, Wells was just as effective as a manager and worked well in instructing younger players and quickly earned their respect. He led by example as well, hitting .361.

A disagreement with the wife of owner Abe Manley led Wells to return to Mexico in 1943, and in 1944 he was playing for Mexico City when manager Rogers Hornsby reportedly issued a ultimatum to the team's owners to get rid of Wells and three other black players. The owners instead fired Hornsby and named Wells to take over the team. Wells stayed in Mexico until 1945, when he returned to the United States.

During the remainder of the 1940s, Wells continued to work with younger players including Robinson. At age 43, Wells hit .328 for Indianapolis in 1948 and spent much of his later years in baseball in Canada before returning to the United States to manage the Birmingham Black Barons in 1954.

After retiring, Wells worked at a delicatessen in New York for 13 years before returning to Austin to care for his ailing mother. Wells continued to live in the same house where he was raised until he died of congestive heart failure in 1989 at age 83.

Wells was elected to the Hall of Fame in 1997.

ZACK WHEAT

Charles Ebbets was skeptical when Larry Sutton revealed that he had purchased a 21-year-old outfielder from Mobile of the Southern Association for $1,200.

"What did he hit?" asked the president of the Brooklyn Dodgers.

"He hit .246," answered the club's one-man scouting staff, "but he'll hit better."

"That's the trouble around here," grumbled Ebbets. "We have too many .246-hitting outfielders."

But Ebbets was smiling before the 1909 season ended. In 26 games, Zack Wheat batted .304 in launching a Brooklyn career that extended through 18 illustrious seasons. Zack finished his big-league career with the Philadelphia A's in 1927.

Wheat batted .312 during the Dodgers' championship season of 1916. Late in the year, he ran off a 29-game batting streak that was snapped by Fred Toney of Cincinnati.

In the World Series against Boston, however, the lefthanded batter collected only four hits and drove in only one run as Brooklyn lost in five games.

Wheat held out stubbornly the following spring. Even a visit by Ebbets to Zack's Missouri home failed to sway the outfielder. Later, when the team was in training, Zack showed up flashing a telegram signed by "C.H. Ebbets" and ordering him to report immediately.

Ebbets denied authorship. The two exchanged heated words before retiring to a room where they ironed out their differences and emerged smiling in due time.

Eventually, the telegram mystery was explained with the revelation that Brooklyn sports editor Abe Yager had sent the wire to provide his scoop of the day.

Wheat won his only batting championship in the war-shortened season of 1918, but it required an executive ruling to clinch the title.

Zack batted .335 in 105 games, Billy Southworth of Pittsburgh hit .341 in 64 games and Edd Roush of Cincinnati posted a .333 mark in 113 games.

Zack Wheat's popularity in New York transcended contemporary Babe Ruth.

National League President John Heydler eliminated Southworth because he had played too few games. He then awarded the crown to Wheat because he had hit for a higher average in only eight fewer games.

The quiet-spoken Wheat was willing to fight for his rights on the field, but he knew the limits of his dissent. He was never ejected from a game.

"I never could see any sense in cursing an umpire," he said of his good conduct. "Most of the time it means you're out of the game. And I came to play nine innings or longer."

Wheat was not only a hero in Brooklyn, but in all New York as well. At a time when Babe Ruth was socking homers for the Yankees and Frank Frisch was sparking the Giants to four straight pennants, Wheat was voted the most popular player in all of Gotham.

Wheat could handle curveballs as well as fastballs and for years John McGraw enforced a rule prohibiting Giants pitchers from feeding Zack curves at the Polo Grounds. McGraw feared that Wheat would pull the breaking pitch into the short right-field stands.

Once, however, Jess Barnes got two strikes on Zack, who sensed that the next pitch would be a curve.

"I hit the ball way up in the upper deck," Zack recalled. "I knew it was a homer when the ball was hit. As I was running to first base, I could hear McGraw shouting, 'Barnes, you blankety-blank pinhead, that'll cost you $500!' "

Zack hit his last National League home run at Ebbets Field in 1926. Rounding first base, he pulled a leg muscle so severely that he was forced to sit on second base for a full five minutes. For a time it was feared he would be unable to complete the trip around the bases, and Rabbit Maranville was suggested as a pinch-runner. Ultimately, however, Zack arose and completed the tour of the bases at a snail's pace.

After retirement, Zack was co-owner of a bowling alley in Kansas City and served on that city's police force for awhile.

Wheat later operated a hunting and fishing lodge at Sunrise Beach, Mo. Death came in Sedalia, Mo., at age 83.

HOYT WILHELM

Hoyt Wilhelm knuckled down and brought relief to numerous major league bullpens.

Progress in professional baseball could be painfully slow in the years immediately following World War II. For instance, a young pitcher who had participated in the Battle of the Bulge not too many months earlier compiled a 21-8 record for Mooresville in 1946 and found himself in the same Class D North Carolina State League in 1947.

A 20-7 record in that second season caught the fancy of a rival manager, who recommended the pitcher to the New York Giants. For a modest $2,000, the National League team acquired future Hall of Famer James Hoyt Wilhelm.

Wilhelm, born July 26, 1923, at Huntersville, N.C., first learned of the freak pitch in 1939 when broadcasts of Washington Senators games into North Carolina reported Dutch Leonard's success with the butterfly pitch. When a local newspaper published an illustrated article on the mechanics of throwing a knuckler, teenager Hoyt studied diagrams closely and developed the pitch to a high degree of efficiency.

By 1950 Wilhelm had advanced to Minneapolis of the Triple-A American Association. Hoyt won 15 games for the Millers in '50 and posted 11 victories in '51, earning an invitation to the Giants' springtraining camp in 1952.

At Phoenix, New York Manager Leo Durocher was smitten by Wilhelm's dancing pitches, particularly after Coach Fred Fitzsimmons, an old knuckleballer himself, suggested that Hoyt abandon his sidearm style and throw with a three-quarter motion in order to improve his control.

Wilhelm was three months from his 29th birthday when he made his major league debut on April 18, 1952, hurling one-third of an inning against Brooklyn. But the game he savored most in his freshman campaign took place on April 23. Relieving in the third inning, Wilhelm hurled 5⅓ innings to gain credit for a 9-5 triumph over Boston. Moreover, on his first trip to the plate as a major leaguer, Hoyt joined an exclusive society by clouting a home run. It not only was his first homer in the majors, but also his last.

Wilhelm won 15 games and lost three as a rookie. His winning percentage (.833), earned-run average (2.43) and total appearances (71) led the N.L.

Although he frequently expressed a desire to become a starting pitcher, Hoyt remained a fireman exclusively in five seasons with the Giants (1952 through 1956) and one season with the Cardinals (1957, a year in which he was sold to Cleveland in the final 10 days of the season). But in 1958, after 363 relief appearances, he was given a starting nod by Indians Manager Bobby Bragan.

Traded to Baltimore in late August of '58, Hoyt started four times for the Orioles and turned one of those assignments into a singular event in his 21-year career. On September 20, he authored his only no-hit game. Making only 99 pitches, 87 of them knuckleballs, Hoyt defeated the Yankees, 1-0.

Wilhelm enjoyed his most active season as a starter in 1959 when he opened 27 games. He reeled off nine straight wins at the start of the season and did not taste defeat until June 15. Although his ERA (2.19) was the lowest in the American League, Wilhelm won only six games after his streak was snapped and finished 15-11 for the sixth-place Orioles.

Hoyt made his final major league start as a member of the White Sox in 1963. The next season, he trudged out of the Chicago bullpen 73 times, his personal high, and compiled an ERA of 1.99. It was one of six times that Hoyt bettered the 2.00 mark as a fireman.

After stints with the Angels, Braves, Cubs and Dodgers, Wilhelm's long, winding trail came to a close on July 21, 1972, when he was released by Los Angeles. That was five days before his 49th birthday.

When the curtain fell, the talented Tar Heel owned lifetime big-league records for relief victories (124), games finished (651), games as a reliever (1,018), most innings in relief (1,870) and most games pitched overall (1,070).

Although saves were not part of the official statistics during most of Wilhelm's career, researchers have determined that he preserved leads 227 times.

His election in 1985 gave Wilhelm the distinction of being the first relief specialist, and the first knuckleballer, to be enshrined at Cooperstown.

BILLY WILLIAMS

Apprehension wreathed the features of the slender young passenger as he alighted from a bus in Ponc City, Okla., in June 1956. The youngster who recently had graduated from his Alabama high school suddenly found himself in an unfamiliar setting, about to embark on his first great adventure as a professional baseball player.

The teenager was a recent addition to the Chicago Cubs' farm system. Without frills or fanfare, he had signed a minor league contract calling for $150 a month in salary and $2.25 in daily meal allowance. As another part of the bargain, his father had received a 15-cent cigar.

Billy Leo Williams was the youngest of five children in the family of Frank Williams of Whistler, Ala., located a few miles from Mobile. The area was a spawning ground for ball players. In recent years, Henry Aaron and Willie McCovey had launched their careers from this section of the country. Now Billy Williams was following in their footsteps, starting on the lowest rung in the professional baseball ladder—the Class D Sooner State League.

Williams' high school did not have a baseball team, so he filled his athletic needs by becoming a 155-pound defensive end. He was good enough that Grambling College offered him a scholarship, which was declined in favor of baseball. Summertime experience with the semi-pro Whistler Cubs and Mobile Black Bears had convinced Billy that his future was on the diamond, not the gridiron.

At the bus terminal in Ponca City, Williams obtained directions to Conover Park, home of the Ponca City Cubs. Upon arrival, the 18-year-old rookie introduced himself to Don Biebel, a young manager, catcher and jack of all trades. "Find a seat in the dugout and watch," the skipper advised the newcomer.

During much of the season that remained, Billy did just that. When the team went on the road, he remained behind. He was left to his own devices as teammates jammed into several station wagons for out-of-town games. The situation bred loneliness and discouragement and Billy was often tempted to chuck it all for the idyllic pleasures of a fisherman along the Mobile River.

Somehow he endured, but played intermittently. When he did play, it was without enthusiasm or merit. One of the reasons for his lackluster performance was an unfamiliar position. An infielder in his semipro days, Billy was converted into an outfielder. On his first chance, he circled under a fly ball, staggered to an unconvincing catch and plunged headlong on his face. He played in only 13 games that season, batting .235. When the season ended, Williams knew that his baseball career

Billy Williams quietly went about his business as one of the top lefthanded hitters in baseball.

would be shortlived if matters didn't improve dramatically.

When he returned to Whistler, Billy received an invitation to join a black team for a barnstorming tour through Florida. He accepted. It was a momentous decision because two of his teammates, Henry Aaron and Satchel Paige, were renowned for their relaxed approach to the game. Their attitude was contagious. Billy Williams was never taut again.

The outfielder returned to Ponca City with a renewed spirit and a more propitious attitude. Free of tensions, he became an integral part of the operation. He made all the trips to out-of-town games, engaged in the spirited clubhouse chatter and batted .310 while leading the league in doubles.

Billy Williams was on his way—Pueblo, Burlington, San Antonio. At the last stop, he was leading the Texas League in hitting when a severe case of homesickness sent Williams on an unlikely course. He went AWOL. He returned to Whistler to visit his future wife and indulge in his favorite summertime passion—fishing. He finished the Texas League season with a .318 batting average, moved up to Fort Worth (American Association) for five games and then joined the Cubs in time to play in 18 late-season contests.

Assigned in 1960 to Houston, then in the American Association, Billy encountered Rogers Hornsby, a batting coach in the Chicago organization. The Rajah made Billy his chief project, advising the 22-year-old lefthanded swinger to choke up on the bat, straighten out his crouch and wait for the right pitch.

Williams was a good pupil. Before long, the Cubs' front office received a telegram from Hornsby: SUGGEST YOU BRING UP WILLIAMS. BEST HITTER ON TEAM.

A Chicago official telephoned Hornsby. "You mean he's the best hitter down there, huh?" he asked.

"He's better than anyone up there," snapped the outspoken Rajah.

The Cubs listened. Williams finished the season in the National League and remained for 14 more years.

With his short, crisp batting stroke, "Sweet Billy" clouted 25 home runs in his freshman season. Two of the blows were grand slams against the San Francisco Giants. He also drove in 86 runs and was acclaimed National League Rookie of the Year.

Frequently, Billy's unspectacular style went unappreciated. One writer compared him to a "book that never gets read because people put it back on the shelf after a couple of pages." Elsewhere, however, he was recognized as a master craftsman. Ted Williams thought Billy "was the best hitter in baseball."

Willie Stargell applauded Billy as "the best lefthanded hitter I ever saw . . . but for all you hear about him, you'd think he was playing in the dark."

Ernie Banks, Billy's exuberant teammate, analyzed his buddy this way: "Billy Williams can hit the *good pitches*. Yeah. For home runs. All of us can hit the *bad pitches*. But Billy Williams can hit the *good pitches*. For home runs."

Williams walloped 392 homers for the Cubs and 34 more in his late-career stint with the Oakland A's. He whacked three homers in one game and five in two consecutive games. He also collected four doubles in one contest and, twice in one season, belted four extra-base hits in a game. In 1972, when he led the league in batting with a .333 mark, Billy was named the Major League Player of the Year by *The Sporting News*. His biggest season was 1970, when he batted .322 with 42 homers and 129 RBIs and finished second in N.L. Most Valuable Player voting.

Williams was extremely durable. Between September 1963 and September 1970, he appeared in 1,117 consecutive games.

Williams engaged in his first and only postseason competition in 1975 when Oakland faced Boston in the A.L. Championship Series. It was not a pleasant experience for the .290 lifetime hitter, who was blanked by the Red Sox in eight trips. He struggled through one more season with the A's before retiring at age 38.

Williams complemented his excellent hitting with good defensive play in the short confines of Wrigley Field.

After leaving Chicago, Williams hooked on with Oakland and experienced his only postseason competition (1975).

SMOKEY JOE WILLIAMS

In a 1952 survey by the Pittsburgh *Courier*, Smokey Joe Williams was named the all-time best pitcher in the Negro Leagues. He received 20 votes, one more than Hall-of-Famer Satchel Paige.

The fact Paige is much better known that Williams has mostly to do with timing. Williams was one of the early pioneers of the Negro Leagues, and by the time Paige came along, the leagues were much more popular and successful. Also, Paige played at a time he still was able to break into the major leagues, even if it was near the end of his career.

Those who saw both pitchers in their prime, however, gave the edge to Williams, who was born in Seguin, Texas, on April 6, 1885. His father was black and his mother a full-blooded Indian. He began his career around San Antonio in 1905 and spent his first five years with the San Antonio Black Bronchos. At one stretch he was credited with 20 consecutive wins.

Williams was 24-years-old in 1910, stood 6-foot-4 and weighed 200 pounds when Rube Foster brought his Leland Giants through San Antonio and got his first look at Williams. The Giants were considered the best black club in the country at the time, and Williams beat them 3-0. When the Giants left town, Williams left with them. That began his long career in the Negro Leagues, which saw the right-handed Williams pitch for 22 years, until 1932.

He was known for not only his blazing fastball, which also earned him the nickname "Cyclone," but as a pitcher with exceptional control and an excellent knowledge of pitching.

From 1912-23, Williams hurled for the New York Lincoln Giants. It was not unusual for him to strike out 20 or more batters in a game. Perhaps one of the best games of his career came in 1930, when he struck out 27 Kansas City Monarchs, allowing only one hit, in a 12-inning night game. His best season was believed to have been 1914 when, pitching against all levels of competition, his combined record was reported to be 41-3.

During his career, Williams frequently pitched in exhibitions against white major leaguers, and his lifetime record in those games was 20-7. Two of his losses came when he was 45 years old. Three times he faced the current National League champions in post-season play. In 1912, he shut out the world-champion New York Giants 6-0. In 1915, he threw a three-hit shutout and struck out 10 as he beat Grover Cleveland Alexander and the Philadelphia Phillies 1-0. Two years later, he struck out 20 members of the New York Giants and pitched a no-hitter, but lost the game 1-0 on an error.

Among Hall of Fame pitchers, Williams defeated Alexander, Walter Johnson, Chief Bender, Rube Marquard, Waite Hoyt and Paige. "If you have ever witnessed the speed of a pebble in a storm you have not seen the equal of the speed possessed by this wonderful Texan," said Frank Leland, the owner of the Leland Giants. "You have but to see him once to exclaim, `That's a plenty.'" Williams also was an effective hitter and, when he wasn't pitching, often played first base or the outfield. He posted a .320 average during the 1912 season.

Said former Negro Leaguer Sam Streeter, "Joe was the only pitcher I ever saw who could tell a man, `They tell me you hit high balls. Well, I'm going to see if you can hit `em. I'm going to throw you a high ball that you're looking for.' And he would throw three of them—three in a row." Williams also served as team captain and manager for several seasons.

In 1924 he played for the Brooklyn Royal Giants, then moved to the Homestead Grays, where he was part of what was generally considered the greatest Negro League team of all-time. Also on the team were Josh Gibson, Oscar Charleston and Jud Wilson. In his first five years with Homestead, Williams was reported to have lost a combined total of five games.

Williams finally retired after the 1932 season and became a bartender in Harlem. He died on March 12, 1946. Williams became the 16th player elected to the Hall of Fame for his accomplishments in the Negro Leagues when he was selected by the Veterans Committee in 1999.

Smokey Joe Williams, nicknamed "Cyclone," was known as a pitcher with exceptional control.

TED WILLIAMS

His mother had hoped that her tall, gangling son would follow in her footsteps and join the Salvation Army, but the kid with the picture-perfect batting stroke respectfully declined. His heart was set on baseball, and no one could deny his ambition.

His eyesight was phenomenal. Opthalmologists reported that they encountered his type of vision only once in 100,000 cases.

While it wasn't true that Ted Williams could read the label of a 78-rpm record while it was spinning, that was about all that exceeded his capabilities. When he returned to the Red Sox from the Korean War and stepped into the batters' box for the first time, Ted told General Manager Joe Cronin that the plate was out of line.

It was impossible, Cronin replied, but to humor the slugger he ordered a check of the alignment. It was off by a fraction of an inch.

A graduate of Herbert Hoover High School in San Diego, Williams was in the major leagues three years after turning professional with his hometown Padres of the Pacific Coast League. He reeked with confidence in his ability as a hitter. When Ted joined the Red Sox and was told, "Wait till you see Jimmie Foxx hit," his instant response was: "Wait til Foxx sees me hit."

It didn't take long for The Kid, or the Splendid Splinter, to start his demonstration. In his first major league game, he struck out twice against Red Ruffing in Yankee Stadium before slamming a double off the right-field fence. That started the hit parade that did not end for 21 years with time out for World War II and the Korean conflict.

Williams gave Tiger fans an early look at his prodigious drives. He hit two homers on May 4, 1939, and on the second smash he became the first player to drive a ball over Detroit's double-decked right-field stands.

In 1935, Ted Williams (left) was a member of the Herbert Hoover High School team in San Diego. Six years later, Williams was the toast of the American League after his ninth-inning homer ended the 1941 All-Star Game.

Williams hits homer Number 500 in 1960, en route to career totals of 2,654 hits and 521 home runs.

In his early major league seasons, Ted ran the emotional gamut. Once, when his line drives were zipping right into waiting gloves, he fumed, "Nuts to baseball, I'd rather be a fireman."

The quote found its way into public print, which gave pixyish Chicago Manager Jimmie Dykes the chance to equip his players with fire helmets and screaming sirens when Ted next visited Comiskey Park.

In the opinion of many, Williams' most dramatic homer occurred in the 1941 All-Star Game when, with two out in the ninth inning, he clouted a three-run homer to give the American League a 7-5 victory.

Entering the final day of the '41 season, Ted was batting .39955, or .400. No major leaguer had attained that magic level since Bill Terry in 1930. Williams was given the option of sitting out the closing doubleheader in Philadelphia to protect his average, but he refused. He rapped six hits in eight at-bats and finished with a .406 average.

When the Most Valuable Player ballots were tabulated at season's end, Ted was edged by Joe DiMaggio, whose .357 average was accompanied by his 56-game hitting streak and a league-leading 125 RBIs. Many regarded the vote as a reflection on Ted's poor relationship with some members of the press.

Williams captured the MVP in 1946, his first season back from a career as a Navy pilot. It also was the season in which Cleveland Manager Lou Boudreau devised the Williams Shift. The alignment invited Ted to try for an opposite-field single, but, proud hitter that he was, the Splinter continued to pull every chance he got.

Williams' inside-the-park homer at Cleveland clinched a tie for the 1946 pennant for the Red Sox, who wrapped up the flag two hours later when the second-place Tigers lost to the Yankees. In the World Series, however, he was held to five singles and one RBI by the Cardinals.

Ted was sidelined for much of the 1950 season after fracturing his elbow in an All-Star Game mishap. Two years later, although he was nearly 34, he was called back to active military duty and missed most of two seasons.

Ted's playing career came to a close on a September afternoon in 1960 when, dramatically as always, Williams homered off Jack Fisher of Baltimore. It was No. 521 and was rapped on his final at-bat.

In 1969, Williams came out of retirement to manage the Washington Senators. He transferred to Texas with the franchise, but retired after a four-year term that produced one Manager of the Year citation.

After turning in his managerial portfolio, Williams went back to his stomping grounds, the Florida Keys, to match wits with the game fish.

Williams' big 1941 season was capped by a .406 batting average, the last .400-plus mark in major league history.

VIC WILLIS

The word "workhorse" was never more appropriately used than to describe the career of pitcher Vic Willis.

Willis, a 6-foot-2, 185-pound righthander, made 471 starts during a 13-year National League career with Boston, Pittsburgh and St. Louis between 1898 and 1910 and completed a remarkable 388 of them. His season total of 45 complete games (out of 46 starts and 51 total appearances) for Boston in 1902 remains the N.L. record for most complete games in a season since 1900.

Willis pitched 410 innings that season, another record, and led the league with 225 strikeouts as he pitched his way to a 27 - 19 record. Willis and teammate Togie Pittinger combined for 54 of third-place Boston's 73 victories that season.

Born in Maryland in 1876, Willis made his major-league debut as a 22-year-old rookie for the Boston Beaneaters in 1898 and won 24 games as he quickly became the anchor around which the Boston staff was built for eight years. On Aug. 7, 1899, he pitched the only no-hitter of his career, a 7-1 victory over Washington.

During his career, Willis topped the 300-inning mark eight times and between 1901 and 1909 pitched at least 278 innings in every season.

As would seem logical for pitchers who worked that many innings, Willis recorded many losses to go with his victories. A seven-time 20-game winner, Willis also lost 20 games in two years. In 1904, pitching for Boston, Willis won 18 games but lost 25 and the next season, he suffered through a 12-29 season that prompted a trade to Pittsburgh.

The 29 losses was a modern major-league record, but Willis had plenty of company. He was one of four pitchers on the Boston staff who each lost 20 or more games that season as Boston limped to a 51–103 record.

Willis rebounded with the change of scenery and reeled off the first of four consecutive 20-win seasons for the Pirates, winning 23, 21, 23 and 22 games while totaling an 89-46 record during that stretch. His performance in 1909 helped lead Pittsburgh to the World Series, where he lost one game, but saw his teammates rally to win the series by defeating Detroit in seven games.

In 1903, both the American League and National League thought they owned the rights to Willis' contract,

On August 7, 1899, righthander Vic Willis pitched the only no-hitter of his career. He joined the Hall of Fame almost 100 years later.

but it was finally decided that he remained the property of Boston.

Tall and graceful, Willis' best pitch was a sweeping curveball which helped him record 50 shutouts among his 247 career victories. He struck out 1,651 batters in his career and compiled an overall ERA of 2.63.

Willis' career ended in 1910, when he went 9-12 for the Cardinals.

Willis died in 1947 at age 71, and was elected to the Hall of Fame in 1995.

HACK WILSON

Tales of the slugging outfielder range from extreme admiration to compassion to extreme sadness. On the field or in all-night roistering, he dispatched high balls with a prowess unknown to lesser mortals. He was a physical oddity, with a size-18 collar, massive shoulders and chest, a protruding abdomen, oak-like legs and size-6 shoes. Nothing about the man conformed to pattern.

When the 5-foot-6, 195-pound player joined the New York Giants in 1923, the clubhouse man complained to John McGraw that he had no uniform to fit the original Mr. Five-by-Five.

Reaching into his locker, the manager extracted a uni-

form which he tossed to the youngster, saying, "Don't disgrace this uniform. It was once worn by a great player."

"Who?" asked the prospect.

"Me."

"Don't worry, a great player will wear it again," Hack Wilson assured Little Napoleon.

In some ways, Wilson was right. In 1930, playing for the Cubs, Hack set a National League record for home runs with 56 and a major league mark for runs batted in with 190. That record held for more than 50 years.

However, in the seventh inning of Game 4 of the previous year's World Series, he lost a fly ball in the sun and the misplay helped Philadelphia score 10 runs and erase an 8-0 Chicago lead.

The Giants lost Wilson through "a clerical error," as McGraw explained. Hack was optioned to Toledo in 1925. When the Giants failed to exercise the option in time, the Mud Hens sold him to the Cubs, for whom he enjoyed his most productive seasons under Manager Joe McCarthy.

A master handler of players, McCarthy knew when to pat Wilson on the back and when to censure him. And he constantly interceded for Wilson when his after-hours adventures offended Owner William Wrigley, an ardent prohibitionist.

McCarthy once tried to demonstrate the evils of liquor to his wayward star.

Hack Wilson (pictured in 1931) was a physical oddity with massive shoulders and chest anchored by size-6 feet.

Wilson is pictured in 1932 with Max Carey, who retired in 1929 after a Hall of Fame career.

By 1933, Wilson was playing in Brooklyn and nearing the end of his major league career.

Wilson was awesome in 1930, when he hit 56 homers and drove in a major league-record 190 runs.

"If I drop a worm in a glass of water it just swims around," said Joe, fitting actions to his words. "But if I drop it in a glass of whiskey, the worm dies. What does that prove?"

"It proves," said Wilson brightly, "that if you drink whiskey you'll never get worms."

The slugger, a onetime printer's devil who swung a sledge hammer in a locomotive factory and also worked in a shipyard after quitting school in the sixth grade, was known as Lew Wilson until he joined the Giants. A New York teammate observed, "You remind me of Hack Miller."

Miller, the son of a circus strongman, had been a big-league outfielder some years earlier. The nickname stuck.

Wilson packed as much punch in his fists as in his bat. One time he decked a teammate with one punch during a card-game argument in the Giant clubhouse. He scored a double knockout in Cincinnati. He dropped pitcher Ray Klop during a game, and that evening—when the Reds and Cubs were about to board a train out of Cincinnati—he leveled Pete Donohue, another hurler.

When Hack sought to take his pugilistic talents into the ring, Commissioner K.M. Landis vetoed the move.

Wilson's star went into decline after McCarthy left the Cubs late in the '30 season. Hack became a Dodger in 1932 and a big press party was scheduled in Brooklyn at the same time the major league owners were in town for the winter meetings. As Wilson was about to sign his contract, he spied McCarthy. "I wish I were going to play for you," Hack told Joe.

"I wish you were, too," said the new Yankee skipper.

After retiring from baseball, Hack held various jobs. He was a master of ceremonies in a Chicago night club and manager of the Druid Hills Park swimming pool in Baltimore, where he spent his last years.

In 1948, he appeared on a network radio show in which he held himself up as an example of the negative effects of demon rum. Shortly thereafter, friends found Hack suffering from a fall. He was 48 when he died of internal hemorrhaging.

The one-time star, who had earned more than $200,000 during his career, died penniless. The hat was passed at a Martinsburg, W. Va., saloon to help defray expenses for internment in that city.

DAVE WINFIELD

Dave Winfield had a decision to make. He had been drafted by the Atlanta Hawks of the NBA, the Utah Stars of the ABA and the Minnesota Vikings of the NFL, in addition to being selected No. 4 overall by the San Diego Padres in baseball's 1973 free-agent amateur draft. It turned out to be an easy decision for the versatile and immensely talented Winfield, who was coming off a standout baseball career at the University of Minnesota. A pitcher/outfielder, he had compiled a 13-1 record and batted .400 for the Gophers as a senior. He had also been named MVP of the 1973 College World Series. Winfield signed a bonus contract estimated to be in the $50,000-$100,000 range, and he joined the Padres immediately out of college in '73.

He played in only 56 games that first season, but as his playing time increased so did his production. He hit 20 home runs in 1974. Three years later, Winfield had a breakout season in which he hit .275, scored 104 runs, hit 25 home runs, drove in 92 runs and stole 16 bases. He played in his first All-Star Game in 1977, going 2-for-2 with two RBIs. Although his run total dropped in 1978, he increased his figures over the previous year in hits, RBIs, batting average and stolen bases. The result: a second consecutive All-Star appearance. In 1979, the massive Winfield—he was a 6'6", 245-pounder—posted career highs in hits (184), triples (10), RBIs (118) and home runs (34).

His numbers fell off markedly in 1980, but by then Winfield was an established and coveted commodity—so much so that teams lined up for his services when he gained free agency. The bids were lavish for that era, with the Mets offering $1.5 million per season for five years. The Yankees, never to be outdone, offered a $1 million signing bonus as part of a 10-year package valued at $23 million. Winfield headed for the Bronx. After a so-so first season in pinstripes, Winfield went on a tear in 1982. He hit a career-best 37 home runs and began a streak of five consecutive seasons with 100-plus RBIs. He batted an eye-popping .340 in 1984, and he finished at .322 four seasons later.

Winfield's years as a Yankee were not without some tough—and even weird—moments. He had numerous run-ins with the boss,

Yankees owner George Steinbrenner. They disagreed on the cost-of-living clause in Winfield's contract and Steinbrenner's contractual obligation to make donations to the David M. Winfield Foundation. The rifts led to notable exchanges of words and lawsuits as well. The cases were settled out of court. Also, Steinbrenner chided Winfield for disappointing postseason play. Winfield hit .154 in the 1981 American League Championship Series, then followed up with a 1-for-22 performance in a World Series loss to the Dodgers.

Beyond the wrangling with the man who signed his checks, Winfield encountered a bizarre problem in Toronto. On a Yankees visit to Exhibition Stadium in 1983, Winfield saw a seagull on the field and tried to scare it away by tossing a ball in its direction. As luck would have it, the ball short-hopped on the artificial turf and struck the bird, killing it. Toronto authorities booked Winfield on a charge of cruelty to animals and briefly held him in jail. The ruckus was short-lived—the charges

Dave Winfield was a versatile athlete who chose baseball as his profession—and he didn't disappoint. He finished his career with 465 home runs and 3,110 hits.

were dropped the next day—but it nonetheless was another bit of grief for the beleaguered Winfield.

Despite the distractions, Winfield regularly put up solid numbers on the field. He also continued his deft outfield play, winning five Gold Gloves as a Yankee to go with the two he had captured with San Diego. Injuries took their toll on Winfield in 1989. He missed the entire season because of a herniated disk. By the start of the 1990 season, he had been reduced to designated-hitter duty and platoon work in the outfield.

On May 11, 1990, New York traded him to the Angels for pitcher Mike Witt. A 10-and-5 player, Winfield held veto power over any trade, and it took five days to hammer out details of the swap. Winfield finally reported to the Angels with a one-year contract extension worth $3.1 million. It turned out that Winfield, 38, still had some gas in his tank. In 112 games with the Angels, he hit 19 homers and knocked in 72 runs—and was named *The Sporting News'* Comeback Player of the Year. Winfield continued to produce in 1991. He enjoyed the only three-homer game of his career, hit for the cycle in another game and finished the season with 28 home runs.

At season's end, he became a free agent. He signed with Toronto. Serving as a designated hitter for most of the 1992 season, Winfield contributed mightily to a Blue Jays team that went on to win the World Series. At age 40, he batted .290 with 26 home runs and 108 RBIs. Although his postseason numbers were modest, he did deliver a World Series-deciding double against the Braves in the 11th inning of Game 6. Said Winfield, "That was the culmination of a perfect year. Every year you come out and practice and prepare and hope you have the right team, you hope nobody gets injured, you hope someone pitches well but you put it all together. We had great team unity, we did it for a club that had never won before. We didn't do it just for a city or state or a province. We did it for the whole country. And it was a great bunch of guys. That sticks out in my memory. It was just a lousy double. That hit, it just made everything right." At last, after nearly two decades as a major leaguer, Winfield had a Series ring.

Once again, Winfield became a free agent at the end of the 1992 season. His career obviously nearing its end, he signed a two-year deal with his hometown Minnesota Twins. After more than a season and a half with the Twins—a stint in which he collected his 3,000th major league hit—he was traded to the Indians in August 1994.

Winfield told ESPN in an interview, "Three thousand hits is a great milestone. . .I'm proud of it. You know what it takes to get 3,000 hits? It takes not only some God-given ability, it takes a tremendous amount of determination, it takes understanding the game as a science, hitting as a science. And what is good for a year or one decade, you may have to make some changes. People who cannot make adjustments can't hang. It's a lot of different things that go into it. . . .They think it's luck but it's a lot of planning."

Due to the players' strike, Winfield didn't play a game for Cleveland until 1995—and he appeared in only 46 games for the Indians before calling it a career. But what a career it was. Over 22 seasons, Winfield batted .283, hit 465 home runs, had 1,833 RBIs and scored 1,669 runs. He appeared in 12 All-Star games. All of these things contributed to Winfield's election to the Hall of Fame in 2001 with 84.5 percent of the vote.

It was during his time with the Minnesota Twins that Winfield made his 3,000th major league hit.

GEORGE WRIGHT

George Wright (right), the man who revolutionized short-stop play in the 19th century, poses with N.L. President Ford Frick at the 1936 All-Star Game.

When Harry Wright launched a search for a short-stop on the first professional baseball team, he looked no farther than his immediate family. Brother George was a perfect choice.

George Wright was not a pure amateur when he was tapped by the Cincinnati Red Stockings of 1869. A native of the Harlem section of New York City, George attained local prominence in baseball circles before accepting an offer from the Washington Nationals in 1867. Allegedly, the Nationals were amateurs, but reason suggests that some inducement was necessary for George to travel so far afield.

A roster of the Washington players listing their occupations and business addresses showed George's occupation as "clerk." However, his address on Pennsylvania Avenue was a public park.

Wright returned to New York in 1868 where, as a member of the Morrisania club, he was recognized as the foremost player in the East.

The son of a onetime English cricket star, Wright was 22 when he heeded the call from Cincinnati in 1869. Brother Harry signed him for $1,400, which was $200 more than Harry was paid to manage the club. In later years, George revealed that his salary actually was $2,000.

As the star of the Red Stockings, George revolutionized shortstop play. Instead of playing on the basepath as had been the style, he played deep from where, with a rifle arm, he was able to retire batters with ease.

In addition, Wright would catch a ball directly in front of his body, with his heels close together, to prevent a batted ball from skipping through his legs. Also, instead of catching a ball stiff-armed, he would relax his arms to deaden the force of the blow.

In the 20th century, former teammate Deacon White said of Wright, "There isn't an infielder in the game today who has anything on George when it came to playing shortstop. George fielded hard-hit balls barehanded, and gathered them up or speared them when in the air with either hand. He was an expert and accurate thrower, being able to throw with either hand."

Wright accompanied his brother to Boston in 1871 and starred on four National Association champions (1872–75) before switching to that city's club in the new National League in 1876.

Boston's N.L. team won flags in 1877 and '78, after which George moved to Providence as shortstop-manager. The Grays captured the pennant in '79, meaning Wright had performed on seven title winners in eight years. After playing only 53 games in the next three years, the standout player retired.

Although primarily a shortstop, George could handle other positions as well. One who observed him in his prime wrote that "while he called shortstop his home position, he was, when called upon, equally at home on any of the bases. He could catch as well as the best catchers of his day and was a fine emergency pitcher."

Wright became interested in the sporting goods business while playing in Washington and opened his own store in Boston in 1871. Later, with a partner, he started to manufacture athletic wear in Boston. The firm gained a worldwide reputation as Wright & Ditson. When the Union Association organized in 1884 as a third major league, it adopted the Wright & Ditson product as its official ball.

Wright became interested in tennis while touring England with two major league baseball teams in 1874 and introduced the game to America. He was a member of the Longwood Cricket Club in Boston. One year, he conducted a tour of young players to the West Coast to familiarize Californians with the game. One of the tour members was Dwight Davis, then a Harvard student and later donor of the Davis Cup, symbol of international tennis supremacy. Beals Wright, one of George's two sons, was a member of the United States Davis Cup team prior to World War I.

Another time, George displayed a set of golf clubs in his store window, strictly as a curiosity item. When a Scotsman stopped by and explained the game to Wright, he became fascinated and shortly thereafter obtained permission to lay out a nine-hole course in Franklin Park near Boston.

For years Wright held the No. 1 pass to National League ball parks. He never lost his enthusiasm for baseball and was a frequent spectator at games in Boston.

The last surviving member of the game's first pro team died in his Boston home in 1937 at age 90.

HARRY WRIGHT

Unquestionably, nobody pioneered in more phases of baseball than Harry Wright, English-born son of a professional cricket player.

Wright was the first to be honored with a special day in all of Organized Baseball, and he was the first supervisor of umpires. As a manager, he was the first to outfit his team in knickers, introduce cooperative team play, take his team on a foreign tour, win four consecutive pennants and use hand signs in coaching.

Harry was a tyke when he came to America with his parents. His first love was cricket, and he gained proficiency as a member of the St. George Club on Long Island. The cricketers played on a field adjoining that of the New York Knickerbockers, baseball's foremost team of that day. Wright watched the Knickerbockers at play and was invited to join them.

Hooked on the game, Wright made his baseball debut in the fall of 1858, making three excellent catches in center field but going hitless against a Brooklyn team. The game also was noteworthy in that it was the first at which admission was charged.

When not engaged in his profession as a jeweler, Wright played with the Knickerbockers for five years before moving to Cincinnati as the pro of the Union Cricket Club. In July of 1866 he helped to organize the Cincinnati Red Stockings—who became a wholly professional team three years later—and dropped his affiliation with cricket.

In 1867, Wright achieved his most remarkable feat as a player. In a game against Newport, Ky., he slugged seven home runs. In June of the same year, he was named manager of the Red Stockings.

At the close of the '67 season, during which the Cincinnati team posted a 41-7 record, Harry was married. As a wedding gift, his players presented him a gold watch wrapped in a $100 government bond.

Wright gained national prominence in 1869 when he masterminded the Red Stockings to 56 consecutive victories. Touring the eastern half of the country, the team traveled more than 21,000 miles and played before more than 200,000 paying customers. The streak was extended to 130 games in 1870 before the team bowed to the Atlantics of Brooklyn, 8-7, in 11 innings.

When the Red Stockings disbanded at the close of the '70 season, Harry accepted an offer to manage the Boston club of the new National Association. He produced four successive pennants from 1872 to '75.

Harry constantly crusaded for the betterment of baseball and was particularly distressed when the

Harry Wright was one of major league baseball's foremost pioneers.

Athletics displayed their championship flag of 1871 in a Philadelphia saloon. He expected his players to be gentlemanly and temperate at all times. In denying a player's request to report two days late for spring training, Wright wrote:

"Professional ballplaying is a business and, as such, I trust you will regard it while the season lasts."

When the National League was founded in February of 1876, Harry served as secretary of the meeting and was lauded highly for his contributions in drafting legislation for the new circuit.

Wright's Boston club failed to win the first N.L. pennant, but it finished No. 1 the next two years. After the 1881 season, Harry switched to Providence for two years and then to Philadelphia where he managed for a decade before failing eyesight forced his retirement. In appreciation for his countless contributions to baseball, the N.L. created the special post of supervisor of umpires for Wright.

After Harry's death from pneumonia in Atlantic City, the 1896 Reach Guide editorialized: "Every magnate in the country is indebted to this man for the establishment of baseball as a business, and every patron for fulfilling him with a systematic recreation. Every player is indebted to him for inaugurating an occupation in which he gains a livelihood, and the country at large for adding one more industry . . . to furnish employment."

On "Harry Wright Day" the following season, more than $3,000 was collected in ball parks throughout the country for a monument to the "Father of Professional Baseball" in West Laurel Hill Cemetery in Philadelphia.

EARLY WYNN

Late in 1936, a chunky kid, clad in overalls and with a battered baseball glove dangling at his side, walked into a Washington Senators tryout camp at Sanford, Fla., and announced that he was a pitcher.

"Let's see you throw some," said Clyde Milan, the camp director whose initial impression was less than favorable.

After a few pitches, however, Milan changed his mind. The kid had a whistling fastball, and his look of determination could not be discounted.

The youngster, uninvited and unscouted, was signed to a Class D contract for $100 a month and one dollar a day meal money.

Nearly 27 years later the same righthander, now 43, took the mound for the Cleveland Indians in the second game of a Saturday doubleheader at Kansas City. He pitched the first five innings, then departed with a 5-4 lead. Jerry Walker shut out the A's the remainder of the game and when the Indians clinched the 7-4 victory,

Early Wynn was in the radio booth ready to be interviewed as baseball's newest 300-game winner.

The date was July 13, 1963, nearly 22 years after Wynn arrived in the majors to stay as a member of the Senators.

Wynn made his big-league debut in 1939, pitching three late-season games for the Senators. He knew he wouldn't be back the next season and explained why.

"In a game against Cleveland I was getting my ears pinned back," he said. "But Washington was making some runs for me and it was still close in the ninth inning. We had men on first and second with none out and they let me bat, to sacrifice. I bunted—into a triple play."

Wynn, nicknamed Gus because, somebody said, "he looks like a Gus," spent 1940 and most of 1941 in the minors. He then pitched for the Senators in six of the next seven seasons, missing only 1945—a year in which the usually also-ran Senators were in the American League pennant race until the last day of the season. Wynn was in the military service in '45.

Traded to Cleveland after the Tribe's world-championship season of 1948, Wynn learned the finer points of his craft from pitching coach Mel Harder. Previously, Early had tried to throw every pitch as hard as he could. Under Harder's guidance, he learned the value of chang-

Early Wynn (left) was the 21-year-old ace for Springfield of the Eastern League when he got the call from Washington. Wynn (center, right photo) looks on during an early career spring training session as coach Benny Bengough returns a throw to a pitcher. Standing to Wynn's left is Calvin Griffith, son of Senators Owner Clark Griffith.

In 1954, Wynn (left) was one of the moving forces of the pennant-winning Indians with 23 victories. Five seasons later, Wynn was on his way to 22 wins as a member of the Chicago White Sox.

ing speeds. Thanks, too, to Harder's advice, Wynn's control improved markedly.

One phase of his game that did not change however, was the fierce determination to win. The one-quarter Cherokee from Alabama dusted off many a batter who took liberties at the plate. He was especially rough on hitters who drove hard smashes through the pitchers' box which, he maintained, "is my office."

In a 1956 game at Washington, Jose Valdivielso drilled the ball up the middle and it struck Wynn on the chin. As Valdivielso stood on base contemplating what might occur on his next at-bat, Al Lopez checked out his pitcher.

"Let me see," said the Cleveland manager.

"I'm fine," replied Gus through clenched jaws.

Lopez repeated the question and Wynn repeated the reply several times until Al said, "Let me see or I'll take you out without looking."

At that, Early yielded, revealing a gash on his chin that would require 16 stitches and a mouth so badly chopped that he would lose seven lower teeth. Under protest, Wynn left the mound—and Valdivielso heaved a sigh of relief.

Truly, Wynn was "the man you would least like to meet in a dark alley on a rainy night."

Gus won 20 or more games four times for the Indians before Bill Veeck, his old boss at Cleveland, acquired him for the White Sox during the winter meetings of 1957.

Wynn was nearly 38, but he had enough of the old cunning, pride and determination to win 14 games in 1958 and a league-leading 22 games for the A.L. champion White Sox of 1959.

At the start of the 1962 season, Wynn still was eight victories short of the coveted 300 mark. He had adopted a strict dietary regimen to prepare himself physically for the final assault. Using a high slider and a knuckleball extensively, he made an admirable effort, but fell one victory short with a 7-15 record. At the end of the season, the White Sox handed Early his release.

The old fighter stayed in shape, although there were no offers. At last, on June 21, 1963, he received a call from his old club. The Indians needed pitching help. Within a month, Wynn had scaled the final peak.

Wynn became a pitching coach for the Indians and Twins, scouted for the Twins and managed a number of minor league clubs. He returned to the scene of many conquests in the early 1980s as a broadcaster for the White Sox. Wynn died in 1999 at the age of 79.

CARL YASTRZEMSKI

Carl Yastrzemski replaced a legend, and in the process, he became a legend. Yastrzemski, who took over in left field for Boston in 1961, one year after Red Sox legend Ted Williams retired, was a steady hitter who compiled a career .285 batting average. More significant were his 3,419 hits and 452 home runs. He is the only A.L. player ever to have both 3,000 hits and 400 homers in his career.

"I'm very pleased and very proud of my accomplishments, but I'm most proud of that," Yastrzemski said. "Not Williams, not (Lou) Gehrig, not (Joe) DiMaggio did that. They were Cadillacs and I'm a Chevrolet."

Three times, he was the leading hitter in the American League. Three times, he was the league's slugging champion. In 1967, he was the A.L's Most Valuable Player and the winner of the Triple Crown. Seven times, he earned Gold Gloves for his defensive work. Seven times, he led the league in assists. And 17 times, he was a member of the A.L. All-Star squad.

The '67 season was Yastrzemski's crowning glory. That year, he enjoyed one of the most remarkable seasons of any professional baseball player. He won the Triple Crown,

In 1967, Yastrzemski won the Triple Crown, leading the A.L. in batting (.326), RBIs (121) and tying for first in home runs (44).

Seventeen-time All-Star Carl Yastrzemski is the only American League player ever to have both 3,000 hits and 400 homers in his career.

leading the A.L. in batting average (.326), RBIs (121) and tying for first in home runs (44). Additionally, he inspired the Red Sox from a ninth-place finish the previous year to a pennant so unlikely in 1967 that that chapter in club history was dubbed the "Impossible Dream." Yastrzemski hit .444 with 26 RBIs in the last 19 games that season and collected 10 hits in his last 13 at-bats.

He also won batting titles in 1963 and 1968, while totalling 40-homer seasons in 1969 and 1970. But nothing compared to his efforts in 1967.

"In my quarter century in baseball, including the two years in the minors, I don't think I could have done any better," he said.

Yastrzemski grew up on a farm on Long Island and went to Notre Dame on a scholarship for one year before entering pro baseball. In 1959, at the age of 19, he accepted a $100,000 bonus to sign with the Red Sox and began his professional career as a shortstop.

He spent his first season in pro baseball with Raleigh (N.C.), where he led the Carolina League with a .377 average, 170 hits and 34 doubles en route to winning league Most Valuable Player honors. He moved to Minneapolis the following season and was switched from shortstop to left field. That year, he compiled a .339 average. After that, it was obvious Yaz was ready for the major leagues.

Yastrzemski singled off Kansas City's Ray Herbert in his first big-league at-bat (at Fenway Park on April 11, 1961).

"It was drizzling rain and cold in Fenway Park," said Yaz, recalling his first major league game. "I had one hit. I threw out a man at home plate. We lost. I was nervous, with all the stuff about my succeeding Ted Williams all during spring training.

"But as much as I remember that day, I remember a day about two months later. I was hitting about .220. The day before, Jim Bunning gave me an 0 for four. Then that day, Frank Lary demolished two or three of my bats with that hard slider of his.

"After the game, I sat there, hitting .220 after hitting .380 and .340 in the minors, and I had doubts about my ability to play. I was ready to cry when Mike Higgins came over, put his hand on my shoulder and said: 'Kid, forget it. You're going to hit.'

"I think that was the day my opening-day jitters finally ended, and I hit about .300 the rest of the season."

Yaz finished his rookie campaign with a .266 average, 11 homers and 80 RBIs. From there, his career continued to gain momentum. He drove in 94 runs and hit .296 the next season, and in 1963 he won his first batting title, hitting .321.

His success continued to mount, and on July 24, 1979, he collected his 400th career home run, hitting it against Mike Morgan of the Oakland A's. That same season, he registered his 3,000th career hit, victimizing the Yankees' Jim Beattie on September 12.

"The 400 home runs had meant a lot because the 3,000-hitting was going to happen," Yastrzemski said. "Those were two things I wanted to get. It was the first time in my career that I really felt individual pressure.

"When I was going for the Triple Crown and all that stuff, it wasn't going through my mind. I didn't even know I'd won the Triple Crown until after the last game because I was so involved in the pennant race.

"But the 3,000-hitting thing was the first time I let individual pressure get to me. I was uptight about it. When I saw the hit going through, I had a sigh of relief more than anything."

During his 23 years in Boston (which tied the major league record for most seasons with one club and most consecutive seasons with one club), Yastrzemski drove in 1,844 runs, scored 1,816 and compiled a .285 batting average. He was the first player in history to get at least 100 hits every season for his first 20 campaigns. He batted 13,990 times and had 11,988 official at-bats, both A.L. records upon his retirement after the 1983 season.

In two World Series, he batted .352 with three homers.

Despite his success in the Fall Classic, Yaz was unable to secure a championship for the Red Sox. In each Series ('67 against St. Louis and '75 against Cincinnati), Yaz and Boston lost in seven games. Those losses left the Red Sox without a world championship since 1918, but it didn't diminish what Yaz did on the field.

"I grew up on a farm," Yastrzemski said. "I just thought I was the same as everybody else. I was lucky enough to have the talent to play baseball. That's how I treated my career. I didn't think I was anybody special, anybody different."

But Yaz was special, and in 1989 he was elected to the baseball Hall of Fame in his first year of eligibility.

"To join Ruth, Williams, (Willie) Mays, (Hank) Aaron, (Stan) Musial, who I grew up idolizing as a player, it's something you don't think about," Yastrzemski said.

"I know in my heart I belong, but in a way if I wasn't voted in, it wouldn't make any difference because I know what I accomplished on the field."

TOM YAWKEY

American League club owners were aghast in 1933 when the new owner of the Boston Red Sox arose at his first meeting and announced that he was prepared to pay handsome prices for established major leaguers.

"Would you be interested in Rick Ferrell and Lloyd Brown?" asked Phil Ball, owner of the St. Louis Browns.

"I would," answered the young millionaire, who started to write a check for a deal in which he gave up catcher Marvyn Shea and cash.

With the acquisition of catcher Ferrell and pitcher Brown, Tom Yawkey—born Thomas Austin—launched a career that carried him through more than four decades and millions of dollars. He built the Red Sox into solid contenders, sometimes known as "Gold Sox" and other times as "Millionaires" because of their owner's generosity in salaries and his free-spending practices in obtaining talent.

For all his efforts, however, Yawkey saw only three A.L. pennants fly from the Fenway Park flagpole—in 1946, 1967 and 1975. And on each occasion, the pennant was followed by a loss in a seven-game World Series.

Thomas Austin was born into a baseball atmosphere. His grandfather, William Clyman Yawkey, founded a lumber and iron-ore empire. He was negotiating for the purchase of the Detroit Tigers in 1904 when he was stricken fatally. His son, William Hoover Yawkey, completed the transaction.

As the brother of young Tom's mother, William Hoover Yawkey became Thomas Austin's foster father and eventually adopted the boy (and Tom took the name Yawkey). Throughout his life, Tom Yawkey always referred to his uncle as Dad.

The elder Yawkey died in 1917, leaving a sizable estate to Tom, who inherited additional millions when he came of age.

As a boy in Detroit, Tom had idolized Ty Cobb and maintained contacts with the old Tiger star into adulthood. At dinner one night, Cobb suggested that Yawkey invest in a major league club. The suggestion

Tom Yawkey's lavish spending finally resulted in a Boston pennant in 1946.

germinated until 1933 when Yawkey, then 30, purchased the Red Sox from Bob Quinn for $1.5 million.

A year later, Yawkey spent an identical sum to refurbish Fenway Park, which had fallen into disrepair since the club's last pennant in 1918.

Yawkey's first move after acquiring the Red Sox was to install Eddie Collins as vice president. Both men had attended the Irving School in Tarrytown, N.Y. They were not contemporaries, but Yawkey formed a lasting admiration for the old second baseman (who had been a coach for the Philadelphia A's in 1932).

By that time Yawkey had earned a degree in the Sheffield Scientific School at Yale and was head of the business empire he had inherited.

With Collins supplying the expertise and Yawkey the money, the Red Sox bought lavisly, obtaining Lefty Grove, Jimmie Foxx, Max Bishop, Roger Cramer, Rube Walberg and John Marcum from the A's. Tom made his most newsworthy transaction in 1934 when he acquired Joe Cronin from the Washington Senators. He gave up $250,000 and shortstop Lyn Lary to get the Nats' manager-shortstop, who was installed as the Red Sox's pilot.

Yawkey never lost the willingness to spend large sums for proven players. Just weeks before his death, he agreed to a $2 million purchase of Rollie Fingers and Joe Rudi from Oakland. The deal was quashed later by Commissioner Bowie Kuhn.

A frustrated athlete himself, Yawkey was a crack shot with a rifle and in his late 30s was able to compete with national handball champions.

While he maintained suites at fashionable hotels in New York and Boston, Yawkey was not considered one of the social elite. He was most comfortable on his 40,000-acre estate in South Carolina where, in battered hat and clothes, he could spend hours hunting with plantation employees.

In his 43 years of club ownership, Tom developed his greatest affection for Ted Williams and Carl Yastrzemski. He cringed when either was booed. But neither was he blind to the faults of his players. He once fined Williams $5,000 for allegedly making an obscene gesture to the crowd.

The worthiest of owners—who spent millions of dollars without a whimper in an effort to produce championships—died of leukemia in 1976 in Boston at age 73.

CY YOUNG

On an August evening in 1890, Cap Anson, manager of the Chicago White Stockings, was relaxing with David Hawley, an official of the Cleveland Spiders, when the conversation turned to that afternoon's game, in which a young farmer had pitched Cleveland to an 8-1 victory in his major league debut.

"That big rube had a lot of luck beating us," said Anson. "He is too green to do your club much good, but I believe I might make a pitcher out of him in a couple of years. Anyway, I'm willing to give you $1,000 for him."

Hawley was not easily deluded.

"If I recall correctly," Hawley responded, "that big rube struck you out twice today, and I believe he can do it again. What's more, I believe he can do us as much good as Chicago, so keep your $1,000 and we'll keep the rube."

The 23-year-old pitcher, who had spaced three hits and did not walk a batter, was Cy Young, destined to be the biggest winner in big-league history. Young had just come off a farm in eastern Ohio and he was, as Anson noted, a rube. When the newcomer reported to the Spiders, Hawley took one glance at his ill-fitting and unfashionable attire and hustled him to a haberdasher before the veterans could crush the youngster's spirits with their ridicule.

When the pitcher left home he was known as Dent Young. Before long, however, he was nicknamed Cy, as in Cyclone, because of his blinding fastball. Or maybe, as some suggested, he got the name because it was a practice of the times to apply it to rural youths.

Young's first stop on the road to national acclaim was Canton in the Tri-State League. The rookie compiled a 15-15 record and soon was being offered to the majors for $500. Only the Spiders were willing to take the gamble. Before long a national sports weekly reported:

"Young, new pitcher of the Cleveland club, is a big, strong countryman who was a rail-splitter before he played ball. He is said to be speedier than Hutchison (Bill Hutchison of Chicago) and has a drop ball that is a killer."

In 1891, Cy Young recorded his first 20-victory season for the Cleveland Spiders. By 1901, Young was pitching for Boston and well on his way to a major league-record 511 career victories.

In 1895, Young (left) recorded the third of five 30-plus victory seasons. When Connie Mack (left, right photo) and Young posed in 1949, the former was 86 years old, the latter 82.

Years later, Tris Speaker rated Young's fastball in the class of Walter Johnson's and Bob Feller's.

During a 22-year career that produced 511 triumphs, Cy reached or topped the 20-victory mark 16 times and exceeded the 30-win plateau five times. Three of his victories were no-hitters, the first a 6-0 decision over Cincinnati in 1897 in which Young walked one batter.

Cy's second no-hitter was a masterpiece. In 1904, he defeated Rube Waddell and the Philadelphia A's, 3-0, without permitting a baserunner. The righthander concentrated so intently on the job at hand that he did not realize he had pitched a perfect game until outfielder Chick Stahl presented him the last ball of the game.

Young was 41 when, in 1908, he hurled his third gem in an 8-0 triumph over New York. Young, who aided his own cause with three hits, allowed only one baserunner (on a walk).

Cy moved with the Spiders franchise to St. Louis in 1899. He was earning the National League's maximum salary of $2,400 a year and was in a receptive mood when Ban Johnson, forming the American League as a new major circuit, offered him a $600-a-year raise to jump to the Boston Red Sox in 1901. Cy accepted.

Young, who had defeated the Baltimore Orioles three times in a five-game Temple Cup Series in 1895, pitched in four games for the Red Sox during the first World Series in 1903. He won two decisions—both coming after the Pittsburgh Pirates had captured three of the first four contests—as Boston took the world championship.

For all his accomplishments, Young's most memorable day was August 13, 1908, when the Boston Post sponsored a "Cy Young Day" unlike any other celebration before or since. All American League activity was suspended for the day so that an all-star team could honor the veteran pitcher by meeting the Red Sox in an exhibition game at the old Huntington Avenue grounds.

The gates opened at 11:30 a.m. Within an hour, 20,000 fans had jammed the ancient park. Another 10,000 were turned away. Young's gifts included a traveling bag from the umpires, a cup from the American League, numerous floral arrangements and a cash donation of at least $6,000.

Young, who pitched the first two innings against the all-stars, was so overcome by emotion—according to the account of the day—that "he could make no response to the presentation speeches."

Cy was a member of the Braves in 1911 when, at 44, he pitched his last game, a loss to Eddie Dent of the Dodgers.

Young returned to his native eastern Ohio where, seated in his favorite armchair and gazing out across the familiar pasture lands, he suffered a fatal heart attack in 1955 at age 88.

ROSS YOUNGS

From the beginning, John McGraw recognized the kid's extraordinary talent. The 20-year-old player would require minor league polish, but the manager of the New York Giants wanted to be certain that nothing was done to harm the prospect's many skills.

The Giants had a working agreement with the Rochester club of the International League in 1917. The Red Wings' manager was Mickey Doolan, a longtime major leaguer.

"I'm going to give you a kid who is going to be a great player," McGraw told Doolan. "Take good care of him because if anything happens to him, I'll hold you responsible."

Doolan followed orders faithfully. Before the season ended, Ross Youngs—after batting .356—was with the Giants, ready for a brilliant career that ended in tragedy.

Youngs' career was still in its infancy when fans nicknamed him Pep. Frequently, the "s" was dropped from his surname.

As a youth, Youngs attended West Texas Military Academy, where he was better known as a halfback and track star than as a baseball player. Football teammate Joe Straus, who later was an outstanding player at Pennsylvania, said if Youngs had attended Penn "as I wanted him to, you never would have heard of me."

But Youngs' heart was set on baseball. He refused to be discouraged when the Austin (Texas) club released him after a lackluster 10-game stint in 1914, and he bounced around the Texas bush leagues for two seasons before he caught on with Sherman (Western Association), where New York scout Dick Kinsella discovered him in 1916.

While Youngs received a major league trial on the infield, McGraw concluded that his arm was not suited to the positions. Ross was switched to right field and almost immediately mastered the position. In all phases of outfield play, Youngs distinguished himself so that McGraw, in his declining years, declared: "He was the greatest outfielder I ever saw. He could do everything that a baseball player should do and do it better than most players. As an outfielder, he had no superiors. And he was the easiest man I ever knew to handle. In all his years with the Giants he never caused one moment's trouble for myself or the club. On top of all that, a gamer player than Youngs never played ball."

Youngs starred on the Giants' four consecutive pennant-winning clubs (1921-24), batting from .327 the first year to .356 the last. In the seventh inning of Game 3 of the 1921 World Series, he sparked an eight-run rally with

Giants star Ross Youngs was only 30 when he succumbed to Bright's disease.

a double and triple to become the first player to register two hits in a Series inning.

When the Giants slipped to second place in 1925, Ross' batting average dropped below .300, plummeting to .264, for the first time. When Youngs reported to training camp in 1926, a physical examination revealed that he was suffering from Bright's disease, a serious kidney ailment. Many observers contended that the disease stemmed from Youngs' habit of diving into bases.

McGraw hired a male nurse to accompany Youngs wherever the Giants went during the '26 season. The player referred to the nurse as "my keeper." Despite failing health, Ross maintained his high spirits throughout the campaign. He batted .306 and taught the fine points of outfield play to his successor, Mel Ott.

Youngs was bed-ridden during the entire 1927 season, and he died on October 22 that year at age 30.

Contemporaries were lavish in their praise of the talented Texan. Waite Hoyt called Youngs "a smaller Ty Cobb." In the onetime pitcher's book, "he was built like Enos Slaughter, had the same hustle—but more ability."

When Ford Frick was asked for his personal all-time, all-star team, the father of the Hall of Fame selected the popular outfield choices of Babe Ruth, Ty Cobb and Tris Speaker. Then he added, "But somehow I've got to find a place for Pep Youngs.

"Don't ask me to take somebody out. I've just got to put Pep in there somewhere."

ROBIN YOUNT

As an 18-year-old rookie shortstop for the Milwaukee Brewers, Robin Yount could have been forgiven for feeling a little intimidated when he went to the plate to bat against Nolan Ryan.

"I remember he choked up the bat and stood up on the plate," Ryan said.

"I can remember after his first at-bat thinking to myself, 'That kid hung in there. He wasn't intimidated.' That's what I found throughout his career."

Yount remembers the at-bat a little differently.

"I must have hid that (being intimidated) well," Yount said. "I know I had no chance, either, to hit off him when I was 18. It took me about three or four years to catch up with his fastball."

The at-bat against Ryan did serve notice on the rest of the baseball world that Yount—who carried the nickname "the Kid" with him for the rest of his career—was going to be a player to watch. He grew from that uncertain, baby-faced rookie to become one of the best players of his era and the most recognizable figure in the history of the Milwaukee Brewers.

No Milwaukee Brewer had more at-bats or more total hits in his career than Robin Yount.

Yount spent his entire 20-year career with Milwaukee and is the first home-grown Brewers player to be elected to the Hall of Fame. That wasn't something many people were predicting when then-manager Del Crandall made the decision to name Yount his starting shortstop in 1974 despite the fact Yount had played only 64 games in the minor leagues.

Yount was born Sept. 16, 1955 in Danville, Ill. He grew up in southern California and was the first-round draft pick by the Brewers in 1973 after graduating from high school. He spent that season at Newark in the Class A New York-Penn League, where he hit .285 with three homers and 25 RBIs. Despite the mediocre offensive numbers, managers did name him as the player most likely to make the major leagues.

Nobody expected that to come so quickly, however. He made his major league debut on April 5, 1974 in the season-opener against Boston. He collected his first career hit off Baltimore's Dave McNally on April 12 and never spent another day in the minor leagues, not even on a rehab assignment.

Yount was able to succeed at that young age because of his excellent work ethic and his ability to make adjustments and understand the game, lessons many older players sometimes are not able to learn. Of all of his accomplishments in the game, Yount ranks at the top in being able to stay focused and competitive in every game.

"The thing I'm most proud of was that I had this attitude that every time I took the field I wanted to play like it was the last time I'd play the game," Yount said. "Because of that, I was able to achieve the things I did."

Yount achieved a great deal during his career. At the time of his retirement in 1994, he was the Brewers' career leader in virtually every offensive category. No Brewer has played more games, had more at-bats, scored more runs, collected more total hits, more singles, more doubles, more triples, more home runs, driven in more runs or stolen more bases.

At the time of his retirement, Yount was 13th on baseball's all-time hit list, and he was the third youngest player in history to reach the 3,000 hit milestone. Yount collected that historic hit on Sept. 9, 1992 off Cleveland's Jose Mesa, a week before his 37th birthday. The only players to get their 3,000th hit at a younger age were Ty Cobb (34) and Hank Aaron (36).

Fellow Hall of Famers Willie Mays and George Brett are the only players besides Yount to compile more than 3,000 hits, 250 home runs, 200 stolen bases and 100 triples in their careers. Yount was only the seventh player in history to hit 250 or more homers and also steal 250 or more bases.

Yount was named the American League Most Valuable Player in 1982 and 1989, becoming only the third player to win the honor while playing different positions. The only other players to do it were Stan Musial and Hank Greenberg, both Hall of Famers.

Yount was the Brewers' shortstop in 1982, when he led the team to the division title and a playoff victory over the California Angels for the American League pennant. They lost to the St. Louis Cardinals in a seven-game World Series, the only World Series appearance in franchise history, but Yount distinguished himself by hitting .414 with three doubles, driving in six runs and scoring six times.

In the 1982 regular season, Yount established career highs with a .331 average, 29 homers, 114 RBI and 129 runs scored. He led the A.L. in hits with 210 and in doubles with 46 and became the first shortstop in league history to lead the league in slugging percentage and total bases. He also was the first shortstop in A.L. history to hit .300 with 20 or more homers and 100 or more RBI and was only the third player in history to collect 40 or more doubles, 10 or more triples, 20 or more homers and 20 or more stolen bases in the same year. The only other players to do that were Chuck Klein and Billy Herman.

He was named the starting shortstop for the A.L. in the All-Star game, his second selection. He also was named to the team in 1980, and in 1983 was the starter after receiving the most votes of any player that season.

Yount won his first Gold Glove for defensive excellence in 1982 and was named Player of the Year by *The Sporting News*.

"That certainly was the highlight of my career," Yount said of 1982.

"The thing I missed most was not having more opportunities to play in the post-season."

After playing at shortstop for the first 11 years of his career, Yount was forced to move to the outfield in 1985 after undergoing surgery on his right (throwing) shoulder following the 1984 season. He played three months in left field, before moving to center field, the position he played for the rest of his career.

In 1989, Yount won his second MVP award on the strength of his .318 average, 21 homers, 103 RBIs, 101 runs scored and 19 stolen bases. He was the only player named on every ballot as he won a close race over Texas' Ruben Sierra and the Orioles' Cal Ripken Jr.

Yount was a free agent after the 1989 season, and came close to leaving the Brewers and signing with the California Angels, whom Yount thought might have a better chance of reaching postseason play. Only a personal visit to Yount's home in Phoenix from Brewers' owner Bud Selig convinced him to stay in Milwaukee.

"I told him, 'Some day you're going to Cooperstown, and what a wonderful thing it would be to say you played your entire career with one team, like Joe DiMaggio of the Yankees, Ted Williams of the Red Sox and Stan Musial of the Cardinals,'" Selig said. "That

"The thing I'm most proud of was that I had this attitude that every time I took the field I wanted to play like it was the last time I'd play the game."

meant so much to me, and those names just popped into my head. I said, 'Sign this contract and you'll go in as Yount of the Brewers.' We both got very emotional, and that was that."

The 6-foot, 185-pound righthanded Yount completed his career with Milwaukee after the 1993 season. He became the only player in history to play more than 1,000 games at shortstop and more than 1,000 additional games in the outfield. He hit .300 or better six times in his career and finished with a .285 average. He drove in more than 100 runs three times, and five times scored more than 100 runs.

He hit for the cycle in a game against the White Sox at Comiskey Park on June 12, 1988. He set the franchise record for most consecutive games played at 276 before sitting out two games in 1989 because of badly bruised knees.

Despite his aggressive style of play and determination, Yount was only on the disabled list twice in his career, in 1978 and in 1991. In 1978, Yount missed the first month of the season with torn ligaments in his foot. He told reporters at the time he was thinking about joining the professional golf tour, but admitted later that was a fabrication because he didn't want people to know he had been hurt while riding a motorcycle before spring training.

"I was scared to death to let anybody know," Yount said. "I was unable to play like I felt I should, so I said to somebody I might have to go and try to play golf."

Yount didn't go on the disabled list again until 1991, when he was suffering from kidney stones.

In 1992, Yount was named the co-winner with George Brett of the Joe Cronin Award for significant achievement after each recorded his 3,000th hit.

Yount was elected to the Hall of Fame in 1999 in his first year of eligibility.

CAREER
RECORDS

Career Records of Hall of Famers

*Denotes led league. ●Denotes tied for league lead.

HENRY LOUIS (HANK) AARON

Year—Club	League	G.	AB.	R.	H.	HR.	RBI.	B.A.
1952—Eau Claire	North.	87	345	79	116	9	61	.336
1953—Jacksonville	Sally	137	574	*115	*208	22	*125	*.362
1954—Milwaukee	Nat.	122	468	58	131	13	69	.280
1955—Milwaukee	Nat.	153	602	105	189	27	106	.314
1956—Milwaukee	Nat.	153	609	106	*200	26	92	*.328
1957—Milwaukee	Nat.	151	615	*118	198	*44	*132	.322
1958—Milwaukee	Nat.	153	601	109	196	30	95	.326
1959—Milwaukee	Nat.	154	629	116	*223	39	123	*.355
1960—Milwaukee	Nat.	153	590	102	172	40	*126	.292
1961—Milwaukee	Nat.	*155	603	115	197	34	120	.327
1962—Milwaukee	Nat.	156	592	127	191	45	128	.323
1963—Milwaukee	Nat.	161	631	*121	201	●44	*130	.319
1964—Milwaukee	Nat.	145	570	103	187	24	95	.328
1965—Milwaukee	Nat.	150	570	109	181	32	89	.318
1966—Atlanta	Nat.	158	603	117	168	*44	*127	.279
1967—Atlanta	Nat.	155	600	●113	184	*39	109	.307
1968—Atlanta	Nat.	160	606	84	174	29	86	.287
1969—Atlanta	Nat.	147	547	100	164	44	97	.300
1970—Atlanta	Nat.	150	516	103	154	38	118	.298
1971—Atlanta	Nat.	139	495	95	162	47	118	.327
1972—Atlanta	Nat.	129	449	75	119	34	77	.265
1973—Atlanta	Nat.	120	392	84	118	40	96	.301
1974—Atlanta	Nat.	112	340	47	91	20	69	.268
1975—Milwaukee	Amer.	137	465	45	109	12	60	.234
1976—Milwaukee	Amer.	85	271	22	62	10	35	.229
American League Totals		222	736	67	171	22	95	.232
National League Totals		3076	11628	2107	3620	733	2202	310
Major League Totals		3298	12364	2174	3771	755	2297	.305

CHAMPIONSHIP SERIES RECORD

Year—Club	League	G.	AB.	R.	H.	HR.	RBI.	B.A.
1969—Atlanta	Nat.	3	14	3	5	3	7	.357

WORLD SERIES RECORD

Year—Club	League	G.	AB.	R.	H.	HR.	RBI.	B.A.
1957—Milwaukee	Nat.	7	28	5	11	3	7	.393
1958—Milwaukee	Nat.	7	27	3	9	0	2	.333
World Series Totals		14	55	8	20	3	9	.364

GROVER CLEVELAND (PETE) ALEXANDER

Year—Club	League	G.	IP.	W.	L.	Pct.	ERA.
1909—Galesburg	Ill.-Mo.	24	219	15	8	.652	......
1910—Syracuse	N.Y. State	*43	245	*29	14	.674	......
1911—Philadelphia	Nat.	48	*366	*28	13	.683	......
1912—Philadelphia	Nat.	46	●310	19	17	.528	2.81
1913—Philadelphia	Nat.	47	306	22	8	.733	2.82
1914—Philadelphia	Nat.	46	*355	●27	15	.643	2.38
1915—Philadelphia	Nat.	49	*376	*31	10	*.756	*1.22
1916—Philadelphia	Nat.	48	*390	*33	12	.733	*1.55
1917—Philadelphia	Nat.	45	*387	*30	13	.698	*1.83
1918—Chicago	Nat.	3	26	2	1	.667	1.73
1919—Chicago	Nat.	30	235	16	11	.593	*1.72
1920—Chicago	Nat.	46	*363	*27	14	.659	*1.91
1921—Chicago	Nat.	31	252	15	13	.536	3.39
1922—Chicago	Nat.	33	246	16	13	.552	3.62
1923—Chicago	Nat.	39	305	22	12	.647	3.19
1924—Chicago	Nat.	21	169	12	5	.706	3.03
1925—Chicago	Nat.	32	236	15	11	.577	3.39
1926—Chicago-St. Louis	Nat.	30	200	12	10	.545	3.06
1927—St. Louis	Nat.	37	268	21	10	.677	2.52
1928—St. Louis	Nat.	34	244	16	9	.640	3.36
1929—St. Louis	Nat.	22	132	9	8	.529	3.89
1930—Philadelphia	Nat.	9	22	0	3	.000	9.00
1930—Dallas	Texas	5	24	1	2	.333	8.25
Major League Totals		696	5188	373	208	.642	2.56

WORLD SERIES RECORD

Year—Club	League	G.	IP.	W.	L.	Pct.	ERA.
1915—Philadelphia	National	2	17⅔	1	1	.500	1.53
1926—St. Louis	National	3	20⅓	2	0	1.000	1.33
1928—St. Louis	National	2	5	0	1	.000	19.80
Major League Totals		7	43	3	2	.600	3.56

WALTER EMMONS ALSTON

RECORD AS MANAGER

Year—Club	League	Position	W.	L.
1940—Portsmouth	Mid. Atl.	Sixth	59	68
1941—Springfield	Mid. Atl.	Fourth	69	57
1942—Springfield	Mid. Atl.	Fifth	59	71
1944—Trenton	Int.-St.	Sixth	31	18
1945—Trenton	Int.-St.	Third	70	69
1946—Nashua	N. Eng.	Second	80	41
1947—Pueblo	West.	Third	70	58
1948—St. Paul	A. A.	Third	86	68
1949—St. Paul	A. A.	First	93	60
1950—Montreal	Int.	Second	86	67
1951—Montreal	Int.	First	95	59
1952—Montreal	Int.	First	95	56
1953—Montreal	Int.	Second	89	63
1954—Brooklyn	Nat.	Second	92	62
1955—Brooklyn	Nat.	First	98	55
1956—Brooklyn	Nat.	First	93	61
1957—Brooklyn	Nat.	Third	84	70
1958—Los Angeles	Nat.	Seventh	71	83
1959—Los Angeles	Nat.	First	88	68
1960—Los Angeles	Nat.	Fourth	82	72
1961—Los Angeles	Nat.	Second	89	65
1962—Los Angeles	Nat.	Second	102	63
1963—Los Angeles	Nat.	First	99	63
1964—Los Angeles	Nat.	Sixth	80	82
1965—Los Angeles	Nat.	First	97	65
1966—Los Angeles	Nat.	First	95	67
1967—Los Angeles	Nat.	Eighth	73	89
1968—Los Angeles	Nat.	Seventh	76	86
1969—Los Angeles	Nat.	Fourth(W)	85	77
1970—Los Angeles	Nat.	Second(W)	87	74
1971—Los Angeles	Nat.	Second(W)	89	73
1972—Los Angeles	Nat.	Third(W)	85	70
1973—Los Angeles	Nat.	Second(W)	95	66
1974—Los Angeles	Nat.	First(W)	102	60
1975—Los Angeles	Nat.	Second(W)	88	74
1976—Los Angeles	Nat.	Second(W)	90	68
Major League Totals			2040	1613

CHAMPIONSHIP SERIES RECORD

Year—Club	League	W.	L.
1974—Los Angeles	National	3	1

WORLD SERIES RECORD

Year—Club	League	W.	L.
1955—Brooklyn	National	4	3
1956—Brooklyn	National	3	4
1959—Los Angeles	National	4	2
1963—Los Angeles	National	4	0
1965—Los Angeles	National	4	3
1966—Los Angeles	National	0	4
1974—Los Angeles	National	1	4

GEORGE LEE (SPARKY) ANDERSON

RECORD AS MANAGER

Year—Club	League	Position	W.	L.
1964—Toronto	Intl.	Fifth	80	72
1965—Rock Hill	W. Carolinas	Eighth	24	40
(Second half)		First	35	23
1966—St. Petersburg	Florida State	Second	42	24
(Second half)		First	49	21
1967—Modesto	California	*Second	38	32
(Second half)		First	41	29
1968—Asheville	Southern	First	86	54
1970—Cincinnati	National	First (W)	102	60
1971—Cincinnati	National	Fourth (E)	79	83
1972—Cincinnati	National	*First (W)	95	59
1973—Cincinnati	National	First (W)	99	63
1974—Cincinnati	National	Second (W)	98	64
1975—Cincinnati	National	First (W)	108	54
1976—Cincinnati	National	First (W)	102	60
1977—Cincinnati	National	Second (W)	88	74
1978—Cincinnati	National	Second (W)	92	69
1979—Detroit	American	Fifth (E)	56	50
1980—Detroit	American	Fifth (E)	84	78
1981—Detroit	American	Fourth (E)	31	26
(Second half)		Third (E)	29	23
1982—Detroit	American	Fourth (E)	83	79
1983—Detroit	American	Second (E)	92	70
1984—Detroit	American	First (E)	104	58
1985—Detroit	American	Third (E)	84	77
1986—Detroit	American	Third (E)	87	75
1987—Detroit	American	First (E)	98	64
1988—Detroit	American	Second (E)	88	74
1989—Detroit	American	Seventh (E)	59	103
1990—Detroit	American	Third (E)	79	83
1991—Detroit	American	*Second (E)	84	78
1992—Detroit	American	Sixth (E)	75	87
1993—Detroit	American	*Third (E)	85	77

Year	Club	League	Position	W.	L.
1994— Detroit	American			53	62
1995— Detroit	American		Fourth (E)	60	84
	Major League Totals			2194	1834

*Tied for position.

CHAMPIONSHIP SERIES RECORD

Year	Club	League	W.	L.
1970— Cincinnati	National	3	0
1972— Cincinnati	National	3	2
1973— Cincinnati	National	2	3
1975— Cincinnati	National	3	0
1976— Cincinnati	National	3	0
1984— Detroit	American	3	0
1987— Detroit	American	1	4

WORLD SERIES RECORD

Year	Club	League	W.	L.
1970— Cincinnati	National	1	4
1972— Cincinnati	National	3	4
1975— Cincinnati	National	4	3
1976— Cincinnati	National	4	0
1984— Detroit	American	4	1

ADRIAN CONSTANTINE (CAP) ANSON

Year	Club	League	G.	AB.	R.	H.	HR.	SB.	B.A.
1870—Marshalltown	Ind.	.....	.....	.....	.....	....	.....	.....
1871—Rockford	N.As'n	25	122	30	43	....	.....	.352
1872—Ath. of Phila	N.As'n	45	231	60	88	....	.....	.381
1873—Ath. of Phila	N.As'n	51	.....	52	103	....	.....	.....
1874—Ath. of Phila	N.As'n	55	267	51	98	....	.....	.367
1875—Ath. of Phila	N.As'n	69	330	83	105	....	.....	.318
1876—Chicago	Nat.	66	321	63	110	2	.....	.343
1877—Chicago	Nat.	47	200	36	67	0	.....	.335
1878—Chicago	Nat.	59	256	54	86	0	.....	.336
1879—Chicago	Nat.	49	221	41	90	0	.....	*.407
1880—Chicago	Nat.	84	346	52	117	1	.....	.338
1881—Chicago	Nat.	84	343	66	*137	1	.....	*.399
1882—Chicago	Nat.	82	348	69	126	1	.....	.362
1883—Chicago	Nat.	98	413	69	127	0	.....	.308
1884—Chicago	Nat.	111	471	108	*159	19	.....	.338
1885—Chicago	Nat.	112	464	100	144	7	.....	.310
1886—Chicago	Nat.	125	504	117	*187	10	29	.371
1887—Chicago	Nat.	122	532	107	224	7	27	*.421
1888—Chicago	Nat.	134	515	101	177	10	28	*.344
1889—Chicago	Nat.	134	518	99	177	7	27	.342
1890—Chicago	Nat.	*139	504	102	157	6	29	.312
1891—Chicago	Nat.	136	537	82	158	8	21	.294
1892—Chicago	Nat.	147	561	62	154	1	15	.275
1893—Chicago	Nat.	101	381	70	123	0	13	.323
1894—Chicago	Nat.	83	347	87	137	5	17	.395
1895—Chicago	Nat.	122	476	88	161	2	16	.338
1896—Chicago	Nat.	106	403	72	135	2	28	.335
1897—Chicago	Nat.	112	423	66	128	3	16	.303
	Major League Totals		2253	9084	1712	3081	92	266	.339

WORLD SERIES RECORD

Year	Club	League	G.	AB.	R.	H.	SB.	B.A.
1885—Chicago	Nat.	7	26	8	11	0	.423
1886—Chicago	Nat.	6	20	3	5	1	.250
	World Series Totals		13	46	11	16	1	.348

LUIS ERNESTO APARICIO

Year	Club	League	G.	AB.	R.	H.	HR.	RBI.	B.A.
1954—Waterloo	I.I.I.	94	390	85	110	4	47	.282
1955—Memphis	South.	150	564	92	154	6	51	.273
1956—Chicago	Amer.	152	533	69	142	3	56	.266
1957—Chicago	Amer.	143	575	82	148	3	41	.257
1958—Chicago	Amer.	145	557	76	148	2	40	.266
1959—Chicago	Amer.	152	612	98	157	6	51	.257
1960—Chicago	Amer.	153	600	86	166	2	61	.277
1961—Chicago	Amer.	156	625	90	170	6	45	.272
1962—Chicago	Amer.	153	581	72	140	7	40	.241
1963—Baltimore	Amer.	146	601	73	150	5	45	.250
1964—Baltimore	Amer.	146	578	93	154	10	37	.266
1965—Baltimore	Amer.	144	564	67	127	8	40	.225
1966—Baltimore	Amer.	151	*659	97	182	6	41	.276
1967—Baltimore	Amer.	134	546	55	127	4	31	.233
1968—Baltimore	Amer.	155	622	55	164	4	36	.264
1969—Chicago	Amer.	156	599	77	168	5	51	.280
1970—Chicago	Amer.	146	552	86	173	5	43	.313
1971—Boston	Amer.	125	491	56	114	4	45	.232
1972—Boston	Amer.	110	436	47	112	3	39	.257
1973—Boston	Amer.	132	499	56	135	0	49	.271
	Major League Totals		2599	10230	1335	2677	83	791	.262

WORLD SERIES RECORD

Year	Club	League	G.	AB.	R.	H.	HR.	RBI.	B.A.
1959—Chicago	Amer.	6	18	1	8	0	0	.308
1966—Baltimore	Amer.	4	16	0	4	0	2	.250
	World Series Totals		10	42	1	12	0	2	.286

LUCIUS BENJAMIN (LUKE) APPLING

Year	Club	League	G.	AB.	R.	H.	HR.	RBI.	B.A.
1930—Atlanta	South.	104	374	63	122	5	75	.326
1930—Chicago	Amer.	6	26	2	8	0	2	.308
1931—Chicago	Amer.	96	297	36	69	1	28	.232
1932—Chicago	Amer.	139	489	66	134	3	63	.274
1933—Chicago	Amer.	151	612	90	197	6	85	.322
1934—Chicago	Amer.	118	452	75	137	2	61	.303
1935—Chicago	Amer.	153	525	94	161	1	71	.307
1936—Chicago	Amer.	138	526	111	204	6	128	*.388
1937—Chicago	Amer.	154	574	98	182	4	77	.317
1938—Chicago	Amer.	81	294	41	89	0	44	.303
1939—Chicago	Amer.	148	516	82	162	0	56	.314
1940—Chicago	Amer.	150	566	96	197	0	79	.348
1941—Chicago	Amer.	154	592	93	186	1	57	.314
1942—Chicago	Amer.	142	543	78	142	3	53	.262
1943—Chicago	Amer.	●155	585	63	192	3	80	*.328
1944—	(In Military Service)							
1945—Chicago	Amer.	18	57	12	21	1	10	.368
1946—Chicago	Amer.	149	582	59	180	1	55	.309
1947—Chicago	Amer.	139	503	67	154	8	49	.306
1948—Chicago	Amer.	139	497	63	156	0	47	.314
1949—Chicago	Amer.	142	492	82	148	5	58	.301
1950—Chicago	Amer.	50	128	11	30	0	13	.234
	Major League Totals		2422	8856	1319	2749	45	1116	.310

DONN RICHARD (RICHIE) ASHBURN

Year	Club	League	G.	AB.	R.	H.	HR.	RBI.	B.A.
1945—Utica	Eastern	106	356	63	111	1	42	.312
1946—Utica	Eastern	(In Military Service)						
1947—Utica	Eastern	137	536	*128	*194	3	52	.362
1948—Philadelphia	National	117	463	78	154	2	40	.333
1949—Philadelphia	National	154	*662	84	188	1	37	.284
1950—Philadelphia	National	151	594	84	180	2	41	.303
1951—Philadelphia	National	154	643	92	*221	4	63	.344
1952—Philadelphia	National	*154	613	93	173	1	42	.282
1953—Philadelphia	National	156	622	110	*205	2	57	.330
1954—Philadelphia	National	153	559	111	175	1	41	.313
1955—Philadelphia	National	140	533	91	180	3	42	*.338
1956—Philadelphia	National	154	628	94	190	3	50	.303
1957—Philadelphia	National	●156	626	93	186	0	33	.297
1958—Philadelphia	National	152	615	98	*215	2	33	*.350
1959—Philadelphia	National	153	564	86	150	1	20	.266
1960—Chicago	National	151	547	99	159	0	40	.291
1961—Chicago	National	109	307	49	79	0	19	.257
1962—New York	National	135	389	60	119	7	28	.306
	Major League Totals		2189	8365	1322	2574	29	586	.308

WORLD SERIES RECORD

Year	Club	League	G.	AB.	R.	H.	HR.	RBI.	B.A.
1950—Philadelphia	National	4	17	0	3	0	1	.176

HOWARD EARL (ROCK) AVERILL

Year	Club	League	G.	AB.	R.	H.	HR.	RBI.	B.A.
1926—San Francisco	P. C.	188	679	131	236	23	119	.348
1927—San Francisco	P. C.	183	754	134	244	20	116	.324
1928—San Francisco	P. C.	189	763	*178	270	36	173	.354
1929—Cleveland	Amer.	152	596	110	198	18	96	.332
1930—Cleveland	Amer.	139	534	102	181	19	119	.339
1931—Cleveland	Amer.	155	*627	140	209	32	143	.333
1932—Cleveland	Amer.	153	631	116	198	32	124	.314
1933—Cleveland	Amer.	151	599	83	180	11	92	.301
1934—Cleveland	Amer.	●154	598	128	187	31	113	.313
1935—Cleveland	Amer.	140	563	109	162	19	79	.288
1936—Cleveland	Amer.	152	614	136	*232	28	126	.378
1937—Cleveland	Amer.	156	609	121	182	21	92	.299
1938—Cleveland	Amer.	134	482	101	159	14	93	.330
1939—Clev.-Detroit	Amer.	111	364	66	96	11	65	.264
1940—Detroit	Amer.	64	118	10	33	2	20	.280
1941—Boston	Nat.	8	17	2	2	0	2	.118
1941—Seattle	P. C.	78	223	24	55	1	17	.247
	American League Totals		1661	6335	1222	2017	238	1162	.318
	National League Totals		8	17	2	2	0	2	.118
	Major League Totals		1669	6352	1224	2019	238	1164	.318

WORLD SERIES RECORD

Year	Club	League	G.	AB.	R.	H.	HR.	RBI.	B.A.
1940—Detroit	Amer.	3	3	0	0	0	0	.000

JOHN FRANKLIN (HOME RUN) BAKER

Year	Club	League	G.	AB.	R.	H.	HR.	RBI.	B.A.
1907	Baltimore	East.	5	15	0	2	0	....	.133
1908	Reading	Tri-State	119	451	65	135	6	....	.299
1908	Philadelphia	Amer.	9	30	5	9	0	4	.300
1909	Philadelphia	Amer.	148	541	73	165	4	89	.305
1910	Philadelphia	Amer.	146	561	83	159	2	73	.283
1911	Philadelphia	Amer.	148	592	96	198	*11	115	.334
1912	Philadelphia	Amer.	149	577	116	200	•10	*133	.347
1913	Philadelphia	Amer.	149	564	116	190	*12	*126	.337
1914	Philadelphia	Amer.	150	570	84	182	*9	97	.319
1915	Philadelphia	Amer.	(Refused to report; played with Upland, Pa.)						
1916	New York	Amer.	100	360	46	97	10	52	.269
1917	New York	Amer.	146	553	57	156	6	70	.282
1918	New York	Amer.	126	504	65	154	6	68	.306
1919	New York	Amer.	•141	567	70	166	10	78	.293
1920	New York	Amer.	(Voluntarily retired; played with Upland, Pa.)						
1921	New York	Amer.	94	330	46	97	9	71	.294
1922	New York	Amer.	69	234	30	65	7	36	.278
1924	Easton	Ea. Shore	43	92	14	27	5	....	.293
	Major League Totals		1575	5983	887	1838	96	1012	.307

WORLD SERIES RECORD

Year	Club	League	G.	AB.	R.	H.	HR.	RBI.	B.A.
1910	Philadelphia	Amer.	5	22	6	9	0	4	.409
1911	Philadelphia	Amer.	6	24	7	9	2	5	.375
1913	Philadelphia	Amer.	5	20	2	9	1	7	.450
1914	Philadelphia	Amer.	4	16	0	4	0	2	.250
1921	New York	Amer.	4	8	0	2	0	0	.250
1922	New York	Amer.	1	1	0	0	0	0	.000
	World Series Totals		25	91	15	33	3	18	.363

DAVID JAMES (BEAUTY) BANCROFT

Year	Club	League	G.	AB.	R.	H.	HR.	RBI.	B.A.
1909	Duluth-Sup	Wis.-Min.	111	367	43	77	1	....	.210
1910	Superior	Wis.-Min.	•127	438	55	117	1	....	.267
1911	Superior	Wis.-Min.	122	524	73	143	....	....	.273
1912	Portland	P. C.	166	565	68	120	0	....	.213
1913	Portland	N. W.	133	483	79	118	2	....	.244
1914	Portland	P. C.	177	668	99	185	2	....	.277
1915	Philadelphia	Nat.	153	563	85	143	7	33	.254
1916	Philadelphia	Nat.	142	477	53	101	3	27	.212
1917	Philadelphia	Nat.	127	478	56	116	4	38	.243
1918	Philadelphia	Nat.	125	499	69	132	0	18	.265
1919	Philadelphia	Nat.	92	335	45	91	0	29	.272
1920	Phila.-N.Y.	Nat.	150	613	102	183	0	36	.299
1921	New York	Nat.	153	606	121	193	6	67	.318
1922	New York	Nat.	•156	651	117	209	4	60	.321
1923	New York	Nat.	107	444	80	135	1	31	.304
1924	Boston	Nat.	79	319	49	89	2	21	.279
1925	Boston	Nat.	128	479	75	153	2	49	.319
1926	Boston	Nat.	127	453	70	141	1	44	.311
1927	Boston	Nat.	111	375	44	91	1	31	.243
1928	Brooklyn	Nat.	149	515	47	127	0	51	.247
1929	Brooklyn	Nat.	104	358	35	99	1	44	.277
1930	New York	Nat.	10	17	0	1	0	0	.059
1936	Sioux City	West.	1	4	1	1	0	0	.250
	Major League Totals		1913	7182	1048	2004	32	579	.279

WORLD SERIES RECORD

Year	Club	League	G.	AB.	R.	H.	HR.	RBI.	B.A.
1915	Philadelphia	Nat.	5	17	2	5	0	1	.294
1921	New York	Nat.	8	33	3	5	0	3	.152
1922	New York	Nat.	5	19	4	4	0	2	.211
1923	New York	Nat.	6	24	1	2	0	1	.083
	World Series Totals		24	93	10	16	0	7	.172

ERNEST BANKS

Year	Club	League	G.	AB.	R.	H.	HR.	RBI.	B.A.
1953	Chicago	Nat.	10	35	3	11	2	6	.314
1954	Chicago	Nat.	•154	593	70	163	19	79	.275
1955	Chicago	Nat.	•154	596	98	176	44	117	.295
1956	Chicago	Nat.	139	538	82	160	28	85	.297
1957	Chicago	Nat.	•156	594	113	169	43	102	.285
1958	Chicago	Nat.	*154	*617	119	193	*47	*129	.313
1959	Chicago	Nat.	•155	589	97	179	45	*143	.304
1960	Chicago	Nat.	*156	597	94	162	*41	117	.271
1961	Chicago	Nat.	138	511	75	142	29	80	.278
1962	Chicago	Nat.	154	610	87	164	37	104	.269
1963	Chicago	Nat.	130	432	41	98	18	64	.227
1964	Chicago	Nat.	157	591	67	156	23	95	.264
1965	Chicago	Nat.	163	612	79	162	28	106	.265
1966	Chicago	Nat.	141	511	52	139	15	75	.272
1967	Chicago	Nat.	151	573	68	158	23	95	.276
1968	Chicago	Nat.	150	552	71	136	32	83	.246
1969	Chicago	Nat.	155	565	60	143	23	106	.253
1970	Chicago	Nat.	72	222	25	56	12	44	.252
1971	Chicago	Nat.	39	83	4	16	3	6	.193
	Major League Totals		2528	9421	1305	2583	512	1636	.274

JACOB PETER (JAKE) BECKLEY

Year	Club	League	G.	AB.	R.	H.	HR.	SB.	B.A.
1886	Leavenworth	West.	....	305	65	104	....	....	.341
1887	Leav.-Lincoln	West.	....	526	....	211	....	....	.401
1888	St. Louis	W. A.	34	145	23	41	....	17	.283
1888	Pittsburgh	Nat.	71	283	35	97	1	20	.343
1889	Pittsburgh	Nat.	123	522	92	157	9	11	.301
1890	Pittsburgh	Play	121	517	109	168	9	19	.325
1891	Pittsburgh	Nat.	129	535	91	156	4	17	.292
1892	Pittsburgh	Nat.	152	603	102	151	10	40	.250
1893	Pittsburgh	Nat.	131	497	108	161	5	24	.324
1894	Pittsburgh	Nat.	132	534	122	184	7	20	.345
1895	Pittsburgh	Nat.	131	536	105	174	5	19	.325
1896	Pitts.-N.Y.	Nat.	99	395	79	106	9	19	.268
1897	N.Y.-Cinn.	Nat.	114	437	84	142	8	22	.325
1898	Cincinnati	Nat.	116	458	86	137	3	7	.299
1899	Cincinnati	Nat.	135	519	87	173	3	18	.333
1900	Cincinnati	Nat.	138	559	99	192	2	22	.343
1901	Cincinnati	Nat.	140	590	80	177	3	6	.300
1902	Cincinnati	Nat.	129	532	82	176	5	16	.331
1903	Cincinnati	Nat.	119	459	85	150	2	23	.327
1904	St. Louis	Nat.	142	551	72	179	1	17	.325
1905	St. Louis	Nat.	134	514	48	147	1	12	.286
1906	St. Louis	Nat.	85	320	29	79	0	3	.247
1907	St. Louis	Nat.	32	115	6	24	0	0	.209
1907	Kansas City	A. A.	100	378	65	138	1	12	.365
1908	Kansas City	A. A.	136	496	66	134	1	13	.270
1909	Kansas City	A. A.	113	428	41	120	1	12	.280
1910	Bartlesville	W. A.	70	249	21	64	0	13	.257
1910	Topeka	West.	63	233	19	60	1	1	.258
1911	Hannibal	C. A.	98	355	50	100	0	22	.282
	National League Totals		2252	8959	1492	2762	78	316	.308
	Players' League Totals		121	517	109	168	9	19	.325
	Major League Totals		2373	9476	1601	2930	87	335	.309

JOHNNY LEE BENCH

Year	Club	League	G.	AB.	R.	H.	HR.	RBI.	B.A.
1965	Tampa	Fla. St.	68	214	29	53	2	35	.248
1966	Peninsula	Carol.	98	350	59	103	22	68	.294
1966	Buffalo	Int.	1	0	0	0	0	0	.000
1967	Buffalo	Int.	98	344	39	89	23	68	.259
1967	Cincinnati	Nat.	26	86	7	14	1	6	.163
1968	Cincinnati	Nat.	154	564	67	155	15	82	.275
1969	Cincinnati	Nat.	148	532	83	156	26	90	.293
1970	Cincinnati	Nat.	158	605	97	177	*45	*148	.293
1971	Cincinnati	Nat.	149	562	80	134	27	61	.238
1972	Cincinnati	Nat.	147	538	87	145	*40	*125	.270
1973	Cincinnati	Nat.	152	557	83	141	25	104	.253
1974	Cincinnati	Nat.	160	621	108	174	33	*129	.280
1975	Cincinnati	Nat.	142	530	83	150	28	110	.283
1976	Cincinnati	Nat.	135	465	62	109	16	74	.234
1977	Cincinnati	Nat.	142	494	67	136	31	109	.275
1978	Cincinnati	Nat.	120	393	52	102	23	73	.260
1979	Cincinnati	Nat.	130	464	73	128	22	80	.276
1980	Cincinnati	Nat.	114	360	52	90	24	68	.250
1981	Cincinnati	Nat.	52	178	14	55	8	25	.309
1982	Cincinnati	Nat.	119	399	44	103	13	38	.258
1983	Cincinnati	Nat.	110	310	32	79	12	54	.255
	Major League Totals		2158	7658	1091	2048	389	1376	.267

CHAMPIONSHIP SERIES RECORD

Year	Club	League	G.	AB.	R.	H.	HR.	RBI.	B.A.
1970	Cincinnati	Nat.	3	9	2	2	1	1	.222
1972	Cincinnati	Nat.	5	18	3	6	1	2	.333
1973	Cincinnati	Nat.	5	19	1	5	1	1	.263
1975	Cincinnati	Nat.	3	13	1	1	0	0	.077
1976	Cincinnati	Nat.	3	12	3	4	1	1	.333
1979	Cincinnati	Nat.	3	12	1	3	1	1	.250
	Championship Series Totals		22	83	11	21	5	6	.253

WORLD SERIES RECORD

Year	Club	League	G.	AB.	R.	H.	HR.	RBI.	B.A.
1970	Cincinnati	Nat.	5	19	3	4	1	3	.211
1972	Cincinnati	Nat.	7	23	4	6	1	1	.261
1975	Cincinnati	Nat.	7	29	5	6	1	4	.207
1976	Cincinnati	Nat.	4	15	4	8	2	6	.533
	World Series Totals		23	86	16	24	5	14	.279

CHARLES ALBERT (CHIEF) BENDER

Year	Club	League	G.	IP.	W.	L.	Pct.	ERA.
1903	Philadelphia	Amer.	36	270	17	15	.531	......
1904	Philadelphia	Amer.	29	205	10	11	.476	......
1905	Philadelphia	Amer.	35	230	18	11	.621	......
1906	Philadelphia	Amer.	36	240	15	10	.600	......
1907	Philadelphia	Amer.	33	222	16	8	.667	......
1908	Philadelphia	Amer.	18	139	8	9	.471	......
1909	Philadephia	Amer.	34	250	18	8	.692	......
1910	Philadelphia	Amer.	30	250	23	5	*.821	......
1911	Philadelphia	Amer.	31	216	17	5	*.773	......
1912	Philadelphia	Amer.	27	171	13	8	.619	......
1913	Philadelphia	Amer.	48	238	21	10	.667	2.19
1914	Philadelphia	Amer.	28	179	17	3	*.850	2.26
1915	Baltimore	Federal	26	179	4	16	.200	4.27
1916	Philadelphia	Nat.	27	123	7	7	.500	3.73
1917	Philadelphia	Nat.	20	113	8	2	.800	1.67
1918	(Voluntarily retired—worked in shipyards)							
1919	Richmond	Va.	34	*280	*29	2	*.935	......
1920	New Haven	East.	*47	*324	*25	12	.676	1.94
1921	New Haven	East.	36	196	13	7	.650	1.93

Year	Club	League	G.	IP.	W.	L.	Pct.	ERA.
1922—Reading		Inter.	30	183	8	13	.381	2.42
1923—Baltimore		Inter.	18	93	6	3	.667	5.03
1924—New Haven		East.	12	91	6	4	.600	3.07
1925—Chicago		Amer.	1	1	0	0	.000	18.00
1927—Johnstown		Mid. Atl.	18	108	7	3	.700	1.33
American League Totals			386	2611	193	103	.652	......
National League Totals			47	236	15	9	.625	2.75
Major League Totals			433	2847	208	112	.650	......

WORLD SERIES RECORD

Year	Club	League	G.	IP.	W.	L.	Pct.	ERA.
1905—Philadelphia		Amer.	2	17	1	1	.500	1.06
1910—Philadelphia		Amer.	2	18⅔	1	1	.500	1.93
1911—Philadelphia		Amer.	3	26	2	1	.667	1.04
1913—Philadelphia		Amer.	2	18	2	0	1.000	4.00
1914—Philadelphia		Amer.	1	5⅓	0	1	.000	10.13
World Series Totals			10	85	6	4	.600	2.44

LAWRENCE PETER (YOGI) BERRA

Year	Club	League	G.	AB.	R.	H.	HR.	RBI.	B.A.
1943—Norfolk		Pied.	111	376	52	95	7	56	.253
1944-45—Kansas City		A. A.	(In Military Service)						
1946—Newark		Int.	77	277	41	87	15	59	.314
1946—New York		Amer.	7	22	3	8	2	4	.364
1947—New York		Amer.	83	293	41	82	11	54	.280
1948—New York		Amer.	125	469	70	143	14	98	.305
1949—New York		Amer.	116	415	59	115	20	91	.277
1950—New York		Amer.	151	597	116	192	28	124	.322
1951—New York		Amer.	141	547	92	161	27	88	.294
1952—New York		Amer.	142	534	97	146	30	98	.273
1953—New York		Amer.	137	503	80	149	27	108	.296
1954—New York		Amer.	151	584	88	179	22	125	.307
1955—New York		Amer.	147	541	84	147	27	108	.272
1956—New York		Amer.	140	521	93	155	30	105	.298
1957—New York		Amer.	134	482	74	121	24	82	.251
1958—New York		Amer.	122	433	60	115	22	90	.266
1959—New York		Amer.	131	472	64	134	19	69	.284
1960—New York		Amer.	120	359	46	99	15	62	.276
1961—New York		Amer.	119	395	62	107	22	61	.271
1962—New York		Amer.	86	232	25	52	10	35	.224
1963—New York		Amer.	64	147	20	43	8	28	.293
1964—New York		Amer.	(Did not play—served as manager.)						
1965—New York		Nat.	4	9	1	2	0	0	.222
American League Totals			2116	7546	1174	2148	358	1430	.285
National League Totals			4	9	1	2	0	0	.222
Major League Totals			2120	7555	1175	2150	358	1430	.285

WORLD SERIES RECORD

Year	Club	League	G.	AB.	R.	H.	HR.	RBI.	B.A.
1947—New York		Amer.	6	19	2	3	1	2	.158
1949—New York		Amer.	4	16	2	1	0	1	.063
1950—New York		Amer.	4	15	2	3	1	2	.200
1951—New York		Amer.	6	23	4	6	0	0	.261
1952—New York		Amer.	7	28	2	6	2	3	.214
1953—New York		Amer.	6	21	3	9	1	4	.429
1955—New York		Amer.	7	24	5	10	1	2	.417
1956—New York		Amer.	7	25	5	9	3	10	.360
1957—New York		Amer.	7	25	5	8	1	2	.320
1958—New York		Amer.	7	27	3	6	0	2	.222
1960—New York		Amer.	7	22	6	7	1	8	.318
1961—New York		Amer.	4	11	2	3	1	3	.273
1962—New York		Amer.	2	2	0	0	0	0	.000
1963—New York		Amer.	1	1	0	0	0	0	.000
World Series Totals			75	259	41	71	12	39	.274

JAMES LEROY (SUNNY JIM) BOTTOMLEY

Year	Club	League	G.	AB.	R.	H.	HR.	RBI.	B.A.
1920—Sioux City		West.	6	14	0	1	0	0	.071
1920—Mitchell		S. Dak.	●97	378	69	118	7	.....	.312
1921—Houston		Tex.	130	459	50	104	4	62	.227
1922—Syracuse		Int.	119	460	78	160	14	94	.348
1922—St. Louis		Nat.	37	151	29	49	5	35	.325
1923—St. Louis		Nat.	134	523	79	194	8	94	.371
1924—St. Louis		Nat.	137	528	87	167	14	111	.316
1925—St. Louis		Nat.	●153	619	92	★227	21	128	.367
1926—St. Louis		Nat.	154	603	98	180	19	★120	.299
1927—St. Louis		Nat.	152	574	95	174	19	124	.303
1928—St. Louis		Nat.	149	576	123	187	●31	★136	.325
1929—St. Louis		Nat.	146	560	108	176	29	137	.314
1930—St. Louis		Nat.	131	487	92	148	15	97	.304
1931—St. Louis		Nat.	108	382	73	133	9	75	.348
1932—St. Louis		Nat.	91	311	45	92	11	48	.296
1933—Cincinnati		Nat.	145	549	57	137	13	83	.250
1934—Cincinnati		Nat.	142	556	72	158	11	78	.284
1935—Cincinnati		Nat.	107	399	44	103	1	49	.258
1936—St. Louis		Amer.	140	544	72	162	12	95	.298
1937—St. Louis		Amer.	65	109	11	26	1	12	.239
1938—Syracuse		Int.	7	14	0	1	0	0	.071

American League Totals			205	653	83	188	13	107	.288
National League Totals			1786	6818	1094	2125	206	1315	.312
Major League Totals			1991	7471	1177	2313	219	1422	.310

WORLD SERIES RECORD

Year	Club	League	G.	AB.	R.	H.	HR.	RBI.	B.A.
1926—St. Louis		National	7	29	4	10	0	5	.345
1928—St. Louis		National	4	14	1	3	1	3	.214
1930—St. Louis		National	6	22	1	1	0	0	.045
1931—St. Louis		National	7	25	2	4	0	2	.160
World Series Totals			24	90	8	18	1	10	.200

LOUIS BOUDREAU

Year	Club	League	G.	AB.	R.	H.	HR.	RBI.	B.A.
1938—Cedar Rapids		I.I.I.	60	231	56	67	3	29	.290
1938—Cleveland		Amer.	1	1	0	0	0	0	.000
1939—Buffalo		Int.	115	481	88	159	17	57	.331
1939—Cleveland		Amer.	53	225	42	58	0	19	.258
1940—Cleveland		Amer.	155	627	97	185	9	101	.295
1941—Cleveland		Amer.	148	579	95	149	10	56	.257
1942—Cleveland		Amer.	147	506	57	143	2	58	.283
1943—Cleveland		Amer.	152	539	69	154	3	67	.286
1944—Cleveland		Amer.	150	584	91	191	3	67	★.327
1945—Cleveland		Amer.	97	345	50	106	3	48	.307
1946—Cleveland		Amer.	140	515	51	151	6	62	.293
1947—Cleveland		Amer.	150	538	79	165	4	67	.307
1948—Cleveland		Amer.	152	560	116	199	18	106	.355
1949—Cleveland		Amer.	134	475	53	135	4	60	.284
1950—Cleveland		Amer.	81	260	23	70	1	29	.269
1951—Boston		Amer.	82	273	37	73	5	47	.267
1952—Boston		Amer.	4	2	1	0	0	2	.000
Major League Totals			1646	6029	861	1779	68	789	.295

WORLD SERIES RECORD

Year	Club	League	G.	AB.	R.	H.	HR.	RBI.	B.A.
1948—Cleveland		Amer.	6	22	1	6	0	0	.273

RECORD AS MANAGER

Year	Club	League	Position	W.	L.
1942—Cleveland		American	Fourth	75	79
1943—Cleveland		American	Third	82	71
1944—Cleveland		American	Fifth	72	82
1945—Cleveland		American	Fifth	73	72
1946—Cleveland		American	Sixth	68	86
1947—Cleveland		American	Fourth	80	74
1948—Cleveland		American	First	97	58
1949—Cleveland		American	Third	89	65
1950—Cleveland		American	Fourth	92	62
1952—Boston		American	Sixth	76	78
1953—Boston		American	Fourth	84	69
1954—Boston		American	Fourth	69	85
1955—Kansas City		American	Sixth	63	91
1956—Kansas City		American	Eighth	52	102
1957—Kansas City		American	Eighth	36	67
1960—Chicago		National	Seventh	54	83
Major League Totals				1162	1224

WORLD SERIES RECORD

Year	Club	League		W.	L.
1948—Cleveland		American		4	2

ROGER PHILLIP (DUKE) BRESNAHAN

Year	Club	League	G.	AB.	R.	H.	HR.	SB.	B.A.
1897—Washington		Nat.	7	18	2	6	0	0	.333
1898—Toledo		Int.-State	4	12	0	5	0	0	.417
1899—Minneapolis		West.	3	1	0	1	0	0	1.000
1900—Chicago		Nat.	1	2	0	0	0	0	.000
1901—Baltimore		Amer.	86	293	40	77	1	10	.263
1902—Baltimore		Amer.	66	234	31	64	4	11	.274
1902—New York		Nat.	50	178	16	52	1	6	.292
1903—New York		Nat.	111	406	87	142	4	34	.350
1904—New York		Nat.	107	402	81	114	5	13	.284
1905—New York		Nat.	95	331	58	100	0	11	.302
1906—New York		Nat.	124	405	69	114	0	25	.281
1907—New York		Nat.	104	328	57	83	4	15	.253
1908—New York		Nat.	139	449	70	127	1	14	.283
1909—St. Louis		Nat.	69	234	27	57	0	11	.244
1910—St. Louis		Nat.	78	234	35	65	0	13	.278
1911—St. Louis		Nat.	78	227	22	63	3	4	.278
1912—St. Louis		Nat.	48	108	8	36	1	4	.333
1913—Chicago		Nat.	69	162	20	39	1	7	.241
1914—Chicago		Nat.	101	248	42	69	0	14	.278
1915—Chicago		Nat.	77	221	19	45	1	19	.204
1916—Toledo		A. A.	44	120	19	29	2	4	.242
1917—Toledo		A. A.	40	80	10	22	0	1	.275
1918—Toledo		A. A.	19	52	4	12	1	0	.231
National League Totals			1258	3953	613	1110	21	190	.281
American League Totals			152	527	71	141	5	21	.268
Major League Totals			1410	4480	684	1251	26	211	.279

PITCHING RECORD

Year—Club	League	G.	W.	L.	Pct.
1897—Washington	National	7	4	0	1.000
1898—Toledo	Inter-State	4	2	2	.500
1899—Minneapolis	Western	3	0	2	.000
1901—Baltimore	American	1	0	0	.000
1910—St. Louis	National	1	0	0	.000
American League Totals		1	0	0	.000
National League Totals		8	4	0	1.000
Major League Totals		9	4	0	1.000

WORLD SERIES RECORD

Year—Club	League	G.	AB.	R.	H.	HR.	SB.	B.A.
1905—New York	Nat.	5	16	3	5	0	1	.313

GEORGE BRETT

Year—Club	League	G.	AB.	R.	H.	HR.	RBI.	B.A.
1971—Billings	Pioneer	68	258	44	75	5	44	.291
1972—San Jose	Calif.	117	431	66	118	10	68	.274
1973—Omaha	A.A.	117	405	66	115	8	64	.284
Kansas City	Amer.	13	40	2	5	0	0	.125
1974—Omaha	A.A.	16	64	9	17	2	14	.266
Kansas City	Amer.	133	457	49	129	2	47	.282
1975—Kansas City	Amer.	159	*634	84	*195	11	89	.308
1976—Kansas City	Amer.	159	*645	94	*215	7	67	*.333
1977—Kansas City	Amer.	139	564	105	176	22	88	.312
1978—Kansas City	Amer.	128	510	79	150	9	62	.294
1979—Kansas City	Amer.	154	645	119	*212	23	107	.329
1980—Kansas City	Amer.	117	449	87	175	24	118	*.390
1981—Kansas City	Amer.	89	347	42	109	6	43	.314
1982—Kansas City	Amer.	144	552	101	166	21	82	.301
1983—Kansas City	Amer.	123	464	90	144	25	93	.310
1984—Kansas City	Amer.	104	377	42	107	13	69	.284
1985—Kansas City	Amer.	155	550	108	184	30	112	.335
1986—Kansas City	Amer.	124	441	70	128	16	73	.290
1987—Kansas City	Amer.	115	427	71	124	22	78	.290
1988—Kansas City	Amer.	157	589	90	180	24	103	.306
1989—Kansas City	Amer.	124	457	67	129	12	80	.282
1990—Kansas City	Amer.	142	544	82	179	14	87	*.329
1991—Kansas City	Amer.	131	505	77	129	10	61	.255
1992—Kansas City	Amer.	152	592	55	169	7	61	.285
1993—Kansas City	Amer.	145	560	69	149	19	75	.266
Major League Totals		2707	10349	1583	3154	317	1595	.305

CHAMPIONSHIP SERIES RECORD

Year—Club	League	G.	AB.	R.	H.	HR.	RBI.	B.A.
1976—Kansas City	Amer.	5	18	4	8	1	5	.444
1977—Kansas City	Amer.	5	20	2	6	0	2	.300
1978—Columbus	Amer.	4	18	7	7	3	3	.389
1980—Kansas City	Amer.	3	11	3	3	2	4	.273
1984—Kansas City	Amer.	3	13	0	3	0	0	.231
1985—Kansas City	Amer.	7	23	6	8	3	5	.348
Championship Series Totals		27	103	22	35	9	19	.340

WORLD SERIES RECORD

Year—Club	League	G.	AB.	R.	H.	HR.	RBI.	B.A.
1980—Kansas City	Amer.	6	24	3	9	1	3	.375
1985—Kansas City	Amer.	7	27	5	10	0	1	.370
World Series Totals		13	51	8	19	1	4	.373

LOUIS CLARK BROCK

Year—Club	League	G.	AB.	R.	H.	HR.	RBI.	B.A.
1961—St. Cloud	Northern	●128	501	*117	*181	14	82	*.361
1961—Chicago	National	4	11	1	1	0	0	.091
1962—Chicago	National	123	434	73	114	9	35	.263
1963—Chicago	National	148	547	79	141	9	37	.258
1964—Chi.-St. Louis	National	155	634	111	200	14	58	.315
1965—St. Louis	National	155	631	107	182	16	69	.288
1966—St. Louis	National	156	643	94	183	15	46	.285
1967—St. Louis	National	159	*689	●113	206	21	76	.299
1968—St. Louis	National	159	660	92	184	6	51	.279
1969—St. Louis	National	157	655	97	195	12	47	.298
1970—St. Louis	National	155	664	114	202	13	57	.304
1971—St. Louis	National	157	640	*126	200	7	61	.313
1972—St. Louis	National	153	621	81	193	3	42	.311
1973—St. Louis	National	160	650	110	193	7	63	.297
1974—St. Louis	National	153	635	105	194	3	48	.306
1975—St. Louis	National	136	528	78	163	3	47	.309
1976—St. Louis	National	133	498	73	150	4	67	.301
1977—St. Louis	National	141	489	69	133	2	46	.272
1978—St. Louis	National	92	298	31	66	0	12	.221
1979—St. Louis	National	120	405	56	123	5	38	.304
Major League Totals		2616	10332	1610	3023	149	900	.293

WORLD SERIES RECORD

Year—Club	League	G.	AB.	R.	H.	HR.	RBI.	B.A.
1964—St. Louis	National	7	30	2	9	1	5	.300
1967—St. Louis	National	7	29	8	12	1	3	.414
1968—St. Louis	National	7	28	6	13	2	5	.464
World Series Totals		21	87	16	34	4	13	.391

DENNIS (DAN) BROUTHERS

Year—Club	League	G.	AB.	R.	H.	HR.	SB.	B.A.
1879—Troy	Nat.	39	168	17	46	4	.....	.274
1880—Troy	Nat.	3	13	0	2	0	.....	.154
1881—Buffalo	Nat.	65	270	60	86	*8	.....	.319
1882—Buffalo	Nat.	84	351	71	*129	6	.....	*.368
1883—Buffalo	Nat.	97	420	83	*156	2	.....	*.371
1884—Buffalo	Nat.	90	381	80	124	14	.....	.325
1885—Buffalo	Nat.	98	407	87	146	7	.....	.359
1886—Detroit	Nat.	121	489	139	181	10	21	.370
1887—Detroit	Nat.	122	570	*153	*239	13	34	.419
1888—Detroit	Nat.	129	522	*118	160	10	34	.306
1889—Boston	Nat.	126	485	105	181	6	22	*.373
1890—Boston	Players	123	464	116	160	1	26	.345
1891—Boston	A. A.	123	458	111	*160	5	33	.349
1892—Brooklyn	Nat.	152	588	121	*197	3	36	●.335
1893—Brooklyn	Nat.	75	267	53	93	2	8	.348
1894—Baltimore	Nat.	123	528	137	182	9	40	.345
1895—Balt.-L'ville.	Nat.	29	121	15	35	2	1	.289
1896—Philadelphia	Nat.	57	218	41	72	1	8	.330
1896—Springfield	East.	51	205	42	82	.....	9	.400
1897—Springfield	East.	126	501	112	*208	14	21	*.415
1898—Spring.-Toronto	East.	50	189	42	63	4	2	.333
1899—Spring.-Roch.	East.	45	170	27	40	3	2	.235
1904—New York	Nat.	2	5	0	0	0	0	.000
1904—Poughkeepsie	Hudson R.	.....	424	.....	158	.....	.....	.373
1905—Poughkeepsie	Hudson R.	.....	308	.....	91	.....	.....	.295
American Association Totals		123	458	111	160	5	33	.349
National League Totals		1412	5803	1280	2029	97	204	.350
Players League Totals		123	464	116	160	1	26	.345
Major League Totals		1658	6725	1507	2349	103	263	.349

MORDECAI PETER CENTENNIAL (THREE FINGER) BROWN

Year—Club	League	G.	IP.	W.	L.	Pct.	ERA.
1901—Terre Haute	I.I.I.	31	.....	*23	8	*.742	.....
1902—Omaha	Western	●43	352	27	15	.643	.....
1903—St. Louis	National	26	201	9	13	.409	.....
1904—Chicago	National	26	212	15	10	.600	.....
1905—Chicago	National	30	249	18	12	.600	.....
1906—Chicago	National	36	278	26	6	.813	.....
1907—Chicago	National	34	233	20	6	.769	.....
1908—Chicago	National	44	312	29	9	.763	.....
1909—Chicago	National	*50	*343	*27	9	.750	.....
1910—Chicago	National	46	295	25	14	.641	.....
1911—Chicago	National	*53	270	21	11	.656	.....
1912—Chicago	National	15	89	5	6	.455	2.63
1913—Cincinnati	National	39	167	11	12	.478	3.02
1914—St.L.-Brooklyn	Federal	35	233	14	11	.560	3.09
1915—Chicago	Federal	35	238	17	8	.680	2.12
1916—Chicago	National	12	48	2	3	.400	3.94
1917—Columbus	Am. Assoc.	30	185	10	12	.455	2.77
1918—Columbus	Am. Assoc.	12	50	3	2	.600	2.70
1919—Terre Haute	I.I.I.	33	175	16	6	.727	2.88
1919—Indianapolis	Am. Assoc.	6	34	0	3	.000	.....
1920—Terre Haute	I.I.I.	13	80	4	6	.400	2.59
Federal League Totals		70	471	31	19	.620	2.60
National League Totals		411	2697	208	111	.652	.....
Major League Totals		411	2697	208	111	.652	.....

WORLD SERIES RECORD

Year—Club	League	G.	IP.	W.	L.	Pct.	ERA.
1906—Chicago	National	3	19⅔	1	2	.333	3.20
1907—Chicago	National	1	9	1	0	1.000	0.00
1908—Chicago	National	2	11	2	0	1.000	0.00
1910—Chicago	National	3	18	1	2	.333	5.50
World Series Totals		9	57⅔	5	4	.556	2.81

JAMES PAUL DAVID BUNNING

Year—Club	League	G.	IP.	W.	L.	Pct.	ERA.
1950 — Richmond	Ohio-Ind.	17	123	7	8	.467	3.22
1951 — Davenport	I.I.I.	22	150	8	10	.444	2.88
1952 — Williamsport	Eastern	20	129	5	9	.357	3.49
1953 — Buffalo	International	3	5	0	0	.000	1.80
1953 — Little Rock	Southern	34	158	5	12	.294	4.56
1954 — Little Rock	Southern	35	193	13	11	.542	4.29
1955 — Buffalo	International	20	129	8	5	.615	3.77
1955 — Detroit	American	15	51	3	5	.375	6.35
1956 — Charleston	Amer. Assoc.	22	163	9	11	.450	3.53
1956 — Detroit	American	15	53	5	1	.833	3.74
1957 — Detroit	American	45	*267	*20	8	.714	2.70
1958 — Detroit	American	35	220	14	12	.538	3.52
1959 — Detroit	American	40	250	17	13	.567	3.89
1960 — Detroit	American	36	252	11	14	.440	2.79
1961 — Detroit	American	38	268	17	11	.607	3.19
1962 — Detroit	American	41	258	19	10	.655	3.59
1963 — Detroit	American	39	248	12	13	.480	3.88
1964 — Philadelphia	National	41	284	19	8	.704	2.63
1965 — Philadelphia	National	39	291	19	9	.679	2.60
1966 — Philadelphia	National	43	314	19	14	.576	2.41
1967 — Philadelphia	National	40	*302	17	15	.531	2.29
1968 — Pittsburgh	National	27	160	4	14	.222	3.88
1969 — Pitts.-L.A.	National	34	212	13	10	.565	3.69
1970 — Philadelphia	National	34	219	10	15	.400	4.11
1971 — Philadelphia	National	29	110	5	12	.294	5.48
American League Totals		304	1867	118	87	.576	3.45
National League Totals		287	1892	106	97	.522	3.10
Major League Totals		591	3759	224	184	.549	3.27

JESSE CAIL (CRAB) BURKETT

Year	Club	League	G.	AB.	R.	H.	HR.	RBI.	B.A.
1888	Scranton	Cent.	35	115	25	26	0	.....	.226
1889	Worcester	Atl. A.	49	175	31	49	3	16	.280
1890	New York	Nat.	101	401	67	124	4	14	.309
1891	Lincoln	W. A.	93	395	78	138	3	.....	.349
1891	Cleveland	Nat.	40	166	30	45	0	2	.271
1892	Cleveland	Nat.	145	605	117	168	3	36	.278
1893	Cleveland	Nat.	124	480	144	179	6	39	.373
1894	Cleveland	Nat.	124	518	134	185	8	32	.357
1895	Cleveland	Nat.	132	555	149	*235	5	47	*.423
1896	Cleveland	Nat.	•133	*585	*159	*240	6	32	*.410
1897	Cleveland	Nat.	128	519	128	199	2	27	.383
1898	Cleveland	Nat.	148	624	115	*215	0	20	.345
1899	St. Louis	Nat.	138	567	115	228	7	22	.402
1900	St. Louis	Nat	•142	560	88	202	7	31	.361
1901	St. Louis	Nat.	•142	*597	*139	*228	10	27	*.382
1902	St. Louis	Amer.	137	549	99	168	5	22	.306
1903	St. Louis	Amer.	133	514	74	152	3	16	.296
1904	St. Louis	Amer.	147	576	72	157	2	12	.273
1905	Boston	Amer.	149	573	78	147	4	13	.257
1906	Worcester	N. Eng.	98	363	59	125	1	.....	*.344
1907	Worcester	N. Eng.	52	195	23	66	1	9	.338
1908	Worcester	N. Eng.	97	375	49	110	1	8	.293
1909	Worcester	N. Eng.	75	218	30	71	1	6	.326
1910	Worcester	N. Eng.	38	72	3	24	0	1	.333
1911	Worcester	N. Eng.	76	243	42	83	1	1	.342
1912	Worcester	N. Eng.	28	60	6	21	0	1	.350
1913	Worcester	N. Eng.	19	42	4	10	0	0	.238
1916	Low.-Law.-Hart.	East.	24	38	5	8	....	0	.211
American League Totals			566	2212	323	624	14	63	.282
National League Totals			1497	6177	1385	2248	58	329	.364
Major League Totals			2063	8389	1708	2872	72	392	.342

PITCHING RECORD

Year	Club	League	G.	IP.	W.	L.	Pct.
1890	New York	National	21	6	116	1	11
1894	Cleveland	National	1	0	4	0	0
1902	St. Louis	American	1	0	1	0	1
National League Totals			22	6	120	1	11
American League Totals			1	0	1	0	1
Major League Totals			23	6	121	1	12

ROY CAMPANELLA

Year	Club	League	G.	AB.	R.	H.	HR.	RBI.	B.A.
1946	Nashua	New Eng.	113	396	75	115	13	96	.290
1947	Montreal	Int.	135	440	64	120	13	75	.273
1948	St. Paul	A.A.	35	123	31	40	13	39	.325
1948	Brooklyn	Nat.	83	279	32	72	9	45	.258
1949	Brooklyn	Nat.	130	436	65	125	22	82	.287
1950	Brooklyn	Nat.	126	437	70	123	31	89	.281
1951	Brooklyn	Nat.	143	505	90	164	33	108	.325
1952	Brooklyn	Nat.	128	468	73	126	22	97	.269
1953	Brooklyn	Nat.	144	519	103	162	41	*142	.312
1954	Brooklyn	Nat.	111	397	43	82	19	51	.207
1955	Brooklyn	Nat.	123	446	81	142	32	107	.318
1956	Brooklyn	Nat.	124	388	39	85	20	73	.219
1957	Brooklyn	Nat.	103	330	31	80	13	62	.242
Major League Totals			1215	4205	627	1161	242	856	.276

WORLD SERIES RECORD

Year	Club	League	G.	AB.	R.	H.	HR.	RBI.	B.A.
1949	Brooklyn	Nat.	5	15	2	4	1	2	.267
1952	Brooklyn	Nat.	7	28	0	6	0	1	.214
1953	Brooklyn	Nat.	6	22	6	6	1	2	.273
1955	Brooklyn	Nat.	7	27	4	7	2	4	.259
1956	Brooklyn	Nat.	7	22	2	4	0	3	.182
World Series Totals			32	114	14	27	4	12	.237

RODNEY CLINE (ROD) CAREW

Year	Club	League	G.	AB.	R.	H.	HR.	RBI.	B.A.
1964	Melbourne Twins	Coc. Rk.	37	123	17	40	0	21	.325
1965	Orlando	Fla. St.	125	439	57	133	1	52	.303
1966	Wilson	Carol.	112	383	64	112	1	30	.292
1967	Minnesota	Amer.	137	514	66	150	8	51	.292
1968	Minnesota	Amer.	127	461	46	126	1	42	.273
1969	Minnesota	Amer.	123	458	79	152	8	56	•.332
1970	Minnesota	Amer.	51	191	27	70	4	28	.366
1971	Minnesota	Amer.	147	577	88	177	2	48	.307
1972	Minnesota	Amer.	142	535	61	170	0	51	•.318
1973	Minnesota	Amer.	149	580	98	•203	6	62	•.350
1974	Minnesota	Amer.	153	599	86	•218	3	55	•.364
1975	Minnesota	Amer.	143	535	89	192	14	80	•.359
1976	Minnesota	Amer.	156	605	97	200	9	90	.331
1977	Minnesota	Amer.	155	616	•128	•239	14	100	•.388
1978	Minnesota	Amer.	152	564	85	188	5	70	•.333
1979	California	Amer.	110	409	78	130	3	44	.318
1980	California	Amer.	144	540	74	179	3	59	.331
1981	California	Amer.	93	364	57	111	2	21	.305
1982	California	Amer.	138	523	88	167	3	44	.319
1983	California	Amer.	129	472	66	160	2	44	.339
1984	California	Amer.	93	329	42	97	3	31	.295
1985	California	Amer.	127	443	69	124	2	39	.280
Major League Totals			2649	9315	1424	3053	92	1015	.328

CHAMPIONSHIP SERIES RECORD

Year	Club	League	G.	AB.	R.	H.	HR.	RBI.	B.A.
1969	Minnesota	Amer.	3	14	0	1	0	0	.071
1970	Minnesota	Amer.	2	2	0	0	0	0	.000
1979	California	Amer.	4	17	4	7	0	1	.412
1982	California	Amer.	5	17	2	3	0	0	.176
Championship Series Totals			14	50	6	11	0	1	.220

MAX GEORGE (SCOOPS) CAREY

Year	Club	League	G.	AB.	R.	H.	HR.	RBI.	B.A.
1909	South Bend	Cent.	48	158	5	25	0	.....	.158
1910	South Bend	Cent.	96	327	39	96	2	.....	.293
1910	Pittsburgh	Nat.	2	6	2	3	0	2	.500
1911	Pittsburgh	Nat.	122	427	77	110	5	41	.258
1912	Pittsburgh	Nat.	150	587	114	177	5	61	.302
1913	Pittsburgh	Nat.	154	*620	•99	172	5	53	.277
1914	Pittsburgh	Nat.	•156	*593	76	144	1	32	.243
1915	Pittsburgh	Nat.	140	564	76	143	3	28	.254
1916	Pittsburgh	Nat.	154	599	90	158	7	42	.264
1917	Pittsburgh	Nat.	155	588	82	174	1	53	.296
1918	Pittsburgh	Nat.	126	468	70	128	3	44	.274
1919	Pittsburgh	Nat.	66	244	41	75	0	9	.307
1920	Pittsburgh	Nat.	130	485	74	140	1	35	.289
1921	Pittsburgh	Nat.	140	521	85	161	7	56	.309
1922	Pittsburgh	Nat.	155	629	140	207	10	70	.329
1923	Pittsburgh	Nat.	153	610	120	188	6	63	.308
1924	Pittsburgh	Nat.	149	599	113	178	7	55	.297
1925	Pittsburgh	Nat.	133	542	109	186	5	44	.343
1926	Pitts.-Brook.	Nat.	113	424	64	98	0	35	.231
1927	Brooklyn	Nat.	144	538	70	143	1	54	.266
1928	Brooklyn	Nat.	108	296	41	73	2	19	.247
1929	Brooklyn	Nat.	19	23	2	7	0	1	.304
Major League Totals			2469	9363	1545	2665	69	797	.285

WORLD SERIES RECORD

Year	Club	League	G.	AB.	R.	H.	HR.	RBI.	B.A.
1925	Pittsburgh	Nat.	7	24	6	11	0	2	.458

STEVEN NORMAN CARLTON

Year	Club	League	G.	IP.	W.	L.	Pct.	ERA.
1964	Rock Hill	W. Carolina	11	79	10	1	.909	1.03
1964	Winnipeg	Northern	12	75	4	4	.500	3.36
1964	Tulsa	Texas	4	24	1	1	.500	2.63
1965	St. Louis	National	15	25	0	0	.000	2.52
1966	Tulsa	Pacific Coast	19	128	9	5	.643	3.59
1966	St. Louis	National	9	52	3	3	.500	3.12
1967	St. Louis	National	30	193	14	9	.609	2.98
1968	St. Louis	National	34	232	13	11	.542	2.99
1969	St. Louis	National	31	236	17	11	.607	2.17
1970	St. Louis	National	34	254	10	*19	.345	3.72
1971	St. Louis	National	37	273	20	9	.690	3.56
1972	Philadelphia	National	41	*346	*27	10	.730	*1.98
1973	Philadelphia	National	40	•293	13	*20	.394	3.90
1974	Philadelphia	National	39	291	16	13	.552	3.22
1975	Philadelphia	National	37	255	15	14	.517	3.56
1976	Philadelphia	National	35	253	20	7	*.741	3.13
1977	Philadelphia	National	36	283	*23	10	.697	2.64
1978	Philadelphia	National	34	247	16	13	.552	2.84
1979	Philadelphia	National	35	251	18	11	.621	3.62
1980	Philadelphia	National	38	*304	*24	9	.727	2.34
1981	Philadelphia	National	24	190	13	4	.765	2.42
1982	Philadelphia	National	38	*295⅔	*23	11	.676	3.10
1983	Philadelphia	National	37	*283⅔	15	16	.484	3.11
1984	Philadelphia	National	33	229	13	7	.650	3.58
1985	Philadelphia	National	16	92	1	8	.111	3.33
1986	Phil.-S.F.	National	22	113	5	11	.313	5.89
1986	Chicago	American	10	63⅓	4	3	.571	3.69
1987	Clev.-Min.	American	32	152	6	14	.300	5.74
1988	Minnesota	American	4	9⅔	0	1	.000	16.76
National League Totals			695	4991⅓	319	226	.585	3.11
American League Totals			46	225	10	18	.357	5.64
Major League Totals			741	5216⅓	329	244	.574	3.22

DIVISION SERIES RECORD

Year	Club	League	G.	IP.	W.	L.	Pct.	ERA.
1981	Philadelphia	National	2	14	0	2	.000	3.86

CHAMPIONSHIP SERIES RECORD

Year	Club	League	G.	IP.	W.	L.	Pct.	ERA.
1976	Philadelphia	National	1	7	0	1	.000	5.14
1977	Philadelphia	National	2	11⅔	0	1	.000	6.94
1978	Philadelphia	National	1	9	1	0	1.000	4.00
1980	Philadelphia	National	2	12⅓	1	0	1.000	2.19
1983	Philadelphia	National	2	13⅔	2	0	1.000	0.66
Championship Series Totals			8	53⅔	4	2	.667	3.52

WORLD SERIES RECORD

Year	Club	League	G.	IP.	W.	L.	Pct.	ERA.
1967	St. Louis	National	1	6	0	1	.000	0.00
1968	St. Louis	National	2	4	0	0	.000	6.75
1980	Philadelphia	National	2	15	2	0	1.000	2.40
1983	Philadelphia	National	1	6⅔	0	1	.000	2.70
World Series Totals			6	31⅔	2	2	.500	2.56

ORLANDO MANUEL CEPEDA

Year	Club	League	G.	AB.	R.	H.	HR.	RBI.	B.A.
1955—	Salem	Appal.	26	93	12	23	1	16	.247
1955—	Kokomo	M.O.V.	92	374	83	147	21	91	*.393
1956—	St. Cloud	Northern	•125	499	100	*177	*26	*112	*.355
1957—	Minneapolis	A.A.	151	563	91	174	25	108	.309
1958—	San Francisco	Nat.	148	603	88	188	25	96	.312
1959—	San Francisco	Nat.	151	605	92	192	27	105	.317
1960—	San Francisco	Nat.	151	569	81	169	24	96	.297
1961—	San Francisco	Nat.	152	585	105	182	*46	*142	.311
1962—	San Francisco	Nat.	162	625	105	191	35	114	.306
1963—	San Francisco	Nat.	156	579	100	183	34	97	.316
1964—	San Francisco	Nat.	142	529	75	161	31	97	.304
1965—	San Francisco	Nat.	33	34	1	6	1	5	.176
1966—	S.F.-St.Louis	Nat.	142	501	70	151	20	73	.301
1967—	St. Louis	Nat.	151	563	91	183	25	*111	.325
1968—	St. Louis	Nat.	157	600	71	149	16	73	.248
1969—	Atlanta	Nat.	154	573	74	147	22	88	.257
1970—	Atlanta	Nat.	148	567	87	173	34	111	.305
1971—	Atlanta	Nat.	71	250	31	69	14	44	.276
1972—	Atlanta	Nat.	28	84	6	25	4	9	.298
1972—	Oakland	Amer.	3	3	0	0	0	0	.000
1973—	Boston	Amer.	142	550	51	159	20	86	.289
1974—	Yucatan	Mex.	28	80	7	17	4	17	.213
1974—	Kansas City	Amer.	33	107	3	23	1	18	.215
	National League Totals		1946	7267	1077	2169	358	1261	.298
	American League Totals		178	660	54	182	21	104	.276
	Major League Totals		2124	7927	1131	2351	379	1365	.297

CHAMPIONSHIP SERIES RECORD

Year	Club	League	G.	AB.	R.	H.	HR.	RBI.	B.A.
1969—	Atlanta	Nat.	3	11	2	5	1	3	.455

WORLD SERIES RECORD

Year	Club	League	G.	AB.	R.	H.	HR.	RBI.	B.A.
1962—	San Francisco	Nat.	5	19	1	3	0	2	.158
1967—	St. Louis	Nat.	7	29	1	3	0	1	.103
1968—	St. Louis	Nat.	7	28	2	7	2	6	.250
	World Series Totals		19	76	4	13	2	9	.171

FRANK LEROY (HUSK) CHANCE

Year	Club	League	G.	AB.	R.	H.	HR.	SB.	B.A.
1898—	Chicago	Nat.	42	146	32	42	1	5	.288
1899—	Chicago	Nat.	57	190	36	55	1	11	.289
1900—	Chicago	Nat.	48	151	26	46	0	9	.305
1901—	Chicago	Nat.	63	228	37	66	0	30	.289
1902—	Chicago	Nat.	67	236	40	67	1	28	.284
1903—	Chicago	Nat.	123	441	83	144	2	*67	.327
1904—	Chicago	Nat.	124	451	89	140	6	42	.310
1905—	Chicago	Nat.	115	392	92	124	2	38	.316
1906—	Chicago	Nat.	136	474	●103	151	3	*57	.319
1907—	Chicago	Nat.	109	382	58	112	1	35	.293
1908—	Chicago	Nat.	126	452	65	123	2	27	.272
1909—	Chicago	Nat.	92	324	53	88	0	29	.272
1910—	Chicago	Nat.	87	295	54	88	0	16	.298
1911—	Chicago	Nat.	29	88	23	21	1	9	.239
1912—	Chicago	Nat.	2	5	2	1	0	1	.200
1913—	New York	Amer.	11	24	3	5	0	1	.208
1914—	New York	Amer.	1	0	0	0	0	0	.000
	American League Totals		12	24	3	5	0	1	.208
	National League Totals		1220	4255	793	1268	20	404	.298
	Major League Totals		1232	4279	796	1273	20	405	.297

WORLD SERIES RECORD

Year	Club	League	G.	AB.	R.	H.	HR.	RBI.	B.A.
1906—	Chicago	Nat.	6	21	3	5	0	2	.238
1907—	Chicago	Nat.	4	14	3	3	0	3	.214
1908—	Chicago	Nat.	5	19	4	8	0	5	.421
1910—	Chicago	Nat.	5	17	1	6	0	0	.353
	World Series Totals		20	71	11	22	0	10	.310

JOHN DWIGHT (HAPPY JACK) CHESBRO

Year	Club	League	G.	IP.	W.	L.	Pct.
1895—	Albany-Johnstown	N.Y.L.	19	156	7	10	.412
1895—	Springfield	Eastern	7	33	3	0	1 000
1896—	Roanoke	Virginia	20	156	7	11	.389
1897—	Richmond	Atlantic	38	283	16	18	.471
1898—	Richmond	Atlantic	40	351	23	15	.605
1899—	Richmond	Atlantic	21	192	17	4	.810
1899—	Pittsburgh	National	19	141	6	10	.375
1900—	Pittsburgh	National	32	213	14	12	.538
1901—	Pittsburgh	National	36	289	21	9	*.700
1902—	Pittsburgh	National	35	286	*28	6	.824
1903—	New York	American	40	325	21	15	.583
1904—	New York	American	●55	*454	*41	13	*.759
1905—	New York	American	41	302	19	13	.594
1906—	New York	American	*49	326	24	16	.600
1907—	New York	American	30	206	10	10	.500
1908—	New York	American	45	289	14	20	.412
1909—	New York-Boston	American	10	55	0	4	.000

			270	1957	129	91	.586
American League Totals			122	929	69	37	.651
National League Totals							
Major League Totals			392	2886	198	128	.607

FRED CLIFFORD CLARKE

Year	Club	League	G.	AB.	R.	H.	HR.	SB.	B.A.
1892—	Hastings	Neb. St.	(No Records Available)						
1893—	St. Joseph	W. Ass'n	(No Records Available)						
1893—	Montgomery	South.	32	120	21	35	0	1	.292
1894—	Savannah	South.	54	219	60	68	2	20	.311
1894—	Louisville	Nat.	76	316	55	87	7	24	.275
1895—	Louisville	Nat.	132	556	94	197	3	36	.354
1896—	Louisville	Nat.	131	517	93	169	9	32	.327
1897—	Louisville	Nat.	129	525	122	213	6	60	.406
1898—	Louisville	Nat.	147	598	115	190	2	*66	.318
1899—	Louisville	Nat.	147	601	124	209	5	47	.348
1900—	Pittsburgh	Nat.	103	398	85	112	3	18	.281
1901—	Pittsburgh	Nat.	128	525	118	166	6	22	.316
1902—	Pittsburgh	Nat.	114	461	104	148	2	34	.321
1903—	Pittsburgh	Nat.	102	427	88	150	5	21	.351
1904—	Pittsburgh	Nat.	70	278	51	85	0	11	.306
1905—	Pittsburgh	Nat.	137	525	95	157	2	24	.299
1906—	Pittsburgh	Nat.	110	417	69	129	1	18	.309
1907—	Pittsburgh	Nat.	144	501	97	145	2	37	.289
1908—	Pittsburgh	Nat.	151	551	83	146	2	24	.265
1909—	Pittsburgh	Nat.	152	550	97	158	3	31	.287
1910—	Pittsburgh	Nat.	118	429	57	113	2	12	.263
1911—	Pittsburgh	Nat.	101	392	73	127	5	10	.324
1913—	Pittsburgh	Nat.	9	13	0	1	0	0	.077
1914—	Pittsburgh	Nat.	2	2	0	0	0	0	.000
1915—	Pittsburgh	Nat.	1	2	0	1	0	0	.500
	Major League Totals		2204	8584	1620	2703	65	527	.315

WORLD SERIES RECORD

Year	Club	League	G.	AB.	R.	H.	HR.	SB.	B.A.
1903—	Pittsburgh	Nat.	8	34	3	9	0	1	.265
1909—	Pittsburgh	Nat.	7	19	7	4	2	3	.211
	World Series Totals		15	53	10	13	2	4	.245

JOHN GIBSON CLARKSON

Year	Club	League	G.	IP.	W.	L.	Pct.
1882—	Worcester	National	3	24	1	2	.333
1883—	Saginaw	Northwestern	23	....	....	....	....
1884—	Saginaw	Northwestern	42	357	31	8	.795
1884—	Chicago	National	14	109	10	3	.769
1885—	Chicago	National	*70	*622	*53	16	.768
1886—	Chicago	National	53	469	35	17	.673
1887—	Chicago	National	*60	*496	*38	21	.644
1888—	Boston	National	53	*485	33	20	.623
1889—	Boston	National	*72	*629	*49	19	*.721
1890—	Boston	National	44	383	26	18	.591
1891—	Boston	National	52	465	34	18	.654
1892—	Boston-Cleveland	National	42	386	24	16	.600
1893—	Cleveland	National	34	296	16	18	.471
1894—	Cleveland	National	22	150	8	8	.500
	Major League Totals		519	4514	327	176	.650

ROBERTO WALKER CLEMENTE

Year	Club	League	G.	AB.	R.	H.	HR.	RBI.	B.A.
1954—	Montreal	Int.	87	148	27	38	2	12	.257
1955—	Pittsburgh	Nat.	124	474	48	121	5	47	.255
1956—	Pittsburgh	Nat.	147	543	66	169	7	60	.311
1957—	Pittsburgh	Nat.	111	451	42	114	4	30	.253
1958—	Pittsburgh	Nat.	140	519	69	150	6	50	.289
1959—	Pittsburgh	Nat.	105	432	60	128	4	50	.296
1960—	Pittsburgh	Nat.	144	570	89	179	16	94	.314
1961—	Pittsburgh	Nat.	146	572	100	201	23	89	*.351
1962—	Pittsburgh	Nat.	144	538	95	168	10	74	.312
1963—	Pittsburgh	Nat.	152	600	77	192	17	76	.320
1964—	Pittsburgh	Nat.	155	622	95	●211	12	87	*.339
1965—	Pittsburgh	Nat.	152	589	91	194	10	65	*.329
1966—	Pittsburgh	Nat.	154	638	105	202	29	119	.317
1967—	Pittsburgh	Nat.	147	585	103	*209	23	110	*.357
1968—	Pittsburgh	Nat.	132	502	74	146	18	57	.291
1969—	Pittsburgh	Nat.	138	507	87	175	19	91	.345
1970—	Pittsburgh	Nat.	108	412	65	145	14	60	.352
1971—	Pittsburgh	Nat.	132	522	82	178	13	86	.341
1972—	Pittsburgh	Nat.	102	378	68	118	10	60	.312
	Major League Totals		2433	9454	1416	3000	240	1305	.317

CHAMPIONSHIP SERIES RECORD

Year	Club	League	G.	AB.	R.	H.	HR.	RBI.	B.A.
1970—	Pittsburgh	Nat.	3	14	1	3	0	1	.214
1971—	Pittsburgh	Nat.	4	18	2	6	0	4	.333
1972—	Pittsburgh	Nat.	5	17	1	4	1	2	.235
	Championship Series Totals		12	49	4	13	1	7	.265

WORLD SERIES RECORD

Year	Club	League	G.	AB.	R.	H.	HR.	RBI.	B.A.
1960—	Pittsburgh	Nat.	7	29	1	9	0	3	.310
1971—	Pittsburgh	Nat.	7	29	3	12	2	4	.414
	World Series Totals		14	58	4	21	2	7	.362

TYRUS RAYMOND (GEORGIA PEACH) COBB

Year	Club	League	G.	AB.	R.	H.	HR.	RBI.	B.A.
1904—Augusta	Sally	37	135	14	32	1	....	.237
1904—Ann.-Shef.	Tn.-Ala.	32	128	22	40	0	....	.313
1905—Augusta	Sally	103	411	60	134	1	....	*.326
1905—Detroit	Amer.	41	150	19	36	1	12	.240
1906—Detroit	Amer.	98	350	45	112	1	41	.320
1907—Detroit	Amer.	150	605	97	*212	5	*116	*.350
1908—Detroit	Amer.	150	581	88	*188	4	*101	*.324
1909—Detroit	Amer.	156	573	*116	*216	*9	*115	*.377
1910—Detroit	Amer.	140	509	*106	196	8	88	*.385
1911—Detroit	Amer.	146	591	*147	*248	8	*144	*.420
1912—Detroit	Amer.	140	553	119	*227	7	90	*.410
1913—Detroit	Amer.	122	428	70	167	4	65	*.390
1914—Detroit	Amer.	97	345	69	127	2	57	*.368
1915—Detroit	Amer.	156	563	*144	*208	3	95	*.369
1916—Detroit	Amer.	145	542	*113	201	5	67	.371
1917—Detroit	Amer.	152	*588	107	*225	6	108	*.383
1918—Detroit	Amer.	111	421	83	161	3	64	*.382
1919—Detroit	Amer.	124	497	92	●191	1	69	*.384
1920—Detroit	Amer.	112	428	86	143	2	63	.334
1921—Detroit	Amer.	128	507	124	197	12	101	.389
1922—Detroit	Amer.	137	526	99	211	4	99	.401
1923—Detroit	Amer.	145	556	103	189	6	88	.340
1924—Detroit	Amer.	●155	625	115	211	4	79	.338
1925—Detroit	Amer.	121	415	97	157	12	102	.378
1926—Detroit	Amer.	79	233	48	79	4	62	.339
1927—Philadelphia	Amer.	133	490	104	175	5	94	.357
1928—Philadelphia	Amer.	95	353	54	114	1	40	.323
Major League Totals		3033	11429	2245	4191	117	1960	.367

WORLD SERIES RECORD

Year	Club	League	G.	AB.	R.	H.	HR.	RBI.	B.A.
1907—Detroit	Amer.	5	20	1	4	0	0	.200
1908—Detroit	Amer.	5	19	3	7	0	4	.368
1909—Detroit	Amer.	7	26	3	6	0	6	.231
World Series Totals		17	65	7	17	0	10	.262

GORDON STANLEY (MICKEY) COCHRANE

Year	Club	League	G.	AB.	R.	H.	HR.	RBI.	B.A.
1923—Dover	East. Sh.	65	245	56	79	5	....	.322
1924—Portland	P. C.	99	300	43	100	7	56	.333
1925—Philadelphia	Amer.	134	420	69	139	6	55	.331
1926—Philadelphia	Amer.	120	370	50	101	8	47	.273
1927—Philadelphia	Amer.	126	432	80	146	12	80	.338
1928—Philadelphia	Amer.	131	468	92	137	10	57	.293
1929—Philadelphia	Amer.	135	514	113	170	7	95	.331
1930—Philadelphia	Amer.	130	487	110	174	10	85	.357
1931—Philadelphia	Amer.	122	459	87	160	17	89	.349
1932—Philadelphia	Amer.	139	518	118	152	23	112	.293
1933—Philadelphia	Amer.	130	429	104	138	15	60	.322
1934—Detroit	Amer.	129	437	74	140	2	76	.320
1935—Detroit	Amer.	115	411	93	131	5	47	.319
1936—Detroit	Amer.	44	126	24	34	2	17	.270
1937—Detroit	Amer.	27	98	27	30	2	12	.306
Major League Totals		1482	5169	1041	1652	119	832	.320

WORLD SERIES RECORD

Year	Club	League	G.	AB.	R.	H.	HR.	RBI.	B.A.
1929—Philadelphia	Amer.	5	15	5	6	0	0	.400
1930—Philadelphia	Amer.	6	18	5	4	2	4	.222
1931—Philadelphia	Amer.	7	25	2	4	0	1	.160
1934—Detroit	Amer.	7	28	2	6	0	1	.214
1935—Detroit	Amer.	6	24	3	7	0	1	.292
World Series Totals		31	110	17	27	2	7	.245

EDWARD TROWBRIDGE (COCKY) COLLINS

Year	Club	League	G.	AB.	R.	H.	HR.	RBI.	B.A.
1906—Philadelphia	Amer.	6	17	1	4	0	0	.235
1907—Philadelphia	Amer.	14	20	0	5	0	3	.250
1907—Newark	East.	4	16	6	7	0	....	.438
1908—Philadelphia	Amer.	102	330	39	90	1	37	.273
1909—Philadelphia	Amer.	153	571	104	198	3	69	.346
1910—Philadelphia	Amer.	153	581	81	188	3	80	.322
1911—Philadelphia	Amer.	132	493	92	180	3	71	.365
1912—Philadelphia	Amer.	153	543	*137	189	0	66	.348
1913—Philadelphia	Amer.	148	534	*125	184	3	75	.345
1914—Philadelphia	Amer.	152	526	*122	181	2	81	.344
1915—Chicago	Amer.	155	521	118	173	4	78	.332
1916—Chicago	Amer.	155	545	87	168	0	56	.308
1917—Chicago	Amer.	156	564	91	163	0	67	.289
1918—Chicago	Amer.	97	330	51	91	2	32	.276
1919—Chicago	Amer.	140	518	87	165	4	73	.319
1920—Chicago	Amer.	153	600	113	220	3	75	.369
1921—Chicago	Amer.	139	526	79	177	2	58	.337
1922—Chicago	Amer.	154	598	92	194	1	69	.324
1923—Chicago	Amer.	145	505	89	182	5	67	.360
1924—Chicago	Amer.	152	556	108	194	6	86	.349
1925—Chicago	Amer.	118	425	80	147	3	80	.346
1926—Chicago	Amer.	106	375	66	129	1	62	.344
1927—Philadelphia	Amer.	95	226	50	76	1	15	.338
1928—Philadelphia	Amer.	36	33	3	10	0	7	.303
1929—Philadelphia	Amer.	9	7	0	0	0	0	.000
1930—Philadelphia	Amer.	3	2	1	1	0	0	.500
Major League Totals		2826	9946	1816	3309	47	1307	.333

WORLD SERIES RECORD

Year	Club	League	G.	AB.	R.	H.	HR.	RBI.	B.A.
1910—Philadelphia	Amer.	5	21	5	9	0	3	.429
1911—Philadelphia	Amer.	6	21	4	6	0	0	.286
1913—Philadelphia	Amer.	5	19	5	8	0	3	.421
1914—Philadelphia	Amer.	4	14	0	3	0	1	.214
1917—Chicago	Amer.	6	22	4	9	0	2	.409
1919—Chicago	Amer.	8	31	2	7	0	1	.226
World Series Totals		34	128	20	42	0	10	.328

JAMES JOSEPH (JIMMY) COLLINS

Year	Club	League	G.	AB.	R.	H.	HR.	SB.	B.A.
1893—Buffalo	East.	76	297	49	85	2	10	.286
1894—Buffalo	East.	125	562	126	*198	8	18	.352
1895—Bos.-L'ville	Nat.	104	410	75	114	7	14	.278
1896—Boston	Nat.	83	303	52	91	1	10	.300
1897—Boston	Nat.	133	529	102	183	6	16	.346
1898—Boston	Nat.	152	600	106	202	*14	10	.337
1899—Boston	Nat.	151	597	98	164	4	16	.275
1900—Boston	Nat.	●142	*585	104	175	6	20	.299
1901—Boston	Amer.	138	563	109	185	5	18	.329
1902—Boston	Amer.	105	425	71	138	6	11	.325
1903—Boston	Amer.	130	541	87	160	5	22	.296
1904—Boston	Amer.	156	633	85	168	3	19	.265
1905—Boston	Amer.	131	508	66	140	4	18	.276
1906—Boston	Amer.	37	142	17	39	1	1	.275
1907—Bos.-Phila.	Amer.	141	523	51	146	0	8	.279
1908—Philadelphia	Amer.	115	433	34	94	0	5	.217
1909—Minneapolis	A. A.	153	556	61	152	2	13	.273
1910—Providence	East.	121	438	35	98	1	12	.224
1911—Providence	East.	8	23	3	4	0	0	.174
American League Totals		953	3768	520	1070	24	102	.284
National League Totals		765	3024	537	929	38	86	.307
Major League Totals		1718	6792	1057	1999	62	188	.294

WORLD SERIES RECORD

Year	Club	League	G.	AB.	R.	H.	HR.	SB.	B.A.
1903—Boston	Amer.	8	36	5	9	0	3	.250

EARLE BRYAN COMBS

Year	Club	League	G.	AB.	R.	H.	HR.	RBI.	B.A.
1922—Louisville	A.A.	130	485	86	167	4	55	.344
1923—Louisville	A.A.	166	634	127	*241	14	145	.380
1924—New York	Amer.	24	35	10	14	0	2	.400
1925—New York	Amer.	150	593	117	203	3	61	.342
1926—New York	Amer.	145	606	113	181	8	56	.299
1927—New York	Amer.	152	*648	137	*231	6	64	.356
1928—New York	Amer.	149	626	118	194	7	56	.310
1929—New York	Amer.	142	586	119	202	3	65	.345
1930—New York	Amer.	137	532	129	183	7	82	.344
1931—New York	Amer.	138	563	120	179	5	58	.318
1932—New York	Amer.	144	591	143	190	9	65	.321
1933—New York	Amer.	122	417	86	125	5	60	.300
1934—New York	Amer.	63	251	47	80	2	25	.319
1935—New York	Amer.	89	298	47	84	3	35	.282
Major League Totals		1455	5746	1186	1866	58	629	.325

WORLD SERIES RECORD

Year	Club	League	G.	AB.	R.	H.	HR.	RBI.	B.A.
1926—New York	Amer.	7	28	3	10	0	2	.357
1927—New York	Amer.	4	16	6	5	0	2	.313
1928—New York	Amer.	1	0	0	0	0	0	.000
1932—New York	Amer.	4	16	8	6	1	4	.375
World Series Totals		16	60	17	21	1	9	.350

CHARLES ALBERT (OLD ROMAN) COMISKEY

Year	Club	League	G.	AB.	R.	H.	HR.	SB.	B.A.
1877—Elgin	Ind.	....	....	....	....	....	....	....
1878—Dubuque	Ind.	21	....	....	....	....	....	.282
1879—Dubuque	N.W.	45	....	....	....	....	....	.235
1880—Dubuque	Ind.	....	....	....	....	....	....	....
1881—Dubuque	Ind.	....	....	....	....	....	....	....
1882—St. Louis	A.A.	78	327	58	80	1	....	.245
1883—St. Louis	A.A.	96	404	76	120	2	....	.297
1884—St. Louis	A.A.	108	461	86	111	2	....	.241
1885—St. Louis	A.A.	83	342	66	89	2	....	.260
1886—St. Louis	A.A.	131	577	94	150	3	47	.260
1887—St. Louis	A.A.	125	563	136	207	4	123	.368
1888—St. Louis	A.A.	137	576	101	156	5	77	.271
1889—St. Louis	A.A.	137	586	105	169	3	71	.288
1890—St. Louis	Players	88	375	53	93	0	35	.248
1891—St. Louis	A.A.	130	532	82	141	3	39	.265
1892—Cincinnati	Nat.	140	554	60	124	4	28	.224
1893—Cincinnati	Nat.	62	253	38	58	0	12	.229
1894—Cincinnati	Nat.	59	230	26	61	0	9	.265
1895—St. Paul	West.	17	67	15	23	....	3	.343
American Association Totals		1025	4368	804	1223	25	356	.280
National League Totals		261	1037	124	243	4	49	.234
Players League Totals		88	375	53	93	0	35	.248
Major League Totals		1374	5780	981	1559	29	440	.270

WORLD SERIES RECORD

Year Club	League	G.	AB.	R.	H.	HR.	SB.	B.A.
1885—St. Louis	A.A.	7	24	6	6	0	0	.250
1886—St. Louis	A.A.	6	23	1	6	0	0	.261
1887—St. Louis	A.A.	15	62	8	20	0	4	.323
1888—St. Louis	A.A.	10	41	6	11	0	5	.268
World Series Totals		38	150	21	43	0	9	.287

ROGER CONNOR

Year Club	League	G.	AB.	R.	H.	HR.	SB.	B.A.
1880—Troy	Nat.	83	340	53	113	3	....	.332
1881—Troy	Nat.	84	361	54	104	2	....	.288
1882—Troy	Nat.	79	339	63	111	4	....	.327
1883—New York	Nat.	96	401	80	145	1	....	.362
1884—New York	Nat.	112	462	93	146	4	....	.316
1885—New York	Nat.	110	455	102	★169	1	....	★.371
1886—New York	Nat.	118	485	105	172	7	17	.355
1887—New York	Nat.	127	546	113	209	17	43	.383
1888—New York	Nat.	134	481	98	140	14	27	.291
1889—New York	Nat.	131	496	117	157	13	21	.317
1890—New York	Players	123	484	134	180	14	23	.372
1891—New York	Nat.	129	477	110	140	7	32	.293
1892—Philadelphia	Nat.	153	558	122	159	11	20	.285
1893—New York	Nat.	●135	490	111	158	11	29	.322
1894—N.Y.-St. Louis	Nat.	121	462	93	145	8	15	.313
1895—St. Louis	Nat.	104	402	78	131	6	8	.326
1896—St. Louis	Nat.	126	485	68	137	8	14	.282
1897—St. Louis	Nat.	22	83	13	19	1	3	.229
1987—Fall River	N. Eng.	47	171	32	49	....	9	.287
1898—Waterbury	Conn.	95						.319
1899—Waterbury	Conn.	92	347	79	136	5	18	★.392
1900—Waterbury	Conn.	83	286	54	82	2	20	.287
1901—Water.-N. Hav.	Conn.	107	411	58	123	....	....	.299
1902—Springfield	Conn.	62	224	25	58	1	15	.259
1903—Springfield	Conn.	75	279	28	76	0	12	272
National League Totals		1864	7323	1473	2355	118	229	.322
Players League Totals		123	484	134	180	14	23	.372
Major League Totals		1987	7807	1607	2535	132	252	.325

WORLD SERIES RECORD

Year Club	League	G.	AB.	R.	H.	HR.	B.A.
1888—New York	National	7	23	7	6	0	.261
1889—New York	National	9	36	9	12	0	.333
World Series Totals		16	59	16	18	0	.305

STANLEY COVELESKI

Year Club	League	G.	IP.	W.	L.	Pct.	ERA.
1908—Shamokin	Atlantic	12	....	6	2	.750	......
1909—Lancaster	Tri-State	43	272	★23	11	.676	......
1910—Lancaster	Tri-State	30		15	8	.652	......
1911—Lancaster	Tri-State	36	272	15	●19	.441	......
1912—Atlantic City	Tri-State	39		20	13	.606	......
1912—Philadelphia	American	5	21	2	1	.667	......
1913—Spokane	N. W.	48	316	17	★20	.459	......
1914—Spokane	N. W.	43	314	20	15	.571	......
1915—Portland	P. C.	●64	293	17	17	.500	2.67
1916—Cleveland	American	45	232	15	12	.556	3.41
1917—Cleveland	American	45	297	19	14	.576	1.81
1918—Cleveland	American	38	311	22	13	.629	1.82
1919—Cleveland	American	43	286	24	12	.667	2.52
1920—Cleveland	American	41	315	24	14	.632	2.49
1921—Cleveland	American	43	316	23	13	.639	3.36
1922—Cleveland	American	35	277	17	14	.548	3.31
1923—Cleveland	American	33	228	13	14	.481	★2.76
1924—Cleveland	American	37	240	15	16	.484	4.05
1925—Washington	American	32	241	20	5	★.800	★2.84
1926—Washington	American	36	245	14	11	.560	3.12
1927—Washington	American	5	14	2	1	.667	3.21
1928—New York	American	12	58	5	1	.833	5.74
Major League Totals		450	3081	215	141	.604	2.88

WORLD SERIES RECORD

Year Club	League	G.	IP.	W.	L.	Pct.	ERA.
1920—Cleveland	Amer.	3	27	3	0	1.000	0.67
1925—Washington	Amer.	2	14⅓	0	2	.000	3.77
World Series Totals		5	41⅓	3	2	.600	1.74

SAMUEL EARL (WAHOO SAM) CRAWFORD

Year Club	League	G.	AB.	R.	H.	HR.	SB.	B.A.
1899—Chatham	Canadian	43	173	34	64	0	7	.370
1899—Col.-Gr. Rapids	Western	60	261	46	87	5	3	.333
1899—Cincinnati	Nat.	31	127	25	39	0	3	.307
1900—Cincinnati	Nat.	96	385	67	104	6	15	.270
1901—Cincinnati	Nat.	124	523	89	175	★16	12	.335
1902—Cincinnati	Nat.	●140	555	94	185	3	15	.333
1903—Detroit	Amer.	137	545	93	181	4	23	.332
1904—Detroit	Amer.	150	571	46	141	2	20	.247
1905—Detroit	Amer.	154	575	73	171	6	22	.297
1906—Detroit	Amer.	145	563	65	166	2	24	.295
1907—Detroit	Amer.	144	582	★102	188	4	18	.323
1908—Detroit	Amer.	152	★591	102	184	★7	15	.311
1909—Detroit	Amer.	156	589	83	185	6	30	.314
1910—Detroit	Amer.	154	588	83	170	5	20	.289

Year Club	League	G.	AB.	R.	H.	HR.	SB.	B.A.
1911—Detroit	Amer.	146	574	109	217	7	37	.378
1912—Detroit	Amer.	149	581	81	189	4	41	.325
1913—Detroit	Amer.	153	★610	78	193	9	13	.316
1914—Detroit	Amer.	157	582	74	183	8	25	.314
1915—Detroit	Amer.	156	612	81	183	4	24	.299
1916—Detroit	Amer.	100	322	41	92	0	10	.286
1917—Detroit	Amer.	61	104	6	18	2	0	.173
1918—Los Angeles	P.C.	96	356	38	104	1	8	.292
1919—Los Angeles	P.C.	173	664	103	★239	14	14	.360
1920—Los Angeles	P.C.	187	719	99	239	12	3	.332
1921—Los Angeles	P.C.	175	626	92	199	9	10	.318
American League Totals		2114	7989	1117	2461	70	322	.308
National League Totals		391	1590	275	503	25	45	.316
Major League Totals		2505	9579	1392	2964	95	367	.309

WORLD SERIES RECORD

Year Club	League	G.	AB.	R.	H.	HR.	SB.	B.A.
1907—Detroit	Amer.	5	21	1	5	0	0	.238
1908—Detroit	Amer.	5	21	2	5	0	0	.238
1909—Detroit	Amer.	7	28	4	7	1	1	.250
World Series Totals		17	70	7	17	1	1	.243

JOSEPH EDWARD CRONIN

Year Club	League	G.	AB.	R.	H.	HR.	RBI.	B.A.
1925—Johnstown	Mid.-Atl.	99	352	64	110	3	....	.313
1926—Pittsburgh	Nat.	38	83	9	22	0	11	.265
1926—New Haven	East.	66	244	61	78	2	....	.320
1927—Pittsburgh	Nat.	12	22	2	5	0	3	.227
1928—Kansas City	A.A.	74	241	34	59	2	32	.245
1928—Washington	Amer.	63	227	23	55	0	25	.242
1929—Washington	Amer.	145	494	72	139	8	60	.281
1930—Washington	Amer.	●154	587	127	203	13	126	.346
1931—Washington	Amer.	★156	611	103	187	12	126	.306
1932—Washington	Amer.	143	557	95	177	6	116	.318
1933—Washington	Amer.	152	602	89	186	5	118	.309
1934—Washington	Amer.	127	504	68	143	7	101	.284
1935—Boston	Amer.	144	556	70	164	9	95	.295
1936—Boston	Amer.	81	295	36	83	2	43	.281
1937—Boston	Amer.	148	570	102	175	18	110	.307
1938—Boston	Amer.	143	530	98	172	17	94	.325
1939—Boston	Amer.	143	520	97	160	19	107	.308
1940—Boston	Amer.	149	548	104	156	24	111	.285
1941—Boston	Amer.	143	518	98	161	16	95	.311
1942—Boston	Amer.	45	79	7	24	4	24	.304
1943—Boston	Amer.	59	77	8	24	5	29	.312
1944—Boston	Amer.	76	191	24	46	5	28	.241
1945—Boston	Amer.	3	8	1	3	0	1	.375
American League Totals		2074	7474	1222	2258	170	1409	.302
National League Totals		50	105	11	27	0	14	.257
Major League Totals		2124	7579	1233	2285	170	1423	.301

WORLD SERIES RECORD

Year Club	League	G.	AB.	R.	H.	HR.	RBI.	B.A.
1933—Washington	Amer.	5	22	1	7	0	2	.318

HAZEN SHIRLEY (KIKI) CUYLER

Year Club	League	G.	AB.	R.	H.	HR.	RBI.	B.A.
1920—Bay City	Mich.-Ont.	69	240	24	62	1	26	.258
1921—Bay City	Mich.-Ont.	116	417	79	132	8	82	.317
1921—Pittsburgh	Nat.	1	3	0	0	0	0	.000
1922—Charleston	Sally	131	489	84	151	12	46	.309
1922—Pittsburgh	Nat.	1	0	0	0	0	0	.000
1923—Nashville	Southern	149	574	114	195	9	108	.340
1923—Pittsburgh	Nat.	11	40	4	10	0	2	.250
1924—Pittsburgh	Nat.	117	466	94	165	9	85	.354
1925—Pittsburgh	Nat.	●153	617	★144	220	18	102	.357
1926—Pittsburgh	Nat.	★157	614	★113	197	8	92	.321
1927—Pittsburgh	Nat.	85	285	60	88	3	31	.309
1928—Chicago	Nat.	133	499	92	142	17	79	.285
1929—Chicago	Nat.	139	509	111	183	15	102	.360
1930—Chicago	Nat.	●156	642	155	228	13	134	.355
1931—Chicago	Nat.	154	613	110	202	9	88	.330
1932—Chicago	Nat.	110	446	58	130	10	77	.291
1933—Chicago	Nat.	70	262	37	83	5	35	.317
1934—Chicago	Nat.	142	559	80	189	6	69	.338
1935—Chi.-Cinc.	Nat.	107	380	58	98	6	40	.258
1936—Cincinnati	Nat.	144	567	96	185	7	74	.326
1937—Cincinnati	Nat.	117	406	48	110	0	32	.271
1938—Brooklyn	Nat.	82	253	45	69	2	23	.273
1939—Chattanooga	Southern	58	159	19	43	0	18	.270
1940—Chattanooga	Southern	1	1	1	1	0	0	1.000
Major League Totals		1879	7161	1305	2299	128	1065	.321

WORLD SERIES RECORD

Year Club	League	G.	AB.	R.	H.	HR.	RBI.	B.A.
1925—Pittsburgh	Nat.	7	26	3	7	1	6	.269
1929—Chicago	Nat.	5	20	4	6	0	4	.300
1932—Chicago	Nat.	4	18	2	5	1	2	.278
World Series Totals		16	64	9	18	2	12	.281

GEORGE STACEY DAVIS

Year Club	League	G.	AB.	R.	H.	HR.	RBI.	B.A.
1889—Albany	(Independent club–no records available)							
1890—Cleveland.........	Nat.	134	526	...	139	6	22	.264
1891—Cleveland.........	Nat.	136	571	115	167	3	43	.292
1892—Cleveland.........	Nat.	143	595	96	151	4	36	.254
1893—New York.........	Nat.	133	533	112	199	11	54	.373
1894—New York.........	Nat.	124	492	124	170	9	37	.346
1895—New York.........	Nat.	110	433	106	143	5	45	.330
1896—New York.........	Nat.	124	495	98	155	3	49	.313
1897—New York.........	Nat.	131	525	114	188	9	64	.358
1898—New York........	Nat.	121	484	80	148	1	22	.306
1899—New York........	Nat.	111	413	69	144	1	38	.349
1900—New York........	Nat.	113	425	70	138	3	32	.325
1901—New York.........	Nat.	130	495	69	153	7	26	.309
1902—Chicago...........	Amer.	132	480	77	143	3	33	.298
1903—New York.........	Nat.	4	15	2	4	0	0	.267
1904—Chicago...........	Amer.	152	558	74	143	1	32	.256
1905—Chicago...........	Amer.	151	550	74	153	1	31	.278
1906—Chicago...........	Amer.	133	484	63	134	0	27	.277
1907—Chicago...........	Amer.	132	466	59	111	1	15	.238
1908—Chicago...........	Amer.	128	419	41	91	0	22	.217
1909—Chicago...........	Amer.	28	68	5	9	0	4	.132
1910—Des Moines.......	West.	32	99	14	19	0	4	.192
American League Totals.........		856	3025	393	784	6	164	.259
National League Totals..........		1514	6002	985	1899	62	468	.316
Major League Totals.............		2370	9027	1378	2683	68	632	.297

WORLD SERIES RECORD

Year Club	League	G.	AB.	R.	H.	HR.	SB.	B.A.
1906—Chicago...........	Amer.	3	13	4	4	0	1	.308

JAY HANNA (DIZZY) DEAN

Year Club	League	G.	IP.	W.	L.	Pct.	ERA.
1930—St. Joseph......................	Western	32	217	17	8	.680	3.69
1930—Houston.........................	Texas	14	85	8	2	.800	2.86
1930—St. Louis.........................	National	1	9	1	0	1.000	1.00
1931—Houston.........................	Texas	41	304	*26	10	.722	*1.57
1932—St. Louis.........................	National	46	*286	18	15	.545	3.30
1933—St. Louis.........................	National	*48	293	20	18	.526	3.04
1934—St. Louis.........................	National	50	312	*30	7	*.811	2.65
1935—St. Louis.........................	National	50	*324	*28	12	.700	3.11
1936—St. Louis.........................	National	•51	*315	24	13	.649	3.17
1937—St. Louis.........................	National	27	197	13	10	.565	2.70
1938—Chicago.........................	National	13	75	7	1	.875	1.80
1939—Chicago.........................	National	19	96	6	4	.600	3.38
1940—Chicago.........................	National	10	54	3	3	.500	5.17
1940—Tulsa.............................	Texas	21	142	8	8	.500	3.17
1941—Chicago.........................	National	1	1	0	0	.000	18.00
1947—St. Louis.........................	American	1	4	0	0	.000	0.00
American League Totals......................		1	4	0	0	.000	0.00
National League Totals.......................		316	1962	150	83	.644	3.04
Major League Totals..............................		317	1966	150	83	.644	3.04

WORLD SERIES RECORD

Year Club	League	G.	IP.	W.	L.	Pct.	ERA.
1934—St. Louis.........................	National	3	26	2	1	.667	1.73
1938—Chicago.........................	National	2	8⅓	0	1	.000	6.48
World Series Totals..............................		5	34⅓	2	2	.500	2.88

EDWARD JAMES (BIG ED) DELAHANTY

Year Club	League	G.	AB.	R.	H.	HR.	SB.	B.A.
1887—Mansfield..............	Ohio St.	73	366	90	130	5	.....	.355
1888—Wheeling..............	Tri. St.	21	98	20	40	5	15	.408
1888—Philadelphia.........	Nat.	74	290	40	66	1	38	.228
1889—Philadelphia.........	Nat.	54	246	37	72	0	19	.293
1890—Cleveland..............	Play.	115	513	106	152	3	24	.296
1891—Philadelphia.........	Nat.	128	545	92	136	5	27	.250
1892—Philadelphia.........	Nat.	120	470	78	147	6	35	.313
1893—Philadelphia.........	Nat.	132	*588	145	218	*19	36	.371
1894—Philadelphia.........	Nat.	114	497	149	199	4	29	.400
1895—Philadelphia.........	Nat.	116	481	148	192	11	46	.399
1896—Philadelphia.........	Nat.	122	505	131	199	•13	37	.394
1897—Philadelphia.........	Nat.	129	530	110	200	4	28	.377
1898—Philadelphia.........	Nat.	142	547	114	183	3	62	.335
1899—Philadelphia.........	Nat.	145	573	133	*234	9	38	*.408
1900—Philadelphia.........	Nat.	130	542	82	173	1	14	.319
1901—Philadelphia.........	Nat.	138	538	106	192	8	28	.357
1902—Washington...........	Amer.	123	474	103	178	10	14	*.376
1903—Washington...........	Amer.	43	154	22	52	1	3	.338
American League Totals............		166	628	125	230	11	17	.366
National League Totals............		1544	6352	1365	2211	84	437	.348
Players League Totals................		115	513	106	152	3	24	.296
Major League Totals....................		1825	7493	1596	2593	98	478	.346

WILLIAM MALCOLM DICKEY

Year Club	League	G.	AB.	R.	H.	HR.	RBI.	B.A.
1925—Little Rock...........	South.	3	10	1	3	0	.....	.300
1926—Muskogee.............	W.A.	61	212	27	60	7	.....	.283
1926—Little Rock...........	South.	21	46	6	18	0	8	.391
1927—Jackson..................	Cot: St.	101	364	46	108	3	.....	.297
1928—Little Rock...........	South.	60	203	22	61	4	32	.300
1928—Buffalo..................	Int.	3	8	0	1	0	0	.125
1928—New York.............	Amer.	10	15	1	3	0	2	.200
1929—New York.............	Amer.	130	447	60	145	10	65	.324
1930—New York.............	Amer.	109	366	55	124	5	65	.339
1931—New York.............	Amer.	130	477	65	156	6	78	.327
1932—New York.............	Amer.	108	423	66	131	15	84	.310
1933—New York.............	Amer.	130	478	58	152	14	97	.318
1934—New York.............	Amer.	104	395	56	127	12	72	.322
1935—New York.............	Amer.	120	448	54	125	14	81	.279
1936—New York.............	Amer.	112	423	99	153	22	107	.362
1937—New York.............	Amer.	140	530	87	176	29	133	.332
1938—New York.............	Amer.	132	454	84	142	27	115	.313
1939—New York.............	Amer.	128	480	98	145	24	105	.302
1940—New York.............	Amer.	106	372	45	92	9	54	.247
1941—New York.............	Amer.	109	348	35	99	7	71	.284
1942—New York.............	Amer.	82	268	28	79	2	37	.295
1943—New York.............	Amer.	85	242	29	85	4	33	.351
1944-45—New York.........	Amer.	(In Military Service)						
1946—New York.............	Amer.	54	134	10	35	2	10	.261
1947—Little Rock...........	South.	8	12	2	4	1	2	.333
Major League Totals....................		1789	6300	930	1969	202	1209	.313

WORLD SERIES RECORD

Year Club	League	G.	AB.	R.	H.	HR.	RBI.	B.A.
1932—New York.............	Amer.	4	16	2	7	0	4	.438
1936—New York.............	Amer.	6	25	5	3	1	5	.120
1937—New York.............	Amer.	5	19	3	4	0	3	.211
1938—New York.............	Amer.	4	15	2	6	1	2	.400
1939—New York.............	Amer.	4	15	2	4	2	5	.267
1941—New York.............	Amer.	5	18	3	3	0	1	.167
1942—New York.............	Amer.	5	19	1	5	0	0	.263
1943—New York.............	Amer.	5	18	1	5	1	4	278
World Series Totals......................		38	145	19	37	5	24	.255

JOSEPH PAUL (YANKEE CLIPPER) DI MAGGIO

Year Club	League	G.	AB.	R.	H.	HR.	RBI.	B.A.
1932—San Francisco......	P. C.	3	9	2	2	0	2	.222
1933—San Francisco......	P. C.	187	762	129	259	28	*169	.340
1934—San Francisco......	P. C.	101	375	58	128	12	69	.341
1935—San Francisco......	P. C.	172	679	*173	270	34	*154	.398
1936—New York.............	Amer.	138	637	132	206	29	125	.323
1937—New York.............	Amer.	151	621	*151	215	*46	167	.346
1938—New York.............	Amer.	145	599	129	194	32	140	.324
1939—New York.............	Amer.	120	462	108	176	30	126	*.381
1940—New York.............	Amer.	132	508	93	179	31	133	*.352
1941—New York.............	Amer.	139	541	122	193	30	*125	.357
1942—New York.............	Amer.	154	610	123	186	21	114	.305
1943-44-45—New York		(In Military Service)						
1946—New York.............	Amer.	132	503	81	146	25	95	.290
1947—New York.............	Amer.	141	534	97	168	20	97	.315
1948—New York.............	Amer.	153	594	110	190	*39	*155	.320
1949—New York.............	Amer.	76	272	58	94	14	67	.346
1950—New York.............	Amer.	139	525	114	158	32	122	.301
1951—New York.............	Amer.	116	415	72	109	12	71	.263
Major League Totals....................		1736	6821	1390	2214	361	1537	.325

WORLD SERIES RECORD

Year Club	League	G.	AB.	R.	H.	HR.	RBI.	B.A.
1936—New York.............	Amer.	6	26	3	9	0	3	.346
1937—New York.............	Amer.	5	22	2	6	1	4	.273
1938—New York.............	Amer.	4	15	4	4	1	2	.267
1939—New York.............	Amer.	4	16	3	5	1	3	.313
1941—New York.............	Amer.	5	19	1	5	0	1	.263
1942—New York.............	Amer.	5	21	3	7	0	3	.333
1947—New York.............	Amer.	7	26	4	6	2	5	.231
1949—New York.............	Amer.	5	18	2	2	1	2	.111
1950—New York.............	Amer.	4	13	2	4	1	2	.308
1951—New York.............	Amer.	6	23	3	6	1	5	.261
World Series Totals......................		51	199	27	54	8	30	.271

LAWRENCE EUGENE DOBY

Year Club	League	G.	AB.	R.	H.	HR.	RBI.	B.A.
1947__Cleveland.........	Amer.	29	32	3	5	0	2	.156
1948—Cleveland.........	Amer.	121	439	83	132	14	66	.301
1949- Cleveland.........	Amer.	147	547	106	153	24	85	.280
1950—Cleveland.........	Amer.	142	503	110	164	25	102	.326
1951—Cleveland.........	Amer.	134	447	84	132	20	69	.295
1952—Cleveland.........	Amer.	140	519	*104	143	*32	104	.276
1953—Cleveland.........	Amer.	149	513	92	135	29	102	.263
1954—Cleveland.........	Amer.	153	577	94	157	*32	*126	.272
1955—Cleveland.........	Amer.	131	491	91	143	26	75	.291
1956—Chicago............	Amer.	140	504	89	135	24	102	.268
1957—Chicago............	Amer.	119	416	57	120	14	79	.288
1958—Cleveland.........	Amer.	89	247	41	70	13	45	.283
1959—Detroit-Chi.......	Amer.	39	113	6	26	0	13	.230
1960—San Diego.........	P.C.	9	27	2	6	0	3	.222
1962—Chunichi..........	Cent.	72	240	27	54	10	35	.225
Major League Totals............		1533	5348	960	1515	253	970	.283

Year	Club	League	G.	AB.	R.	H.	HR.	RBI.	B.A.
1948—Cleveland		Amer.	6	22	7	7	1	2	.318
1954—Cleveland		Amer.	4	16	0	2	0	0	.125
World Series Totals			10	38	1	9	11	2	.237

ROBERT PERSHING (BOBBY) DOERR

Year	Club	League	G.	AB.	R.	H.	HR.	RBI.	B.A.
1934—Hollywood	P.C.	67	201	12	52	0	11	.259
1935—Hollywood	P.C.	172	647	87	205	4	74	.317
1936—San Diego	P.C.	175	695	100	•238	2	77	.342
1937—Boston	Amer.	55	147	22	33	2	14	.224
1938—Boston	Amer.	145	509	70	147	5	80	.289
1939—Boston	Amer.	127	525	75	167	12	73	.318
1940—Boston	Amer.	151	595	87	173	22	105	.291
1941—Boston	Amer.	132	500	74	141	16	93	.282
1942—Boston	Amer.	144	545	71	158	15	102	.290
1943—Boston	Amer.	•155	604	78	163	16	75	.270
1944—Boston	Amer.	125	468	95	152	15	81	.325
1945—Boston	Amer.			(In Military Service)				
1946—Boston	Amer.	151	583	95	158	18	116	.271
1947—Boston	Amer.	146	561	79	145	17	95	.258
1948—Boston	Amer.	140	527	94	150	27	111	.285
1949—Boston	Amer.	139	541	91	167	18	109	.309
1950—Boston	Amer.	149	586	103	172	27	120	.294
1951—Boston	Amer.	106	402	60	116	13	73	.289
Major League Totals		1865	7093	1094	2042	223	1247	.288

WORLD SERIES RECORD

Year	Club	League	G.	AB.	R.	H.	HR.	RBI.	B.A.
1946—Boston		Amer.	6	22	1	9	1	3	.409

DONALD SCOTT (BIG D) DRYSDALE

Year	Club	League	G.	IP.	W.	L.	Pct.	ERA.
1954—Bakersfield	Calif.	15	112	8	5	.615	3.45
1955—Montreal	Int.	28	173	11	11	.500	3.33
1956—Brooklyn	Nat.	25	99	5	5	.500	2.64
1957—Brooklyn	Nat.	34	221	17	9	.654	2.69
1958—Los Angeles	Nat.	44	212	12	13	.480	4.16
1959—Los Angeles	Nat.	44	271	17	13	.567	3.45
1960—Los Angeles	Nat.	41	269	15	14	.517	2.84
1961—Los Angeles	Nat.	40	244	13	10	.565	3.69
1962—Los Angeles	Nat.	43	*314	*25	9	.735	2.84
1963—Los Angeles	Nat.	42	315	19	17	.528	2.63
1964—Los Angeles	Nat.	40	*321	18	16	.529	2.19
1965—Los Angeles	Nat.	44	308	23	12	.657	2.78
1966—Los Angeles	Nat.	40	274	13	16	.448	3.42
1967—Los Angeles	Nat.	38	282	13	16	.448	2.74
1968—Los Angeles	Nat.	31	239	14	12	.538	2.15
1969—Los Angeles	Nat.	12	63	5	4	.556	4.43
Major League Totals		518	3432	209	166	.557	2.95

WORLD SERIES RECORD

Year	Club	League	G.	IP.	W.	L.	Pct.	ERA.
1956—Brooklyn	Nat.	1	2	0	0	.000	9.00
1959—Los Angeles	Nat.	1	7	1	0	1.000	1.29
1963—Los Angeles	Nat.	1	9	1	0	1.000	0.00
1965—Los Angeles	Nat.	2	11⅔	1	1	.500	3.86
1966—Los Angeles	Nat.	2	10	0	2	.000	4.50
World Series Totals		7	39⅔	3	3	.500	2.95

HUGH DUFFY

Year	Club	League	G.	AB.	R.	H.	HR.	RBI.	B.A.
1886—Hartford	East.	7	18	3	5	0	1	.278
1887—Springfield	East.	17	80	20	28	1	17	.350
1887—Salem-Lowell	N. Eng.	78	325	103	139	16	16	.428
1888—Chicago	Nat.	71	298	60	84	7	13	.282
1889—Chicago	Nat.	•136	*584	144	182	12	52	.312
1890—Chicago	Play.	137	591	*161	194	7	79	.328
1891—Boston	A. A.	121	511	124	174	10	83	.341
1892—Boston	Nat.	146	609	125	184	5	61	.302
1893—Boston	Nat.	131	537	*149	203	6	50	*.378
1894—Boston	Nat.	124	539	160	*236	•18	49	*.438
1895—Boston	Nat.	131	540	113	190	8	42	.352
1896—Boston	Nat.	131	533	93	161	5	45	.302
1897—Boston	Nat.	134	554	131	189	8	45	.341
1898—Boston	Nat.	151	561	97	179	8	32	.319
1899—Boston	Nat.	147	588	102	164	5	18	.279
1900—Boston	Nat.	50	181	28	54	2	12	.298
1901—Milwaukee	Amer.	78	286	41	88	2	13	.308
1902—Milwaukee	West.	140	505	79	147	2	37	.291
1903—Milwaukee	West.	71	257	45	77	0	30	.300
1904—Philadelphia	Nat.	18	46	10	13	0	3	.283
1905—Philadelphia	Nat.	15	40	7	12	0	0	.300
1906—Philadelphia	Nat.	1	1	0	0	0	0	.000
1907—Providence	East.	35	73	9	22	0	5	.301
1908—Providence	East.	37	57	10	19	1	5	.333
American Association Totals		121	511	124	174	10	83	.340
American League Totals		78	286	41	88	2	13	.308
National League Totals		1386	5611	1219	1851	84	422	.330
Players League Totals		137	591	161	194	7	79	.328
Major League Totals		1722	6999	1545	2307	103	597	.330

LEO ERNEST (THE LIP) DUROCHER

RECORD AS MANAGER

Year	Club	League	Position	W.	L.
1939 — Brooklyn	National	Third	84	69
1940 — Brooklyn	National	Second	88	65
1941 — Brooklyn	National	First	100	54
1942 — Brooklyn	National	Second	104	50
1943 — Brooklyn	National	Third	81	72
1944 — Brooklyn	National	Seventh	63	91
1945 — Brooklyn	National	Third	87	67
1946 — Brooklyn	National	Second	96	60
1947 — Brooklyn	National	(Suspended from baseball)		
1948 — Brooklyn	National	Fifth	36	37
1948 — New York	National	Fifth	41	38
1949 — New York	National	Fifth	73	81
1950 — New York	National	Third	86	68
1951 — New York	National	First	98	59
1952 — New York	National	Second	92	62
1953 — New York	National	Fifth	70	84
1954 — New York	National	First	97	57
1955 — New York	National	Third	80	74
1966 — Chicago	National	Tenth	59	103
1967 — Chicago	National	Third	87	74
1968 — Chicago	National	Third	84	78
1969 — Chicago	National	Second (E)	92	70
1970 — Chicago	National	Second (E)	84	78
1971 — Chicago	National	Third (E)	83	79
1972 — Houston	National	Second (W)	16	15
1973 — Houston	National	Fourth (W)	82	80
Major League Totals			2008	1709

WORLD SERIES RECORD

Year	Club	League	W.	L.
1941 — Brooklyn	National	1	4
1951 — New York	National	2	4
1954 — New York	National	4	0

JOHN JOSEPH (CRAB) EVERS

Year	Club	League	G.	AB.	R.	H.	HR.	RBI.	B.A.
1902—Troy	N.Y.S.	84	333	50	95	10		.285
1902—Chicago	Nat.	25	89	7	20	0		.225
1903—Chicago	Nat.	123	464	70	136	0		.293
1904—Chicago	Nat.	152	532	49	141	0		.265
1905—Chicago	Nat.	99	340	44	94	1		.276
1906—Chicago	Nat.	154	533	65	136	1		.255
1907—Chicago	Nat.	151	508	66	127	2	55	.250
1908—Chicago	Nat.	123	416	83	125	0	35	.300
1909—Chicago	Nat.	126	463	88	122	1	20	.263
1910—Chicago	Nat.	125	433	87	114	0	25	.263
1911—Chicago	Nat.	44	155	29	35	0	9	.226
1912—Chicago	Nat.	143	478	73	163	1	56	.341
1913—Chicago	Nat.	136	446	81	127	3	48	.285
1914—Boston	Nat.	139	491	81	137	1	33	.279
1915—Boston	Nat.	83	278	38	73	1	23	.263
1916—Boston	Nat.	71	241	33	52	0	15	.216
1917—Bos.-Phila.	Nat.	80	266	25	57	1	11	.214
1922—Chicago	Amer.	1	3	0	0	0	1	.000
1929—Boston	Nat.	1	0	0	0	0	0	.000
Major League Totals		1776	6136	919	1659	12		.270

WORLD SERIES RECORD

Year	Club	League	G.	AB.	R.	H.	HR.	RBI.	B.A.
1906—Chicago	Nat.	6	20	2	3	0	1	.150
1907—Chicago	Nat.	5	20	2	7	0	1	.350
1908—Chicago	Nat.	5	20	5	7	0	2	.350
1914—Boston	Nat.	4	16	2	7	0	2	.438
World Series Totals		20	76	11	24	0	6	.316

WILLIAM BUCKINGHAM (BUCK) EWING

Year	Club	League	G.	AB.	R.	H.	HR.	RBI.	B.A.
1878—Mohawk Browns	Ind.							
1879—Mohawk Browns	Ind.							
1880—Cin. Buckeyes	Ind.							
1880—Rochester	N. Assn.	13						.148
1880—Troy	Nat.	13	46	1	8	0		.174
1881—Troy	Nat	65	267	38	65	0		.243
1882—Troy	Nat.	72	318	65	87	2		.274
1883—New York	Nat.	85	369	88	113	*10		.306
1884—New York	Nat.	88	374	87	104	3		.278
1885—New York	Nat.	81	342	81	104	6		.304
1886—New York	Nat.	70	275	59	85	4	18	.309
1887—New York	Nat.	76	348	81	127	6	36	.365
1888—New York	Nat.	103	415	83	127	5	53	.306
1889—New York	Nat.	96	407	91	133	4	34	.327
1890—New York	Play.	83	349	99	122	7	39	.350
1891—New York	Nat.	14	49	8	17	0	3	.347
1892—New York	Nat.	97	394	58	126	8	53	.320
1893—Cleveland	Nat.	114	477	116	177	6	53	.371
1894—Cleveland	Nat.	53	212	32	54	2	19	.255
1895—Cincinnati	Nat.	103	439	90	139	3	34	.317
1896—Cincinnati	Nat.	67	266	41	75	1	47	.282
1897—Cincinnati	Nat.	1	0	0	0	0	0	.000
National League Totals		1198	4999	1019	1541	59		.308
Players League Totals		83	349	99	122	7	39	.350
Major League Totals		1281	5348	1118	1663	66		.311

WORLD SERIES RECORD

Year	Club	League	G.	AB.	R.	H.	HR.	RBI.	B.A.
1888—New York	Nat.	7	26	5	9	1	5	.346
1889—New York	Nat.	8	36	5	9	0	2	.250
World Series Totals		15	62	10	18	1	7	.290

URBAN CLARENCE (RED) FABER

Year	Club	League	G.	IP.	W.	L.	Pct.	ERA.
1909—Dubuque	I.I.I.	15	114	7	6	.538	......
1910—Dubuque	I.I.I.	44	334	18	19	.486	......
1911—Minneapolis	Amer. Assn.	2	6	0	0	.000	......
1911—Pueblo	Western	29	180	12	8	.600	......
1912—Des Moines	Western	43	304	21	14	.600	......
1913—Des Moines	Western	50	*373	20	17	.541	2.49
1914—Chicago	American	40	181	10	9	.526	2.69
1915—Chicago	American	●50	300	24	14	.632	2.55
1916—Chicago	American	35	205	17	9	.654	2.02
1917—Chicago	American	41	248	16	13	.552	1.92
1918—Chicago	American	11	81	4	1	.800	1.22
1919—Chicago	American	25	162	11	9	.550	3.83
1920—Chicago	American	40	319	23	13	.639	2.99
1921—Chicago	American	43	331	25	15	.625	*2.47
1922—Chicago	American	43	*353	21	17	.553	*2.80
1923—Chicago	American	32	234	14	11	.560	3.41
1924—Chicago	American	21	161	9	11	.450	3.86
1925—Chicago	American	34	238	12	11	.522	3.78
1926—Chicago	American	27	185	15	8	.652	3.55
1927—Chicago	American	18	111	4	7	.364	4.54
1928—Chicago	American	27	201	13	9	.591	3.76
1929—Chicago	American	31	234	13	13	.500	3.88
1930—Chicago	American	29	169	8	13	.381	4.21
1931—Chicago	American	44	184	10	14	.417	3.82
1932—Chicago	American	42	106	2	11	.154	3.74
1933—Chicago	American	36	86	3	4	.429	3.45
Major League Totals		669	4089	254	212	.545	3.15

WORLD SERIES RECORD

Year	Club	League	G.	IP.	W.	L.	Pct.	ERA.
1917—Chicago	American	4	27	3	1	.750	2.33

ROBERT WILLIAM ANDREW FELLER

Year	Club	League	G.	IP.	W.	L.	Pct.	ERA.
1936—Cleveland	American	14	62	5	3	.625	3.34
1937—Cleveland	American	26	149	9	7	.563	3.38
1938—Cleveland	American	39	278	17	11	.607	4.08
1939—Cleveland	American	39	*297	*24	9	.727	2.85
1940—Cleveland	American	*43	*320	*27	11	.711	*2.62
1941—Cleveland	American	*44	*343	*25	13	.658	3.15
1942-43-44—Cleveland	American		(In Military Service)				
1945—Cleveland	American	9	72	5	3	.625	2.50
1946—Cleveland	American	*48	*371	●26	15	.634	2.18
1947—Cleveland	American	42	*299	*20	11	.645	2.68
1948—Cleveland	American	44	280	19	15	.559	3.57
1949—Cleveland	American	36	211	15	14	.517	3.75
1950—Cleveland	American	35	247	16	11	.593	3.43
1951—Cleveland	American	33	250	*22	8	*.733	3.49
1952—Cleveland	American	30	192	9	13	.409	4.73
1953—Cleveland	American	25	176	10	7	.588	3.58
1954—Cleveland	American	19	140	13	3	.813	3.09
1955—Cleveland	American	25	83	4	4	.500	3.47
1956—Cleveland	American	19	58	0	4	.000	4.97
Major League Totals		570	3828	266	162	.621	3.25

WORLD SERIES RECORD

Year	Club	League	G.	IP.	W.	L.	Pct.	ERA.
1948—Cleveland	American	2	14⅓	0	2	.000	5.02

RICK FERRELL

Year	Club	League	G.	AB.	R.	H.	HR.	RBI.	B.A.
1926—Kinston	Virginia	64	192	24	51	2	20	.266
1926—Columbus	A. A.	5	14	2	4	0	....	.286
1927—Columbus	A. A.	104	345	42	86	2	44	.249
1928—Columbus†	A. A.	126	339	51	113	2	65	.333
1929—St. Louis	Amer.	64	144	21	33	0	20	.229
1930—St. Louis	Amer.	101	314	43	84	1	41	.268
1931—St. Louis	Amer.	117	386	47	118	3	57	.306
1932—St. Louis	Amer.	126	438	67	138	2	65	.315
1933—St. L.‡-Boston	Amer.	140	493	58	143	4	77	.290
1934—Boston	Amer.	132	437	50	130	1	48	.297
1935—Boston	Amer.	133	458	54	138	3	61	.301
1936—Boston§-Wash.	Amer.	121	410	59	128	8	55	.312
1937—Boston§-Wash.	Amer.	104	344	39	84	2	36	.244
1938—Washington	Amer.	135	411	55	120	1	58	.292
1939—Washington	Amer.	87	274	32	77	0	31	.281
1940—Washington	Amer.	103	326	35	89	0	28	.273
1941—Wash'ton x-St.L.	Amer.	121	387	38	99	2	36	.256
1942—St. Louis	Amer.	99	273	20	61	0	26	.223
1943—St. Louis y	Amer.	74	209	12	50	0	20	.239
1944—Washington	Amer.	99	339	14	94	0	25	.277
1945—Washington	Amer.	91	286	33	76	1	38	.266
1947—Washington	Amer.	37	99	10	30	0	12	.303
Major League Totals		1884	6028	687	1692	28	734	.281

ROLLIE FINGERS

Year	Club	League	G.	IP.	W.	L.	Pct.	ERA.	SV.
1965—Leesburg	Fl. State	25	175	8	15	.348	2.98	...
1966—Modesto	Calif.	22	159	11	6	.647	2.77	...
1967—Birmingham	Southern	18	102	6	5	.545	2.21	...
1968—Birmingham	Southern	18	108	10	4	.714	3.00	...
—Oakland	American	1	1	0	0	...	36.00	...
1969—Oakland	American	60	119	6	7	.462	3.71	12
1970—Oakland	American	45	148	7	9	.438	3.65	2
1971—Oakland	American	48	129	4	6	.400	3.00	17
1972—Oakland	American	65	111	11	9	.550	2.51	21
1973—Oakland	American	62	127	7	8	.467	1.91	22
1974—Oakland	American	*76	119	9	5	.643	2.65	18
1975—Oakland	American	*75	127	10	6	.625	2.98	24
1976—Oakland	American	70	135	13	11	.542	2.47	20
1977—San Diego	National	*78	132	8	9	.471	3.00	*35
1978—San Diego	National	67	107	6	13	.316	2.52	*37
1979—San Diego	National	54	84	9	9	.500	4.50	13
1980—San Diego	National	66	103	11	9	.550	2.80	23
1981—Milwaukee	American	47	78	6	3	.667	1.04	*28
1982—Milwaukee	American	50	79 ²/₃	5	6	.455	2.60	29
1983—		Did not play					
1984—Milwaukee	American	33	46	1	2	.333	1.96	23
1985—Milwaukee	American	47	55 ¹/₃	1	6	.143	5.04	.17
American League Totals		679	1275	80	78	.506	2.83	233
National League Totals		265	426	34	40	.459	3.13	108
Major League Totals		944	1701	114	118	.491	2.90	341

DIVISION SERIES RECORD

Year	Club	League	G.	IP.	W.	L.	Pct.	ERA.	SV.
1981—Milwaukee	American	3	4 ²/₃	1	0	1.000	.386	1

CHAMPIONSHIP SERIES RECORD

Year	Club	League	G.	IP.	W.	L.	PCT.	ERA.	SV.
1971—Oakland	American	2	2 ¹/₃	0	0	...	7.71	0
1972—Oakland	American	3	5 ¹/₃	1	0	1.000	1.69	0
1973—Oakland	American	3	4 ²/₃	0	1	.000	1.93	1
1974—Oakland	American	2	3	0	0	...	3.00	1
1975—Oakland	American	4	4	0	1	.000	6.75	0
1982—Milwaukee	American		Did not play					
Championship Series Totals		14	19 ¹/₃	1	2	.333	3.72	2

WORLD SERIES RECORD

Year	Club	League	G.	IP.	W.	L.	Pct.	ERA.	SV.
1972—Oakland	American	6	10 ¹/₃	1	1	.500	1.74	2
1973—Oakland	American	6	13 ²/₃	0	1	.000	0.66	2
1974—Oakland	American	4	9 ¹/₃	1	0	1.000	1.93	2
1982—Milwaukee	American		Did not play					
World Series Totals		16	33 ¹/₃	2	2	.500	1.35	6

CARLTON ERNEST FISK

Year	Club	League	G.	AB.	R.	H.	HR.	RBI.	B.A.
1968—Waterloo	Midwest	62	195	31	66	12	34	.338
1969—Pittsfield	Eastern	97	309	38	75	10	41	.243
1969—Boston	American	2	5	0	0	0	0	.000
1970—Pawtucket	Eastern	93	284	43	65	12	44	.229
1971—Louisville	Intl.	94	308	45	81	10	43	.263
1971—Boston	American	14	48	7	15	2	6	.313
1972—Boston	American	131	457	74	134	22	61	.293
1973—Boston	American	135	508	65	125	26	71	.246
1974—Boston	American	52	187	36	56	11	26	.299
1975—Boston	American	79	263	47	87	10	52	.331
1976—Boston	American	134	487	76	124	17	58	.255
1977—Boston	American	152	536	106	169	26	102	.315
1978—Boston	American	157	571	94	162	20	88	.284
1979—Boston	American	91	320	49	87	10	42	.272
1980—Boston	American	131	478	73	138	18	62	.289
1981—Chicago	American	96	338	44	89	7	45	.263
1982—Chicago	American	135	476	66	127	14	65	.267
1983—Chicago	American	138	488	85	141	26	86	.289
1984—Chicago	American	102	359	54	83	21	43	.231
1985—Chicago	American	153	543	85	129	37	107	.238
1986—Chicago	American	125	457	42	101	14	63	.221
1987—Chicago	American	135	454	68	116	23	71	.256
1988—Chicago	American	76	253	37	70	19	50	.277
1989—Chicago	American	103	375	47	110	13	68	.293
1990—Chicago	American	137	452	65	129	18	65	.285
1991—Chicago	American	134	460	42	111	18	74	.241
1992—South Bend	Midwest	1	2	1	1	1	3	.500
1992—Sarasota	Fla. State	7	25	3	3	1	2	.120
1992—Chicago	American	62	188	12	43	3	21	.229
1993—Chicago	American	25	53	2	10	1	4	.189
Major League Totals		2499	8756	1276	2356	376	1330	.269

CHAMPIONSHIP SERIES RECORD

Year	Club	League	G.	AB.	R.	H.	HR.	RBI.	B.A.
1975—Boston	American	3	12	4	5	0	2	.417
1983—Chicago	American	4	17	0	3	0	0	.176
Championship Series Totals		7	29	4	8	0	2	.276

WORLD SERIES RECORD

Year	Club	League	G.	AB.	R.	H.	HR.	RBI.	B.A.
1975—Boston	American	7	25	5	6	2	4	.240

ELMER HARRISON FLICK

Year Club	League	G.	AB.	R.	H.	HR.	SB.	B.A.
1896—Youngstown	Int. St.	31	130	34	57	....	....	.438
1897—Dayton	Int. St.	126	474	135	183	....	....	.386
1898—Philadelphia	Nat.	133	447	84	142	7	29	.318
1899—Philadelphia	Nat.	125	486	101	167	2	31	.344
1900—Philadelphia	Nat.	138	547	106	207	11	37	.378
1901—Philadelphia	Nat.	138	542	111	182	8	26	.336
1902—Phil.-Cleve	Amer.	121	464	83	137	2	24	.295
1903—Cleveland	Amer.	*142	529	84	158	2	27	.299
1904—Cleveland	Amer.	149	575	95	174	5	•42	.303
1905—Cleveland	Amer.	131	500	72	154	4	35	*.308
1906—Cleveland	Amer.	*157	*624	*98	194	1	•39	.311
1907—Cleveland	Amer.	147	549	80	166	3	41	.302
1908—Cleveland	Amer.	9	35	4	8	0	0	.229
1909—Cleveland	Amer.	66	235	28	60	0	9	.255
1910—Cleveland	Amer.	24	68	5	18	1	1	.265
1911—Toledo	A. A.	84	313	63	102	3	10	.326
1912—Toledo	A. A.	115	382	60	100	2	28	.262
American League Totals		946	3579	549	1069	18	218	.299
National League Totals		534	2022	402	698	28	123	.345
Major League Totals		1480	5601	951	1767	46	341	.315

EDWARD CHARLES (WHITEY) FORD

Year Club	League	G.	IP.	W.	L.	Pct.	ERA.
1947—Butler	Mid. Atl.	24	157	13	4	.765	3.84
1948—Norfolk	Pied.	30	216	16	8	.667	2.58
1949—Binghamton	East.	26	168	16	5	.762	*1.61
1950—Kansas City	A. A.	12	95	6	3	.667	3.22
1950—New York	Amer.	20	112	9	1	.900	2.81
1951-52—New York	Amer.	(In Military Service)					
1953—New York	Amer.	32	207	18	6	.750	3.00
1954—New York	Amer.	34	211	16	8	.667	2.82
1955—New York	Amer.	39	254	•18	7	.720	2.62
1956—New York	Amer.	31	226	19	6	*.760	*2.47
1957—New York	Amer.	24	129	11	5	.688	2.58
1958—New York	Amer.	30	219	14	7	.667	*2.01
1959—New York	Amer.	35	204	16	10	.615	3.04
1960—New York	Amer.	33	193	12	9	.571	3.08
1961—New York	Amer.	39	*283	*25	4	*.862	3.21
1962—New York	Amer.	38	258	17	8	.680	2.90
1963—New York	Amer.	38	*269	*24	7	*.774	2.74
1964—New York	Amer.	39	245	17	6	.739	2.13
1965—New York	Amer.	37	244	16	13	.552	3.25
1966—New York	Amer.	22	73	2	5	.286	2.47
1967—New York	Amer.	7	44	2	4	.333	1.64
Major League Totals		498	3171	236	106	.690	2.74

WORLD SERIES RECORD

Year Club	League	G.	IP.	W.	L.	Pct.	ERA.
1950—New York	Amer.	1	8⅔	1	0	1.000	0.00
1953—New York	Amer.	2	8	0	1	.000	4.50
1955—New York	Amer.	2	17	2	0	1.000	2.12
1956—New York	Amer.	2	12	1	1	.500	5.25
1957—New York	Amer.	2	16	1	1	.500	1.13
1958—New York	Amer.	3	15⅓	0	1	.000	4.11
1960—New York	Amer.	2	18	2	0	1.000	0.00
1961—New York	Amer.	2	14	2	0	1.000	0.00
1962—New York	Amer.	3	19⅔	1	1	.500	4.12
1963—New York	Amer.	2	12	0	2	.000	4.50
1964—New York	Amer.	1	5⅓	0	1	.000	8.44
World Series Totals		22	146	10	8	.556	2.71

JACOB NELSON (NELLIE) FOX

Year Club	League	G.	AB.	R.	H.	HR.	RBI.	B.A.
1944 — Lancaster	Int.-St.	24	77	11	25	0	12	.325
1944 — Jamestown	Pony	56	230	40	70	0	18	.304
1945 — Lancaster	Int.-St.	•140	*573	*128	*180	1	68	.314
1946 — Philadelphia	American	(In Military Service)						
1947 — Lancaster	Int.-St.	55	228	42	64	1	22	.281
1947 — Philadelphia	American	7	3	2	0	0	0	.000
1948 — Lincoln	West.	136	*576	97	*179	5	67	.311
1948 — Philadelphia	American	3	13	0	2	0	0	.154
1949 — Philadelphia	American	88	247	42	63	0	21	.255
1950 — Chicago	American	130	457	45	113	0	30	.247
1951 — Chicago	American	147	604	93	189	4	55	.313
1952 — Chicago	American	152	*648	76	*192	0	39	.296
1953 — Chicago	American	154	624	92	178	3	72	.285
1954 — Chicago	American	•155	631	111	•201	2	47	.319
1955 — Chicago	American	•154	*636	100	198	6	59	.311
1956 — Chicago	American	154	*649	109	192	4	52	.296
1957 — Chicago	American	*155	619	110	*196	6	61	.317
1958 — Chicago	American	•155	623	82	*187	0	49	.300
1959 — Chicago	American	*156	*624	84	191	2	70	.306
1960 — Chicago	American	150	*605	85	175	2	59	.289
1961 — Chicago	American	159	606	67	152	2	51	.251
1962 — Chicago	American	157	621	79	166	2	54	.267
1963 — Chicago	American	137	539	54	140	2	42	.260
1964 — Houston	National	133	442	45	117	0	28	.265
1965 — Houston	National	21	41	3	11	0	1	.268
American League Totals		2213	8749	1231	2535	35	761	.290
National League Totals		154	483	48	128	0	29	.265
Major League Totals		2367	9232	1279	2663	35	790	.288

WORLD SERIES RECORD

Year Club	League	G.	AB.	R.	H.	HR.	RBI.	B.A.
1959 — Chicago	American	6	24	4	9	0	0	.375

JAMES EMORY (JIMMIE) FOXX

Year Club	League	G.	AB.	R.	H.	HR.	RBI.	B.A.
1924—Easton	East. Sh.	76	260	33	77	10	....	.296
1925—Philadelphia	Amer.	10	9	2	6	0	0	.667
1925—Providence	Int.	41	101	12	33	1	15	.327
1926—Philadelphia	Amer.	26	32	8	10	0	5	.313
1927—Philadelphia	Amer.	61	130	23	42	3	20	.323
1928—Philadelphia	Amer.	118	400	85	131	13	79	.328
1929—Philadelphia	Amer.	149	517	123	183	33	117	.354
1930—Philadelphia	Amer.	153	562	127	188	37	156	.335
1931—Philadelphia	Amer.	139	515	93	150	30	120	.291
1932—Philadelphia	Amer.	154	585	*151	213	*58	*169	.364
1933—Philadelphia	Amer.	149	573	125	204	*48	*163	*.356
1934—Philadelphia	Amer.	150	539	120	180	44	130	.334
1935—Philadelphia	Amer.	147	535	118	185	•36	115	.346
1936—Boston	Amer.	•155	585	130	198	41	143	.338
1937—Boston	Amer.	150	569	111	162	36	127	.285
1938—Boston	Amer.	149	565	139	197	50	*175	*.349
1939—Boston	Amer.	124	467	130	168	*35	105	.360
1940—Boston	Amer.	144	515	106	153	36	119	.297
1941—Boston	Amer.	135	487	87	146	19	105	.300
1942—Boston	Amer.	30	100	18	27	5	14	.270
1942—Chicago	Nat.	70	205	25	42	3	19	.205
1943—Chicago	Nat.	(Did not play)						
1944—Chicago	Nat.	15	20	0	1	0	2	.050
1944—Portsmouth	Pied.	5	2	0	0	0	0	.000
1945—Philadelphia	Nat.	89	224	30	60	7	38	.268
1946—		(Out of Organized Ball)						
1947—St. Petersburg	Fla. Int.	6	6	0	1	....	......	.167
American League Totals		2143	7685	1696	2543	524	1862	.331
National League Totals		174	449	55	103	10	59	.229
Major League Totals		2317	8134	1751	2646	534	1921	.325

PITCHING RECORD

Year Club	League	G.	IP.	W.	L.	Pct.	ERA.
1939—Boston	Amer.	1	1	0	0	.000	0.00
1945—Philadelphia	Nat.	9	23	1	0	1.000	1.57
Major League Totals		10	24	1	0	1.000	1.50

WORLD SERIES RECORD

Year Club	League	G.	AB.	R.	H.	HR.	RBI.	B.A.
1929—Philadelphia	Amer.	5	20	5	7	2	5	.350
1930—Philadelphia	Amer.	6	21	3	7	1	3	.333
1931—Philadelphia	Amer.	7	23	3	8	1	3	.348
World Series Totals		18	64	11	22	4	11	.344

FRANK FRANCIS (FORDHAM FLASH) FRISCH

Year Club	League	G.	AB.	R.	H.	HR.	RBI.	B.A.
1919—New York	Nat.	54	190	21	43	2	22	.226
1920—New York	Nat.	110	440	57	123	4	77	.280
1921—New York	Nat.	153	618	121	211	8	100	.341
1922—New York	Nat.	132	514	101	168	5	51	.327
1923—New York	Nat.	151	641	116	*223	12	111	.348
1924—New York	Nat.	145	603	•121	198	7	69	.328
1925—New York	Nat.	120	502	89	166	11	48	.331
1926—New York	Nat.	135	535	75	171	5	44	.314
1927—St. Louis	Nat.	153	617	112	208	10	78	.337
1928—St. Louis	Nat.	141	547	107	164	10	86	.300
1929—St. Louis	Nat.	138	527	93	176	5	74	.334
1930—St. Louis	Nat.	133	540	121	187	10	114	.346
1931—St. Louis	Nat.	131	518	96	161	4	82	.311
1932—St. Louis	Nat.	115	486	59	142	3	60	.292
1933—St. Louis	Nat.	147	585	74	177	4	66	.303
1934—St. Louis	Nat.	140	550	74	168	3	75	.305
1935—St. Louis	Nat.	103	354	52	104	1	55	.294
1936—St. Louis	Nat.	93	303	40	83	1	26	.274
1937—St. Louis	Nat.	17	32	3	7	0	4	.219
Major League Totals		2311	9112	1532	2880	105	1242	.316

WORLD SERIES RECORD

Year Club	League	G.	AB.	R.	H.	HR.	RBI.	B.A.
1921—New York	Nat.	8	30	5	9	0	1	.300
1922—New York	Nat.	5	17	3	8	0	2	.471
1923—New York	Nat.	6	25	2	10	0	1	.400
1924—New York	Nat.	7	30	1	10	0	0	.333
1928—St. Louis	Nat.	4	13	1	3	0	1	.231
1930—St. Louis	Nat.	6	24	0	5	0	0	.208
1931—St. Louis	Nat.	7	27	2	7	0	1	.259
1934—St. Louis	Nat.	7	31	2	6	0	4	.194
World Series Totals		50	197	16	58	0	10	.294

JAMES F. (PUD or GENTLE JAMES) GALVIN

Year Club	League	G.	IP.	W.	L.	Pct.	ShO.
1875—St. Louis	National Assn.	9	....		4	2	....
1876—St. Louis Red Stockings		(Independent Ball)					
1877—Allegheny	Int. Assn.	19	....	....	....	96	4
1878—Buffalo	Int. Assn.	38	....	....	....	......	....
1879—Buffalo	National	66	592	37	27	.578	6
1880—Buffalo	National	58	462	20	37	.351	5
1881—Buffalo	National	56	470	29	24	.547	5
1882—Buffalo	National	52	437	28	22	.560	3
1883—Buffalo	National	76	*656	46	29	.613	•5
1884—Buffalo	National	72	636	46	22	.676	*12
1885—Buffalo	National	33	287	13	19	.406	3
1885—Allegheny	American Assn.	11	89	3	7	.300	0
1886—Allegheny	American Assn.	50	443	29	21	.580	2
1887—Pittsburgh	National	49	440	28	21	.571	3
1888—Pittsburgh	National	50	436	23	25	.479	6

Year Club	League	G.	IP.	W.	L.	Pct.	ShO.
1889—Pittsburgh	National	41	347	23	16	.590	4
1890—Pittsburgh	Players	26	216	12	13	.480	1
1891—Pittsburgh	National	33	260	14	13	.519	2
1892—Pitt.-St. L.	National	24	188	10	13	.435	0
1894—Buffalo	Eastern	2	....	0	2	.000	.....
National League Totals		610	5211	317	268	.542	54
American Association Totals		61	532	32	28	.533	2
Players League Totals		26	216	12	13	.480	1
Major League Totals		697	5959	361	309	.539	57

HENRY LOUIS (LOU or IRON HORSE) GEHRIG

Year Club	League	G.	AB.	R.	H.	HR.	RBI.	B.A.
1921—Hartford	East.	12	46	5	12	0	.....	.261
1922—				(Not in Organized Ball)				
1923—New York	Amer.	13	26	6	11	1	9	.423
1923—Hartford	East.	59	227	54	69	24	.....	.304
1924—New York	Amer.	10	12	2	6	0	5	.500
1924—Hartford	East.	134	504	111	186	37		.369
1925—New York	Amer.	126	437	73	129	20	68	.295
1926—New York	Amer.	155	572	135	179	16	107	.313
1927—New York	Amer.	*155	584	149	218	47	*175	.373
1928—New York	Amer.	154	562	139	210	27	●142	.374
1929—New York	Amer.	154	553	127	166	35	126	.300
1930—New York	Amer.	●154	581	143	220	41	*174	.379
1931—New York	Amer.	155	619	*163	*211	●46	*184	.341
1932—New York	Amer.	*156	596	138	208	34	151	.349
1933—New York	Amer.	152	593	*138	198	32	139	.334
1934—New York	Amer.	●154	579	128	210	*49	*165	*.363
1935—New York	Amer.	149	535	*125	176	30	119	.329
1936—New York	Amer.	●155	579	*167	205	*49	152	.354
1937—New York	Amer.	*157	569	138	200	37	159	.351
1938—New York	Amer.	●157	576	115	170	29	114	.295
1939—New York	Amer.	8	28	2	4	0	1	.143
Major League Totals		2164	8001	1888	2721	493	1990	.340

WORLD SERIES RECORD

Year Club	League	G.	AB.	R.	H.	HR.	RBI.	B.A.
1926—New York	Amer.	7	23	1	8	0	3	.348
1927—New York	Amer.	4	13	2	4	0	4	.308
1928—New York	Amer.	4	11	5	6	4	9	.545
1932—New York	Amer.	4	17	9	9	3	8	.529
1936—New York	Amer.	6	24	5	7	2	7	.292
1937—New York	Amer.	5	17	4	5	1	3	.294
1938—New York	Amer.	4	14	4	4	0	0	.286
World Series Totals		34	119	30	43	10	34	.361

CHARLES LEONARD (MECHANICAL MAN) GEHRINGER

Year Club	League	G.	AB.	R.	H.	HR.	RBI.	B.A.
1924—London	Mich.-Ont.	112	401	60	117	3	60	.292
1924—Detroit	Amer.	5	13	2	6	0	1	.462
1925—Toronto	Int.	155	633	128	206	25	108	.325
1925—Detroit	Amer.	8	18	3	3	0	0	.167
1926—Detroit	Amer.	123	459	62	127	1	48	.277
1927—Detroit	Amer.	133	508	110	161	4	61	.317
1928—Detroit	Amer.	154	603	108	193	6	74	.320
1929—Detroit	Amer.	●155	634	*131	●215	13	106	.339
1930—Detroit	Amer.	●154	610	144	201	16	98	.330
1931—Detroit	Amer.	101	383	67	119	4	53	.311
1932—Detroit	Amer.	152	618	112	184	19	107	.298
1933—Detroit	Amer.	●155	628	103	204	12	105	.325
1934—Detroit	Amer.	●154	601	*134	*214	11	127	.356
1935—Detroit	Amer.	150	610	123	201	19	108	.330
1936—Detroit	Amer.	154	641	144	227	15	116	.354
1937—Detroit	Amer.	144	564	133	209	14	96	*.371
1938—Detroit	Amer.	152	568	133	174	20	107	.306
1939—Detroit	Amer.	118	406	86	132	16	86	.325
1940—Detroit	Amer.	139	515	108	161	10	81	.313
1941—Detroit	Amer.	127	436	65	96	3	46	.220
1942—Detroit	Amer.	45	45	6	12	1	7	.267
Major League Totals		2323	8860	1774	2839	184	1427	.320

WORLD SERIES RECORD

Year Club	League	G.	AB.	R.	H.	HR.	RBI.	B.A.
1934—Detroit	Amer.	7	29	5	11	1	2	.379
1935—Detroit	Amer.	6	24	4	9	0	4	.375
1940—Detroit	Amer.	7	28	3	6	0	1	.214
World Series Totals		20	81	12	26	1	7	.321

ROBERT GIBSON

Year Club	League	G.	IP.	W.	L.	Pct.	ERA.
1957—Omaha	Amer. Assoc.	10	42	2	1	.667	4.29
1957—Columbus	Sally	8	43	4	3	.571	3.77
1958—Omaha	Amer. Assoc.	13	87	3	4	.429	3.31
1958—Rochester	International	20	103	5	5	.500	2.45
1959—Omaha	Amer. Assoc.	24	135	9	9	.500	3.07
1959—St. Louis	National	13	76	3	5	.375	3.32
1960—St. Louis	National	27	87	3	6	.333	5.59
1960—Rochester	International	6	41	2	3	.400	2.85
1961—St. Louis	National	35	211	13	12	.520	3.24
1962—St. Louis	National	32	234	15	13	.536	2.85
1963—St. Louis	National	36	255	18	9	.667	3.39
1964—St. Louis	National	40	287	19	12	.613	3.01
1965—St. Louis	National	38	299	20	12	.625	3.07
1966—St. Louis	National	35	280	21	12	.636	2.44
1967—St. Louis	National	24	175	13	7	.650	2.98
1968—St. Louis	National	34	305	22	9	.710	*1.12
1969—St. Louis	National	35	314	20	13	.606	2.18
1970—St. Louis	National	34	294	●23	7	.767	3.12
1971—St. Louis	National	31	246	16	13	.552	3.04
1972—St. Louis	National	34	278	19	11	.633	2.46
1973—St. Louis	National	25	195	12	10	.545	2.77
1974—St. Louis	National	33	240	11	13	.458	3.83
1975—St. Louis	National	22	109	3	10	.231	5.04
Major League Totals		528	3885	251	174	.591	2.91

WORLD SERIES RECORD

Year Club	League	G.	IP.	W.	L.	Pct.	ERA.
1964—St. Louis	National	3	27	2	1	.667	3.00
1967—St. Louis	National	3	27	3	0	1.000	1.00
1968—St. Louis	National	3	27	2	1	.667	1.67
World Series Totals		9	81	7	2	.778	1.89

VERNON (LEFTY) GOMEZ

Year Club	League	G.	IP.	W.	L.	Pct.	ERA.
1928—Salt Lake	Utah-Idaho	*39	194	12	*14	.462	3.48
1929—San Francisco	Pacific Coast	41	267	18	11	.621	*3.44
1930—New York	American	15	60	2	5	.286	5.55
1930—St. Paul	Amer. Assn.	17	86	8	4	.667	4.08
1931—New York	American	40	243	21	9	.700	2.63
1932—New York	American	37	265	24	7	.774	4.21
1933—New York	American	35	235	16	10	.615	3.18
1934—New York	American	38	*282	*26	5	*.839	*2.33
1935—New York	American	34	246	12	15	.444	3.18
1936—New York	American	31	189	13	7	.650	4.38
1937—New York	American	34	278	*21	11	.656	*2.33
1938—New York	American	32	239	18	12	.600	3.35
1939—New York	American	26	198	12	8	.600	3.41
1940—New York	American	9	27	3	3	.500	6.67
1941—New York	American	23	156	15	5	*.750	3.75
1942—New York	American	13	80	6	4	.600	4.28
1943—Washington	American	1	5	0	1	.000	5.40
1946—Binghamton	Eastern	1	3	0	0	.000	9.00
1947—Binghamton	Eastern	1	1	0	0	.000	0.00
Major League Totals		368	2503	189	102	.649	3.34

WORLD SERIES RECORD

Year Club	League	G.	IP.	W.	L.	Pct.	ERA.
1932—New York	American	1	9	1	0	1.000	1.00
1936—New York	American	2	15⅓	2	0	1.000	4.70
1937—New York	American	2	18	2	0	1.000	1.50
1938—New York	American	1	7	1	0	1.000	3.86
1939—New York	American	1	1	0	0	.000	9.00
World Series Totals		7	50⅓	6	0	1.000	2.86

LEON ALLEN (GOOSE) GOSLIN

Year Club	League	G.	AB.	R.	H.	HR.	RBI.	B.A.
1920—Columbia	Sally	90	319	52	101	4	65	.317
1921—Columbia	Sally	142	549	*124	*214	16	*131	*.390
1921—Washington	Amer.	14	50	8	13	1	6	.260
1922—Washington	Amer.	101	358	44	116	3	53	.324
1923—Washington	Amer.	150	600	86	180	9	99	.300
1924—Washington	Amer.	154	579	100	199	12	*129	.344
1925—Washington	Amer.	150	601	116	201	18	113	.334
1926—Washington	Amer.	147	568	105	201	17	108	.354
1927—Washington	Amer.	148	581	96	194	13	120	.334
1928—Washington	Amer.	135	456	80	173	17	102	*.379
1929—Washington	Amer.	145	553	82	159	18	91	.288
1930—Wash.-St. L.	Amer.	148	584	115	180	37	138	.308
1931—St. Louis	Amer.	151	591	114	194	24	105	.328
1932—St. Louis	Amer.	150	572	88	171	17	104	.299
1933—Washington	Amer.	132	549	97	163	10	64	.297
1934—Detroit	Amer.	151	614	106	187	13	100	.305
1935—Detroit	Amer.	147	590	88	172	9	109	.292
1936—Detroit	Amer.	147	572	122	180	24	125	.315
1937—Detroit	Amer.	79	181	30	43	4	35	.238
1938—Washington	Amer.	38	57	6	9	2	8	.158
1939—Trenton	Int.-St.	99	349	65	113	3	58	.324
1940—Trenton	Int.-St.	49	128	24	32	1	16	.250
Major League Totals		2287	8656	1483	2735	248	1609	.316

WORLD SERIES RECORD

Year Club	League	G.	AB.	R.	H.	HR.	RBI.	B.A.
1924—Washington	Amer.	7	32	4	11	3	7	.344
1925—Washington	Amer.	7	26	6	8	3	6	.308
1933—Washington	Amer.	5	20	2	5	1	1	.250
1934—Detroit	Amer.	7	29	2	7	0	2	.241
1935—Detroit	Amer.	6	22	2	6	0	3	.273
World Series Totals		32	129	16	37	7	19	.287

HENRY BENJAMIN (HANK) GREENBERG

Year Club	League	G.	AB.	R.	H.	HR.	RBI.	B.A.
1930—Hartford	East.	17	56	10	12	2	6	.214
1930—Raleigh	Pied.	122	452	88	142	19	93	.314
1930—Detroit	Amer.	1	1	0	0	0	0	.000
1931—Evansville	I.I.I.	●126	487	88	155	15	85	.318
1931—Beaumont	Texas	3	2	0	0	0	0	.000
1932—Beaumont	Texas	154	600	*123	174	*39	131	.290
1933—Detroit	Amer.	117	449	59	135	12	87	.301
1934—Detroit	Amer.	153	593	118	201	26	139	.339
1935—Detroit	Amer.	152	619	121	203	●36	*170	.328

Year—Club	League	G.	AB.	R.	H.	HR.	RBI.	B.A.
1936—Detroit	Amer.	12	46	10	16	1	16	.348
1937—Detroit	Amer.	154	594	137	200	40	*183	.337
1938—Detroit	Amer.	155	556	*144	175	*58	146	.315
1939—Detroit	Amer.	138	500	112	156	33	112	.312
1940—Detroit	Amer.	148	573	129	195	*41	*150	.340
1941—Detroit	Amer.	19	67	12	18	2	12	.269
1942-43-44—Detroit	Amer.			(In Military Service)				
1945—Detroit	Amer.	78	270	47	84	13	60	.311
1946—Detroit	Amer.	142	523	91	145	*44	*127	.277
1947—Pittsburgh	Nat.	125	402	71	100	25	74	.249
American League Totals		1269	4791	980	1528	306	1202	.319
National League Totals		125	402	71	100	25	74	.249
Major League Totals		1394	5193	1051	1628	331	1276	.313

WORLD SERIES RECORD

Year—Club	League	G.	AB.	R.	H.	HR.	RBI.	B.A.
1934—Detroit	Amer.	7	28	4	9	1	7	.321
1935—Detroit	Amer.	2	6	1	1	1	2	.167
1940—Detroit	Amer.	7	28	5	10	1	6	.357
1945—Detroit	Amer.	7	23	7	7	2	7	.304
World Series Totals		23	85	17	27	5	22	.318

CLARK CALVIN (OLD FOX) GRIFFITH

Year—Club	League	G.	IP.	W.	L.	Pct.
1888—Bloomington	Cent.-Int. St.	14	.....	10	4	.714
1888—Milwaukee	Western	23	.....	12	10	.545
1889—Milwaukee	Western	31	.....	18	13	.581
1890—Milwaukee	Western	34	.....	27	7	.794
1891—St. Louis-Boston	Amer. Assn.	24	225	17	7	.708
1892—Tacoma	P. N. W.	24	.....	13	7	.650
1893—Oakland	Pacific Coast	48	.....	30	18	.625
1893—Chicago	National	3	22	1	1	.500
1894—Chicago	National	32	274	21	11	.656
1895—Chicago	National	39	352	25	13	.658
1896—Chicago	National	35	319	22	13	.629
1897—Chicago	National	46	344	21	19	.525
1898—Chicago	National	37	316	26	10	.722
1899—Chicago	National	39	319	22	13	.629
1900—Chicago	National	27	249	14	13	.519
1901—Chicago	American	32	257	24	7	*.774
1902—Chicago	American	25	216	15	9	.625
1903—New York	American	24	214	14	10	.583
1904—New York	American	12	92	7	5	.583
1905—New York	American	16	100	9	6	.600
1906—New York	American	17	61	2	2	.500
1907—New York	American	4	6	0	0	.000
1909—Cincinnati	National	1	1	0	0	.000
1910—Cincinnati	National			(One game as pinch-hitter)		
1912—Washington	American	1	1	0	0	.000
1913—Washington	American	1	1	0	0	.000
1914—Washington	American	1	1	0	0	.000
American League Totals		133	949	71	39	.645
National League Totals		259	2196	152	94	.618
American Association Totals		24	225	17	7	.708
Major League Totals		416	3370	240	140	.632

BURLEIGH ARLAND (OLD STUBBLEBEARD) GRIMES

Year—Club	League	G.	IP.	W.	L.	Pct.	ERA.
1912—Eau Claire	Minn.-Wis.		(League disbanded July 1)				
1913—Ottumwa	Cent. Assn.	9	70	6	2	.750	....
1913—Chattanooga	Southern	17	112	6	7	.462	....
1914—Chat.-Birm.	Southern	4	10	0	2	.000	....
1914—Richmond	Virginia	39	296	23	13	.639	....
1915—Birmingham	Southern	41	296	17	13	.567	....
1916—Birmingham	Southern	40	276	20	11	.645	....
1916—Pittsburgh	National	6	46	2	3	.400	2.35
1917—Pittsburgh	National	37	194	3	16	.158	3.53
1918—Brooklyn	National	*40	270	19	9	.679	2.13
1919—Brooklyn	National	25	181	10	11	.476	3.48
1920—Brooklyn	National	40	304	23	11	*.676	2.22
1921—Brooklyn	National	37	302	●22	13	.629	2.83
1922—Brooklyn	National	35	256	17	14	.548	4.75
1923—Brooklyn	National	39	*327	21	18	.538	3.58
1924—Brooklyn	National	38	*311	22	13	.629	3.82
1925—Brooklyn	National	33	247	12	*19	.387	5.03
1926—Brooklyn	National	30	225	12	13	.480	3.72
1927—New York	National	39	260	19	8	.704	3.53
1928—Pittsburgh	National	*48	*331	●25	14	.641	2.99
1929—Pittsburgh	National	33	233	17	7	.708	3.13
1930—Bos.-St.L.	National	33	201	16	11	.593	4.07
1931—St. Louis	National	29	212	17	9	.654	3.65
1932—Chicago	National	30	141	6	11	.353	4.79
1933—Chi.-St.L.	National	21	84	3	7	.300	3.75
1934—St.L.-Pitt.	National	12	35	3	3	.500	6.43
1934—New York	American	10	18	1	2	.333	5.50
1935—Bloomington	I.I.I.	21	119	10	5	.667	......
American League Totals		10	18	1	2	.333	5.50
National League Totals		605	4160	269	210	.562	3.52
Major League Totals		615	4178	270	212	.560	3.52

WORLD SERIES RECORD

Year—Club	League	G.	IP.	W.	L.	Pct.	ERA.
1920—Brooklyn	National	3	19⅓	1	2	.333	4.19
1930—St. Louis	National	2	17	0	2	.000	3.71
1931—St. Louis	National	2	17⅔	2	0	1.000	2.04
1932—Chicago	National	2	2⅔	0	0	.000	23.63
World Series Totals		9	56⅔	3	4	.429	4.05

ROBERT MOSES (LEFTY) GROVE

Year—Club	League	G.	IP.	W.	L.	Pct.	ERA.
1920—Martinsburg	Blue Ridge	6	59	3	3	.500	......
1920—Baltimore	International	19	123	12	2	.857	3.80
1921—Baltimore	International	47	313	25	10	.714	2.56
1922—Baltimore	International	41	209	18	8	.692	2.80
1923—Baltimore	International	*52	303	27	10	.730	3.12
1924—Baltimore	International	47	236	*27	6	*.813	3.01
1925—Philadelphia	American	45	197	10	12	.455	4.75
1926—Philadelphia	American	45	258	13	13	.500	*2.51
1927—Philadelphia	American	51	262	20	13	.606	3.19
1928—Philadelphia	American	39	262	●24	8	.750	2.58
1929—Philadelphia	American	42	275	20	6	*.769	*2.81
1930—Philadelphia	American	*50	291	*28	5	*.848	*2.54
1931—Philadelphia	American	41	289	*31	4	*.886	*2.06
1932—Philadelphia	American	44	292	25	10	.714	*2.84
1933—Philadelphia	American	45	275	●24	8	*.750	3.21
1934—Boston	American	22	109	8	8	.500	6.52
1935—Boston	American	35	273	20	12	.625	*2.70
1936—Boston	American	35	253	17	12	.586	*2.81
1937—Boston	American	32	262	17	9	.654	3.02
1938—Boston	American	24	164	14	4	.778	*3.07
1939—Boston	American	23	191	15	4	*.789	*2.54
1940—Boston	American	22	153	7	6	.538	4.00
1941—Boston	American	21	134	7	7	.500	4.37
Major League Totals		616	3940	300	141	.680	3.06

WORLD SERIES RECORD

Year—Club	League	G.	IP.	W.	L.	Pct.	ERA.
1929—Philadelphia	American	2	6⅓	0	0	.000	0.00
1930—Philadelphia	American	3	19	2	1	.667	1.42
1931—Philadelphia	American	3	26	2	1	.667	2.42
World Series Totals		8	51⅓	4	2	.667	1.75

CHARLES JAMES (CHICK) HAFEY

Year—Club	League	G.	AB.	R.	H.	HR.	RBI.	B.A.
1923—Fort Smith	W. Assn.	141	573	83	163	16		.284
1924—Houston	Tex.	126	481	82	173	9	90	.360
1924—St. Louis	Nat.	24	91	10	23	2	22	.253
1925—Syracuse	Int.	21	84	17	24	2	8	.286
1925—St. Louis	Nat.	93	358	36	108	5	57	.302
1926—St. Louis	Nat.	78	225	30	61	4	38	.271
1927—St. Louis	Nat.	103	346	62	114	18	63	.329
1928—St. Louis	Nat.	138	520	101	175	27	111	.337
1929—St. Louis	Nat.	134	517	101	175	29	125	.338
1930—St. Louis	Nat.	120	446	108	150	26	107	.336
1931—St. Louis	Nat.	122	450	94	157	16	95	*.349
1932—Cincinnati	Nat.	83	253	34	87	2	36	.344
1933—Cincinnati	Nat.	144	568	77	172	7	62	.303
1934—Cincinnati	Nat.	140	535	75	157	18	67	.293
1935—Cincinnati	Nat.	15	59	10	20	1	9	.339
1936—Cincinnati	Nat.			(Voluntarily Retired)				
1937—Cincinnati	Nat.	89	257	39	67	9	41	.261
Major League Totals		1283	4625	777	1466	164	833	.317

WORLD SERIES RECORD

Year—Club	League	G.	AB.	R.	H.	HR.	RBI.	B.A.
1926—St. Louis	Nat.	7	27	2	5	0	0	.185
1928—St. Louis	Nat.	4	15	0	3	0	0	.200
1930—St. Louis	Nat.	6	22	2	6	0	2	.273
1931—St. Louis	Nat.	6	24	1	4	0	0	.167
World Series Totals		23	88	5	18	0	2	.205

JESSE JOSEPH (POP) HAINES

Year—Club	League	G.	IP.	W.	L.	Pct.	ERA.
1913—Dayton	Central		(Pitched one game, last day of season vs. Evansville)				
1914—Saginaw	S. Mich.	33	258	17	14	.548	......
1914—Fort Wayne	Central		(No records available)				
1915—Saginaw	S. Mich. (League disbanded July 1—no records available)						
1916—Springfield	Central	41	310	23	12	.657	1.68
1917—Springfield	Central	35	275	19	10	.655	
1918—Topeka-Hutch'on	Western	16	132	12	4	.750	
1918—Cincinnati	National	1	5	0	0	.000	1.80
1919—Tulsa	Western	14	101	5	9	.357	......
1919—Kansas City	Amer. Assn.	28	213	21	5	.808	2.11
1920—St. Louis	National	*47	302	13	20	.394	2.98
1921—St. Louis	National	37	244	18	12	.600	3.50
1922—St. Louis	National	29	183	11	9	.550	3.84
1923—St. Louis	National	37	266	20	13	.606	3.11
1924—St. Louis	National	35	223	8	19	.296	4.40
1925—St. Louis	National	29	207	13	14	.481	4.57
1926—St. Louis	National	33	183	13	4	.765	3.25
1927—St. Louis	National	38	301	24	10	.706	2.72
1928—St. Louis	National	33	240	20	8	.714	3.19
1929—St. Louis	National	28	180	13	10	.565	5.70
1930—St. Louis	National	29	182	13	8	.619	4.30
1931—St. Louis	National	19	120	12	3	.800	3.02
1932—St. Louis	National	20	85	3	5	.375	4.76
1933—St. Louis	National	32	115	9	6	.600	2.50
1934—St. Louis	National	37	90	4	4	.500	3.50
1935—St. Louis	National	30	115	6	5	.545	3.60
1936—St. Louis	National	25	99	7	5	.583	3.91
1937—St. Louis	National	16	66	3	3	.500	4.50
Major League Totals		555	3208	210	158	.571	3.64

Year	Club	League	G.	IP.	W.	L.	Pct.	ERA.
1926—St. Louis	National	3	16⅔	2	0	1.000	1.08
1928—St. Louis	National	1	6	0	1	.000	4.50
1930—St. Louis	National	1	9	1	0	1.000	1.00
1934—St. Louis	National	1	⅔	0	0	.000	0.00
World Series Totals		6	32⅓	3	1	.750	1.67

WILLIAM ROBERT (SLIDING BILLY) HAMILTON

Year	Club	League	G.	AB.	R.	H.	HR.	SB.	B.A.
1888—Worcester	N. Eng.	61	247	76	87	...	70	.352
1888—Kansas City	A. A.	35	128	17	32	0	23	.250
1889—Kansas City	A. A.	137	532	145	160	3	*117	.301
1890—Philadelphia	Nat.	123	496	131	161	2	*102	.325
1891—Philadelphia	Nat.	133	529	*142	*179	2	*115	*.338
1892—Philadelphia	Nat.	136	539	131	178	3	56	.330
1893—Philadelphia	Nat.	82	349	111	138	5	41	.395
1894—Philadelphia	Nat.	131	559	*196	223	4	*99	.399
1895—Philadelphia	Nat.	121	517	*166	203	5	*95	.393
1896—Boston	Nat.	131	523	153	190	2	93	.363
1897—Boston	Nat.	125	506	*153	174	3	70	.344
1898—Boston	Nat.	109	417	111	153	3	59	.367
1899—Boston	Nat.	81	294	62	90	1	19	.306
1900—Boston	Nat.	135	524	103	174	1	29	.332
1901—Boston	Nat.	99	349	70	102	3	19	.292
1902—Haverhill	N. Eng.	66	243	67	82	2	26	.337
1903—Haverhill	N. Eng.	37	132	37	60	4	27	.446
1904—Haverhill	N. Eng.	113	408	*113	*168	0	*74	*.412
1905—Harrisburg	Tri-St.			(No Record Available)				
1906—Haverhill	N.Eng.	14	51	1	10	0	...	.196
1906—Harrisburg	Tri.-St.	43	155	33	43	0	16	.278
1907—Haverhill	N. Eng.	91	324	50	108	0	29	*.333
1908—Haverhill	N. Eng.	85	300	63	87	1	39	.290
1909—Lynn	N. Eng.	109	376	61	125	0	23	*.332
1910—Lynn	N. Eng.	41	112	14	28	0	5	.250
American Association Totals		172	660	162	192	3	140	.291
National League Totals		1406	5602	1529	1965	34	797	.351
Major League Totals		1578	6262	1690	2157	37	937	.344

EDWARD HUGH (NED) HANLON

RECORD AS MANAGER

Year	Club	League	Position	W.	L.
1889 — Pittsburgh	National	Fifth	26	18
1890 — Pittsburgh	Players	Sixth	60	68
1891 — Pittsburgh	National	Eighth	31	47
1892 — Baltimore	National	Twelfth	17	39
(Second half)		Tenth	26	46
1893 — Baltimore	National	Eighth	60	70
1894 — Baltimore	National	First	89	39
1895 — Baltimore	National	First	87	43
1896 — Baltimore	National	First	90	39
1897 — Baltimore	National	Second	90	40
1898 — Baltimore	National	Second	96	53
1899 — Brooklyn	National	First	101	47
1900 — Brooklyn	National	First	82	54
1901 — Brooklyn	National	Third	79	57
1902 — Brooklyn	National	Second	75	63
1903 — Brooklyn	National	Fifth	70	66
1904 — Brooklyn	National	Sixth	56	97
1905 — Brooklyn	National	Eighth	48	104
1906 — Cincinnati	National	Sixth	64	87
1907 — Cincinnati	National	Sixth	66	87
Major League Totals			1313	1164

STANLEY RAYMOND (BUCKY) HARRIS

Year	Club	League	G.	AB.	R.	H.	HR.	RBI.	B.A.
1916—Muskegon	Central	55	169	8	28	....	....	.166
1917—Norfolk	Virginia	15	50	4	6	0	2	.120
1917—Reading	N.Y.S.	75	280	44	70	....	....	.250
1918—Buffalo	Int.	85	320	51	77	0	....	.241
1919—Buffalo	Int.	120	447	68	126	2	....	.282
1919—Washington	Amer.	8	28	0	6	0	4	.214
1920—Washington	Amer.	137	506	76	152	1	68	.300
1921—Washington	Amer.	154	584	82	169	0	54	.289
1922—Washington	Amer.	154	602	95	162	2	40	.269
1923—Washington	Amer.	145	532	60	150	2	70	.282
1924—Washington	Amer.	143	544	88	146	1	58	.268
1925—Washington	Amer.	144	551	91	158	1	66	.287
1926—Washington	Amer.	141	537	94	152	1	63	.283
1927—Washington	Amer.	128	475	98	127	1	55	.267
1928—Washington	Amer.	99	358	34	73	0	28	.204
1929—Detroit	Amer.	7	11	3	1	0	0	.091
1930—Detroit	Amer.			(Did not play)				
1931—Detroit	Amer.	4	8	1	1	0	0	.125
Major League Totals		1264	4736	722	1297	9	506	.274

WORLD SERIES RECORD

Year	Club	League	G.	AB.	R.	H.	HR.	RBI.	B.A.
1924—Washington	Amer.	7	33	5	11	2	7	.333
1925—Washington	Amer.	7	23	2	2	0	0	.087
World Series Totals		14	56	7	13	2	7	.232

RECORD AS MANAGER

Year	Club	League	Position	W.	L.
1924—Washington	American	First	92	62
1925—Washington	American	First	96	55
1926—Washington	American	Fourth	81	69
1927—Washington	American	Third	85	69
1928—Washington	American	Fourth	75	79
1929—Detroit	American	Sixth	70	84
1930—Detroit	American	Fifth	75	79
1931—Detroit	American	Seventh	61	93
1932—Detroit	American	Fifth	76	75
1933—Detroit	American	Fifth	75	79
1934—Boston	American	Fourth	76	76
1935—Washington	American	Sixth	67	86
1936—Washington	American	Fourth	82	71
1937—Washington	American	Sixth	73	80
1938—Washington	Americcn	Fifth	75	76
1939—Washington	Americcan	Sixth	65	87
1940—Washington	American	Seventh	64	90
1941—Washington	American	*Sixth	70	84
1942—Washington	American	Seventh	62	89
1943—Philadelphia†	National	Sixth	39	52
1944—Buffalo	International	Fourth	78	76
1945—Buffalo	International	*Sixth	64	89
1947—New York	American	First	97	57
1948—New York	American	Third	94	60
1949—San Diego	Pacific Coast	*Fourth	96	92
1950—Washington	American	Fifth	67	87
1951—Washington	American	Seventh	62	92
1952—Washington	American	Fifth	78	76
1953—Washington	American	Fifth	76	76
1954—Washington	American	Sixth	66	88
1955—Detroit	American	Fifth	79	75
Major League Totals			2078	2146

*Tied for position.
†Replaced as manager by Fred Fitzsimmons, July 28, 1943.

WORLD SERIES RECORD

Year	Club	League	W.	L.
1924—Washington	American	4	3
1925—Washington	American	3	4
1947—New York	American	4	3

CHARLES LEO (GABBY) HARTNETT

Year	Club	League	G.	AB.	R.	H.	HR.	RBI.	B.A.
1921—Worcester	East.	100	345	38	91	3	....	.264
1922—Chicago	Nat.	31	72	4	14	0	4	.194
1923—Chicago	Nat.	85	231	28	62	8	39	.268
1924—Chicago	Nat.	111	354	56	106	16	67	.299
1925—Chicago	Nat.	117	398	61	115	24	67	.289
1926—Chicago	Nat.	93	284	35	78	8	41	.275
1927—Chicago	Nat.	127	449	56	132	10	80	.294
1928—Chicago	Nat.	120	388	61	117	14	57	.302
1929—Chicago	Nat.	25	22	2	6	1	9	.273
1930—Chicago	Nat.	141	508	84	172	37	122	.339
1931—Chicago	Nat.	116	380	53	107	8	70	.282
1932—Chicago	Nat.	121	406	52	110	12	52	.271
1933—Chicago	Nat.	140	490	55	135	16	88	.276
1934—Chicago	Nat.	130	438	58	131	22	90	.299
1935—Chicago	Nat.	116	413	67	142	13	91	.344
1936—Chicago	Nat.	121	424	49	130	7	64	.307
1937—Chicago	Nat.	110	356	47	126	12	82	.354
1938—Chicago	Nat.	88	299	40	82	10	59	.274
1939—Chicago	Nat.	97	306	36	85	12	59	.278
1940—Chicago	Nat.	37	64	3	17	1	12	.266
1941—New York	Nat.	64	150	20	45	5	26	.300
1942—Indianapolis	A. A.	72	186	17	41	4	24	.220
1943—Jersey City	Int.	16	16	0	4	0	5	.250
1944—Jersey City	Int.	31	11	1	2	0	6	.182
Major League Totals		1990	6432	867	1912	236	1179	.297

WORLD SERIES RECORD

Year	Club	League	G.	AB.	R.	H.	HR.	RBI.	B.A.
1929—Chicago	Nat.	3	3	0	0	0	0	.000
1932—Chicago	Nat.	4	16	2	5	1	1	.313
1935—Chicago	Nat.	6	24	1	7	1	2	.292
1938—Chicago	Nat.	3	11	0	1	0	0	.091
World Series Totals		16	54	3	13	2	3	.241

HARRY EDWIN HEILMANN

Year	Club	League	G.	AB.	R.	H.	HR.	RBI.	B.A.
1913—Portland	N. W.	122	417	55	127	11	....	.305
1914—Detroit	Amer.	66	182	25	41	2	22	.225
1915—San Francisco	P. C.	98	371	57	135	12	....	.364
1916—Detroit	Amer.	136	451	57	127	2	76	.282
1917—Detroit	Amer.	150	556	57	156	5	84	.281
1918—Detroit	Amer.	79	286	34	79	5	44	.276
1919—Detroit	Amer.	140	537	74	172	8	95	.320
1920—Detroit	Amer.	145	543	66	168	9	90	.309
1921—Detroit	Amer.	149	602	114	*237	19	139	*.394
1922—Detroit	Amer.	118	455	92	162	21	92	.356
1923—Detroit	Amer.	144	524	121	211	18	115	*.403
1924—Detroit	Amer.	153	570	107	197	10	114	.346
1925—Detroit	Amer.	150	573	97	225	13	134	*.393
1926—Detroit	Amer.	141	502	90	184	9	103	.367
1927—Detroit	Amer.	141	505	106	201	14	120	*.398
1928—Detroit	Amer.	151	558	83	183	14	107	.328

Year	Club	League	G.	AB.	R.	H.	HR.	RBI.	B.A.
1929—	Detroit	Amer.	125	453	86	156	15	120	.344
1930—	Cincinnati	Nat.	142	459	79	153	19	91	.333
1931—	Cincinnati	Nat.	(Out of game all season)						
1932—	Cincinnati	Nat.	15	31	3	8	0	6	.258
	American League Totals		1988	7297	1209	2499	164	1455	.343
	National League Totals		157	490	82	161	19	97	.329
	Major League Totals		2145	7787	1291	2660	183	1552	.342

WILLIAM JENNINGS HERMAN

Year	Club	League	G.	AB.	R.	H.	HR.	RBI.	B.A.
1928—	Vicksburg	Cot.St.	106	364	63	121	4	....	.332
1928—	Louisville	A. A.	4	15	3	5	0	4	.333
1929—	Dayton	Cent.	138	529	96	174	13	79	.329
1929—	Louisville	A. A.	24	93	17	30	1	13	.323
1930—	Louisville	A. A.	143	617	108	188	8	86	.305
1931—	Louisville	A. A.	118	486	100	170	7	59	.350
1931—	Chicago	Nat.	25	98	14	32	0	16	.327
1932—	Chicago	Nat.	•154	656	102	206	1	51	.314
1933—	Chicago	Nat.	153	619	82	173	0	44	.279
1934—	Chicago	Nat.	113	456	79	138	3	42	.303
1935—	Chicago	Nat.	154	666	113	*227	7	83	.341
1936—	Chicago	Nat.	153	632	101	211	5	93	.334
1937—	Chicago	Nat.	138	564	106	189	8	65	.335
1938—	Chicago	Nat.	•152	624	86	173	1	56	.277
1939—	Chicago	Nat.	156	623	111	191	7	70	.307
1940—	Chicago	Nat.	135	558	77	163	5	57	.292
1941—	Chi.-Brook	Nat.	144	572	81	163	3	41	.285
1942—	Brooklyn	Nat.	*155	571	76	146	2	65	.256
1943—	Brooklyn	Nat.	153	585	76	193	2	100	.330
1944-45—	Brooklyn	Nat.	(In Military Service)						
1946—	Brk.-Bos.	Nat.	122	436	56	130	3	50	.298
1947—	Pittsburgh	Nat.	15	47	3	10	0	6	.213
1948—	Minneapolis	A. A.	10	31	9	14	2	9	.452
1949—			(Out of Organized Ball)						
1950—	Oakland	P. C.	71	202	32	62	4	29	.307
	Major League Totals		1922	7707	1163	2345	47	839	.304

WORLD SERIES RECORD

Year	Club	League	G.	AB.	R.	H.	HR.	RBI.	B.A.
1932—	Chicago	Nat.	4	18	5	4	0	1	.222
1935—	Chicago	Nat.	6	24	3	8	1	6	.333
1938—	Chicago	Nat.	4	16	1	3	0	0	.188
1941—	Brooklyn	Nat.	4	8	0	1	0	0	.125
	World Series Totals		18	66	9	16	1	7	.242

HARRY BARTHOLOMEW HOOPER

Year	Club	League	G.	AB.	R.	H.	HR.	RBI.	B.A.
1907—	Oak.-Sacra'to	Calif. St.	36	139	26	43	1	....	.309
1908—	Sacramento	Calif. St.	77	294	47	101	....	....	.344
1909—	Boston	Amer.	81	255	29	72	0	16	.282
1910—	Boston	Amer.	155	584	81	156	2	33	.267
1911—	Boston	Amer.	130	524	93	163	4	43	.311
1912—	Boston	Amer.	147	590	98	143	2	46	.242
1913—	Boston	Amer.	148	585	100	169	4	40	.289
1914—	Boston	Amer.	141	530	85	137	1	44	.258
1915—	Boston	Amer.	149	566	90	133	2	48	.235
1916—	Boston	Amer.	151	575	75	156	1	33	.271
1917—	Boston	Amer.	151	559	89	143	3	43	.256
1918—	Boston	Amer.	126	474	81	137	1	46	.289
1919—	Boston	Amer.	128	491	76	131	3	48	.267
1920—	Boston	Amer.	139	536	91	167	7	53	.312
1921—	Chicago	Amer.	108	419	74	137	8	58	.327
1922—	Chicago	Amer.	152	602	111	183	11	80	.304
1923—	Chicago	Amer.	145	576	87	166	10	65	.288
1924—	Chicago	Amer.	130	476	107	156	10	62	.328
1925—	Chicago	Amer.	127	442	62	117	6	55	.265
1926—			(Out of Organized Ball)						
1927—	Missions	P. C.	78	218	35	62	1	19	.284
	Major League Totals		2308	8784	1429	2466	75	813	.281

WORLD SERIES RECORD

Year	Club	League	G.	AB.	R.	H.	HR.	RBI.	B.A.
1912—	Boston	Amer.	8	31	3	9	0	2	.290
1915—	Boston	Amer.	5	20	4	7	2	3	350
1916—	Boston	Amer.	5	21	6	7	0	1	.333
1918—	Boston	Amer.	6	20	0	4	0	0	.200
	World Series Totals		24	92	13	27	2	6	.293

ROGERS (RAJAH) HORNSBY

Year	Club	League	G.	AB.	R.	H.	HR.	RBI.	B.A.
1914—	Hugo-Denison	Tex.-Ok	113	393	47	91	3	....	.232
1915—	Denison	W. A.	119	429	75	119	4	....	.277
1915—	St. Louis	Nat.	18	57	5	14	0	4	.246
1916—	St. Louis	Nat.	139	495	63	155	6	60	.313
1917—	St. Louis	Nat.	145	523	86	171	8	70	.327
1918—	St. Louis	Nat.	115	416	51	117	5	59	.281
1919—	St. Louis	Nat.	138	512	68	163	8	68	.318
1920—	St. Louis	Nat.	149	589	96	*218	9	•94	*.370
1921—	St. Louis	Nat.	*154	592	*131	*235	21	*126	*.397
1922—	St. Louis	Nat.	154	623	*141	*250	*42	*152	*.401
1923—	St. Louis	Nat.	107	424	89	163	17	83	*.384
1924—	St. Louis	Nat.	143	536	•121	*227	25	94	*.424
1925—	St. Louis	Nat.	138	504	133	203	*39	*143	*.403
1926—	St. Louis	Nat.	134	527	96	167	11	93	.317
1927—	New York	Nat.	•155	568	•133	205	26	125	.361
1928—	Boston	Nat.	140	486	99	188	21	94	*.387
1929—	Chicago	Nat.	*156	602	*156	229	39	149	.380
1930—	Chicago	Nat.	42	104	15	32	2	18	.308
1931—	Chicago	Nat.	100	357	64	118	16	90	.331
1932—	Chicago	Nat.	19	58	10	13	1	7	.224
1933—	St. Louis	Nat.	46	83	9	27	2	21	.325
1933—	St. Louis	Amer.	11	9	2	3	1	2	.333
1934—	St. Louis	Amer.	24	23	2	7	1	11	.304
1935—	St. Louis	Amer	10	24	1	5	0	3	.208
1936—	St. Louis	Amer.	2	5	1	2	0	2	.400
1937—	St. Louis	Amer.	20	56	7	18	1	11	.321
1938—	Baltimore	Int.	16	27	2	2	0	0	.074
1939—	Chattanooga	South.	3	3	1	2	1	2	.667
1940—	Oklahoma City	Tex.	1	1	0	1	0	0	1.000
1942—	Ft. Worth	Tex.	1	4	0	1	0	2	.250
	National League Totals		2192	8056	1566	2895	298	1550	.359
	American League Totals		67	117	13	35	3	29	.299
	Major League Totals		2259	8173	1579	2930	301	1579	.358

WORLD SERIES RECORD

Year	Club	League	G.	AB.	R.	H.	HR.	RBI.	B.A.
1926—	St. Louis	Nat	7	28	2	7	0	4	.250
1929—	Chicago	Nat.	5	21	4	5	0	1	.238
	World Series Totals		12	49	6	12	0	5	.245

WAITE CHARLES (SCHOOLBOY) HOYT

Year	Club	League	G.	IP.	W.	L.	Pct.	ERA.
1916—	Mt. Carmel	Pa. State	6	....	5	1	.833	......
1916—	Hartford-Lynn	Eastern	10	71	4	5	.444	......
1917—	Memphis	Southern	17	103	3	9	.250	......
1917—	Montreal	International	28	215	7	17	.292	2.51
1918—	Nashville	Southern	19	137	5	10	.333	......
1918—	New York	National	1	1	0	0	.000	0.00
1918—	Newark	International	5	43	2	3	.400	2.09
1919—	Boston	American	13	105	4	6	.400	3.26
1920—	Boston	American	22	121	6	6	.500	4.39
1921—	New York	American	44	282	19	13	.594	3.10
1922—	New York	American	37	265	19	12	.613	3.43
1923—	New York	American	37	239	17	9	.654	3.01
1924—	New York	American	46	247	18	13	.581	3.79
1925—	New York	American	46	243	11	14	.440	4.00
1926—	New York	American	40	218	16	12	.571	3.84
1927—	New York	American	36	256	•22	7	*.759	2.64
1928—	New York	American	42	273	23	7	.767	3.36
1929—	New York	American	30	202	10	9	.526	4.23
1930—	N.Y.-Detroit	American	34	183	11	10	.524	4.72
1931—	Detroit-Phila.	American	32	203	13	13	.500	4.97
1932—	Brooklyn-N.Y.	National	26	124	6	10	.375	4.35
1933—	Pittsburgh	National	36	117	5	7	.417	2.92
1934—	Pittsburgh	National	48	191	15	6	.714	2.92
1935—	Pittsburgh	National	39	164	7	11	.389	3.40
1936—	Pittsburgh	National	22	117	7	5	.583	2.69
1937—	Pittsburgh-Brooklyn	National	38	195	8	9	.471	3.42
1938—	Brooklyn	National	6	16	0	3	.000	5.06
	American League Totals		459	2837	189	131	.591	3.68
	National League Totals		216	925	48	51	.485	3.31
	Major League Totals		675	3762	237	182	.566	3.59

WORLD SERIES RECORD

Year	Club	League	G.	IP.	W.	L.	Pct.	ERA.
1921—	New York	American	3	27	2	1	.667	0.00
1922—	New York	American	2	8	0	1	.000	1.13
1923—	New York	American	1	2⅓	0	0	.000	15.43
1926—	New York	American	2	15	1	1	.500	1.20
1927—	New York	American	1	7⅓	1	0	1.000	4.91
1928—	New York	American	2	18	2	0	1.000	1.50
1931—	Philadelphia	American	1	6	0	1	.000	4.50
	World Series Totals		12	83⅔	6	4	.600	1.83

CARL OWEN (KING CARL) HUBBELL

Year	Club	League	G.	IP.	W.	L.	Pct.	ERA.
1923—	Cushing	Oklahoma State	(No records available)					
1924—	Cushing	Oklahoma State	(No records available)					
1924—	Ardmore	West Assn.	2	12	1	0	1.000	......
1924—	Oklahoma City	Western	2	15	1	1	.500	......
1925—	Oklahoma City	Western	45	284	17	13	.567	......
1926—	Toronto	Int.	31	93	7	7	.500	3.77
1927—	Decatur	I.I.I.	23	185	14	7	.667	2.53
1927—	Fort Worth	Texas	2	3	0	1	.000	......
1928—	Beaumont	Texas	21	185	12	9	.571	2.97
1928—	New York	National	20	124	10	6	.625	2.83
1929—	New York	National	39	268	18	11	.621	3.69
1930—	New York	National	37	242	17	12	.586	3.87
1931—	New York	National	36	248	14	12	.538	2.65
1932—	New York	National	40	284	18	11	.621	2.50
1933—	New York	National	45	*309	*23	12	.657	*1.66
1934—	New York	National	49	313	21	12	.636	*2.30
1935—	New York	National	42	303	23	12	.657	3.27
1936—	New York	National	42	304	*26	6	*.813	*2.31

Year	Club	League	G.	IP.	W.	L.	Pct.	ERA.
1937—New York	National		39	262	*22	8	*.733	3.19
1938—New York	National		24	179	13	10	.565	3.07
1939—New York	National		29	154	11	9	.550	2.75
1940—New York	National		31	214	11	12	.478	3.66
1941—New York	National		26	164	11	9	.550	3.57
1942—New York	National		24	157	11	8	.579	3.96
1943—New York	National		12	66	4	4	.500	4.91
Major League Totals			535	3591	253	154	.622	2.98

WORLD SERIES RECORD

Year	Club	League	G.	IP.	W.	L.	Pct.	ERA.
1933—New York	National		2	20	2	0	1.000	0.00
1936—New York	National		2	16	1	1	.500	2.25
1937—New York	National		2	14⅓	1	1	.500	3.77
World Series Totals			6	50⅓	4	2	.667	1.79

MILLER JAMES HUGGINS

Year	Club	League	G.	AB.	R.	H.	HR.	SB.	B.A.
1899—Mansfield	Int. St.				(No Records available)				
1900					(Played semi-pro baseball)				
1901—St. Paul	West.		129	474	79	153	2	17	.322
1902—St. Paul	A. A.		129	466	75	153	0	34	.328
1903—St. Paul	A. A.		124	444	91	137	0	48	.308
1904—Cincinnati	Nat.		140	491	96	129	2	13	.263
1905—Cincinnati	Nat.		149	564	117	154	1	27	.273
1906—Cincinnati	Nat.		146	545	81	159	0	41	.292
1907—Cincinnati	Nat.		*156	561	64	139	1	28	.248
1908—Cincinnati	Nat.		135	498	65	119	0	30	.239
1909—Cincinnati	Nat.		46	159	18	34	0	11	.213
1910—St. Louis	Nat.		151	547	101	145	1	34	.265
1911—St. Louis	Nat.		136	509	106	133	1	37	.261
1912—St. Louis	Nat.		120	431	82	131	0	35	.304
1913—St. Louis	Nat.		121	382	74	109	0	23	.285
1914—St. Louis	Nat.		148	509	85	134	1	32	.263
1915—St. Louis	Nat.		107	353	57	85	2	13	.241
1916—St. Louis	Nat.		18	9	2	3	0	0	.333
Major League Totals			1573	5558	948	1474	9	324	.265

RECORD AS MANAGER

Year	Club	League	Position	W.	L.
1913—St. Louis	National		Eighth	51	99
1914—St. Louis	National		Third	81	72
1915—St. Louis	National		Sixth	72	81
1916—St. Louis	National		Seventh†	60	93
1917—St. Louis	National		Third	82	70
1918—New York	American		Fourth	60	63
1919—New York	American		Third	80	59
1920—New York	American		Third	95	59
1921—New York	American		First	98	55
1922—New York	American		First	94	60
1923—New York	American		First	98	54
1924—New York	American		Second	89	63
1925—New York	American		Seventh	69	85
1926—New York	American		First	91	63
1927—New York	American		First	110	44
1928—New York	American		First	101	53
1929—New York	American		Second	88	66
Major League Totals				1419	1139

†Tied for position.

WORLD SERIES RECORD

Year	Club	League	W.	L.
1921—New York	American		3	5
1922—New York	American		0	4
1923—New York	American		4	2
1926—New York	American		3	4
1927—New York	American		4	0
1928—New York	American		4	0

JAMES AUGUSTUS (CATFISH) HUNTER

Year	Club	League	G.	IP.	W.	L.	Pct.	ERA.
1964—Daytona Beach	Florida St.				(Did not play)			
1965—Kansas City	American		32	133	8	8	.500	4.26
1966—Kansas City	American		30	177	9	11	.450	4.02
1967—Kansas City	American		35	260	13	17	.433	2.80
1968—Oakland	American		36	234	13	13	.500	3.35
1969—Oakland	American		38	247	12	15	.444	3.35
1970—Oakland	American		40	262	18	14	.563	3.81
1971—Oakland	American		37	274	21	11	.656	2.96
1972—Oakland	American		38	295	21	7	*.750	2.04
1973—Oakland	American		36	256	21	5	*.808	3.34
1974—Oakland	American		41	318	●25	12	.676	*2.49
1975—New York	American		39	*328	●23	14	.622	2.58
1976—New York	American		36	299	17	15	.531	3.52
1977—New York	American		22	143	9	9	.500	4.72
1978—New York	American		21	118	12	6	.667	3.58
1979—New York	American		19	105	2	9	.182	5.31
Major League Totals			500	3449	224	166	.574	3.26

WORLD SERIES RECORD

Year	Club	League	G.	IP.	W.	L.	Pct.	ERA.
1972—Oakland	American		3	16	2	0	1.000	2.81
1973—Oakland	American		2	13⅓	1	0	1.000	2.03
1974—Oakland	American		2	7⅔	1	0	1.000	1.17
1976—New York	American		1	8⅔	0	1	.000	3.12
1977—New York	American		2	4⅓	1	1	.000	10.38
1978—New York	American		2	13	1	1	.500	4.15
World Series Totals			12	63	5	3	.625	3.29

MONFORD MERRILL (MONTE) IRVIN
ORGANIZED BALL PLAYING RECORD

Year	Club	League	G.	AB.	R.	H.	HR.	RBI.	B.A.
1949—Jersey City	Int.		63	204	55	76	9	52	.373
1949—New York	Nat.		36	76	7	17	0	7	.224
1950—Jersey City	Int.		18	51	28	26	10	33	.510
1950—New York	Nat.		110	374	61	112	15	66	.299
1951—New York	Nat.		151	558	94	174	24	*121	.312
1952—New York	Nat.		46	126	10	39	4	21	.310
1953—New York	Nat.		124	444	72	146	21	97	.329
1954—New York	Nat.		135	432	62	113	19	64	.262
1955—New York	Nat.		51	150	16	38	1	17	.253
1955—Minneapolis	A. A.		75	250	57	88	14	52	.352
1956—Chicago	Nat.		111	339	44	92	15	50	.271
Major League Totals			764	2499	366	731	99	443	.293

WORLD SERIES RECORD

Year	Club	League	G.	AB.	R.	H.	HR.	RBI.	B.A.
1951—New York	Nat.		6	24	3	11	0	2	.458
1954—New York	Nat.		4	9	1	2	0	2	.222
World Series Totals			10	33	4	13	0	4	*.394

REGGIE JACKSON

Year	Club	League	G.	AB.	R.	H.	HR.	RBI.	B.A.
1966—Lewiston	N'west		12	48	14	14	2	11	.292
1966—Modesto	Calif.		56	221	50	66	21	60	.299
1967—Birmingham	South.		114	413	*84	121	17	58	.293
1967—Kansas City	Amer.		35	118	13	21	1	6	.178
1968—Oakland	Amer.		154	553	82	138	29	74	.250
1969—Oakland	Amer.		152	549	*123	151	47	118	.275
1970—Oakland	Amer.		149	426	57	101	23	66	.237
1971—Oakland	Amer.		150	567	87	157	32	80	.277
1972—Oakland	Amer.		135	499	72	132	25	75	.265
1973—Oakland	Amer.		151	539	*99	158	*32	*117	.293
1974—Oakland	Amer.		148	506	90	146	29	93	.289
1975—Oakland	Amer.		157	593	91	150	●36	104	.253
1976—Baltimore	Amer.		134	498	84	138	27	91	.277
1977—New York	Amer.		146	525	93	150	32	110	.286
1978—New York	Amer.		139	511	82	140	27	97	.274
1979—New York	Amer.		131	465	78	138	29	89	.297
1980—New York	Amer.		143	514	94	154	●41	111	.300
1981—New York	Amer.		94	334	33	79	15	54	.237
1982—California	Amer.		153	530	92	146	●39	101	.275
1983—California	Amer.		116	397	43	77	14	49	.194
1984—California	Amer.		143	525	67	117	25	81	.223
1985—California	Amer.		143	460	64	116	27	85	.252
1986—California	Amer.		132	419	65	101	18	58	.241
1987—Oakland	Amer.		115	336	42	74	15	43	.220
Major League Totals			2820	9864	1551	2584	563	1702	.262

DIVISION SERIES RECORD

Year	Club	League	G.	AB.	R.	H.	HR.	RBI.	B.A.
1981—New York	Amer.		5	20	4	6	2	4	.300

CHAMPIONSHIP SERIES RECORD

Year	Club	League	G.	AB.	R.	H.	HR.	RBI.	B.A.
1971—Oakland	Amer.		3	12	2	4	2	2	.333
1972—Oakland	Amer.		5	18	1	5	0	2	.278
1973—Oakland	Amer.		5	21	0	3	0	0	.143
1974—Oakland	Amer.		4	12	0	2	0	1	.167
1975—Oakland	Amer.		3	12	1	5	1	3	.417
1977—New York	Amer.		5	16	1	2	0	1	.125
1978—New York	Amer.		4	13	5	6	2	6	.462
1980—New York	Amer.		3	11	1	3	0	0	.273
1981—New York	Amer.		2	4	1	0	0	1	.000
1982—California	Amer.		5	18	2	2	1	2	.111
1986—California	Amer.		6	26	2	5	0	2	.192
LCS Totals			45	163	16	37	6	20	.227

WORLD SERIES RECORD

Year	Club	League	G.	AB.	R.	H.	HR.	RBI.	B.A.
1973—Oakland	Amer.		7	29	3	9	1	6	.310
1974—Oakland	Amer.		5	14	3	4	1	1	.286
1977—New York	Amer.		6	20	10	9	5	8	.450
1978—New York	Amer.		6	23	2	9	2	8	.391
1981—New York	Amer.		3	12	3	4	1	1	.333
World Series Totals			27	98	21	35	10	24	.357

TRAVIS CALVIN (STONEWALL or JAX) JACKSON

Year	Club	League	G.	AB.	R.	H.	HR.	RBI.	B.A.
1921—Little Rock	South.		39	130	11	26	1	12	.200
1922—Little Rock	South.		147	521	59	146	7	....	.280
1922—New York	Nat.		3	8	1	0	0	0	.000
1923—New York	Nat.		96	327	45	90	4	37	.275
1924—New York	Nat.		151	596	81	180	11	76	.302
1925—New York	Nat.		112	411	51	117	9	59	.285
1926—New York	Nat.		111	385	64	126	8	51	.327
1927—New York	Nat.		127	469	67	149	14	98	.318
1928—New York	Nat.		150	537	73	145	14	77	.270
1929—New York	Nat.		149	551	92	162	21	94	.294
1930—New York	Nat.		116	431	70	146	13	82	.339
1931—New York	Nat.		145	555	65	172	5	71	.310
1932—New York	Nat.		52	195	23	50	4	38	.256
1933—New York	Nat.		53	122	11	30	0	12	.246
1934—New York	Nat.		137	523	75	140	16	101	.268
1935—New York	Nat.		128	511	74	154	9	80	.301
1936—New York	Nat.		126	465	41	107	7	53	.230

Year Club	League	G.	AB.	R.	H.	HR.	RBI.	B.A.
1937—Jersey City	Int.	6	20	0	5	0	1	.250
1938—Jersey City	Int.	10	17	0	5	0	2	.294
Major League Totals		1656	6086	833	1768	135	929	.291

WORLD SERIES RECORD

Year Club	League	G.	AB.	R.	H.	HR.	RBI.	B.A.
1923—New York	Nat.	1	1	0	0	0	0	.000
1924—New York	Nat.	7	27	3	2	0	1	.074
1933—New York	Nat.	5	18	3	4	0	2	.222
1936—New York	Nat.	6	21	1	4	0	1	.190
World Series Totals		19	67	7	10	0	4	.149

FERGUSON ARTHUR (FERGIE) JENKINS

Year Club	League	G.	IP.	W.	L.	Pct.	ERA.
1962—Miami	Florida St.	11	65	7	2	.778	0.97
1962—Buffalo	International	3	13	1	1	.500	5.54
1963—Arkansas	International	4	10	0	1	.000	6.30
1963—Miami	Florida St.	20	140	12	5	.706	3.41
1964—Chattanooga	Southern	21	139	10	6	.625	3.11
1964—Arkansas	P. Coast	11	57	5	5	.500	3.16
1965—Arkansas	P. Coast	32	122	8	6	.571	2.95
1965—Philadelphia	National	7	12	2	1	.667	2.25
1966—Philadelphia-Chicago	National	61	184	6	8	.429	3.33
1967—Chicago	National	38	289	20	13	.606	2.80
1968—Chicago	National	40	308	20	15	.571	2.63
1969—Chicago	National	43	311	21	15	.583	3.21
1970—Chicago	National	40	313	22	16	.579	3.39
1971—Chicago	National	39	∗325	∗24	13	.649	2.77
1972—Chicago	National	36	289	20	12	.625	3.21
1973—Chicago	National	38	271	14	16	.467	3.89
1974—Texas	American	41	328	●25	12	.676	2.83
1975—Texas	American	37	270	17	18	.486	3.93
1976—Boston	American	30	209	12	11	.522	3.27
1977—Boston	American	28	193	10	10	.500	3.68
1978—Texas	American	34	249	18	8	.692	3.04
1979—Texas	American	37	259	16	14	.533	4.07
1980—Texas	American	29	198	12	12	.500	3.77
1981—Texas	American	19	106	5	8	.385	4.50
1982—Chicago	National	34	217⅓	14	15	.483	3.15
1983—Chicago	National	33	167⅓	6	9	.400	4.30
American League Totals		255	1812	115	93	.553	3.54
National League Totals		409	2686⅔	169	133	.560	3.20
Major League Totals		664	4498⅔	284	226	.557	3.34

HUGH AMBROSE (EE-YAH) JENNINGS

Year Club	League	G.	AB.	R.	H.	HR.	SB.	B.A.
1890—Allentown	E. Int.-St.	13	50	8	16	....	....	.320
1891—Louisville	A. A.	81	316	46	95	1	14	.300
1892—Louisville	Nat.	152	584	66	137	2	24	.232
1893—Louis.-Balt.	Nat.	38	135	12	25	2	1	.192
1894—Baltimore	Nat.	128	505	136	168	4	36	.332
1895—Baltimore	Nat.	131	528	159	204	4	60	.385
1896—Baltimore	Nat.	129	523	125	208	0	73	.398
1897—Baltimore	Nat.	115	436	131	154	2	60	.353
1898—Baltimore	Nat.	143	533	136	173	0	31	.325
1899—Brkn.-Balt.	Nat.	63	223	44	67	0	18	.300
1900—Brooklyn	Nat.	112	440	62	119	2	35	.270
1901—Philadelphia	Nat.	81	302	38	83	1	13	.274
1902—Philadelphia	Nat.	78	289	31	80	1	8	.277
1903—Brooklyn	Nat.	6	17	2	4	0	0	.235
1903—Baltimore	East.	32	122	26	40	0	9	.328
1904—Baltimore	East.	92	332	65	97	1	23	.292
1905—Baltimore	East.	56	179	24	45	0	3	.251
1906—Baltimore	East.	75	242	24	60	0	2	.248
1907—Detroit	Amer.	2	4	0	1	0	0	.250
1908—Detroit	Amer.	1	0	0	0	0	0	.000
1909—Detroit	Amer.	2	4	1	2	0	0	.500
1912—Detroit	Amer.	1	1	0	0	0	0	.000
1918—Detroit	Amer.	1	0	0	0	0	0	.000
American Association Totals		81	316	46	95	1	14	.300
American League Totals		7	9	1	3	0	0	.333
National League Totals		1176	4515	942	1422	18	359	.315
Major League Totals		1264	4840	989	1520	19	373	.314

WALTER PERRY (BARNEY) JOHNSON

Year Club	League	G.	IP.	W.	L.	Pct.	ERA.
1907—Washington	Amer.	14	110	5	9	.357	....
1908—Washington	Amer.	36	257	14	14	.500	....
1909—Washington	Amer.	40	297	13	25	.342	....
1910—Washington	Amer.	●45	∗374	25	17	.595	....
1911—Washington	Amer.	40	322	25	13	.658	....
1912—Washington	Amer.	50	368	32	12	.727	....
1913—Washington	Amer.	48	∗346	∗36	7	.837	∗1.14
1914—Washington	Amer.	∗51	∗372	∗28	18	.609	1.72
1915—Washington	Amer.	47	∗337	∗27	13	.675	1.55
1916—Washington	Amer.	48	∗371	∗25	20	.556	1.89
1917—Washington	Amer.	47	328	23	16	.590	2.28
1918—Washington	Amer.	39	325	∗23	13	.639	∗1.27
1919—Washington	Amer.	39	290	20	14	.588	∗1.49
1920—Washington	Amer.	21	144	8	10	.444	3.13
1921—Washington	Amer.	35	264	17	14	.548	3.51

Year Club	League	G.	IP.	W.	L.	Pct.	ERA.
1922—Washington	Amer.	41	280	15	16	.484	2.99
1923—Washington	Amer.	42	261	17	12	.586	3.48
1924—Washington	Amer.	38	278	∗23	7	∗.767	∗2.72
1925—Washington	Amer.	30	229	20	7	.741	3.07
1926—Washington	Amer.	33	262	15	16	.484	3.61
1927—Washington	Amer.	18	108	5	6	.455	5.08
1928—Newark	Int.	1	0	0	0	.000	0.00
Major League Totals		802	5923	416	279	.599	....

WORLD SERIES RECORD

Year Club	League	G.	IP.	W.	L.	Pct.	ERA.
1924—Washington	American	3	24	1	2	.333	2.25
1925—Washington	American	3	26	2	1	.667	2.08
World Series Totals		6	50	3	3	.500	2.16

ADRIAN (ADDIE) JOSS

Year Club	League	G.	IP.	W.	L.	Pct.
1900—Toledo	Inter-State	49	....	19	16	.543
1901—Toledo	Western Assn.	41	353	25	15	.625
1902—Cleveland	American	32	269	17	13	.567
1903—Cleveland	American	32	284	18	13	.581
1904—Cleveland	American	25	192	14	10	.583
1905—Cleveland	American	33	289	20	12	.625
1906—Cleveland	American	34	282	21	9	.700
1907—Cleveland	American	42	339	27	10	.730
1908—Cleveland	American	42	324	24	12	.667
1909—Cleveland	American	33	243	14	13	.519
1910—Cleveland	American	13	107	5	5	.500
Major League Totals		286	2329	160	97	.623

ALBERT WILLIAM KALINE

Year Club	League	G.	AB.	R.	H.	HR.	RBI.	B.A.
1953—Detroit	Amer.	30	28	9	7	1	2	.250
1954—Detroit	Amer.	138	504	42	139	4	43	.276
1955—Detroit	Amer.	152	588	121	∗200	27	102	∗.340
1956—Detroit	Amer.	153	617	96	194	27	128	.314
1957—Detroit	Amer.	149	577	83	170	23	90	.295
1958—Detroit	Amer.	146	543	84	170	16	85	.313
1959—Detroit	Amer.	136	511	86	167	27	94	.327
1960—Detroit	Amer.	147	551	77	153	15	68	.278
1961—Detroit	Amer.	153	586	116	190	19	82	.324
1962—Detroit	Amer.	100	398	78	121	29	94	.304
1963—Detroit	Amer.	145	551	89	172	27	101	.312
1964—Detroit	Amer.	146	525	77	154	17	68	.293
1965—Detroit	Amer.	125	399	72	112	18	72	.281
1966—Detroit	Amer.	142	479	85	138	29	88	.288
1967—Detroit	Amer.	131	458	94	141	25	78	.308
1968—Detroit	Amer.	102	327	49	94	10	53	.287
1969—Detroit	Amer.	131	456	74	124	21	69	.272
1970—Detroit	Amer.	131	467	64	130	16	71	.278
1971—Detroit	Amer.	133	405	69	119	15	54	.294
1972—Detroit	Amer.	106	278	46	87	10	32	.313
1973—Detroit	Amer.	91	310	40	79	10	45	.255
1974—Detroit	Amer.	147	558	71	146	13	64	.262
Major League Totals		2834	10116	1622	3007	399	1583	.297

CHAMPIONSHIP SERIES RECORD

Year Club	League	G.	AB.	R.	H.	HR.	RBI.	B.A.
1972—Detroit	Amer.	5	19	3	5	1	1	.263

WORLD SERIES RECORD

Year Club	League	G.	AB.	R.	H.	HR.	RBI.	B.A.
1968—Detroit	Amer.	7	29	6	11	2	8	.379

TIMOTHY J. (TIM) KEEFE

Year Club	League	G.	IP.	W.	L.	Pct.	ShO.
1879—Utica-New Bedford	Nat. Assn.	24	....	....	....	....	....
1880—Albany	Nat. Assn.	18	....	....	....	....	....
1880—Troy	National	12	105	6	6	.500	0
1881—Troy	National	45	404	18	27	.400	4
1882—Troy	National	43	376	17	26	.395	1
1883—Metropolitan	Amer. Assn.	∗68	∗619	41	27	.603	5
1884—Metropolitan	Amer. Assn.	56	483	37	17	.685	4
1885—New York	National	46	400	32	13	.711	7
1886—New York	National	∗64	∗535	●42	20	.677	2
1887—New York	National	56	476	35	19	.648	2
1888—New York	National	51	434	∗35	11	∗.761	●8
1889—New York	National	47	363	28	13	.683	3
1890—New York	Players	30	227	17	11	.607	1
1891—N.Y.-Philadelphia	National	19	131	5	11	.313	0
1892—Philadelphia	National	39	312	19	16	.543	3
1893—Philadelphia	National	22	178	10	7	.588	0
American Association Totals		124	1102	78	44	.639	9
National League Totals		444	3714	247	169	.594	30
Players League Totals		30	227	17	11	.607	1
Major League Totals		598	5043	342	224	.604	40

WORLD SERIES RECORD

Year Club	League	G.	IP.	W.	L.	Pct.	ShO.
1884—Metropolitan	American Assn.	2	15	0	2	.000	0
1888—New York	National	4	35	4	0	1.000	0
1889—New York	National	2	11	0	1	.000	0
World Series Totals		8	61	4	3	.571	0

WILLIAM H. (WEE WILLIE) KEELER

Year	Club	League	G.	AB.	R.	H.	HR.	SB.	B.A.
1892—Binghamton	East.	93	410	109	153	2	12	*.373
1892—Binghamton	East.	93	410	109	153	2	12	*.373
1892—N.Y.	Nat.	13	49	6	15	0	5	.306
1893—N.Y.-Brooklyn	Nat.	29	90	19	30	2	7	.333
1893—Binghamton	East.	15	68	9	20	1	3	.294
1894—Baltimore	Nat.	128	593	164	218	5	30	.368
1895—Baltimore	Nat.	131	560	161	221	4	57	.395
1896—Baltimore	Nat.	127	546	154	214	4	73	.392
1897—Baltimore	Nat.	128	562	147	*243	0	63	*.432
1898—Baltimore	Nat.	128	564	126	214	0	26	*.379
1899—Brooklyn	Nat.	143	571	*141	215	1	44	.377
1900—Brooklyn	Nat.	137	568	106	*208	4	39	.366
1901—Brooklyn	Nat.	136	589	124	209	2	31	.355
1902—Brooklyn	Nat.	132	550	84	188	0	23	.342
1903—New York	Amer.	132	515	98	164	0	25	.318
1904—New York	Amer.	143	539	76	185	2	22	.343
1905—New York	Amer.	149	560	81	169	4	19	.302
1906—New York	Amer.	152	592	96	180	2	23	.304
1907—New York	Amer.	107	423	50	99	0	7	.234
1908—New York	Amer.	91	323	38	85	1	14	.263
1909—New York	Amer.	99	360	44	95	1	10	.264
1910—New York	Nat.	19	10	5	3	0	1	.300
1911—Toronto	East.	39	155	26	43	0	4	.277
American League Totals		873	3312	483	977	10	120	.295
National League Totals		1251	5252	1237	1978	22	399	.377
Major League Totals		2124	8564	1720	2955	32	519	.345

GEORGE CLYDE KELL

Year	Club	League	G.	AB.	R.	H.	HR.	RBI.	B.A.
1940—Newport	NE. Ark.	48	169	14	27	0	14	.160
1941—Newport	NE. Ark.	118	462	71	*143	1	75	.310
1942—Lancaster	Int.-St.	127	465	56	139	0	30	.299
1943—Lancaster	Int.-St.	138	555	*120	*220	1	79	*.396
1943—Philadelphia	Amer.	1	5	1	1	0	1	.200
1944—Philadelphia	Amer.	139	514	51	138	0	44	.268
1945—Philadelphia	Amer.	147	567	50	154	4	56	.272
1946—Phila.-Detroit	Amer.	131	521	70	168	4	52	.322
1947—Detroit	Amer.	152	588	75	188	5	93	.320
1948—Detroit	Amer.	92	368	47	112	2	44	.304
1949—Detroit	Amer.	134	522	97	179	3	59	*.343
1950—Detroit	Amer.	●157	*641	114	*218	8	101	.340
1951—Detroit	Amer.	147	598	92	*191	2	59	.319
1952—Det.-Boston	Amer.	114	428	52	133	7	57	.311
1953—Boston	Amer.	134	460	68	141	12	73	.307
1954—Bos.-Chicago	Amer.	97	326	40	90	5	58	.276
1955—Chicago	Amer.	128	429	44	134	8	81	.312
1956—Chi.-Balt.	Amer.	123	425	52	115	9	48	.271
1957—Baltimore	Amer.	99	310	28	92	9	44	.297
Major League Totals		1795	6702	881	2054	78	870	.306

JOSEPH JAMES KELLEY

Year	Club	League	G.	AB.	R.	H.	HR.	SB.	B.A.
1891—Lowell	N. Eng.	57	245	50	81	...	21	.331
1891—Bos.-Pittsburgh	Nat.	14	52	8	12	0	0	.231
1892—Omaha	West.	49	203	32	67	...	18	.330
1892—Pitts.-Balt.	Nat.	66	232	30	57	0	7	.246
1893—Baltimore	Nat.	124	490	120	153	9	38	.312
1894—Baltimore	Nat.	129	509	167	199	6	45	.391
1895—Baltimore	Nat.	131	510	148	189	10	59	.371
1896—Baltimore	Nat.	130	516	147	191	8	90	.370
1897—Baltimore	Nat.	129	503	113	196	5	50	.390
1898—Baltimore	Nat.	124	467	71	153	3	22	.328
1899—Brooklyn	Nat.	144	540	107	178	6	31	.330
1900—Brooklyn	Nat.	118	453	92	144	6	26	.318
1901—Brooklyn	Nat.	120	493	77	152	4	20	.308
1902—Baltimore	Amer.	60	222	50	69	1	12	.311
1902—Cincinnati	Nat.	37	156	24	51	1	3	.327
1903—Cincinnati	Nat.	104	383	85	121	3	18	.316
1904—Cincinnati	Nat.	123	449	75	126	0	15	.281
1905—Cincinnati	Nat.	87	321	43	89	1	8	.277
1906—Cincinnati	Nat.	127	465	43	106	1	9	.228
1907—Toronto	East.	91	314	32	101	1	5	.322
1908—Boston	Nat.	62	228	25	59	2	5	.259
1909—Toronto	East.	107	357	49	96	1	11	.269
1910—Toronto	East.	46	110	13	31	0	4	.282
American League Totals		60	222	50	69	1	12	.311
National League Totals		1769	6767	1375	2176	65	446	.322
Major League Totals		1829	6989	1425	2245	66	458	.321

PITCHING RECORD

Year	Club	League	G.	I.P.	W.	L.	Pct.
1891—Lowell	New England	14	121	10	3	.769

GEORGE LANGE (HIGH POCKETS) KELLY

Year	Club	League	G.	AB.	R.	H.	HR.	RBI.	B.A.
1914—Victoria	N. W.	141	436	45	109	7	.....	.250
1915—Victoria	N. W.	94	361	57	107	5	.....	.297
1915—New York	Nat.	17	38	2	6	1	5	.158
1916—New York	Nat.	49	76	4	12	0	2	.158
1917—N.York-Pitts.	Nat.	19	30	2	2	0	0	.067
1917—Rochester	Int.	32	120	16	36	4	.....	.300
1918—New York	Nat.	(In Military Service)						

Year	Club	League	G.	AB.	R.	H.	HR.	RBI.	B.A.
1919—Rochester	Int.	103	376	72	134	15	.....	.356
1919—New York	Nat.	32	107	12	31	1	13	.290
1920—New York	Nat.	155	590	69	157	11	●94	.266
1921—New York	Nat.	149	587	95	181	*23	122	.308
1922—New York	Nat.	151	592	96	194	17	107	.328
1923—New York	Nat.	145	560	82	172	16	103	.307
1924—New York	Nat.	144	571	91	185	21	●136	.324
1925—New York	Nat.	147	586	87	181	20	99	.309
1926—New York	Nat.	136	499	70	151	13	80	.303
1927—Cincinnati	Nat.	61	222	27	60	5	21	.270
1928—Cincinnati	Nat.	116	402	46	119	3	58	.296
1929—Cincinnati	Nat.	147	577	73	169	5	103	.293
1930—Cin.-Chicago	Nat.	90	354	40	109	8	54	.308
1930—Minneapolis	A. A.	34	147	25	53	6	38	.361
1931—Minneapolis	A. A.	155	606	84	194	20	112	.320
1932—Brooklyn	Nat.	64	202	23	49	4	22	.243
1932—Jersey City	Int.	47	153	18	45	6	31	.294
1933—Oakland	P. C.	21	56	5	13	1	6	.232
Major League Totals		1622	5993	819	1778	148	1019	.297

WORLD SERIES RECORD

Year	Club	League	G.	AB.	R.	H.	HR.	RBI.	B.A.
1921—New York	Nat.	8	30	3	7	0	3	.233
1922—New York	Nat.	5	18	0	5	0	2	.278
1923—New York	Nat.	6	22	1	4	0	1	.182
1924—New York	Nat.	7	31	7	9	1	4	.290
World Series Totals		26	101	11	25	1	10	.248

MICHAEL JOSEPH (KING) KELLY

Year	Club	League	G.	AB.	R.	H.	HR.	SB.	B.A.
1878—Cincinnati	Nat.	59	231	29	65	0	.....	.281
1879—Cincinnati	Nat.	76	342	78	119	3	.....	.348
1880—Chicago	Nat.	82	335	71	98	1	.....	.293
1881—Chicago	Nat.	80	353	84	114	2	.....	.323
1882—Chicago	Nat.	84	377	81	115	1	.....	.305
1883—Chicago	Nat.	98	430	92	109	3	.....	.253
1884—Chicago	Nat.	107	448	*120	153	12	.....	.341
1885—Chicago	Nat.	107	438	*124	126	9	.....	.288
1886—Chicago	Nat.	118	451	*155	175	4	53	*.388
1887—Boston	Nat.	114	525	119	207	8	84	.394
1888—Boston	Nat.	105	440	85	140	9	56	.318
1889—Boston	Nat.	125	507	120	149	7	68	.293
1890—Boston	Players	90	352	89	114	3	40	.324
1891—Cin.-Bos.(N.L.)	A. A.	77	264	50	73	2	16	.276
1891—Boston	Nat.	24	96	14	23	0	24	.240
1892—Boston	Nat.	72	279	40	56	1	24	.201
1893—New York	Nat.	16	54	8	17	0	5	.315
1894—Allentown	Pa. State	75	325	82	99	3	.....	.305
1894—Allen.-Yonkers	Eastern	15	61	11	23	0	.....	.377
American Association Totals		77	264	50	73	2	16	.276
Players League Totals		90	352	89	114	3	40	.324
National League Totals		1267	5306	1220	1666	60	.....	.314
Major League Totals		1434	5922	1359	1853	65	.....	.313

HARMON CLAYTON (KILLER) KILLEBREW, JR.

Year	Club	League	G.	AB.	R.	H.	HR.	RBI.	B.A.
1954—Washington	Amer.	9	13	1	4	0	3	.308
1955—Washington	Amer.	38	80	12	16	4	7	.200
1956—Washington	Amer.	44	99	10	22	5	13	.222
1956—Charlotte	Sally	70	249	61	81	15	63	.325
1957—Chattanooga	South.	142	519	90	145	*29	101	.279
1957—Washington	Amer.	9	31	4	9	2	5	.290
1958—Washington	Amer.	13	31	2	6	0	2	.194
1958—Indianapolis	A. A.	38	121	14	26	2	10	.215
1958—Chattanooga	South.	86	299	58	92	17	54	.308
1959—Washington	Amer.	153	546	98	132	●42	105	.242
1960—Washington	Amer.	124	442	84	122	31	80	.276
1961—Minnesota	Amer.	150	541	94	156	46	122	.288
1962—Minnesota	Amer.	155	552	85	134	*48	*126	.243
1963—Minnesota	Amer.	142	515	88	133	*45	96	.258
1964—Minnesota	Amer.	158	577	95	156	*49	111	.270
1965—Minnesota	Amer.	113	401	78	108	25	75	.269
1966—Minnesota	Amer.	162	569	89	160	39	110	.281
1967—Minnesota	Amer.	163	547	105	147	●44	113	.269
1968—Minnesota	Amer.	100	295	40	62	17	40	.210
1969—Minnesota	Amer.	●162	555	106	153	*49	*140	.276
1970—Minnesota	Amer.	157	527	96	143	41	113	.271
1971—Minnesota	Amer.	147	500	61	127	28	*119	.254
1972—Minnesota	Amer.	139	433	53	100	26	74	.231
1973—Minnesota	Amer.	69	248	29	60	5	32	.242
1974—Minnesota	Amer.	122	333	28	74	13	54	.222
1975—Kansas City	Amer.	106	312	25	62	14	44	.199
Major League Totals		2435	8147	1283	2086	573	1584	.256

WORLD SERIES RECORD

Year	Club	League	G.	AB.	R.	H.	HR.	RBI.	B.A.
1965—Minnesota	Amer.	7	21	2	6	1	2	.286

RALPH McPHERRAN KINER

Year	Club	League	G.	AB.	R.	H.	HR.	RBI.	B.A.
1941—Albany	East.	●141	509	94	142	11	66	.279
1942—Albany	East.	*141	483	84	124	*14	75	.257

Year	Club	League	G.	AB.	R.	H.	HR.	RBI.	B.A.
1943—Toronto	Int.		43	144	22	34	2	13	.236
1943-44-45—Pittsburgh	Nat.				(In Military Service)				
1946—Pittsburgh	Nat.		144	502	63	124	*23	81	.247
1947—Pittsburgh	Nat.		152	565	118	177	●51	127	.313
1948—Pittsburgh	Nat.		●156	555	104	147	●40	123	.265
1949—Pittsburgh	Nat.		152	549	116	170	*54	*127	.310
1950—Pittsburgh	Nat.		150	547	112	149	*47	118	.272
1951—Pittsburgh	Nat.		151	531	●124	164	*42	109	.309
1952—Pittsburgh	Nat.		149	516	90	126	●37	87	.244
1953—Pitts.-Chi.	Nat.		*158	562	100	157	35	116	.279
1954—Chicago	Nat.		147	557	88	159	22	73	.285
1955—Cleveland	Amer.		113	321	56	73	18	54	.243
	National League Totals		1359	4884	915	1373	351	961	.281
	American League Totals		113	321	56	73	18	54	.243
	Major League Totals		1472	5205	971	1451	369	1015	.279

CHARLES HERBERT (CHUCK) KLEIN

Year	Club	League	G.	AB.	R.	H.	HR.	RBI.	B.A.
1927—Evansville	I.I.I.		14	49	10	16	2	....	.327
1928—Fort Wayne	Cent.		88	359	85	119	26	....	.331
1928—Philadelphia	Nat.		64	253	41	91	11	34	.360
1929—Philadelphia	Nat.		149	616	126	219	*43	145	.356
1930—Philadelphia	Nat.		●156	648	*158	250	40	170	.386
1931—Philadelphia	Nat.		148	594	●121	200	*31	*121	.337
1932—Philadelphia	Nat.		●154	650	*152	*226	*38	137	.348
1933—Philadelphia	Nat.		152	606	101	*223	*28	*120	*.368
1934—Chicago	Nat.		115	435	78	131	20	80	.301
1935—Chicago	Nat.		119	434	71	127	21	73	.293
1936—Chi.-Phil.	Nat.		146	601	102	184	25	104	.306
1937—Philadelphia	Nat.		115	406	74	132	15	57	.325
1938—Philadelphia	Nat.		129	458	53	113	8	61	.247
1939—Phi.-Pit.	Nat.		110	317	45	90	12	56	.284
1940—Philadelphia	Nat.		116	354	39	77	7	37	.218
1941—Philadelphia	Nat.		50	73	6	9	1	3	.123
1942—Philadelphia	Nat.		14	14	0	1	0	0	.071
1943—Philadelphia	Nat.		12	20	0	2	0	3	.100
1944—Philadelphia	Nat.		4	7	1	1	0	0	.143
	Major League Totals		1753	6486	1168	2076	300	1201	.320

WORLD SERIES RECORD

Year	Club	League	G.	AB.	R.	H.	HR.	RBI.	B.A.
1935—Chicago	Nat.		5	12	2	4	1	2	.333

SANFORD (SANDY) KOUFAX

Year	Club	League	G.	IP.	W.	L.	Pct.	ERA.
1955—Brooklyn	National	12	42	2	2	.500	3.00
1956—Brooklyn	National	16	59	2	4	.333	4.88
1957—Brooklyn	National	34	104	5	4	.556	3.89
1958—Los Angeles	National	40	159	11	11	.500	4.47
1959—Los Angeles	National	35	153	8	6	.571	4.06
1960—Los Angeles	National	37	175	8	13	.381	3.91
1961—Los Angeles	National	42	256	18	13	.581	3.52
1962—Los Angeles	National	28	184	14	7	.667	*2.54
1963—Los Angeles	National	40	311	●25	5	.833	*1.88
1964—Los Angeles	National	29	223	19	5	*.792	*1.74
1965—Los Angeles	National	43	*336	*26	8	*.765	*2.04
1966—Los Angeles	National	41	*323	*27	9	.750	*1.73
	Major League Totals	397	2325	165	87	.655	2.76

WORLD SERIES RECORD

Year	Club	League	G.	IP.	W.	L.	Pct.	ERA.
1959—Los Angeles	National	2	9	0	1	.000	1.00
1963—Los Angeles	National	2	18	2	0	1.000	1.50
1965—Los Angeles	National	3	24	2	1	.667	0.38
1966—Los Angeles	National	1	6	0	1	.000	1.50
	World Series Totals	8	57	4	3	.571	0.95

NAPOLEON (LARRY) LAJOIE

Year	Club	League	G.	AB.	R.	H.	HR.	SB.	B.A.
1896—Fall River	N. Eng.		80	380	94	163	16	....	*.429
1896—Philadelphia	Nat.		39	174	37	57	4	6	.328
1897—Philadelphia	Nat.		126	545	107	198	*10	22	.363
1898—Philadelphia	Nat.		147	610	113	200	5	33	.328
1899—Philadelphia	Nat.		72	308	70	117	6	14	.380
1900—Philadelphia	Nat.		102	451	95	156	7	25	.346
1901—Philadelphia	Amer.		131	543	*145	*229	*14	27	*.422
1902—Phila.-Cleveland	Amer.		87	352	81	129	7	19	.366
1903—Cleveland	Amer.		126	488	90	173	7	22	*.355
1904—Cleveland	Amer.		140	554	92	*211	5	31	*.381
1905—Cleveland	Amer.		65	249	29	82	2	11	.329
1906—Cleveland	Amer.		152	602	88	*214	0	20	.355
1907—Cleveland	Amer.		137	509	53	153	2	24	.301
1908—Cleveland	Amer.		*157	581	77	168	2	15	.289
1909—Cleveland	Amer.		128	469	56	152	1	13	.324
1910—Cleveland	Amer.		*159	*591	94	*227	4	27	*.384
1911—Cleveland	Amer.		90	315	36	115	2	13	.365
1912—Cleveland	Amer.		117	448	66	165	0	18	.368
1913—Cleveland	Amer.		137	465	67	156	1	17	.335
1914—Cleveland	Amer.		121	419	37	108	0	14	.258
1915—Philadelphia	Amer.		129	490	40	137	1	10	.280
1916—Philadelphia	Amer.		113	426	33	105	2	15	.246
1917—Toronto	Int.		151	581	83	*221	5	4	*.380
1918—Indianapolis	A. A.		78	291	39	82	2	10	.282

American League Totals		1989	7501	1084	2524	50	296	.336
National League Totals		486	2088	422	728	32	100	.349
Major League Totals		2475	9589	1506	3252	82	396	.339

THOMAS CHARLES LASORDA
RECORD AS MANAGER

Year	Club	League	Position	W.	L.
1965 — Pocatello	Pioneer	*Second	33	33
1966 — Ogden	Pioneer	First	39	27
1967 — Ogden	Pioneer	First	41	25
1968 — Ogden	Pioneer	First	39	25
1969 — Spokane	Pacific Coast	Second (N)	71	73
1970 — Spokane	Pacific Coast	First (N)	94	52
1971 — Spokane	Pacific Coast	Third (N)	69	76
1972 — Albuquerque	Pacific Coast	First (E)	92	56
1976 — Los Angeles	National	Second (W)	2	2
1977 — Los Angeles	National	First (W)	98	64
1978 — Los Angeles	National	First (W)	95	67
1979 — Los Angeles	National	Third (W)	79	83
1980 — Los Angeles	National	Second (W)	92	71
1981 — Los Angeles	National	First (W)	36	21
....	(Second half)		Fourth (W)	27	26
1982 — Los Angeles	National	Second (W)	88	74
1983 — Los Angeles	National	First (W)	91	71
1984 — Los Angeles	National	Fourth (W)	79	83
1985 — Los Angeles	National	First (W)	95	67
1986 — Los Angeles	National	Fifth (W)	73	89
1987 — Los Angeles	National	Fourth (W)	73	89
1988 — Los Angeles	National	First (W)	94	67
1989 — Los Angeles	National	Fourth (W)	77	83
1990 — Los Angeles	National	Second (W)	86	76
1991 — Los Angeles	National	Second (W)	93	69

Year	Club	League	Position	W.	L.
1992 — Los Angeles	National	Sixth (W)	63	99
1993 — Los Angeles	National	Fourth (W)	81	81
1994 — Los Angeles	National	... ...	58	56
1995 — Los Angeles	National	First (W)	78	66
1996 — Los Angeles	National	First (W)	41	35
	Major League Totals			1599	1439

*Tied for position

DIVISION SERIES RECORD

Year	Club	League	W.	L.
1981 — Los Angeles	National	3	2
1995 — Los Angeles	National	0	3

CHAMPIONSHIP SERIES RECORD

Year	Club	League	W.	L.
1977 — Los Angeles	National	3	1
1978 — Los Angeles	National	3	1
1981 — Los Angeles	National	3	2
1983 — Los Angeles	National	1	3
1985 — Los Angeles	National	2	4
1988 — Los Angeles	National	4	3

WORLD SERIES RECORD

Year	Club	League	W.	L.
1977 — Los Angeles	National	2	4
1978 — Los Angeles	National	2	4
1981 — Los Angeles	National	4	2
1988 — Los Angeles	National	4	1

ANTHONY MICHAEL (TONY) LAZZERI

Year	Club	League	G.	AB.	R.	H.	HR.	RBI.	B.A.
1922 — Salt Lake	P.C.		45	78	9	15	1	8	.192
1923 — Peoria	I.I.I.		135	436	63	108	14	...	.248
1923 — Salt Lake	P.C.		39	130	25	46	7	21	.354
1924 — Lincoln	West.		82	316	65	104	28	...	.329
1924 — Salt Lake	P.C.		85	293	51	83	16	61	.283
1925 — Salt Lake	P.C.		197	710	202	252	60	222	.355
1926 — New York	Amer.		155	589	79	162	18	114	.275
1927 — New York	Amer.		153	570	92	176	18	102	.309
1928 — New York	Amer.		116	404	62	134	10	82	.332
1929 — New York	Amer.		147	545	101	193	18	106	.354
1930 — New York	Amer.		143	571	109	173	9	121	.303
1931 — New York	Amer.		135	484	67	129	8	83	.267
1932 — New York	Amer.		142	511	78	154	15	113	.301
1933 — New York	Amer.		139	523	94	154	18	104	.294
1934 — New York	Amer.		123	438	59	117	14	71	.267
1935 — New York	Amer.		130	477	72	130	13	63	.273
1936 — New York	Amer.		150	537	82	154	14	109	.287
1937 — New York	Amer.		126	446	56	109	14	70	.244
1938 — Chicago	Nat.		54	120	21	32	5	23	.267
1939 — Brooklyn-N.Y.	Nat.		27	83	13	24	4	14	.289
1939 — Toronto	Int.		39	97	19	22	1	20	.227
1940 — Toronto	Int.		13	17	0	3	0	0	.176
1941 — San Francisco	P.C.		102	315	40	78	3	39	.248
1942 — Portsmouth	Pied.		98	310	32	75	2	40	.242
1943 — Wilkes-Barre	East.		58	181	25	49	3	21	.271
	American League Totals		1659	6095	951	1785	169	1138	.293
	National League Totals		81	203	34	56	9	37	.276
	Major League Totals		1740	6298	985	1841	178	1175	.292

WORLD SERIES RECORD

Year	Club	League	G.	AB.	R.	H.	HR.	RBI.	B.A.
1926 — New York	Amer.		7	26	2	5	0	3	.192
1927 — New York	Amer.		4	15	1	4	0	2	.267

Year	Club	League	G.	AB.	R.	H.	HR.	RBI.	B.A.
1928— New York	Amer.		4	12	2	3	0	0	.250
1932— New York	Amer.		4	17	4	5	2	5	.294
1936— New York	Amer.		6	25	4	5	1	7	.200
1937— New York	Amer.		5	15	3	6	1	2	.400
1938— Chicago	Nat.		2	2	0	0	0	0	.000
World Series Totals			32	112	16	28	4	19	.250

ROBERT GRANVILLE LEMON

PITCHING RECORD

Year	Club	League	G.	IP.	W.	L.	Pct.	ERA.
1938—Oswego	Can.-Amer.	1	1	0	0	.000	0.00
1941—Wilkes-Barre	Eastern	1	1	0	1	.000	9.00
1946—Cleveland	American	32	94	4	5	.444	2.49
1947—Cleveland	American	37	167	11	5	.688	3.45
1948—Cleveland	American	43	*294	20	14	.588	2.82
1949—Cleveland	American	37	280	22	10	.688	2.99
1950—Cleveland	American	44	*288	*23	11	.676	3.84
1951—Cleveland	American	42	263	17	14	.548	3.52
1952—Cleveland	American	42	*310	22	11	.667	2.50
1953—Cleveland	American	41	*287	21	15	.583	3.36
1954—Cleveland	American	36	258	●23	7	.767	2.72
1955—Cleveland	American	35	211	●18	10	.643	3.88
1956—Cleveland	American	39	255	20	14	.588	3.04
1957—Cleveland	American	21	117	6	11	.353	4.62
1958—Cleveland	American	11	25	0	1	.000	5.40
1958—San Diego	P. Coast	12	56	2	5	.286	4.34
Major League Totals		460	2849	207	128	.618	3.23

WORLD SERIES RECORD

Year	Club	League	G.	IP.	W.	L.	Pct.	ERA.
1948—Cleveland	American	2	16⅓	2	0	1.000	1.65
1954—Cleveland	American	2	13⅓	0	2	.000	6.75
World Series Totals		4	29⅔	2	2	.500	3.94

BATTING RECORD

Year	Club	League	G.	AB.	R.	H.	HR.	RBI.	B.A.
1938—Springfield	M.-Atl.	7	18	1	4	0	2	.222
1938—Oswego	C.-A	75	282	44	88	7	34	.312
1939—Springfield	M.-Atl.	80	307	44	90	3	39	.293
1939—New Orleans	South.	52	207	30	64	0	22	.309
1940—Wilkes-Barre	East.	92	321	37	82	2	53	.255
1941—Wilkes-Barre	East.	*141	*562	*109	*169	4	43	.301
1941—Cleveland	Amer.	5	4	0	1	0	0	.250
1942—Baltimore	Int.	148	596	95	160	21	80	.268
1942—Cleveland	Amer.	5	5	0	0	0	0	.000
1943-44-45—Cleveland	Amer.	(In Military Service)						
1946—Cleveland	Amer.	55	89	9	16	1	4	.180
1947—Cleveland	Amer.	47	56	11	18	2	5	.321
1948—Cleveland	Amer.	52	119	20	34	5	21	.286
1949—Cleveland	Amer.	46	108	17	29	7	19	.269
1950—Cleveland	Amer.	72	136	21	37	6	26	.272
1951—Cleveland	Amer.	56	102	11	21	3	13	.206
1952—Cleveland	Amer.	54	124	14	28	2	9	.226
1953—Cleveland	Amer.	51	112	12	26	2	17	.232
1954—Cleveland	Amer.	40	98	11	21	2	10	.214
1955—Cleveland	Amer.	49	78	11	19	1	9	.244
1956—Cleveland	Amer.	43	93	8	18	5	12	.194
1957—Cleveland	Amer.	25	46	2	3	1	1	.065
1958—Cleveland	Amer.	15	13	1	3	0	1	.231
1958—San Diego	P.C.	32	69	2	18	0	7	.261
Major League Totals		615	1183	148	274	37	147	.232

FREDERICK CHARLES (LINDY) LINDSTROM

Year	Club	League	G.	AB.	R.	H.	HR.	RBI.	B.A.
1922—Toledo	A. A.	18	23	3	7	0	1	.304
1923—Toledo	A. A.	147	581	77	157	1	39	.270
1924—New York	Nat.	52	79	19	20	0	4	.253
1925—New York	Nat.	104	356	43	102	4	33	.287
1926—New York	Nat.	140	543	90	164	9	76	.302
1927—New York	Nat.	138	562	107	172	7	58	.306
1928—New York	Nat.	153	646	99	*231	14	107	.358
1929—New York	Nat.	130	549	99	175	15	91	.319
1930—New York	Nat.	148	609	127	231	22	106	.379
1931—New York	Nat.	78	303	39	91	5	36	.300
1932—New York	Nat.	144	595	83	161	15	92	.271
1933—Pittsburgh	Nat.	138	538	70	167	5	55	.310
1934—Pittsburgh	Nat.	97	383	59	111	4	49	.290
1935—Chicago	Nat.	90	342	49	94	3	62	.275
1936—Brooklyn	Nat.	26	106	12	28	0	10	.264
Major League Totals		1438	5611	895	1747	103	779	.311

WORLD SERIES RECORD

Year	Club	League	G.	AB.	R.	H.	HR.	RBI.	B.A.
1924—New York	Nat.	7	30	1	10	0	4	.333
1935—Chicago	Nat.	4	15	0	3	0	0	.200
World Series Totals		11	45	1	13	0	4	.289

ERNEST NATALI (SCHNOZ) LOMBARDI

Year	Club	League	G.	AB.	R.	H.	HR.	RBI.	B.A.
1926—Oakland	P. C.	4	6	.....	2	0	.....	.333
1927—Oakland	P. C.	16	20	2	3	1	6	.150
1927—Ogden	Utah-Idaho	50	186	29	74	4	47	.398
1928—Oakland	P. C.	120	318	39	120	8	47	.377

Year	Club	League	G.	AB.	R.	H.	HR.	RBI.	B.A.
1929—Oakland	P. C.	164	516	70	189	24	109	.366
1930—Oakland	P. C.	146	473	76	175	22	105	.370
1931—Brooklyn	Nat.	73	182	20	54	4	23	.297
1932—Cincinnati	Nat.	118	413	43	125	11	68	.303
1933—Cincinnati	Nat.	107	350	30	99	4	47	.283
1934—Cincinnati	Nat.	132	417	42	127	9	62	.305
1935—Cincinnati	Nat.	120	332	36	114	12	64	.343
1936—Cincinnati	Nat.	121	387	42	129	12	68	.333
1937—Cincinnati	Nat.	120	368	41	123	9	59	.334
1938—Cincinnati	Nat.	129	489	60	167	19	95	*.342
1939—Cincinnati	Nat.	130	450	43	129	20	85	.287
1940—Cincinnati	Nat.	109	376	50	120	14	74	.319
1941—Cincinnati	Nat.	117	398	33	105	10	60	.264
1942—Boston	Nat.	105	309	32	102	11	46	*.330
1943—New York	Nat.	104	295	19	90	10	51	.305
1944—New York	Nat.	117	373	37	95	10	58	.255
1945—New York	Nat.	115	368	46	113	19	70	.307
1946—New York	Nat.	88	238	19	69	12	39	.290
1947—New York	Nat.	48	110	8	31	4	21	.282
1948—Sacra.-Oak.	P. C.	102	284	25	75	11	55	.264
Major League Totals		1853	5855	601	1792	190	990	.306

ALFONSO RAMON (SENOR) LOPEZ

Year	Club	League	G.	AB.	R.	H.	HR.	RBI.	B.A.
1925—Tampa	Fla. St.	51	134	13	30	0	0	.224
1926—Tampa	Fla. St.	116	419	64	132	1	....	.315
1927—Jacksonville	So'East	128	416	58	115	3	....	276
1928—Macon	Sally	114	389	67	127	14	64	.326
1928—Brooklyn	Nat.	3	12	0	0	0	0	.000
1929—Atlanta	South.	143	490	70	160	10	85	.327
1930—Brooklyn	Nat.	128	421	60	130	6	57	.309
1931—Brooklyn	Nat.	111	360	38	97	0	40	.269
1932—Brooklyn	Nat.	126	404	44	111	1	43	.275
1933—Brooklyn	Nat.	126	372	39	112	3	41	.301
1934—Brooklyn	Nat.	140	439	58	120	7	54	.273
1935—Brooklyn	Nat.	128	379	50	95	3	39	.251
1936—Boston	Nat.	128	426	46	103	8	50	.242
1937—Boston	Nat.	105	334	31	68	3	38	.205
1938—Boston	Nat.	71	236	19	63	1	14	.267
1939—Boston	Nat.	131	412	32	104	8	49	.252
1940—Bos.-Pitts.	Nat.	95	293	35	80	3	41	.273
1941—Pittsburgh	Nat.	114	317	33	84	5	43	.265
1942—Pittsburgh	Nat.	103	289	17	74	1	26	.256
1943—Pittsburgh	Nat.	118	372	40	98	1	39	.263
1944—Pittsburgh	Nat.	115	331	27	76	1	34	.230
1945—Pittsburgh	Nat.	91	243	22	53	0	18	.218
1946—Pittsburgh	Nat.	56	150	13	46	1	12	.307
1947—Cleveland	Amer.	61	126	9	33	0	14	.262
1948—Indianapolis	A. A.	43	127	13	34	2	21	.268
American League Totals		61	126	9	33	0	14	.262
National League Totals		1889	5790	604	1514	52	638	.261
Major League Totals		1950	5916	613	1547	52	652	.261

RECORD AS MANAGER

Year	Club	League	Position	W.	L.
1948—Indianapolis	Amer. Assoc.	First	100	54
1949—Indianapolis	Amer. Assoc.	Second	93	61
1950—Indianapolis	Amer. Assoc.	Second	85	67
1951—Cleveland	American	Second	93	61
1952—Cleveland	American	Second	93	61
1953—Cleveland	American	Second	92	62
1954—Cleveland	American	First	111	43
1955—Cleveland	American	Second	93	61
1956—Cleveland	American	Second	88	66
1957—Chicago	American	Second	90	64
1958—Chicago	American	Second	82	72
1959—Chicago	American	First	94	60
1960—Chicago	American	Third	87	67
1961—Chicago	American	Fourth	86	76
1962—Chicago	American	Fifth	85	77
1963—Chicago	American	Second	94	68
1964—Chicago	American	Second	98	64
1965—Chicago	American	Second	95	67
1968—Chicago	American	Eighth†	33	48
1969—Chicago	American	Fourth	8	9
Major League Totals			1422	1026

†Tied for position.

WORLD SERIES RECORD

Year	Club	League	W.	L.
1954—Cleveland	American	0	4
1959—Chicago	American	2	4

THEODORE AMAR (TED) LYONS

Year	Club	League	G.	IP.	W.	L.	Pct.	ERA.
1923—Chicago	American	9	23	2	1	.667	6.26
1924—Chicago	American	41	216	12	11	.522	4.88
1925—Chicago	American	43	263	●21	11	.656	3.25
1926—Chicago	American	39	284	18	16	.529	3.01
1927—Chicago	American	39	●308	●22	14	.611	2.83
1928—Chicago	American	39	240	15	14	.517	3.98
1929—Chicago	American	37	259	14	20	.412	4.10
1930—Chicago	American	42	*298	22	15	.595	3.78
1931—Chicago	American	22	101	4	6	.400	4.01

Year	Club		G.	IP.	W.	L.	Pct.	ERA.
1932—Chicago	American		33	231	10	15	.400	3.27
1933—Chicago	American		36	228	10	*21	.323	4.38
1934—Chicago	American		30	205	11	13	.458	4.87
1935—Chicago	American		23	191	15	8	.652	3.02
1936—Chicago	American		26	182	10	13	.435	5.14
1937—Chicago	American		22	169	12	7	.632	4.15
1938—Chicago	American		23	195	9	11	.450	3.69
1939—Chicago	American		21	173	14	6	.700	2.76
1940—Chicago	American		22	186	12	8	.600	3.24
1941—Chicago	American		22	187	12	10	.545	3.71
1942—Chicago	American		20	180	14	6	.700	*2.10
1943-44-45—Chicago	American			(In Military Service)				
1946—Chicago	American		5	43	1	4	.200	2.30
Major League Totals			594	4162	260	230	.531	3.67

MICKEY CHARLES MANTLE

Year	Club	League	G.	AB.	R.	H.	HR.	RBI.	B.A.
1949—Independence	K-O-M	89	323	54	101	7	63	.313
1950—Joplin	W. A.	137	519	*141	*199	26	136	*.383
1951—New York	Amer.	96	341	61	91	13	65	.267
1951—Kansas City	A. A.	40	166	32	60	11	50	.361
1952—New York	Amer.	142	549	94	171	23	87	.311
1953—New York	Amer.	127	461	105	136	21	92	.295
1954—New York	Amer.	146	543	*129	163	27	102	.300
1955—New York	Amer.	147	517	121	158	*37	99	.306
1956—New York	Amer.	150	533	*132	188	*52	*130	*.353
1957—New York	Amer.	144	474	*121	173	34	94	.365
1958—New York	Amer.	150	519	*127	158	*42	97	.304
1959—New York	Amer.	144	541	104	154	31	75	.285
1960—New York	Amer.	153	527	*119	145	*40	94	.275
1961—New York	Amer.	153	514	●132	163	54	128	.317
1962—New York	Amer.	123	377	96	121	30	89	.321
1963—New York	Amer.	65	172	40	54	15	35	.314
1964—New York	Amer.	143	465	92	141	35	111	.303
1965—New York	Amer.	122	361	44	92	19	46	.255
1966—New York	Amer.	108	333	40	96	23	56	.288
1967—New York	Amer.	144	440	63	108	22	55	.245
1968—New York	Amer.	144	435	57	103	18	54	.237
Major League Totals			2401	8102	1677	2415	536	1509	.298

WORLD SERIES RECORDS

Year	Club	League	G.	AB.	R.	H.	HR.	RBI.	B.A.
1951—New York	Amer.	2	5	1	1	0	0	.200
1952—New York	Amer.	7	29	5	10	2	3	.345
1953—New York	Amer.	6	24	3	5	2	7	.208
1955—New York	Amer.	3	10	1	2	1	1	.200
1956—New York	Amer.	7	24	6	6	3	4	.250
1957—New York	Amer.	6	19	3	5	1	2	.263
1958—New York	Amer.	7	24	4	6	2	3	.250
1960—New York	Amer.	7	25	8	10	3	11	.400
1961—New York	Amer.	2	6	0	1	0	0	.167
1962—New York	Amer.	7	25	2	3	0	0	.120
1963—New York	Amer.	4	15	1	2	1	1	.133
1964—New York	Amer.	7	24	8	8	3	8	.333
World Series Totals			65	230	42	59	18	40	.257

HENRY EMMETT (HEINIE) MANUSH

Year	Club	League	G.	AB.	R.	H.	HR.	RBI.	B.A.
1921—Edmonton	W. Can.	83	327	52	105	*9	....	.321
1922—Omaha	West.	167	652	148	245	20	....	.376
1923—Detroit	Amer.	109	308	59	103	4	54	.334
1924—Detroit	Amer.	120	422	83	122	9	68	.289
1925—Detroit	Amer.	99	278	46	84	5	47	.303
1926—Detroit	Amer.	136	498	95	188	14	86	*.378
1927—Detroit	Amer.	151	593	102	177	6	90	.298
1928—St. Louis	Amer.	154	638	104	*241	13	108	.378
1929—St. Louis	Amer.	142	574	85	204	6	81	.355
1930—St. L.-Wash.	Amer.	137	554	100	194	9	94	.350
1931—Washington	Amer.	146	616	110	189	6	70	.307
1932—Washington	Amer.	149	625	121	214	14	116	.342
1933—Washington	Amer.	153	658	115	*221	5	95	.336
1934—Washington	Amer.	137	556	88	194	11	89	.349
1935—Washington	Amer.	119	479	68	131	4	56	.273
1936—Boston	Amer.	82	313	43	91	0	45	.291
1937—Brooklyn	Nat.	132	466	57	155	4	73	.333
1938—Brook.-Pitts.	Nat.	32	64	11	16	0	10	.250
1938—Toronto	Int.	81	277	38	86	3	39	.310
1939—Pittsburgh	Nat.	10	12	0	0	0	1	.000
1939—Toronto	Int.	66	228	32	55	0	19	.241
1940—Rocky Mount	Pied.	32	107	13	30	1	16	.280
1941—Greensboro	Pied.	12	32	7	10	0	7	.313
1942—Greensboro	Pied.		(Less than ten games)					
1943—Roanoke	Pied.	10	8	0	0	0	1	.000
1944—Scranton	East.		(Less than ten games)					
1945—Martinsville	Car.		(Less than ten games)					
American League Totals			1834	7112	1219	2353	106	1099	.331
National League Totals			174	542	68	171	4	84	.315
Major League Totals			2008	7654	1287	2524	110	1183	.330

WORLD SERIES RECORD

Year	Club	League	G.	AB.	R.	H.	HR.	RBI.	B.A.
1933—Washington	Amer.	5	18	2	2	0	0	.111

JAMES WALTER VINCENT (RABBIT) MARANVILLE

Year	Club	League	G.	AB.	R.	H.	HR.	RBI.	B.A.
1911—New Bedford	N. Eng.	117	422	41	96	2	....	.227
1912—New Bedford	N. Eng.	122	452	65	128	4	....	.283
1912—Boston	Nat.	26	86	8	18	0	7	.209
1913—Boston	Nat.	143	571	68	141	2	44	.247
1914—Boston	Nat.	●156	586	74	144	4	72	.246
1915—Boston	Nat.	149	509	51	124	4	47	.244
1916—Boston	Nat.	155	604	79	142	4	36	.235
1917—Boston	Nat.	142	561	69	146	3	41	.260
1918—Boston	Nat.	11	38	3	12	0	3	.316
1919—Boston	Nat.	131	480	44	128	5	43	.267
1920—Boston	Nat.	134	493	48	131	1	43	.266
1921—Pittsburgh	Nat.	153	612	90	180	1	70	.294
1922—Pittsburgh	Nat.	155	*672	115	198	0	63	.295
1923—Pittsburgh	Nat.	141	581	78	161	3	41	.277
1924—Pittsburgh	Nat.	152	594	62	158	2	71	.266
1925—Chicago	Nat.	75	266	37	62	0	23	.233
1926—Brooklyn	Nat.	78	234	32	55	0	24	.235
1927—Rochester	Int.	135	507	81	151	1	63	.298
1927—St. Louis	Nat.	9	29	0	7	0	1	.241
1928—St. Louis	Nat.	112	366	40	88	1	34	.240
1929—Boston	Nat.	146	560	87	159	0	55	.284
1930—Boston	Nat.	142	558	85	157	2	43	.281
1931—Boston	Nat.	145	562	69	146	0	33	.260
1932—Boston	Nat.	149	571	67	134	0	37	.235
1933—Boston	Nat.	143	478	46	104	0	38	.218
1934—Boston	Nat.		(Broke leg in exhibition game and did not play)					
1935—Boston	Nat.	23	67	3	10	0	5	.149
1936—Elmira	NYP	123	427	65	138	0	54	.323
1939—Albany	East.	6	17	3	2	0	2	.118
Major League Totals			2670	10078	1255	2605	28	874	.258

WORLD SERIES RECORD

Year	Club	League	G.	AB.	R.	H.	HR.	RBI.	B.A.
1914—Boston	Nat.	4	13	1	4	0	3	.308
1928—St. Louis	Nat.	4	13	2	4	0	0	.308
World Series Totals			8	26	3	8	0	3	.308

JUAN ANTONIO MARICHAL (SANCHEZ)

Year	Club	League	G.	IP.	W.	L.	Pct.	ERA.
1958—Michigan City	Midwest	35	*245	*21	8	.724	*1.87
1959—Springfield	Eastern	37	*271	18	13	.581	2.39
1960—Tacoma	P. Coast	18	139	11	5	.688	3.11
1960—San Francisco	National	11	81	6	2	.750	2.67
1961—San Francisco	National	29	185	13	10	.565	3.89
1962—San Francisco	National	37	263	18	11	.621	3.35
1963—San Francisco	National	41	*321	●25	8	.758	2.41
1964—San Francisco	National	33	269	21	8	.724	2.48
1965—San Francisco	National	39	295	22	13	.629	2.14
1966—San Francisco	National	37	307	25	6	.806	2.23
1967—San Francisco	National	26	202	14	10	.583	2.76
1968—San Francisco	National	38	*326	*26	9	.743	2.43
1969—San Francisco	National	37	300	21	11	.656	*2.10
1970—San Francisco	National	34	243	12	10	.545	4.11
1971—San Francisco	National	37	279	13	11	.621	2.94
1972—San Francisco	National	25	165	6	16	.273	3.71
1973—San Francisco	National	34	207	11	15	.423	3.83
1974—Boston	American	11	57	5	1	.833	4.89
1975—Los Angeles	National	2	6	0	1	.000	13.50
National League Totals			460	3449	238	141	.628	2.86
American League Totals			11	57	5	1	.833	4.89
Major League Totals			471	3506	243	142	.631	2.89

CHAMPIONSHIP SERIES RECORD

Year	Club	League	G.	IP.	W.	L.	Pct.	ERA.
1971—San Francisco	National	1	8	0	1	.000	2.25

WORLD SERIES RECORD

Year	Club	League	G.	IP.	W.	L.	Pct.	ERA.
1962—San Francisco	National	1	4	0	0	.000	0.00

RICHARD W. (RUBE) MARQUARD

Year	Club	League	G.	IP.	W.	L.	Pct.	ERA.
1907—Canton	Central	40	....	*23	13	.639	......
1908—Indianapolis	Amer. Assn.	*47	*367	*28	19	.596	......
1908—New York	National	1	5	0	1	.000	......
1909—New York	National	29	173	5	13	.278	......
1910—New York	National	13	69	4	4	.500	......
1911—New York	National	45	278	24	7	*.774	......
1912—New York	National	43	295	●26	11	.703	2.56
1913—New York	National	42	288	23	10	.697	2.50
1914—New York	National	39	268	12	22	.353	3.06
1915—N.Y.-Brooklyn	National	33	194	11	10	.524	4.04
1916—Brooklyn	National	36	205	13	6	.684	1.58
1917—Brooklyn	National	37	233	19	12	.613	2.55
1918—Brooklyn	National	34	239	9	●18	.333	2.64
1919—Brooklyn	National	8	59	3	3	.500	2.29
1920—Brooklyn	National	28	190	10	7	.588	3.22
1921—Cincinnati	National	39	266	17	14	.548	3.38
1922—Boston	National	39	198	11	15	.423	5.09
1923—Boston	National	38	239	11	14	.440	3.73
1924—Boston	National	6	36	1	2	.333	3.00
1925—Boston	National	26	72	2	8	.200	5.75
1926—Providence	Eastern	7	44	3	1	.750	3.68

Year	Club	League	G.	IP.	W.	L.	Pct.	ERA.
1927—Baltimore	Intenational	6	30	1	2	.333	
1927—Birmingham	Southern	3	11	0	1	.000	
1928—		(Out of Organized Ball)					
1929—Jacksonville	Southeastern	3	3	0	0	.000	
1930—Jacksonville	Southeastern	15	114	5	4	.556	2.13
1931—		(Umpire, Eastern League)					
1932—Atlanta	Southern	6	42	1	3	.250	
Major League Totals		536	3307	201	177	.532	3.13	

WORLD SERIES RECORD

Year	Club	League	G.	IP.	W.	L.	Pct.	ERA.
1911—New York	National	3	11⅔	0	1	.000	1.54
1912—New York	National	2	18	2	0	1.000	0.50
1913—New York	National	2	9	0	1	.000	7.00
1916—Brooklyn	National	2	11	0	2	.000	6.55
1920—Brooklyn	National	2	9	0	1	.000	1.00
World Series Totals		11	58⅔	2	5	.286	2.91

EDWIN LEE MATHEWS, JR.

Year	Club	League	G.	AB.	R.	H.	HR.	RBI.	B.A.
1949—H. Point-Th'ville	N.C. St.	63	240	62	87	17	56	.363
1950—Atlanta	South.	146	552	103	158	32	106	.286
1951—Atlanta	South.	37	128	23	37	6	29	.289
1951—Milwaukee	A. A.	12	9	2	3	1	5	.333
1952—Boston	Nat.	145	528	80	128	25	58	.242
1953—Milwaukee	Nat.	157	579	110	175	*47	135	.302
1954—Milwaukee	Nat.	138	476	96	138	40	103	.290
1955—Milwaukee	Nat.	141	499	108	144	41	101	.289
1956—Milwaukee	Nat.	151	552	103	150	37	95	.272
1957—Milwaukee	Nat.	148	572	109	167	32	94	.292
1958—Milwaukee	Nat.	149	546	97	137	31	77	.251
1959—Milwaukee	Nat.	148	594	118	182	*46	114	.306
1960—Milwaukee	Nat.	153	548	108	152	39	124	.277
1961—Milwaukee	Nat.	152	572	103	175	32	91	.306
1962—Milwaukee	Nat.	152	536	106	142	29	90	.265
1963—Milwaukee	Nat.	158	547	82	144	23	84	.263
1964—Milwaukee	Nat.	141	502	83	117	23	74	.233
1965—Milwaukee	Nat.	156	546	77	137	32	95	.251
1966—Atlanta	Nat.	134	452	72	113	16	53	.250
1967—Houston	Nat.	101	328	39	78	10	38	.238
1967—Detroit	Amer.	36	108	14	25	6	19	.231
1968—Detroit	Amer.	31	52	4	11	3	8	.212
National League Totals		2324	8377	1491	2279	503	1426	.272
American League Totals		67	160	18	36	9	27	.225
Major League Totals		2391	8537	1509	2315	512	1453	.271

WORLD SERIES RECORD

Year	Club	League	G.	AB.	R.	H.	HR.	RBI.	B.A.
1957—Milwaukee	Nat.	7	22	4	5	1	4	.227
1958—Milwaukee	Nat.	7	25	3	4	0	3	.160
1968—Detroit	Amer.	2	3	0	1	0	0	.333
World Series Totals		16	50	7	10	1	7	.200

CHRISTOPHER (BIG SIX) MATHEWSON

Year	Club	League	G.	IP.	W.	L.	Pct.	ERA.
1899—Taunton	New England	17	....	5	2	.714	
1900—Norfolk	Virginia	22	187	20	2	.909	
1900—New York	National	6	34	0	3	.000	
1901—New York	National	40	336	20	17	.541	
1902—New York	National	34	276	14	17	.452	
1903—New York	National	45	367	30	13	.698	
1904—New York	National	48	368	33	12	.733	
1905—New York	National	43	339	*31	9	.775	
1906—New York	National	38	267	22	12	.647	
1907—New York	National	41	315	*24	12	.667	
1908—New York	National	*56	*391	*37	11	.771	
1909—New York	National	37	274	25	6	.806	
1910—New York	National	38	319	*27	9	.750	
1911—New York	National	45	307	26	13	.667	
1912—New York	National	43	●310	23	12	.657	2.12
1913—New York	National	40	306	25	11	.694	*2.06
1914—New York	National	41	312	24	13	.648	3.00
1915—New York	National	27	186	8	14	.364	3.58
1916—N.Y.-Cinn	National	13	74	4	4	.500	3.04
Major League Totals		635	4781	373	188	.665	

WORLD SERIES RECORD

Year	Club	League	G.	IP.	W.	L.	Pct.	ERA.
1905—New York	National	3	27	3	0	.000	0.00
1911—New York	National	3	27	1	2	.333	2.00
1912—New York	National	3	28	0	2	.000	1.57
1913—New York	National	2	19	1	1	.500	0.95
World Series Totals		11	101	5	5	.500	1.15

WILLIE HOWARD MAYS, JR.

Year	Club	League	G.	AB.	R.	H.	HR.	RBI.	B.A.
1950—Trenton	Int. St.	81	306	50	108	4	55	.353
1951—Minneapolis	A. A.	35	149	38	71	8	30	.477
1951—New York	Nat.	121	464	59	127	20	68	.274
1952—New York	Nat.	34	127	17	30	4	23	.236
1953—New York	Nat.				(In Military Service)			

Year	Club	League	G.	AB.	R.	H.	HR.	RBI.	B.A.
1954—New York	Nat.	151	565	119	195	41	110	*.345
1955—New York	Nat.	152	580	123	185	*51	127	.319
1956—New York	Nat.	152	578	101	171	36	84	.296
1957—New York	Nat.	152	585	112	195	35	97	.333
1958—San Francisco	Nat.	152	600	*121	208	29	96	.347
1959—San Francisco	Nat.	151	575	125	180	34	104	.313
1960—San Francisco	Nat.	153	595	107	*190	29	103	.319
1961—San Francisco	Nat.	154	572	*129	176	40	123	.308
1962—San Francisco	Nat.	162	621	130	189	*49	141	.304
1963—San Francisco	Nat.	157	596	115	187	38	103	.314
1964—San Francisco	Nat.	157	578	121	171	*47	111	.296
1965—San Francisco	Nat.	157	558	118	177	*52	112	.317
1966—San Francisco	Nat.	152	552	99	159	37	103	.288
1967—San Francisco	Nat.	141	486	83	128	22	70	.263
1968—San Francisco	Nat.	148	498	84	144	23	79	.289
1969—San Francisco	Nat.	117	403	64	114	13	58	.283
1970—San Francisco	Nat.	139	478	94	139	28	83	.291
1971—San Francisco	Nat.	136	417	82	113	18	61	.271
1972—S. F.-N.Y.	Nat.	88	244	35	61	8	22	.250
1973—New York	Nat.	66	209	24	44	6	25	.211
Major League Totals		2992	10881	2062	3283	660	1903	.302

CHAMPIONSHIP SERIES RECORD

Year	Club	League	G.	AB.	R.	H.	HR.	RBI.	B.A.
1971—San Francisco	Nat.	4	15	2	4	1	3	.267
1973—New York	Nat.	1	3	1	1	0	1	.333
Championship Series Totals		5	18	3	5	1	4	.278

WORLD SERIES RECORD

Year	Club	League	G.	AB.	R.	H.	HR.	RBI.	B.A.
1951—New York	Nat.	6	22	1	4	0	1	.182
1954—New York	Nat.	4	14	4	4	0	3	.286
1962—San Francisco	Nat.	7	28	3	7	0	1	.250
1973—New York	Nat.	3	7	1	2	0	1	.286
World Series Totals		20	71	9	17	0	6	.239

WILLIAM STANLEY MAZEROSKI

Year	Club	League	G.	AB.	R.	H.	HR.	RBI.	B.A.
1954—Williamsport	Eastern	93	315	35	74	3	28	.235
1955—Hollywood	P.C.	21	47	4	8	1	3	.170
1955—Williamsport	Eastern	114	413	68	121	11	65	.293
1956—Hollywood	P.C.	80	284	47	87	9	36	.306
1956—Pittsburgh	National	81	255	30	62	3	14	.243
1957—Pittsburgh	National	148	526	59	149	8	54	.283
1958—Pittsburgh	National	152	567	69	156	19	68	.275
1959—Pittsburgh	National	135	493	50	119	7	59	.241
1960—Pittsburgh	National	151	538	58	147	11	64	.273
1961—Pittsburgh	National	152	558	71	148	13	59	.265
1962—Pittsburgh	National	159	572	55	155	14	81	.271
1963—Pittsburgh	National	142	534	43	131	8	52	.245
1964—Pittsburgh	National	162	601	66	161	10	64	.268
1965—Pittsburgh	National	130	494	52	134	6	54	.271
1966—Pittsburgh	National	●162	621	56	163	16	82	.262
1967—Pittsburgh	National	*163	639	62	167	9	77	.261
1968—Pittsburgh	National	143	506	36	127	3	42	.251
1969—Pittsburgh	National	67	227	13	52	3	25	.229
1970—Pittsburgh	National	112	367	29	84	7	39	.229
1971—Pittsburgh	National	70	193	17	49	1	16	.254
1972—Pittsburgh	National	34	64	3	12	0	3	.188
Major League Totals		2163	7755	769	2016	138	853	.260

WORLD SERIES RECORD

Year	Club	League	G.	AB.	R.	H.	HR.	RBI.	B.A.
1960—Pittsburgh	National	7	25	4	8	2	5	.320
1971—Pittsburgh	National	1	1	0	0	0	0	.000
World Series Totals		8	26	4	8	2	5	.308

JOSEPH VINCENT (MARSE JOE) McCARTHY
RECORD AS MANAGER

Year	Club	League	Position	W.	L.
1913—Wilkes-Barre	New York State	Second	84	56
1919—Louisville*	Amer. Assoc.	Third	39	30
1920—Louisville	Amer. Assoc.	Second	88	79
1921—Louisville	Amer. Assoc.	First	98	70
1922—Louisville	Amer. Assoc.	Sixth	77	91
1923—Louisville	Amer. Assoc.	Third	91	77
1924—Louisville	Amer. Assoc.	Third	90	75
1925—Louisville	Amer. Assoc.	First	102	61
1926—Chicago	National	Fourth	82	72
1927—Chicago	National	Fourth	85	68
1928—Chicago	National	Third	91	63
1929—Chicago	National	First	98	54
1930—Chicago†	National	Second	86	64
1931—New York	American	Second	94	59
1932—New York	American	First	107	47
1933—New York	American	Second	91	59
1934—New York	American	Second	94	60
1935—New York	American	Second	89	60
1936—New York	American	First	102	51
1937—New York	American	First	102	52
1938—New York	American	First	99	53
1939—New York	American	First	106	45

Year Club	League	Position	W.	L.
1940—New York	American	Third	88	66
1941—New York	American	First	101	53
1942—New York	American	First	103	51
1943—New York	American	First	98	56
1944—New York	American	Third	83	71
1945—New York	American	Fourth	81	71
1946—New York‡	American	Second	22	13
1948—Boston x	American	Second	96	59
1949—Boston	American	Second	96	58
1950—Boston y	American	Fourth	32	30
Major League Totals			2126	1335

WORLD SERIES RECORD

Year Club	League	W.	L.
1929—Chicago	National	1	4
1932—New York	American	4	0
1936—New York	American	4	2
1937—New York	American	4	1
1938—New York	American	4	0
1939—New York	American	4	0
1941—New York	American	4	1
1942—New York	American	1	4
1943—New York	American	4	1

*Replaced Pat Flaherty as manager, July 22, with club in third place.
†Resigned as manager, September 24, 1930, replaced by Rogers Hornsby.
‡Resigned as manager, May 24, 1946, replaced by William Dickey.
xIncludes game lost in playoff for league championship.
yResigned as manager, June 23, 1950, replaced by Steve O'Neill.

THOMAS FRANCIS MICHAEL McCARTHY

Year Club	League	G.	AB.	R.	H.	HR.	SB.	B.A.
1884—Boston	U.A.	53	218	37	45	0	....	.206
1885—Boston	Nat.	40	148	16	27	...	....	.182
1886—Philadelphia	Nat.	8	27	6	5	...	0	.185
1887—Philadelphia	Nat.	18	72	7	15	...	15	.208
1888—St. Louis	A.A.	131	510	106	141	...	109	.276
1889—St. Louis	A.A.	140	603	136	179	2	59	.297
1890—St. Louis	A.A.	132	539	*134	189	6	91	.351
1891—St. Louis	A.A.	125	527	115	163	8	37	.309
1892—Boston	Nat.	152	602	116	147	4	59	.244
1893—Boston	Nat.	116	441	108	159	5	49	.361
1894—Boston	Nat.	126	536	118	187	13	40	.349
1895—Boston	Nat.	116	454	89	132	2	24	.291
1896—Brooklyn	Nat.	101	378	62	96	3	23	.254
Union Association Totals		53	218	37	45	0	....	.206
American Association Totals		528	2179	491	672	16	296	.308
National League Totals		677	2658	522	768	27	210	.289
Major League Totals		1258	5055	1050	1485	43	506	.294

WORLD SERIES RECORD

Year Club	League	G.	AB.	R.	H.	HR.	SB.	B.A.
1888—St. Louis	A.A.	10	41	9	10	1	6	.244

WILLIE LEE McCOVEY

Year Club	League	G.	AB.	R.	H.	HR.	RBI.	B.A.
1955—Sandersville	Ga. St.	107	410	82	125	19	*113	.305
1956—Danville	Carol.	152	519	119	161	29	89	.310
1957—Dallas	Texas	115	395	63	111	11	65	.281
1958—Phoenix	P. C.	146	527	91	168	14	89	.319
1959—Phoenix	P. C.	95	349	84	130	*29	●92	.372
1959—San Francisco	Nat.	52	192	32	68	13	38	.354
1960—San Francisco	Nat.	101	260	37	62	13	51	.238
1960—Tacoma	P. C.	17	63	14	18	3	16	.286
1961—San Francisco	Nat.	106	328	59	89	18	50	.271
1962—San Francisco	Nat.	91	229	41	67	20	54	.293
1963—San Francisco	Nat.	152	564	103	158	●44	102	.280
1964—San Francisco	Nat.	130	364	55	80	18	54	.220
1965—San Francisco	Nat.	160	540	93	149	39	92	.276
1966—San Francisco	Nat.	150	502	85	148	36	96	.295
1967—San Francisco	Nat.	135	456	73	126	31	91	.276
1968—San Francisco	Nat.	148	523	81	153	*36	*105	.293
1969—San Francisco	Nat.	149	491	101	157	*45	*126	.320
1970—San Francisco	Nat.	152	495	98	143	39	126	.289
1971—San Francisco	Nat.	105	329	45	91	18	70	.277
1972—San Francisco	Nat.	81	263	30	56	14	35	.213
1973—San Francisco	Nat.	130	383	52	102	29	75	.266
1974—San Diego	Nat.	128	344	53	87	22	63	.253
1975—San Diego	Nat.	122	413	43	104	23	68	.252
1976—San Diego	Nat.	71	202	20	41	7	36	.203
1976—Oakland	Amer.	11	24	0	5	0	0	.208
1977—San Francisco	Nat.	141	478	54	134	28	86	.280
1978—San Francisco	Nat.	108	351	32	80	12	64	.228
1979—San Francisco	Nat.	117	353	34	88	15	57	.249
1980—San Francisco	Nat.	48	113	8	23	1	16	.204
National League Totals		2577	8173	1229	2206	521	1555	.270
American League Totals		11	24	0	5	0	0	.208
Major League Totals		2588	8197	1229	2211	521	1555	.270

WORLD SERIES RECORD

Year Club	League	G.	AB.	R.	H.	HR.	RBI.	B.A.
1962—San Francisco	Nat.	4	15	2	3	1	1	.200

CORNELIUS (CONNIE MACK) McGILLICUDDY
RECORD AS MANAGER

Year Club	League	Position	W.	L.
1894—Pittsburgh†	National	Seventh	11	11
1895—Pittsburgh	National	Seventh	71	61
1896—Pittsburgh	National	Sixth	66	63
1897—Milwaukee‡	Western	Fourth	85	51
1898—Milwaukee	Western	Third	82	57
1889—Milwaukee	Western	Sixth	55	68
1900—Milwaukee	American	Second	79	58
1901—Philadelphia	American	Fourth	74	62
1902—Philadelphia	American	First	83	53
1903—Philadelphia	American	Second	75	60
1904—Philadelphia	American	Fifth	81	70
1905—Philadelphia	American	First	92	56
1906—Philadelphia	American	Fourth	78	67
1907—Philadelphia	American	Second	88	57
1908—Philadelphia	American	Sixth	68	84
1909—Philadelphia	American	Second	95	58
1910—Philadelphia	American	First	102	48
1911—Philadelphia	American	First	101	50
1912—Philadelphia	American	Third	90	62
1913—Philadelphia	American	First	96	57
1914—Philadelphia	American	First	99	53
1915—Philadelphia	American	Eighth	43	109
1916—Philadelphia	American	Eighth	36	117
1917—Philadelphia	American	Eighth	55	98
1918—Philadelphia	American	Eighth	52	76
1919—Philadelphia	American	Eighth	36	104
1920—Philadelphia	American	Eighth	48	106
1921—Philadelphia	American	Eighth	53	100
1922—Philadelphia	American	Seventh	65	89
1923—Philadelphia	American	Sixth	69	83
1924—Philadelphia	American	Fifth	71	81
1925—Philadelphia	American	Second	88	64
1926—Philadelphia	American	Third	83	67
1927—Philadelphia	American	Second	91	63
1928—Philadelphia	American	Second	98	55
1929—Philadelphia	American	First	104	46
1930—Philadelphia	American	First	102	52
1931—Philadelphia	American	First	107	45
1932—Philadelphia	American	Second	94	60
1933—Philadelphia	American	Third	79	72
1934—Philadelphia	American	Fifth	68	82
1935—Philadelphia	American	Eighth	58	91
1936—Philadelphia	American	Eighth	53	100
1937—Philadelphia	American	Seventh	54	97
1938—Philadelphia	American	Eighth	53	99
1939—Philadelphia	American	Seventh	55	97
1940—Philadelphia	American	Eighth	54	100
1941—Philadelphia	American	Eighth	64	90
1942—Philadelphia	American	Eighth	55	99
1943—Philadelphia	American	Eighth	49	105
1944—Philadelphia	American	*Fifth	72	82
1945—Philadelphia	American	Eighth	52	98
1946—Philadelphia	American	Eighth	49	105
1947—Philadelphia	American	Fifth	78	76
1948—Philadelphia	American	Fourth	84	70
1949—Philadelphia	American	Fifth	81	73
1950—Philadelphia	American	Eighth	52	102
Major League Totals			3775	4025

WORLD SERIES RECORD

Year Club	League	W.	L.
1905—Philadelphia	American	1	4
1910—Philadelphia	American	4	1
1911—Philadelphia	American	4	2
1913—Philadelphia	American	4	1
1914—Philadelphia	American	0	4
1929—Philadelphia	American	4	1
1930—Philadelphia	American	4	2
1931—Philadelphia	American	3	4

*Tied for position.
†Replaced Al Buckenberger as manager, September 3, with club in seventh place.

JOSEPH JEROME (IRON MAN) McGINNITY

Year Club	League	G.	IP.	W.	L.	Pct.	ShO.
1893—Montgomery	Southern	31	193	10	19	.345	....
1894—Kansas City	Western	20	124	8	10	.444	....
1898—Peoria	West. Assn.	16	104	10	3	.769	....
1899—Baltimore	National	49	380	●28	17	.622	4
1900—Brooklyn	National	*45	347	*29	9	*.763	1
1901—Baltimore	American	*48	*378	26	21	.553	1
1902—Baltimore	American	25	199	13	10	.565	0
1902—New York	National	19	153	8	8	.500	1
1903—New York	National	*55	*434	*31	20	.608	3
1904—New York	National	*51	*408	*35	8	*.814	*9
1905—New York	National	●46	320	21	15	.588	2
1906—New York	National	*45	340	*27	12	.692	3
1907—New York	National	*47	310	18	18	.500	3
1908—New York	National	37	186	11	7	.611	5
1909—Newark	Eastern	*55	*422	*29	16	.644	....
1910—Newark	Eastern	*61	*408	*30	19	.612	....
1911—Newark	Eastern	43	278	12	19	.387	....
1912—Newark	International	37	261	16	10	.615	....

Year Club	League	G.	IP.	W.	L.	Pct.	ShO.
1913—Tacoma	Northwestern	*68	*436	22	19	.537	....
1914—Tacoma	Northwestern	49	326	20	*21	.488	....
1914—Venice	Pacific Coast	8	37	1	4	.200	....
1915—Tacoma	Northwestern	45	*355	21	15	.583	....
1916—Butte	Northwestern	43	291	20	13	.606	....
1917—Butte-Great Falls	Northwestern	16	119	7	6	.538	....
1918—Vancouver	P. C.-Int.	9	....	2	6	.250	....
1922—Danville	I. I. I.	16	79	1	6	.143	....
1922—Dubuque	Miss. Valley	19	91	5	8	.385	....
1923—Dubuque	Miss. Valley	42	206	15	12	.556	....
1925—Dubuque	Miss. Valley	15	85	6	6	.500	....
American League Totals		73	577	39	31	.557	1
National League Totals		394	2878	208	114	.646	31
Major League Totals		467	3455	247	145	.630	32

WORLD SERIES RECORD

Year Club	League	G.	IP.	W.	L.	Pct.	ERA.
1905—New York	National	2	17	1	1	.500	0.00

JOHN JOSEPH (LITTLE NAPOLEON) McGRAW
RECORD AS MANAGER

Year Club	League	Position	W.	L.
1899—Baltimore	National	Fourth	86	62
1901—Baltimore	American	Fifth	68	65
1902—Baltimore	American	Seventh	28	34
1902—New York	National	Eighth	25	38
1903—New York	National	Second	84	55
1904—New York	National	First	106	47
1905—New York	National	First	105	48
1906—New York	National	Second	96	56
1907—New York	National	Fourth	82	71
1908—New York	National	Second	98	56
1909—New York	National	Third	92	61
1910—New York	National	Second	91	63
1911—New York	National	First	99	54
1912—New York	National	First	103	48
1913—New York	National	First	101	51
1914—New York	National	Second	84	70
1915—New York	National	Eighth	69	83
1916—New York	National	Fourth	86	66
1917—New York	National	First	98	56
1918—New York	National	Second	71	53
1919—New York	National	Second	87	53
1920—New York	National	Second	86	68
1921—New York	National	First	94	59
1922—New York	National	First	93	61
1923—New York	National	First	95	58
1924—New York	National	First	93	60
1925—New York	National	Second	86	66
1926—New York	National	Fifth	74	77
1927—New York	National	Third	92	62
1928—New York	National	Second	93	61
1929—New York	National	Third	84	67
1930—New York	National	Third	87	67
1931—New York	National	Second	87	65
1932—New York	National	Eighth	17	23
Major League Totals			2840	1984

WORLD SERIES RECORD

Year Club	League	W.	L.
1905—New York	National	4	1
1911—New York	National	2	4
1912—New York	National	3	4
1913—New York	National	1	4
1917—New York	National	2	4
1921—New York	National	5	3
1922—New York	National	4	0
1923—New York	National	2	4
1924—New York	National	3	4

WILLIAM BOYD (DEACON) McKECHNIE
RECORD AS MANAGER

Year Club	League	Position	W.	L.
1915—Newark†	Federal	Fifth	53	45
1922—Pittsburgh‡	National	Fourth	47	26
1923—Pittsburgh	National	Third	87	67
1924—Pittsburgh	National	Third	90	63
1925—Pittsburgh	National	First	95	58
1926—Pittsburgh	National	Third	84	69
1928—St. Louis	National	First	95	59
1929—Rochester§	International	First	60	20
1929—St. Louis x	National	Fourth	35	29
1930—Boston	National	Sixth	70	84
1931—Boston	National	Seventh	64	90
1932—Boston	National	Fifth	77	77
1933—Boston	National	Fourth	83	71
1934—Boston	National	Fourth	78	73
1935—Boston	National	Eighth	38	115
1936—Boston	National	Sixth	71	83
1937—Boston	National	Fifth	79	73
1938—Cincinnati	National	Fourth	82	68
1939—Cincinnati	National	First	97	57
1940—Cincinnati	National	First	100	53
1941—Cincinnati	National	Third	88	66

Year Club	League	Position	W.	L.
1942—Cincinnati	National	Fourth	76	76
1943—Cincinnati	National	Second	87	67
1944—Cincinnati	National	Third	89	65
1945—Cincinnati	National	Seventh	61	93
1946—Cincinnati	National	Sixth	67	87
Major League Totals			1840	1669

WORLD SERIES RECORD

Year Club	League	W.	L.
1925—Pittsburgh	National	4	3
1928—St. Louis	National	0	4
1939—Cincinnati	National	0	4
1940—Cincinnati	National	4	3

†Replaced Bill Phillips as manager with club tied for fifth place, June 19.
‡Replaced George Gibson as manager with club in sixth place, July 15.
§xSwapped jobs with Billy Southworth, taking over Cardinals in fourth place, July 23.

JOHN ALEXANDER (BID) McPHEE

Year Club	League	G.	AB.	R.	H.	HR.	SB.	B.A.
1879—Davenport	Northwest	(No records available)						
1880—Akron	Independent	(No records available)						
1881—Akron	Independent	(No records available)						
1882—Cincinnati	Amer. Assoc.	78	311	43	71	1	...	.228
1883—Cincinnati	Amer. Assoc.	96	367	61	90	2	...	.245
1884—Cincinnati	Amer. Assoc.	112	450	107	125	5	...	.278
1885—Cincinnati	Amer. Assoc.	110	431	78	114	0	...	.265
1886—Cincinnati	Amer. Assoc.	140	560	139	150	8	40	.268
1887—Cincinnati	Amer. Assoc.	129	595	137	211	2	95	.355
1888—Cincinnati	Amer. Assoc.	111	458	88	110	4	54	.240
1889—Cincinnati	Amer. Assoc.	135	540	109	145	5	63	.269
1890—Cincinnati	National	132	528	125	135	3	55	.256
1891—Cincinnati	National	138	562	107	144	6	33	.256
1892—Cincinnati	National	144	573	111	157	4	44	.274
1893—Cincinnati	National	127	491	101	138	3	25	.281
1894—Cincinnati	National	128	483	113	151	5	33	.313
1895—Cincinnati	National	115	432	107	129	1	30	.299
1896—Cincinnati	National	117	433	81	132	1	48	.305
1897—Cincinnati	National	81	282	45	85	1	9	.301
1898—Cincinnati	National	133	486	72	121	1	21	.249
1899—Cincinnati	National	112	376	60	105	1	18	.279
American Association Totals		911	3712	762	1016	27	252	.274
National League Totals		1227	4646	922	1297	26	316	.279
Major League Totals		2138	8358	1684	2313	53	568	.277

JOSEPH MICHAEL (DUCKY) MEDWICK

Year Club	League	G.	AB.	R.	H.	HR.	RBI.	B.A.
1930—Scottdale	Mid. Atl.	75	332	75	139	22	100	.419
1931—Houston	Texas	*161	616	99	188	*19	*126	.305
1932—Houston	Texas	139	560	113	198	26	111	.354
1932—St. Louis	Nat.	26	106	13	37	2	12	.349
1933—St. Louis	Nat.	148	595	92	182	18	98	.306
1934—St. Louis	Nat.	149	620	110	198	18	106	.319
1935—St. Louis	Nat.	154	634	132	224	23	126	.353
1936—St. Louis	Nat.	155	636	115	*223	18	*138	.351
1937—St. Louis	Nat.	*156	*633	*111	*237	●31	*154	*.374
1938—St. Louis	Nat.	146	590	100	190	21	*122	.322
1939—St. Louis	Nat.	150	606	98	201	14	117	.332
1940—St. L.-Brook.	Nat.	143	581	83	175	17	86	.301
1941—Brooklyn	Nat.	133	538	100	171	18	88	.318
1942—Brooklyn	Nat.	142	553	69	166	4	96	.300
1943—Brook.-N.Y.	Nat.	126	497	54	138	5	70	.278
1944—New York	Nat.	128	490	64	165	7	85	.337
1945—N.Y.-Bos.	Nat.	92	310	31	90	3	37	.290
1946—Brooklyn	Nat.	41	77	7	24	2	18	.312
1947—St. Louis	Nat.	75	150	19	46	4	28	.307
1948—St. Louis	Nat.	20	19	0	4	0	2	.211
1948—Houston	Texas	35	87	8	24	2	20	.276
1949—Miami Beach	Fla. Int.	106	375	53	121	10	72	.323
1951—Raleigh	Carolina	60	158	22	45	4	33	.285
1952—Tampa	Fla. Int.	11	9	0	3	0	6	.333
Major League Totals		1984	7635	1198	2471	205	1383	.324

JOHN ROBERT (BIG CAT) MIZE

Year Club	League	G.	AB.	R.	H.	HR.	RBI.	B.A.
1930—Greensboro	Pied.	12	31	5	6	0	2	.194
1931—Greensboro	Pied.	94	341	69	115	9	64	.337
1932—Elmira	NYP	106	405	60	132	8	78	.326
1933—Greensboro	Pied.	98	378	108	136	22	104	.360
1933—Rochester	Int.	42	159	27	56	8	32	.352
1934—Rochester	Int.	90	313	49	106	17	66	.339
1935—Rochester	Int.	65	252	37	80	12	44	.317
1936—St. Louis	Nat.	126	414	76	136	19	93	.329
1937—St. Louis	Nat.	145	560	103	204	25	113	.364
1938—St. Louis	Nat.	149	531	85	179	27	102	.337
1939—St. Louis	Nat.	153	564	104	197	*28	108	*.349
1940—St. Louis	Nat.	155	579	111	182	*43	*137	.314
1941—St. Louis	Nat.	126	473	67	150	16	100	.317
1942—New York	Nat.	142	541	97	165	26	*110	.305
1943-44-45—New York	Nat.	(In Military Service)						
1946—New York	Nat.	101	377	70	127	22	70	.337
1947—New York	Nat.	154	586	*137	177	●51	*138	.302

Year	Club	League	G.	AB.	R.	H.	HR.	RBI.	B.A.
1948—New York	Nat.		152	560	110	162	●40	125	.289
1949—New York	Nat.		106	388	59	102	18	62	.263
1949—New York	Amer.		13	23	4	6	1	2	.261
1950—Kansas City	A.A.		26	94	18	28	5	18	.298
1950—New York	Amer.		90	274	43	76	25	72	.277
1951—New York	Amer.		113	332	37	86	10	49	.259
1952—New York	Amer.		78	137	9	36	4	29	.263
1953—New York	Amer.		81	104	6	26	4	27	.250
American League Totals			375	870	99	230	44	179	.264
National League Totals			1509	5573	1019	1781	315	1158	.320
Major League Totals			1884	6443	1118	2011	359	1337	.312

WORLD SERIES RECORD

Year	Club	League	G.	AB.	R.	H.	HR.	RBI.	B.A.
1949—New York	Amer.		2	2	0	2	0	2	1.000
1950—New York	Amer.		4	15	0	2	0	0	.133
1951—New York	Amer.		4	7	2	2	0	1	.286
1952—New York	Amer.		5	15	3	6	3	6	.400
1953—New York	Amer.		3	3	0	0	0	0	.000
World Series Totals			18	42	5	12	3	9	.286

JOE LEONARD MORGAN

Year	Club	League	G.	AB.	R.	H.	HR.	RBI.	B.A.
1963— Modesto	Calif.		45	152	42	40	5	27	.263
1963— Durham	Carol.		95	322	74	107	13	43	.332
1963— Houston	Nat.		8	25	5	6	0	3	.240
1964— San Antonio	Texas		●140	496	113	160	12	90	.323
1964— Houston	Nat.		10	37	4	7	0	0	.189
1965— Houston	Nat.		157	601	100	163	14	40	.271
1966— Houston	Nat.		122	425	60	121	5	42	.285
1967— Houston	Nat.		133	494	73	136	6	42	.275
1968— Houston	Nat		10	20	6	5	0	0	.250
1969— Houston	Nat		147	535	94	126	15	43	.236
1970— Houston	Nat.		144	548	102	147	8	52	.268
1971— Houston	Nat.		160	583	87	149	13	56	.256
1972— Cincinnati	Nat.		149	552	•122	161	16	73	.292
1973— Cincinnati	Nat.		157	576	116	167	26	82	.290
1974— Cincinnati	Nat.		149	512	107	150	22	67	.293
1975— Cincinnati	Nat.		146	498	107	163	17	94	.327
1976— Cincinnati	Nat.		141	472	113	151	27	111	.320
1977— Cincinnati	Nat.		153	521	113	150	22	78	.288
1978— Cincinnati	Nat.		132	441	68	104	13	75	.236
1979— Cincinnati	Nat.		127	436	70	109	9	32	.250
1980— Houston	Nat.		141	461	66	112	11	49	.243
1981— San Francisco	Nat.		90	308	47	74	8	31	.240
1982— San Francisco	Nat.		134	463	68	134	14	61	.289
1983— Philadelphia	Nat.		123	404	72	93	16	59	.230
1984— Oakland	Amer.		116	365	50	89	6	43	.244
National League Totals			2533	8912	1600	2428	262	1090	.272
American League Totals			116	365	50	89	6	43	.244
Major League Totals			2649	9277	1650	2517	268	1133	.271

CHAMPIONSHIP SERIES RECORD

Year	Club	League	G.	AB.	R.	H.	HR.	RBI.	B.A.
1972— Cincinnati	Nat.		5	19	5	5	2	3	.263
1973— Cincinnati	Nat.		5	20	1	2	0	1	.100
1975— Cincinnati	Nat.		3	11	2	3	0	1	.273
1976— Cincinnati	Nat.		3	7	2	0	0	0	.000
1979— Cincinnati	Nat.		3	11	0	0	0	0	.000
1980— Houston	Nat.		4	13	1	2	0	0	.154
1983— Philadelphia	Nat.		4	15	1	1	0	0	.067
Championship Series Totals			27	96	12	13	2	5	.135

WORLD SERIES RECORD

Year	Club	League	G.	AB.	R.	H.	HR.	RBI.	B.A.
1972— Cincinnati	Nat.		7	24	4	3	0	1	.125
1975— Cincinnati	Nat.		7	27	4	7	0	3	.259
1976— Cincinnati	Nat.		4	15	3	5	1	2	.333
1983— Philadelphia	Nat.		5	19	3	5	2	2	.263
World Series Totals			23	85	14	20	3	8	.235

STANLEY FRANK (THE MAN) MUSIAL

Year	Club	League	G.	AB.	R.	H.	HR.	RBI.	B.A.
1938—Williamson	Mt. St.		26	62	5	16	1	6	.258
1939—Williamson	Mt. St.		23	71	10	25	1	9	.352
1940—Daytona Beach	Fla. St.		113	405	55	126	1	70	.311
1941—Springfield	W. Assoc.		87	348	100	132	*26	94	.379
1941—Rochester	Int.		54	221	43	72	3	21	.326
1941—St. Louis	Nat.		12	47	8	20	1	7	.426
1942—St. Louis	Nat.		140	467	87	147	10	72	.315
1943—St. Louis	Nat.		●157	617	108	●220	13	81	*.357
1944—St. Louis	Nat.		146	568	112	●197	12	94	.347
1945—St. Louis	Nat.	(In Military Service)							
1946—St. Louis	Nat.		●156	*624	*124	*228	16	103	*.365
1947—St. Louis	Nat.		149	587	113	183	19	95	.312
1948—St. Louis	Nat.		155	611	*135	*230	39	*131	*.376
1949—St. Louis	Nat.		*157	612	128	*207	36	123	.338
1950—St. Louis	Nat.		146	555	105	192	28	109	*.346
1951—St. Louis	Nat.		152	578	●124	205	32	108	*.355
1952—St. Louis	Nat.		●154	578	●105	•194	21	91	*.336
1953—St. Louis	Nat.		157	593	127	200	30	113	.337
1954—St. Louis	Nat.		153	591	●120	195	35	126	.330
1955—St. Louis	Nat.		●154	562	97	179	33	108	.319
1956—St. Louis	Nat.		156	594	87	184	27	*109	.310
1957—St. Louis	Nat.		134	502	82	176	29	102	*.351
1958—St. Louis	Nat.		135	472	64	159	17	62	.337
1959—St. Louis	Nat.		115	341	37	87	14	44	.255
1960—St. Louis	Nat.		116	331	49	91	17	63	.275
1961—St. Louis	Nat.		123	372	46	107	15	70	.288
1962—St. Louis	Nat.		135	433	57	143	19	82	.330
1963—St. Louis	Nat.		124	337	34	86	12	58	.255
Major League Totals			3026	10972	1949	3630	475	1951	.331

WORLD SERIES RECORD

Year	Club	League	G.	AB.	R.	H.	HR.	RBI.	B.A.
1942—St. Louis	Nat.		5	18	2	4	0	2	.222
1943—St. Louis	Nat.		5	18	2	5	0	0	.278
1944—St. Louis	Nat.		6	23	2	7	1	2	.304
1946—St. Louis	Nat.		7	27	3	6	0	4	.222
World Series Totals			23	86	9	22	1	8	.256

PITCHING RECORD

Year	Club	League	G.	IP.	W.	L.	Pct.	ERA.
1938—Williamson	Mt. State		20	110	6	6	.500	4.66
1939—Williamson	Mt. State		13	92	9	2	.818	4.30
1940—Daytona Beach	Fla. State		28	223	18	5	*.783	2.62
1952—St. Louis	National		1	0	0	0	.000	0.00
Major League Totals			1	0	0	0	.000	0.00

HAL NEWHOUSER

Year	Club	League	G.	IP.	W.	L.	Pct.	ERA.
1939— Alexandria	Evangeline		12	96	8	4	.667	2.34
— Beaumont	Texas		22	134	5	14	.263	3.83
— Detroit	American		1	5	0	1	.000	5.40
1940— Detroit	American		28	133	9	9	.500	4.87
1941— Detroit	American		33	173	9	11	.450	4.79
1942— Detroit	American		38	184	8	14	.364	2.45
1943— Detroit	American		37	196	8	17	.320	3.03
1944— Detroit	American		47	312	•29	9	.763	2.22
1945— Detroit	American		40	•313	•25	9	*.735	•1.81
1946— Detroit	American		37	293	●26	9	.743	•1.94
1947— Detroit	American		40	285	17	•17	.500	2.87
1948— Detroit	American		39	272	•21	12	.636	3.01
1949— Detroit	American		38	292	18	11	.621	3.36
1950— Detroit	American		35	214	15	13	.536	4.33
1951— Detroit	American		15	96	6	6	.500	3.94
1952— Detroit	American		25	154	9	9	.500	3.74
1953— Detroit	American		7	22	0	1	.000	6.95
1954— Cleveland	American		26	47	7	2	.778	2.49
1955— Cleveland	American		2	2	0	0	...	0.00
Major League Totals			488	2993	207	150	.580	3.06

WORLD SERIES RECORD

Year	Club	League	G.	IP.	W.	L.	Pct.	ERA.
1945— Detroit	American		3	20⅔	2	1	.667	6.10
1954— Cleveland	American		1	0	0	0	...	....
World Series Totals			4	20⅔	2	1	.667	6.53

CHARLES AUGUSTUS (KID) NICHOLS

Year	Club	League	G.	CG.	IP.	W.	L.	Pct.	ShO.
1887—Kansas City	Western		...	...	...		12	...	
1888—Memphis	Southern		15	...	...		8	...	
1888—Kansas City	West. Assn.		18	...					
1889—Omaha	West. Assn.		48	...		36	12	.750	...
1890—Boston	National		48	47	424	27	19	.587	*7
1891—Boston	National		52	45	423	30	17	.638	5
1892—Boston	National		53	49	454	35	16	.686	5
1893—Boston	National		52	43	414	34	14	.708	1
1894—Boston	National		50	40	417	32	13	.711	●3
1895—Boston	National		47	37	394	26	16	.619	1
1896—Boston	National		49	37	375	30	14	.682	3
1897—Boston	National		*46	37	358	31	11	.738	2
1898—Boston	National		50	40	388	31	12	.721	5
1899—Boston	National		42	37	349	21	19	.525	4
1900—Boston	National		29	25	226	13	16	.448	●4
1901—Boston	National		38	33	326	19	16	.543	4
1902—Kansas City	Western		37	...	...	27	7	.794	...
1903—Kansas City	Western		35	...	...	21	12	.636	...
1904—St. Louis	National		36	35	317	21	13	.618	3
1905—St. Louis-Phila	National		24	20	191	11	11	.500	1
1906—Philadelphia	National		4	1	11	0	1	.000	0
Major League Totals			620	531	5067	361	208	.634	48

PHILIP HENRY NIEKRO

Year	Club	League	G.	IP.	W.	L.	Pct.	ERA.
1959 — Wellsville	NY-Penn.		10	35	2	1	.667	7.46
1959 — McCooke	Nebraska State		*23	52	7	1	.875	3.12
1960 — Jacksonville	SAL		38	84	6	4	.600	2.79
1960 — Louisville	A. A.		6	10	1	0	1.000	3.60
1961 — Austin	Texas		*51	110	4	4	.500	2.95
1962 — Louisville	A. A.		49	98	9	6	.600	3.86
1963	(In Military Service)							
1964 — Milwaukee	National		10	15	0	0	.000	4.80

Year	Club	League	G.	IP.	W.	L.	Pct.	ERA.
1964	Denver	Pacific	29	172	11	5	.688	3.45
1965	Milwaukee	National	41	75	2	3	.400	2.88
1966	Atlanta	National	28	50	4	3	.571	4.14
1966	Richmond	International	17	54	3	4	.429	3.67
1967	Atlanta	National	46	207	11	9	.550	*1.87
1968	Atlanta	National	37	257	14	12	.538	2.59
1969	Atlanta	National	40	284	23	13	.639	2.57
1970	Atlanta	National	34	230	12	18	.400	4.27
1971	Atlanta	National	42	269	15	14	.517	2.98
1972	Atlanta	National	38	282	16	12	.571	3.06
1973	Atlanta	National	42	245	13	10	.565	3.31
1974	Atlanta	National	41	*302	•20	13	.606	2.38
1975	Atlanta	National	39	276	15	15	.500	3.20
1976	Atlanta	National	38	271	17	11	.607	3.29
1977	Atlanta	National	44	*330	16	•20	.444	4.04
1978	Atlanta	National	44	*334	19	*18	.514	2.88
1979	Atlanta	National	44	*342	•21	*20	.512	3.39
1980	Atlanta	National	40	275	15	*18	.455	3.63
1981	Atlanta	National	22	139	7	7	.500	3.11
1982	Atlanta	National	35	234⅓	17	4	*.810	3.61
1983	Atlanta	National	34	201⅔	11	10	.524	3.97
1984	New York	American	32	215⅔	16	8	.667	3.09
1985	New York	American	33	220	16	12	.571	4.09
1986	Cleveland	American	34	210⅓	11	11	.500	4.32
1987	Cleve.-Tor.	American	25	135⅔	7	13	.350	6.10
1987	Atlanta	National	1	3	0	0	.000	15.00
	National League Totals		740	4622	268	230	.538	3.20
	American League Totals		124	781⅔	50	44	.532	4.23
	Major League Totals		864	5403⅔	318	274	.537	3.35

CHAMPIONSHIP SERIES RECORD

Year	Club	League	G.	IP.	W.	L.	Pct.	ERA.
1969	Atlanta	National	1	8	0	1	.000	4.50
1982	Atlanta	National	1	6	0	0	.000	3.00
	Championship Series Totals		2	14	0	1	.000	3.86

JAMES HENRY (ORATOR JIM) O'ROURKE

Year	Club	League	G.	AB.	R.	H.	HR.	SB.	B.A.
1872	Mansfield	Nat. Assn.	....	....	....	....	...	....	......
1873	Boston	Nat. Assn.	57	297	79	103	...	....	.347
1874	Boston	Nat. Assn.	70	334	80	115	...	....	.344
1875	Boston	Nat. Assn.	69	....	....	....	...	....	.306
1876	Boston	Nat.	70	327	61	102	2	....	.312
1877	Boston	Nat.	49	211	54	74	0	....	.351
1878	Boston	Nat.	60	255	44	70	1	....	.275
1879	Providence	Nat.	80	359	69	126	4	....	.351
1880	Boston	Nat.	84	355	70	100	●6	....	.282
1881	Buffalo	Nat.	83	348	71	105	0	....	.302
1882	Buffalo	Nat.	84	370	62	104	2	....	.281
1883	Buffalo	Nat.	93	430	99	141	1	....	.328
1884	Buffalo	Nat.	104	448	112	157	4	.....	*.350
1885	New York	Nat.	112	477	119	143	4	.....	.300
1886	New York	Nat.	104	440	106	136	1	14	.309
1887	New York	Nat.	103	433	73	149	2	46	.344
1888	New York	Nat.	107	409	50	112	4	25	.274
1889	New York	Nat.	128	502	89	161	3	33	.321
1890	New York	Play.	111	469	112	172	8	26	.367
1891	New York	Nat.	136	554	94	167	5	25	.301
1892	New York	Nat.	112	447	63	133	0	23	.298
1893	Washington	Nat.	129	527	76	161	2	19	.306
1904	New York	Nat.	1	4	1	1	0	0	.250
1904	Bridgeport	Conn.	65	245	28	70	0	2	.286
1905	Bridgeport	Conn.	68	238	15	60	1	3	.252
1906	Bridgeport	Conn.	93	348	26	85	0	5	.244
1907	Bridgeport	Conn.	24	83	3	16	....	....	.193
	National League Totals		1639	6896	1313	2142	41	....	.311
	Players League Totals		111	469	112	172	8	26	.367
	Major League Totals		1750	7365	1425	2314	49	....	.314

MELVIN THOMAS OTT

Year	Club	League	G.	AB.	R.	H.	HR.	RBI.	B.A.
1926	New York	Nat.	35	60	7	23	0	4	.383
1927	New York	Nat.	82	163	23	46	1	19	.282
1928	New York	Nat.	124	435	69	140	18	77	.322
1929	New York	Nat.	150	545	138	179	42	151	.328
1930	New York	Nat.	148	521	122	182	25	119	.349
1931	New York	Nat.	138	497	104	145	29	115	.292
1932	New York	Nat.	●154	566	119	180	●38	123	.318
1933	New York	Nat.	152	580	98	164	23	103	.283
1934	New York	Nat.	153	582	119	190	●35	*135	.326
1935	New York	Nat.	152	593	113	191	31	114	.322
1936	New York	Nat.	150	534	120	175	*33	135	.328
1937	New York	Nat	151	545	99	160	●31	95	.294
1938	New York	Nat.	150	527	*116	164	*36	116	.311
1939	New York	Nat.	125	396	85	122	27	80	.308
1940	New York	Nat.	151	536	89	155	19	79	.289
1941	New York	Nat.	148	525	89	150	27	90	.286
1942	New York	Nat.	152	549	*118	162	*30	93	.295
1943	New York	Nat.	125	380	65	89	18	47	.234
1944	New York	Nat.	120	399	91	115	26	82	.288
1945	New York	Nat.	135	451	73	139	21	79	.308
1946	New York	Nat.	31	68	2	5	1	4	.074
1947	New York	Nat.	4	4	0	0	0	0	.000
	Major League Totals		2730	9456	1859	2876	511	1860	.304

WORLD SERIES RECORD

Year	Club	League	G.	AB.	R.	H.	HR.	RBI.	B.A.
1933	New York	Nat.	5	18	3	7	2	4	.389
1936	New York	Nat.	6	23	4	7	1	3	.304
1937	New York	Nat.	5	20	1	4	1	3	.200
	World Series Totals		16	61	8	18	4	10	.295

LEROY ROBERT (SATCHEL) PAIGE

Year	Club	League	G.	IP.	W.	L.	Pct.	ERA.
1948	Cleveland	American	21	73	6	1	.857	2.47
1949	Cleveland	American	31	83	4	7	.364	3.04
1950			(Out of Organized Ball)					
1951	St. Louis	American	23	62	3	4	.429	4.79
1952	St. Louis	American	46	138	12	10	.545	3.07
1953	St. Louis	American	57	117	3	9	.250	3.54
1954-55			(Out of Organized Ball)					
1956	Miami	International	37	111	11	4	.733	1.86
1957	Miami	International	40	119	10	8	.556	2.42
1958	Miami	International	28	110	10	10	.500	2.95
1959-60			(Out of Organized Ball)					
1961	Portland	Pacific Coast	5	25	0	0	.000	2.88
1962-63-64			(Out of Organized Ball)					
1965	Kansas City	American	1	3	0	0	.000	0.00
1966	Peninsula	Carolinas	1	2	0	0	.000	9.00
	Major League Totals		179	476	28	31	.475	3.29

WORLD SERIES RECORD

Year	Club	League	G.	IP.	W.	L.	Pct.	ERA.
1948	Cleveland	American	1	⅔	0	0	.000	0.00

JAMES ALVIN (JIM) PALMER

Year	Club	League	G.	IP.	W.	L.	Pct.	ERA.
1964	Aberdeen	Northern	19	129	11	3	.786	2.51
1965	Baltimore	American	27	92	5	4	.556	3.72
1966	Baltimore	American	30	208	15	10	.600	3.46
1967	Baltimore	American	9	49	3	1	.750	2.94
1967	Rochester	International	2	7	0	0	.000	11.57
1967	Miami	Florida St.	5	27	1	1	.500	2.00
1968	Miami	Florida St.	2	8	0	0	.000	0.00
1968	Rochester	International	2	4	0	0	.000	13.50
1968	Elmira	Eastern	6	25	0	2	.000	4.32
1969	Baltimore	American	26	181	16	4	•.800	2.34
1970	Baltimore	American	39	●305	20	10	.667	2.71
1971	Baltimore	American	37	282	20	9	.690	2.68
1972	Baltimore	American	36	274	21	10	.677	2.07
1973	Baltimore	American	38	296	22	9	.710	•2.40
1974	Baltimore	American	26	179	7	12	.368	3.27
1975	Baltimore	American	39	323	●23	11	.676	•2.09
1976	Baltimore	American	40	•315	•22	13	.629	2.51
1977	Baltimore	American	39	•319	●20	11	.645	2.91
1978	Baltimore	American	38	•296	21	12	.636	2.46
1979	Baltimore	American	23	156	10	6	.625	3.29
1980	Baltimore	American	34	224	16	10	.615	3.98
1981	Baltimore	American	22	127	7	8	.467	3.76
1982	Baltimore	American	36	227	15	5	●.750	3.13
1983	Baltimore	American	14	76⅔	5	4	.556	4.23
1983	Hagerstown	Carolina	2	13	2	0	1.000	3.46
1984	Baltimore	American	5	17⅔	0	3	.000	9.17
	Major League Totals		558	3947⅔	268	152	.638	2.86

CHAMPIONSHIP SERIES RECORD

Year	Club	League	G.	IP.	W.	L.	Pct..	ERA.
1969	Baltimore	American	1	9	1	0	1.000	2.00
1970	Baltimore	American	1	9	1	0	1.000	1.00
1971	Baltimore	American	1	9	1	0	1.000	3.00
1973	Baltimore	American	3	14⅔	1	0	1.000	1.84
1974	Baltimore	American	1	9	0	1	.000	1.00
1979	Baltimore	American	1	9	0	0	.000	3.00
	Championship Series Totals		8	59⅔	4	1	.800	1.96

WORLD SERIES RECORD

Year	Club	League	G.	IP.	W.	L.	Pct..	ERA.
1966	Baltimore	American	1	9	1	0	1.000	0.00
1969	Baltimore	American	1	6	0	1	.000	6.00
1970	Baltimore	American	2	15⅔	1	0	1.000	4.60
1971	Baltimore	American	2	17	1	0	1.000	2.65
1979	Baltimore	American	2	15	0	1	.000	3.60
1983	Baltimore	American	1	2	1	0	1.000	0.00
	World Series Totals		9	64⅔	4	2	.667	3.20

HERBERT JEFFERIS PENNOCK

Year	Club	League	G.	IP.	W.	L.	Pct.	ERA.
1912	Philadelphia	American	17	50	1	2	.333	......
1913	Philadelphia	American	14	33	2	1	.667	5.13
1914	Philadelphia	American	28	152	11	4	.733	2.78
1915	Providence	International	13	90	6	4	.600	......
1915	Phila.-Boston	American	16	58	3	6	.333	6.36
1916	Boston	American	9	27	0	2	.000	3.00
1916	Buffalo	International	15	113	7	6	.538	1.67
1917	Boston	American	24	101	5	5	.500	3.30
1918	Boston	American	(In Military Service)					
1919	Boston	American	32	219	16	8	.667	2.71

Year	Club	League	G.	IP.	W.	L.	Pct.	ERA.
1920—Boston	American		37	242	16	13	.552	3.68
1921—Boston	American		32	223	12	14	.462	4.04
1922—Boston	American		32	202	10	17	.370	4.32
1923—New York	American		35	238	19	6	*.760	3.14
1924—New York	American		40	286	21	9	.700	2.83
1925—New York	American		47	*277	16	17	.485	2.96
1926—New York	American		40	266	23	11	.676	3.62
1927—New York	American		34	210	19	8	.704	3.00
1928—New York	American		28	211	17	6	.739	2.56
1929—New York	American		27	158	9	11	.450	4.90
1930—New York	American		25	156	11	7	.611	4.33
1931—New York	American		25	189	11	6	.647	4.29
1932—New York	American		22	147	9	5	.643	4.59
1933—New York	American		23	65	7	4	.636	5.54
1934—Boston	American		30	62	2	0	1.000	3.05
Major League Totals			617	3572	240	162	.597	3.54

WORLD SERIES RECORD

Year	Club	League	G.	IP.	W.	L.	Pct.	ERA.
1914—Philadelphia	American		1	3	0	0	.000	0.00
1923—New York	American		3	17⅓	2	0	1.000	3.63
1926—New York	American		3	22	2	0	1.000	1.23
1927—New York	American		1	9	1	0	1.000	1.00
1932—New York	American		2	4	0	0	.000	2.25
World Series Totals			10	55⅓	5	0	1.000	1.95

ATANASIO RIGAL (TONY) PEREZ

Year	Club	League	G.	AB.	R.	H.	HR.	RBI.	B.A.
1960— Geneva	NYP	104	384	82	107	6	43	.279
1961— Geneva	NYP	121	460	110	•160	27	*132	*.348
1962— Rocky Mount	Carolina	100	384	72	112	18	74	.292
1963—San Diego	P.C.	8	29	4	11	1	5	.379
1963—Macon	Sally	69	256	44	79	11	48	.309
1964—San Diego	P.C.	124	479	96	148	34	107	.309
1964—Cincinnati	National	12	25	1	2	0	1	.080
1965—Cincinnati	National	104	281	40	73	12	47	.260
1966—Cincinnati	National	99	257	25	68	4	39	.265
1967—Cincinnati	National	156	600	78	174	26	102	.290
1968—Cincinnati	National	160	625	93	176	18	92	.282
1969—Cincinnati	National	160	629	103	185	37	122	.294
1970—Cincinnati	National	158	587	107	186	40	129	.317
1971—Cincinnati	National	158	609	72	164	25	91	.269
1972—Cincinnati	National	136	515	64	146	21	90	.283
1973—Cincinnati	National	151	564	73	177	27	101	.314
1974—Cincinnati	National	158	596	81	158	28	101	.265
1975—Cincinnati	National	137	511	74	144	20	109	.282
1976—Cincinnati	National	139	527	77	137	19	91	.260
1977—Montreal	National	154	559	71	158	19	91	.283
1978—Montreal	National	148	544	63	158	14	78	.290
1979—Montreal	National	132	489	58	132	13	73	.270
1980—Boston	American	151	585	73	161	25	105	.275
1981—Boston	American	84	306	35	77	9	39	.252
1982—Boston	American	69	196	18	51	6	31	.260
1983—Philadelphia	National	91	253	18	61	6	43	.241
1984—Cincinnati	National	71	137	9	33	2	15	.241
1985—Cincinnati	National	72	183	25	60	6	33	.328
1986—Cincinnati	National	77	200	14	51	2	29	.255
National League Totals		2473	8691	1146	2443	339	1477	.281
American League Totals		304	1087	126	289	40	175	.266
Major League Totals		2777	9778	1272	2732	379	1652	.279

CHAMPIONSHIP SERIES RECORD

Year	Club	League	G.	AB.	R.	H.	HR.	RBI.	B.A.
1970—Cincinnati	National	3	12	1	4	1	2	.333
1972—Cincinnati	National	5	20	0	4	0	2	.200
1973—Cincinnati	National	5	22	1	2	1	2	.091
1975—Cincinnati	National	3	12	3	5	1	4	.417
1976—Cincinnati	National	3	10	1	2	0	3	.200
1983—Philadelphia	National	1	1	0	1	0	0	1.000
Championship Series Totals		20	77	6	18	3	13	.234

WORLD SERIES RECORD

Year	Club	League	G.	AB.	R.	H.	HR.	RBI.	B.A.
1970—Cincinnati	National	5	18	2	1	0	0	.056
1972—Cincinnati	National	7	23	3	10	0	2	.435
1975—Cincinnati	National	7	28	4	5	3	7	.179
1976—Cincinnati	National	4	16	1	5	0	2	.313
1983—Philadelphia	National	4	10	0	2	0	0	.200
World Series Totals		27	95	10	23	3	11	.242

GAYLORD JACKSON PERRY

Year	Club	League	G.	IP.	W.	L.	Pct.	ERA.
1958— St. Cloud	Northern	17	128	9	5	.643	2.39
1959— Corpus Christi	Texas	41	191	10	11	.476	4.05
1960— Tacoma	P. Coast	1	1	0	0	.000	9.00
1960— Rio Gr. Vally	Texas	31	188	9	13	.409	•2.82
1961— Tacoma	P. Coast	33	•219	●16	10	.615	2.55
1962— San Francisco	National	13	43	3	1	.750	5.23
1962— Tacoma	P. Coast	22	156	10	7	.588	•2.48
1963— San Francisco	National	31	76	1	6	.143	4.03
1963— Tacoma	P. Coast	1	9	1	0	1.000	1.00
1964— San Francisco	National	44	206	12	11	.522	2.75
1965— San Francisco	National	47	196	8	12	.400	4.18
1966— San Francisco	National	36	256	21	8	.724	2.99
1967— San Francisco	National	39	293	15	17	.469	2.61
1968— San Francisco	National	39	291	16	15	.516	2.44
1969— San Francisco	National	40	•325	19	14	.576	2.49
1970— San Francisco	National	41	•329	●23	13	.639	3.20
1971— San Francisco	National	37	280	16	12	.571	2.76
1972— Cleveland	American	41	343	●24	16	.600	1.92
1973— Cleveland	American	41	344	19	19	.500	3.38
1974— Cleveland	American	37	322	21	13	.618	2.52
1975— Cleveland-Texas	American	37	306	18	17	.514	3.24
1976— Texas	American	32	250	15	14	.517	3.24
1977— Texas	American	34	238	15	12	.556	3.37
1978— San Diego	National	37	261	•21	6	.778	2.72
1979— San Diego	National	32	233	12	11	.522	3.05
1980— Texas-New York	American	34	206	10	13	.435	3.67
1981— Atlanta	National	23	151	8	9	.471	3.93
1982— Seattle	American	32	216⅔	10	12	.455	4.40
1983— Seattle-K.C.	American	30	186⅓	7	14	.333	4.64
National League Totals		459	2940	175	135	.565	3.00
American League Totals		318	2412	139	130	.517	3.24
Major League Totals		777	5352	314	265	.542	3.10

CHAMPIONSHIP SERIES RECORD

Year	Club	League	G.	IP.	W.	L.	Pct.	ERA.
1971— San Francisco	National	2	14⅔	1	1	.500	6.14

EDWARD S. PLANK

Year	Club	League	G.	IP.	W.	L.	Pct.	ERA.
1901—Philadelphia	American	33	262	17	11	.607	.....
1902—Philadelphia	American	36	295	20	15	.571	.....
1903—Philadelphia	American	*43	338	23	16	.590	.....
1904—Philadelphia	American	44	365	26	17	.605	.....
1905—Philadelphia	American	41	●346	25	12	.676	.....
1906—Philadelphia	American	26	211	19	6	*.760	.....
1907—Philadelphia	American	43	344	24	16	.600	.....
1908—Philadelphia	American	34	245	14	16	.467	.....
1909—Philadelphia	American	34	265	19	10	.655	.....
1910—Philadelphia	American	38	250	16	10	.615	.....
1911—Philadelphia	American	40	257	22	8	.733	.....
1912—Philadelphia	American	37	266	26	6	.813	.....
1913—Philadelphia	American	41	244	18	10	.643	2.59
1914—Philadelphia	American	34	185	15	7	.682	2.87
1915—St. Louis	Federal	42	269	21	11	.656	*2.01
1916—St. Louis	American	37	236	16	15	.516	2.33
1917—St. Louis	American	20	131	5	6	.455	1.79
Major League Totals		581	4234	305	181	.628	.....

WORLD SERIES RECORD

Year	Club	League	G.	IP.	W.	L.	Pct.	ERA.
1905—Philadelphia	American	2	17	0	2	.000	1.06
1911—Philadelphia	American	2	9⅔	1	1	.500	1.86
1913—Philadelphia	American	2	19	1	1	.500	0.95
1914—Philadelphia	American	1	9	0	1	.000	1.00
World Series Totals		7	54⅔	2	5	.286	1.15

KIRBY PUCKETT

Year	Club	League	G.	AB.	R.	H.	HR.	RBI.	B.A.
1982—Elizabethton	Appal.	65	*275	*65	*105	3	35	*.382
1983—Visalia	Calif.	138	*548	105	172	9	97	.314
1984—Toledo	Intl.	21	80	9	21	1	5	.263
1984—Minnesota	American	128	557	63	165	0	31	.296
1985—Minnesota	American	161	*691	80	199	4	74	.288
1986—Minnesota	American	161	680	119	223	31	96	.328
1987—Minnesota	American	157	624	96	•207	28	99	.332
1988—Minnesota	American	158	*657	109	•234	24	121	.356
1989—Minnesota	American	159	635	75	*215	9	85	*.339
1990—Minnesota	American	146	551	82	164	12	80	.298
1991—Minnesota	American	152	611	92	195	15	89	.319
1992—Minnesota	American	160	639	104	*210	19	110	.329
1993—Minnesota	American	156	622	89	184	22	89	.296
1994—Minnesota	American	108	439	79	139	20	*112	.317
1995—Minnesota	American	137	538	83	169	23	99	.314
Major League Totals		1783	7244	1071	2304	207	1085	.318

CHAMPIONSHIP SERIES RECORD

Year	Club	League	G.	AB.	R.	H.	HR.	RBI.	B.A.
1987—Minnesota	American	5	24	3	5	1	3	.208
1991—Minnesota	American	5	21	4	9	2	6	.429
Championship Series Totals		10	45	7	14	3	9	.311

WORLD SERIES RECORD

Year	Club	League	G.	AB.	R.	H.	HR.	RBI.	B.A.
1987	Minnesota	American	7	28	5	10	0	3	.357
1991	Minnesota	American	7	24	4	6	2	4	.250
World Series Totals			14	52	9	16	2	7	.308

CHARLES (OLD HOSS) RADBOURN

Year	Club	League	G.	IP.	W.	L.	Pct.	ShO.
1878	Peoria Reds	Independent	Batted .289 and fielded .810 in 28 games					
1879	Dubuque	N.W.L.	Batted .387 and fielded .916 in 47 games					
1880	Buffalo	National	Batted .143 and fielded .937 in 6 games					
1881	Providence	National	41	327	25	11	*.694	3
1882	Providence	National	52	471	31	19	.620	*6
1883	Providence	National	*76	642	*49	25	.662	4
1884	Providence	National	*74	*679	*60	12	*.833	11
1885	Providence	National	49	448	26	20	.565	2
1886	Boston	National	57	511	27	30	.474	3
1887	Boston	National	47	429	24	23	.511	1
1888	Boston	National	24	209	7	16	.304	1
1889	Boston	National	32	276	20	11	.645	1
1890	Boston	Players	40	347	27	12	.692	1
1891	Cincinnati	National	25	204	12	12	.500	2
National League Totals			477	4196	281	179	.611	34
Players League Totals			40	347	27	12	.692	1
Major League Totals			517	4543	308	191	.617	35

WORLD SERIES RECORD

Year	Club	League	G.	IP.	W.	L.	Pct.	ShO.
1884	Providence	National	3	22	3	0	1.000	0

PEE WEE REESE

Year	Club	League	G.	AB.	R.	H.	HR.	RBI.	B.A.
1938	Louisville	A. A.	138	483	68	134	3	54	.277
1939	Louisville	A. A.	149	506	78	141	4	57	.279
1940	Brooklyn	Nat.	84	312	58	85	5	28	.272
1941	Brooklyn	Nat.	152	595	76	136	2	46	.229
1942	Brooklyn	Nat.	151	564	87	144	3	53	.255
1943-44-45	Brooklyn	Nat.	(In Military Service)						
1946	Brooklyn	Nat.	152	542	79	154	5	60	.284
1947	Brooklyn	Nat.	142	476	81	135	12	73	.284
1948	Brooklyn	Nat.	151	566	96	155	9	75	.274
1949	Brooklyn	Nat.	155	617	*132	172	16	73	.279
1950	Brooklyn	Nat.	141	531	97	138	11	52	.260
1951	Brooklyn	Nat.	154	616	94	176	10	84	.286
1952	Brooklyn	Nat.	149	559	94	152	6	58	.272
1953	Brooklyn	Nat.	140	524	108	142	13	61	.271
1954	Brooklyn	Nat.	141	554	98	171	10	69	.309
1955	Brooklyn	Nat.	145	553	99	156	10	61	.282
1956	Brooklyn	Nat.	147	572	85	147	9	46	.257
1957	Brooklyn	Nat.	103	330	33	74	1	29	.224
1958	Los Angeles	Nat.	59	147	21	33	4	17	.224
Major League Totals			2166	8058	1338	2170	126	885	.269

WORLD SERIES RECORD

Year	Club	League	G.	AB.	R.	H.	HR.	RBI.	B.A.
1941	Brooklyn	Nat.	5	20	1	4	0	2	.200
1947	Brooklyn	Nat.	7	23	5	7	0	4	.304
1949	Brooklyn	Nat.	5	19	2	6	1	2	.316
1952	Brooklyn	Nat.	7	29	4	10	1	4	.345
1953	Brooklyn	Nat.	6	24	0	5	0	0	.278
1955	Brooklyn	Nat.	7	27	5	8	0	2	.296
1956	Brooklyn	Nat.	7	27	3	6	0	2	.222
World Series Totals			44	169	20	46	2	16	.272

EDGAR CHARLES (SAM) RICE

Year	Club	League	G.	AB.	R.	H.	HR.	RBI.	B.A.
1914	Petersburg	Va.	31	71	9	22	0	....	.310
1915	Petersburg	Va.	62	156	16	47	0	....	.301
1915	Washington	Amer.	4	8	0	3	0	0	.375
1916	Washington	Amer.	58	197	26	59	1	16	.299
1917	Washington	Amer.	155	586	77	177	0	68	.302
1918	Washington	Amer.	7	23	3	8	0	3	.348
1919	Washington	Amer.	•141	557	80	179	3	72	.321
1920	Washington	Amer.	153	624	83	211	3	80	.336
1921	Washington	Amer.	143	561	83	185	4	79	.330
1922	Washington	Amer.	154	*633	91	187	6	69	.295
1923	Washington	Amer.	148	595	117	188	3	75	.316
1924	Washington	Amer.	154	*646	106	*216	1	76	.334
1925	Washington	Amer.	152	649	111	227	1	87	.350
1926	Washington	Amer.	152	*641	98	•216	3	76	.337
1927	Washington	Amer.	142	603	98	179	2	65	.297
1928	Washington	Amer.	148	616	95	202	2	55	.328
1929	Washington	Amer.	150	616	119	199	1	62	.323
1930	Washington	Amer.	147	593	121	207	1	73	.349
1931	Washington	Amer.	120	413	81	128	0	42	.310
1932	Washington	Amer.	106	288	58	93	1	34	.323
1933	Washington	Amer.	73	85	19	25	1	12	.294
1934	Cleveland	Amer.	97	335	48	98	1	33	.293
Major League Totals			2404	9269	1514	2987	34	1077	.322

WORLD SERIES RECORD

Year	Club	League	G.	AB.	R.	H.	HR.	RBI.	B.A.
1924	Washington	Amer.	7	29	2	6	0	1	.207
1925	Washington	Amer.	7	33	5	12	0	3	.364
1933	Washington	Amer.	1	1	0	1	0	0	1.000
World Series Totals			15	63	7	19	0	4	.302

PITCHING RECORD

Year	Club	League	G.	IP.	W.	L.	Pct.	ERA.
1914	Petersburg	Virginia	15	123	9	2	.818	....
1915	Petersburg	Virginia	29	233	11	12	.478	....
1915	Washington	American	4	18	1	0	.000	2.00
1916	Washington	American	5	21⅓	0	1	.000	2.94
Major League Totals			9	39⅓	1	1	.500	2.52

EPPA (JEPTHA) RIXEY

Year	Club	League	G.	IP.	W.	L.	Pct.	ERA.
1912	Philadelphia	National	23	162	10	10	.500	2.50
1913	Philadelphia	National	35	156	9	5	.643	3.12
1914	Philadelphia	National	24	103	2	11	.154	4.37
1915	Philadelphia	National	29	177	11	12	.478	2.39
1916	Philadelphia	National	38	287	22	10	.688	1.85
1917	Philadelphia	National	39	281	16	•21	.432	2.27
1918	Philadelphia	National	(In Military Service)					
1919	Philadelphia	National	23	154	6	12	.333	3.97
1920	Philadelphia	National	41	284	11	*22	.333	3.49
1921	Cincinnati	National	40	301	19	18	.514	2.78
1922	Cincinnati	National	40	*313	*25	13	.658	3.54
1923	Cincinnati	National	42	309	20	15	.571	2.80
1924	Cincinnati	National	35	238	15	14	.517	2.76
1925	Cincinnati	National	39	287	21	11	.656	2.89
1926	Cincinnati	National	37	233	14	8	.636	3.40
1927	Cincinnati	National	34	220	12	10	.545	3.48
1928	Cincinnati	National	43	291	19	18	.514	3.43
1929	Cincinnati	National	35	201	10	13	.435	4.16
1930	Cincinnati	National	32	164	9	13	.409	5.10
1931	Cincinnati	National	22	127	4	7	.364	3.90
1932	Cincinnati	National	25	112	5	5	.500	2.65
1933	Cincinnati	National	16	94	6	3	.667	3.16
Major League Totals			692	4494	266	251	.515	3.15

WORLD SERIES RECORD

Year	Club	League	G.	IP.	W.	L.	Pct.	ERA.
1915	Philadelphia	National	1	6⅔	0	1	.000	2.70

PHILIP FRANCIS (SCOOTER) RIZZUTO

Year	Club	League	G.	AB.	R.	H.	HR.	RBI.	B.A.
1937	Bassett	Bi-State	67	284	53	88	5	...	.310
1938	Norfolk	Pied.	112	446	97	150	9	58	.336
1939	Kansas City	A. A.	135	503	99	159	5	64	.316
1940	Kansas City	A.A.	148	579	124	201	10	73	.347
1941	New York	American	133	515	65	158	3	46	.307
1942	New York	American	144	553	79	157	4	68	.284
1943-5	New York	American	(In Military Service)						
1946	New York	American	126	471	53	121	2	38	.257
1947	New York	American	153	549	78	150	2	60	.273
1948	New York	American	128	464	65	117	6	50	.252
1949	New York	American	153	614	110	169	5	65	.275
1950	New York	American	155	617	125	200	7	66	.324
1951	New York	American	144	540	87	148	2	43	.274
1952	New York	American	152	578	89	147	2	43	.254
1953	New York	American	134	413	54	112	2	54	.271
1954	New York	American	127	307	47	60	2	15	.195
1955	New York	American	81	143	19	37	1	9	.259
1956	New York	American	31	52	6	12	0	6	.231
Major League Totals			1661	5816	877	1588	38	563	.273

WORLD SERIES RECORD

Year	Club	League	G.	AB.	R.	H.	HR.	RBI.	B.A.
1941	New York	American	5	18	0	2	0	0	.111
1942	New York	American	5	21	2	8	1	1	.381
1947	New York	American	7	26	3	8	0	2	.308
1949	New York	American	5	18	2	3	0	1	.167
1950	New York	American	4	14	1	2	0	0	.143
1951	New York	American	6	25	5	8	1	3	.320
1952	New York	American	7	27	2	4	0	0	.148
1953	New York	American	6	19	4	6	0	0	.316
1955	New York	American	7	15	2	4	0	1	.267
World Series Totals			52	183	21	45	2	8	.246

ROBIN EVAN ROBERTS

Year	Club	League	G.	IP.	W.	L.	Pct.	ERA.
1948	Wilmington	Int. State	11	96	9	1	*.900	*2.06
1948	Philadelphia	National	20	147	7	9	.438	3.18
1949	Philadelphia	National	43	227	15	15	.500	3.69
1950	Philadelphia	National	40	304	20	11	.645	3.02
1951	Philadelphia	National	44	*315	21	15	.583	3.03
1952	Philadelphia	National	39	*330	*28	7	.800	2.59
1953	Philadelphia	National	44	*347	•23	16	.590	2.75
1954	Philadelphia	National	45	*337	*23	15	.605	2.96
1955	Philadelphia	National	41	*305	*23	14	.622	3.28
1956	Philadelphia	National	43	297	19	•18	.514	4.45
1957	Philadelphia	National	39	250	10	*22	.313	4.07
1958	Philadelphia	National	35	270	17	14	.548	3.23
1959	Philadelphia	National	35	257	15	17	.469	4.27
1960	Philadelphia	National	35	237	12	16	.429	4.03
1961	Philadelphia	National	26	117	1	10	.091	5.85
1962	Baltimore	American	27	191	10	9	.526	2.78
1963	Baltimore	American	35	251	14	13	.519	3.33
1964	Baltimore	American	31	204	13	7	.650	2.91
1965	Baltimore	American	20	115	5	7	.417	3.37
1965	Houston	National	10	76	5	2	.714	1.89
1966	Houston-Chicago	National	24	112	5	8	.385	4.82
1967	Reading	Eastern	11	80	5	3	.625	2.48
American League Totals			113	761	42	36	.538	3.09
National League Totals			563	3928	244	209	.539	3.45
Major League Totals			676	4689	286	245	.539	3.40

Year	Club	League	G.	IP.	W.	L.	Pct.	ERA.
1950—Philadelphia		National	2	11	0	1	.000	1.64

BROOKS CALBERT ROBINSON, JR.

Year	Club	League	G.	AB.	R.	H.	HR.	RBI.	B.A.
1955—York		Pied.	95	354	72	117	11	67	.331
1955—Baltimore		Amer.	6	22	0	2	0	1	.091
1956—San Antonio		Texas	154	577	72	157	9	74	.272
1956—Baltimore		Amer.	15	44	5	10	1	1	.227
1957—San Antonio		Texas	33	124	10	33	1	9	.266
1957—Baltimore		Amer.	50	117	13	28	2	14	.239
1958—Baltimore		Amer.	145	463	31	110	3	32	.238
1959—Vancouver		P. C.	42	163	20	54	6	30	.331
1959—Baltimore		Amer.	88	313	29	89	4	24	.284
1960—Baltimore		Amer.	152	595	74	175	14	88	.294
1961—Baltimore		Amer.	●163	*668	89	192	7	61	.287
1962—Baltimore		Amer.	●162	634	77	192	23	86	.303
1963—Baltimore		Amer.	*161	589	67	148	11	67	.251
1964—Baltimore		Amer.	●163	612	82	194	28	*118	.317
1965—Baltimore		Amer.	144	559	81	166	18	80	.297
1966—Baltimore		Amer.	157	620	91	167	23	100	.269
1967—Baltimore		Amer.	158	610	88	164	22	77	.269
1968—Baltimore		Amer.	●162	608	65	154	17	75	.253
1969—Baltimore		Amer.	156	598	73	140	23	84	.234
1970—Baltimore		Amer.	158	608	84	168	18	94	.276
1971—Baltimore		Amer.	156	589	67	160	20	92	.272
1972—Baltimore		Amer.	153	556	48	139	8	64	.250
1973—Baltimore		Amer.	155	549	53	141	9	72	.257
1974—Baltimore		Amer.	153	553	46	159	7	59	.288
1975—Baltimore		Amer.	144	482	50	97	6	53	.201
1976—Baltimore		Amer.	71	218	16	46	3	11	.211
1977—Baltimore		Amer.	24	47	3	7	1	4	.149
Major League Totals			2896	10654	1232	2848	268	1357	.267

CHAMPIONSHIP SERIES RECORD

Year	Club	League	G.	AB.	R.	H.	HR.	RBI.	B.A.
1969—Baltimore		Amer.	3	14	1	7	0	0	.500
1970—Baltimore		Amer.	3	12	3	7	0	1	.583
1971—Baltimore		Amer.	3	11	2	4	1	3	.364
1973—Baltimore		Amer.	5	20	1	5	0	2	.250
1974—Baltimore		Amer.	4	12	1	1	1	1	.083
Championship Series Totals			18	69	8	24	2	7	.348

WORLD SERIES RECORD

Year	Club	League	G.	AB.	R.	H.	HR.	RBI.	B.A.
1966—Baltimore		Amer.	4	14	2	3	1	1	.214
1969—Baltimore		Amer.	5	19	0	1	0	2	.053
1970—Baltimore		Amer.	5	21	5	9	2	6	.429
1971—Baltimore		Amer.	7	22	2	7	0	5	.318
World Series Totals			21	76	9	20	3	14	.263

FRANK ROBINSON

Year	Club	League	G.	AB.	R.	H.	HR.	RBI.	B.A.
1953—Ogden		Pion.	72	270	70	94	17	83	.348
1954—Tulsa		Tex.	8	30	4	8	0	1	.267
1954—Columbia		Sally	132	491	*112	165	25	110	.336
1955—Columbia		Sally	80	243	50	64	12	52	.263
1956—Cincinnati		Nat.	152	572	*122	166	38	83	.290
1957—Cincinnati		Nat.	150	611	97	197	29	75	.322
1958—Cincinnati		Nat.	148	554	90	149	31	83	.269
1959—Cincinnati		Nat.	146	540	106	168	36	125	.311
1960—Cincinnati		Nat.	139	464	86	138	31	83	.297
1961—Cincinnati		Nat.	153	545	117	176	37	124	.323
1962—Cincinnati		Nat.	162	609	*134	208	39	136	.342
1963—Cincinnati		Nat.	140	482	79	125	21	91	.259
1964—Cincinnati		Nat.	156	568	103	174	29	96	.306
1965—Cincinnati		Nat.	156	582	109	172	33	113	.296
1966—Baltimore		Am.	155	576	*122	182	*49	*122	.316
1967—Baltimore		Am.	129	479	83	149	30	94	.311
1968—Baltimore		Am.	130	421	69	113	15	52	.268
1969—Baltimore		Am.	148	539	111	166	32	100	.308
1970—Baltimore		Am.	132	471	88	144	25	78	.306
1971—Baltimore		Am.	133	455	82	128	28	99	.281
1972—Los Angeles		Nat.	103	342	41	86	19	59	.251
1973—California		Amer.	147	534	85	142	30	97	.266
1974—Calif.-Cleve.		Amer.	144	477	81	117	22	68	.245
1975—Cleveland		Amer.	49	118	19	28	9	24	.237
1976—Cleveland		Amer.	36	67	5	15	3	10	.224
National League Totals			1605	5869	1084	1759	343	1068	.300
American League Totals			1203	4137	745	1184	243	744	.286
Major League Totals			2808	10006	1829	2943	586	1812	.294

CHAMPIONSHIP SERIES RECORD

Year	Club	League	G.	AB.	R.	H.	HR.	RBI.	B.A.
1969—Baltimore		Amer.	3	12	1	4	1	2	.333
1970—Baltimore		Amer.	3	10	3	2	1	2	.200
1971—Baltimore		Amer.	3	12	2	1	0	1	.083
Championship Series Totals			9	34	6	7	2	5	.206

WORLD SERIES RECORD

Year	Club	League	G.	AB.	R.	H.	HR.	RBI.	B.A.
1961—Cincinnati		Nat.	5	15	3	3	1	4	.200
1966—Baltimore		Amer.	4	14	4	4	2	3	.286

Year	Club	League	G.	AB.	R.	H.	HR.	RBI.	B.A.
1969—Baltimore		Amer.	5	16	2	3	1	1	.188
1970—Baltimore		Amer.	5	22	5	6	2	4	.273
1971—Baltimore		Amer.	7	25	5	7	2	2	.280
World Series Totals			26	92	19	23	8	14	.250

JACK ROOSEVELT ROBINSON

Year	Club	League	G.	AB.	R.	H.	HR.	RBI.	B.A.
1946—Montreal		Int.	124	444	●113	155	3	66	*.349
1947—Brooklyn		Nat.	151	590	125	175	12	48	.297
1948—Brooklyn		Nat.	147	574	108	170	12	85	.296
1949—Brooklyn		Nat.	156	593	122	203	16	124	*.342
1950—Brooklyn		Nat.	144	518	99	170	14	81	.328
1951—Brooklyn		Nat.	153	548	106	185	19	88	.338
1952—Brooklyn		Nat.	149	510	104	157	19	75	.308
1953—Brooklyn		Nat.	136	484	109	159	12	95	.329
1954—Brooklyn		Nat.	124	386	62	120	15	59	.311
1955—Brooklyn		Nat.	105	317	51	81	8	36	.256
1956—Brooklyn		Nat.	117	357	61	98	10	43	.275
Major League Totals			1382	4877	947	1518	137	734	.311

WORLD SERIES RECORD

Year	Club	League	G.	AB.	R.	H.	HR.	RBI.	B.A.
1947—Brooklyn		Nat.	7	27	3	7	0	3	.259
1949—Brooklyn		Nat.	5	16	2	3	0	2	.188
1952—Brooklyn		Nat.	7	23	4	4	1	2	.174
1953—Brooklyn		Nat.	6	25	3	8	0	2	.320
1955—Brooklyn		Nat.	6	22	5	4	0	1	.182
1956—Brooklyn		Nat.	7	24	5	6	1	2	.250
World Series Totals			38	137	22	32	2	12	.234

WILBERT (ROBBY) ROBINSON

RECORD AS MANAGER

Year	Club	League	Position	W.	L.
1902—Baltimore		American	Eighth	22	54
1914—Brooklyn		National	Fifth	75	79
1915—Brooklyn		National	Third	80	72
1916—Brooklyn		National	First	94	60
1917—Brooklyn		National	Seventh	70	81
1918—Brooklyn		National	Fifth	57	69
1919—Brooklyn		National	Fifth	69	71
1920—Brooklyn		National	First	93	61
1921—Brooklyn		National	Fifth	77	75
1922—Brooklyn		National	Sixth	76	78
1923—Brooklyn		National	Sixth	76	78
1924—Brooklyn		National	Second	92	62
1925—Brooklyn		National	Sixth†	68	85
1926—Brooklyn		National	Sixth	71	82
1927—Brooklyn		National	Sixth	65	88
1928—Brooklyn		National	Sixth	77	76
1929—Brooklyn		National	Sixth	70	83
1930—Brooklyn		National	Fourth	86	68
1931—Brooklyn		National	Fourth	79	73
Major League Totals				1397	1395

†Tied for position

WORLD SERIES RECORD

Year	Club	League	W.	L.
1916—Brooklyn		National	1	4
1920—Brooklyn		National	2	5

EDD J. ROUSH

Year	Club	League	G.	AB.	R.	H.	HR.	RBI.	B.A.
1912—Evansville		Kitty	41	148	17	43	2	.....	.284
1913—Evansville		Central	89	344	42	109	5	.....	.317
1913—Chicago		Amer.	9	10	2	1	0	0	.100
1913—Lincoln		West.	10	35		6	0	.....	.171
1914—Indianapolis		Federal	74	165	26	55	1	.....	.333
1915—Newark		Federal	145	550	73	164	3	.....	.298
1916—N.Y.-Cin.		Nat.	108	341	38	91	0	19	.267
1917—Cincinnati		Nat.	136	522	82	178	4	62	*.341
1918—Cincinnati		Nat.	113	435	61	145	5	61	.333
1919—Cincinnati		Nat.	133	504	73	162	3	69	*.321
1920—Cincinnati		Nat.	149	579	81	196	4	90	.339
1921—Cincinnati		Nat.	112	418	68	147	4	71	.352
1922—Cincinnati		Nat.	49	165	29	58	1	24	.352
1923—Cincinnati		Nat.	138	527	88	185	6	88	.351
1924—Cincinnati		Nat.	121	483	67	168	3	72	.348
1925—Cincinnati		Nat.	134	540	91	183	8	83	.339
1926—Cincinnati		Nat.	144	563	95	182	7	70	.323
1927—New York		Nat.	140	570	83	173	7	58	.304
1928—New York		Nat.	46	163	20	41	2	13	.252
1929—New York		Nat.	115	450	76	146	8	52	.324
1930—New York					(Out of Organized Ball)				
1931—Cincinnati		Nat.	101	376	46	102	1	41	.271
American League Totals			9	10	2	1	0	0	.100
National League Totals			1739	6636	998	2157	63	882	.325
Major League Totals			1748	6646	1000	2158	63	882	.325

WORLD SERIES RECORD

Year	Club	League	G.	AB.	R.	H.	HR.	RBI.	B.A.
1919—Cincinnati		Nat.	8	28	6	6	0	7	.214

CHARLES HERBERT (RED) RUFFING

Year	Club	League	G.	IP.	W.	L.	Pct.	ERA.
1923—Danville		I.I.I.	39	239	12	16	.429	.....
1924—Boston		Amer.	8	23	0	0	.000	6.65
1924—Dover		East. Shore	15	94	4	7	.364	.....
1925—Boston		Amer.	37	217	9	18	.333	5.02
1926—Boston		Amer.	37	166	6	15	.286	4.39
1927—Boston		Amer.	26	158	5	13	.278	4.67
1928—Boston		Amer.	42	289	10	*25	.286	3.89
1929—Boston		Amer.	35	244	9	*22	.290	4.87
1930—Boston-New York		Amer.	38	222	15	8	.652	4.38
1931—New York		Amer.	37	237	16	14	.533	4.41
1932—New York		Amer.	35	259	18	7	.720	3.09
1933—New York		Amer.	35	235	9	14	.391	3.91
1934—New York		Amer.	36	256	19	11	.633	3.94
1935—New York		Amer.	30	222	16	11	.593	3.12
1936—New York		Amer.	33	271	20	12	.625	3.85
1937—New York		Amer.	31	256	20	7	.741	2.99
1938—New York		Amer.	31	247	*21	7	*.750	3.32
1939—New York		Amer.	28	233	21	7	.750	2.94
1940—New York		Amer.	30	226	15	12	.556	3.38
1941—New York		Amer.	23	186	15	6	.714	3.53
1942—New York		Amer.	24	194	14	7	.667	3.20
1943-44—New York		Amer.			(In Military Service)			
1945—New York		Amer.	11	87	7	3	.700	2.90
1946—New York		Amer.	8	61	5	1	.833	1.77
1947—Chicago		Amer.	9	53	3	5	.375	6.11
Major League Totals			624	4342	273	225	.548	3.80

WORLD SERIES RECORD

Year	Club	League	G.	IP.	W.	L.	Pct.	ERA.
1932—New York		Amer.	1	9	1	0	1.000	4.00
1936—New York		Amer.	2	14	0	1	.000	4.50
1937—New York		Amer.	1	9	1	0	1.000	1.00
1938—New York		Amer.	2	18	2	0	1.000	1.50
1939—New York		Amer.	1	9	1	0	1.000	1.00
1941—New York		Amer.	1	9	1	0	1.000	1.00
1942—New York		Amer.	2	17⅔	1	1	.500	4.08
World Series Totals			10	85⅔	7	2	.778	2.63

AMOS WILSON RUSIE

Year	Club	League	G.	W.	L.	Pct.	ShO.
1889—Indianapolis		National	23	13	10	.565	1
1890—New York		National	60	29	30	.492	4
1891—New York		National	54	32	19	.627	*6
1892—New York		National	62	31	28	.525	2
1893—New York		National	*48	29	18	.617	●4
1894—New York		National	49	*36	13	.735	●3
1895—New York		National	43	22	21	.512	●4
1896—New York		National			(Holdout all season)		
1897—New York		National	37	29	8	*.784	●3
1898—New York		National	33	20	10	.667	4
1899-1900—New York		National			(Under suspension)		
1901—Cincinnati		National	3	0	1	.000	0
Major League Totals			412	241	158	.604	31

TEMPLE CUP RECORD

Year	Club	League	G.	I.P.	W.	L.	Pct.
1894—New York		National	2	18	2	0	1.000

GEORGE HERMAN (BABE) RUTH

Year	Club	League	G.	AB.	R.	H.	HR.	RBI.	B.A.
1914—Balt.-Prov		Int.	46	121	22	28	1	.....	.231
1914—Boston		Amer.	5	10	1	2	0	0	.200
1915—Boston		Amer.	42	92	16	29	4	20	.315
1916—Boston		Amer.	67	136	18	37	3	16	.272
1917—Boston		Amer.	52	123	14	40	2	10	.325
1918—Boston		Amer.	95	317	50	95	●11	64	.300
1919—Boston		Amer.	130	432	*103	139	*29	*112	.322
1920—New York		Amer.	142	458	*158	172	*54	*137	.376
1921—New York		Amer.	152	540	*177	204	*59	*171	.378
1922—New York		Amer.	110	406	94	128	35	99	.315
1923—New York		Amer.	152	520	*151	205	*41	*131	.394
1924—New York		Amer.	153	529	*143	200	*46	121	*.378
1925—New York		Amer.	98	359	61	104	25	66	.290
1926—New York		Amer.	152	495	*139	184	*47	*145	.372
1927—New York		Amer.	151	540	*158	192	*60	164	.356
1928—New York		Amer.	154	536	*163	173	*54	●142	.323
1929—New York		Amer.	135	499	121	172	*46	154	.345
1930—New York		Amer.	145	518	150	186	*49	153	.359
1931—New York		Amer.	145	534	149	199	●46	163	.373
1932—New York		Amer.	133	457	120	156	41	137	.341
1933—New York		Amer.	137	459	97	138	34	103	.301
1934—New York		Amer.	125	365	78	105	22	84	.288
1935—Boston		Nat.	28	72	13	13	6	12	.181
American League Totals			2475	8325	2161	2860	708	2192	.344
National League Totals			28	72	13	13	6	12	.181
Major League Totals			2503	8397	2174	2873	714	2204	.342

WORLD SERIES RECORD

Year	Club	League	G.	AB.	R.	H.	HR.	RBI.	B.A.
1915—Boston		Amer.	1	1	0	0	0	0	.000
1916—Boston		Amer.	1	5	0	0	0	1	.000
1918—Boston		Amer.	3	5	0	1	0	2	.200
1921—New York		Amer.	6	16	3	5	1	4	.313
1922—New York		Amer.	5	17	1	2	0	1	.118
1923—New York		Amer.	6	19	8	7	3	3	.368
1926—New York		Amer.	7	20	6	6	4	5	.300
1927—New York		Amer.	4	15	4	6	2	7	.400
1928—New York		Amer.	4	16	9	10	3	4	.625
1932—New York		Amer.	4	15	6	5	2	6	.333
World Series Totals			41	129	37	42	15	33	.326

PITCHING RECORD

Year	Club	League	G.	IP.	W.	L.	Pct.	ERA.
1914—Balti.-Providence		International	35	245	22	9	.710	......
1914—Boston		American	4	23	2	1	.667	3.91
1915—Boston		American	32	218	18	8	.692	2.44
1916—Boston		American	44	324	23	12	.657	*1.75
1917—Boston		American	41	326	24	13	.649	2.02
1918—Boston		American	20	166	13	7	.650	2.22
1919—Boston		American	17	133	9	5	.643	2.97
1920—New York		American	1	4	1	0	1.000	4.50
1921—New York		American	2	9	2	0	1.000	9.00
1930—New York		American	1	9	1	0	1.000	3.00
1933—New York		American	1	9	1	0	1.000	5.00
Major League Totals			163	1221	94	46	.671	2.28

WORLD SERIES PITCHING RECORD

Year	Club	League	G.	IP.	W.	L.	Pct.	ERA.
1916—Boston		American	1	14	1	0	1.000	0.64
1918—Boston		American	2	17	2	0	1.000	1.06
World Series Totals			3	31	3	0	1.000	0.87

LYNN NOLAN RYAN

Year	Club	League	G.	IP.	W.	L.	Pct.	ERA.
1965—Marion		Appal.	13	78	3	6	.333	4.38
1966—Greenville		W.Car	29	183	*17	2	.895	2.51
Williamsport		East.	3	19	0	2	.000	0.95
New York		Nat.	2	3	0	1	.000	15.00
1967—Winter Haven		F.S.L.	1	4	0	0	...	2.25
Jacksonville		Int.	3	7	1	0	1.000	0.00
1968—New York		Nat.	21	134	6	9	.400	3.09
1969—New York		Nat.	25	89	6	3	.667	3.54
1970—New York		Nat.	27	132	7	11	.389	3.41
1971—New York		Nat.	30	152	10	14	.417	3.97
1972—California		Amer.	39	284	19	16	.543	2.28
1973—California		Amer.	41	326	21	16	.568	2.87
1974—California		Amer.	42	*333	22	16	.579	2.89
1975—California		Amer.	28	198	14	12	.538	3.45
1976—California		Amer.	39	284	17	*18	.486	3.36
1977—California		Amer.	37	299	19	16	.543	2.77
1978—California		Amer.	31	235	10	13	.435	3.71
1979—California		Amer.	34	223	16	14	.533	3.59
1980—Houston		Nat.	35	234	11	10	.524	3.35
1981—Houston		Nat.	21	149	11	5	.688	*1.69
1982—Houston		Nat.	35	250-1/3	16	12	.571	3.16
1983—Houston		Nat.	29	196-1/3	14	9	.609	2.98
1984—Houston		Nat.	30	183-2/3	12	11	.522	3.04
1985—Houston		Nat.	35	232	10	12	.455	3.80
1986—Houston		Nat.	30	178	12	8	.600	3.34
1987—Houston		Nat.	34	211-2/3	8	16	.333	*2.76
1988—Houston		Nat.	33	220	12	11	.522	3.52
1989—Texas		Amer.	32	239-1/3	16	10	.615	3.20
1990—Texas		Amer.	30	204	13	9	.591	3.44
1991—Texas		Amer.	27	173	12	6	.667	2.91
1992—Texas		Amer.	27	157-1/3	5	9	.357	3.72
1993—Texas		Amer.	13	66-1/3	5	5	.500	4.88
American League Totals			420	3022	189	160	.542	3.17
National League Totals			387	2365	135	132	.506	3.23
Major League Totals			807	5387	324	292	.526	3.19

CHAMPIONSHIP SERIES RECORD

Year	Club	League	G.	IP.	W.	L.	Pct.	ERA.
1969—New York		Nat.	1	7	1	0	1.000	2.57
1979—California		Amer.	1	7	0	0	...	1.29
1980—Houston		Nat.	2	13-1/3	0	0	...	5.40
1986—Houston		Nat.	2	14	0	1	.000	3.86
Championship Series Totals			6	41-1/3	1	1	.500	3.70

WORLD SERIES RECORD

Year	Club	League	G.	IP.	W.	L.	Pct.	ERA.
1969—New York		Nat.	1	2-1/3	0	0	...	0.00

RAYMOND WILLIAM (CRACKER) SCHALK

Year	Club	League	G.	AB.	R.	H.	HR.	RBI.	B.A.
1911—Taylorville		Ill.-Mo.	47	161	27	64		.....	.398
1911—Milwaukee		A. A.	31	76	9	18	0	.....	.237
1912—Milwaukee		A. A.	80	266	19	72	3	.....	.271
1912—Chicago		Amer.	23	63	7	18	0	6	.286
1913—Chicago		Amer.	128	401	38	98	1	42	.244

Year	Club	League	G.	AB.	R.	H.	HR.	RBI.	B.A.
1914	Chicago	Amer.	135	392	30	106	0	37	.270
1915	Chicago	Amer.	135	413	46	110	1	48	.266
1916	Chicago	Amer.	129	410	36	95	0	36	.232
1917	Chicago	Amer.	140	424	48	96	3	53	.226
1918	Chicago	Amer.	108	333	35	73	0	24	.219
1919	Chicago	Amer.	131	394	57	111	0	40	.282
1920	Chicago	Amer.	151	485	64	131	1	61	.270
1921	Chicago	Amer.	128	416	32	105	0	47	.252
1922	Chicago	Amer.	142	442	57	124	4	60	.281
1923	Chicago	Amer.	123	382	42	87	1	44	.228
1924	Chicago	Amer.	57	153	15	30	1	11	.196
1925	Chicago	Amer.	125	343	44	94	0	52	.274
1926	Chicago	Amer.	82	226	26	60	0	32	.265
1927	Chicago	Amer.	16	26	2	6	0	2	.231
1928	Chicago	Amer.	2	1	0	1	0	1	1.000
1929	New York	Nat.	5	2	0	0	0	0	.000
1932	Buffalo	Int.	1	3	1	2	0	0	.667
	American League Totals		1755	5304	579	1345	12	596	.254
	National League Totals		5	2	0	0	0	0	.000
	Major League Totals		1760	5306	579	1345	12	596	.253

WORLD SERIES RECORD

Year	Club	League	G.	AB.	R.	H.	HR.	RBI.	B.A.
1917	Chicago	Amer.	6	19	1	5	0	0	.263
1919	Chicago	Amer.	8	23	1	7	0	2	.304
	World Series Totals		14	42	2	12	0	2	.286

MICHAEL JACK SCHMIDT

Year	Club	League	G.	AB.	R.	H.	HR.	RBI.	B.A.
1971	Reading	Eastern	74	237	27	50	8	31	.211
1972	Eugene	Pacific Coast	131	436	80	127	26	91	.291
1972	Philadelphia	National	13	34	2	7	1	3	.206
1973	Philadelphia	National	132	367	43	72	18	52	.196
1974	Philadelphia	National	162	568	108	160	*36	116	.282
1975	Philadelphia	National	158	562	93	140	*38	95	.249
1976	Philadelphia	National	160	584	112	153	*38	107	.262
1977	Philadelphia	National	154	544	114	149	38	101	.274
1978	Philadelphia	National	145	513	93	129	21	78	.251
1979	Philadelphia	National	160	541	109	137	45	114	.253
1980	Philadelphia	National	150	548	104	157	*48	*121	.286
1981	Philadelphia	National	102	354	*78	112	*31	*91	.316
1982	Philadelphia	National	148	514	108	144	35	87	.280
1983	Philadelphia	National	154	534	104	136	*40	109	.255
1984	Philadelphia	National	151	528	93	146	•36	•106	.277
1985	Philadelphia	National	158	549	89	152	33	93	.277
1986	Philadelphia	National	160	552	97	160	*37	*119	.290
1987	Philadelphia	National	147	522	88	153	35	113	.293
1988	Philadelphia	National	108	390	52	97	12	62	.249
1989	Philadelphia	National	42	148	19	30	6	28	.203
	Major League Totals		2404	8352	1506	2234	548	1595	.267

DIVISION SERIES RECORD

Year	Club	League	G.	AB.	R.	H.	HR.	RBI.	B.A.
1981	Philadelphia	National	5	16	3	4	1	2	.250

CHAMPIONSHIP SERIES RECORD

Year	Club	League	G.	AB.	R.	H.	HR.	RBI.	B.A.
1976	Philadelphia	National	3	13	1	4	0	2	.308
1977	Philadelphia	National	4	16	2	1	0	1	.063
1978	Philadelphia	National	4	15	1	3	0	1	.200
1980	Philadelphia	National	5	24	1	5	0	1	.208
1983	Philadelphia	National	4	15	5	7	1	2	.467
	Championship Series Totals		20	83	10	20	1	7	.241

WORLD SERIES RECORD

Year	Club	League	G.	AB.	R.	H.	HR.	RBI.	B.A.
1980	Philadelphia	National	6	21	6	8	2	7	.381
1983	Philadelphia	National	5	20	0	1	0	0	.050
	World Series Totals		11	41	6	9	2	7	.220

ALBERT FRED (RED) SCHOENDIENST

Year	Club	League	G.	AB.	R.	H.	HR.	RBI.	B.A.
1942	Union City	Kitty	6	27	4	11	0	4	.407
1942	Albany	Ga.-Fla.	68	264	41	71	1	28	.269
1943	Lynchburg	Pied.	9	36	8	17	0	5	.472
1943	Rochester	Int.	136	555	81	•187	6	37	•.337
1944	Rochester	Int.	25	102	26	38	2	14	.373
1945	St. Louis	Nat.	137	565	89	157	1	47	.278
1946	St. Louis	Nat.	142	606	94	170	0	34	.281
1947	St. Louis	Nat.	151	•659	91	167	3	48	.253
1948	St. Louis	Nat.	119	408	64	111	4	36	.272
1949	St. Louis	Nat.	151	640	102	190	3	54	.297
1950	St. Louis	Nat.	153	•642	81	177	7	63	.276
1951	St. Louis	Nat.	135	553	88	160	6	54	.289
1952	St. Louis	Nat.	152	620	91	188	7	67	.303
1953	St. Louis	Nat.	146	564	107	193	15	79	.342
1954	St. Louis	Nat.	148	610	98	192	5	79	.315
1955	St. Louis	Nat.	145	553	68	148	11	51	.268
1956	St. L. - N. Y.	Nat.	132	487	61	147	2	29	.302
1957	N. Y. - Milw.	Nat.	150	648	91	•200	15	65	.309
1958	Milwaukee	Nat.	106	427	47	112	1	24	.262
1959	Milwaukee	Nat.	5	3	0	0	0	0	.000
1960	Milwaukee	Nat.	68	226	21	58	1	19	.257
1961	St. Louis	Nat.	72	120	9	36	1	12	.300
1962	St. Louis	Nat.	98	143	21	43	2	12	.301
1963	St. Louis	Nat.	6	5	0	0	0	0	.000
	Major League Totals		2216	8479	1223	2449	84	773	.289

WORLD SERIES RECORD

Year	Club	League	G.	AB.	R.	H.	HR.	RBI.	B.A.
1946	St. Louis	Nat.	7	30	3	7	0	1	.233
1957	Milwaukee	Nat.	5	18	0	5	0	2	.278
1958	Milwaukee	Nat.	7	30	5	9	0	0	.300
	World Series Totals		19	78	8	21	0	3	.269

RECORD AS MANAGER

Year	Club	League	Position	W.	L.
1965	St. Louis	Nat.	Seventh	80	81
1966	St. Louis	Nat.	Sixth	83	79
1967	St. Louis	Nat.	First	101	60
1968	St. Louis	Nat.	First	97	65
1969	St. Louis	Nat.	Fourth(E)	87	75
1970	St. Louis	Nat.	Fourth(E)	76	86
1971	St. Louis	Nat.	Second(E)	90	72
1972	St. Louis	Nat.	Fourth(E)	75	81
1973	St. Louis	Nat.	Second(E)	81	81
1974	St. Louis	Nat.	Second(E)	86	75
1975	St. Louis	Nat.	†Third(E)	82	80
1976	St. Louis	Nat.	Fifth(E)	72	90
1980	St. Louis‡	Nat.	Fourth(E)	18	19
	Major League Totals			1028	944

†Tied for position.
‡Served as interim manager when Whitey Herzog named general manager, August 28 through October 5, 1980.
Coach, St. Louis Cardinals, 1963, 1964, and since 1979; Oakland A's 1977 and 1978.

WORLD SERIES RECORD

Year	Club	League	W.	L.
1967	St. Louis	Nat.	4	3
1968	St. Louis	Nat.	3	4
	World Series Totals		7	7

GEORGE THOMAS SEAVER

Year	Club	League	G.	IP.	W.	L.	Pct.	ERA.
1966	Jacksonville	Intl.	34	210	12	12	.500	3.13
1967	New York	National	35	251	16	13	.552	2.76
1968	New York	National	36	278	16	12	.571	2.20
1969	New York	National	36	273	•25	7	•.781	2.21
1970	New York	National	37	291	18	12	.600	•2.81
1971	New York	National	36	286	20	10	.667	•1.76
1972	New York	National	35	262	21	12	.636	2.92
1973	New York	National	36	290	19	10	.655	•2.08
1974	New York	National	32	236	11	11	.500	3.20
1975	New York	National	36	280	•22	9	.710	2.38
1976	New York	National	35	271	14	11	.560	2.59
1977	New York-Cinn.	National	33	261	21	6	.778	2.59
1978	Cincinnati	National	36	260	16	14	.533	2.87
1979	Cincinnati	National	32	215	16	6	•.727	3.14
1980	Cincinnati	National	26	168	10	8	.556	3.64
1981	Cincinnati	National	23	166	14	2	•.875	2.55
1982	Cincinnati	National	21	111⅓	5	13	.278	5.50
1983	New York	National	34	231	9	14	.391	3.55
1984	Chicago	American	34	236⅔	15	11	.577	3.95
1985	Chicago	American	35	238⅔	16	11	.593	3.17
1986	Chicago-Boston	American	28	176⅓	7	13	.350	4.03
	American League Totals		97	651⅔	38	35	.521	3.69
	National League Totals		559	4130⅓	273	170	.616	2.73
	Major League Totals		656	4782	311	205	.603	2.86

CHAMPIONSHIP SERIES RECORD

Year	Club	League	G.	IP.	W.	L.	Pct.	ERA.
1969	New York	National	1	7	1	0	1.000	6.43
1973	New York	National	2	16⅔	1	1	.500	1.62
1979	Cincinnati	National	1	8	0	0	...	2.25
	Championship Series Totals		4	31⅔	2	1	.667	2.84

WORLD SERIES RECORD

Year	Club	League	G.	IP.	W.	L.	Pct.	ERA.
1969	New York	National	2	15	1	1	.500	3.00
1973	New York	National	2	15	0	1	.000	2.40
	World Series Totals		4	30	1	2	.333	2.70

FRANK GIBSON SELEE

RECORD AS MANAGER

Year	Club	League	W.	L.
1886	Haverhill	New England	••	••
1887	Oshkosh	Northwestern	76	41
1888	Omaha	Western Assoc.	55	48
1889	Omaha	Western Assoc.	83	38
1890	Boston	Nat.	76	57
1891	Boston	Nat.	87	51
1892	Boston	Nat.	52	22
1892	Boston	Nat.	50	26

Year	Club	League	W.	L.
1893—Boston	Nat.		86	43
1894—Boston	Nat.		83	49
1895—Boston	Nat.		71	60
1896—Boston	Nat.		74	57
1897—Boston	Nat.		93	39
1898—Boston	Nat.		102	47
1899—Boston	Nat.		95	57
1900—Boson	Nat.		66	72
1901—Boston	Nat.		69	69
1902—Chicago	Nat.		68	69
1903—Chicago	Nat.		82	56
1904—Chicago	Nat.		93	60
1905—Chicago	Nat.		37	28
Major League Totals			1284	862

JOSEPH WHEELER SEWELL

Year	Club	League	G.	AB.	R.	H.	HR.	RBI.	B.A.
1920—New Orleans	South.	92	346	58	100	2	.....	.289
1920—Cleveland	Amer.	22	70	14	23	0	12	.329
1921—Cleveland	Amer.	154	572	101	182	4	91	.318
1922—Cleveland	Amer.	153	558	80	167	2	83	.299
1923—Cleveland	Amer.	153	553	98	195	3	109	.353
1924—Cleveland	Amer.	153	594	99	188	4	106	.316
1925—Cleveland	Amer.	155	608	78	204	1	98	.336
1926—Cleveland	Amer.	154	578	91	187	4	85	.324
1927—Cleveland	Amer.	153	569	83	180	1	92	.316
1928—Cleveland	Amer.	●155	588	79	190	4	70	.323
1929—Cleveland	Amer.	152	578	90	182	7	73	.315
1930—Cleveland	Amer.	109	353	44	102	0	48	.289
1931—New York	Amer.	130	484	102	146	6	64	.302
1932—New York	Amer.	125	503	95	137	11	68	.272
1933—New York	Amer.	135	524	87	143	2	54	.273
Major League Totals		1903	7132	1141	2226	49	1053	.312

WORLD SERIES RECORD

Year	Club	League	G.	AB.	R.	H.	HR.	RBI.	B.A.
1920—Cleveland	Amer.	7	23	0	4	0	0	.174
1932—Cleveland	Amer.	4	15	4	5	0	3	.333
World Series Totals		11	38	4	9	0	3	.237

ALOYSIUS HARRY (BUCKETFOOT) SIMMONS

Year	Club	League	G.	AB.	R.	H.	HR.	RBI.	B.A.
1922—Milwaukee	A. A.	19	50	9	11	1	7	.220
1922—Aberdeen	Dakota	99	395	91	*144	10	.....	.365
1923—Shreveport	Tex.	144	525	96	189	12	99	.360
1923—Milwaukee	A. A.	24	98	20	39	0	16	.398
1924—Philadelphia	Amer.	152	594	69	183	8	102	.308
1925—Philadelphia	Amer.	153	*658	122	*253	24	129	.384
1926—Philadelphia	Amer.	147	581	90	199	19	109	.343
1927—Philadelphia	Amer.	106	406	86	159	15	108	.392
1928—Philadelphia	Amer.	119	464	78	163	15	107	.351
1929—Philadelphia	Amer.	143	581	114	212	34	*157	.365
1930—Philadelphia	Amer.	138	554	*152	211	36	165	*.381
1931—Philadelphia	Amer.	128	513	105	200	22	128	*.390
1932—Philadelphia	Amer.	154	*670	144	*216	35	151	.322
1933—Chicago	Amer.	146	605	85	200	14	119	.331
1934—Chicago	Amer.	138	558	102	192	18	104	.344
1935—Chicago	Amer.	128	525	68	140	16	79	.267
1936—Detroit	Amer.	143	568	96	186	13	112	.327
1937—Washington	Amer.	103	419	60	117	8	84	.279
1938—Washington	Amer.	125	470	79	142	21	95	.302
1939—Bos.-Cin.	Nat.	102	351	39	96	7	44	.274
1940—Philadelphia	Amer.	37	81	7	25	1	19	.309
1941—Philadelphia	Amer.	9	24	1	3	0	1	.125
1942—Philadelphia	Amer.	(Served as coach.)						
1943—Boston	Amer.	40	133	9	27	1	12	.203
1944—Philadelphia	Amer.	4	6	1	3	0	2	.500
American League Totals		2113	8410	1468	2831	300	1783	.337
National League Totals		102	351	39	96	7	44	.274
Major League Totals		2215	8761	1507	2927	307	1827	.334

WORLD SERIES RECORD

Year	Club	League	G.	AB.	R.	H.	HR.	RBI.	B.A.
1929—Philadelphia	Amer.	5	20	6	6	2	5	.300
1930—Philadelphia	Amer.	6	22	4	8	2	4	.364
1931—Philadelphia	Amer.	7	27	4	9	2	8	.333
1939—Cincinnati	Nat.	1	4	1	1	0	0	.250
World Series Totals		19	73	15	24	6	17	.329

GEORGE HAROLD (GORGEOUS GEORGE) SISLER

Year	Club	League	G.	AB.	R.	H.	HR.	RBI.	B.A.
1915—St. Louis	Amer.	81	274	28	78	3	29	.285
1916—St. Louis	Amer.	151	580	83	177	4	74	.305
1917—St. Louis	Amer.	135	539	60	190	2	55	.353
1918—St. Louis	Amer.	114	452	69	154	2	45	.341
1919—St. Louis	Amer.	132	511	96	180	10	83	.352
1920—St. Louis	Amer.	●154	*631	137	*257	19	122	*.407
1921—St. Louis	Amer.	138	582	125	216	12	104	.371
1922—St. Louis	Amer.	142	586	*134	*246	8	105	*.420
1923—St. Louis	Amer.	(Out with eye trouble)						
1924—St. Louis	Amer.	151	636	94	194	9	74	.305
1925—St. Louis	Amer.	150	649	100	224	12	105	.345
1926—St. Louis	Amer.	150	613	78	178	7	71	.289
1927—St. Louis	Amer.	149	614	87	201	5	97	.327
1928—Washington	Amer.	20	49	1	12	0	2	.245
1928—Boston	Nat.	118	491	71	167	4	68	.340
1929—Boston	Nat.	154	629	67	205	2	79	.326
1930—Boston	Nat.	116	431	54	133	3	67	.309

Year	Club	League	G.	AB.	R.	H.	HR.	RBI.	B.A.
1931—Rochester	Int.	159	613	86	186	3	81	.303
1932—Shrev.-Tyler	Texas	70	258	28	74	1	23	.287
American League Totals		1667	6716	1092	2307	93	966	.344
National League Totals		388	1551	192	505	9	214	.326
Major League Totals		2055	8267	1284	2812	102	1180	.340

PITCHING RECORD

Year	Club	League	G.	IP.	W.	L.	Pct.	ERA.
1915—St. Louis	American	15	70	4	4	.500	2.83
1916—St. Louis	American	3	27	1	2	.333	1.00
1920—St. Louis	American	1	1	0	0	.000	0.00
1925—St. Louis	American	1	2	0	0	.000	0.00
1926—St. Louis	American	1	2	0	0	.000	0.00
1928—Boston	National	1	1	0	0	.000	0.00
Major League Totals		22	103	5	6	.455	2.13

ENOS BRADSHER SLAUGHTER

Year	Club	League	G.	AB.	R.	H.	HR.	RBI.	B.A.
1935—Martinsville	Bi-State	109	422	68	115	18	.....	.273
1936—Columbus	Sally	151	569	106	185	9	118	.325
1937—Columbus	A. A.	154	642	*147	*245	26	122	*.382
1938—St. Louis	Nat.	112	395	59	109	8	58	.276
1939—St. Louis	Nat.	149	604	95	193	12	86	.320
1940—St. Louis	Nat.	140	516	96	158	17	73	.306
1941—St. Louis	Nat.	113	425	71	132	13	76	.311
1942—St. Louis	Nat.	152	591	100	*188	13	98	.318
1943-44-45—St. Louis	Nat.	(In Military Service)						
1946—St. Louis	Nat.	●156	609	100	183	18	*130	.300
1947—St. Louis	Nat.	147	551	100	162	10	86	.294
1948—St. Louis	Nat.	146	549	91	176	11	90	.321
1949—St. Louis	Nat.	151	568	92	191	13	96	.336
1950—St. Louis	Nat.	148	556	82	161	10	101	.290
1951—St. Louis	Nat.	123	409	48	115	4	64	.281
1952—St. Louis	Nat.	140	510	73	153	11	101	.300
1953—St. Louis	Nat.	143	492	64	143	6	89	.291
1954—New York	Amer.	69	125	19	31	1	19	.248
1955—N.Y.-K.C.	Amer.	118	276	50	87	5	35	.315
1956—K.C.-N.Y.	Amer.	115	306	52	86	2	27	.281
1957—New York	Amer.	96	209	24	53	5	34	.254
1958—New York	Amer.	77	138	21	42	4	19	.304
1959—New York	Amer.	74	99	10	17	6	21	.172
1959—Milwaukee	Nat.	11	18	0	3	0	1	.167
1960—Houston	A. A.	40	45	7	13	1	8	.289
1961—Raleigh	Car.	42	41	8	14	0	9	.341
American League Totals		549	1153	176	316	23	155	.274
National League Totals		1831	6793	1071	2067	146	1149	.304
Major League Totals		2380	7946	1247	2383	169	1304	.300

WORLD SERIES RECORD

Year	Club	League	G.	AB.	R.	H.	HR.	RBI.	B.A.
1942—St. Louis	Nat.	5	19	3	5	1	2	.263
1946—St. Louis	Nat.	7	25	5	8	1	2	.320
1956—New York	Amer.	6	20	6	7	1	4	.350
1957—New York	Amer.	5	12	2	3	0	0	.250
1958—New York	Amer.	4	3	1	0	0	0	.000
World Series Totals		27	79	17	23	3	8	.291

EDWIN DONALD (DUKE) SNIDER

Year	Club	League	G.	AB.	R.	H.	HR.	RBI.	B.A.
1944—Montreal	Int.	2	2	0	0	0	0	.000
1944—Newport News	Pied.	131	507	87	149	*9	50	.294
1945—Newport News	Pied.	(In Military Service)						
1946—Fort Worth	Tex.	68	232	36	58	5	30	.250
1947—St. Paul	A.A.	66	269	59	85	12	46	.316
1947—Brooklyn	Nat.	40	83	6	20	0	5	.241
1948—Montreal	Int.	77	275	67	90	17	77	.327
1948—Brooklyn	Nat.	53	160	22	39	5	21	.244
1949—Brooklyn	Nat.	146	552	100	161	23	92	.292
1950—Brooklyn	Nat.	152	620	109	*199	31	107	.321
1951—Brooklyn	Nat.	150	606	96	168	29	101	.277
1952—Brooklyn	Nat.	144	534	80	162	21	92	.303
1953—Brooklyn	Nat.	153	590	*132	198	42	126	.336
1954—Brooklyn	Nat.	149	584	●120	199	40	130	.341
1955—Brooklyn	Nat.	148	538	*126	166	42	*136	.309
1956—Brooklyn	Nat.	151	542	112	158	*43	101	.292
1957—Brooklyn	Nat.	139	508	91	139	40	92	.274
1958—Los Angeles	Nat.	106	327	45	102	15	58	.312
1959—Los Angeles	Nat.	126	370	59	114	23	88	.308
1960—Los Angeles	Nat.	101	235	38	57	14	36	.243
1961—Los Angeles	Nat.	85	233	35	69	16	56	.296
1962—Los Angeles	Nat.	80	158	28	44	5	30	.278
1963—New York	Nat.	129	354	44	86	14	45	.243
1964—San Francisco	Nat.	91	167	16	35	4	17	.210
Major League Totals		2143	7161	1259	2116	407	1333	.295

WORLD SERIES RECORD

Year	Club	League	G.	AB.	R.	H.	HR.	RBI.	B.A.
1949—Brooklyn	Nat.	5	21	2	3	0	0	.143
1952—Brooklyn	Nat.	7	29	5	10	4	8	.345
1953—Brooklyn	Nat.	6	25	3	8	1	5	.320
1955—Brooklyn	Nat.	7	25	5	8	4	7	.320
1956—Brooklyn	Nat.	7	23	5	7	1	4	.304
1959—Los Angeles	Nat.	4	10	1	2	1	2	.200
World Series Totals		36	133	21	38	11	26	.286

WARREN EDWARD SPAHN

Year	Club	League	G.	IP.	W.	L.	Pct.	ERA.
1940—Bradford	Pony	12	66	5	4	.556	2.73
1941—Evansville	I.I.I.	28	212	*19	6	*.760	*1.83

Year	Club	League	G.	IP.	W.	L.	Pct.	ERA.
1942—Hartford	Eastern		33	248	17	12	.586	1.96
1942—Boston	National		4	16	0	0	.000	5.63
1943-44-45—Boston	National			(In Military Service)				
1946—Boston	National		24	126	8	5	.615	2.93
1947—Boston	National		40	*290	21	10	.677	*2.33
1948—Boston	National		36	257	15	12	.556	3.71
1949—Boston	National		38	*302	*21	14	.600	3.07
1950—Boston	National		41	293	*21	17	.553	3.16
1951—Boston	National		39	311	22	14	.611	2.98
1952—Boston	National		40	290	14	19	.424	2.98
1953—Milwaukee	National		35	266	●23	7	.767	*2.10
1954—Milwaukee	National		39	283	21	12	.636	3.15
1955—Milwaukee	National		39	246	17	14	.548	3.26
1956—Milwaukee	National		39	281	20	11	.645	2.79
1957—Milwaukee	National		39	271	*21	11	.656	2.69
1958—Milwaukee	National		38	*290	●22	11	●.667	3.07
1959—Milwaukee	National		40	*292	●21	15	.583	2.96
1960—Milwaukee	National		40	268	●21	10	.677	3.49
1961—Milwaukee	National		38	263	●21	13	.618	*3.01
1962—Milwaukee	National		34	269	18	14	.563	3.04
1963—Milwaukee	National		33	260	23	7	.767	2.60
1964—Milwaukee	National		38	174	6	13	.316	5.28
1965—N.Y.-San Fran.	National		36	198	7	16	.304	4.00
1966—Mexico City Tigers	Mexican		3	10	1	1	.500	4.50
1967—Tulsa	Pacific Coast		3	7	0	1	.000	6.43
Major League Totals			750	5246	363	245	.597	3.08

WORLD SERIES RECORD

Year	Club	League	G.	IP.	W.	L.	Pct.	ERA.
1948—Boston	Nat.		3	12	1	1	.500	3.00
1957—Milwaukee	Nat.		2	15⅓	1	1	.500	4.70
1958—Milwaukee	Nat.		3	28⅔	2	1	.667	1.88
World Series Totals			8	56	4	3	.571	2.89

TRISTRAM (SPOKE or GRAY EAGLE) SPEAKER

Year	Club	League	G.	AB.	R.	H.	HR.	RBI.	B.A.
1906—Cleburne	No. Tex.		84	287	35	77	....	....	.268
1907—Houston	Texas		118	468	70	147	....	....	*.314
1907—Boston	Amer.		7	20	0	3	0	0	.150
1908—Little Rock	South.		127	471	*81	*165	3	....	*.350
1908—Boston	Amer.		31	116	12	26	0	10	.224
1909—Boston	Amer.		143	544	73	168	7	79	.309
1910—Boston	Amer.		141	538	92	183	7	62	.340
1911—Boston	Amer.		141	500	88	167	8	80	.334
1912—Boston	Amer.		153	580	136	222	10	98	.383
1913—Boston	Amer.		141	520	94	190	3	81	.365
1914—Boston	Amer.		●158	571	100	*193	4	86	.338
1915—Boston	Amer.		150	547	108	176	0	63	.322
1916—Cleveland	Amer.		151	546	102	*211	2	83	*.386
1917—Cleveland	Amer.		142	523	90	184	2	65	.352
1918—Cleveland	Amer.		128	475	73	151	0	61	.318
1919—Cleveland	Amer.		134	494	83	146	2	69	.296
1920—Cleveland	Amer.		150	552	137	214	8	107	.388
1921—Cleveland	Amer.		132	506	107	183	3	74	.362
1922—Cleveland	Amer.		131	426	85	161	11	71	.378
1923—Cleveland	Amer.		150	574	133	218	17	130	.380
1924—Cleveland	Amer.		136	486	94	167	9	65	.344
1925—Cleveland	Amer.		117	429	79	167	12	87	.389
1926—Cleveland	Amer.		150	539	96	164	7	86	.304
1927—Washington	Amer.		141	523	71	171	2	73	.327
1928—Philadelphia	Amer.		64	191	28	51	3	32	.267
1929—Newark	Int.		48	138	36	49	5	20	.355
1930—Newark	Int.		11	31	3	13	0	3	.419
Major League Totals			2791	10200	1881	3516	117	1562	.345

WORLD SERIES RECORD

Year	Club	League	G.	AB.	R.	H.	HR.	RBI.	B.A.
1912—Boston	Amer.		8	30	4	9	0	2	.300
1915—Boston	Amer.		5	17	2	5	0	0	.294
1920—Cleveland	Amer.		7	25	6	8	0	1	.320
World Series Totals			20	72	12	22	0	3	.306

WILVER DORNEL STARGELL

Year	Club	League	G.	AB.	R.	H.	HR.	RBI.	B.A.
1959—S. A'gelo-R'well	Soph.		118	431	66	118	7	87	.274
1960—Grand Forks	North.		107	396	63	103	11	61	.260
1961—Asheville	Sally		130	453	78	131	22	89	.289
1962—Columbus	Int.		138	497	97	137	27	82	.276
1962—Pittsburgh	Nat.		10	31	1	9	0	4	.290
1963—Pittsburgh	Nat.		108	304	34	74	11	47	.243
1964—Pittsburgh	Nat.		117	421	53	115	21	78	.273
1965—Pittsburgh	Nat.		144	533	68	145	27	107	.272
1966—Pittsburgh	Nat.		140	485	84	153	33	102	.315
1967—Pittsburgh	Nat.		134	462	54	125	20	73	.271
1968—Pittsburgh	Nat.		128	435	57	103	24	67	.237
1969—Pittsburgh	Nat.		145	522	89	160	29	92	.307
1970—Pittsburgh	Nat.		136	474	70	125	31	85	.264
1971—Pittsburgh	Nat.		141	511	104	151	*48	125	.295
1972—Pittsburgh	Nat.		138	495	75	145	33	112	.293
1973—Pittsburgh	Nat.		148	522	106	156	*44	*119	.299
1974—Pittsburgh	Nat.		140	508	90	153	25	96	.301
1975—Pittsburgh	Nat.		124	461	71	136	22	90	.295
1976—Pittsburgh	Nat.		117	428	54	110	20	65	.257
1977—Pittsburgh	Nat.		63	186	29	51	13	35	.274
1978—Pittsburgh	Nat.		122	390	60	115	28	97	.295
1979—Pittsburgh	Nat.		126	424	60	119	32	82	.281
1980—Pittsburgh	Nat.		67	202	28	53	11	38	.262

Year	Club	League	G.	AB.	R.	H.	HR.	RBI.	B.A.
1981—Pittsburgh	Nat.		38	60	2	17	0	9	.283
1982—Pittsburgh	Nat.		74	73	6	17	3	17	.233
Major League Totals			2360	7927	1195	2232	475	1540	.282

WORLD SERIES RECORD

Year	Club	League	G.	AB.	R.	H.	HR.	RBI	B.A.
1971—Pittsburgh	Nat.		7	24	3	5	0	1	.208
1979—Pittsburgh	Nat.		7	30	7	12	3	7	.400
World Series Totals			14	54	10	17	3	8	.315

CHARLES DILLON (CASEY) STENGEL

Year	Club	League	G.	AB.	R.	H.	HR.	RBI.	B.A.
1910—Kankakee	No. Assn.			(League disbanded in July)					
1910—Shelb.-Mays.	Bl.Grass		69	233	27	52	2	....	.223
1911—Aurora	Wis.-Ill.		121	420	76	*148	4	....	.352
1912—Montgomery	South.		136	479	85	139	....	....	.290
1912—Brooklyn	Nat.		17	57	9	18	1	13	.316
1913—Brooklyn	Nat.		124	438	60	119	7	44	.272
1914—Brooklyn	Nat.		126	412	55	130	4	56	.316
1915—Brooklyn	Nat.		132	459	52	109	3	43	.237
1916—Brooklyn	Nat.		127	462	66	129	8	53	.279
1917—Brooklyn	Nat.		150	549	69	141	6	69	.257
1918—Pittsburgh	Nat.		39	122	18	30	1	13	.246
1919—Pittsburgh	Nat.		89	321	38	94	4	40	.293
1920—Philadelphia	Nat.		129	445	53	130	9	50	.292
1921—Phila.-N.Y.	Nat.		42	81	11	23	0	6	.284
1922—New York	Nat.		84	250	48	92	7	48	.368
1923—New York	Nat.		75	218	39	74	5	43	.339
1924—Boston	Nat.		131	461	57	129	5	39	.280
1925—Boston	Nat.		12	13	0	1	0	2	.077
1925—Worcester	East.		100	334	73	107	10	....	.320
1926—Toledo	A.A.		88	201	40	66	0	27	.328
1927—Toledo	A.A.		18	17	3	3	1	3	.176
1928—Toledo	A.A.		26	32	5	14	0	12	.438
1929—Toledo	A.A.		20	31	2	7	0	9	.226
1931—Toledo	A.A.		2	8	1	3	0	0	.375
Major League Totals			1277	4288	575	1219	60	518	.284

WORLD SERIES RECORD

Year	Club	League	G.	AB.	R.	H.	HR.	RBI.	B.A.
1916—Brooklyn	Nat.		4	11	2	4	0	0	.364
1922—New York	Nat.		2	5	0	2	0	0	.400
1923—New York	Nat.		6	12	3	5	2	4	.417
World Series Totals			12	28	5	11	2	4	.393

RECORD AS MANAGER

Year	Club	League	Position	W.	L.
1925—Worcester†	Eastern		Third	70	55
1926—Toledo	Amer. Assoc.		Fourth	87	77
1927—Toledo	Amer. Assoc.		First	101	67
1928—Toledo	Amer. Assoc.		Sixth	79	88
1929—Toledo	Amer. Assoc.		Eighth	67	100
1930—Toledo	Amer. Assoc.		Third	88	66
1931—Toledo	Amer. Assoc.		Eighth	68	100
1934—Brooklyn	National		Sixth	71	81
1935—Brooklyn	National		Fifth	70	83
1936—Brooklyn‡	National		Seventh	67	87
1938—Boston	National		Fifth	77	75
1939—Boston	National		Seventh	63	88
1940—Boston	National		Seventh	65	87
1941—Boston	National		Seventh	62	92
1942—Boston	National		Seventh	59	89
1943—Boston§	National		Sixth	68	85
1944—Milwaukee x	Amer. Assoc.		First	91	49
1945—Kansas City	Amer. Assoc.		Seventh	65	86
1946—Oakland	Pacific Coast		Second	111	72
1947—Oakland	Pacific Coast		Fourth	96	90
1948—Oakland	Pacific Coast		First	114	74
1949—New York	American		First	97	57
1950—New York	American		First	98	56
1951—New York	American		First	98	56
1952—New York	American		First	95	59
1953—New York	American		First	99	52
1954—New York	American		Second	103	51
1955—New York	American		First	96	58
1956—New York	American		First	97	57
1957—New York	American		First	98	56
1958—New York	American		First	92	62
1959—New York	American		Third	79	75
1960—New York	American		First	97	57
1962—New York	National		Tenth	40	120
1963—New York	National		Tenth	51	111
1964—New York	National		Tenth	53	109
1965—New York y	National		Tenth	31	64
Major League Totals				1926	1867

†Named president-manager when Boston Braves purchased club, while in eighth place, May 22, 1925.

‡Ousted as manager at close of 1936 season, but continued to draw salary in 1937 under terms of contract.

§Struck by an auto while crossing street in Boston on April 20, suffering a broken leg, returning to bench in July. Released as manager in December, 1943.

xReplaced Charlie Grimm, who moved up to Chicago Cubs, as manager with club in first place, May 5, 1944.

yRetired, July 24, 1965; replaced by Wes Westrum.

WORLD SERIES RECORD

Year	Club	League	W.	L.
1949	New York	American	4	1
1950	New York	American	4	0
1951	New York	American	4	2
1952	New York	American	4	3
1953	New York	American	4	2
1955	New York	American	3	4
1956	New York	American	4	3
1957	New York	American	3	4
1958	New York	American	4	3
1960	New York	American	3	4

DONALD HOWARD SUTTON

Year	Club	League	G.	IP.	W.	L.	Pct.	ERA.
1965	Santa Barbara	California	10	84	8	1	.889	1.50
1965	Albuquerque	Texas	21	165	15	6	*.714	2.78
1966	Los Angeles	Nat.	37	226	12	12	.500	2.99
1967	Los Angeles	Nat.	37	233	11	15	.423	3.94
1968	Spokane	P. Coast	2	16	1	1	.500	1.13
1968	Los Angeles	Nat.	35	208	11	15	.423	2.60
1969	Los Angeles	Nat.	41	293	17	18	.486	3.47
1970	Los Angeles	Nat.	38	260	15	13	.536	4.08
1971	Los Angeles	Nat.	38	265	17	12	.586	2.55
1972	Los Angeles	Nat.	33	273	19	9	.679	2.08
1973	Los Angeles	Nat.	33	256	18	10	.643	2.43
1974	Los Angeles	Nat.	40	276	19	9	.679	3.23
1975	Los Angeles	Nat.	35	254	16	13	.552	2.87
1976	Los Angeles	Nat.	35	268	21	10	.677	3.06
1977	Los Angeles	Nat.	33	240	14	8	.636	3.19
1978	Los Angeles	Nat.	34	238	15	11	.577	3.55
1979	Los Angeles	Nat.	33	226	12	15	.444	3.82
1980	Los Angeles	Nat.	32	212	13	5	.722	*2.21
1981	Houston	Nat.	23	159	11	9	.550	2.60
1982	Houston	Nat.	27	195	13	8	.619	3.00
1982	Milwaukee	Amer.	7	54-2/3	4	1	.800	3.29
1983	Milwaukee	Amer.	31	220-1/3	8	13	.381	4.08
1984	Milwaukee	Amer.	33	212-2/3	14	12	.538	3.77
1985	Oakland-Calif.	Amer.	34	226	15	10	.600	3.86
1986	California	Amer.	34	207	15	11	.577	3.74
1987	California	Amer.	35	191-2/3	11	11	.500	4.70
1988	Los Angeles	Nat.	16	87-1/3	3	6	.333	3.92
	National League Totals		600	4169-1/3	257	198	.565	3.07
	American League Totals		174	1112-1/3	67	58	.536	3.98
	Major League Totals		774	5281-2/3	324	256	.559	3.26

CHAMPIONSHIP SERIES RECORD

Year	Club	League	G.	IP.	W.	L.	Pct.	ERA.
1974	Los Angeles	Nat.	2	17	2	0	1.000	0.53
1977	Los Angeles	Nat.	1	9	1	0	1.000	1.00
1978	Los Angeles	Nat.	1	5-2/3	0	1	.000	6.35
1982	Milwaukee	Amer.	1	7-2/3	1	0	1.000	3.52
1986	California	Amer.	2	9-2/3	0	0	.000	1.86
	Championship Series Totals		7	49	4	1	.800	2.02

WORLD SERIES RECORD

Year	Club	League	G.	IP.	W.	L.	Pct.	ERA.
1974	Los Angeles	Nat.	2	13	1	0	1.000	2.77
1977	Los Angeles	Nat.	2	16	1	0	1.000	3.94
1978	Los Angeles	Nat.	2	12	0	2	.000	7.50
1982	Milwaukee	Amer.	2	10-1/3	0	1	.000	7.84
	World Series Totals		8	51-1/3	2	3	.400	5.26

WILLIAM HAROLD TERRY

Year	Club	League	G.	AB.	R.	H.	HR.	RBI.	B.A.
1915	Newnan	Ga.-Ala.	8	....	....	....	....	....	.....
1916	Shreveport	Tex.	19	29	3	7	0	....	.241
1917	Shreveport	Tex.	95	208	15	48	4	....	.231
1918-19-20-21				(Played semi-pro ball)					
1922	Toledo	A. A.	88	235	41	79	14	61	.336
1923	Toledo	A. A.	109	427	73	161	15	82	.377
1923	New York	Nat.	3	7	1	1	0	0	.143
1924	New York	Nat.	77	163	26	39	5	24	.239
1925	New York	Nat.	133	489	75	156	11	70	.319
1926	New York	Nat.	98	225	26	65	5	43	.289
1927	New York	Nat.	150	580	101	189	20	121	.326
1928	New York	Nat.	149	568	100	185	17	101	.326
1929	New York	Nat.	150	607	103	226	14	117	.372
1930	New York	Nat.	154	633	139	*254	23	129	*.401
1931	New York	Nat.	153	611	•121	213	9	112	.349
1932	New York	Nat.	•154	643	124	225	28	117	.350
1933	New York	Nat.	123	475	68	153	6	58	.322
1934	New York	Nat.	153	602	109	213	8	83	.354
1935	New York	Nat.	145	596	91	203	6	64	.341
1936	New York	Nat.	79	229	36	71	2	39	.310
	Major League Totals		1721	6428	1120	2193	154	1078	.341

PITCHING RECORD

Year	Club	League	G.	IP.	W.	L.	Pct.	ERA.
1915	Newnan	Ga.-Ala.	8	....	7	1	.875	......
1916	Shreveport	Texas	19	84	6	2	.750	1.07
1917	Shreveport	Texas	40	246	14	11	.560	3.00
1922	Toledo	Amer. Assn.	26	127	9	9	.500	4.26

WORLD SERIES RECORD

Year	Club	League	G.	AB.	R.	H.	HR.	RBI.	B.A.
1924	New York	Nat.	5	14	3	6	1	1	.429
1933	New York	Nat.	5	22	3	6	1	1	.273
1936	New York	Nat.	6	25	1	6	0	5	.240
	World Series Totals		16	61	7	18	2	7	.295

SAMUEL L. (BIG SAM) THOMPSON

Year	Club	League	G.	AB.	R.	H.	HR.	SB.	B.A.
1884	Evansville	N.W.	5	23	5	9	0	0	.391
1885	Indianapolis	West.	30	136	38	43	1	....	.316
1885	Detroit	Nat.	63	254	58	77	7	....	.303
1886	Detroit	Nat.	122	503	100	156	8	13	.310
1887	Detroit	Nat.	127	576	118	234	10	22	.406
1888	Detroit	Nat.	55	238	51	67	6	5	.282
1889	Philadelphia	Nat.	128	533	103	158	*20	24	.296
1890	Philadelphia	Nat.	132	549	114	•172	4	25	.313
1891	Philadelphia	Nat.	133	551	108	163	7	33	.296
1892	Philadelphia	Nat.	151	602	109	183	9	30	.304
1893	Philadelphia	Nat.	130	583	130	*220	11	18	.377
1894	Philadelphia	Nat.	102	458	115	185	13	29	.404
1895	Philadelphia	Nat.	118	533	131	210	16	24	.394
1896	Philadelphia	Nat.	119	517	103	158	•13	11	.306
1897	Philadelphia	Nat.	3	13	2	3	0	0	.231
1898	Philadelphia	Nat.	14	63	13	23	2	1	.365
1906	Detroit	Amer.	8	31	4	7	0	0	.226
	American League Totals		8	31	4	7	0	0	.226
	National League Totals		1397	5973	1255	2009	126	235	.336
	Major League Totals		1405	6004	1259	2016	126	235	.336

WORLD SERIES RECORD

Year	Club	League	G.	AB.	R.	H.	BA.
1887	Detroit	Nat.	15	61	9	23	.377

JOSEPH BERT TINKER

Year	Club	League	G.	AB.	R.	H.	HR.	SB.	B.A.
1900	Denver	West.	32	137	18	30	...	8	.219
1900	Gr't F'ls-Helena	Mont. St.	57	236	39	76	...	12	.322
1901	Portland	P. NW.	106	424	74	123	...	37	.290
1902	Chicago	Nat.	133	501	54	137	2	28	.273
1903	Chicago	Nat.	124	460	67	134	2	27	.291
1904	Chicago	Nat.	141	488	55	108	3	41	.221
1905	Chicago	Nat.	149	547	70	135	2	31	.247
1906	Chicago	Nat.	148	523	75	122	1	30	.233
1907	Chicago	Nat.	113	402	36	89	1	20	.221
1908	Chicago	Nat.	•157	548	67	146	6	30	.266
1909	Chicago	Nat.	143	516	56	132	4	23	.256
1910	Chicago	Nat.	132	473	48	136	3	20	.288
1911	Chicago	Nat.	143	536	61	149	4	30	.278
1912	Chicago	Nat.	142	550	80	155	0	25	.282
1913	Cincinnati	Nat.	110	382	47	121	1	10	.317
1914	Chicago	Fed.	127	440	53	114	2	24	.259
1915	Chicago	Fed.	30	69	7	19	0	3	.275
1916	Chicago	Nat.	7	10	0	1	0	0	.100
1917	Columbus	A. A.	22	51	5	6	0	4	.118
1921	Orlando	Fla. St.	2	3	1	1	0	0	.333
	Major League Totals		1642	5936	716	1565	29	315	.264

WORLD SERIES RECORD

Year	Club	League	G.	AB.	R.	H.	HR.	SB.	B.A.
1906	Chicago	Nat.	6	18	4	3	0	2	.167
1907	Chicago	Nat.	5	13	4	2	0	3	.154
1908	Chicago	Nat.	5	19	2	5	1	5	.263
1910	Chicago	Nat.	5	18	2	6	0	0	.333
	World Series Totals		21	68	12	16	1	10	.235

HAROLD JOSEPH (PIE) TRAYNOR

Year	Club	League	G.	AB.	R.	H.	HR.	RBI.	B.A.
1920	Portsmouth	Va.	104	392	50	106	8	57	.270
1920	Pittsburgh	Nat.	17	52	6	11	0	2	.212
1921	Birmingham	South.	131	527	101	177	5	53	.336
1921	Pittsburgh	Nat.	7	19	0	5	0	2	.263
1922	Pittsburgh	Nat.	142	571	89	161	4	81	.282
1923	Pittsburgh	Nat.	153	616	108	208	12	101	.338
1924	Pittsburgh	Nat.	142	545	86	160	5	82	.294
1925	Pittsburgh	Nat.	150	591	114	189	6	106	.320
1926	Pittsburgh	Nat.	152	574	83	182	3	92	.317
1927	Pittsburgh	Nat.	149	573	93	196	5	106	.342
1928	Pittsburgh	Nat.	144	569	91	192	3	124	.337
1929	Pittsburgh	Nat.	130	540	94	192	4	108	.356
1930	Pittsburgh	Nat.	130	497	90	182	9	119	.366
1931	Pittsburgh	Nat.	155	615	81	183	2	103	.298
1932	Pittsburgh	Nat.	135	513	74	169	2	68	.329
1933	Pittsburgh	Nat.	•154	624	85	190	1	82	.304
1934	Pittsburgh	Nat.	119	444	62	137	1	61	.309
1935	Pittsburgh	Nat.	57	204	24	57	1	36	.279
1936	Pittsburgh	Nat.			(Did not play)				
1937	Pittsburgh	Nat.	5	12	3	2	0	0	.167
	Major League Totals		1941	7559	1183	2416	58	1273	.320

WORLD SERIES RECORD

Year	Club	League	G.	AB.	R.	H.	HR.	RBI.	B.A.
1925	Pittsburgh	Nat.	7	26	2	9	1	4	.346
1927	Pittsburgh	Nat.	4	15	1	3	0	0	.200
	World Series Totals		11	41	3	12	1	4	.293

ARTHUR CHARLES (DAZZY) VANCE

Year Club	League	G	IP	W	L	Pct.	ERA.
1912—Red Cloud	Neb. State	36	....	11	15	.423	
1913—Superior	Neb. State	25	....	11	14	.440	
1914—Hastings	Neb. State	26	....	17	4	*.810	
1914—St. Joseph	Western	21	134	9	8	.529	2.96
1915—Pittsburgh	National	1	3	0	1	.000	6.00
1915—St. Joseph	Western	39	264	17	15	.531	2.93
1915—New York	American	8	28	0	3	.000	3.54
1916—Columbus	Amer. Assn.	14	50	2	2	.500	4.50
1917—Toledo	Amer. Assn.	15	71	2	6	.250	2.28
1917—Memphis	Southern	16	122	6	8	.429	......
1918—Memphis	Southern	16	117	8	6	.571	......
1918—Rochester	International	9	72	3	5	.375	3.88
1918—New York	American	2	2	0	0	.000	18.00
1919—Sacramento	Pacific Coast	48	294	10	18	.357	2.82
1920—Mem.-New Orleans	Southern	45	284	16	17	.485	......
1921—New Orleans	Southern	38	253	21	11	.656	3.52
1922—Brooklyn	National	36	246	18	12	.600	3.70
1923—Brooklyn	National	37	280	18	15	.545	3.50
1924—Brooklyn	National	35	309	*28	6	.824	*2.16
1925—Brooklyn	National	31	265	*22	9	.710	3.53
1926—Brooklyn	National	24	169	9	10	.474	3.89
1927—Brooklyn	National	34	273	16	15	.516	2.70
1928—Brooklyn	National	38	280	22	10	.688	*2.09
1929—Brooklyn	National	31	231	14	13	.519	3.90
1930—Brooklyn	National	35	259	17	15	.531	*2.61
1931—Brooklyn	National	30	219	11	13	.458	3.37
1932—Brooklyn	National	27	176	12	11	.522	4.19
1933—St. Louis	National	28	99	6	2	.750	3.55
1934—Cincinnati-St.L.	National	25	77	1	3	.250	4.56
1935—Brooklyn	National	20	51	3	2	.600	4.41
American League Totals		10	30	0	3	.000	4.50
National League Totals		432	2937	197	137	.590	3.23
Major League Totals		442	2967	197	140	.585	3.24

WORLD SERIES RECORD

Year Club	League	G	IP	W	L	Pct.	ERA.
1934—St. Louis	National	1	1⅓	0	0	.000	0.00

JOSEPH FLOYD (ARKY) VAUGHAN

Year Club	League	G	AB	R	H	HR	RBI	B.A.
1931—Wichita	West.	132	494	*145	167	21	81	.338
1932—Pittsburgh	Nat.	129	497	71	158	4	61	.318
1933—Pittsburgh	Nat.	152	573	85	180	9	97	.314
1934—Pittsburgh	Nat.	149	558	115	186	12	94	.333
1935—Pittsburgh	Nat.	137	499	108	192	19	99	*.385
1936—Pittsburgh	Nat.	●156	568	*122	190	9	78	.335
1937—Pittsburgh	Nat.	126	469	71	151	5	72	.322
1938—Pittsburgh	Nat.	148	541	88	174	7	68	.322
1939—Pittsburgh	Nat.	152	595	94	182	6	62	.306
1940—Pittsburgh	Nat.	*156	594	*113	178	7	95	.300
1941—Pittsburgh	Nat.	106	374	69	118	6	38	.316
1942—Brooklyn	Nat.	128	495	82	137	2	49	.277
1943—Brooklyn	Nat.	149	610	*112	186	5	66	.305
1944-45-46—Brooklyn	Nat.		(Voluntarily retired)					
1947—Brooklyn	Nat.	64	126	24	41	2	25	.325
1948—Brooklyn	Nat.	65	123	19	30	3	22	.244
1949—San Francisco	P.C.L.	97	281	50	81	2	26	.288
Major League Totals		1817	6622	1173	2103	96	926	.318

WORLD SERIES RECORD

Year Club	League	G	AB	R	H	HR	RBI	B.A.
1947—Brooklyn	Nat.	3	2	0	1	0	0	.500

GEORGE EDWARD (RUBE) WADDELL

Year Club	League	G	IP	W	L	Pct.	ShO.
1897—Louisville	National	2	13	0	1	.000	0
1898—Detroit	Western	9	....	4	4	.500	....
1899—Col.-Grand Rapids	American	42	330	27	13	.675	....
1899—Louisville	National	10	80	7	2	.778	1
1900—Pittsburgh	National	29	212	9	11	.450	2
1900—Milwaukee	American	15	129	10	3	.769	2
1901—Pittsburgh-Chicago	National	31	250	13	16	.448	0
1902—Los Angeles	Pacific Coast	20	178	12	8	.600	2
1902—Philadelphia	American	33	275	23	7	.767	3
1903—Philadelphia	American	39	323	21	16	.568	4
1904—Philadelphia	American	46	384	25	19	.568	8
1905—Philadelphia	American	*46	324	*26	11	.703	7
1906—Philadelphia	American	43	272	15	17	.469	8
1907—Philadelphia	American	44	285	19	13	.594	7
1908—St. Louis	American	43	286	19	14	.576	5
1909—St. Louis	American	31	220	11	14	.440	5
1910—St. Louis	American	10	34	3	1	.750	0
1910—Newark	Eastern	15	97	5	3	.625	....
1911—Minneapolis	Amer. Assn.	54	300	20	17	.541	....
1912—Minneapolis	Amer. Assn.	33	151	12	6	.667	....
1913—Virginia	Northern	15	84	3	9	.250	....
American League Totals		335	2403	162	112	.591	47
National League Totals		72	555	29	30	.492	3
Major League Totals		407	2958	191	142	.574	50

JOHN PETER (HONUS) WAGNER

Year Club	League	G	AB	R	H	HR	RBI	B.A.
1895—Steubenville	Int. St.	44	.....	.....	.....	.....	.....	.402
1895—Mansfield	Ohio St.		(No records available)					
1895—Adrian	Mich. St.	20	.....	.....	.....	.....	.....	.365
1895—Warren	Iron-Oil	65	.....	.....	.....	.....	.....	.369
1896—Paterson	Atl.	109	416	106	145	.....	.....	.349
1897—Paterson	Atlantic	74	301	61	114	.....	.....	.379
1897—Louisville	Nat.	61	241	38	83	2	.....	.344
1898—Louisville	Nat.	148	591	80	180	10	.....	.305
1899—Louisville	Nat.	144	549	102	197	7	.....	.359
1900—Pittsburgh	Nat.	134	528	107	201	4	.....	*.381
1901—Pittsburgh	Nat.	141	556	100	196	6	.....	.353
1902—Pittsburgh	Nat.	137	538	*105	177	3	.....	.329
1903—Pittsburgh	Nat.	129	512	97	182	5	.....	*.355
1904—Pittsburgh	Nat.	132	490	97	171	4	.....	*.349
1905—Pittsburgh	Nat.	147	548	114	199	6	.....	.363
1906—Pittsburgh	Nat.	140	516	●103	175	2	.....	*.339
1907—Pittsburgh	Nat.	142	515	98	180	6	*91	.350
1908—Pittsburgh	Nat.	151	568	100	*201	10	*106	*.354
1909—Pittsburgh	Nat.	137	495	92	168	5	*102	*.339
1910—Pittsburgh	Nat.	150	556	90	●178	4	84	.320
1911—Pittsburgh	Nat.	130	473	87	158	9	108	*.334
1912—Pittsburgh	Nat.	145	558	91	181	7	94	.324
1913—Pittsburgh	Nat.	114	413	51	124	3	55	.300
1914—Pittsburgh	Nat.	150	552	60	139	1	46	.252
1915—Pittsburgh	Nat.	156	566	68	155	6	78	.274
1916—Pittsburgh	Nat.	123	432	45	124	1	38	.287
1917—Pittsburgh	Nat.	74	230	15	61	0	22	.265
Major League Totals		2785	10427	1740	3430	101	.....	.329

WORLD SERIES RECORD

Year Club	League	G	AB	R	H	HR	RBI	B.A.
1903—Pittsburgh	Nat.	8	27	2	6	0	3	.222
1909—Pittsburgh	Nat.	7	24	4	8	0	7	.333
World Series Totals		15	51	6	14	0	10	.275

RODERICK JOHN (BOBBY) WALLACE

Year Club	League	G	AB	R	H	HR	SB	B.A.
1894—Cleveland	Nat.	4	13	0	2	0	0	.154
1895—Cleveland	Nat.	27	97	16	21	0	3	.216
1896—Cleveland	Nat.	33	130	17	30	1	1	.231
1897—Cleveland	Nat.	131	522	99	177	4	17	.339
1898—Cleveland	Nat.	153	591	81	159	3	9	.269
1899—St. Louis	Nat.	151	576	90	174	12	11	.302
1900—St. Louis	Nat.	129	489	72	133	5	10	.272
1901—St. Louis	Nat.	135	556	69	179	2	17	.322
1902—St. Louis	Amer.	133	495	71	142	1	19	.287
1903—St. Louis	Amer.	136	519	63	127	1	11	.245
1904—St. Louis	Amer.	139	550	57	150	2	19	.273
1905—St. Louis	Amer.	*156	587	67	159	1	13	.271
1906—St. Louis	Amer.	139	476	64	123	2	24	.258
1907—St. Louis	Amer.	147	538	56	138	0	16	.257
1908—St. Louis	Amer.	137	487	59	123	1	5	.253
1909—St. Louis	Amer.	116	403	36	96	1	7	.238
1910—St. Louis	Amer.	138	508	47	131	0	12	.258
1911—St. Louis	Amer.	125	410	35	95	0	8	.232
1912—St. Louis	Amer.	99	323	39	78	0	3	.241
1913—St. Louis	Amer.	52	147	11	31	0	2	.211
1914—St. Louis	Amer.	26	73	3	16	0	1	.219
1915—St. Louis	Amer.	9	13	1	3	0	0	.231
1916—St. Louis	Amer.	14	18	0	5	0	0	.278
1917—Wichita	West.	33	123	9	34	0	0	.276
1917—St. Louis	Nat.	8	10	0	1	0	0	.100
1918—St. Louis	Nat.	32	98	3	15	0	1	.153
American League Totals		1566	5547	609	1417	9	140	.255
National League Totals		803	3082	447	891	27	69	.289
Major League Totals		2369	8629	1056	2308	36	209	.267

PITCHING RECORD

Year Club	League	G	CG	ShO.	IP	W	L	Pct.
1894—Cleveland	National	4	2	0	26	2	1	.667
1895—Cleveland	National	27	21	1	222	12	13	.480
1896—Cleveland	National	22	12	2	144	10	7	.588
1902—St. Louis	American	1	0	0	0	0	0	.000
Major League Totals		54	35	3	392	24	21	.534

TEMPLE CUP PITCHING RECORD

Year Club	League	G	CG	ShO.	IP	W	L	Pct.
1896—Cleveland	National	1	1	0	8	0	1	.000

TEMPLE CUP BATTING RECORD

Year Club	League	G	AB	R	H	HR	SB	B.A.
1896—Cleveland	National	3	5	1	1	0	0	.200

EDWARD AUGUSTIN WALSH

Year Club	League	G	IP	W	L	Pct.	ShO.
1902—Wilkes-Barre	Pa. State	4	36	1	2	.333	....
1902—Meriden	Connecticut	21	182	15	5	.750	....
1903—Meriden	Connecticut	23	182	11	10	.524	....
1903—Newark	Eastern	19	117	9	5	.643	....
1904—Chicago	American	18	113	6	3	.667	1
1905—Chicago	American	22	138	8	3	.727	1
1906—Chicago	American	42	281	17	13	.567	*10
1907—Chicago	American	*56	*419	24	18	.600	5
1908—Chicago	American	*66	*465	*40	15	*.727	*12
1909—Chicago	American	31	230	15	11	.577	*8
1910—Chicago	American	●45	370	18	*20	.474	7
1911—Chicago	American	*56	*369	27	18	.600	5
1912—Chicago	American	*62	*393	27	17	.614	6
1913—Chicago	American	16	98	8	3	.727	1
1914—Chicago	American	9	45	2	3	.400	1
1915—Chicago	American	3	27	3	0	1.000	1

Year Club	League	G.	IP.	W.	L.	Pct.	ShO.
1916—Chicago	American	2	3	0	1	1.000	0
1917—Boston	National	4	18	0	1	.000	0
1919—Milwaukee	Amer. Assn.	4	21	2	2	.500	....
1920—Bridgeport	Eastern	3	22	1	1	.500	....
American League Totals		428	2951	195	125	.609	58
National League Totals		4	18	0	1	.000	0
Major League Totals		432	2969	195	126	.607	58

WORLD SERIES RECORD

Year Club	League	G.	IP.	W.	L.	Pct.	ShO.
1906—Chicago	American	2	15	2	0	1.000	1

LLOYD JAMES (LITTLE POISON) WANER

Year Club	League	G.	AB.	R.	H.	HR.	RBI.	B.A.
1925—San Francisco	P.C.	31	44	7	11	0	1	.250
1926—San Francisco	P.C.	6	20	0	4	0	....	.200
1926—Columbia	So. Atl.	121	498	95	172	6	33	.345
1927—Pittsburgh	Nat.	150	629	●133	223	2	27	.355
1928—Pittsburgh	Nat.	152	*659	121	221	5	61	.335
1929—Pittsburgh	Nat.	151	*662	134	234	5	74	.353
1930—Pittsburgh	Nat.	68	260	32	94	1	36	.362
1931—Pittsburgh	Nat.	154	*681	90	*214	4	57	.314
1932—Pittsburgh	Nat.	134	565	90	188	2	38	.333
1933—Pittsburgh	Nat.	121	500	59	138	0	26	.276
1934—Pittsburgh	Nat.	140	611	95	173	1	48	.283
1935—Pittsburgh	Nat.	122	537	83	166	0	46	.309
1936—Pittsburgh	Nat.	106	414	67	133	1	31	.321
1937—Pittsburgh	Nat.	129	537	80	177	1	45	.330
1938—Pittsburgh	Nat.	147	619	79	194	5	57	.313
1939—Pittsburgh	Nat.	112	379	49	108	0	24	.285
1940—Pittsburgh	Nat.	72	166	30	43	0	3	.259
1941—Pitt.-Bos.-Cinn.	Nat.	77	219	26	64	0	11	.292
1942—Philadelphia	Nat.	101	287	23	75	0	10	.261
1943—Brooklyn	Nat.			(Voluntarily retired)				
1944—Brook.-Pitts.	Nat.	34	28	5	9	0	3	.321
1945—Pittsburgh	Nat.	23	19	5	5	0	1	.263
Major League Totals		1993	7772	1201	2459	27	598	.316

WORLD SERIES RECORD

Year Club	League	G.	AB.	R.	H.	HR.	RBI.	B.A.
1927—Pittsburgh	Nat.	4	15	5	6	0	0	.400

PAUL GLEE (BIG POISON) WANER

Year Club	League	G.	AB.	R.	H.	HR.	RBI.	B.A.
1923—San Francisco	P.C.	112	325	54	120	3	39	.369
1924—San Francisco	P.C.	160	587	113	209	8	97	.356
1925—San Francisco	P.C.	174	699	167	280	11	130	*.401
1926—Pittsburgh	Nat.	144	536	101	180	8	79	.336
1927—Pittsburgh	Nat.	●155	623	114	*237	9	*131	*.380
1928—Pittsburgh	Nat.	152	602	*142	223	6	86	.370
1929—Pittsburgh	Nat.	151	596	131	200	15	100	.336
1930—Pittsburgh	Nat.	145	589	117	217	8	77	.368
1931—Pittsburgh	Nat.	150	559	88	180	6	70	.322
1932—Pittsburgh	Nat.	●154	630	107	215	8	82	.341
1933—Pittsburgh	Nat.	●154	618	101	191	7	70	.309
1934—Pittsburgh	Nat.	146	599	*122	*217	14	90	*.362
1935—Pittsburgh	Nat.	139	549	98	176	11	78	.321
1936—Pittsburgh	Nat.	148	585	107	218	5	94	*.373
1937—Pittsburgh	Nat.	154	619	94	219	2	74	.354
1938—Pittsburgh	Nat.	148	625	77	175	6	69	.280
1939—Pittsburgh	Nat.	125	461	62	151	3	45	.328
1940—Pittsburgh	Nat.	89	238	32	69	1	32	.290
1941—Brook.-Bost.	Nat.	106	329	45	88	2	50	.267
1942—Boston	Nat.	114	333	43	86	1	39	.258
1943—Brooklyn	Nat.	82	225	29	70	1	26	.311
1944—Brooklyn	Nat.	83	136	16	39	0	16	.287
1944—New York	Amer.	9	7	1	1	0	1	.143
1945—New York	Amer.	1	0	0	0	0	0	.000
1946—Miami	Fla. Int.	62	80	12	26	0	12	.325
American League Totals		10	7	1	1	0	1	.143
National League Totals		2539	9452	1626	3151	113	1308	.333
Major League Totals		2549	9459	1627	3152	113	1309	.333

WORLD SERIES RECORD

Year Club	League	G.	AB.	R.	H.	HR.	RBI.	B.A.
1927—Pittsburgh	Nat.	4	15	0	5	0	3	.333

JOHN MONTGOMERY WARD

Year Club	League	G.	AB.	R.	H.	HR.	SB.	B.A.
1877—Athletics		League Alliance club—no record available						
1878—Providence	Nat.	35	128	14	26	1	....	.203
1879—Providence	Nat.	82	362	71	104	2	....	.287
1880—Providence	Nat.	82	340	49	77	0	....	.226
1881—Providence	Nat.	83	352	56	85	0	....	.241
1882—Providence	Nat.	83	355	58	87	0	....	.245
1883—New York	Nat.	88	379	76	98	7	....	.259
1884—New York	Nat.	109	466	99	116	2	....	.249
1885—New York	Nat.	111	446	72	101	0	....	.226
1886—New York	Nat.	122	491	82	134	2	36	.273
1887—New York	Nat.	129	574	113	213	1	*111	.371
1888—New York	Nat.	122	510	70	128	2	38	.251
1889—New York	Nat.	114	479	86	143	1	62	.299

Year Club	League	G.	AB.	R.	H.	HR.	SB.	B.A.
1890—Brooklyn	Play.	128	558	135	*207	4	71	.371
1891—Brooklyn	Nat.	104	438	85	126	0	80	.288
1892—Brooklyn	Nat.	148	610	109	167	2	*94	.274
1893—New York	Nat.	134	557	129	194	2	*72	.348
1894—New York	Nat.	136	552	99	145	0	41	.262
National League Total		1682	7039	1268	1944	22	534	.276
Players League Totals		128	558	135	207	4	71	.371
Major League Totals		1810	7597	1403	2151	26	605	.283

PITCHING RECORD

Year Club	League	G.	CG.	W.	L.	Pct.	ShO.
1878—Providence	National	35	35	22	13	.629	6
1879—Providence	National	65	58	*44	18	*.710	2
1880—Providence	National	63	58	40	23	.635	*9
1881—Providence	National	36	33	18	18	.500	3
1882—Providence	National	32	30	19	13	.594	4
1883—New York	National	33	24	12	14	.462	1
1884—New York	National	9	5	3	3	.500	0
Major League Totals		273	243	158	102	.608	25

WORLD SERIES RECORD

Year Club	League	G.	AB.	R.	H.	HR.	SB.	B.A.
1888—New York	Nat.	8	29	4	11	0	6	.379
1889—New York	Nat.	9	37	10	15	0	8	.405
World Series Totals		17	66	14	26	0	14	.394

EARL SIDNEY WEAVER
RECORD AS MANAGER

Year Club	League	Position	W.	L.
1956 — Knoxville	Sally	Eighth	10	24
1957 — Fitzgerald	Georgia-Florida	Fourth	37	33
	(Second half)	Sixth	28	41
1958 — Dublin	Georgia-Florida	Third	37	28
	(Second half)	Third	35	28
1959 — Aberdeen	Northern	Second	69	55
1960 — Fox Cities	I.I.I.	First	82	56
1961 — Fox Cities	I.I.I.	Fourth	67	62
1962 — Elmira	Eastern	Second	72	68
1963 — Elmira	Eastern	Second	76	64
1964 — Elmira	Eastern	First	82	58
1965 — Elmira	Eastern	Second	83	55
1966 — Rochester	International	First	83	64
1967 — Rochester	International	Second	80	61
1968 — Baltimore	American	Second	48	34
1969 — Baltimore	American	First (E)	109	53
1970 — Baltimore	American	First (E)	108	54
1971 — Baltimore	American	First (E)	101	57
1972 — Baltimore	American	Third (E)	80	74
1973 — Baltimore	American	First (E)	97	65
1974 — Baltimore	American	First (E)	91	71
1975 — Baltimore	American	Second (E)	90	69
1976 — Baltimore	American	Second (E)	88	74
1977 — Baltimore	American	Second (E)	97	64
1978 — Baltimore	American	Fourth (E)	90	71
1979 — Baltimore	American	First (E)	102	57
1980 — Baltimore	American	Second (E)	100	62
1981 — Baltimore	American	.....	59	46
1982 — Baltimore	American	Second (E)	94	68
1985 — Baltimore	American	Fourth (E)	53	52
1986 — Baltimore	American	Seventh (E)	73	89
Major League Totals			1480	1060

CHAMPIONSHIP SERIES RECORD

Year Club	League	W.	L.
1969 — Baltimore	American	3	0
1970 — Baltimore	American	3	0
1971 — Baltimore	American	3	0
1973 — Baltimore	American	2	3
1974 — Baltimore	American	1	3
1979 — Baltimore	American	3	1

WORLD SERIES RECORD

Year Club	League	W.	L.
1969 — Baltimore	American	1	4
1970 — Baltimore	American	4	1
1971 — Baltimore	American	3	4
1979 — Baltimore	American	3	4

MICHAEL FRANCIS (MICKEY) WELCH

Year Club	League	G.	IP.	W.	L.	Pct.	ShO.
1878—Auburn	National Assn.	...	...	...	...	.....	..
1879—Holyoke	National Assn.	...	...	...	...	.....	..
1880—Troy	National	65	574	34	30	.531	4
1881—Troy	National	40	362	21	18	.538	4
1882—Troy	National	34	292	14	16	.467	5
1883—New York	National	54	422	25	23	.521	4
1884—New York	National	65	555	39	21	.650	4
1885—New York	National	56	496	44	11	.800	7
1886—New York	National	59	499	33	22	.600	1
1887—New York	National	41	346	22	15	.595	2
1888—New York	National	47	425	26	19	.578	5
1889—New York	National	45	364	27	12	.692	3
1890—New York	National	37	294	17	13	.567	2
1891—New York	National	22	160	5	9	.357	0
1892—New York	National	1	5	0	0	.000	0
1892—Troy	Eastern	31	...	17	14	.548	..
Major League Totals		566	4794	307	209	.595	41

ZACHARIAH DAVIS (ZACK) WHEAT

Year	Club	League	G.	AB.	R.	H.	HR.	RBI.	B.A.
1908—Shreveport	Texas	92	239	49	91	1	....	.268
1909—Mobile	South.	129	460	58	112	2	....	.246
1909—Brooklyn	Nat.	26	102	15	31	0	4	.304
1910—Brooklyn	Nat.	●156	606	78	172	2	54	.284
1911—Brooklyn	Nat.	136	534	55	153	5	76	.287
1912—Brooklyn	Nat.	123	453	70	138	8	62	.305
1913—Brooklyn	Nat.	138	535	64	161	7	71	.301
1914—Brooklyn	Nat.	145	533	66	170	9	88	.319
1915—Brooklyn	Nat.	146	528	64	136	5	70	.258
1916—Brooklyn	Nat.	149	568	76	177	9	76	.312
1917—Brooklyn	Nat.	109	362	38	113	1	40	.312
1918—Brooklyn	Nat.	105	409	39	137	0	48	★.335
1919—Brooklyn	Nat.	137	536	70	159	5	68	.297
1920—Brooklyn	Nat.	148	583	89	191	9	73	.328
1921—Brooklyn	Nat.	148	568	91	182	14	85	.320
1922—Brooklyn	Nat.	152	600	92	201	16	112	.335
1923—Brooklyn	Nat.	98	349	63	131	8	65	.375
1924—Brooklyn	Nat.	141	566	92	212	14	97	.375
1925—Brooklyn	Nat.	150	616	125	221	14	103	.359
1926—Brooklyn	Nat.	111	411	68	119	5	35	.290
1927—Philadelphia	Amer.	88	247	34	80	1	38	.324
1928—Minneapolis	A.A.	82	194	17	60	5	30	.309
American League Totals		88	247	34	80	1	38	.324
National League Totals		2318	8859	1255	2804	131	1227	.317
Major League Totals		2406	9106	1289	2884	132	1265	.317

WORLD SERIES RECORD

Year	Club	League	G.	AB.	R.	H.	HR.	RBI.	B.A.
1916—Brooklyn	Nat.	5	19	2	4	0	1	.211
1920—Brooklyn	Nat.	7	27	2	9	0	2	.333
World Series Totals		12	46	4	13	0	3	.283

JAMES HOYT WILHELM

Year	Club	League	G.	IP.	W.	L.	Pct.	ERA.
1942—Mooresville	N.C. St.	23	108	10	3	.769	4.25
1943-44-45—Mooresville	N.C. St.	(In Military Service)					
1946—Mooresville	N.C. St.	★34	233	21	8	.724	2.47
1947—Mooresville	N.C. St.	31	★250	★20	7	.741	3.38
1948—Jacksonville	Sally	6	11	0	0	.000	8.18
1948—Knoxville	Tri-State	24	189	13	9	.591	3.62
1949—Jacksonville	Sally	33	223	17	12	.586	2.66
1950—Minneapolis	Am. Assoc.	35	180	15	11	.577	4.95
1951—Minneapolis	Am. Assoc.	40	●210	11	14	.440	3.94
1952—New York	National	★71	159	15	3	★.833	★2.43
1953—New York	National	★68	145	7	8	.467	3.04
1954—New York	National	57	111	12	4	●.750	2.11
1955—New York	National	59	103	4	1	.800	3.93
1956—New York	National	64	89	4	9	.308	3.84
1957—St. Louis	National	40	55	1	4	.200	4.25
1957—Cleveland	American	2	4	1	0	1.000	2.25
1958—Cleveland-Baltimore	American	39	131	3	10	.231	2.34
1959—Baltimore	American	32	226	15	11	.577	★2.19
1960—Baltimore	American	41	147	11	8	.579	3.31
1961—Baltimore	American	51	110	9	7	.563	2.29
1962—Baltimore	American	52	93	7	10	.412	1.94
1963—Chicago	American	55	136	5	8	.385	2.65
1964—Chicago	American	73	131	12	9	.571	1.99
1965—Chicago	American	66	144	7	7	.500	1.81
1966—Chicago	American	46	81	5	2	.714	1.67
1967—Chicago	American	49	89	8	3	.727	1.31
1968—Chicago	American	72	94	4	4	.500	1.72
1969—California	American	44	66	5	7	.417	2.45
1969—Atlanta	National	8	12	2	0	1.000	0.75
1970—Atlanta-Chicago	National	53	82	6	5	.545	3.40
1971—Spokane	Pac. Coast	8	37	2	3	.400	3.89
1971—Atlanta-Los Angeles	National	12	20	0	1	.000	2.70
1972—Los Angeles	National	16	25	0	1	.000	4.68
American League Totals		622	1452	92	86	.517	2.19
National League Totals		448	801	51	36	.586	3.12
Major League Totals		1070	2253	143	122	.540	2.52

WORLD SERIES RECORD

Year	Club	League	G.	IP.	W.	L.	Pct.	ERA.
1954—New York	National	2	2⅓	0	0	.000	0.00

BILLY LEO WILLIAMS

Year	Club	League	G.	AB.	R.	H.	HR.	RBI.	B.A.
1956—Ponca City	Soo. St.	13	17	4	4	0	4	.235
1957—Ponca City	Soo. St.	●126	451	87	140	17	95	.310
1958—Pueblo	West.	21	80	9	20	2	11	.250
1958—Burlington	I.I.I.	61	214	38	65	10	38	.304
1959—San Antonio	Tex.	94	371	57	118	10	79	.318
1959—Fort Worth	A.A.	5	21	7	10	1	5	.476
1959—Chicago	Nat.	18	33	0	5	0	2	.152
1960—Houston	A.A.	126	473	74	153	26	80	.323
1960—Chicago	Nat.	12	47	4	13	2	7	.277
1961—Chicago	Nat.	146	529	75	147	25	86	.278
1962—Chicago	Nat.	159	618	94	184	22	92	.298
1963—Chicago	Nat.	161	612	87	175	25	95	.286
1964—Chicago	Nat.	162	645	100	201	33	98	.312
1965—Chicago	Nat.	●164	645	115	203	34	108	.315
1966—Chicago	Nat.	●162	648	100	179	29	91	.276
1967—Chicago	Nat.	162	634	92	176	28	84	.278
1968—Chicago	Nat.	★163	642	91	185	30	98	.288
1969—Chicago	Nat.	★163	642	103	188	21	95	.293
1970—Chicago	Nat.	●161	636	★137	●205	42	129	.322
1971—Chicago	Nat.	157	594	86	179	28	93	.301
1972—Chicago	Nat.	150	574	95	191	37	122	★.333
1973—Chicago	Nat.	156	576	72	166	20	86	.288
1974—Chicago	Nat.	117	404	55	113	16	68	.280
1975—Oakland	Amer.	155	520	68	127	23	81	.244
1976—Oakland	Amer.	120	351	36	74	11	41	.211
National League Totals		2213	8479	1306	2510	392	1354	.296
American League Totals		275	871	104	201	34	122	.231
Major League Totals		2488	9350	1410	2711	426	1476	.290

THEODORE SAMUEL (THE KID) WILLIAMS

Year	Club	League	G.	AB.	R.	H.	HR.	RBI.	B.A.
1936—San Diego	P.C.	42	107	18	29	0	11	.271
1937—San Diego	P.C.	138	454	66	132	23	98	.291
1938—Minneapolis	A.A.	148	528	★130	193	★43	★142	★.366
1939—Boston	Amer.	149	565	131	185	31	★145	.327
1940—Boston	Amer.	144	561	★134	193	23	113	.344
1941—Boston	Amer.	143	456	★135	185	★37	120	★.406
1942—Boston	Amer.	150	522	★141	186	★36	★137	★.356
1943-44-45—Boston	Amer.	(In Military Service)						
1946—Boston	Amer.	150	514	★142	176	38	123	.342
1947—Boston	Amer.	156	528	★125	181	★32	★114	.343
1948—Boston	Amer.	137	509	124	188	25	127	★.369
1949—Boston	Amer.	●155	566	★150	194	★43	●159	.343
1950—Boston	Amer.	89	334	82	106	28	97	.317
1951—Boston	Amer.	148	531	109	169	30	126	.318
1952—Boston	Amer.	6	10	2	4	1	3	.400
1953—Boston	Amer.	37	91	17	37	13	34	.407
1954—Boston	Amer.	117	386	93	133	29	89	.345
1955—Boston	Amer.	98	320	77	114	28	83	.356
1956—Boston	Amer.	136	400	71	138	24	82	.345
1957—Boston	Amer.	132	420	96	163	38	87	★.388
1958—Boston	Amer.	129	411	81	135	26	85	★.328
1959—Boston	Amer.	103	272	32	69	10	43	.254
1960—Boston	Amer.	113	310	56	98	29	72	.316
Major League Totals		2292	7706	1798	2654	521	1839	.344

PITCHING RECORD

Year	Club	League	G.	IP.	W.	L.	Pct.	ERA.
1936—San Diego	Pacific Coast	1	1⅓	0	0	.000	13.50
1940—Boston	American	1	2	0	0	.000	4.50

WORLD SERIES RECORD

Year	Club	League	G.	AB.	R.	H.	HR.	RBI.	B.A.
1946—Boston	Amer.	7	25	2	5	0	1	.200

VICTOR GAZAWAY WILLIS

Year	Club	League	G.	IP.	W.	L.	Pct.	ShO.
1895 — Harrisburg	Pa. State	16	....	....	....	....	....
1896 — Syracuse	Eastern	17	....	10	6	.625	....
1897 — Syracuse	Eastern	40	....	21	16	.568	....
1898 — Boston	National	41	316	23	12	.657	1
1899 — Boston	National	41	343	27	10	.730	★5
1900 — Boston	National	31	225	9	16	.360	2
1901 — Boston	National	38	307	18	17	.514	●6
1902 — Boston	National	★51	★411	27	19	.587	4
1903 — Boston	National	33	278	12	18	.400	2
1904 — Boston	National	43	350	18	●25	.419	2
1905 — Boston	National	41	342	12	★29	.293	4
1906 — Pittsburgh	National	41	322	23	13	.639	6
1907 — Pittsburgh	National	39	293	21	11	.656	6
1908 — Pittsburgh	National	41	305	23	11	.676	7
1909 — Pittsburgh	National	39	290	22	11	.667	4
1910 — St. Louis	National	33	212	9	12	.429	1
Major League Totals		512	3994	244	204	.545	50

WORLD SERIES RECORD

Year	Club	League	G.	IP.	W.	L.	Pct.	ShO.
1909 — Pittsburgh	National	2	11⅔	0	1	.000	0

LEWIS ROBERT (HACK) WILSON

Year	Club	League	G.	AB.	R.	H.	HR.	RBI.	B.A.
1921—Martinsburg	B. Ridge	30	101	17	36	5	....	.356
1922—Martinsburg	B. Ridge	84	322	66	118	★30	....	.366
1923—Portsmouth	Va.	115	448	96	174	★19	★101	★.388
1923—New York	Nat.	3	10	0	2	0	0	.200
1924—New York	Nat.	107	383	62	113	10	57	.295
1925—New York	Nat.	62	180	28	43	6	30	.239
1925—Toledo	A.A.	55	210	42	72	4	36	.343
1926—Chicago	Nat.	142	529	97	170	★21	109	.321
1927—Chicago	Nat.	146	551	119	175	●30	129	.318
1928—Chicago	Nat.	145	520	89	163	●31	120	.313
1929—Chicago	Nat.	150	574	135	198	39	★159	.345
1930—Chicago	Nat.	155	585	146	208	★56	★190	.356
1931—Chicago	Nat.	112	395	66	103	13	61	.261
1932—Brooklyn	Nat.	135	481	77	143	23	123	.297
1933—Brooklyn	Nat.	117	360	41	96	9	54	.267
1934—Brook.-Phila.	Nat.	74	192	24	47	6	30	.245
1935—Albany	Int.	59	175	30	46	3	29	.263
Major League Totals		1348	4760	884	1461	244	1062	.307

WORLD SERIES RECORD

Year Club	League	G.	AB.	R.	H.	HR.	RBI.	B.A.
1924—New York	Nat.	7	30	1	7	0	3	.233
1929—Chicago	Nat.	5	17	2	8	0	0	.471
World Series Totals		12	47	3	15	0	3	.319

DAVID MARK WINFIELD

Year Club	League	G.	AB.	R.	H.	HR.	RBI.	B.A.
1973—San Diego	National	56	141	9	39	3	12	.277
1974—San Diego	National	145	498	57	132	20	75	.265
1975—San Diego	National	143	509	74	136	15	76	.267
1976—San Diego	National	137	492	81	139	13	69	.283
1977—San Diego	National	157	615	104	169	25	92	.275
1978—San Diego	National	158	587	88	181	24	97	.308
1979—San Diego	National	159	597	97	184	34	*118	.308
1980—San Diego	National	162	558	89	154	20	87	.276
1981—New York	American	105	388	52	114	13	68	.294
1982—New York	American	140	539	84	151	37	106	.280
1983—New York	American	152	598	99	169	32	116	.283
1984—New York	American	141	567	106	193	19	100	.340
1985—New York	American	155	633	105	174	26	114	.275
1986—New York	American	154	565	90	148	24	104	.262
1987—New York	American	156	575	83	158	27	97	.275
1988—New York	American	149	559	96	180	25	107	.322
1989—New York	American				(Did not play: injured)			
1990—New York	American	20	61	7	13	2	6	.213
1990—California	American	112	414	63	114	19	72	.275
1991—California	American	150	568	75	149	28	86	.262
1992—Toronto	American	156	583	92	169	26	108	.290
1993—Minnesota	American	143	547	72	148	21	76	.271
1994—Minnesota	American	77	294	35	74	10	43	.252
1995—Cleveland	American	46	115	11	22	2	4	.191
American League Totals		1856	7006	1070	1976	311	1207	.282
National League Totals		1117	3997	599	1134	154	626	.284
Major League Totals		2973	11003	1669	3110	465	1833	.283

DIVISION SERIES RECORD

Year Club	League	G.	AB.	R.	H.	HR.	RBI.	B.A.
1981—New York	American	5	20	2	7	0	0	.350

CHAMPIONSHIP SERIES

Year Club	League	G.	AB.	R.	H.	HR.	RBI.	B.A.
1981—New York	American	3	13	2	2	0	2	.154
1992—Toronto	American	6	24	7	6	2	3	.250
Championship Series Totals		9	37	9	8	2	5	.216

WORLD SERIES RECORD

Year Club	League	G.	AB.	R.	H.	HR.	RBI.	B.A
1981—New York	American	6	22	0	1	0	1	.045
1992—Toronto	American	6	22	0	5	0	3	.227
World Series Totals		12	44	0	6	0	4	.136

EARLY (GUS) WYNN, JR.

Year Club	League	G.	IP.	W.	L.	Pct.	ERA.
1937—Sanford	Florida State	35	235	16	11	.593	3.41
1938—Charlotte	Piedmont	29	179	10	11	.476	5.28
1939—Charlotte	Piedmont	34	243	15	14	.517	3.96
1939—Washington	American	3	20	0	2	.000	5.85
1940—Charlotte	Piedmont	31	144	9	7	.563	4.25
1941—Springfield	Eastern	34	257	16	12	.571	2.56
1941—Washington	American	5	40	3	1	.750	1.58
1942—Washington	American	30	190	10	16	.385	5.12
1943—Washington	American	37	257	18	12	.600	2.91
1944—Washington	American	33	208	8	*17	.320	3.38
1945—Washington	American			(In Military Service)			
1946—Washington	American	17	107	8	5	.615	3.11
1947—Washington	American	33	247	17	15	.531	3.64
1948—Washington	American	33	198	8	19	.296	5.82
1949—Cleveland	American	26	165	11	7	.611	4.15
1950—Cleveland	American	32	214	18	8	.692	*3.20
1951—Cleveland	American	37	*274	20	13	.606	3.02
1952—Cleveland	American	42	286	23	12	.657	2.90
1953—Cleveland	American	36	252	17	12	.586	3.93
1954—Cleveland	American	40	*271	●23	11	.676	2.72
1955—Cleveland	American	32	230	17	11	.607	2.82
1956—Cleveland	American	38	278	20	9	.690	2.72
1957—Cleveland	American	40	263	14	17	.452	4.31
1958—Chicago	American	40	240	14	16	.467	4.13
1959—Chicago	American	37	*256	*22	10	.688	3.16
1960—Chicago	American	36	237	13	12	.520	3.49
1961—Chicago	American	17	110	8	2	.800	3.52
1962—Chicago	American	27	168	7	15	.318	4.45
1963—Cleveland	American	20	55	1	2	.333	2.29
Major League Totals		691	4566	300	244	.551	3.54

WORLD SERIES RECORD

Year Club	League	G.	IP.	W.	L.	Pct.	ERA.
1954—Cleveland	American	1	7	0	1	.000	3.86
1959—Chicago	American	3	13	1	1	.500	5.54
World Series Totals		4	20	1	2	.333	4.95

CARL MICHAEL (YAZ) YASTRZEMSKI

Year Club	League	G.	AB.	R.	H.	HR.	RBI.	B.A.
1959—Raleigh	Carol.	120	451	87	•170	15	100	•.377
1960—Minneapolis	A.A.	148	570	84	•193	7	69	.339
1961—Boston	Amer.	148	583	71	155	11	80	.266
1962—Boston	Amer.	160	646	99	191	19	94	.296
1963—Boston	Amer.	151	570	91	•183	14	68	•.321
1964—Boston	Amer.	151	567	77	164	15	67	.289
1965—Boston	Amer.	133	494	78	154	20	72	.312
1966—Boston	Amer.	160	594	81	165	16	80	.278
1967—Boston	Amer.	161	579	•112	•189	●44	•121	•.326
1968—Boston	Amer.	157	539	90	162	23	74	•.301
1969—Boston	Amer.	●162	603	96	154	40	111	.255
1970—Boston	Amer.	161	566	•125	186	40	102	.329
1971—Boston	Amer.	148	508	75	129	15	70	.254
1972—Boston	Amer.	125	455	70	120	12	68	.264
1973—Boston	Amer.	152	540	82	160	19	95	.296
1974—Boston	Amer.	148	515	•93	155	15	79	.301
1975—Boston	Amer.	149	543	91	146	14	60	.269
1976—Boston	Amer.	155	546	71	146	21	102	.267
1977—Boston	Amer.	150	558	99	165	28	102	.296
1978—Boston	Amer.	144	523	70	145	17	81	.277
1979—Boston	Amer.	147	518	69	140	21	87	.270
1980—Boston	Amer.	105	364	49	100	15	50	.275
1981—Boston	Amer.	91	338	36	83	7	53	.246
1982—Boston	Amer.	131	459	53	126	16	72	.275
1983—Boston	Amer.	119	380	38	101	10	56	.266
Major League Totals		3308	11988	1816	3419	452	1844	.285

CHAMPIONSHIP SERIES RECORD

Year Club	League	G.	AB.	R.	H.	HR.	RBI.	B.A.
1975—Boston	Amer.	3	11	4	5	.1	2	.455

WORLD SERIES RECORD

Year Club	League	G.	AB.	R.	H.	HR.	RBI.	B.A.
1967—Boston	Amer.	7	25	4	10	3	5	.400
1975—Boston	Amer.	7	29	7	9	0	4	.310
World Series Totals		14	54	11	19	3	9	.352

DENTON TRUE (CY) YOUNG

Year Club	League	G.	IP.	W.	L.	Pct.	ShO.
1890—Canton	Tri-State	31	260	15	15	.500	0
1890—Cleveland	National	17	150	9	7	.563	0
1891—Cleveland	National	54	430	27	20	.574	0
1892—Cleveland	National	53	455	36	11	*.766	*9
1893—Cleveland	National	53	426	32	16	.667	1
1894—Cleveland	National	52	409	25	22	.532	2
1895—Cleveland	National	47	373	*35	10	.778	●4
1896—Cleveland	National	51	414	29	16	.644	●5
1897—Cleveland	National	●47	338	21	18	.538	2
1898—Cleveland	National	46	378	25	14	.641	1
1899—St. Louis	National	44	369	26	15	.634	4
1900—St. Louis	National	41	321	20	18	.526	●4
1901—Boston	American	43	371	*33	10	.767	●5
1902—Boston	American	*45	*386	*32	10	.762	3
1903—Boston	American	40	*342	*28	10	.737	*7
1904—Boston	American	43	380	26	16	.619	*10
1905—Boston	American	38	321	18	19	.486	5
1906—Boston	American	39	288	13	●21	.382	0
1907—Boston	American	43	343	22	15	.595	6
1908—Boston	American	36	299	21	11	.656	3
1909—Cleveland	American	35	295	19	15	.559	3
1910—Cleveland	American	21	163	7	10	.412	1
1911—Cleveland	American	7	46	3	4	.429	0
1911—Boston	National	11	80	4	5	.444	2
American League Totals		390	3234	222	141	.612	43
National League Totals		516	4143	289	172	.627	34
Major League Totals		906	7377	511	313	.620	77

TEMPLE CUP RECORD

Year Club	League	G.	IP.	W.	L.	Pct.	ShO.
1895—Cleveland	National	3	27	3	0	1.000	0
1896—Cleveland	National	1	9	0	1	.000	0
Temple Cup Totals		4	36	3	1	.750	0

WORLD SERIES RECORD

Year Club	League	G.	IP.	W.	L.	Pct.	ShO.
1903—Boston	American	4	34	2	1	.667	0

ROSS MIDDLEBROOK (PEP) YOUNGS

Year Club	League	G.	AB.	R.	H.	HR.	RBI.	B.A.
1914—Austin	Tex.	10	31	.....	3	0	.....	.097
1915—Brenham	Mid. Tex.	No averages. League disbanded June 19.						
1915—Waxahachie	Cent. Tex.	League disbanded in July. No averages.						
1916—Sherman	W. A.	137	*539	*103	*195	4	.....	*.362
1917—Rochester	Int.	140	506	85	180	1	.....	.356
1917—New York	Nat.	7	26	5	9	0	1	.346
1918—New York	Nat.	121	474	70	143	1	29	.302
1919—New York	Nat.	130	489	73	152	2	43	.311
1920—New York	Nat.	153	581	92	204	6	78	.351
1921—New York	Nat.	141	504	90	165	3	102	.327
1922—New York	Nat.	149	559	105	185	7	86	.331
1923—New York	Nat.	152	596	*121	200	3	87	.336
1924—New York	Nat.	133	526	112	187	10	74	.356
1925—New York	Nat.	130	500	82	132	6	53	.264
1926—New York	Nat.	95	372	62	114	4	43	.306
Major League Totals		1211	4627	812	1491	42	596	.322

WORLD SERIES RECORD

Year Club	League	G.	AB.	R.	H.	HR.	RBI.	B.A.
1921—New York	Nat.	8	25	3	7	0	4	.280
1922—New York	Nat.	5	16	2	6	0	2	.375
1923—New York	Nat.	6	23	2	8	1	3	.348
1924—New York	Nat.	7	27	3	5	0	2	.185
World Series Totals		26	91	10	26	1	11	.286

ROBIN R. YOUNT

Year Club	League	G.	AB.	R.	H.	HR.	RBI.	B.A.
1973— Newark	N.Y.-P.	64	242	29	69	3	25	.285
1974— Milwaukee	Amer.	107	344	48	86	3	26	.250
1975— Milwaukee	Amer.	147	558	67	149	8	52	.267
1976— Milwaukee	Amer.	•161	638	59	161	2	54	.252
1977— Milwaukee	Amer.	154	605	66	174	4	49	.288
1978— Milwaukee	Amer.	127	502	66	147	9	71	.293
1979— Milwaukee	Amer.	149	577	72	154	8	51	.267
1980— Milwaukee	Amer.	143	611	121	179	23	87	.293
1981— Milwaukee	Amer.	96	377	50	103	10	49	.273
1982— Milwaukee	Amer.	156	635	129	*210	29	114	.331
1983— Milwaukee	Amer.	149	578	102	178	17	80	.308
1984— Milwaukee	Amer.	160	624	105	186	16	80	.298
1985— Milwaukee	Amer.	122	466	76	129	15	68	.277
1986— Milwaukee	Amer.	140	522	82	163	9	46	.312
1987— Milwaukee	Amer.	158	635	99	198	21	103	.312
1988— Milwaukee	Amer.	*162	621	92	190	13	91	.306
1989— Milwaukee	Amer.	160	614	101	195	21	103	.318
1990— Milwaukee	Amer.	158	587	981	45	17	77	.247
1991— Milwaukee	Amer.	130	503	66	131	10	77	.260
1992— Milwaukee	Amer.	150	557	71	147	8	77	.264
1993— Milwaukee	Amer.	127	454	62	117	8	51	.258
Major League Totals		2856	11008	1632	3142	251	1406	.285

CHAMPIONSHIP SERIES RECORD

Year Club	League	G.	AB.	R.	H.	HR.	RBI.	B.A.
1982— Milwaukee	Amer.	5	16	1	4	0	0	.250

WORLD SERIES RECORD

Year Club	League	G.	AB.	R.	H.	HR.	RBI.	B.A.
1982— Milwaukee	Amer.	7	29	6	12	1	6	.414

This book does not include the Negro league records of the black baseball greats who have been added to the Hall of Fame over the years, or the playing records of those Hall of Famers whose enshrinement was based on a successful managerial career. Those inducted for off-the-field contributions —the game's founders, pioneers and executives—are covered solely in profile form.

Major league records of all players in this book are based on performances in the following leagues:

National League—1876 through 1982
American Association—1882 through 1891
Union Association—1884
Players League—1890
American League—1901 through 1982

Federal League records of 1914–1915, although carried in the players' year-by-year performances. are not included in the players' major league career totals. This league was not recognized at that time by *The Sporting News*, the commissioner, Kenesaw Mountain Landis, or the American and National leagues as a major league.

AUTOGRAPHS

AUTOGRAPHS